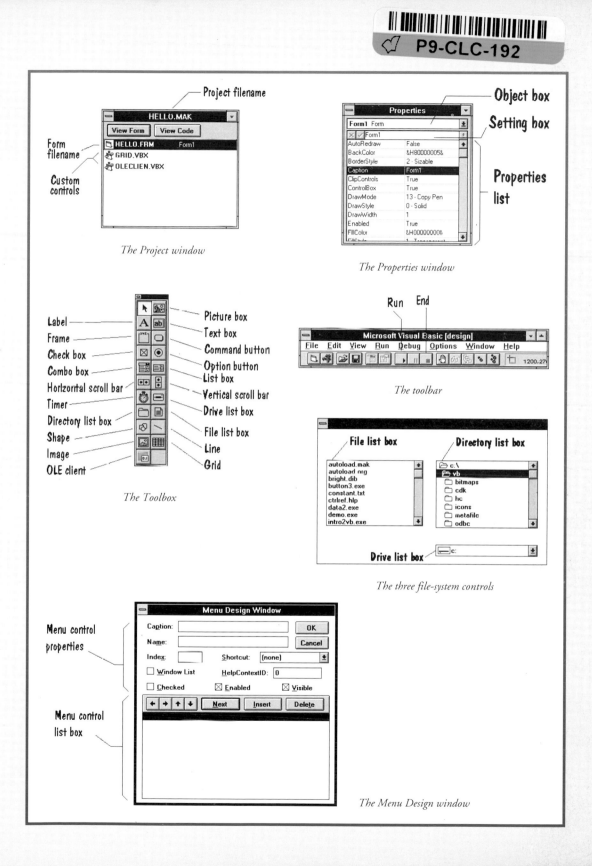

Project filename

Object box

Setting box

HELLO.MAK

View Form   View Code

HELLO.FRM   Form1
GRID.VBX
OLECLIEN.VBX

Form filename

Custom controls

The Project window

Properties

Form1 Form

Form1

AutoRedraw	False
BackColor	&H80000005&
BorderStyle	2 - Sizable
Caption	Form1
ClipControls	True
ControlBox	True
DrawMode	13 - Copy Pen
DrawStyle	0 - Solid
DrawWidth	1
Enabled	True
FillColor	&H00000000&

Properties list

The Properties window

Label
Frame
Check box
Combo box
Horizontal scroll bar
Timer
Directory list box
Shape
Image
OLE client

Picture box
Text box
Command button
Option button
List box
Vertical scroll bar
Drive list box
File list box
Line
Grid

The Toolbox

Run   End

Microsoft Visual Basic [design]

File   Edit   View   Run   Debug   Options   Window   Help

1200.27

The toolbar

File list box

autoload.mak
autoload.org
bright.dib
button3.exe
constant.txt
ctrlref.hlp
data2.exe
demo.exe
intro2vb.exe

Directory list box

c:\
vb
bitmaps
cdk
hc
icons
metafile
odbc

Drive list box   c:

The three file-system controls

Menu Design Window

Caption: OK

Name: Cancel

Index: Shortcut: [none]

Window List   HelpContextID: 0

Checked   Enabled   Visible

Next   Insert   Delete

Menu control properties

Menu control list box

The Menu Design window

Naming conventions for controls.

Control	Control Name Starts with the Characters	Example
Form	frm	frmMyForm
Check Box	chk	chkSound
Combo Box	cbo	cboSelection
Command Button	cmd	cmdExit
Directory List	dir	dirFiles
Drive List	drv	drvSource
File List	fil	filTarget
Frame	fra	fraChoices
Grid	grd	grdTV
Horizontal Scroll Bar	hsb	hsbSpeed
Image	img	imgMyImage
Label	lbl	lblInfo
Line	lin	linDiagonal
List Box	lst	lstChapters
Menu	mnu	mnuFile
Option Button	opt	optLevel1
Picture Box	pic	picMyPicture
Shape	shp	shpMyShape
Text Box	txt	txtUserArea
Timer	tmr	tmrMoveIt
Vertical Scroll Bar	vsb	vsbSpeed

QBColor() function numbers.

Color	Number
Black	0
Blue	1
Green	2
Cyan	3
Red	4
Magenta	5
Yellow	6
White	7
Gray	8
Light blue	9
Light green	10
Light cyan	11
Light red	12
Light magenta	13
Light yellow	14
Bright white	15

The data types that Visual Basic supports.

Data Type	Number of Bytes	Shortcut Notation	Range
Integer	2	%	-32,768 to 32,767
Long	4	&	-2,147,483,648 to 2,147,483,647
Single positive	4	!	1.401298E-45 to 3.402823E38
Single negative	4	!	-3.402823E38 to -1.401298E-45
Double positive	8	#	4.94065645841247D-24 to 1.79769313486232D308
Double negative	8	#	1.79769313486232D308 to -4.94065645841247D-324
Currency	8	[064]	-922337203685477.5808 to 922337203685466.5807
String	Depends on the number of characters in the string	$	A string may hold up to approximately 65,000 characters
Variant	Date, time, floating point, or string	(none)	Range of Date: from January 1, 0000 to December 31, 9999

The code of the special keys when used with the SendKeys statement.

Key	Use in SendKeys
Shift	+
Ctrl	^ (Above the 6 key)
Alt	%
Backspace	{BACKSPACE}
Break	{BREAK}
Caps Lock	{CAPLOCKS}
Clear	{CLEAR}
Del	{DELETE}
Down arrow	{DOWN}
End	{END}
Enter	{ENTER}
Esc	{ESCAPE}
Help	{HELP}
Home	{HOME}
Ins	{INSERT}
Left arrow	{LEFT}
Num Lock	{NUMLOCK}
Page Down	{PGDN}
Page Up	{PGUP}
Print Screen	{PRTSC}
Right arrow	{RIGHT}
Scroll Lock	{SCROLLLOCK}
Tab	{TAB}
Up arrow	{UP}
F1	{F1}
...	...
...	...
...	...
F16	{F16}

What's New in This Edition

- **Multimedia.** Multimedia is very popular, and nowadays PC vendors ship their PCs with multimedia equipment already installed in the PC. As you'll see, writing multimedia applications with Visual Basic is easy. You'll write programs that play MIDI files, CD audio, and movie AVI files.

- **Animation.** You'll learn how to create programs that display cartoon movies, and you'll learn how to synchronize sound with animation. In this chapter you'll also learn how to create programs that have animated icons.

- **Networks.** You'll learn how to write Visual Basic network-based programs and you'll get a basic understanding of how networks work.

- **Virtual reality–based programs.** You'll learn how to create virtual reality–based programs with Visual Basic.

- **Games.** You'll write impressive game programs with Visual Basic and you'll learn basic algorithms to build your own games.

- **VBX controls.** You'll learn about interesting VBX controls such as three-dimensional buttons and gauge controls.

- **Dynamic linked libraries (DLLs).** You'll learn how to write your own DLLs for Visual Basic.

Some of the programs you'll design in the bonus chapters require additional hardware and software. Even if you don't have the hardware and software necessary to run the programs, it is highly recommended that you read these chapters. This way, you'll gain an understanding of how things are done, and you might even consider upgrading your software/hardware. For example, on Bonus Day 3 you'll learn about networking. Even if you currently don't have a network, browse through this chapter. This chapter explains how you can connect your old PC to your new PC via a network (instead of throwing away or selling the old PC). Similarly, Bonus Day 1 discusses various hardware and software topics as they are related to multimedia technology. As another example, Bonus Day 5 teaches how to design game programs by using some of the VBXs of the Borland Visual Solutions Pack. Even if you don't own this package, it is a good idea to read the material in this chapter, because you'll understand how to design some interesting games with Visual Basic, and you might even get your own ideas regarding building your own DLLs or VBXs for designing game programs.

Teach Yourself
Visual Basic

in 21 Days,
Bestseller Edition

Teach Yourself
Visual Basic
in 21 Days,
Bestseller Edition

Nathan Gurewich
Ori Gurewich

SAMS
PUBLISHING

201 West 103rd Street
Indianapolis, Indiana 46290

Overview

Contents

Acknowledgments

We would like to thank Angelique Brittingham, the development editor of this book; Bruce Graves, Sr., and Keith Brophy, the technical editors; and Kitty Wilson, the production editor.

We would also like to thank all the other people at Sams who contributed to this book.

Thanks also to Microsoft Corporation, which supplied us with technical information and various betas and upgrades of the software product.

About the Authors

Nathan Gurewich and Ori Gurewich are the authors of several best-selling books in the areas of Visual Basic for Windows, C/C++ programming, multimedia programming, database design and programming, and other topics.

Nathan Gurewich

Nathan Gurewich holds a master's degree in electrical engineering from Columbia University, New York, and a bachelor's degree in electrical engineering from Hofstra University, Long Island, New York. Since the introduction of the PC, the author has been involved in the design and implementation of commercial software packages for the PC. He is an expert in the field of PC programming and in providing consulting services in the area of local area networks, wide area networks, database management and design, and software marketing.

Nathan Gurewich can be contacted via CompuServe (CompuServe ID 75277,2254).

Ori Gurewich

Ori Gurewich holds a bachelor's degree in electrical engineering from Stony Brook University, Stony Brook, New York. His background includes working as a senior software engineer and as a software consultant engineer for companies, and developing professional multimedia and Windows applications. He is an expert in the field of PC programming and network communications, and has developed various multimedia algorithms for the PC. Ori Gurewich can be contacted via CompuServe (CompuServe ID 72072,312).

Introduction

This book teaches you how to use the Microsoft Visual Basic for Windows package. After reading this book you'll be able to write advanced Windows programs using the Visual Basic programming language.

The word *Basic* in Visual Basic may be misleading. You might think that all serious Windows applications should be written using the C/C++ compiler and SDK for Windows. However, this is *not* the case. After reading this book you'll be able to write advanced Windows programs in a fraction of the time it takes to write the same programs using other programming languages.

As its name suggests, a big portion of the programming with Visual Basic is accomplished visually. This means that during design time you are able to see how your program will look during runtime. This is a great advantage over other programming languages, because you are able to change and experiment with your design until you are satisfied with the colors, sizes, and images that are included in your program.

Perhaps the most powerful feature of Visual Basic is its capability to use dynamic linked libraries (DLLs). If you are unfamiliar with the concept of DLLs, be patient—the topic is covered in this book. For now, however, just remember that DLLs extend the capabilities of Visual Basic. No matter what application you are developing, if the programming feature you need is not included in the out-of-the-box Visual Basic package, you'll be able to add the feature by using a DLL. For example, in this book you'll learn how to use DLLs to extend the capability of Visual Basic so your program will be able to play music through the PC speaker without any additional hardware.

The book is divided into 28 days, 7 of which are bonus days, and you are expected to read and learn a chapter each day. However, many readers may feel confident enough to work through two (or more) chapters in a day. The number of chapters you should read each day depends on your previous programming experience with Windows and/or any other programming language.

The book assumes no prior experience with Visual Basic. So take your time when reading the chapters, and be sure to learn and enter the code of all the programs covered in each chapter. Once you understand the programs, experiment with them for a while. That is, change and modify the code to see what happens when you alter the programs in some way. Remember, the only way to learn a programming language is to actually write programs.

At the end of each chapter you'll find quizzes and exercises, as well as the solutions to them. Be sure to perform these quizzes and exercises.

Visual Basic is interesting and fun because it enables you to write sophisticated professional programs for Windows in a very short time.

So relax, and prepare yourself for a very enjoyable journey.

How to Use This Book

This book starts at the beginning, taking people who know nothing about Visual Basic and stepping them through 21 lessons plus 7 bonus lessons on to programming proficiency.

Within this book you'll find hands-on tutorials, timely tips, and easy-to-understand technical information to help you get your footing with Visual Basic. You begin by writing simple programs and progress to complex, useful programs that you can apply to your day-to-day situations.

Special features that you'll see throughout the book are the following:

DO/DON'T boxes give you specific guidance on what to do and what to avoid doing when programming in Visual Basic.

Notes: These provide essential background information so that you not only do things with Visual Basic, but have a good understanding of what you are doing and why.

Tips: These provide useful information on improving your programming.

Who Should Read This Book

Teach Yourself Visual Basic in 21 Days, Bestseller Edition has you, the beginner, in mind when explaining concepts and techniques within programming. No prior programming experience is required; however, knowing how to program in other languages certainly helps.

Conventions

This book uses various typefaces to help you differentiate between Visual Basic code and regular English, and also to help you identify important concepts. Actual Visual Basic code is typeset in a special monospace font. When new terms are introduced in the text, they are typeset in *italics*.

With this book you will write many Visual Basic programs. Therefore, you must install the Visual Basic package (if you haven't installed it yet). Use the following steps to install the package:

☐ Insert Disk 1 into your A: or B: drive.

☐ Start Windows.

☐ Select Run from the File Manager of Windows.

Windows responds by displaying the Run dialog box.

☐ Click the Browse button.

Windows responds by displaying the Browse dialog box.

☐ Change the content of the Drives list box to A: (or B:). (The Drives list box appears in the bottom-right portion of the Browse dialog box. To change the content of the Drives list box, click the arrow icon and select the drive. Windows responds by displaying a list of files that reside in the A:, or B:, drive. One of these files is SETUP.EXE, the file that installs the Visual Basic package.)

☐ Click the file SETUP.EXE and click the OK button.

Windows responds by executing the SETUP.EXE program of Visual Basic.

☐ Follow the instructions the SETUP program gives you during the installation of Visual Basic.

Where You're Going

Okay, you've installed Visual Basic successfully. Now what? In Chapter 1, "Writing Your First Program," you'll write your first Visual Basic program. This will give you insight into how easy it is to write a real Windows program with Visual Basic and why the package is called Visual Basic.

During the rest of the first week, you'll learn to write many more programs. Each program teaches you a new concept in Visual Basic and shows you how to apply the concept in your programs (as always, the only way to learn programming is to actually write programs, and Visual Basic is no exception).

Writing Your First Program

In this chapter you'll write your first Visual Basic program. Writing Visual Basic programs involves two steps: the visual programming step and the code programming step.

During the visual programming step, you design your programs by using the tools that come with the Visual Basic package. These tools let you design your programs by using the mouse and the keyboard. To perform the visual programming portion, you do not have to do any code writing! All you have to know is how to operate and use the software tools of Visual Basic. This chapter concentrates on learning how to use the visual tools of Visual Basic.

In the code programming step, you write programs using a text editor. The programs are composed of statements written in the Visual Basic programming language. The process of writing such code is similar to the process of writing code for other programming languages.

About This Chapter

If you browse through subsequent chapters of this book, you may notice that this chapter is not a typical chapter. This chapter concentrates on the visual programming aspect of Visual Basic. As such, it mainly concentrates on teaching you how to use the Visual Basic software tools. It is the job of subsequent chapters to teach you how to write code in the Visual Basic programming language.

Creating a Working Directory

Before starting the process of writing Visual Basic programs, create a directory that will contain the files of your programs. This chapter assumes that you already have a directory called C:\VBPROG\CH01. You will be instructed to save files into this directory.

Use the following steps to create the working directory:

☐ Use the DOS command MD (or use the File Manager program of Windows) to create the directory C:\VBPROG\CH01.

The Hello Program

When you write the Visual Basic program called Hello, it should do the following:

☐ Upon startup of the program, the window shown in Figure 1.1 appears. As you can see, the window of the program contains three command buttons (Display Hello, Clear, and Exit) and an empty text box.

Figure 1.1.
The Hello program.

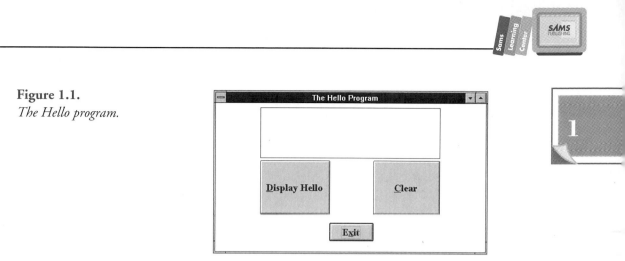

☐ When you click the Display Hello button, the text Hello World! is displayed in the text box (see Figure 1.2).

Figure 1.2.
Displaying text inside the text box.

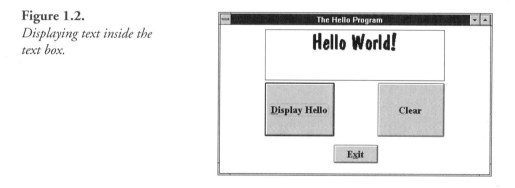

☐ When you click the Clear button, the text in the text box disappears.

☐ To terminate the program, click the Exit button.

Creating a New Project

Now that you know what the Hello program is supposed to do, you can write the program.

The very first thing that you need to do is open a new project.

Use the following steps to create a new project for the Hello program:

☐ Start Visual Basic.

☐ Select New project from the File menu.

> *Visual Basic responds by displaying various windows on the desktop. One of the windows that is displayed is a blank form with a caption, Form1 (see Figure 1.3). Your job is to use the various tools of Visual Basic until the blank form looks like the form shown in Figure 1.1.*

Figure 1.3.
The blank form.

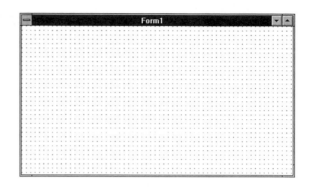

Saving the New Project

Although you haven't yet made any changes or modifications to the blank form, you should save the project at this early stage of the design. When you save the project, two files are saved:

- The make file. This file has the .MAK file extension, and it contains information that Visual Basic uses for building the project.
- The form file. This file has the .FRM file extension, and it contains information about the form.

Now use the following steps to save the two files of the Hello project HELLO.MAK (the make file) and HELLO.FRM (the form file):

☐ Select Save Project As from the File menu.

   Visual Basic displays the dialog box shown in Figure 1.4, asking you if you want to save the form.

Figure 1.4.
Saving the form.

☐ Select the Yes button to indicate that you want to save the form.

   Visual Basic responds by displaying a Save File As dialog box.

☐ Select the directory C:\VBPROG\CH01 as the directory where the file will be saved, and change the default filename of the form from Form1.frm to HELLO.FRM (see Figure 1.5).

Figure 1.5.
Saving the form as Hello.frm.

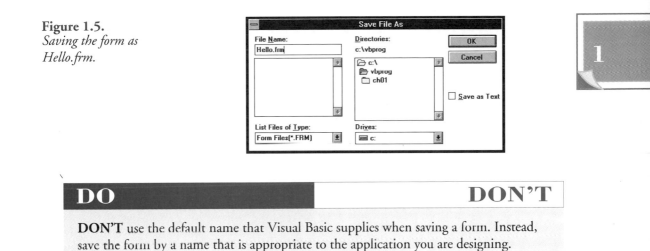

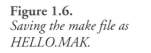

> **DON'T** use the default name that Visual Basic supplies when saving a form. Instead, save the form by a name that is appropriate to the application you are designing.

☐ Visual Basic now displays the Save Project As dialog box. The default filename that Visual Basic supplies is Project1.mak. However, you need to name the make file with a name that is more appropriate to the particular application you are developing. Save the make file as HELLO.MAK in the directory C:\VBPROG\CH01 (see Figure 1.6).

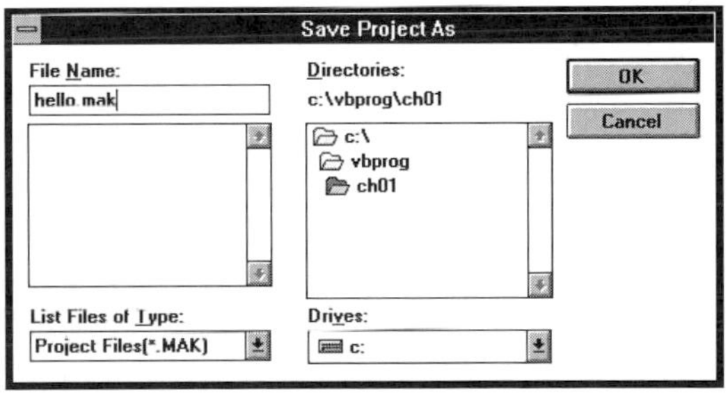

Figure 1.6.
Saving the make file as HELLO.MAK.

> **DON'T** use the default name Visual Basic supplies when saving a make file. Instead, save the file by a name that is appropriate to the application you are designing.

Now you have saved two files: HELLO.MAK (the make file) and HELLO.FRM (the form file).

Examining the Project Window

At this point, your project is called HELLO.MAK, and it consists of a single form file: the HELLO.FRM file. However, in subsequent chapters your project will contain many more files. One of the tools that Visual Basic offers is the project window, which enables you to see the various files that are included in the project. (You'll learn to appreciate this feature as your projects get more complicated.)

Use the following steps to examine the project window:

☐ Select Project from the Window menu.

> *The project window pops up, as shown in Figure 1.7. (If you are using the Professional Edition of Visual Basic, your project window should look like the one shown in Figure 1.8.) Depending on the particular version you are using, the project window may have more (or fewer) items in it.*

Figure 1.7.

The project window.

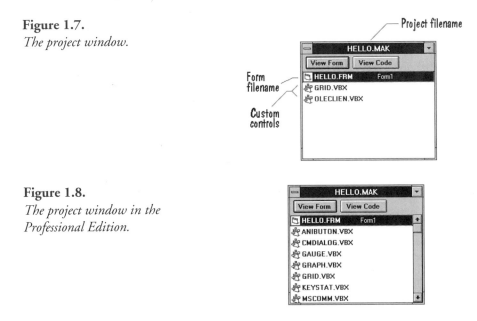

Figure 1.8.

The project window in the Professional Edition.

The title of the project window contains the name of the project. Because you saved the project as HELLO.MAK, the title of the project window contains this name.

The first file that appears in the project window contains the name of the form. Because you saved the form as HELLO.FRM, this is the first file that appears in the project window.

The project window also contains files with .VBX extensions, called custom controls, which are not covered in this chapter.

Changing the Caption Property of the Form

The blank form that was created by Visual Basic has the caption Form1 (see Figure 1.3). This is the default caption that Visual Basic assigned to the blank form. Although you may leave the caption of the form as Form1, it is a good idea to assign a friendlier caption to the form. As shown in Figure 1.1, the caption of the finished form should be The Hello Program.

Here is how you change the caption of the blank form to The Hello Program:

☐ Make sure that the blank form is selected. You can easily recognize whether the form is selected by examining its caption. If the caption is highlighted, the form is selected.

If the form is not selected, simply click anywhere inside the form. An alternate method of selecting the form is to select Project from the Window menu, highlight the form item in the project window, and click the View Form button that appears in the project window.

☐ Select properties from the Window menu.

Visual Basic responds by displaying the properties window (see Figure 1.9).

Figure 1.9.
The properties window.

☐ Highlight the Caption item in the properties window, then click inside the setting box of the properties window (see Figure 1.9 for the location of the setting box). Visual Basic now lets you edit the Caption property.

☐ In the setting box of the properties window, type The Hello Program (see Figure 1.10).

Congratulations! You have finished changing the Caption property of the form. Take a look at the blank form. Now its caption is The Hello Program.

Figure 1.10.
Changing the Caption property of the form.

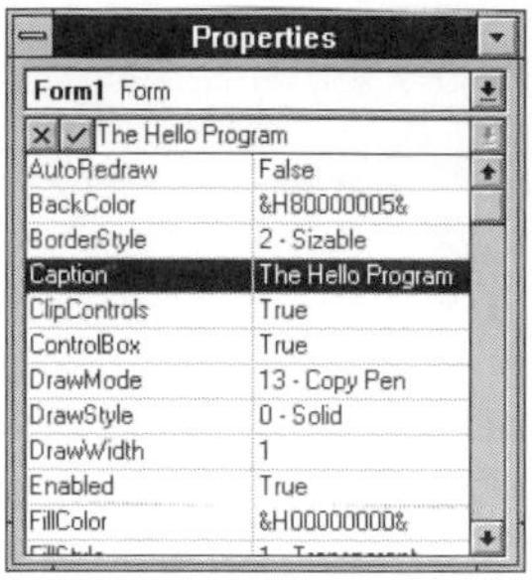

What Is a Property?

The caption is just one of the properties of the form. As you can see from the properties window, the form has many other properties. To understand what a property is, you have to understand that Visual Basic programs deal with objects. Examples of objects are forms, command buttons, scroll bars, and pictures.

The properties of an object define how the object looks and behaves. For example, a form is an object. The Caption property of the form defines the text that appears in the title of the form. Another property of the form object is BackColor. As implied by its name, this property defines the background color of the form. Change the BackColor property of the form:

☐ Make sure that the form is selected by clicking anywhere inside the form.

☐ To display the properties window, select Properties from the Window menu.

☐ Click the BackColor property that appears in the properties window.

☐ Click the three-dots box that appears in the setting box (see Figure 1.11).

> *Visual Basic responds by displaying a color palette window (see Figure 1.12).*

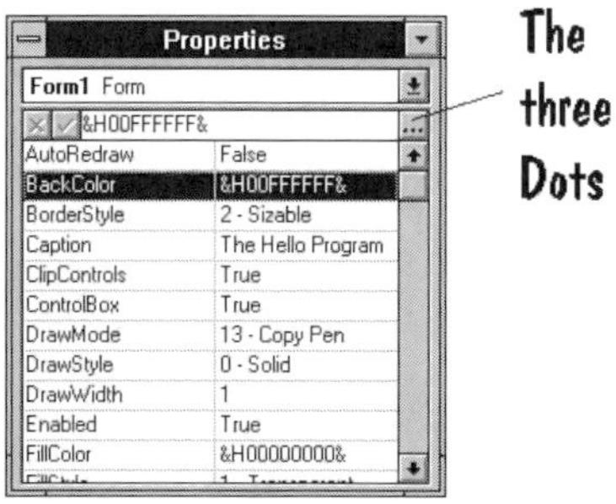

Figure 1.11.
The BackColor property.

The three Dots

☐ Select the color of your choice by clicking on the desired color.

Figure 1.12.
The color palette.

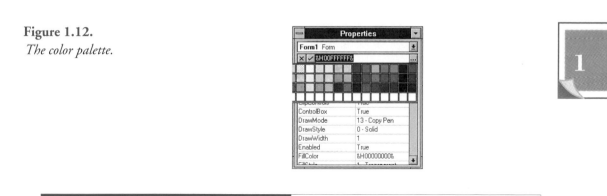

DO	DON'T

DO examine the setting box when changing a property. If the setting box has three dots, clicking the three dots displays a window that lets you select a value with the mouse.

Try a few colors by repeating the process until you are happy with your color selection.

Changing the Name Property of the Form

Each object in Visual Basic must have a name. The name of the object is defined in the Name property of the object. When you created the new project of the Hello program, Visual Basic automatically set the Name property of the form to Form1.

Now change the Name property of the form:

☐ Make sure that the form is selected by clicking anywhere inside the form.

☐ Select Properties from the Window menu.

☐ Highlight the Name property in the properties window, then click inside the setting box of the properties window. Visual Basic now lets you edit the Name property.

☐ In the setting box of the properties window, type frmHello.

In the preceding step, you changed the Name property of the form from Form1 to frmHello. Throughout this book, the first three characters of the Name property of objects are three letters that indicate the type of object. Therefore, the first three characters of the Name property of a form are *frm*, as in frmHello.

11

DO	**DON'T**

DO rename objects so that their names reflect their purposes in the program. For example, frmHello is the name of a form that is used by the Hello program.

Saving Your Work

You have not yet finished preparing the form. (Remember that upon completion, the form should look like the one shown in Figure 1.1.) Nevertheless, it is a good idea to save the work you have done so far, because you'll have to start designing the form all over again if for some reason your PC system collapses before you save your work. This is especially true when working in the Windows environment. And as you'll see in subsequent chapters, designing forms may involve opening and executing other Windows applications such as Paintbrush and Word for Windows. If one of these other applications collapses, it may take down the whole system with it. So be safe—save your work from time to time.

Use the following step to save your work:

☐ Select Save Project from the File menu.

Adding the Exit Button to the frmHello Form

As shown in Figure 1.1, the final form should have three command buttons in it: Display Hello, Clear, and Exit.

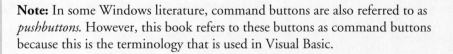

Note: In some Windows literature, command buttons are also referred to as *pushbuttons*. However, this book refers to these buttons as command buttons because this is the terminology that is used in Visual Basic.

To place a command button inside your form, you have to pick it up from the Toolbox.

The Toolbox

The Toolbox is a window that contains control objects. It is your job to pick up a control from the Toolbox and place it inside your form. Figure 1.13 shows the Toolbox. (This figure shows the control objects that come with the Standard Edition of Visual Basic.) Depending on the particular version you are using, the Toolbox may have fewer (or more) items in it.

Figure 1.13.
The Toolbox.

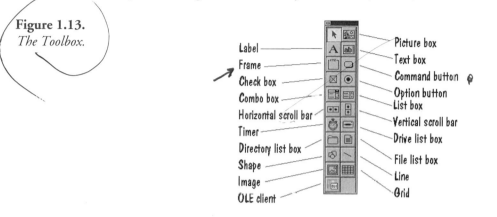

Placing the Exit Button Inside the Form

Use the following steps to place a command button inside the form:

☐ Double-click the command button control. As you can see from Figure 1.13, the command button is the third object from the top in the right column of the Toolbox.

Visual Basic responds by placing a command button at the center of the form (see Figure 1.14).

Visual Basic assigns various default properties to the command button that you placed on the form. For example, the default Caption property of this command button is Command1.

Visual Basic also assigns the default name Command1 to the Name property of the command button.

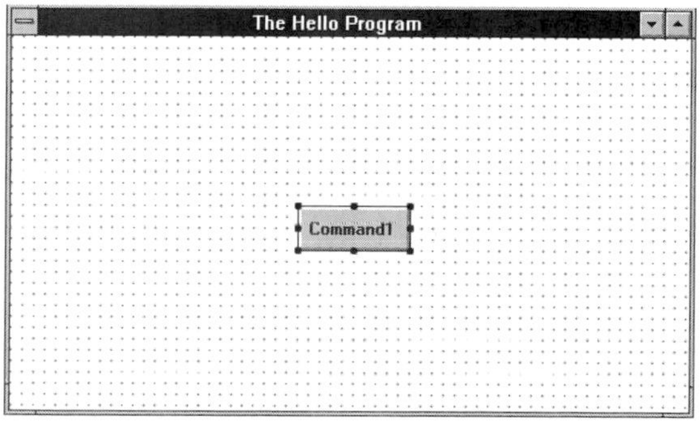

Figure 1.14.
Placing a command button.

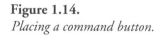

Changing the Name Property of the Exit Button

Because the command button that you just created serves as the Exit button, change its Name property to cmdExit:

☐ Select Properties from the Window menu.

☐ Make sure that the object box of the properties window displays the Command1 command button. (See Figure 1.9 for the location of the object box.)

> **Note:** Currently, the form has two objects: the form frmHello and the command button Command1. The properties window lists the properties of the object whose name currently appears in the object box (see Figure 1.9). To switch to another object, click on the arrow of the object box, and select the desired object (see Figure 1.15).

☐ Change the Name property of Command1 from Command1 to cmdExit.

Note the naming convention for the Name property of the command button. Because the object is a command button, the first three characters of its name are *cmd*. Also, because this command button serves as the Exit button, its full name is cmdExit.

Figure 1.15.

The properties of the command button.

Click here to switch to another object.

Changing the Caption Property of the Exit Button

The default caption that Visual Basic assigns to the command button is Command1. Because this command button serves as the Exit button, a more appropriate caption is Exit.

☐ Change the Caption property of cmdExit from Command1 to E&xit.

The & character before the *x* in E&xit causes Visual Basic to display the *x* underlined (see Figure 1.1). Upon execution of the program, pressing Alt+x produces the same result as clicking the Exit button.

Note: When assigning a caption to a button, always prefix one of the characters with the & character. This underlines the prefixed character, and during execution time your users will be able to either click the button or press Alt+*key* (where *key* is the underlined character).

Changing the Location of the Exit Button

As you can see from Figure 1.1, the Exit button should be near the bottom of the form.

☐ Drag the Exit button to the desired location. (To drag the button, click anywhere inside the button, and without releasing the mouse's left button, move the mouse.)

Changing the Font Properties of the Exit Button

As shown in Figure 1.1, the font of the Exit button is different from the default font that Visual Basic assigned to the caption of the button you created. Use the following steps to change the font:

☐ Change the FontName property of the cmdExit button to Times New Roman.

☐ Change the size of the font by changing the FontSize property of the cmdExit button. (In Figure 1.1, the FontSize property of the cmdExit button is 13.5.)

Note: One of the main advantages of Visual Basic programming is that you instantaneously see the results of your visual programming. Always experiment and try different options (that is, try different fonts, different sizes, and so on) until you are satisfied with the results.

Adding the Other Buttons to the frmHello Form

Now it's time to add two more command buttons to the form: the Display Hello button and the Clear button.

Placing the Buttons

☐ Add the Display Hello button to the form by double-clicking the command button in the Toolbox. Now drag the new command button to the left. (This button serves as the Display Hello button.)

☐ Double-click the command button in the Toolbox again, then drag the new command button to the right. (This button serves as the Clear button.)

Resizing the Buttons

The default sizes of the Display Hello and the Clear buttons are smaller than the buttons shown in Figure 1.1.

☐ Enlarge these buttons. To enlarge/shrink an object, select the object by clicking on it and dragging one of its sizing handles until the object reaches the required size. For example, to resize an object in the horizontal direction, drag one of its horizontal sizing handles (see Figure 1.16). Likewise, to resize an object in the vertical direction, drag one of its vertical sizing handles.

Figure 1.16.
Resizing horizontally.

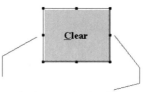

Drag a horizontal size handle
to enlarge/shrink the size of
the object horizontally.

Changing the Name Properties

The default names that Visual Basic assigned to the command buttons that you just created are Command1 and Command2. More appropriate names are cmdHello and cmdClear.

☐ Change the Name property of the left command button to cmdHello.

☐ Change the Name property of the right command button to cmdClear.

Changing the Caption Properties

As shown in Figure 1.1, the left button should have the caption Display Hello, and the right button should have the caption Clear.

☐ Change the Caption property of the left button to &Display Hello.

☐ Change the Caption property of the right button to &Clear.

Changing the Font Properties

As shown in Figure 1.1, the Display Hello and Clear buttons should have a different font and font size from the default font that Visual Basic assigns to your command buttons.

☐ Change the FontName property of the cmdHello button to Times New Roman.

☐ Change the FontSize property of the cmdHello button to 13.5.

☐ Change the FontName property of the cmdClear button to Times New Roman.

☐ Change the FontSize property of the cmdClear button to 13.5.

Adding the Text Box Object to the frmHello Form

There is one more object to add to the form: the text box object. A text box object is a rectangular area in which text is displayed. The text may be inserted into the text box during design time, as well as during execution time.

Placing the Text Box Inside the Form

The text box object is the second object in the right column of the Toolbox (see Figure 1.13). Depending on your particular version of Visual Basic, the locations of the objects inside the Toolbox may be different from the locations shown in Figure 1.13.

Use the following steps to place the text box inside the form:

☐ Double-click its icon in the Toolbox.

☐ Move and resize the text box until it looks like the text box shown in Figure 1.1.

Changing the Properties of the Text Box

Use the following steps to modify several properties of the text box:

☐ Change the Name property of the text box from the default name Text1 to txtDisplay.

☑ The default Text property of the text box is Text1. This means that upon execution of the Hello program, the text Text1 appears in the text box. Because you want the text box to be empty upon startup of the program, delete the text of this property.

☐ The default FontName property of the text box is MS Sans Serif. Change the FontName property to Dom Casual. (If your PC is not equipped with the Dom Casual font, use another font.)

☐ The default FontSize property of the text box is 8.25. Change the FontSize property to 30. (If your PC does not support this font size, use a different font size.)

☐ The default Alignment property of the text box is 0-Left Justify, which means that the text in the text box is aligned to the left. Because you want the text to appear at the center of the text box, change the Alignment property to 2-Center.

☐ As it turns out, Visual Basic refuses to place the text in the center unless the MultiLine property of the text box is set to True. So, in addition to having the Alignment property set to 2-Center, you must also change the MultiLine property of the text box to True. By setting the MultiLine property to True, Visual Basic is able to display more than one line in the text box, so go ahead and change the MultiLine property of the txtDisplay text box to True.

Building Forms from Figures and Tables

The visual programming portion is now completed. To save your work, select Save Project from the File menu.

Throughout this book you will be instructed to build many other forms. However, this book does not instruct you to construct the form in the same way that you were instructed to build the Hello form. Instead, you have to build the form by looking at the figure of the completed form (such as Figure 1.1) and following a properties table. A properties table is a table that contains all the objects that are included in the form. The table also lists objects' properties that are different from the default properties. Your job is to follow the table, line by line, and to change the properties' values to the values that appear in the table. Table 1.1 is the properties table of the Hello form.

Table 1.1. The properties table of the Hello program.

Object	Property	Setting
Form	**Name**	**frmHello**
	Caption	The Hello Program

Object	Property	Setting
Command Button	**Name**	**cmdExit**
	Caption	E&xit
	FontName	Times New Roman
	FontSize	13.5
Command Button	**Name**	**cmdHello**
	Caption	&Display Hello
	FontName	Times New Roman
	FontSize	13.5
Command Button	**Name**	**cmdClear**
	Caption	&Clear
	FontName	Times New Roman
	FontSize	13.5
Text Box	**Name**	**txtDisplay**
	Text	(empty)
	FontName	Dom Casual
	FontSize	30
	Alignment	2-Center
	MultiLine	True

Attaching Code to the Objects

Because you placed the objects inside the form and set the properties of the objects, the visual programming portion of the job is complete. Now it is time to attach some code to the objects.

Visual Basic is an event-driven programming language. This means that code is executed as a response to an event. For example, if you click the Exit button, the code that corresponds to this event is executed. Likewise, if you click the Display Hello button, the code that corresponds to this event is executed. Your job is to write the appropriate code and attach it to the appropriate object and event. Does this sound complicated? Well, it is actually very easy! Start by attaching some code to the Exit button.

Attaching Code to the Exit Button

Use the following steps to attach code to the Exit button:

☐ Double-click the Exit button.

> *Visual Basic responds by displaying the code window (you write code inside this window), which is shown in Figure 1.17.*

Figure 1.17.
Attaching code to the cmdExit button.

Visual Basic makes it very easy for you to recognize which code is currently being displayed in the code window. As shown in Figure 1.17, the top-left combo box and the top-right combo box display the name of the object and the name of the event that the code will be attached to.

As you can see from Figure 1.17, Visual Basic already placed two lines of code inside the code window:

```
Sub cmdExit_Click ()

End Sub
```

Code can be written between these two lines. When you're finished writing the code, the code window looks like this:

```
Sub cmdExit_Click ()
        .................
        .................
        .... Your code....
        .................
        .................
End Sub
```

The First and Last Lines of the Code

As stated, Visual Basic already wrote the first and last lines of code for you. The first line of code starts with the word Sub. Sub is a keyword that indicates that a procedure starts here. A procedure is a code dedicated for a particular event. The name of the procedure is cmdExit_Click().

The last line of code is End Sub. End Sub marks the end of the procedure.

The Name of the Procedure

The name of the procedure is cmdExit_Click(). Why did Visual Basic assign this name to the procedure? Because you double-clicked the cmdExit button, Visual Basic knows that you are attempting to attach code to the Exit button. Therefore, the first half of the subroutine name is cmdExit_.

The second half of the name is _Click(). Why did Visual Basic assign this name? Because the event for which you are now writing code is the click event.

The Code of the *cmdExit_Click()* Procedure

What code should you write inside the cmdExit_Click() procedure? Because this procedure is executed whenever you click the Exit button, the code to be inserted in this procedure is code that should cause the program to terminate. The code that causes a Visual Basic program to terminate is the End statement.

☐ Type End inside the cmdExit_Click() procedure:

```
Sub cmdExit_Click()

    End

End Sub
```

(Note that in Visual Basic the code you type is not case sensitive.) You have finished attaching code to the cmdExit_Click() procedure.

Executing the Hello Program

Although you have not yet finished attaching code to the rest of the objects, you can now execute the Hello program and see how the code you attached to the Exit button works for you.

☐ Save your work by selecting Save Project from the File menu.

☐ Select Start from the Run menu.

> *Visual Basic responds by executing your program. The window of the application pops up, as shown in Figure 1.1.*

You may now click the Display Hello button, but nothing happens. Why? You have not yet attached any code to this button. You may click the Clear button, but again nothing happens, because you have not attached any code to this object.

Now click the Exit button. As a response to the clicking, the code in the procedure cmdExit_Click() is executed. Because the code inside this procedure consists of code that causes the program to terminate, the Hello program terminates.

Attaching More Code to the *cmdExit_Click()* Procedure

Use the following steps to attach more code inside the cmdExit_Click() procedure.

☐ Double-click the cmdExit button.

> *Visual Basic responds by displaying the* cmdExit_Click() *procedure.*

☐ Add the Beep statement before the End statement as follows:

```
Sub cmdExit_Click()

    Beep
    End

End Sub
```

☐ Save your work (select Save Project from the File menu).

☐ Execute the Hello program (select Start from the Run menu).

The Beep statement causes the PC to beep. So whenever you click the Exit button, the PC beeps and then the End statement is executed, causing the Hello program to terminate.

Attaching Code to the Display Hello Button

Use the following steps to attach code to the Display Hello button.

☐ Make sure that the frmHello form is selected.

☐ Double-click the Display Hello button.

> *Visual Basic responds by displaying the* cmdHello_Click() *procedure, with two lines of code already written:*

```
Sub cmdHello_Click ()

End Sub
```

The preceding procedure is executed whenever you click the Display Hello button during the execution of the Hello program.

1

So what code should you insert inside this procedure? It depends on what you want to happen when you click the Display Hello button. In the Hello program, you want the program to display the words Hello World! in the text box.

☐ Type the following code:

```
txtDisplay.Text = "Hello World!"
```

inside the cmdHello_Click() procedure. When you finish, the procedure should look like this:

```
Sub cmdHello_Click ()

    txtDisplay.Text = "Hello World!"

End Sub
```

txtDisplay is the name of the text box object (the text box in which the words Hello World! are displayed).

This statement:

```
txtDisplay.Text = "Hello World!"
```

assigns the value Hello World! to the Text property of txtDisplay. (The Text property of a text box contains the text that the text box displays.)

DO	DON'T

DO assign a new value to a property from within the code of the program, using the following format:

```
ObjectName.Property = "The new value of the property"
```

For example, to change the Text property of the txtDisplay text box to Hello World! use this:

```
txtDisplay.Text = "Hello World!"
```

Attaching Code to the Clear Button

Use the following steps to attach code to the Clear button.

☐ Double-click the Clear button.

Visual Basic responds by displaying the code window with the cmdClear_Click() procedure in it.

The code of this procedure should clear the text box. In other words, the Text property of the txtDisplay text box should change to null. You accomplish this by inserting the following statement inside the procedure:

```
txtDisplay.Text = ""
```

☐ Type this statement:

```
txtDisplay.Text - ""
```

inside the procedure so that the procedure looks like this:

```
Sub cmdClear_Click ()

    txtDisplay.Text = ""

End Sub
```

☐ Save your work by selecting Save Project from the File menu.

Executing the Hello Program

The Hello program is complete. Use the following steps to execute the program:

☐ Select Start from the Run menu.

☐ Click the Display Hello and Clear buttons to display and clear the words `Hello World!` in the text box.

☐ You may use the keys Alt+D and Alt+C. Using these keys has the same effect as clicking the Display Hello and Clear buttons.

☐ To terminate the program, click the Exit button.

Note that the text box displays the text centered in Dom Casual font, because during design time you set the FontName property of the text box to Dom Casual, and the Alignment property to 2-Center.

Other Events

The Hello program makes use of the `Click` event for the Command buttons. There are other events that a Visual Basic program may use. Each event has its own procedure.

The *KeyDown* Event

Now look at the procedure that corresponds to the `KeyDown` event. The `KeyDown` event occurs whenever you press a key on the keyboard.

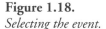

To see the KeyDown procedure of the Exit button do the following:

☐ Select the frmHello form.

☐ Double-click the Exit button.

By default, Visual Basic displays the procedure that corresponds to the Click event.

Because you want to look at the procedure that corresponds to the KeyDown event, switch to the KeyDown procedure by clicking the Proc combo box (see Figure 1.18).

Figure 1.18.
Selecting the event.

```
┌──────────────────── HELLO.FRM ────────────────────┐
│  Object: cmdExit      ▲  Proc: Click          ▲    │
│                                   ┌───────────────┐ │
│  Sub cmdExit_Click ()             │Click          │ │
│                                   │DragDrop       │ │
│  End Sub                          │DragOver       │ │
│                                   │GotFocus       │ │
│                                   │KeyDown      ✓ │ │
│                                   │KeyPress       │ │
│                                   │KeyUp          │ │
│                                   │LostFocus      │ │
│                                   └───────────────┘ │
└────────────────────────────────────────────────────┘
```

Visual Basic responds by dropping down a list that contains all the possible events that are associated with the cmdExit object.

☐ Click the KeyDown item in the list.

Visual Basic responds by displaying the cmdExit_KeyDown procedure:

```
Sub cmdExit_KeyDown (KeyCode As Integer,
                     Shift   As Integer)

End Sub
```

The first line of the procedure that Visual Basic automatically writes for the KeyDown event is a little different from the first line that Visual Basic automatically writes for the Click event.

At this point, do not add any code to the cmdExit_KeyDown procedure. (You went through this exercise to become familiar with accessing the procedures of other events.)

Creating an Executable File (HELLO.EXE)

Earlier you executed the Hello program by selecting Start from the Run menu. You don't want your users to execute the program in this manner (your users may not even own the Visual Basic package).

To be able to distribute the Hello program, you need to generate the EXE file HELLO.EXE:

☐ Select Make EXE File from the File menu.

Visual Basic responds by displaying the Make EXE File dialog box (see Figure 1.19).

Figure 1.19.

The Make EXE file dialog box.

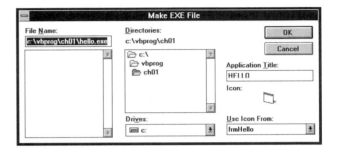

☐ Save the file as HELLO.EXE in the directory C:\VBPROG\CH01.

You now have the file HELLO.EXE in the directory C:\VBPROG\CH01. You may execute HELLO.EXE just as you would any other Windows program.

Summary

In this chapter you wrote your first Visual Basic program. You learned about the steps necessary to write a Visual Basic program: the visual programming step and the code programming step.

In the visual programming step, you placed objects inside the form and set their properties.

In the code programming step you selected a procedure by selecting the object and the event, and then you inserted code inside the procedure. This code is executed during runtime whenever the event occurs.

Q&A

Q The title of this book is *Teach Yourself Visual Basic in 21 Days.* **Can I read and learn the book in fewer (or more) days?**

A Yes. Some people work through a couple chapters each day. You should learn at your own pace.

Q **Can I write professional programs using Visual Basic?**

A Yes. Visual Basic is designed so you can write fancy, advanced Windows applications in a very short time.

Q **What is the difference between a command button and a pushbutton?**

A Pushbuttons and command buttons are the same thing. Visual Basic literature refers to this object as a command button (other Windows literature sometimes refers to this object as a pushbutton).

Q **I get confused! There are many windows on the desktop: form, project, properties, Toolbox, the color palette, and so on. Is there any good trick for finding and selecting a particular window?**

A At any point during your design, you may select Project from the Window menu. This pops up the project window.

You may then highlight the Form item in the project window, then click either the View Form button or the View Code button. If you click View Form, the form is selected. You can pop up the properties window by selecting Properties from the Window menu, or you can pop up the Toolbox by selecting the Toolbox item from the Window menu.

After practicing for a while, you'll be able to maneuver among the various windows without any difficulty.

Quiz

1. What are the two steps in the design process of a Visual Basic program?
2. What is the first thing that you have to do when writing a new Visual Basic program?
3. Give several examples of objects and their properties.
4. Which of the following is not a Visual Basic object?

   a. command button
   b. form
   c. variable
   d. text box

5. Describe how you attach code to an object.
6. BUG BUSTER. There is something wrong in the following statement:

   ```
   txtDisplay.Text = Hi there!
   ```

   What's wrong with it?

Exercise

Build the form shown in Figure 1.20 from Table 1.2.

Table 1.2. The properties table of Exercise 1.

Object	Property	Setting
Form	Name	frmExercise1
	Caption	Exercise 1.1
Horizontal Scroll Bar	Name	hsbSpeed
	Min	20
	Max	100
Vertical Scroll Bar	Name	vsbAmount
	Min	-10
	Max	10
Command Button	Name	cmdExit
	Caption	E&xit
Check Box	Name	chkSound
	Caption	Sound
Check Box	Name	chkColor
	Caption	Color
Option Button	Name	optYellow
	Caption	Yellow
Option Button	Name	optWhite
	Caption	White
Option Button	Name	optBlue
	Caption	Blue
Option Button	Name	optGreen
	Caption	Green

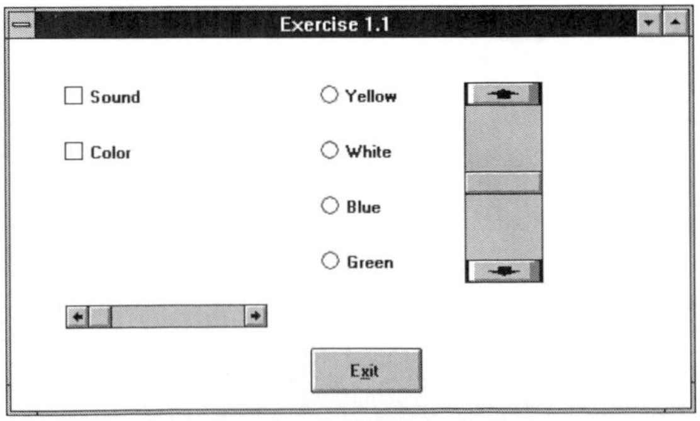

Figure 1.20.
The form of Exercise 1.

Quiz Answers

1. The two steps are:

    a. The visual programming step. In this step you place objects inside the form and set their properties.

    b. The code programming step. In this step you write and attach code to objects and events.

2. The first thing you have to do when writing a Visual Basic program is open a new project.

3. Here is how you can see the properties of the command button:

    ☐ Open a new project.

    ☐ Double-click the command button icon in the Toolbox.

    > *Visual Basic responds by placing the button inside the form.*

    ☐ Open the Property window for the command button and browse through its properties. As you can see, the command button has many properties.

    Repeat this process for other controls.

4. A variable is not an object (variables are discussed in later chapters).

5. To attach a code to an object do the following:

    ☐ Double-click the object.

    > *Visual Basic responds by displaying the code window for this object.*

    ☐ Select the event by clicking the Proc combo box (see Figure 1.18).

    You may now attach code to the object by typing the code between `Sub` and `End Sub`.

6. The correct syntax is this:

    ```
    txtDisplay.Text = "Hi there!"
    ```

    You must enclose the text within double quotes.

Exercise Answer

☐ Start a new project.

☐ Select Save Project As from the File menu.

> *Visual Basic responds by asking you if you want to save the form.*

☐ Click the Yes button (that is, you want to save the form).

> *Visual Basic responds by displaying the Save File As dialog box.*

☐ Save the form as EX1.FRM.

Visual Basic responds by saving the file and displaying another dialog box that lets you save the make file.

☐ Save the make file as EX1.MAK.

The first item in Table 1.2 is the form. As you can see from Table 1.2, you need to set two properties for the form. To set the Name property of the form to frmExercise1 do the following:

☐ Make sure that the form is selected (make sure that the title of the form is highlighted). (To select the form, click anywhere inside the form.)

☐ Select Properties from the Window menu.

Visual Basic responds by displaying the properties window of the form.

☐ Select the Name property in the properties window and set its value to frmExercise1.

Use the following step to change the Caption property of the form:

☐ Select the Caption property from the properties window and set its value to Exercise 1.

The next item in the properties table of Table 1.2 is the horizontal scroll bar.

Use the following steps to place the horizontal scroll bar inside the form:

☐ Double-click the horizontal scroll bar icon inside the Toolbox. (Figure 1.13 shows how the icon of the horizontal scroll bar looks.)

Visual Basic responds by placing the horizontal scroll bar inside the form.

☐ Drag the scroll bar so that it will be located as shown in Figure 1.20

☐ Make sure that the scroll bar is selected and then select Properties from the Window menu.

Visual Basic responds by displaying the properties window of the scroll bar.

You may now set the Name, Min, and Max properties of the horizontal scroll bar according to the specifications in Table 1.2.

In a similar manner, place all the other controls that appear in Table 1.2 and set their properties.

Properties and Controls

This chapter focuses on *controls* in Visual Basic—objects such as scroll bars, text boxes, and command buttons—and how to include these controls in your programs, how to change their properties, and how to attach code to them.

Most programs output information to the user and get information from the user. The process of outputting and inputting information is called the *user interface* aspect of the program. Windows programs use controls for providing easy and pleasant user interface (that's the reason for the popularity of Windows). In this chapter you'll learn that implementing fancy user interface is very easy in Visual Basic.

The Scroll Bar

A commonly used control in Windows programs is the scroll bar. Using this object enables the user to select a value by positioning the thumb tab of the scroll bar at a desired position (instead of typing the desired value).

The Speed Program

The Speed program illustrates how a scroll bar is used for obtaining a value from the user.

The Speed program should do the following things:

☐ When the Speed program is started, the form shown in Figure 2.1 pops up. The thumb tab of the scroll bar is positioned at the center of the scroll bar (the default position), and the text box displays a speed value of 50 mph (the default value).

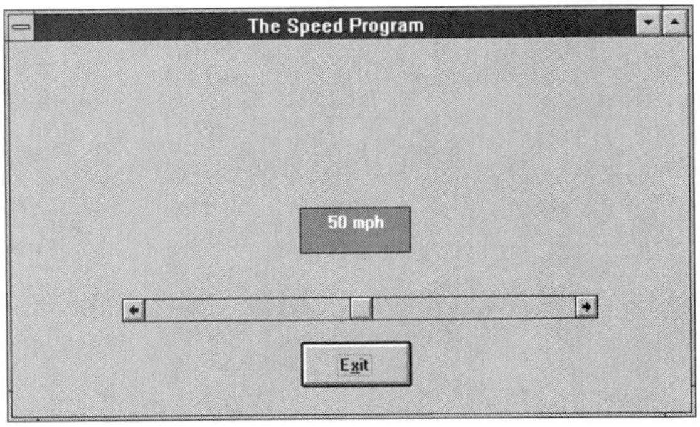

Figure 2.1.
The Speed program.

☐ When you change the thumb tab position of the scroll bar, the text box reflects the change. For example, when the thumb tab is placed at the extreme left, the text box displays the value 0; when the thumb tab is placed at the extreme right, the text box displays the value 100.

☐ To exit the program, click the Exit button.

The Visual Implementation of the Speed Program

The Speed program uses the horizontal scroll bar control. To see which item in the Toolbox represents the horizontal scroll bar, refer to Figure 1.13 in Chapter 1, "Writing Your First Program." The exact location of the icon in the Toolbox varies from version to version.

☐ Open a new project (select New Project from the File menu).

☐ Save the form of the project as SPEED.FRM, and save the make file of the project as SPEED.MAK. (Select Save Project As from the File menu. When Visual Basic asks you if you want to save the form, click the Yes button, and when the Save File As dialog box pops up, save the file as SPEED.FRM. When Visual Basic displays the Save As dialog box for saving the make file of the project, save it as SPEED.MAK.)

☐ Build the frmSpeed form according to the specifications in Table 2.1.

The completed form should look like the one shown in Figure 2.1.

From Chapter 1 you should recall that to place a control inside a form you have to double-click the icon of the desired control inside the Toolbox. Visual Basic responds by placing the control in the middle of the form. You then move the control by dragging it with the mouse. You enlarge or shrink the control by dragging its handles. To access the properties of the control, be sure that the control is selected, and select Properties from the Window menu. Visual Basic responds by displaying the properties window of the control. You may then change the properties of the control.

☐ Save the project (select Save Project from the File menu).

Table 2.1. The properties table of frmSpeed form.

Object	Property	Setting
Form	**Name**	**frmScroll**
	BackColor	(gray)
	Caption	The Speed Program
	Height	4425
	Left	1035
	Top	1140
	Width	7485
Text Box	**Name**	**txtSpeed**
	Alignment	2-Center
	BackColor	(red)

Table 2.1. continued

Object	Property	Setting
	ForeColor	(white)
	Height	495
	Left	3120
	MultiLine	True
	Text	50 mph
	Top	1800
	Width	1215
Horizontal Scroll Bar	**Name**	**hsbSpeed**
	Height	255
	Left	1200
	Max	100
	Top	2760
	Value	50
	Width	5175
Command Button	**Name**	**cmdExit**
	Caption	E&xit
	Height	495
	Left	3120
	Top	3240
	Width	1215

Entering the Code of the Speed Program

Now enter the code of the Speed program:

☐ Enter the following code inside the cmdExit_Click() procedure of the frmSpeed form:

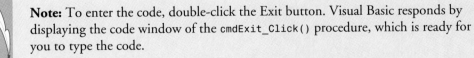

Note: To enter the code, double-click the Exit button. Visual Basic responds by displaying the code window of the cmdExit_Click() procedure, which is ready for you to type the code.

```
Sub cmdExit_Click ()

    End

End Sub
```

☐ Save the project (select Save Project from the File menu).

Executing the Speed Program

Although you have not finished writing the code of the Speed program yet, execute the Speed program to see what you have accomplished so far:

☐ To execute the Speed program, you may press F5, or select Start from the Run menu, or click the Run icon. (See Figure 2.2 for the location of the Run icon.) The form of the Speed program pops up, as shown in Figure 2.1.

Figure 2.2.
The toolbar.

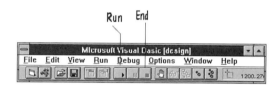

☐ Change the scroll bar position by clicking the right and left arrows of the scroll bar.

As you can see, nothing is happening! Why? You have not attached any code to the scroll bar.

☐ Click the Exit button to terminate the program.

The Min, Max, and Value Properties of the Scroll Bar

Table 2.1 contains some new properties not covered in Chapter 1. The following sections review these properties.

The Min and Max Properties

A scroll bar represents a set of values. The Min property represents the minimum value, and the Max property represents the maximum value. As shown in Table 2.1, the Min property is set to 0 and the Max property is set to 100. This means that the scroll bar may be set to any value between 0 and 100.

The Value Property

The Value property of the scroll bar represents the current value of the scroll bar. Therefore, the Value property of the scroll bar may be any number between 0 and 100. Upon execution of the Speed program, the thumb tab of the scroll bar is set to the position that corresponds to the Value property. Because you set the Value property to 50 when starting the Speed program, the thumb tab of the scroll bar is positioned at the middle of the bar (that is, 50 is midway between 0 and 100).

Note that the Text property of the text box is set to 50 mph in Table 2.1. When you start the program, the value displayed inside the text box reflects the current setting of the scroll bar.

The Keyboard Focus

You may press the Tab key on your keyboard to move the focus from object to object. Each time the Tab key is pressed, the focus shifts from one object to another. You may easily recognize which object has the focus. When the text box has the focus, a cursor inside the text box blinks. When the Exit button has the focus, a dashed rectangular shape surrounds its caption. When the scroll bar has the focus, its thumb tab is blinking.

What does it mean when an object has the focus? While an object has the focus, you may use the keyboard to control this object. To understand the keyboard focus concept, try the following:

☐ Execute the program.

☐ Press the Tab key until the scroll bar has the focus (that is, until you see the thumb tab of the scroll bar blinking).

☐ While the scroll bar has the focus, use the right and left arrow keys of the keyboard to move the thumb tab of the scroll bar. Because the scroll bar now has the focus, pressing the arrow keys on the keyboard has the identical effect as clicking the right and left arrow icons of the scroll bar.

☐ Press the Tab key until the Exit button has the focus.

☐ While the Exit button has the focus, press the space bar (or Enter). Pressing the space bar (or Enter) while the button has the focus has the identical effect as clicking the button.

Note the richness of the Speed program! You may change the scroll bar position, shrink and enlarge the window of the program, move the window of the program (by dragging its caption area), and do many other Windows operations. The beauty of it is that you didn't have to write any code to implement these features. Indeed, this is one of the main advantages of writing Windows programs.

Enhancing the Speed Program

Now enhance the Speed program by attaching more code to it.

☐ Enter the following code inside the hsbSpeed_Change() procedure:

> **Note:** To access the hsbSpeed_Change() procedure, double-click the scroll bar. Visual Basic responds by displaying the hsbSpeed_Change() procedure, in which you can type code.

```
Sub hsbSpeed_Change ()

    txtSpeed.Text - hsbSpeed.Value + " mph"

End Sub
```

As implied by the name hsbSpeed_Change(), this procedure is executed whenever you change the position of the scroll bar thumb tab. As you change the position of the thumb tab, the Value property of the scroll bar changes automatically. For example, if you place the thumb tab at the extreme left, the Value property of the scroll bar is automatically set to 0.

Whenever you change the position of the scroll bar, the text box should display the new position of the scroll bar thumb tab. In other words, you need to assign the Value property of the scroll bar to the Text property of the text box. This is accomplished in the hsbSpeed_Change() procedure with the following statement:

```
txtSpeed.Text = hsbSpeed.Value + " mph"
```

For example, if the Value property of the scroll bar is 20, the Text property of the text box is set to 20 mph.

Now look at your code in action:

☐ Save the project (select Save Project from the File menu).

☐ Execute the Speed program.

☐ Play with the scroll bar. As you change the scroll bar thumb tab position, the content of the text box changes accordingly.

There is, however, a cosmetic problem in the current version of the Speed program. Can you tell what the problem is? You are able to type text inside the text box. This creates a problem because you may type inside the text box a number that does not correspond to the position of the scroll bar.

☐ While the Speed program is running, click inside the text box and type Blah Blah Blah.

Because the text box should always display the current speed as indicated by the scroll bar, your program must not allow you to enter text inside the text box.

To prevent the user from entering text into the text box, you need to change the Enable property of the text box:

☐ Terminate the Speed program (click the Exit button or click the End icon that appears on the toolbar, as shown in Figure 2.2).

☐ Display the property table and change the Enabled property of the text box object to False.

> **Note:** To prevent the user from entering text inside a text box, set the Enable property of the text box to False.

☐ Execute the program again (the text box cannot be edited).

Changing the Text Box While Dragging the Scroll Bar Thumb Tab

You are almost done with the Speed program. There is, however, one more problem to solve. To see the problem, use the following steps:

☐ Try to drag the thumb tab of the scroll bar. As you drag the thumb tab, the text box content does not change! It changes only after you release the thumb tab.

It would be nice if the text box would change its content while the thumb tab of the scroll bar is dragged.

☐ To take care of this feature, enter the following code inside the hsbSpeed_Scroll() procedure:

```
Sub hsbSpeed_Scroll ()

    txtSpeed.Text = hsbSpeed.Value + " mph"

End Sub
```

To place code inside the hsbSpeed_Scroll() event procedure, double-click the scroll bar. Visual Basic responds by displaying the code window with the procedure hsbSpeed_Change() in it. Because you need to enter code inside the hsbSpeed_Scroll() procedure, select the Scroll item from the Proc list box that appears on the top-right portion of the code window.

As implied by the name hsbSpeed_Scroll(), this procedure is executed whenever you change the position of the scroll bar. As you change the position of the scroll bar, the Value property of the scroll bar is updated automatically.

Table 2.2. continued

Object	Property	Setting
Option Button	**Name**	**optLevel1**
	BackColor	&H0000FFFF&
	Caption	Level &1
	Height	495
	Left	4080
	Top	360
	Width	1215
Option Button	**Name**	**optLevel2**
	BackColor	&H00FF00FF&
	Caption	Level &2
	Height	495
	Left	4080
	Top	840
	Width	1215
Option Button	**Name**	**optLevel3**
	BackColor	&H00C0C0C0&
	Caption	Level &3
	Height	495
	Left	4080
	Top	1320
	Width	1215
Check Box	**Name**	**chkColors**
	BackColor	&H000000FF&
	Caption	&Colors
	Height	495
	Left	360
	Top	1320
	Width	1215

Object	Property	Setting
Check Box	**Name**	**chkMouse**
	BackColor	&H000000FF&
	Caption	&Mouse
	Height	495
	Left	360
	Top	840
	Width	1215
Check Box	**Name**	**chkSound**
	BackColor	&H000000FF&
	Caption	&Sound
	Height	495
	Left	360
	Top	360
	Width	1215
Command Button	**Name**	**cmdExit**
	Caption	&Exit
	Height	495
	Left	5880
	Top	3360
	Width	1215
Label	**Name**	**lblChoice**
	Alignment	2-Center
	Height	1095
	Left	600
	Top	2400
	Width	3495
	Caption	(empty)

Figure 2.3.
The frmOption form.

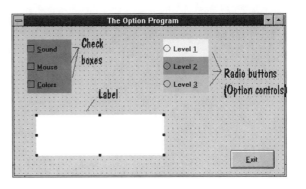

Entering the Code of the Option Program

☐ Enter the following code inside the general declarations area of the frmOption form:

```
' All variables MUST be declared.
Option Explicit
```

To access the general declaration area double-click anywhere inside the form, click the arrow icon of the Object list, and select (general).

☐ Enter the following code inside the cmdExit_Click() procedure of the frmOption form:

```
Sub cmdExit_Click()

    End

End Sub
```

Executing the Option Program

Although there is more code to be entered, execute the Option program now:

☐ Execute the Option program.

☐ Click the Level 1 option button.

> *The program responds by selecting the Level 1 option button (a dot appears inside the Level 1 option button).*

☐ Click the Level 2 option button.

> *The program responds by deselecting the Level 1 button and selecting the Level 2 button.*

☐ Click the Level 3 option button.

> *The program responds by deselecting the Level 2 button and selecting the Level 3 button.*

Only one option button is selected at any time. Option buttons are used in programs when you want your user to select a single option out of several options.

☐ Click the Sound check box.

The program responds by checking the check box.

☐ Click the other check boxes.

As you can see, it is possible to check more than one check box. You use check boxes when you want the user to be able to select various options. For example, if the program is a game application, you may select to play with or without sound, with or without mouse, and with or without colors.

To deselect a check box, click it again. (When a check box is not selected, it does not have an × in it.)

☐ Terminate the program by clicking the Exit button.

Entering More Code Inside the Option Program

Now enter more code inside the Option program. This code detects which check boxes are selected and which option button is selected and responds to the selection.

☐ Enter the following code inside the chkColors_Click() procedure of the frmOption form:

```
Sub chkColors_Click ()

    UpdateLabel

End Sub
```

☐ Enter the following code inside the chkMouse_Click() procedure of the frmOption form:

```
Sub chkMouse_Click ()

    UpdateLabel

End Sub
```

☐ Enter the following code inside the chkSound_Click() procedure of the frmOption form:

```
Sub chkSound_Click ()

    UpdateLabel

End Sub
```

☐ Enter the following code inside the optLevel1_Click() procedure of the frmOption form:

```
Sub optLevel1_Click ()

    UpdateLabel

End Sub
```

☐ Enter the following code inside the optLevel2_Click() procedure of the frmOption form:

```
Sub optLevel2_Click ()

    UpdateLabel

End Sub
```

☐ Enter the following code inside the optLevel3_Click() procedure of the frmOption form:

```
Sub optLevel3_Click ()

    UpdateLabel

End Sub
```

Now add a new procedure and name it UpdateLabel.

Use the following steps to add a new procedure:

☐ Select Project from the Window menu.

Visual Basic responds by displaying the project window.

☐ Be sure that the frmOption form is highlighted in the project window and click the View Code button that appears at the top of the project window.

Visual Basic responds by displaying the code window.

☐ Select New Procedure from the View menu.

Visual Basic responds by displaying the New Procedure dialog box (see Figure 2.4).

☐ Be sure the Sub option button in the dialog box is selected (because you are adding a Sub, not a Function). Type UpdateLabel in the Name field (see Figure 2.5).

☐ Click the OK button of the New Procedure dialog box.

Visual Basic responds by creating a new procedure with the name UpdateLabel, and it displays the code of the procedure in the code window (see Figure 2.6).

Figure 2.4.
*The New Procedure
dialog box.*

Figure 2.5.
Adding a new procedure.

Figure 2.6.
*Adding code to the
UpdateLabel procedure.*

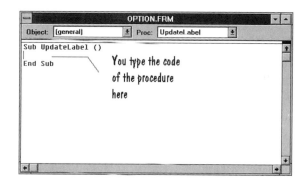

☐ Enter the following code inside the UpdateLabel() procedure:

```
Sub UpdateLabel ()

    Dim Info

    ' Sound
    If chkSound.Value = 1 Then
        Info = "Sound: ON"
    Else
        Info = "Sound: OFF"
    End If

    ' Mouse
    If chkMouse.Value = 1 Then
        Info = Info + Chr(13) + "Mouse: ON"
    Else
        Info = Info + Chr(13) + "Mouse: OFF"
    End If

    ' Colors
    If chkColors.Value = 1 Then
        Info = Info + Chr(13) + "Colors: ON"
    Else
        Info = Info + Chr(13) + "Colors: OFF"
    End If
```

```
' Level
If optLevel1.Value = True Then
    Info = Info + Chr(13) + "Level:1"
End If

If optLevel2.Value = True Then
    Info = Info + Chr(13) + "Level:2"
End If

If optLevel3.Value = True Then
    Info = Info + Chr(13) + "Level:3"
End If

lblChoice.Caption = Info

End Sub
```

☐ Save the project (select Save Project from the File menu).

Executing the Option Program

☐ Execute the Option program.

☐ Click the various check boxes and option buttons.

> *The program responds by displaying the status of the check boxes and radio buttons in the* lblChoice *label (see Figure 2.7).*

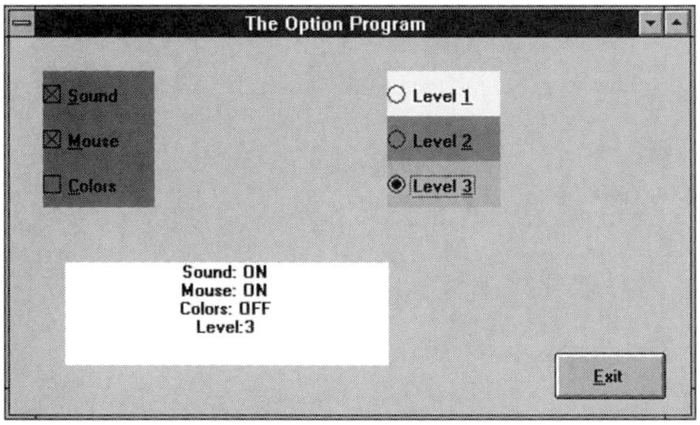

Figure 2.7.
The Option program.

☐ Terminate the program by clicking the Exit button.

How the Option Program Works

The Option program executes the UpdateLabel procedure whenever you click any of the check boxes or any of the radio buttons.

The Code Inside the *chkColors_Click()* Event Procedure of the frmOption Form

The `chkColors_Click()` procedure is executed whenever you click the chkColors check box:

```
Sub chkColors_Click ()

    UpdateLabel

End Sub
```

Who causes this procedure to be executed? It is executed automatically whenever you click the chkColors check box. That's how programs written with Visual Basic work!

The code inside the `chkColors_Click()` procedure executes the `UpdateLabel` procedure. The code inside the `UpdateLabel` procedure is covered later in this chapter.

The Code Inside the *chkMouse_Click()* Event Procedure of the frmOption Form

The `chkMouse_Click()` procedure is executed whenever you click the chkMouse check box:

```
Sub chkMouse_Click ()

    UpdateLabel

End Sub
```

Just like the `chkColors_Click()` procedure, this procedure also executes the `UpdateLabel` procedure.

The Code Inside the *chkSound_Click()* Event Procedure of the frmOption Form

The `chkSound_Click()` procedure is executed whenever you click the chkSound check box:

```
Sub chkSound_Click ()

    UpdateLabel

End Sub
```

Just like the `chkColors_Click()` and `chkMouse_Click()` procedures, this procedure also executes the `UpdateLabel` procedure.

The Code Inside the *optLevel1_Click()* Event Procedure of the frmOption Form

The `optLevel1_Click()` procedure is executed whenever you click the optLevel1 procedure:

```
Sub optLevel1_Click ()

    UpdateLabel

End Sub
```

This procedure also executes the UpdateLabel procedure.

The optLevel2_Click() and optLevel3_Click() procedures are executed whenever you click the optLevel2 and optLevel3 option buttons. These procedures also execute the UpdateLabel() procedure.

The Code Inside the *UpdateLabel()* Procedure

As discussed, whenever you click a check box or an option button, the UpdateLabel() procedure is executed.

The UpdateLabel() procedure is not an event procedure. (This procedure is created by selecting New Procedure from the View menu.)

Declaring the *Info* Variable

The first statement in this procedure declares the Info variable:

```
Dim Info
```

The word Dim is an instruction to Visual Basic that the following word (the Info word) is a name of a variable. The variable Info is used as a string variable during the execution of the UpdateLabel() procedure. Therefore, you also may declare this variable as follows:

```
Dim Info As String
```

However, Visual Basic is liberal in this respect, and it does not force you to declare the type of variable at the time of the declaration.

If you have experience with other programming languages, you probably know that some programming languages do not require you to declare variables. However, it is a good programming habit to declare all variables. To see why this is a good habit, assume that your procedure includes the following calculations:

```
Time = 10
Velocity = 50
Distance  = Velocity * Time
lblDistance.Caption = "Distance = " + Distance
```

The preceding four statements assign 10 to the Time variable, assign 50 to the Velocity variable, calculate the distance by multiplying Velocity by Time, and display the Distance by assigning its value to the Caption property of the lblDistance label.

Now suppose that by mistake you typed the following (that is, there is an *a* missing after the *t* in `Distance`):

```
lblDistance.Caption = "Distance = " + Distnce
```

Visual Basic considers `Distnce` as a new variable, and it automatically assigns the value 0 to it. Therefore, the lblVelocity label displays the following:

```
Distance: 0
```

This, of course, is an error.

You may avoid such foolish errors by instructing Visual Basic to complain whenever a variable is not declared. In the preceding example, the statements that calculate and display the distance should be the following:

```
Dim Time
Dim Velocity
Dim Distance

Time = 10
Velocity - 50
Distance  = Velocity * Time
lblDistance.Caption = "Distance = " + Distnce
```

If Visual Basic is set to complain whenever your code includes a variable that is not declared, Visual Basic beeps and prompts you with an error message telling you that the variable (in this case `Distnce`) is unknown. Visual Basic highlights the variable `Distnce`, letting you know that there is something wrong with this variable.

To instruct Visual Basic to complain whenever there is a variable in the code that is not declared, place the following statement inside the general declarations section of the form:

```
Option Explicit
```

To make Visual Basic automatically place the `Option Explicit` statement in every form, use the following steps:

☐ Select Environment from the Options menu.

Visual Basic responds by displaying the Environment Options dialog box (see Figure 2.8).

Figure 2.8 shows that the item Require Variable Declaration is marked as No. This means that you are not forced to declare variables (when you make a mistake such as typing `Distnce` instead of `Distance`, Visual Basic will not complain).

☐ Double-click the Require Variable Declaration item in the list.

Visual Basic responds by changing the setting of this item to Yes, as shown in Figure 2.9.

Figure 2.8.
The Environment Options dialog box.

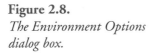

Figure 2.9.
Forcing declaration of variables.

☐ Click the OK button of the Environment Options dialog box to save the setting.

From now on, every form has the following statement in its general declarations section:

```
Option Explicit
```

From now on, you must declare each variable that your code uses. If you misspell the name of a certain variable, Visual Basic will complain.

> **Note:** In this book, you'll be instructed to add the `Option Explicit` statement in the general declarations section of the forms. If you set the Required Variable Declaration item to Yes, the `Option Explicit` statement is inserted automatically in the code of your form.

Checking the Value Property of the Check Box

The statements after the Dim declaration in the `UpdateLabel()` procedure are a block of `If…Else…End If` statements:

```
' Sound
If chkSound.Value = 1 Then
    Info = "Sound: ON"
Else
    Info = "Sound: OFF"
End If
```

In Visual Basic, you may insert comments in the code using the apostrophe (') character or the Rem word. The following line:

```
' Sound
```

is identical to this line:

```
Rem Sound
```

This book uses the apostrophe as the character that starts a comment line. Comments also may be inserted in a line of code, as follows:

```
A = 1 ' Initialize the variable.
```

It is a good programming habit to insert comments that give a brief description of the code. This makes the program easier to read and debug.

The `UpdateLabel()` procedure checks whether the Value property of the chkSound check box is equal to 1. If the Value property is equal to 1, the statements between If and Else are executed. In this case, you have only one statement between the If and the Else, so if the Value property of the chkSound box is equal to 1, the following statement is executed:

```
Info = "Sound: ON"
```

This statement assigns the string "Sound: ON" to the variable Info.

Note that Then in the If statement must be included.

The Value property of the check box is equal to 1 when there is an × inside the check box. Therefore, whenever there is an × inside the check box, the variable Info is set to "Sound: ON".

The statements between Else and End If are executed if the Value property of the chkSound Check property is not equal to 1. The Value property of a check box may be equal to either 1 or 0. Whenever there is no × inside the check box, the Value property is equal to 0. If there is no × inside the chkSound check box, the statement between Else and End If is executed, which sets the contents of the Info variable to "Sound: OFF".

To summarize, the Info variable is set either to this:

```
Sound: ON
```

or to this:

```
Sound: OFF
```

In a similar way, the next `If...Else...End If` block checks the Value property of the chkMouse check box:

```
' Mouse
If chkMouse.Value = 1 Then
    Info = Info + Chr(13) + "Mouse: ON"
Else
    Info = Info + Chr(13) + "Mouse: OFF"
End If
```

`Chr(13)` is the carriage return character (Enter). For example, if the chkSound check box has an × in it, and the chkMouse check box does not have an × in it, the first two `If...Else...End If` blocks in the `UpdateLabel()` procedure assign the following string to the `Info` variable:

```
Sound: ON Chr(13) Mouse: OFF
```

This is displayed as the following:

```
Sound: ON
Mouse: OFF
```

The next `If...Else...End If` block in the `UpdateLabel()` procedure checks the Value property of the chkColors check box and updates the `Info` variable accordingly:

```
' Colors
If chkColors.Value = 1 Then
    Info = Info + Chr(13) + "Colors: ON"
Else
    Info = Info + Chr(13) + "Colors: OFF"
End If
```

The next `If...End If` block in the `UpdateLabel()` procedure checks the Value property of the optLevel1 option button:

```
' Level
If optLevel1.Value = True Then
    Info = Info + Chr(13) + "Level:1"
End If
```

Again, the Value property of the control specifies its status. However, for the option button control, a Value property that equals True means that the option button is selected, and hence the `Info` variable is updated accordingly. If the Value property of the optLevel1 is not equal to True, it means that this option button is not selected. In Visual Basic, True is defined as -1, and False is defined as 0. Therefore, the state of the option button may be either True (that is, -1) or False (that is, 0).

Note: The Value property of a check box may be 0, 1, or 2. The Value property of a check box that is checked is 1. The Value property of a check box that is not checked is 0. The Value property of a check box is 2 whenever the check box is grayed (unavailable). To make the check box gray, set its Enabled property to False.

> **Note:** The Value property of an option button may be True or False. The Value property of an option button that is selected is True. The Value property of an option button that is not selected is False. In Visual Basic, True is defined as -1, and False is defined as 0.

2

The next two If...End If blocks update the Info variable in accordance with the Value properties of the optLevel2 and optLevel3 option buttons:

```
If optLevel2.Value = True Then
   Info = Info + Chr(13) + "Level:2"
End If

If optLevel3.Value = True Then
   Info = Info + Chr(13) + "Level:3"
End If
```

The last statement in the UpdateLabel() procedure updates the Caption property of the lblChoice label with the contents of the Info variable:

```
lblChoice.Caption = Info
```

This causes the contents of the Info variable to be displayed in the lblIChoice label, as shown in Figure 2.7.

What Else?

As you may realize by now, programming with Visual Basic amounts to understanding the meaning of each of the controls in the Toolbox and the meaning and purpose of the properties of the controls. A property means different things for different controls. For example, the Caption property of the form contains the text content that is displayed in the title of the form, while the Caption property of the label control contains the text that is being displayed inside the label. Likewise, the Value property of the check box indicates whether the check box has an × in it, while the Value property of the option button indicates whether the option button is selected, and the Value property of the scroll bar indicates the current position of the scroll bar.

The Toolbox contains the icons of the controls, and each control has its own set of properties. Some of the controls that appear in the Toolbox are standard Windows controls such as the horizontal scroll bars, vertical scroll bars, text boxes, labels, check boxes, option buttons, and command buttons. On the other hand, some of the controls in the Toolbox are very special (the grid control, for example), and this book dedicates full chapters to these special controls.

The code inside the `hsbScroll_Scroll()` procedure is identical to the code inside the `hsbSpeed_Change()` procedure.

☐ Execute the Speed program.

☐ Drag the thumb tab of the scroll bar (the text inside the text box changes in accordance with the position of the scroll bar).

Final Words About the Speed Program

The Speed program illustrates how you can create an elegant user interface for entering numbers.

The Option Program

The Option program demonstrates how you can write programs that let you select an option.

The Visual Implementation of the Option Program

The Option program uses the option button control. To see which item in the Toolbox represents the option button, refer to Figure 1.13 in Chapter 1. The exact location of the icon in the Toolbox varies from version to version.

☐ Open a new project (select New Project from the File menu).

☐ Save the form of the project as OPTION.FRM. Save the make file of the project as OPTION.MAK.

☐ Build the frmOption form according to the specifications in Table 2.2.

When the form is complete, it should look like the one shown in Figure 2.3.

Table 2.2. The properties table of the frmOption form.

Object	Property	Setting
Form	**Name**	**frmOption**
	BackColor	&H0000FF00&
	Caption	The Option Program
	Height	4425
	Left	1035
	Top	1140
	Width	7485

Generally speaking, Visual Basic is not a difficult programming language to learn, but there is a lot to learn. The key to success is to practice and experiment. After writing and experimenting with the book's programs, you are expected to master Visual Basic. After you enter the code of the book's programs and understand their code, we recommend that you perform your own experiments. Try to change the properties of the control during design time (during the time you implement the visual portion of the program), and try to change properties during runtime. Changing properties during runtime means that the value of the property changes from within the code of the program. For example, the last statement in the UpdateLabel() procedures updates the Caption property of the lblChoice label during runtime. On the other hand, the Caption property of the form was set to The Option Program during design time.

Some properties may be changed during runtime, some properties may be set only during design time, and some properties may be set only during runtime. For example, the Caption property of the label control may be set during design time as well as at runtime.

Chapter 3, "Programming Building Blocks," explores programming topics such as loops, decision statements, and others. You'll make extensive use of these topics in subsequent chapters. The chapters that follow Chapter 3 discuss special controls, special properties, and special programming topics.

Naming Conventions Used in This Book

In this book the controls are named according to the specifications in Table 2.3. For example, the names of the command buttons start with the characters *cmd*, and the names of the text boxes start with the characters *txt*.

Table 2.3. Naming conventions for the controls.

Control	Control Name Starts with the Characters	Example
Form	frm	frmMyForm
Check Box	chk	chkSound
Combo Box	cbo	cboSelection
Command Button	cmd	cmdExit
Directory List	dir	dirFiles
Drive List	drv	drvSource
File List	fil	filTarget
Frame	fra	fraChoices

Control	Control Name Starts with the Characters	Example
Grid	grd	grdTV
Horizontal Scroll Bar	hsb	hsbSpeed
Image	img	imgMyImage
Label	lbl	lblInfo
Line	lin	linDiagonal
List Box	lst	lstChapters
Menu	mnu	mnuFile
Option Button	opt	optLevel1
Picture Box	pic	picMyPicture
Shape	shp	shpMyShape
Text Box	txt	txtUserArea
Timer	tmr	tmrMoveIt
Vertical Scroll Bar	vsb	vsbSpeed

Statements That Cannot Fit on a Single Line in This Book

In Visual Basic, a statement must be typed all on one line (you can't spread the statement on more than one line). However, some statements in Visual Basic tend to be long! In fact, some statements were so long that no matter what font the graphic designers of this book used, the statement would not fit on a single line. To overcome this problem, this book uses the symbol ➡ as an indication that the line is a continuation from the previous line. For example, the following line might appear in this book:

```
Info = "This is a string " +
          ➡ txtUserArea.Text
```

If you try to type that line in Visual Basic, Visual Basic will complain because it does not recognize the ➡ symbol.

Therefore, when you see the ➡ symbol, remember to type the statement on a single line. The preceding statement must be typed in Visual Basic as the following:

```
Info = "This is a string" + txtUserArea.Text
```

Similarly, this statement:

```
MyProcedyre ( Arg1 As Integer,
        ➥   Arg2 As Integer,
        ➥   Arg3 As Integer)
```

must be typed in Visual Basic as this:

```
MyProcedyre ( Arg1 As Integer, Arg2 As Integer,  Arg3 As Integer )
```

Summary

In this chapter you jumped into the water! Yes, you actually built a true Windows program that includes a scroll bar, a text box, a command button, check boxes, and option buttons. You learned how to incorporate these controls into your Visual Basic program, how to determine their Value properties, and how to insert code in the event procedures that correspond to these controls.

Q&A

Q The visual implementation portion took me a long time to implement. Any suggestions?

A Yes, practice. You should be fluent with the visual implementation portion of the programs, and the only way to be fluent with the visual implementation is to practice.

Q I can't recognize the icons in the Toolbox. Any suggestions?

A Consult Figure 1.13 in Chapter 1. After practicing for a while, you won't need to refer to Figure 1.13!

Quiz

1. A certain statement appears in this book as follows:

   ```
   Info = "ABC" +
              ➥  "DEF" + "GH" +
              ➥  "IJK"
              ➥  + "L"
   ```

   How would you type it inside your Visual Basic program?

   a. `Info = "ABC" + "DEF" + "GH" +"IJK" + "L"`

   b. Exactly as shown in the book

2. Suppose that your program includes a vertical scroll bar with the name vsbVolume. Write a statement that places the thumb tab of the scroll bar at position 37.

3. Suppose that your program includes a horizontal scroll bar with the name hsbDistance. How do you change the Min and Max properties of the scroll bar to 10 and 200, respectively?

Exercise

Enhance the Option program so that it accomplishes the following:

a. Whenever you check the chkSound check box, the PC beeps.

b. Whenever you uncheck the chkColors check box, the background color of the form changes to purple, and whenever you check the chkColors check box, the background color of the form changes to yellow.

> **Note:** To cause the PC to beep, use the Beep statement.
>
> To change the background of the form to purple, use the following statement:
>
> `frmOption.BackColor = QBColor(13)`
>
> To change the background of the form to yellow, use the following statement:
>
> `frmOption.BackColor = QBColor(14)`

Quiz Answers

1. a. `Info = "ABC" + "DEF" + "GH" +"IJK" + "L"`

2. To place the thumb tab of the vsbVolume to position 37, use the following statement:

   `vsbVolume.Value = 37`

3. You may change the Min and Max properties of the scroll bar at design time and at runtime.

To change the properties at design time do the following:

☐ Select the scroll bar.

☐ Select Properties from the Window menu.

   Visual Basic responds by displaying the Properties table of the scroll bar.

☐ Select the Min property, and change its value to 10.

☐ Select the Max property, and change its value to 200.

Alternatively, you may set these properties at runtime by using the following statements:

```
hsbDistance.Min = 10
hsbDistance.Max = 200
```

Exercise Answer

Change the chkSound_Click() procedure so that it looks like this:

```
Sub chkSound_Click ()

    If chkSound.Value = 1 Then
      Beep
    End If

    UpdateLabel

End Sub
```

Change the chkColors_Click() procedure so that it looks like this:

```
Sub chkColors_Click ()

    If chkColors.Value = 1 Then
        frmOption.BackColor = QBColor(13)
    Else
        frmOption.BackColor = QBColor(14)
    End If

    UpdateLabel

End Sub
```

The If…End If block in the chkSound_Click() procedure checks the Value property of the check box. If it is 1, you checked the box (put an × inside this check box), and the Beep statement is executed.

The If…Else…End If block checks the Value property of the chkColors check box. If the Value property is equal to 1, you checked the box, and the BackColor property of the form is set to QBColor(13). If the Value property of the check box is not equal to 1, it means that you unchecked the check box, and the BackColor property of the form is set to QBColor(14).

Programming Building Blocks

This chapter focuses on the programming building blocks of Visual Basic. Just like any other programming language, Visual Basic uses programming building blocks such as procedures, functions, If statements, Do loops, variables, and other important programming language concepts.

The Multiply Program

The Multiply program illustrates how to use procedures and functions in your programs.

The Visual Implementation of the Multiply Program

☐ Open a new project, save the form of the project as MULTIPLY.FRM, and save the make file of the project as MULTIPLY.MAK.

☐ Build the frmMultiply form according to the specifications in Table 3.1.

The completed form should look like the one shown in Figure 3.1.

Table 3.1. The properties table of frmMultiply form.

Object	Property	Setting
Form	**Name**	**frmMultiply**
	Caption	The Multiply Program
	Height	4440
	Left	1572
	Top	1416
	Width	7464
Command Button	**Name**	**cmdCalculate**
	Caption	&Calculate
	Height	1815
	Left	1800
	Top	1800
	Width	2295
Command Button	**Name**	**cmdExit**
	Caption	&Exit
	Height	495

Object	Property	Setting
	Left	5760
	Top	3360
	Width	1215
Text Box	**Name**	**txtResult**
	Height	855
	Left	360
	Top	480
	Width	6495
	Text	(empty)
Label	**Name**	**lblResult**
	Caption	Result:
	Height	255
	Left	360
	Top	240
	Width	735

Figure 3.1.
The frmMultiply form.

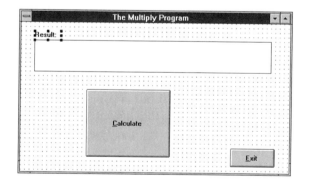

Entering the Code of the Multiply Program

☐ Enter the following code inside the general declarations section of frmMultiply:

```
' All variables MUST be declared.
Option Explicit
```

☐ Enter the following code inside the cmdCalculate_Click() procedure of the frmMultiply form:

```
Sub cmdCalculateClick ()

    Multiply 2, 3

End Sub
```

☐ Enter the following code inside the cmdExit_Click() procedure of the frmMultiply form:

```
Sub cmdExit_Click ()

    End

End Sub
```

☐ Add a new procedure to the form and name it Multiply. (If you have forgotten how to create a new procedure, refer to Chapter 2, "Properties and Controls," which shows you how to create a new procedure called UpdateLabel in the Option program).

Visual Basic responds by displaying the code window of the Multiply() procedure.

☐ Change the heading of the procedures so it looks like the following:

```
Sub Multiply (X As Integer, Y As Integer)

End Sub
```

☐ Enter the following code inside the Multiply() procedure:

```
Sub Multiply (X As Integer, Y As Integer)

    DIM Z
        Z = X * Y
        txtResult.Text = Z

End Sub
```

Executing the Multiply Program

☐ Execute the Multiply program.

☐ Click the Calculate button.

The program responds by displaying the number 6 in the text box. (When you press the Calculate button, the program multiplies 2 by 3 and displays the result in the text box.)

How the Multiply Program Works

The Multiply program executes the Multiply() procedure to multiply two numbers.

The Code Inside the *cmdCalculate_Click()* Event Procedure of the frmMultiply Form

The `cmdCalculate_Click()` procedure is executed whenever the user clicks the cmdCalculate button:

```
Sub cmdCalculate_Click ()

    Multiply 2, 3

End Sub
```

The statement inside this procedure executes the `Multiply()` procedure with two arguments: 2 and 3.

The Code Inside the *Multiply()* Procedure

The `Multiply()` procedure has two arguments:

```
Sub Multiply (X As Integer, Y As Integer)

    Dim Z

    Z = X*Y
    txtResult.Text = Z

End Sub
```

The first argument is called X and it is declared As Integer. The second argument is called Y and it is also declared As Integer.

The `Multiply()` procedure declares a variable called Z, and then assigns to it the result of the X*Y multiplication.

The procedure then assigns the value of the Z variable to the Text property of txtResult.

Note that the `UpdateLabel()` procedure used in the Option program in Chapter 2 does not have any arguments. Therefore, the heading of the `UpdateLabel()` procedure was used as follows:

```
Sub UpdateLabel ()

End Sub
```

To execute the `UpdateLabel()` procedure, the following statement was used:

```
UpdateLabel
```

On the other hand, the `Multiply()` procedure has two arguments (both are integers), and hence the heading of this procedure is the following:

```
Sub Multiply (X As Integer, Y As Integer)

End Sub
```

To execute the `Multiply()` procedure, the following statement was used:

```
Multiply 2, 3
```

In Visual Basic, you may also execute procedures using the `Call` statement. For example, you may rewrite the `cmdMultiply_Click()` procedures as follows:

```
Sub cmdCalculate_Click ()

    Call Multiply (2, 3)

End Sub
```

When using the Call word, you must include the arguments in parentheses. (It does not matter which method you use to execute procedures.)

Using a Function in the Multiply Program

The `Multiply()` procedure is called a procedure because it does not return any value.

A function is similar to a procedure, but a function returns a value. To see a function in action, use the following steps. Remove the `Multiply()` procedure from the Multiply program as follows:

☐ Display the code window. (To display the code window, highlight the frmMultiply form in the project window and click the View Code button in the project window.)

☐ Click the arrow that appears in the Object list box (the Object list box appears at the top-left side of the code window).

☐ Select the (general) item from the Object list.

☐ Click the arrow that appears in the Proc list box (the Proc list box appears at the top-right side of the code window).

☐ Select the Multiply item from the Proc list.

   Visual Basic responds by displaying the `Multiply()` procedure.

☐ Highlight the whole procedure (including its heading and its very last line) and press Delete.

That's it—you don't have the `Multiply()` procedure in your code anymore.

Use the following steps to add a new function to the Multiply program:

☐ Display the code window (by selecting the View Code button from the project window).

☐ Select New Procedure from the View menu.

   Visual Basic responds by displaying the New Procedure dialog box.

☐ Select the Function option button of the New Procedure dialog box (because you are adding a new function).

☐ Type Multiply in the Name field of the New Procedure dialog box.

☐ Click the OK button of the New Procedure dialog box.

Visual Basic responds by displaying the code window of the Multiply() function:

```
Function Multiply ()

End Function
```

☐ Change the heading of the Multiply() function so that it looks like the following:

```
Function Multiply (X As Integer, Y As Integer)

End Function
```

☐ Add the following code inside the Multiply() function:

```
Function Multiply (X As Integer, Y As Integer)

        Dim Z

        Z = X * Y
        Multiply = Z

End Function
```

☐ Change the cmdCalculate_Click() procedure so that it looks like the following:

```
Sub cmdCalculate_Click ()

    txtResult.Text = Multiply(2, 3)

End Sub
```

☐ Save the project (select Save Project from the File menu).

☐ Execute the Multiply program.

☐ Click the Calculate button.

As you can see, the program behaves the same way it did when the Multiply() procedure was used.

☐ Click the Exit button to terminate the program.

The Code Inside the *Multiply()* Function

The code inside the `Multiply()` function declares the Z variable and assigns the result of the X*Y multiplication to the Z variable:

```
Function Multiply (X As Integer, Y As Integer)

    Dim Z

    Z = X * Y
    Multiply = Z

End Function
```

The last statement in the `Multiply()` procedure assigns the value of Z to `Multiply`:

```
Multiply = Z
```

`Multiply` is the returned value of the `Multiply()` function. Whoever executed the `Multiply()` function is able to use the returned value of the `Multiply()` function, as explained in the next section.

The Code Inside the *cmdCalculate_Click()* Event Procedure

The code inside the `cmdCalculate_Click()` procedure assigns the returned value from the `Multiply()` function to the Text property of the txtResult text box:

```
Sub cmdCalculate_Click ()

    txtResult.Text = Multiply(2, 3)

End Sub
```

As you can see, using this function is a little bit more complicated than using procedures, but after using them for a while, you'll get used to them and you'll learn to appreciate them, because they make your program easy to read and understand. Consider the following statement:

```
txtResult.Text = Multiply(2, 3)
```

This statement says the following: Execute the `Multiply()` function with two arguments, 2 and 3, and assign the returned value to the Text property of the txtResult text box.

Procedures, Functions, and Methods

As discussed earlier in this chapter, the difference between a procedure and a function is that a procedure does not return a value, and a function returns a value. In subsequent chapters of this book you will also encounter the term *method*. A method works similarly to how procedures and

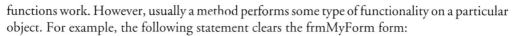

functions work. However, usually a method performs some type of functionality on a particular object. For example, the following statement clears the frmMyForm form:

```
frmMyForm.Cls
```

Note that in the preceding statement Cls is the name of the method. From a programmer's point of view, you may view the method as procedures with a strange syntax.

Specifying Controls

As you may have noticed by now, you may refer to a property of a control by typing the name of the control, a dot (.), and then the name of the property. For example, you refer to the Text property of the txtResult text box control as txtResult.Text.

You may also refer to the property by including the name of the form on which the control is located. For example, you may refer to the Text property of the txtResult text box that is located inside the frmMultiply form as frmMultiply.txtResult.Text.

In most cases, you may omit the name of the form (this saves you some typing). However, if your program includes more than one form, you may want to specify the name of the form for clarity.

The *If* Statement

You already encountered the If…End If block of statements in Chapter 2. For example, in the following If…End If block, the statements in between the If line and the End If line are executed only if A is equal to 1:

```
If A = 1 Then

.........................................
... This code is executed only if A ...
... is equal to 1.              ...
.........................................

End If
```

The following statements illustrate the If…Else…End If statements:

```
If A = 1
    .........................................
    ... This code is executed only if A ...
    ... is equal to 1.              ...
    .........................................

else
    .........................................
    ... This code is executed only if A ...
    ... is NOT equal to 1.          ...
    .........................................

End If
```

The *Select Case* Statement

Select Case is sometimes more convenient to use than If…Else…End If.

The following block of statements illustrates how the Select Case statement works:

```
Select Case X
      Case 0
            ......................................
            ... Write here a code that will be ...
            ... executed if X = 0.            ...
            ......................................
Case 1
      ......................................
      ... Write here a code that will be ...
      ... executed if X = 1.            ...
      ......................................
Case 2
      ......................................
      ... Write here a code that will be ...
      ... executed if X = 2.            ...
End  Select
```

As you can see, Select Case works in a similar way to the If statement.

The *Do While…Loop* Loop

The Do…Loop is used to execute statements until certain conditions occur. The following Do…Loop counts from 1 to 1000:

```
Counter = 1
Do While Counter < 1001
   Counter = Counter + 1
Loop
```

The variable Counter is initialized to 1, and then the Do…While loop starts.

The first line of the loop checks whether the Counter variable is less than 1001. If this is the case, the statements between the Do While line and the Loop line are executed. In the preceding example, there is only one statement between these lines:

```
Counter = Counter + 1
```

which increases the Counter variable by 1.

The program then returns to the Do While line and examines the value of the Counter variable again. Now Counter is equal to 2, so again, the statement between the Do While line and the Loop line is executed. This process continues until Counter equals 1001. In this case, the Do While line finds that Counter is no longer less than 1001, and the program continues with the statement after the Loop line.

The *Do...Loop While* Loop

The statements inside the Do...While loop described in the previous section may or may not be executed. For example, in the following Do...While loop, the statements between the Do While line and the Loop line are never executed:

```
Counter = 2000
Do While Counter < 1001
    Counter = Counter + 1
Loop
```

This is the case because when the program reaches the Do While line, it discovers that Counter is equal to 2000, and, therefore, the statement between the Do While line and the Loop line is not executed.

Sometimes, you may want the program to enter the loop at least once. In this case, use the Do...Loop While statements:

```
Counter = 2000
Do
    txtUserArea.Text = Counter
    Counter = Counter + 1
Loop While Counter < 1001
```

The program executes the statements in between the Do line and the Loop While line in any case. Then the program determines whether Counter is less then 1001. If Counter is less then 1001, the program again executes the statements between the Do line and the Loop While line.

When the program discovers that the Counter variable is no longer less than 1001, the program continues with the execution, executing the statement that appears after the Loop While line.

The following Do...Loop While statements count from 50 to 300:

```
Counter = 50
Do
    Counter = Counter + 1
Loop While Counter < 301
```

The *For...Next* Loop

The For...Next loop is an alternate way to implement loops in Visual Basic. The following loop counts from 1 to 100:

```
For I =1 to 100 Step 1
    txtMyTextArea.Text = I
Next
```

To count from 1 to 100 in steps of 2, you may use the following For...Next loop:

```
For I =1 to 100 Step 2
    txtMyTextArea.Text = I
Next
```

The preceding loop counts as follows: 1,3,5,....

If you omit the Step word, Visual Basic uses `Step 1` as the default.

The following two `For...Next` blocks produce the same results:

```
For I =1 to 100 Step 1
    txtMyTextArea.Text = I
Next

For I =1 to 100
    txtMyTextArea.Text = I
Next
```

The *Exit For* Statement

You may exit a `For...Next` loop by executing the `Exit For` statement as follows:

```
For I = 1 To 1000
    txtResult.Text = I
    If I = 500 Then
      Exit For
    End If
Next
```

The preceding code counts in increments of 1, starting from 1. When I equals 500, the `For` loop terminates.

The *Exit Do* Statement

The `While...Do` loop may be terminated using the `Exit Do` statement as follows:

```
I = 1
Do While I < 10001
    txtResult.Text = I
    I = I + 2
    If I > 500 Then
      Exit Do
    End If
Loop
```

The preceding loops count in increments of 2, starting from 1. When I is greater than 500, the `Do While...Loop` terminates.

Oops...

Occasionally, you may make errors like the one shown in the following loop:

```
I = 1
Do While I < 10001
    txtResult.Text = I
```

```
    If I > 500 Then
        Exit Do
    End If
Loop
```

That is, you might forget to include the following statement:

```
I = I + 2
```

In the preceding Do While...Loop, the Counter variable remains at its current value (Counter = 1) because you forgot to increment its value. In this case, the program stays in the loop forever because I is less than 1001 and it never increases. To get out of the loop, press Ctrl+Break to stop the program, and then click the End icon on the toolbar (see Figure 2.2 in Chapter 2 for the location of the End icon).

The Sum Program

The Sum program enables the user to select a number, and then adds all the integers from 1 to the selected number. For example, if the user selects the number 5, the program makes the following calculations:

```
1+2+3+4+5   = 15
```

and displays the result.

The Visual Implementation of the Sum Program

☐ Open a new project, save the form of the project as SUM.FRM, and save the make file of the file as SUM.MAK.

☐ Build the frmSum form according to the specifications in Table 3.2.

The completed form should look like the one shown in Figure 3.2.

Table 3.2. The properties table of the frmSum form.

Object	Property	Setting
Form	**Name**	**frmSum**
	Caption	The Sum Program
	Height	3708
	Left	1416
	Top	1512
	Width	6516

Table 3.2. continued

Object	Property	Setting
Command Button	**Name**	**cmdSumIt**
	Caption	&Sum It
	Height	1692
	Left	3600
	Top	480
	Width	2052
Vertical Scroll Bar	**Name**	**vsbNum**
	Height	2652
	Left	240
	Max	500
	Min	1
	Top	240
	Value	1
	Width	252
Text Box	**Name**	**txtResult**
	Alignment	2-Center
	Enabled	False
	Height	612
	Left	600
	MultiLine	True
	Top	720
	Width	2292
	Text	(empty)
Command Button	**Name**	**cmdExit**
	Caption	&Exit
	Height	372
	Left	4080
	Top	2400
	Width	972

Object	Property	Setting
Label	**Name**	**lblNum**
	Caption	Selected number:
	Height	372
	Left	600
	Top	2040
	Width	2412

Figure 3.2.
The frmSum form.

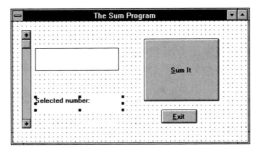

Entering the Code of the Sum Program

☐ Enter the following code inside the general declarations section of the frmSum form:

```
' All variables MUST be declared.
Option Explicit
```

☐ Enter the following code inside the cmdExit_Click() procedure of the frmSum form:

```
Sub cmdExit_Click ()

    End

End Sub
```

☐ Enter the following code inside the cmdSumIt_Click() procedure of the frmSum form:

```
Sub cmdSumIt_Click ()

    Dim I
    Dim R

    For I = 1 To vsbNum.Value Step 1
        R = R + I
    Next

    txtResult.Text = R

End Sub
```

☐ Enter the following code inside the vsbNum_Change() procedure of the frmSum form:

```
Sub vsbNum_Change ()

    lblNum = "Selected number: " + vsbNum.Value

End Sub
```

☐ Enter the following code inside the vsbNum_Scroll() procedure of the frmSum form:

```
Sub vsbNum_Scroll ()

    lblNum = "Selected number: " + vsbNum.Value

End Sub
```

Executing the Sum Program

☐ Execute the Sum program.

☐ Select a number by clicking the arrow icons of the vertical scroll bar or by dragging the thumb tab of the scroll bar.

The program responds by displaying the selected number (see Figure 3.3).

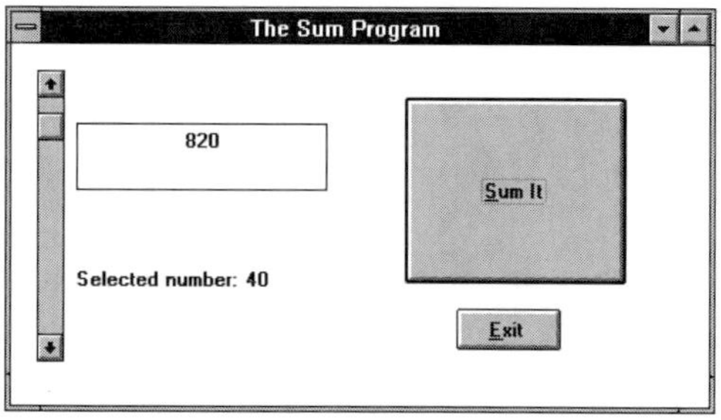

Figure 3.3.
The Sum program.

☐ Click the Sum It button.

The program responds by making the calculations and displaying the result in the text box (see Figure 3.3).

For example, select the number 5 with the scroll bar and click the Sum It button. The program should display the number 15 (that is, 1+2+3+4+5=15).

☐ Terminate the program by clicking the Exit button.

How the Sum Program Works

The Sum program uses a For...Next loop to perform the calculations.

The Code Inside the *cmdSumIt_Click()* Event Procedure of the frmSum Form

The cmdSumIt_Click() procedure is executed whenever the user clicks the cmdSumIt button:

```
Sub cmdSumIt_Click ()

    Dim I
    Dim R

    For I = 1 To vsbNum.Value Step 1
      R = R + I
    Next

    txtResult.Text = R

End Sub
```

The procedure declares two variables: I and R.

The For...Next loop then calculates the summation:

```
1 + 2 + 3 + ...+ vsbNum.Value
```

Initially, the R variable is equal to 0, because Visual Basic initializes variables to 0 at the time of the declaration. Some programmers like to include this redundant statement:

```
R = 0
```

before the For statement for the purpose of making the code easier to read.

The last statement in this procedure updates the Text property of the text box with the content of the R variable.

The Code Inside the *vsbNum_Change()* Event Procedure of the frmSum Form

The vsbNum_Change() procedure is executed whenever the user changes the scroll bar position:

```
Sub vsbNum_Change ()

    lblNum = "Selected number: " + vsbNum.Value

End Sub
```

The procedure updates the Text property of the lblNum label with the Value property of the scroll bar. This enables the user to read the position of the scroll bar.

The Code Inside the *vsbNum_Scroll()* Event Procedure of the frmSum Form

The vsbNum_Scroll() procedure is executed when the user drags the thumb tab of the scroll bar:

```
Sub vsbNum_Scroll ()

    lblNum = "Selected number: " + vsbNum.Value

End Sub
```

This procedure's code is identical to that of the vsbSum_Change() procedure.

The Timer Program

The Timer program illustrates the concept of variable visibility. This program also introduces a new control: the Timer control.

The Visual Implementation of the Timer Program

☐ Open a new project, save the form of the project as TIMER.FRM, and save the make file of the project as TIMER.MAK.

☐ Build the frmTimer form according to the specifications in Table 3.3.

The completed form should look like the one shown in Figure 3.4.

Table 3.3. The properties table of the frmTimer form.

Object	Property	Setting
Form	Name	frmTimer
	Caption	The Timer Program
	Height	2640
	Left	1896
	Top	2016
	Width	6516
Timer	Name	tmrTimer
	Interval	2000
	Left	960
	Top	240

Object	Property	Setting
Command Button	**Name**	**cmdExit**
	Caption	&Exit
	Height	372
	Left	5280
	Top	1680
	Width	972

Figure 3.4.
The frmTimer form.

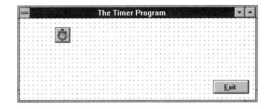

Entering the Code of the Timer Program

☐ Enter the following code inside the general declarations section of the frmTimer form:

```
' All variables MUST be declared.
Option Explicit
```

☐ Enter the following code inside the cmdExit_Click() procedure of the frmTimer form:

```
Sub cmdExit_Click ()

    End

End Sub
```

☐ Enter the following code inside the tmrTimer_Timer() procedure of the frmTimer form:

```
Sub tmrTimer_Timer ()

    Beep

End Sub
```

Executing the Timer Program

☐ Execute the Timer program.

> *The Timer program beeps every 2 seconds. During the execution of the Timer program, the timer control icon is not shown.*

☐ Click the Exit button to terminate the program.

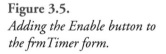

How the Timer Program Works

The Timer program uses the timer control. The program automatically executes the `tmrTimer_Timer()` procedure every 2000 milliseconds.

The Code Inside the *tmrTimer_Timer()* Event Procedure

The Interval property of `tmrTimer` was set to 2000 at design time. This means that the `tmrTimer_Timer()` procedure is executed every 2000 milliseconds (2 seconds):

```
Sub tmrTimer_Timer ()

    Beep

End Sub
```

Therefore, every 2 seconds the PC beeps.

Because the timer control icon is not shown during the execution of the program, its position inside the form is not important, and you may place it anywhere inside the form.

Enhancing the Timer Program

☐ Add a command button to the frmTimer form, as shown in Figure 3.5. The command button should have the following properties: The Name property should be cmdEnableDisable and the Caption property should be &Enable.

Figure 3.5.
Adding the Enable button to the frmTimer form.

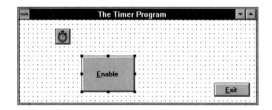

☐ Modify the general declarations section of the frmTimer form so that it looks like the following:

```
' All variables MUST be declared.
Option Explicit

' Declare the KeepTrack variable
Dim KeepTrack
```

☐ Modify the `tmrTimer_Timer()` procedure so that it looks like the following:

```
Sub tmrTimer_Timer ()

    ' If the KeepTrack variable is equal to 1,
    ' then enable beeping.
    If KeepTrack = 1 Then
        Beep
    End If

End Sub
```

☐ Add the following code inside the `cmdEnableDisable_Click()` procedure:

```
Sub cmdEnableDisable_Click ()

    If KeepTrack = 1 Then
        KeepTrack = 0
        cmdEnableDisable.Caption = "&Enable"
    Else
        KeepTrack = 1
        cmdEnableDisable.Caption = "&Disable"
    End If

End Sub
```

Executing the Timer Program

☐ Execute the Timer program.

The program does not beep every 2 seconds.

To enable the beeping, click the Enable button (see Figure 3.6).

Figure 3.6.
The cmdEnableDisable button as an Enable button.

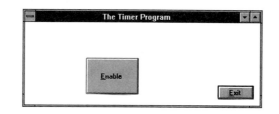

☐ Click the Enable button.

The caption of the Enable button changes to Disable, and the program now beeps every 2 seconds (see Figure 3.7).

☐ Click the Disable button.

The caption of the Disable button changes to Enable, and the program does not beep every 2 seconds.

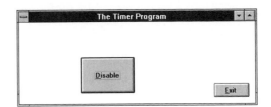

Figure 3.7.
*The cmdEnableDisable
button as a Disable button.*

☐ You may keep clicking the Enable/Disable button to enable or disable the beeping.

☐ Click the Exit button to terminate the program.

The Code Inside the General Declarations Section of the frmTimer Form

The code inside the general declarations section of the frmTimer form includes the declaration of the `KeepTrack` variable:

```
' Declare the KeepTrack variable
Dim KeepTrack
```

Why do you declare this variable in the general declarations section? You want this variable to be visible by all the procedures of this form. If you declare this variable inside the `tmrTimer_Timer()` procedure, you are able to access this variable from inside the code of the `tmrTimer_Timer()` procedure, but you are not able to access this variable from any other procedure. By declaring this variable inside the general declarations section of the form, you make this variable accessible by all the procedures and functions that exist in this form.

The Code Inside the *tmrTimer_Timer()* Event Procedure of the frmTimer Form

The `tmrTimer_Timer()` procedure is executed every 2 seconds (because you set the Interval property of the tmrTimer control to 2000):

```
Sub tmrTimer_Timer ()

    ' If the KeepTrack variable is equal to 1,
    ' then enable beeping.
    If KeepTrack = 1 Then
      Beep
    End If

End Sub
```

If the variable `KeepTrack` is equal to 1, the statement between the `If` line and the `End If` line is executed, and the `Beep` statement is executed. If, however, the variable `KeepTrack` is not equal to 1, the `Beep` statement is not executed. Note that the `KeepTrack` variable is not declared in this procedure; nevertheless, this procedure recognizes this variable because it was declared in the general declarations section of the form.

Upon startup of the program, the variable KeepTrack is created and its value is set to 0.

The Code Inside the *cmdEnableDisable_Click()* Event Procedure of the frmTimer Form

The cmdEnableDisable_Click() procedure is executed whenever the user clicks the cmdEnableDisable button:

```
Sub cmdEnableDisable_Click ()

    If KeepTrack = 1 Then
       KeepTrack = 0
       cmdEnableDisable.Caption = "&Enable"
    Else
       KeepTrack = 1
       cmdEnableDisable.Caption = "&Disable"
    End If

End Sub
```

If the current value of the KeepTrack variable is 1, the statements between the If line and the Else line change its value to 0 and change the Caption property of the cmdEnableDisable button to Enable.

If, however, the current value of the KeepTrack variable is not equal to 1, the statements between the Else line and the End If line are executed. These statements toggle the value of the KeepTrack variable to 1 and change the Caption property of the cmdEnableDisable button to Disable.

The cmdEnableDisable_Click() procedure recognizes the KeepTrack variable because this variable was declared in the general declarations section of the frmTimer form.

Modifying the Timer Program

The reason the KeepTrack variable was used was to demonstrate how a variable may be declared in the general declarations section, and, hence, may be accessed by all the procedures of the form. However, you may implement the Timer program without the use of the KeepTrack variable. Use the following steps to see how this is accomplished:

☐ Remove the declaration of the KeepTrack variable from the general declarations section of the frmTimer form (that is, the program will not use this variable). The following is the only code that should be in the general declarations section of the form:

```
' All variables MUST be declared.
Option Explicit
```

As shown in the properties table of the tmrTimer control, Visual Basic assigns the value True as the default value for the Enabled property. Now change the setting of this property:

☐ Change the Enabled property of the tmrTimer control to False.

☐ Change the cmdEnableDisable_Click() procedure so it looks like the following:

```
Sub cmdEnableDisable_Click ()

    If tmrTimer.Enabled = True Then
        tmrTimer.Enabled = False
        cmdEnableDisable.Caption = "&Enable"
    Else
        tmrTimer.Enabled = True
        cmdEnableDisable.Caption = "&Disable"
    End If

End Sub
```

☐ Change the tmrTimer_Timer() procedure so that it looks like the following:

```
Sub tmrTimer_Timer ()

    Beep

End Sub
```

☐ Save the project.

Executing the Timer Program

☐ Execute the Timer program and verify that it works the same way it worked when the KeepTrack variable was used.

☐ Terminate the program by clicking the Exit button.

The Code Inside the *tmrTimer_Timer()* Procedure

The code inside the tmrTimer_Timer() procedure is executed every 2000 milliseconds provided that the Enabled property of the tmrTimer control is set to True.

Because you set the Enabled property of this timer to False, upon startup of the program this procedure is not executed every 2 seconds.

The Code Inside the *cmdEnableDisable_Click()* Procedure

The cmdEnableDisable_Click() procedure is executed whenever the user clicks the cmdEnableDisable button:

```
Sub cmdEnableDisable_Click ()

    If tmrTimer.Enabled = True Then
        tmrTimer.Enabled = False
        cmdEnableDisable.Caption = "&Enable"
    Else
        tmrTimer.Enabled = True
        cmdEnableDisable.Caption = "&Disable"
    End If

End Sub
```

The If statement checks the value of the Enabled property of the timer control. If the timer is enabled, the statements between the If line and the Else line are executed. These statements set the Enabled property of the timer to False and change the Caption property of the cmdEnableDisable button to Enable.

If, however, the current value of the Enabled property of the timer control is not True, the statements between the Else line and the End If line are executed. These statements set the Enabled property of the timer to True and change the Caption property of the cmdEnableDisable button to Disable.

Many Windows programs use the preceding technique for changing the Caption of the button in accordance with the current status of the program.

Summary

This chapter discusses the decision maker statements of Visual Basic and the various loop statements. These statements are considered the programming building blocks of Visual Basic, which together with your knowledge about controls and properties, enable you to write Visual Basic programs for Windows.

This chapter also focuses on the timer control, the visibility of the variables, and procedures, functions, and methods.

Q&A

Q The Timer program illustrates that I can implement the program by using the variable KeepTrack that was declared in the general declarations section, as well as without the KeepTrack variable. Which way is the preferred way?

A Generally speaking, if you can implement a program without using variables that are declared in the general declarations section, this is the preferred way because the program is easier to read and understand.

However, when writing programs, if you find that it is necessary to use such variables, then use them. The problem with such variables is that if you have many variables declared in the general declarations section, you might lose track of the purpose of these variables, and the program will become difficult to read and to understand.

Quiz

1. What is wrong with the following If…End If statement:

```
If B = 3
   B = 2
End If
```

2. Suppose that currently the variable MyVariable is equal to 3. What will be the contents of the lblMyLabel label after the following code is executed:

```
Select Case MyVariable

        Case 0
            lblMyLabel.Caption = "Hi, Have a nice day"

        Case 1
            lblMyLabel.Caption = ""

        Case 2
            lblMyLabel.Caption = "Are you having fun?"

        Case 3
            lblMyLabel.Caption = "Good-bye"

        Case 4
            lblMyLabel.Caption = "Good morning"

    End Select
```

Exercises

1. Change the Sum program so that it uses the Do While…Loop statements instead of the For…Next loop.

2. Enhance the Sum program as follows:

   Add a command button. The command button should have the following properties: the Name property should be cmdSqr and the Caption property should be Square Root.

   Whenever the user clicks the Square Root button, the program should calculate and display the square root of the number that is selected by the scroll bar.

> ✓ **Tip:** Use the Sqr() function to calculate the square root of a number.

Quiz Answers

1. You must include the Then word. The correct syntax is the following:

```
If B = 3 Then
    B = 2
End If
```

2. Because the current value of MyVariable is 3, the statements under Case 3 are executed. In this example, there is only one statement under the Case 3 line:

```
Case 3
    lblMyLabel.Caption = "Good-bye"
```

The lblMyLabel label contains the text Good-bye.

Exercise Answers

1. Change the cmdSumIt_Click() procedure so that it looks like the following:

```
Sub cmdSumIt_Click ()

    Dim I
    Dim R

    I = 1
    Do While I <= vsbNum.Value
        R = R + I
        I = I + 1
    Loop

    txtResult.Text = R

End Sub
```

The procedure initializes the variable I to 1 and starts the Do While loop. The statements between the Do While line and the Loop line are executed as long as I is less than or equal to the Value property of the vsbNum scroll bar.

2. Use the following steps:

☐ Add the command button to the form.

☐ Add the following code inside the cmdSqr_Click() procedure:

```
Sub cmdSqr_Click ()

    txtResult.Text = Sqr(vsbNum.Value)
```

End Sub

☐ Save the project.

☐ Execute the Sum program.

☐ Select the number 4 by clicking the scroll bar.

☐ Click the Square Root button.

The program responds by displaying the result.

☐ Terminate the program by clicking the Exit button.

The cmdSqr_Click() procedure is executed whenever the user clicks the Square Root button. The statement inside this procedure executes the Sqr() function:

```
txtResult.Text = Sqr(vsbNum.Value)
```

The returned value of the Sqr() function is assigned to the Text property of the txtResult text box. The Sqr() function returns the square root of the number that is specified as its argument.

The Sqr() function is one of the many functions that Visual Basic includes. Therefore, you do not have to write the Sqr() function yourself.

The Mouse

Many Windows programs make heavy use of the mouse device. In this chapter you'll learn how to detect and make use of the various events that occur due to mouse movements, mouse clicking, and the combination of mouse clicking and keyboard pressing. You'll also learn about dragging and dropping objects with the mouse.

Moving Objects

The Move program moves objects by responding to mouse events.

The Visual Implementation of the Move Program

To build the Move program, use the following steps:

☐ Start a new project.

☐ Save the form of the project as MOVE.FRM and save the make file of the project as MOVE.MAK.

☐ Build the form of the Move program according to the specifications in Table 4.1.

The completed form should look like the one shown in Figure 4.1.

Table 4.1. The properties table of the Move program.

Object	Property	Setting
Form	**Name**	**frmMove**
	BackColor	(yellow)
	Caption	The Move Program
	Height	4425
	Left	1035
	Top	1140
	Width	7485
Option Button	**Name**	**optCup**
	BackColor	(yellow)
	Caption	Cup
	Height	495
	Left	480
	Top	1800
	Width	1215

Object	Property	Setting
Option Button	**Name**	**optClock**
	BackColor	(yellow)
	Caption	Clock
	Height	495
	Left	480
	Top	1320
	Width	1215
Option Button	**Name**	**optBell**
	BackColor	(yellow)
	Caption	Bell
	Height	495
	Left	480
	Top	840
	Width	1215
Command Button	**Name**	**cmdExit**
	Caption	E&xit
	Height	495
	Left	3120
	Top	3240
	Width	1215
Image	**Name**	**imgCup**
	Height	330
	Left	3840
	Picture	C:\VB\BITMAPS\ASSORTED\CUP.BMP
	Top	240
	Width	360
Image	**Name**	**imgClock**
	Height	330
	Left	3360
	Picture	C:\VB\BITMAPS\ASSORTED\CLOCK.BMP

continues

Table 4.1. continued

Object	Property	Setting
	Top	240
	Width	360
Image	**Name**	**imgBell**
	Height	330
	Left	2880
	Picture	C:\VB\BITMAPS\ASSORTED\BELL.BMP
	Top	240
	Width	360

Depending on which version of Visual Basic you are using, the BMP files listed in Table 4.1 may not appear in your Visual Basic directory. If your Visual Basic directory doesn't contain these files, use any other small BMP files.

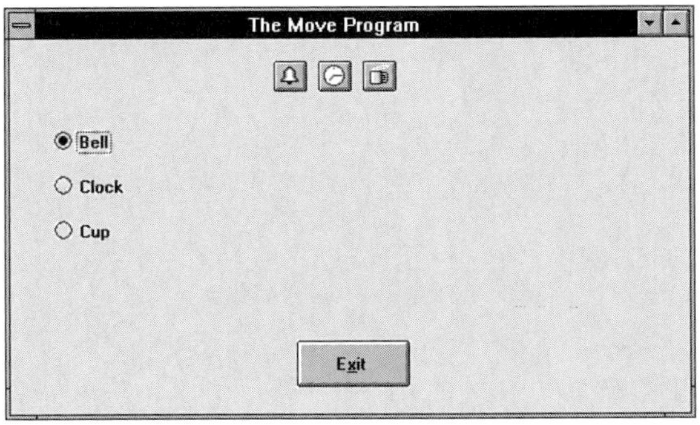

Figure 4.1.
The Move program.

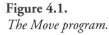

Entering the Code of the Move Program

☐ Enter the following code inside the general declarations section of the frmMove form:

```
' All variables MUST be declared.
Option Explicit
```

☐ Enter the following code in the Form_MouseDown() event procedure:

```
Sub Form_MouseDown    (Button As Integer,
                    ➥ Shift  As Integer,
                    ➥ X      As Single,
                    ➥ Y      As Single)
```

```
    ' Move the checked object to coordinate X,Y
    If optBell.Value = True Then
        imgBell.Move X, Y
    ElseIf optClock.Value = True Then
        imgClock.Move X, Y
    Else
        imgCup.Move X, Y
    End If
End Sub
```

☐ Enter the following code inside the cmdExit_Click() event procedure:

```
Sub cmdExit_Click ()

    End

End Sub
```

Executing the Move Program

☐ Execute the Move program.

As shown in Figure 4.1, the Move program displays three images: a bell, a clock, and a cup. It also displays three option buttons labeled Bell, Clock, and Cup. When you click the mouse inside the form of the program, one of the images moves to the location where the mouse is clicked. You select which image moves by selecting one of the option buttons. For example, if the bell's option button is currently checked, clicking the mouse anywhere inside the form moves the bell image to the position where the mouse was clicked (see Figure 4.2).

To terminate the Move program click the Exit button.

Figure 4.2.
The Move program after you
move the bell.

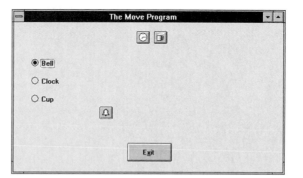

How the Move Program Works

During the discussion of the Move program, you'll encounter the term *form coordinates*. Therefore, the discussion of the Move program starts with the form coordinates topic.

Form Coordinates

The coordinates of a form may be specified in various units. The units used are specified by the ScaleMode property of the form. The default value Visual Basic sets for this property is twip (there are 1440 twips in one inch).

> **Note:** The ScaleMode property may be set to any of the following units:
> - Twips (there are 1440 twips in one inch)
> - Points (there are 72 points in one inch)
> - Pixels (the number of pixels in one inch depends on the resolution of the monitor)
> - Inches
> - Millimeters
> - Centimeters

The origin of the form coordinate system is defined by the ScaleTop and ScaleLeft properties of the form. The default values that Visual Basic assigns to the ScaleTop and ScaleLeft properties are 0. This means that the upper-left corner of the form's area has the coordinate 0,0. As you know, a form has borders and a title bar. However, the term *form's area* means the usable area of the form. The usable area of the form does not include its borders or its title.

The Code of the *cmdExit_Click()* Event Procedure

Whenever you click the Exit button, the cmdExit_Click() procedure is executed. The End statement in this procedure causes the program to terminate:

```
Sub cmdExit_Click ()

    End

End Sub
```

The Code of the *Form_MouseDown()* Event Procedure

Mouse devices may have one to three buttons. Whenever you push down any of the mouse buttons inside the form's area, the Form_MouseDown() procedure is executed.

Because the form's area does not include the title area of the form, this procedure is not executed if the mouse is clicked inside the title area. The procedure is executed only if the mouse button is pushed inside a free area of the form. For example, if the mouse button is pushed down inside the area of the option buttons, or inside the area of the Exit button, the `Form_MouseDown()` procedure is not executed.

The Arguments of the *Form_MouseDown()* Event Procedure

The `Form_MouseDown()` procedure has four arguments: `Button`, `Shift`, `X`, and `Y`. These arguments contain information regarding the state of the mouse at the moment the mouse button was pushed down:

```
Sub Form_MouseDown (Button As Integer,
              ➥ Shift  As Integer,
              ➥ X      As Single,
              ➥ Y      As Single)

    If optBell.Value = True Then
        imgBell.Move X, Y
    ElseIf optClock.Value = True Then
        imgClock.Move X, Y
    Else
        imgCup.Move X, Y
    End If

End Sub
```

The first argument of the `Form_MouseDown()` procedure is an integer called `Button`. The value of this argument indicates whether the pushed button was the left, right, or middle button. The Move program does not care which button was pushed, so the value of this argument is not used in the procedure.

The second argument of the `Form_MouseDown()` procedure is an integer called `Shift`. The value of this argument indicates whether the mouse button was pushed simultaneously with the Shift key, the Ctrl key, or the Alt key. The Move program does not care whether the mouse button was pushed down simultaneously with any of these keys, so the value of this argument is not used in the procedure.

The third and fourth arguments of the `Form_MouseDown()` procedure are the `X` and `Y` variables. These variables contain the coordinates of the mouse location at the time the mouse button was pushed. Because the `Form_MouseDown()` procedure is executed whenever the mouse button is pushed inside the form's area, the X, Y coordinates are referenced to the form (for example, X=0, Y=0 means that the mouse button was pushed down on the upper-left corner of the form).

The *If...Else* Statements of the *Form_MouseDown()* Event Procedure

The `If...Else` statements check which option button is currently checked.

For example, if the currently checked option button is the Bell button, the first `If` condition

```
If optBell.Value = True Then
    imgBell.Move X, Y
```

is met, and this statement:

```
imgBell.Move X, Y
```

is executed. This statement uses the Move method to move the bell image from its current position to the X,Y coordinate. Recall that the X,Y coordinate is the location at which the mouse button was pushed.

The Move Method

You use the Move method to move objects. The objects that can be moved with the Move method are forms and controls.

To move the Cup object from its current location to a specific X,Y coordinate, use this statement:

```
imgCup.Move X, Y
```

> **Note:** After using the following statement:
>
> ```
> imgCup.Move X, Y
> ```
>
> the new location of the upper-left corner of the image is at coordinate X,Y.
>
> To move the image so that its center has the X,Y coordinate, you may use the following statement:
>
> ```
> imgCup.Move(X-imgCup.Width/2),(Y-imgCup.Height/2)
> ```

Drawing

The Draw program illustrates how your program may use various mouse events to implement a simple drawing program.

The Visual Implementation of the Draw Program

☐ Start a new project. Save the form of the project as DRAW.FRM and save the make file of the project as DRAW.MAK.

☐ Build the form of the Draw program according to the specifications in Table 4.2. The completed form should look like the one shown in Figure 4.3.

Table 4.2. The properties table of the Draw program.

Object	Property	Setting
Form	**Name**	**frmDraw**
	Caption	The Draw Program
	Height	4425
	Left	1035
	Top	1140
	Width	7485
Command Button	**Name**	**cmdExit**
	Caption	E&xit
	Height	495
	Left	6000
	Top	3360
	Width	1215

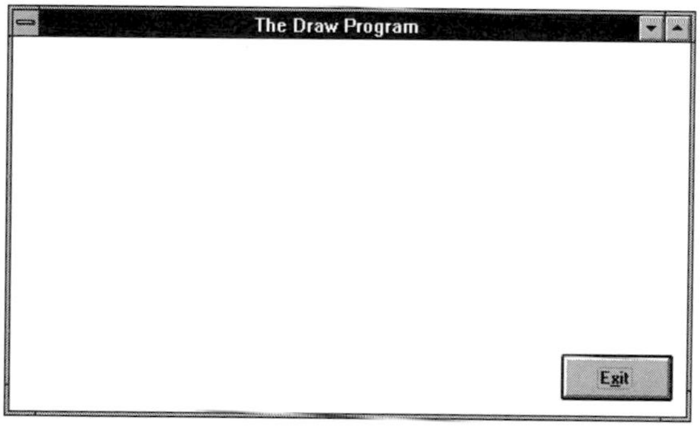

Figure 4.3.
The Draw program.

Entering the Code of the Draw Program

☐ Enter the following code in the general declarations section of the frmDraw form:

```
' All variables MUST be declared.
Option Explicit
```

☐ Enter the following code in the Form_MouseDown() event procedure:

```
Sub Form_MouseDown (Button As Integer,
                  ➡ Shift  As Integer,
                  ➡ X      As Single,
                  ➡ Y      As Single)

    ' Change CurrentX and CurrentY to the coordinate
    ' where the mouse button was just pushed.
    frmDraw.CurrentX = X
    frmDraw.CurrentY = Y

End Sub
```

☐ Enter the following code in the `Form_MouseMove()` event procedure:

```
Sub Form_MouseMove (Button As Integer,
                  ➡ Shift  As Integer,
                  ➡ X      As Single,
                  ➡ Y      As Single)

    ' If the left mouse button is currently pushed
    ' then draw a line.
    If Button = 1 Then
      Line(frmDraw.CurrentX,frmDraw.CurrentY)-(X,Y),QBColor(0)
    End If

End Sub
```

☐ Enter the following code in the `cmdExit_Click()` event procedure:

```
Sub cmdExit_Click ()

    End

End Sub
```

Executing the Draw Program

☐ Start the Draw program.

Upon startup of the Draw program, an empty form pops up, as shown in Figure 4.3.

When you push down the mouse button inside the form of the program and move the mouse (while the mouse button is down), a line is drawn in accordance with the mouse movement. Releasing the mouse button stops the drawing process. Figure 4.4 is an example of a drawing done with the Draw program.

Figure 4.4.
Drawing with the Draw program.

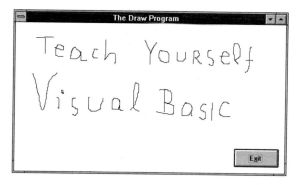

To terminate the Draw program click the Exit button.

How the Draw Program Works

The Draw program uses two graphics-related Visual Basic concepts: the Line method and the CurrentX and CurrentY properties. To understand the Draw program, you first need to understand these graphics-related concepts.

The Line Method

To draw a line inside a form, use the Line method. For example, to draw a line from the coordinate 2000, 3000 to 5000, 2500, you use the following statement:

```
Line (2000,3000) - (5000,2500)
```

Figure 4.5 shows the line that is drawn by this Line method statement. The line starts 2000 twips from the left side of the form and 3000 twips from the top of the form. The line ends 5000 twips from the left side of the form and 2500 twips from the top of the form.

Figure 4.5.
Drawing a line with the Line method.

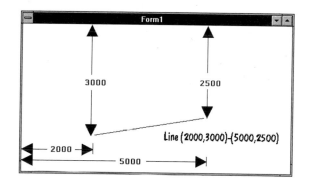

You may also specify the color in which you want the line to be drawn. The color may be specified by using the QBColor() function. The QBColor() function uses the numbers shown in Table 4.3.

Table 4.3. Numbers used in the QBColor() function.

Color	Number
Black	0
Blue	1
Green	2
Cyan	3
Red	4
Magenta	5
Yellow	6
White ✓	7
Gray	8
Light blue	9
Light green	10
Light cyan	11
Light red	12
Light magenta	13
Light yellow	14
Bright white ✓	15

For example, to draw the line of Figure 4.5 in black use this statement:

```
Line (2000,3000) - (5000,2500), QBColor(0)
```

To draw the line of Figure 4.5 in red use this statement:

```
Line (2000,3000) - (5000,2500), QBColor(4)
```

The CurrentX and CurrentY Properties of a Form

If you examine the Properties window of a form, you will not find the CurrentX and CurrentY properties, because Visual Basic does not let you set these properties at design time. You may change the values of these properties only at runtime.

The CurrentX and CurrentY properties are automatically updated by Visual Basic after using various graphics methods. For example, after using the Line method to draw a line inside a form, Visual Basic automatically assigns the coordinate of the endpoint of the line to the CurrentX and CurrentY properties of the form on which the line was drawn. Therefore, after this statement is executed CurrentX equals 5000, and CurrentY equals 2500:

```
Line (2000,3000) - (5000,2500), QBColor(0)
```

The Code of the *Form_MouseDown()* Event Procedure

Whenever the mouse button is pushed inside the form's area, the Form_MouseDown() procedure is executed:

```
Sub Form_MouseDown (Button As Integer,
              ➡ Shift  As Integer,
              ➡ X      As Single,
              ➡ Y      As Single)

    frmDraw.CurrentX = X
    frmDraw.CurrentY = Y

End Sub
```

The Form_MouseDown() procedure assigns the values of the X and Y arguments to the CurrentX and CurrentY properties of the Draw form. Therefore, after you push the mouse button, the CurrentX and CurrentY properties are updated with the coordinate of the mouse at the time you pushed the mouse button.

The Code of the *Form_MouseMove()* Event Procedure

The procedure Form_MouseMove() is executed whenever you move the mouse over the form.

The X and Y arguments of this procedure have identical meanings to the X and Y arguments of the Form_MouseDown() procedure:

```
Sub Form_MouseMove (Button As Integer,
              ➡ Shift  As Integer,
              ➡ X      As Single,
              ➡ Y      As Single)

' If the left mouse button is currently pushed
' then draw a black line.
If Button = 1 Then
  Line(frmDraw.CurrentX,frmDraw.CurrentY)-(X,Y),QBColor(0)
End If

End Sub
```

The code inside the Form_MouseMove() procedure checks whether the left mouse button is currently pushed down. This checking is accomplished by examining the value of the Button argument. If the Button argument is equal to 1, it means that the left mouse button is pushed. (A more detailed discussion of the Button argument is presented later in this chapter.)

If the left button is pushed down, the Line method statement is executed:

```
Line(frmDraw.CurrentX,frmDraw.CurrentY)-(X,Y),QBColor(0)
```

This Line statement draws a line from the location specified by the CurrentX and CurrentY properties to the current location of the mouse.

Recall that Visual Basic automatically updates the CurrentX and CurrentY properties with the endpoint of the line after the Line method is executed. This means that the next time the Form_MouseMove() procedure is executed, the starting point of the line is already updated. So on the next execution of the Form_MouseMove() procedure a line is drawn, starting from the endpoint of the previous line.

As you move the mouse, Visual Basic executes the Form_MouseMove() procedure, and if the mouse button is held down, a new line is drawn from the end of the previous line to the current location of the mouse.

The Code of the *cmdExit_Click()* Event Procedure

Whenever you click the Exit button, the cmdExit_Click() procedure is executed. The End statement in this procedure causes the program to terminate:

```
Sub cmdExit_Click ()

    End

End Sub
```

The AutoRedraw Property

There is a small flaw in the Draw program. Use the following steps to see the problem:

☐ Execute the Draw program, and draw several lines with it.

☐ Minimize the window of the program. (Click the minus icon that appears on the upper-left corner of the form, and choose Minimize from the menu that pops up.)

The Draw program responds by closing its window and displaying itself as an icon on the desktop.

☐ Restore the window of the Draw program. (Click the icon of the program and select Restore from the menu that pops up.)

As you can see, your drawing disappeared!

The same problem occurs if you hide part of the Draw window by placing another window on top of it. To solve this problem, at design time simply set the AutoRedraw property of the form to True. As implied by the name of this property, if it is set to True, Visual Basic automatically redraws the window whenever necessary.

The HowOften Program

Visual Basic cannot occupy itself by constantly executing the Form_MouseMove() procedure whenever the mouse is moved. In fact, if this were the case, Visual Basic would not be able to execute any other procedure while you moved the mouse. To be able to execute other tasks while the mouse is moving, Visual Basic checks the status of the mouse only at fixed intervals. If Visual Basic finds that the mouse was moved since the last check, the Form_MouseMove() procedure is executed. The HowOften program illustrates how often Form_MouseMove() is executed.

The Visual Implementation of the HowOften Program

☐ Start a new project. Save the form of the project as HOWOFTEN.FRM and save the make file of the project as HOWOFTEN.MAK.

☐ Build the form according to the specifications in Table 4.4.

The completed form should look like the one shown in Figure 4.6.

Table 4.4. The properties table of the HowOften program.

Object	Property	Setting
Form	**Name**	**frmHowOften**
	Caption	The HowOften Program
	Height	4425
	Left	1035
	Top	1140
	Width	7485
Command Button	**Name**	**cmdExit**
	Caption	E&xit
	Height	495
	Left	6000
	Top	3360
	Width	1215

Figure 4.6.
The HowOften program.

Entering the Code of the HowOften Program

☐ Enter the following code in the general declarations section of the frmHowOften form:

```
' All variables MUST be declared.
Option Explicit
```

☐ Enter the following code in the `Form_MouseMove()` event procedure:

```
Sub Form_MouseMove (Button As Integer,
            ➡ Shift  As Integer,
            ➡ X      As Single,
            ➡ Y      As Single)

    Circle (X, Y), 40

End Sub
```

☐ Enter the following code in the `cmdExit_Click()` event procedure:

```
Sub cmdExit_Click ()

    End

End Sub
```

Executing the HowOften Program

☐ Execute the HowOften program.

When you execute the HowOften program, the window shown in Figure 4.6 is displayed. As you move the mouse, the `Form_MouseMove()` procedure draws small circles at the current location of the mouse. As you move the mouse, you realize that the `Form_MouseMove()` procedure is not executed for each and every movement of the mouse (see Figure 4.7). In particular, when you move the mouse quickly, the trail of small circles that the `Form_MouseMove()` procedure draws consists of only several locations along the path of the mouse. However, if you move the mouse slowly, the `Form_MouseMove()` procedure leaves a dense trail of circles. Remember, each small circle is an indication that the `MouseMove` event occurred and the `Form_MouseMove()` procedure was executed.

Figure 4.7.
Moving the mouse in the HowOften program.

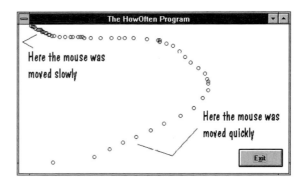

How the HowOften Program Works

The HowOften program uses the `Form_MouseMove()` procedure for performing the work.

The Code of the *Form_MouseMove()* Event Procedure

Whenever Visual Basic checks the mouse status and finds that the mouse moved since the last check, the `Form_MouseMove()` procedure is executed:

```
Sub Form_MouseMove (Button As Integer,
              ➥ Shift  As Integer,
              ➥ X      As Single,
              ➥ Y      As Single)

    Circle (X, Y), 40

End Sub
```

The `Form_MouseMove()` procedure simply draws a small circle at the current location of the mouse. The circle is drawn by using the Circle method.

The Circle Method

As implied by its name, the Circle method draws a circle. To draw a circle with a radius of 40 units at coordinate X, Y use the following statement:

```
Circle (X, Y), 40
```

The units used by the Circle method are the units indicated by the ScaleMode property. Because the ScaleMode property of the form is Twip, the Circle method uses the twip units (that is, radius in units of twips, and center at X,Y, where X,Y are in units of twips).

103

The Code of the *cmdExit_Click()* Event Procedure

Whenever you click the Exit button, the cmdExit_Click() procedure is executed. The End statement in this procedure causes the program to terminate:

```
Sub cmdExit_Click ()

    End

End Sub
```

The *Button* Argument

The Button argument of the mouse event procedures specifies which mouse button was pushed at the time of the event.

Now you'll write a program called Button. This program uses the Button argument of the MouseDown and MouseUp event procedures for determining which of the mouse buttons was pushed or released.

The Visual Implementation of the Button Program

☐ Start a new project. Save the form of the project as BUTTON.FRM and save the make file of the project as BUTTON.MAK.

☐ Build the form of the Button program according to the specifications in Table 4.5.

The completed form should look like the one shown in Figure 4.8.

Table 4.5. The properties table of the Button program.

Object	Property	Setting
Form	**Name**	**frmButton**
	Caption	The Button Program
	Height	4425
	Left	1035
	Top	1140
	Width	7485
Text Box	**Name**	**txtResult**
	Alignment	2-Center
	Enabled	False

Object	Property	Setting
	Height	495
	Left	1800
	MultiLine	True
	Text	(empty)
	Top	1440
	Width	3615
Command Button	**Name**	**cmdExit**
	Caption	E&xit
	Height	495
	Left	3000
	Top	3360
	Width	1215
Image	**Name**	**imgMouse**
	Height	975
	Left	480
	Picture	C:\VB\ICONS\COMPUTER \MOUSE04.ICO
	Stretch	True
	Top	600
	Width	1095
Label	**Name**	**lblInstruction**
	Alignment	2-Center
	Caption	Push any of the mouse buttons
	ForeColor	(red)
	Height	255
	Left	1680
	Top	840
	Width	3615
Label	**Name**	**lblHeading**
	Caption	Instructions:
	FontUnderline	True
	FontSize	13.5

Table 4.5. continued

Object	Property	Setting
	Height	495
	Left	2760
	Top	240
	Width	1935

Figure 4.8.
The Button program.

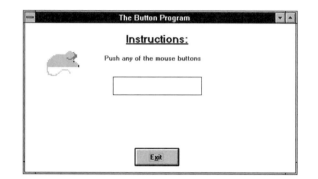

Entering the Code of the Button Program

☐ Enter the following code in the general declarations section of the frmButton form:

```
Option Explicit
```

☐ Enter the following code in the Form_MouseDown() event procedure:

```
Sub Form_MouseDown (Button As Integer,
             ➥ Shift  As Integer,
             ➥ X      As Single,
             ➥ Y      As Single)

' Is the left mouse button down?
If Button = 1 Then
   txtResult.Text="Left button is currently pushed"
End If

' Is the right mouse button down?
If Button = 2 Then
  txtResult.Text="Right button is currently pushed"
End If

' Is the middle mouse button down?
If Button = 4 Then
 txtResult.Text="Middle button is currently pushed"
End If
```

```
End Sub
```

☐ Enter the following code in the Form_MouseUp() event procedure:

```
Sub Form_MouseUp (Button As Integer,
            ➥ Shift  As Integer,
            ➥ X      As Single,
            ➥ Y      As Single)

    ' Clear the content of the text box
    txtResult.Text = ""

End Sub
```

☐ Enter the following code in the cmdExit_Click() event procedure:

```
Sub cmdExit_Click ()

    End

End Sub
```

Executing the Button Program

☐ Execute the Button program.

Upon startup of the Button program, the window of Figure 4.8 is shown.

Whenever you push any of the mouse buttons in a free area of the form, the text box displays the name of the currently pushed button. For example, Figure 4.9 shows the content of the text box when the left button is pushed. The Button program displays the status of the mouse button only if the button is pushed in a free area of the form.

Figure 4.9.
Displaying the pushed button.

Note: A *free area* of the form is an area inside the form that is not covered by an enabled control. For example, the Enabled property of the lblInstruction label is True. Therefore, the area that this label occupies is not considered a free area of the

form. On the other hand, the Enabled property of the txtResult text box is False.
Therefore, the area that this text box occupies is considered a free area of the form.

Even if your mouse has three buttons, but it is not installed as a three-button mouse, the Button
program does not respond if you push the middle mouse button.

How the Button Program Works

The Button program responds to the MouseDown event in the Form_MouseDown() procedure and
to the MouseUp event in the Form_MouseUp() procedure.

The Code of the *Form_MouseDown()* Event Procedure

Whenever you push any of the mouse buttons in a free area of the form, the Form_MouseDown()
procedure is executed. This procedure detects which button was pushed by examining the value
of the Button argument. When the Button argument equals 1, it means that the left button is
pushed. When the Button argument equals 2, it means that the right button is down. When the
Button argument equals 4, it means that the middle button is pushed:

```
Sub Form_MouseDown (Button As Integer,
                 ➥ Shift  As Integer,
                 ➥ X       As Single,
                 ➥ Y       As Single)

' Is the left mouse button down?
If Button = 1 Then
   txtResult.Text="Left button is currently pushed"
End If

' Is the right mouse button down?
If Button = 2 Then
   txtResult.Text="Right button is currently pushed"
End If

' Is the middle mouse button down?
If Button = 4 Then
   txtResult.Text="Middle button is currently pushed"
End If

End Sub
```

The Code of the *Form_MouseUp()* Event Procedure

Whenever the mouse button is released, the Form_MouseUp() procedure is executed. The code
inside this procedure clears the content of the text box:

```
Sub Form_MouseUp (Button As Integer,
              ➥ Shift  As Integer,
              ➥ X       As Single,
              ➥ Y       As Single)

    ' Clear the content of the text box
    txtResult.Text = ""

End Sub
```

The *Button* Argument

The Button argument that is used in the mouse event procedures indicates which mouse button is pushed. This argument is declared as an integer and therefore consists of 2 bytes. These 2 bytes are shown in Figure 4.10.

Also shown in Figure 4.10 are the three least significant bits of the integer (the bits at the right), which represent the status of the mouse button.

For example, if the left mouse button is pushed, the binary number that represents the Button argument is the decimal number 1:

`00000000 00000001`

If the right mouse button is pushed, the binary number that represents the Button argument is the decimal number 2:

`00000000 00000010`

If the middle mouse button is pushed, the binary number that represents the Button argument is which is the decimal number 4:

`00000000 00000100`

The Button argument in the Form_MouseDown() procedure reflects the last status of the mouse button. For example, if you push two buttons together, the Button argument reports that only one button is pushed: the last button that was pushed. In other words, the value of the Button argument in the Form_MouseDown() procedures may be either 1, 2, or 4, but it cannot have any other values.

Figure 4.10.
The Button *argument.*

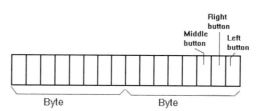

The *Button* Argument of the *MouseMove* Event

As stated, the Button argument in the Form_MouseDown() procedure may be either 1, 2, or 4, but it cannot have any other values. This means that you can't use the MouseDown event to detect whether there is more than one mouse button pushed. In contrast, the Button argument of the Form_MouseMove() procedure may have any value between 0 and 7, indicating all the possible combinations of pushing the mouse buttons.

For example, when the Button argument of the Form_MouseMove() procedure is equal to 3, the equivalent binary number is

00000000 00000011

which means that both the left and right buttons are pushed (see Figure 4.10).

The Button2 program illustrates how to use the Button argument of the Form_MouseMove() procedure.

The Visual Implementation of the Button2 Program

☐ Start a new project. Save the form of the project as BUTTON2.FRM and save the make file of the project as BUTTON2.MAK.

☐ Build the form of the Button2 program according to the specifications in Table 4.6.

The completed form should look like the one shown in Figure 4.11.

Table 4.6. The properties table of the Button2 program.

Object	Property	Setting
Form	Name	frmButton
	Caption	The Button2 Program
	Height	4425
	Left	1035
	Top	1200
	Width	7485
Check Box	Name	chkRight
	Caption	Right
	Enabled	False

Object	Property	Setting
	FontSize	13.5
	Height	495
	Left	4560
	Top	2520
	Width	1215
Check Box	**Name**	**chkMiddle**
	Caption	Middle
	Enabled	False
	FontSize	13.5
	Height	495
	Left	3120
	Top	1920
	Width	1215
Check Box	**Name**	**chkLeft**
	Caption	Left
	Enabled	False
	FontSize	13.5
	Height	495
	Left	1920
	Top	2520
	Width	1095
Command Button	**Name**	**cmdExit**
	Caption	E&xit
	Height	495
	Left	3000
	Top	3360
	Width	1215
Image	**Name**	**imgMouse**
	Height	975
	Left	480
	Picture	C:\VB\ICONS\COMPUTER \MOUSE04.ICO

Table 4.6. continued

Object	Property	Setting
	Stretch	True
	Top	600
	Width	1095
Label	**Name**	**lblInstruction**
	Alignment	2-Center
	Caption	Push any of the mouse button(s) and move the mouse
	ForeColor	(red)
	Height	255
	Left	1680
	Top	840
	Width	4815
Label	**Name**	**lblHeading**
	FontUnderline	True
	Caption	Instructions:
	FontSize	13.5
	Height	495
	Left	2760
	Top	240
	Width	1935

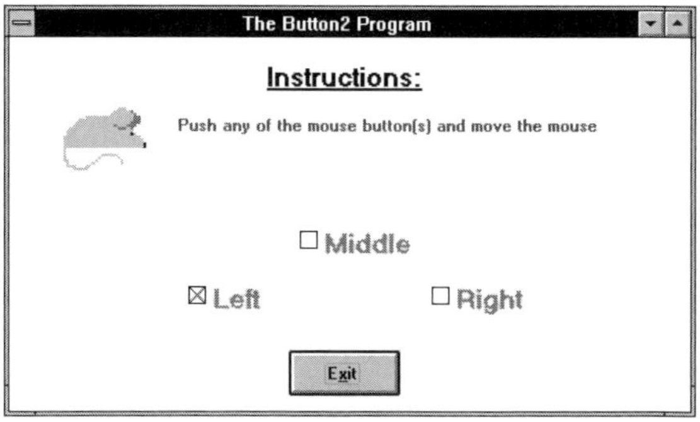

Figure 4.11.
The Button2 program.

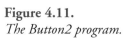

Entering the Code of the Button2 Program

☐ Enter the following code inside the general declarations section of the frmButton2 form:

```
' All variables MUST be declared.
Option Explicit
```

☐ Enter the following code in the Form_MouseMove() event procedure:

```
Sub Form_MouseMove (Button As Integer,
               ➥ Shift  As Integer,
               ➥ X      As Single,
               ➥ Y      As Single)

    ' Is the left button pushed?
    If (Button And 1) = 1 Then
        chkLeft.Value = 1
    Else
        chkLeft.Value = 0
    End If

    ' Is the right button pushed?
    If (Button And 2) = 2 Then
        chkRight.Value = 1
    Else
        chkRight.Value = 0
    End If

    ' Is the middle button pushed?
    If (Button And 4) = 4 Then
        chkMiddle.Value = 1
    Else
        chkMiddle.Value = 0
    End If

End Sub
```

☐ Enter the following code in the Form_MouseUp() event procedure:

```
Sub Form_MouseUp (Button As Integer,
             ➥ Shift  As Integer,
             ➥ X      As Single,
             ➥ Y      As Single)

    ' Was the left button just released?
    If Button = 1 Then
        chkLeft.Value = 0
    End If

    ' Was the right button just released?
    If Button = 2 Then
        chkRight.Value = 0
    End If

    ' Was the middle button just released?
    If Button = 4 Then
        chkMiddle.Value = 0
```

```
        End If

End Sub
```

☐ Enter the following code in the cmdExit_Click() event procedure:

```
Sub cmdExit_Click ()

    End

End Sub
```

Executing the Button2 Program

☐ Execute the Button2 program.

As shown in Figure 4.11, the window of the Button2 program includes three check boxes: the Left check box, the Middle check box, and the Right check box.

The Button2 program checks and unchecks the check boxes in accordance with the status of the mouse buttons while the mouse is moving.

For example, if you push the left and right mouse buttons together and move the mouse, the program checks the Left and Right check boxes.

How the Button2 Program Works

The Button2 program makes use of the Button argument in the Form_MouseMove() procedure, taking advantage of the fact that in this procedure the Button argument may report any combination of mouse button(s) pushed.

The Code of the *Form_MouseMove()* Event Procedure

Whenever you move the mouse, the Form_MouseMove() procedure is executed:

```
Sub Form_MouseMove (Button As Integer,
              ➥ Shift  As Integer,
              ➥ X      As Single,
              ➥ Y      As Single)

    ' Is the left button pushed?
    If (Button And 1) = 1 Then
        chkLeft.Value = 1
    Else
        chkLeft.Value = 0
    End If
```

```
    ' Is the right button pushed?
    If (Button And 2) = 2 Then
        chkRight.Value = 1
    Else
        chkRight.Value = 0
    End If

    ' Is the middle button pushed?
    If (Button And 4) - 4 Then
        chkMiddle.Value = 1
    Else
        chkMiddle.Value = 0
    End If

End Sub
```

The code inside this procedure checks and unchecks the check boxes based on the value of the Button argument. For example, the first If...Else statement determines whether the left button is pushed by ANDing the Button argument with 1. If the result of the AND operation is 1, the left mouse is pushed.

The Code of the *Form_MouseUp()* Event Procedure

4

Whenever any of the mouse buttons is released, the Form_MouseUp() procedure is executed:

```
Sub Form_MouseUp (Button As Integer,
            ➥ Shift  As Integer,
            ➥ X      As Single,
            ➥ Y      As Single)

    ' Was the left button just released?
    If Button = 1 Then
      chkLeft.Value = 0
    End If

    ' Was the right button just released?
    If Button = 2 Then
      chkRight.Value = 0
    End If

    ' Was the middle button just released?
    If Button = 4 Then
      chkMiddle.Value = 0
    End If

End Sub
```

This code checks which mouse button was released and accordingly unchecks the corresponding check box. For example, if the mouse button that was just released is the left button, the first If condition is met, and therefore the Left check box is unchecked.

Pressing the Shift, Ctrl, and Alt Keys Together with the Mouse Buttons

The `MouseDown`, `MouseUp`, and `MouseMove` event procedures have the `Shift` integer as their second argument. This argument is an indication of whether the Shift, Ctrl, or Alt keys were pressed together with the mouse button(s).

The `Shift` argument is an integer, and therefore consists of 2 bytes (see Figure 4.12).

Figure 4.12.

The `Shift` *argument.*

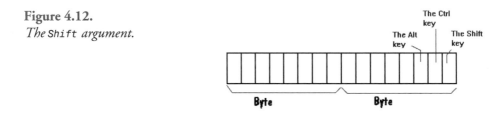

The three least significant bits of the `Shift` argument represent the status of the Shift, Ctrl, and Alt keys at the time you pushed the mouse button(s).

Table 4.7 shows the meaning of the eight possible values that the `Shift` argument may have.

Table 4.7. The `Shift` argument.

Binary Value of the `Shift` Argument	Decimal Value of the `Shift` Argument	Alt Key Pressed	Ctrl Key Pressed	Shift Key Pressed
00000000 00000000	0	No	No	No
00000000 00000001	1	No	No	Yes
00000000 00000010	2	No	Yes	No
00000000 00000011	3	No	Yes	Yes
00000000 00000100	4	Yes	No	No
00000000 00000101	5	Yes	No	Yes
00000000 00000110	6	Yes	Yes	No
00000000 00000111	7	Yes	Yes	Yes

For example, when the `Shift` argument in the `Form_MouseDown()`, `Form_MouseUp()`, or `Form_MouseMove()` procedures is equal to 6, you pressed the mouse button(s) together with the Alt and Ctrl keys. Note that the `Button` argument of the `Form_MouseDown()` procedure may have the value 1, 2, or 4. In contrast, the `Shift` argument of the `Form_MouseDown()` procedure may have any of the values listed in Table 4.7.

Dragging

Until now you have learned how to use mouse events that occur due to pushing the mouse button (MouseDown), releasing the mouse button (MouseUp), and moving the mouse (MouseMove). You'll now learn how to use mouse events that are related to dragging and dropping controls with the mouse. Dragging is the process of pushing the left mouse button inside a control and moving the mouse while holding down the mouse button. The action of releasing the mouse button after the dragging is called *dropping*.

Now write a program called Drag. This program illustrates how easy it is to implement dragging in a program.

The Visual Implementation of the Drag Program

☐ Start a new project. Save the form of the project as DRAG.FRM and save the make file of the project as DRAG.MAK.

☐ Build the form of the Drag program according to the specifications in Table 4.8.

The completed form should look like the one shown in Figure 4.13.

Table 4.8. The properties table of the Drag program.

Object	Property	Setting
Form	Name	frmDrag
	BackColor	(yellow)
	Caption	The Drag Program
	Height	4425
	Left	1035
	Top	1140
	Width	7485
Command Button	Name	cmdDragMe
	Caption	Drag Me
	DragMode	1-Automatic
	Height	495
	Left	3120
	Top	1800

continues

Table 4.8. continued

Object	Property	Setting
	Width	1215
Command Button	**Name**	**cmdExit**
	Caption	E&xit
	Height	495
	Left	3120
	Top	2880
	Width	1215

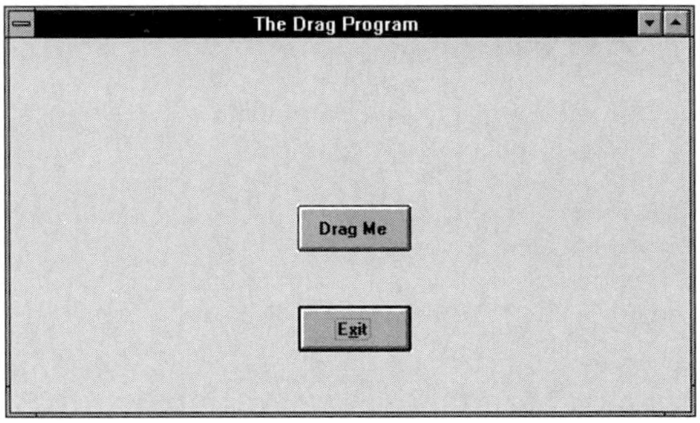

Figure 4.13.
The Drag program.

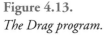

Entering the Code of the Drag Program

☐ Enter the following code in the general declarations area of the frmDrag form:

```
' All variables MUST be declared.
Option Explicit
```

☐ Enter the following code in the cmdExit_Click() event procedure:

```
Sub cmdExit_Click ()

    End

End Sub
```

Executing the Drag Program

During design time you set the DragMode property of the Drag Me button to 1-Automatic, so the Drag Me button may be dragged.

Use the following steps to see how the Drag Me button is dragged:

☐ Execute the Drag program.

☐ Push the left mouse button inside the Drag Me button and while holding the mouse button down move the mouse. As you can see, a rectangle that has the size of the Drag Me button pops up and follows the mouse movements.

☐ Try to drag the Drag Me button outside the form. The program responds by displaying the illegal icon, an indication that you dragged the control to a forbidden zone.

When you release the mouse button (called *dropping*), the rectangle disappears. Note that the Drag Me button remains in its original position.

Enhancing the Drag Program

As was demonstrated with the Drag program, while you move a control that has its DragMode property set to 1-Automatic, a rectangle that is the size of the control moves in accordance with the mouse movements. This rectangle enables you to see where the control is being dragged.

To produce a different image while the control is being dragged, use the following steps:

☐ Select the Properties window.

☐ Change the DragIcon property of the cmdDragMe button to c:\vb\icons\dragdrop\drag1pg.ico.

Use the following steps to see the effect of setting the DragIcon property:

☐ Execute the Drag program.

☐ Drag the Drag Me button.

> *The program responds by displaying the drag1pg.ico icon while the Drag Me button is dragged.*

Dropping

As previously stated, dropping is the action of releasing the mouse button at the end of the dragging process. The Drop program illustrates how dropping is used in a program.

The Visual Implementation of the Drop Program

☐ Start a new project. Save the form of the project as DROP.FRM and save the make file of the project as DROP.MAK.

☐ Build the form of the Drop program according to the specifications in Table 4.9. The completed form should look like the one shown in Figure 4.14.

Table 4.9. The properties table of the Drop program.

Object	Property	Setting
Form	**Name**	**frmDrop**
	BackColor	(yellow)
	Caption	The Drop Program
	Height	4425
	Left	1035
	Top	1140
	Width	7485
Text Box	**Name**	**txtInfo**
	Alignment	2-Center
	Enabled	False
	Height	495
	Left	840
	MultiLine	True
	Text	(empty)
	Top	480
	Width	5655
Command Button	**Name**	**cmdExit**
	BackColor	(yellow)
	Caption	E&xit
	Height	495
	Left	3120
	Top	3120
	Width	1215
Image	**Name**	**imgWater**
	DragMode	1-Automatic
	Height	1095
	Left	3120
	Picture	C:\VB\ICONS\ELEMENTS\WATER.ICO

Object	Property	Setting
	Stretch	True
	Tag	The Water image
	Top	1680
	Width	1215

Figure 4.14.
The Drop program.

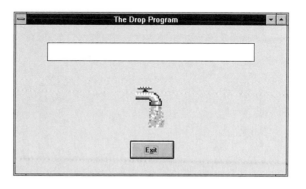

Entering the Code of the Drop Program

☐ Enter the following code in the general declarations area of the frmDrop form:

```
' All variables MUST be declared.
Option Explicit
```

☐ Enter the following code in the Form_DragOver() event procedure:

```
Sub Form_DragOver (Source As Control,
              ➡ X       As Single,
              ➡ Y       As Single,
              ➡ State   As Integer)

    Dim sInfo As String
    ' Display the dragging information.
    sInfo = "Now dragging "
    sInfo = sInfo + Source.Tag
    sInfo = sInfo + " over the Form."
    sInfo = sInfo + " State = "
    sInfo = sInfo + Str$(State)
    txtInfo.Text = sInfo

End Sub
```

☐ Enter the following code in the cmdExit_DragOver() event procedure:

```
Sub cmdExit_DragOver (Source As Control,
                 ➡ X       As Single,
                 ➡ Y       As Single,
                 ➡ State   As Integer)
```

```
Dim sInfo As String
' Display the dragging information.
sInfo = "Now dragging "
sInfo = sInfo + Source.Tag
sInfo = sInfo + " over the Exit button."
sInfo = sInfo + " State = "
sInfo = sInfo + Str$(State)
txtInfo.Text = sInfo

End Sub
```

☐ Enter the following code in the `Form_DragDrop()` event procedure:

```
Sub Form_DragDrop (Source As Control,
➡ X       As Single,
➡ Y       As Single)

    ' Clear the text box.
    txtInfo.Text = ""
    ' Move the control.
    Source.Move X, Y

End Sub
```

☐ Enter the following code in the `cmdExit_Click()` event procedure:

```
Sub cmdExit_Click ()

    End

End Sub
```

Executing the Drop Program

☐ Execute the Drop program.

☐ Drag the water image.

As you drag the water image, the text box displays a message that indicates the status of the dragging.

Upon releasing the mouse button, or dropping, the water image moves to the point of the drop.

How the Drop Program Works

The Drop program uses the `Form_DragOver()`, `cmdExit_DragOver()`, and `Form_DragDrop()` event procedures.

The Code of the *Form_DragOver()* Event Procedure

The `Form_DragOver()` procedure is executed whenever you drag a control over the form.

In the Drop program, the control being dragged is the water image. Therefore, whenever you drag the water image over the form, the Form_DragOver() procedure is executed. This procedure has four arguments: Source, X, Y, and State:

```
Sub Form_DragOver (Source As Control,
            ➡   X       As Single,
            ➡   Y       As Single,
            ➡   State   As Integer)
    . . . . . . . . . . . . . . .
    . . . . . . . . . . . . . . .
    . . . . . . . . . . . . . . .

End Sub
```

The Source argument is the control that is being dragged. Because the dragged control is the water image, the Source argument is equal to the imgWater control.

The X and Y arguments are the current X,Y coordinate of the mouse (referenced to the form coordinate system).

The State argument is an integer that has a value of 0, 1, or 2:

- When the State argument equals 2, the water image was dragged from one free point on the form to another free point on the form.

- When the State argument equals 1, it means that the water image was dragged from a free point on the form to an illegal point (such as to a point outside the free area of the form).

- When the State argument equals 0, it means that the water image was dragged from an illegal point to a free point in the form.

The Form_DragOver() procedure prepares a string called sInfo and displays this string in the txtInfo text box:

```
Sub Form_DragOver (Source As Control,
            ➡   X       As Single,
            ➡   Y       As Single,
            ➡   State   As Integer)

Dim sInfo As String

sInfo = "Now dragging "
sInfo = sInfo + Source.Tag
sInfo = sInfo + " over the Form."
sInfo = sInfo + " State = "
sInfo = sInfo + Str$(State)
txtInfo.Text = sInfo

End Sub
```

For example, when the water image is dragged from one free point in the form to another free point in the form, the content of the sInfo string is this:

Now dragging The Water image over the Form. State=2.

One of the statements that is used in preparing the sInfo string is this:

sInfo = sInfo + Source.Tag

During design time, you set the Tag property of the water image to The Water image. Therefore, the value of Source.Tag is equal to The Water image whenever the imgWater control is dragged over the form.

The Tag Property

The Tag property is often used as a storage area for data and strings. For example, the Tag property of imgWater contains a string that identifies the control. In the Form_DragOver() procedure, you use this string to identify the dragged control.

The Code of the *cmdExit_DragOver()* Event Procedure

The cmdExit_DragOver() procedure is executed whenever you drag a control over the Exit button. Therefore, whenever you drag the water image over the Exit button, this procedure is executed.

The code inside this procedure is similar to the code inside the Form_DragOver() procedure, only now the sInfo string reflects the fact that the water image is dragged over the Exit button:

```
Sub cmdExit_DragOver (Source As Control,
              ➡   X       As Single,
              ➡   Y       As Single,
              ➡   State   As Integer)

     Dim sInfo As String

     sInfo = "Now dragging "
     sInfo = sInfo + Source.Tag
     sInfo = sInfo + " over the Exit button."
     sInfo = sInfo + " State = "
     sInfo = sInfo + Str$(State)
     txtInfo.Text = sInfo

End Sub
```

For example, when you drag the water image from a point in the form to the Exit button, sInfo is filled with this string:

Now dragging The Water image over the Exit button. State = 0

State is 0 because in this example the water image is dragged from outside the Exit button into the Exit button. From the point of view of the Exit button, any point outside the Exit button is an illegal point.

The Code of the *Form_DragDrop()* Event Procedure

The Form_DragDrop() procedure is executed whenever you drop the control inside the form. There are two things to do when this occurs: clear the txtInfo text box and move the water image to the drop point. This is accomplished with the following two statements:

```
Sub Form_DragDrop (Source As Control,
            ➥ X      As Single,
            ➥ Y      As Single)

    ' Clear the text box.
    txtInfo.Text = ""

    ' Move the control.
    Source.Move X, Y

End Sub
```

The water image is moved to the drop point by using the Move method. The drop point is specified by the X,Y arguments of the procedure.

Summary

This chapter covers mouse events. You have learned about the MouseDown, MouseUp, MouseMove, DragOver, and DragDrop events. The arguments of the procedures of the mouse events provide you with information regarding the state of the mouse at the time of the event. The Button argument tells you which mouse button was pushed/released; the Shift argument tells you whether the Shift, Ctrl, or Alt keys were pressed together with the mouse button(s); and the X and Y arguments tell you where the mouse was at the time of the event.

Q&A

Q Dragging and dropping a control is nice. But where can I use it?

A Suppose you are developing a program that lets your user design forms. In such a program, the user should be able to drag and move controls. (Of course, there are many other applications for the drag and drop features.)

Q During the execution of the Button program of this chapter, I pushed down the mouse button on the lbHeading label, but the program did not recognize this push. Why?

A The Form_MouseDown() procedure is executed only if the mouse button is pushed inside a free area of the form. During design time, you left the Enabled property of the label in its default value (True). This means that the area occupied by this label belongs to the label and it is not considered part of the free area of the form.

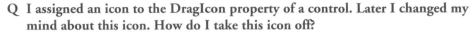
Q I assigned an icon to the DragIcon property of a control. Later I changed my mind about this icon. How do I take this icon off?

A During design time, you may select the DragIcon property in the Properties window and then click on the three dots in the setting box of the Properties window to select another icon. Visual Basic lets you select another icon.

If you want to return the default icon (an empty rectangle), click on the setting box and press the Del key. The DragIcon property changes from (icon) to (none).

Quiz

1. When is the `Form_MouseDown()` event procedure executed?

   a. When the user clicks the mouse on the Exit button

   b. When any of the mouse buttons is pushed inside a free area of the form

   c. Whenever the mouse moves inside a free area of the form

2. What is the ScaleMode property?

3. What method is used for moving objects during runtime?

   a. The Move method

   b. The Line method

   c. The Circle method

4. What is the meaning of the X and Y arguments in mouse event procedures?

5. When is the `Form_MouseMove()` event procedure executed?

   a. When the user moves the mouse inside a free area of the form

   b. When any of the mouse buttons is released

   c. When the left mouse button is released

6. When is the `Form_DragDrop()` event procedure executed?

   a. When the mouse device drops down on the floor

   b. When the user releases the mouse button over a free area of the form after the dragging

   c. When a control is dragged outside the form

7. What is the value of the `Source` argument of the `Form_DragDrop()` procedure?

   a. 0

   b. The control that was dropped

   c. The Tag property of the control that was dropped

Exercises

1. Enhance the Drag program so that whenever the user drags the Drag Me button outside the free area of the form the speaker beeps.

2. Currently, the Draw program uses the left mouse button for drawing in black. Enhance the Draw program so the right mouse button is used for drawing in red.

Quiz Answers

1. b

2. The ScaleMode property defines the units of the coordinate system of the object. For example, if the ScaleMode property of a form is set to twips, the width, height, and all other length-related properties are measured in twips.

3. a

4. The X and Y arguments contain the values of the mouse location when the event occurred.

5. a

6. b

7. b

Exercise Answers

1. The program may detect that the user dragged the control to a point outside the free area of the form by using the State argument of the Form_DragOver() procedure. If the State argument is equal to 1, the control was dragged outside the free area of the form:

```
Sub Form_DragOver (Source As Control,
              ➡ X       As Single,
              ➡ Y       As Single,
              ➡ State   As Integer)

    If State = 1 Then
        Beep
    End If

End Sub
```

2. Modify the Form_MouseMove() procedure as follows:

```
Sub Form_MouseMove (Button As Integer,
             ➡ Shift    As Integer,
             ➡ X        As Single,
             ➡ Y        As Single)
```

```
If Button = 1 Then
 ' Draw the line in black.
 Line(frmDraw.CurrentX,frmDraw.CurrentY)-(X,Y),QBColor(0)
End If

If Button = 2 Then
  ' Draw the line in red.
  Line(frmDraw.CurrentX,frmDraw.CurrentY)-(X,Y),QBColor(4)
End If


End Sub
```

The first If statement checks whether the left mouse button is currently pushed. If this is the case, a line is drawn in black. The second If statement checks whether the right mouse button is currently pushed. If this is the case, a line is drawn in red.

5

Menus

This chapter focuses on incorporating a menu into a program. You'll learn how to visually design the menu and how to attach code to it.

Writing a Program That Includes a Menu

In this chapter you will write a program that includes a menu. The program, called Colors, lets you choose a color from a menu and fill the form of the program with the selected color. The program also lets you set the size of the program's form by selecting the desired size from a menu.

Before you start writing the Colors program, specify how the menu system of the program should look and what it should do:

☐ Upon startup of the program, a menu bar with two menu titles appears: Colors and Size (see Figure 5.1).

Figure 5.1.
The Colors program.

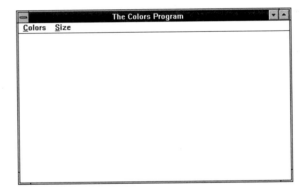

☐ The Colors menu has two items: Set color and Exit (see Figure 5.2).

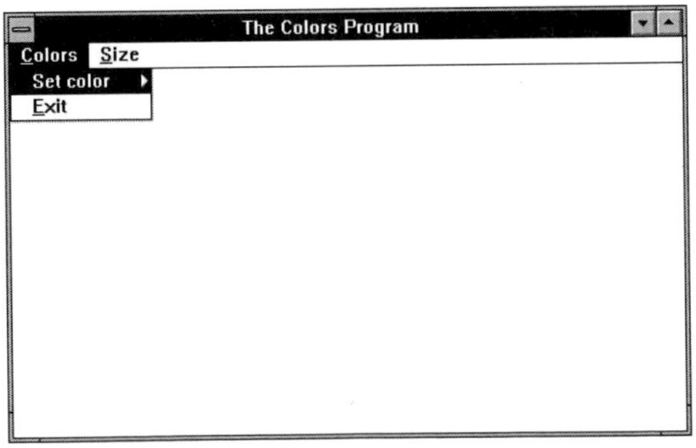

Figure 5.2.
The Colors menu.

☐ The Size menu has two items: Small and Large (see Figure 5.3).

Figure 5.3.
The Size menu.

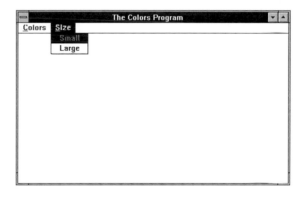

☐ When you select Set color from the Colors menu, another menu pops up. This menu lets you select a color from a list of colors (see Figure 5.4). Once you select a color, the form of the program is filled with that color.

Figure 5.4.
The submenu of Set colors.

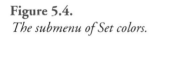

☐ When you select any of the sizes from the Size menu, the Window of the program is sized to the selected size.

☐ When you select Exit from the Colors menu, the program terminates.

The Visual Implementation
of the Colors Program

☐ Start a new project. Save the form of the project as COLORS.FRM and save the make file of the project as COLORS.MAK.

☐ Build the form of the Colors program according to the specifications in Table 5.1.

Table 5.1. The properties table of the Colors program.

Object	Property	Value
Form	Name	frmColors
	Caption	The Colors Program

Creating the Menu of the Colors Program

Now create the menu of the Colors program.

In Visual Basic, a menu is attached to a form. So before creating the menu you must first select the form.

☐ Select the Colors.frm form (highlight COLORS.FRM in the Project window, then click the View Form button in the Project window).

COLORS.FRM is now selected, so in the following steps Visual Basic attaches the menu to the COLORS.FRM form.

☐ Select Menu Design from the Window menu.

Visual Basic responds by displaying the Menu Design window (see Figure 5.5).

Figure 5.5.
The Menu Design window.

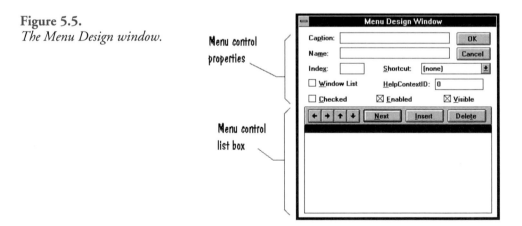

Menu control
properties

Menu control
list box

Your objective is to use the Menu Design window to create the menu system shown in Figures 5.1 through 5.4.

Creating Menu Controls

As you can see from Figure 5.5, the Menu Design window is composed of two parts: the menu control list box (the lower part of the window) and the menu control properties (the upper part of the window).

When you finish creating the menus of the Colors program, the menu control list box contains all the menu controls of the Colors program. What are menu controls? Menu controls could be menu titles (such as the Colors and Size menu titles shown in Figure 5.1) or menu items (such as the Set color and Exit items shown in Figure 5.2).

The Colors program has two pull-down menus: the Colors menu (see Figure 5.2) and the Size menu (see Figure 5.3).

As you can see from Figure 5.2, the Colors menu has three menu controls:

- Colors (the menu title)
- Set color (a menu item)
- Exit (a menu item)

At this point, a blank row is highlighted in the Menu Control list box of the Menu Design window. This means that Visual Basic is ready for you to create a menu control.

Use the following steps to create the Colors menu title:

☐ In the Caption text box of the Menu Design window type &Colors.

☐ In the Name text box of the Menu Design window type mnuColors.

The & character in &Colors causes Visual Basic to display the *C* underlined (see Figure 5.1). Upon execution of the program, pressing Alt+C has the same result as clicking the Colors menu title.

You have just created the menu title of the Colors menu. The Menu Design window should now look like the one shown in Figure 5.6.

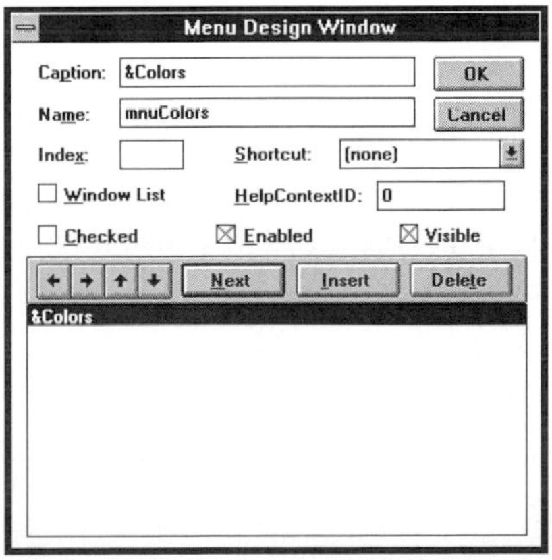

Figure 5.6.
Creating the Colors menu title.

The next thing to do is to create the two menu items of the Colors menu.

Use the following steps to create the Set color menu item:

☐ Click the Next button.

Visual Basic responds by highlighting the next row in the menu control list.

☐ In the Caption text box type `&Set Color`.

☐ In the Name text box type `mnuSetColor`.

Because Set color is an item of the Colors menu, it must be indented. Use the following step to indent Set color:

☐ Click the right arrow button.

The Menu Design window should now look like the one shown in Figure 5.7.

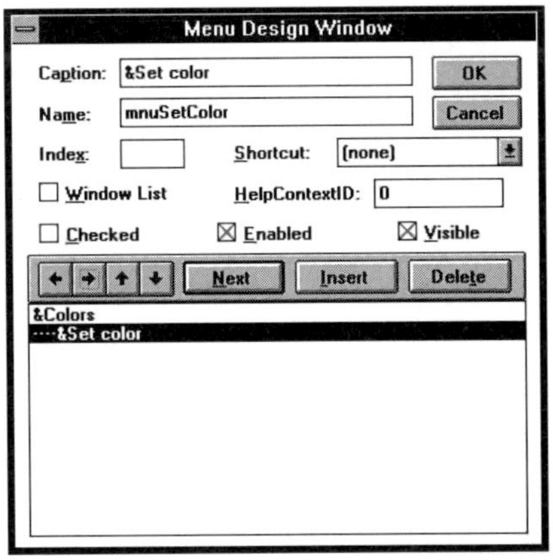

Figure 5.7.
Creating the Set color
menu item.

The & character in &Set Color causes Visual Basic to display the *S* underlined. Upon execution of the program, whenever the Colors menu is displayed, pressing S has identical results as clicking the Set color item.

Use the following steps to create the second item of the Colors menu:

☐ Click the Next button.

Visual Basic responds by highlighting the next row in the menu control list.

☐ In the Caption text box type `&Exit`.

☐ In the Name text box type `mnuExit`.

Visual basic indented this item for you automatically, so you don't need to indent it.

That's it for the Colors menu. Now create the Size menu. As you can see from Figure 5.3, the Size menu has three menu controls:

- Size (the menu title)
- Small (a menu item)
- Large (a menu item)

Use the following steps to create the Size menu title:

☐ Click the Next button.

Visual Basic responds by highlighting the next row in the menu control list.

☐ In the Caption text box type &Size.

☐ In the Name text box type mnuSize.

Visual basic indented this item for you automatically. But because Size is a menu title and not a menu item, it must not be indented. So you must un-indent it.

Use the following step to un-indent Size:

☐ Click the left arrow button.

The Menu Design window should now look like the one shown in Figure 5.8.

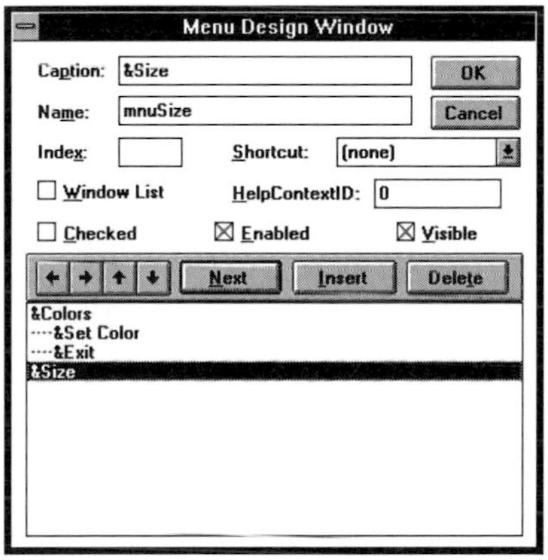

Figure 5.8.
Creating the Size menu title.

```
═                    Menu Design Window
  Caption:  &Size                           OK
  Name:     mnuSize                         Cancel
  Index:            Shortcut:  (none)            ▼
  ☐ Window List     HelpContextID:  0
  ☐ Checked     ☒ Enabled       ☒ Visible
  ← → ↑ ↓    Next    Insert    Delete
  &Colors
  ····&Set Color
  ····&Exit
  &Size
```

Now create the two menu items of the Size menu.

Use the following steps to create the Small menu item:

☐ Click the Next button.

Visual Basic responds by highlighting the next row in the menu control list.

☐ In the Caption text box type &Small.

☐ In the Name text box type mnuSmall.

Because Small is an item of the Size menu, it must be indented. Use the following step to indent Small:

☐ Click the right arrow button.

Use the following steps to create the second item of the Size menu:

☐ Click the Next button.

☐ In the Caption text box type &Large.

☐ In the Name text box type mnuLarge.

Visual basic indented this item for you automatically, so you don't need to indent it.

The Size menu is now ready! The Menu Design window should now look like the one shown in Figure 5.9.

Figure 5.9.
*Creating the items of the
Size menu.*

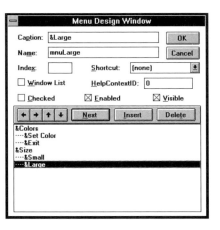

You have finished creating the Colors menu and the Size menu. There is one more menu to be created: the Set color menu.

When you select Set color from the Colors menu, a submenu should pop up (see Figure 5.4). This submenu has three items: Red, Blue, and White.

Because the submenu is displayed whenever Set color is selected, you should insert the three items of the submenu below the Set color item.

Use the following steps to insert Red below Set color:

☐ Select the Exit item (because you are about to insert an item in the line above the Exit item).

☐ Click the Insert button.

Visual Basic responds by inserting a blank row below Set color.

☐ In the Caption text box type &Red.

☐ In the Name text box type mnuRed.

Currently, Red is indented at the same level as Set color. But because Red is an item of the Set color submenu, it should be further indented.

Use the following step to further indent Red:

☐ Click the right arrow button.

Use the following steps to insert the Blue menu item:

☐ Insert a blank row below the Red menu item.

☐ In the Caption text box type &Blue.

☐ In the Name text box type mnuBlue.

☐ Indent Blue so that it is at the same level as Red.

Use the following steps to insert the White menu item:

☐ Insert a blank row below the Blue menu item.

☐ In the Caption text box type &White.

☐ In the Name text box type mnuWhite.

☐ Indent White so that it is at the same level as Red and Blue.

The menu of the Colors program is complete!

The Menu Design window should now look like the one shown in Figure 5.10.

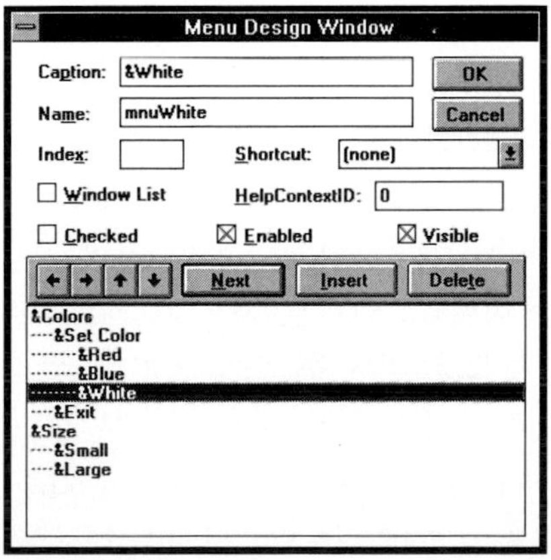

Figure 5.10.
The Menu Design window after the menu design is complete.

Use the following step to exit the Menu Design window:

☐ Click the OK button.

> *Visual Basic responds by closing the Menu Design window, and the frmColors form is displayed onscreen. As you can see, the menu that you just designed is attached to the form.*

The visual implementation of the Colors program is done. Save your work:

☐ Select Save Project from the File menu.

Following a Menu Table

Because the Colors program is your first menu program, the preceding instructions were step-by-step tutorials of how to create a menu. Later in this chapter and in subsequent chapters, you will be instructed to create other menus. However, you will not be instructed to create the menus in the same way you were instructed here. Instead, you will be instructed to follow a menu table.

A menu table is made up of two columns. The left column lists the captions and indentation levels of the menu controls, and the right column lists the names of the menu controls.

A typical menu table is shown in Table 5.2. This table is the menu table of the Colors program.

Table 5.2. The menu table of the Colors program.

Caption	Name
&Colors	mnuColors
...&Set Color	mnuSetColor
......&Red	mnuRed
......&Blue	mnuBlue
......&White	mnuWhite
...&Exit	mnuExit
&Size	mnuSize
...&Small	mnuSmall
...&Large	mnuLarge

Entering the Code of the Colors Program

Each of the menu controls that you designed has a `Click` event procedure. The `Click` event procedure of a menu item is executed whenever you select that menu item. For example, when you select the Exit menu item of the Colors menu, the event procedure `mnuExit_Click()` is executed. The name of this procedure starts with the characters `mnuExit_`, because `mnuExit` is the name you assigned to the Exit menu item.

Although the event procedure is called Click (for example, mnuExit_Click), the procedure is executed whenever you select the menu item by either clicking the menu item or by selecting the item using the keyboard.

As you can see, the menu of the program is displayed on the screen during design time. To display the event procedure of a menu item, simply click on the desired menu item. For example, to see the procedure that is executed whenever you select the Exit menu item, simply click this item.

Another way to display the procedure of a menu item is to display the Code window of the form by double-clicking anywhere inside the form and selecting the desired menu object from the Object combo box.

Now enter the code of the Colors program.

☐ Enter the following code inside the general declarations section of the frmColors form:

```
' All variables MUST be declared.
Option Explicit
```

☐ Enter the following code inside the Form_Load() event procedure:

```
Sub Form_Load ()

    'Because initially the window is white,
    'disable the White menu item.
    mnuWhite.Enabled = False

    'Because initially the window is small,
    'disable the Small menu item.
    mnuSmall.Enabled = False

End Sub
```

☐ Enter the following code inside the mnuRed_Click() event procedure:

```
Sub mnuRed_Click ()

    ' Set the color of the form to red.
    frmColors.BackColor = QBColor(4)

    ' Disable the Red menu item.
    mnuRed.Enabled = False

    ' Enable the Blue and White menu items.
    mnuBlue.Enabled = True
    mnuWhite.Enabled = True

End Sub
```

☐ Enter the following code inside the mnuBlue_Click event() procedure:

```
Sub mnuBlue_Click ()

    ' Set the color of the form to blue.
```

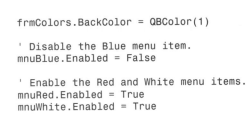
```
frmColors.BackColor = QBColor(1)

' Disable the Blue menu item.
mnuBlue.Enabled = False

' Enable the Red and White menu items.
mnuRed.Enabled = True
mnuWhite.Enabled = True
```

End Sub

☐ Enter the following code in the mnuWhite_Click() event procedure:

Sub mnuWhite_Click ()

```
' Set the color of the form to bright white.
frmColors.BackColor = QBColor(15)

' Disable the White menu item.
mnuWhite.Enabled = False

' Enable the Red and Blue menu items.
mnuRed.Enabled = True
mnuBlue.Enabled = True
```

End Sub

☐ Enter the following code inside the mnuSmall_Click() event procedure:

Sub mnuSmall_Click ()

```
' Set the size of the form to small.
frmColors.WindowState = 0

' Disable the Small menu item.
mnuSmall.Enabled = False

' Enable the Large menu item.
mnuLarge.Enabled = True
```

End Sub

☐ Enter the following code inside the mnuLarge_Click() event procedure:

Sub mnuLarge_Click ()

```
' Set the size of the form to large.
frmColors.WindowState = 2

' Disable the Large menu item.
mnuLarge.Enabled = False

' Enable the Small menu item.
mnuSmall.Enabled = True
```

End Sub

☐ Enter the following code inside the `mnuExit_Click()` event procedure:

```
Sub mnuExit_Click ()

    End

End Sub
```

Executing the Colors Program

Execute the Colors program and select the various items of the menu. While you run the program, notice the following features:

- Upon execution of the program, the menu item White of the Set color submenu is dimmed (that is, not available). This menu item is dimmed because initially the color of the form is white, so it makes no sense to let you change white to white. Similarly, the Small menu item of the Size menu is dimmed because initially the form is small.

- After you select Large from the Size menu, the form becomes large and the menu item Large becomes dimmed.

- After you select any color from the Set color submenu, the form changes its color to the selected color, and the menu item of the selected color becomes dimmed.

Use the following step to terminate the Colors program:

☐ Select Exit from the Colors menu.

How the Colors Program Works

The Colors program uses the `Form_Load()` procedure and the `Click` event procedures of the various menu items.

The Code Inside the *Form_Load()* Procedure

Whenever you start the program, the `Form_Load()` procedure is executed. In this procedure, the menu item White of the Set color submenu and the menu item Small of the Size menu are disabled.

The `Form_Load()` procedure disables the White and Small menu items by setting their Enabled properties to False:

```
Sub Form_Load ()

    ' Because initially the window is white,
    ' disable the White menu item.
    mnuWhite.Enabled = False
```

```
' Because initially the window is small,
' disable the Small menu item.
mnuSmall.Enabled = False
```

End Sub

The Code Inside the *mnuRed_Click()* Event Procedure

Whenever you select Red from the Set color submenu, the `mnuRed_Click()` procedure is executed. The code inside this procedure changes the color of the form to red and disables the Red menu item:

```
Sub mnuRed_Click ()

    ' Set the color of the form to red.
    frmColors.BackColor = QBColor(4)

    'Disable the Red menu item.
    mnuRed.Enabled = False

    'Enable the Blue and White menu items.
    mnuBlue.Enabled = True
    mnuWhite.Enabled = True

End Sub
```

After the procedure disables the Red menu item, the procedure enables the Blue and White menu items. The Blue and White menu items are enabled because now the color of the form is red, and you should be able to change it to either blue or white.

The `mnuBlue_Click()` and `mnuWhite_Click()` procedures are similar to the `mnuRed_Click()` procedure.

The Code Inside the *mnuSmall_Click()* Event Procedure

When you select Small from the Size menu the `mnuSmall_Click()` procedure is executed. The code inside this procedure changes the size of the form to small and disables the Small menu item:

```
Sub mnuSmall_Click ()

    ' Set the size of the form to small.
    frmColors.WindowState = 0

    ' Disable the Small menu item.
    mnuSmall.Enabled = False
```

```
' Enable the Large menu item.
mnuLarge.Enabled = True
```

End Sub

You change the size of the form by setting the WindowState property of the form. When the WindowState property of the form is set to 0, the form is sized to its default normal size (the size that is set at design time). When it is set to 2, the form is sized to its maximum size.

When the procedure disables the Small menu item, it enables the Large menu item. This is done because now the size of the form is small, and you should be able to change it to large.

The mnuLarge_Click() procedure is similar to the mnuSmall_Click() procedure.

The Code Inside the *mnuExit_Click()* Event Procedure

Whenever you select Exit from the Colors menu the mnuExit_Click() procedure is executed. This procedure terminates the program:

```
Sub mnuExit_Click ()

    End

End Sub
```

Shortcut Keys

You may enhance the Colors program by adding *shortcut keys*. A shortcut key enables you to execute a menu item by pressing a combination of keys on the keyboard.

For example, in the Colors program you may assign the shortcut key Ctrl+R to the Red menu item of the Set Color submenu. By doing so, whenever you press Ctrl+R, the form changes its color to red.

Use the following steps to assign the shortcut key Ctrl+R to the Red menu item:

☐ Select the frmColors form (that is, click anywhere inside the form or highlight frmColors in the Project window and click View Form).

☐ Select Menu Design from the Window menu.

Visual Basic responds by displaying the Menu Design window.

☐ Highlight the Red menu item.

Visual Basic responds by displaying the properties of the Red menu item.

As you can see, the Shortcut combo box of the Red menu item currently is set to none.

Use the following steps to set the shortcut key to Ctrl+R:

☐ Click the Shortcut combo box and select the shortcut Ctrl+R.

☐ Click the OK button to close the Menu Design window.

Use the following steps to see how the shortcut key works in the program:

☐ Execute the Colors program.

☐ Press Ctrl+R.

The Colors program responds by changing the color of the form to red.

In a similar manner, you may now assign the shortcut key Ctrl+B to the Blue menu item, and the shortcut key Ctrl+W to the White menu item.

Adding a Separator Bar to a Menu

A separator bar is a line that is displayed between menu items. Its only purpose is cosmetic.

Figure 5.11 shows the Colors menu of the Colors program after a separator bar was inserted between the Set Color item and the Exit item.

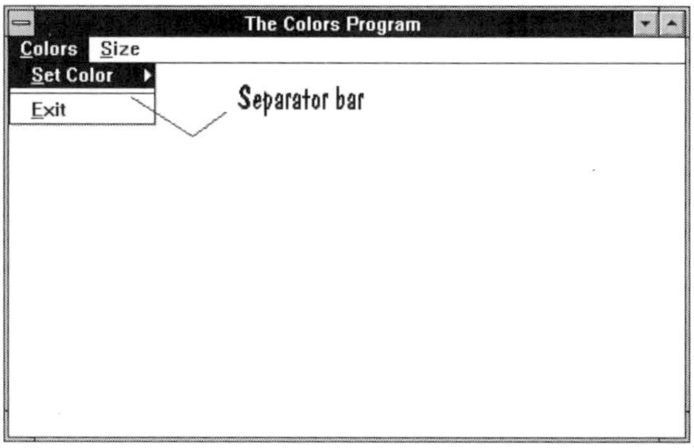

Figure 5.11.

A separator bar.

Use the following steps to insert a separator bar between the Set Color item and the Exit item:

☐ Select the frmColors form (that is, click anywhere inside the form, or highlight frmColors in the Project window and click View Form).

☐ Select Menu Design from the Window menu.

Visual Basic responds by displaying the Menu Design window.

☐ Highlight the Exit menu item and click the Insert button.

Visual Basic responds by inserting a blank row above the Exit item.

☐ In the Caption text box type -.

☐ In the Name text box type mnuSep1.

☐ Click the OK button to close the Menu Design window.

The hyphen character (-) entered in the Caption text box is the symbol for a separator bar.

You named the separator bar mnuSep1. In the future, if you have to add more separator bars to the menu, you could name them mnuSep2, mnuSep3, and so on. Of course, you may give a separator bar any name you wish, but it is a good idea to give it a name that distinguishes it as a separator. You cannot select the separator bar during runtime, so the mnuSep1_Click() procedure is never executed. (Why do you need a name for it? Visual Basic requires that you name all menu controls.)

☐ Execute the Colors program.

As you can see, the separator bar that you just created appears.

Making a Menu Control Invisible

In the Colors program you enabled and disabled menu items at runtime by setting the Enabled property of the item to True or False. When the item is disabled (that is, when the Enabled property is False), it becomes dimmed and you may not select it. However, you can still see the menu item.

In some programs you may need to hide a menu item completely (not just dim it). You need to use the Visible property to do this. For example, to make a menu item called mnuMyItem invisible during runtime, use the following statement:

Change color selected items

```
mnuMyItem.Visible = False
```

After you issue this statement, the MyItem menu item disappears, and all the menu items under it move up to fill its space.

To make a whole menu invisible, you need to set the Visible property of the title of the menu to False. After you make a menu invisible, it disappears and all the menus to its right move to the left to fill its space.

Check Marks

In some programs you may need to mark menu items. You can use check marks to do this. Figure 5.12 shows a menu item with a check mark next to it.

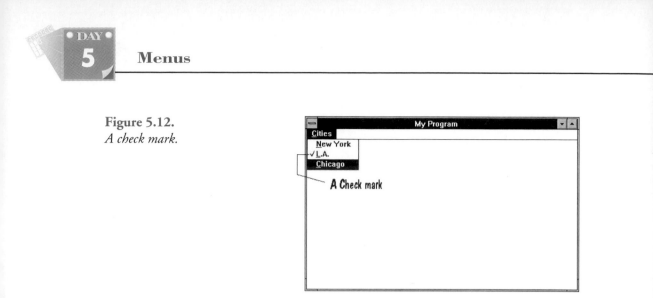

Figure 5.12.
A check mark.

To place a check mark next to a menu item, use the Checked property. To place the check mark, set the Checked property to True. To remove the check mark, set the Checked property to False.

For example, to place a check mark next to the L.A. menu item shown in Figure 5.12, you need to issue the following statement:

```
mnuLA.Checked = True
```

To uncheck the L.A. menu item, issue the following statement:

```
mnuLA.Checked = False
```

Adding Items to a Menu During Runtime

Now write a program that illustrates how items can be added to a menu (or removed from a menu) during runtime. The program Grow lets you add items to and remove items from a menu.

Before you start writing the Grow program, specify what the program should do:

☐ Upon startup of the program, a menu bar with the menu title Grow appears, as shown in Figure 5.13.

☐ The Grow menu initially has three menu items (Add, Remove, Exit), and a separator bar (see Figure 5.14).

☐ Every time you select Add, a new item is added to the Grow menu. For example, after you select Add three times, the Grow menu should look like the one shown in Figure 5.15.

☐ Every time you select Remove, the last item of the Grow menu is removed.

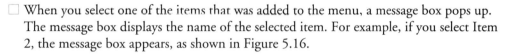

☐ When you select one of the items that was added to the menu, a message box pops up. The message box displays the name of the selected item. For example, if you select Item 2, the message box appears, as shown in Figure 5.16.

Figure 5.13.
The Grow program.

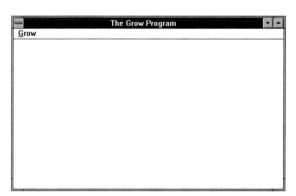

Figure 5.14.
The Grow menu (without added items).

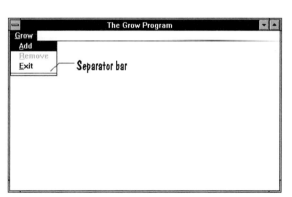

Figure 5.15.
The Grow menu with three added items.

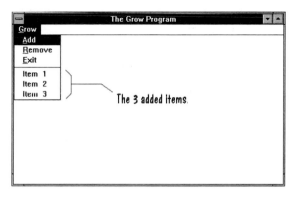

Figure 5.16.

The message box after you select Item 2 from the Grow menu.

The Visual Implementation of the Grow Program

☐ Start a new project. Save the form of the project as GROW.FRM and save the make file of the project as GROW.MAK.

☐ Build the form according to the specifications in Table 5.3.

Table 5.3. The properties table of the Grow program.

Object	Property	Value
Form	**Name**	**frmGrow**
	Caption	The Grow Program

Creating the Menu of the Grow Program

Now attach a menu to the frmGrow form:

☐ Select the frmGrow form (that is, click anywhere inside the form or highlight frmColors in the Project window and click View Form).

☐ Select Menu Design from the Window menu.

Visual Basic responds by displaying the Menu Design window.

☐ Fill the Menu Design window according to the specifications in Table 5.4.

Table 5.4. The menu table of the frmGROW form.

Caption	Name
&Grow	mnuGrow
...&Add	mnuAdd
...&Remove	mnuRemove
...&Exit	mnuExit
...-	mnuItems

☐ Highlight the last item of the menu (that is, the separator bar) and type 0 in the Index text box (see Figure 5.17).

☐ Click the OK button.

The visual implementation of the Grow program is complete!

Figure 5.17.
Setting the Index property of the separator bar.

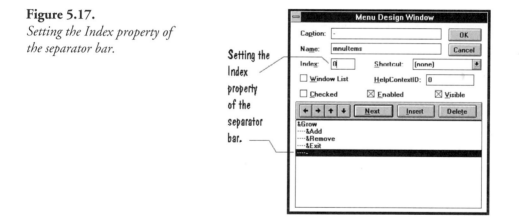

Menu Control Array

By setting the Index property of the separator bar to 0, you created a menu control array. Because you set the Name property to mnuItems, the control array that you created is called mnuItems.

So far, the mnuItems array has only one element: the separator bar (that is, mnuItems(0) is the separator bar). During runtime, every time you select Add from the menu, the code of the program adds a new element to the mnuItems array. As a result, more menu items appear below the separator bar.

Entering the Code of the Grow Program

☐ Enter the following code inside the general declarations section of the frmGROW form:

```
' All variables MUST be declared.
Option Explicit

' Declare the LastElement variable as integer.
Dim LastElement As Integer
```

☐ Enter the following code inside the Form_Load() event procedure:

```
Sub Form_Load ()

    ' Initially the last element in the
    ' mnuItems[] array is 0.
    LastElement = 0

    ' Initially no items are added to the
    ' Grow menu, so disable the Remove option.
    mnuRemove.Enabled = False

End Sub
```

☐ Enter the following code inside the mnuAdd_Click() event procedure:

```
Sub mnuAdd_Click ()

    ' Increment the LastElement variable.
    LastElement = LastElement + 1

    ' Add a new element to the mnuItems[] array.
    Load mnuItems(LastElement)

    ' Assign a caption to the item that
    ' was just added.
    mnuItems(LastElement).Caption = "Item
              ➥ "+Str$(LastElement)

    ' Because an element was just added to the
    ' mnuItems array, the Remove option should be
    ' enabled.
    mnuRemove.Enabled = True

End Sub
```

☐ Enter the following code inside the mnuRemove_Click() event procedure:

```
Sub mnuRemove_Click ()

    ' Remove the last element of the mnuItems array.
    Unload mnuItems(LastElement)

    ' Decrement the LastElement variable.
    LastElement = LastElement - 1

    ' If only element 0 is left in the array,
```

```
   ' disable the Remove option.
   If LastElement = 0 Then
       mnuRemove.Enabled = False
   End If

End Sub
```

☐ Enter the following code inside the mnuItems_Click() event procedure:

```
Sub mnuItems_Click (Index As Integer)

   ' Display the item that was selected.
   MsgBox "You selected Item " + Str$(Index)

End Sub
```

☐ Enter the following code inside the mnuExit_Click() event procedure:

```
Sub mnuExit_Click ()

   End

End Sub
```

Executing the Grow Program

Execute the Grow program and select the various items of the menu. While you run the program, notice the following features:

- Upon execution of the program, the menu item Remove is dimmed (that is, not available). This menu item is dimmed because at this point no items are added to the menu so there is nothing to remove.

- Every time Add is selected, a new item is added to the menu. Whenever there is at least one added item in the menu, the Remove option is available.

- Every time Remove is selected, the last added menu item is removed. When there are no more added items in the menu, the Remove option is dimmed.

Use the following step to terminate the Grow program:

☐ Select Exit from the menu.

How the Grow Program Works

The Grow program uses the variable LastElement to keep count of the number of elements in the mnuItems array. Because this variable should be visible in all the procedures of the form, it is declared in the general declarations area of the form.

The Code of the *Form_Load()* Procedure

Upon startup of the program the Form_Load() procedure is executed.

In this procedure, LastElement is initialized to 0 and the Remove menu item is disabled:

```
Sub Form_Load ()

    ' Initially the last element in the
    ' mnuItems[] array is 0.
    LastElement = 0

    ' Initially, no items are added to the
    ' Grow menu, so disable the Remove option.
    mnuRemove.Enabled = False

End Sub
```

The first statement in this procedure initializes the LastElement variable to 0, because at this point, the mnuItems array has only one element in it: the 0th element. You created the 0th element of the array at design time (the separator bar).

The next statement in this procedure disables the Remove menu item (because at this point you have not added any items to the menu).

The Code of the *Add_Click()* Event Procedure

The Add_Click() procedure is executed whenever you select Add from the menu. This procedure is responsible for adding a new element to the mnuItems array and setting the Caption property of the new element:

```
Sub mnuAdd_Click ()

    ' Increment the LastElement variable.
    LastElement = LastElement + 1

    ' Add a new element to the mnuItems[] array.
    Load mnuItems(LastElement)

    ' Assign a caption to the item that
    ' was just added.
    mnuItems(LastElement).Caption = "Item "+Str$(LastElement)

    ' Because an element was just added to the
    ' mnuItems array, the Remove option should be
    ' enabled.
    mnuRemove.Enabled = True

End Sub
```

The first thing that the procedure does is increment the value of the variable LastElement:

```
LastElement = LastElement + 1
```

Then a new element is added to the `mnuItems` array with the `Load` statement:

```
Load mnuItems(LastElement)
```

The Caption property of the new element is set with the following statement:

```
mnuItems(LastElement).Caption = "Item " + Str$(LastElement)
```

Finally, the Remove menu item is enabled:

```
mnuRemove.Enabled = True
```

The Remove item is enabled because the procedure just added an item to the menu, and you should be able to remove it.

The Code of the *Remove_Click()* Event Procedure

The `Remove_Click()` procedure is executed whenever you select Remove from the menu:

```
Sub mnuRemove_Click ()

    ' Remove the last element of the mnuItems array.
    Unload mnuItems(LastElement)

    ' Decrement the LastElement variable.
    LastElement = LastElement - 1

    ' If only element 0 is left in the array,
    ' disable the Remove option.
    If LastElement = 0 Then
        mnuRemove.Enabled = False
    End If

End Sub
```

In this procedure, the last element of the `mnuItems` array is removed with the `Unload` statement:

```
Unload mnuItems(LastElement)
```

Then the variable `LastElement` is decremented.

If, after the last element of the array is removed (that is, the array is left with only element 0), the Remove menu item is disabled:

```
If LastElement = 0 Then
    mnuRemove.Enabled = False
End If
```

The Code of the *mnuItems_Click()* Event Procedure

The `mnuItems_Click()` procedure is executed whenever you select any of the added items from the Grow menu:

```
Sub mnuItems_Click (Index As Integer)

    ' Display the item that was selected.
    MsgBox "You selected Item " + Str$(Index)

End Sub
```

The Index argument of this procedure indicates which item was selected. For example, if you selected Item 1, the Index argument is equal to 1 (that is, Item 1 is element number 1 in the mnuItems array). If you selected Item 2, the Index argument is equal to 2.

Summary

In this chapter you have learned how to write programs that include a menu. You have learned how to attach a menu to a form using the Menu Design window, and you have learned how to attach code to the menu controls. The different properties of the menu controls give you power and flexibility in changing the appearance of the menu during runtime (for example, the Visible property, the Checked property). By creating a menu control array, you may even add and remove items to a menu during runtime.

Q&A

Q In the Colors program, the Enabled properties of the White and Small menu items were set to False in the Form_Load() procedure. Can I set these properties at design time?

A Yes, you can set these properties during design time.

Q I learned how to disable menu items during runtime from the examples of this chapter. How can I disable a complete menu?

A You need to set the Enabled property of the menu title to False to disable a complete menu. By doing so, the disabled title becomes dimmed, and you will not be able to pop the menu. For example, to disable the Size menu of the Colors program you need to issue the following statement:

```
mnuSize.Enabled = False
```

The entire Size menu is disabled after this statement is issued.

Q How many levels of submenus can a menu include?

A A menu can include a maximum of four levels of submenus. Figure 5.18 shows four levels of submenus.

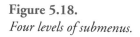

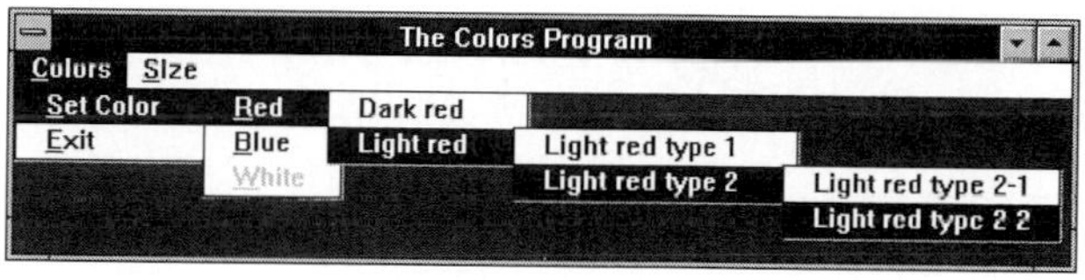

Figure 5.18.
Four levels of submenus.

> **The Colors Program**
>
> <u>C</u>olors <u>S</u>ize
>
> <u>S</u>et Color   <u>R</u>ed   Dark red
> <u>E</u>xit   <u>B</u>lue   Light red   Light red type 1
>   White   Light red type 2   Light red type 2-1
>   Light red type 2 2

Quiz

1. What is the difference between the Enabled property and the Visible property of a menu control?
2. How do you create a menu control array, and what is it used for?
3. What are shortcut keys and how do you create them?
4. What are check marks and how do you use them in a program?
5. What is a separator bar?

Exercises

1. Enhance the Colors program so that when a color is selected a check mark is placed next to the selected color menu item.
2. Enhance the Grow program so that you will be limited to adding a maximum of 15 items to the Grow menu (at this point, you can add an unlimited number of items).

Quiz Answers

1. When the Enabled property of a menu item is set to False, the menu item is disabled (dimmed), but you can still see it. When the Visible property of a menu item is set to False, the menu item completely disappears (that is, it is not just dimmed). You may have a need to completely hide a menu item or a menu in some programs.
2. You create a menu control array during design time by setting the Index property of a menu item to 0. This menu item becomes element number 0 of the array. During runtime the program may add items to the menu by adding more elements to the array. (The items are added below the item that was created in design time.)
3. A shortcut key enables you to execute a menu item by pressing a combination of keys on the keyboard (for example, Ctrl+C, Ctrl+A). You assign a shortcut key to a menu item during design time by setting the Shortcut property of the menu item to the desired keys combination.
4. A check mark is used to mark menu items. To place a check mark next to a menu item during runtime, set the Checked property of the item to True. To remove a check mark, set the Checked property of the item to False.

5. A separator bar is a horizontal line that is used to separate menu items. The Caption property of a separator bar is the hyphen character (-).

Exercise Answers

1. To enhance the Colors program so that it will place a check mark next to the selected color menu item, modify the procedures mnuRed_Click(), mnuBlue_Click(), and mnuWhite_Click() as follows:

   ☐ Add the following statements to the mnuRed_Click() procedure:

   ```
   ' Put a check mark next to the Red menu item.
   mnuRed.Checked = True

   ' Un-check the Blue and White menu items.
   mnuWhite.Checked = False
   mnuBlue.Checked = False
   ```

   ☐ Add the following statements to the mnuBlue_Click() procedure:

   ```
   ' Put a check mark next to the Blue menu item.
   mnuBlue.Checked = True

   ' Un-check the White and Red menu items.
   mnuWhite.Checked = False
   mnuRed.Checked = False
   ```

   ☐ Add the following statements to the mnuWhite_Click() procedure:

   ```
   ' Put a check mark next to the White menu item.
   mnuWhite.Checked = True

   ' Un-check the Blue and Red menu items.
   mnuBlue.Checked = False
   mnuRed.Checked = False
   ```

2. To limit the number of items that you may add to the Grow menu to 15, insert the following code to the beginning of the mnuAdd_Click() procedure:

   ```
   Sub mnuAdd_Click ()

       ' If the last element is 15 then beep and end
       ' this procedure.
       If LastElement = 15 Then
          Beep
          Exit Sub
       End IF


       ...................................
       ... The rest of the procedure ...
       ... remains the same.        ...
       ...................................

   End Sub
   ```

Dialog Boxes

This chapter shows you how to incorporate dialog boxes into your programs. Dialog boxes are used to display information to the user and to get information from the user. In Visual Basic there are three types of dialog boxes: predefined dialog boxes, custom dialog boxes, and common dialog boxes.

Predefined Dialog Boxes

As the name implies, predefined dialog boxes are predefined by Visual Basic. To display a predefined dialog box, you use a Visual Basic statement with parameters that specify how the dialog box should appear. You may display a predefined dialog box by using one of the following:

- The MsgBox statement and the MsgBox() function
- The InputBox() function

The *MsgBox* Statement and the *MsgBox()* Function

You can use the MsgBox statement and MsgBox() function to display messages to the user and to get the user's response to yes/no types of questions. The Message program shows how the MsgBox statement and MsgBox() function are used in a program.

The Visual Implementation of the Message Program

☐ Start a new project.

☐ Save the form of the project as MESSAGE.FRM and save the make file of the project as MESSAGE.MAK.

☐ Build the form according to the specifications in Table 6.1.

The completed form should look like the one shown in Figure 6.1.

Table 6.1. The properties table of the MESSAGE.FRM form.

Object	Property	Value
Form	**Name**	**frmMessage**
	Caption	The Message Program
	Height	4425
	Left	1035

Object	Property	Value
	Top	1140
	Width	7485
Command Button	**Name**	**cmdMessage**
	Caption	Message
	Height	1335
	Left	2280
	Top	1080
	Width	2415
Command Button	**Name**	**cmdExit**
	Caption	Exit
	Height	495
	Left	2880
	Top	3120
	Width	1215

Figure 6.1.
The form of the Message program.

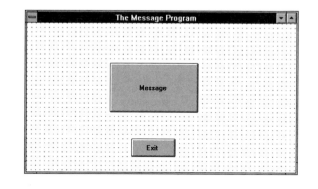

Entering the Code of the Message Program

☐ Enter the following code inside the general declarations area of the frmMessage form:

```
' All variables must be declared.
Option Explicit

' Define button constants for the MsgBox statement
' and MsgBox() function.
Const MB_OK = 0
Const MB_YESNO = 4

' Define icon constants for the MsgBox statement
```

```
' and MsgBox() function.
Const MB_ICONEXCLAMATION = 48
Const MB_ICONQUESTION = 32

' Define output constant for the MsgBox() function.
Const IDYES = 6
```

☐ Enter the following code inside the cmdMessage_Click() event procedure:

```
Sub cmdMessage_Click ()

    Dim Message As String
    Dim DialogType As Integer
    Dim Title As String

    ' The message of the dialog box.
    Message = "This is a sample message!"

    ' The dialog box should have an OK button and
    ' an exclamation icon.
    DialogType = MB_OK + MB_ICONEXCLAMATION

    ' The title of the dialog box.
    Title = "Dialog Box Demonstration"

    ' Display the dialog box.
    MsgBox Message, DialogType, Title

End Sub
```

☐ Enter the following code inside the cmdExit_Click() event procedure:

```
Sub cmdExit_Click ()

    Dim Message As String
    Dim DialogType As Integer
    Dim Title As String
    Dim Response As Integer

    ' The message of the dialog box.
    Message = "Are you sure you want to quit?"

    ' The dialog box should have Yes and No buttons,
    ' and a question icon.
    DialogType = MB_YESNO + MB_ICONQUESTION

    ' The title of the dialog box.
    Title = "The Message Program"

    ' Display the dialog box and get user's response.
    Response = MsgBox(Message, DialogType, Title)

    ' Evaluate the user's response.
    If Response = IDYES Then
        End
    End If

End Sub
```

Executing the Message Program

☐ Execute the Message program.

While you run the Message program, note the following features:

- When you click the Message button, a dialog box with a sample message, an OK button, and an exclamation icon is displayed (see Figure 6.2). This message box is modal, which means that the program does not continue until you close the dialog box. For example, if you try to click the mouse on the Exit button while the dialog box is displayed, the program beeps.

Figure 6.2.
A dialog box with an OK button and an exclamation icon.

- When you click the Exit button, a dialog box with a question, a Yes button, a No button, and a question mark icon is displayed (see Figure 6.3). This dialog box asks you to confirm that you want to exit the program. If you press the Yes button, the program terminates. If you press the No button, the dialog box closes and the program does not terminate. This dialog box is also modal (that is, you must click the Yes or No button before the program continues).

Figure 6.3.
A dialog box with Yes and No buttons and a question mark icon.

How the Message Program Works

The Message program uses the MsgBox statement and MsgBox() function to display message boxes.

Declaring Constants

The MsgBox statement and the MsgBox() function use constants. To make these constants visible in all the procedures of the form, these constants are declared in the general declarations area of the form:

```
' Define button constants for the MsgBox statement
' and MsgBox() function.
Const MB_OK = 0
Const MB_YESNO = 4

' Define icon constants for the MsgBox statement
' and MsgBox() function.
Const MB_ICONEXCLAMATION = 48
Const MB_ICONQUESTION = 32

' Define output constant for the MsgBox() function.
Const IDYES = 6
```

These constants are used later by the MsgBox statement and MsgBox() function to display message boxes.

Displaying a Dialog Box with the *MsgBox* Statement

Whenever the user clicks the Message button, the cmdMessage_Click() procedure is executed. The code inside this procedure uses the MsgBox statement to display a dialog box with an OK button and an exclamation icon:

```
Sub cmdMessage_Click ()

    Dim Message As String
    Dim DialogType As Integer
    Dim Title As String

    ' The message of the dialog box.
    Message = "This is a sample message!"

    ' The dialog box should have an OK button and
    ' an exclamation icon.
    DialogType = MB_OK + MB_ICONEXCLAMATION

    ' The title of the dialog box.
    Title = "Dialog Box Demonstration"

' Display the dialog box.
MsgBox Message, DialogType, Title

End Sub
```

The MsgBox statement takes three parameters:

- The message to be displayed (a string)
- The dialog box type (an integer)
- The title of the dialog box (a string)

Before executing the MsgBox statement, the cmdMessage_Click() procedure updates three variables that will be used as the parameters of the MsgBox statement.

The first variable the cmdMessage() procedure updates is the string variable Message. Message is updated with the message of the dialog box:

```
Message = "This is a sample message!"
```

Message is used as the first parameter of the MsgBox statement.

The second variable that is updated by the cmdMessage_Click() procedure is the integer variable DialogType. DialogType is updated with a number that determines the dialog box type:

```
DialogType = MB_OK + MB_ICONEXCLAMATION
```

DialogType is used as the second parameter of the MsgBox statement.

The constants MB_OK and MB_ICONEXCLAMATION were declared in the general declarations area of the form. MB_OK is a constant that represents a button, and MB_ICONEXCLAMATION is a constant that represents an icon. By specifying DialogType as the sum of MB_OK and MB_ICONEXCLAMATION, you specify that the dialog box should have an OK button and an exclamation icon (see Figure 6.2). Tables 6.2 and 6.3 list all the button constants and icon constants that may be used to specify a dialog type. For example, to specify a dialog box with an OK button and a Stop icon, the second parameter of the MsgBox statement should be the sum of the two constants MB_OK and MB_ICONSTOP.

Table 6.2. Button constants.

Constant Name	Value	Displayed Buttons
MB_OK	0	OK
MB_OKCANCEL	1	OK, Cancel
MB_ABORTRETRYIGNORE	2	Abort, Retry, Ignore
MB_YESNOCANCEL	3	Yes, No, Cancel
MB_YESNO	4	Yes, No
MB_RETRYCANCEL	5	Retry, Cancel

Table 6.3. Icon constants.

Constant Name	Value	Displayed Icon
MB_ICONSTOP	16	The stop sign icon
MB_ICONQUESTION	32	The question mark icon
MB_ICONEXCLAMATION	48	The exclamation point icon
MB_ICONINFORMATION	64	The information icon

6

The third variable that the `cmdMessage_Click()` procedure updates is `Title`. `Title` is updated with the title of the dialog box:

```
Title = "Dialog Box Demonstration"
```

Finally, the variables `Message`, `DialogType`, and `Title` are used as the parameters of the `MsgBox` statement:

```
MsgBox Message, DialogType, Title
```

As a result, the message box shown in Figure 6.2 is displayed.

Displaying a Dialog Box with the *MsgBox()* Function

Whenever the user clicks the Exit button, the `cmdExit_Click()` procedure is executed. The code inside this procedure uses the `MsgBox()` function to display a dialog box with a question message, Yes and No buttons, and a question mark icon:

```
Sub cmdExit_Click ()

    Dim Message As String
    Dim DialogType As Integer
    Dim Title As String
    Dim Response As Integer

    ' The message of the dialog box.
    Message = "Are you sure you want to quit?"

    ' The dialog box should have Yes and No buttons,
    ' and a question icon.
    DialogType = MB_YESNO + MB_ICONQUESTION

    ' The title of the dialog box.
    Title = "The Message Program"

    ' Display the dialog box and get user's response.
    Response = MsgBox(Message, DialogType, Title)

    ' Evaluate the user's response.
    If Response = IDYES Then
      End
    End If

End Sub
```

The `MsgBox()` function takes the same three parameters as the `MsgBox` statement (that is, the message, the dialog type, and the title of the dialog box). The only difference between the `MsgBox` statement and the `MsgBox()` function is that the `MsgBox()` function returns a value. The returned value of the `MsgBox()` function indicates which button in the dialog box was clicked by the user.

Before executing the `MsgBox()` function, the `cmdExit_Click()` procedure updates the three variables `Message`, `DialogType`, and `Title`:

```
Message = "Are you sure you want to quit?"
DialogType = MB_YESNO + MB_ICONQUESTION
Title = "The Message Program"
```

The variable `DialogType` is updated with the sum of the constants `MB_YESNO` and `MB_ICONQUESTION`, because the dialog box should have Yes and No buttons and a question mark icon.

Once the variables `Message`, `DialogType`, and `Title` are updated, the `MsgBox()` function is executed and its returned value is assigned to the variable `Response`:

```
Response = MsgBox(Message, DialogType, Title)
```

The returned value of the `MsgBox()` function indicates which button was clicked by the user. Table 6.4 lists all the possible constants that may be returned by the `MsgBox()` function. For example, if the returned value of the `MsgBox()` function is the constant `IDYES`, the user clicked the Yes button of the message box.

Table 6.4. The output constants of the `MsgBox()` function.

Constant Name	Value	Clicked Button
IDOK	1	OK button was clicked
IDCANCEL	2	Cancel button was clicked
IDABORT	3	Abort button was clicked
IDRETRY	4	Retry button was clicked
IDIGNORE	5	Ignore button was clicked
IDYES	6	Yes button was clicked
IDNO	7	No button was clicked

To determine which button the user clicked (the Yes button or the No button), the value of the `Response` variable is examined with an `If` statement:

```
If Response = IDYES Then
    End
End If
```

The `IDYES` constant was declared in the general declarations area of the form. If the user clicked the Yes button, `Response` is equal to `IDYES`. If this is the case, the program is terminated with the `End` statement—the user answered Yes to the question Are you sure you want to quit? and so the program terminated.

Application Modal Versus System Modal

Dialog boxes that are displayed with the MsgBox statement and MsgBox() function are modal. However, a modal dialog box can be either application modal or system modal.

If the dialog box is application modal, the user cannot continue working with the current application until a response is given to the dialog box. However, the user may continue working in other applications.

If the dialog box is system modal, the user cannot continue working with any application until a response is given to the dialog box. As long as the dialog box is displayed, the user cannot continue working with the current application or with any other application.

The dialog boxes of the Message program are application modal. To verify that these dialog boxes are indeed application modal, use the following steps:

☐ Execute the Message program.

☐ Click the Message button.

The program responds by displaying the dialog box shown in Figure 6.2.

☐ While the dialog box is displayed, try to click the Exit button of the Message program.

The program responds by beeping, which is an indication that you must respond to the dialog box.

While the dialog box is displayed, try to switch to another application:

☐ Press Ctrl+Esc.

Windows responds by displaying the Task List window. When you select Program Manager from the Task List window, Windows responds by switching to the Program Manager.

As you can see, the dialog box of the Message program is application modal. It is not system modal. That is, while the dialog box is displayed, you cannot continue with the Message program, but you can switch to other applications.

Is it possible to make the dialog box system modal? Yes. The following steps show you how to modify the Message program so that the displayed dialog box is system modal:

☐ Switch back to the Message program, close the dialog box, and terminate the program.

☐ Add the following constant declaration inside the general declarations area of the frmMessage form:

```
Const MB_SYSTEMMODAL = 4096
```

☐ Change the line in the `cmdMessage_Click` procedure that updates the `DialogType` variable from this:

```
' The dialog box should have an OK button and
' an exclamation icon.
DialogType = MB_OK + MB_ICONEXCLAMATION
```

to this:

```
' The dialog box should have an OK button,
' an exclamation icon, and it should be system-modal.
DialogType = MB_OK + MB_ICONEXCLAMATION + MB_SYSTEMMODAL
```

☐ Save the project.

By adding the constant `MB_SYSTEMMODAL` to the `DialogType` variable, you are specifying that the dialog type should be system modal. You may now verify that the dialog box is system modal by using the following steps:

☐ Execute the Message program.

☐ Click the Message button.

The program responds by displaying the dialog box shown in Figure 6.2.

☐ While the dialog box is displayed, try to click the Exit button of the Message program. The program responds by doing nothing! The program does not even beep.

☐ While the dialog box is displayed, try to switch to another application by pressing Ctrl+Esc. Again, nothing happens.

As you can see, the dialog box is now system modal. While the dialog box is displayed, you cannot continue with the current application, and you can't switch to other applications. As long as the dialog box is displayed, all the applications of the system are suspended.

The Dialogs Program

The Message program illustrates how you can use the `MsgBox` statement and the `MsgBox()` function to display a dialog box with an OK button and a dialog box with Yes and No buttons. As you can see from Table 6.2, you may display other standard buttons in the dialog box.

The Dialogs program illustrates how you can use the `MsgBox()` function to display various buttons in dialog boxes and how you can use the returned value of the `MsgBox()` function to determine which button the user clicked.

In the Message program, the constants of the `MsgBox()` function were declared in the general declarations area of the form of the program. As a result, the constants were visible in all the procedures of the form. However, if an application has more than one form, declaring the constants in the general declarations area of one of the forms will not make the constants visible in the other form.

To make the constants visible to all the procedures in all the forms, you need to declare the constants as global. This is done by creating a new module in the project (for example, CONST.BAS) and defining the constants as global inside the general declarations area of the module.

The following discussion shows you how to add a module to the Dialogs program step-by-step, and how to declare global constants inside the module's general declarations area.

The Visual Implementation of the Dialogs Program

☐ Start a new project.

☐ Save the form of the project as DIALOGS.FRM and save the make file of the project as DIALOGS.MAK.

☐ Build the form according to the specifications in Table 6.5.

The completed form should look like the one shown in Figure 6.4.

Table 6.5. The properties table of the DIALOGS.FRM form.

Object	Property	Value
Form	**Name**	**frmDialogs**
	Caption	The Dialogs Program
Menu	**(see Table 6.6)**	**(see Table 6.6)**

Table 6.6. The menu table of the frmDialogs form.

Caption	Name
Dialogs	mnuDialogs
...OK-Cancel dialog	mnuOkCancel
...Abort-Retry-Ignore dialog	mnuAbortRetryIgnore
...Yes-No-Cancel dialog	mnuYesNoCancel
...Yes-No dialog	mnuYesNo
...Retry-Cancel dialog	mnuRetryCancel
...-	mnuSep1
...Exit	mnuExit

Figure 6.4.
The frmDialogs form.

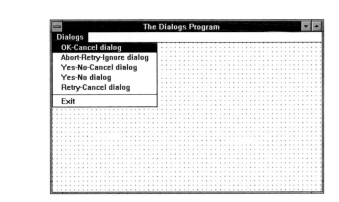

Entering the Code of the Dialogs Program

The Dialogs program has global declarations. Because global declarations cannot be made inside the general declarations section of a form, you need to create a module and put the global declarations inside the general declarations area of the module.

To create a new module in the Dialogs program use the following steps:

☐ Select Project from the Window menu.

  Visual Basic responds by displaying the project window.

☐ Select New Module from the File menu.

  Visual Basic responds by displaying the code window of the new module.

☐ Select Save File As from the File menu and save the module as CONST.BAS.

  Now that you have a new module, you can enter global declarations inside its general declarations section.

☐ Enter the following code inside the general declarations section of the CONST.BAS module:

```
Option Explicit

' Define the button constants of the MsgBox() function.
Global Const MB_OK = 0, MB_OKCANCEL = 1,
                        ➥ MB_ABORTRETRYIGNORE=2

Global Const MB_YESNOCANCEL = 3, MB_YESNO = 4,
                        ➥ MB_RETRYCANCEL=5

' Define the icon constants of the MsgBox() function.
Global Const MB_ICONSTOP = 16, MB_ICONQUESTION = 32
Global Const MB_ICONEXCLAMATION = 48, MB_ICONINFORMATION = 64
```

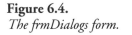

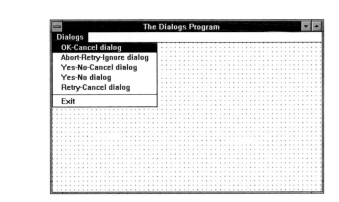

6

169

```
' Define the output constants of the MsgBox() function.
Global Const IDOK = 1, IDCANCEL = 2, IDABORT = 3, IDRETRY = 4
Global Const IDIGNORE = 5, IDYES = 6, IDNO = 7
```

☐ Enter the following code inside the `mnuAbortRetryIgnore_Click()` event procedure of the frmDialogs form:

```
Sub mnuAbortRetryIgnore_Click ()

    Dim DialogType As Integer
    Dim DialogTitle As String
    Dim DialogMsg As String
    Dim Response As Integer

    ' Dialog should have Abort, Retry, Ignore buttons,
    ' and an EXCLAMATION icon.
    DialogType = MB_ABORTRETRYIGNORE + MB_ICONEXCLAMATION

    ' The dialog title.
    DialogTitle = "MsgBox Demonstration"

    ' The dialog message.
    DialogMsg = "This is a sample message!"

    ' Display the dialog box, and get user's response.
    Response = MsgBox(DialogMsg, DialogType, DialogTitle)

    ' Evaluate the user's response.
    Select Case Response
        Case IDABORT
            MsgBox "You clicked the Abort button!"
        Case IDRETRY
            MsgBox "You clicked the Retry button!"
        Case IDIGNORE
            MsgBox "You clicked the Ignore button!"
    End Select

End Sub
```

☐ Enter the following code inside the `mnuExit_Click()` event procedure of the frmDialogs form:

```
Sub mnuExit_Click ()

    Dim DialogType As Integer
    Dim DialogTitle As String
    Dim DialogMsg As String
    Dim Response As Integer

    ' Dialog should have Yes & No buttons, and a STOP icon.
    DialogType = MB_YESNO + MB_ICONSTOP

    ' The dialog title.
    DialogTitle = "The Dialogs Program"
```

```
' The dialog message.
DialogMsg = "Are you sure you want to exit?"

' Display the dialog box, and get user's response.
Response = MsgBox(DialogMsg, DialogType, DialogTitle)

' Evaluate the user's response.
If Response = IDYES Then
   End
End If

End Sub
```

☐ Enter the following code inside the `mnuOkCancel_Click()` event procedure of the frmDialogs form:

```
Sub mnuOkCancel_Click ()

   Dim DialogType As Integer
   Dim DialogTitle As String
   Dim DialogMsg As String
   Dim Response As Integer

   ' Dialog should have OK & Cancel buttons,
   ' and an EXCLAMATION icon.
   DialogType = MB_OKCANCEL + MB_ICONEXCLAMATION

   ' The dialog title.
   DialogTitle = "MsgBox Demonstration"

   ' The dialog message.
   DialogMsg = "This is a sample message!"

   ' Display the dialog box, and get user's response.
   Response = MsgBox(DialogMsg, DialogType, DialogTitle)

   ' Evaluate the user's response.
   If Response = IDOK Then
      MsgBox "You clicked the OK button!"
   Else
      MsgBox "You clicked the Cancel button!"
   End If

End Sub
```

6

☐ Enter the following code inside the `mnuRetryCancel_Click()` event procedure of the frmDialogs form:

```
Sub mnuRetryCancel_Click ()

   Dim DialogType As Integer
   Dim DialogTitle As String
   Dim DialogMsg As String
   Dim Response As Integer
```

```
' Dialog should have Retry & Cancel buttons,
' and an EXCLAMATION icon.
DialogType = MB_RETRYCANCEL + MB_ICONEXCLAMATION

' The dialog title.
DialogTitle = "MsgBox Demonstration"

' The dialog message.
DialogMsg = "This is a sample message!"

' Display the dialog box, and get user's response.
Response = MsgBox(DialogMsg, DialogType, DialogTitle)

' Evaluate the user's response.
If Response = IDRETRY Then
   MsgBox "You clicked the Retry button!"
Else
   MsgBox "You clicked the Cancel button!"
End If

End Sub
```

☐ Enter the following code inside the `mnuYesNo_Click()` event procedure of the frmDialogs form:

```
Sub mnuYesNo_Click ()

   Dim DialogType As Integer
   Dim DialogTitle As String
   Dim DialogMsg As String
   Dim Response As Integer

   ' Dialog should have Yes & No buttons,
   ' and a question mark icon.
   DialogType = MB_YESNO + MB_ICONQUESTION

   ' The dialog title.
   DialogTitle = "MsgBox Demonstration"

   ' The dialog message.
   DialogMsg = "Is this is a sample message?"

   ' Display the dialog box, and get user's response.
   Response = MsgBox(DialogMsg, DialogType, DialogTitle)

   ' Evaluate the user's response.
   If Response = IDYES Then
      MsgBox "You clicked the Yes button!"
   Else
      MsgBox "You clicked the No button!"
   End If

End Sub
```

☐ Enter the following code inside the `mnuYesNoCancel_Click()` event procedure of the frmDialogs form:

```
Sub mnuYesNoCancel_Click ()

    Dim DialogType As Integer
    Dim DialogTitle As String
    Dim DialogMsg As String
    Dim Response As Integer

    ' Dialog should have Yes, No, and Cancel buttons,
    ' and an EXCLAMATION icon.
    DialogType = MB_YESNOCANCEL + MB_ICONEXCLAMATION

    ' The dialog title.
    DialogTitle = "MsgBox Demonstration"

    ' The dialog message.
    DialogMsg = "This is a sample message!"

    ' Display the dialog box, and get user's response.
    Response = MsgBox(DialogMsg, DialogType, DialogTitle)

    ' Evaluate the user's response.
    Select Case Response
        Case IDYES
            MsgBox "You clicked the Yes button!"
        Case IDNO
            MsgBox "You clicked the No button!"
        Case IDCANCEL
            MsgBox "You clicked the Cancel button!"
    End Select

End Sub
```

Executing the Dialogs Program

Execute the Dialogs program and experiment with the various dialog boxes. For example, to display the Abort-Retry-Ignore dialog box do the following:

☐ Select Abort-Retry-Ignore dialog from the Dialogs menu.

> *The program responds by displaying a dialog box with Abort, Retry, and Ignore buttons (see Figure 6.5).*

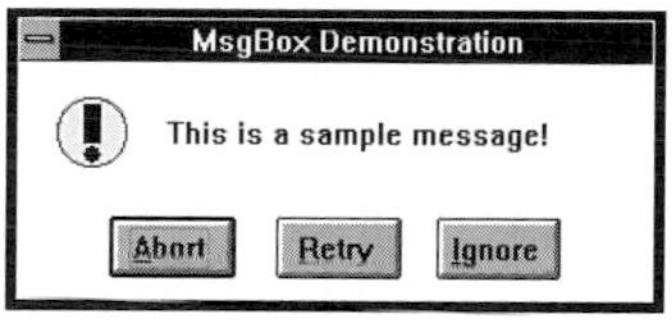

Figure 6.5.
A dialog box with Abort, Retry, and Ignore buttons.

☐ Click one of the buttons of the dialog box.

The program responds by displaying a message that indicates the name of the button that you clicked.

Use the following steps to terminate the Dialogs program:

☐ Select Exit from the Dialogs menu.

The program responds by displaying a Yes/No dialog box, asking you if you are sure you want to quit.

☐ Click the Yes button.

How the Dialogs Program Works

The Dialogs program uses the MsgBox() function to display various dialog boxes with different buttons. The program uses the returned value of the MsgBox() function to determine which button the user clicked.

Declaring the Constants as Global

To make the constants of the MsgBox() function visible in all the procedures of the program, the constants are declared as global inside the general declarations section of the CONST.BAS module:

```
' Define the button constants of the MsgBox() function.
Global Const MB_OK = 0, MB_OKCANCEL = 1,
                        ➥ MB_ABORTRETRYIGNORE=2
Global Const MB_YESNOCANCEL = 3, MB_YESNO = 4,
                        ➥ MB_RETRYCANCEL=5

' Define the icon constants of the MsgBox() function.
Global Const MB_ICONSTOP = 16, MB_ICONQUESTION = 32
Global Const MB_ICONEXCLAMATION = 48, MB_ICONINFORMATION = 64

' Define the output constants of the MsgBox() function.
Global Const IDOK = 1, IDCANCEL = 2, IDABORT = 3, IDRETRY = 4
Global Const IDIGNORE = 5, IDYES = 6, IDNO = 7
```

These declarations correspond to the values listed in Tables 6.2, 6.3, and 6.4.

The *mnuAbortRetryIgnore_Click()* Procedure

Whenever the user selects Abort-Retry-Ignore dialog from the Dialogs menu, the mnuAbortRetryIgnore_Click() procedure is executed. The code inside this procedure uses the MsgBox() function to display a dialog box with Abort, Retry, and Ignore buttons:

```
Sub mnuAbortRetryIgnore_Click ()

    Dim DialogType As Integer
    Dim DialogTitle As String
    Dim DialogMsg As String
    Dim Response As Integer

    ' Dialog should have Abort, Retry, Ignore buttons,
    ' and an EXCLAMATION icon.
    DialogType = MB_ABORTRETRYIGNORE + MB ICONEXCLAMATION

    ' The dialog title.
    DialogTitle = "MsgBox Demonstration"

    ' The dialog message.
    DialogMsg = "This is a sample message!"

    ' Display the dialog box, and get user's response.
    Response = MsgBox(DialogMsg, DialogType, DialogTitle)

    ' Evaluate the user's response.
    Select Case Response
      Case IDABORT
        MsgBox "You clicked the Abort button!"
      Case IDRETRY
        MsgBox "You clicked the Retry button!"
      Case IDIGNORE
        MsgBox "You clicked the Ignore button!"
    End Select

End Sub
```

Before executing the `MsgBox()` function, the `mnuAbortRetryIgnore_Click()` procedure updates the variables `DialogType`, `DialogMsg`, and `DialogTitle`:

```
DialogType = MB_ABORTRETRYIGNORE + MB_ICONEXCLAMATION
DialogTitle = "MsgBox Demonstration"
DialogMsg = "This is a sample message!"
```

`DialogType` is updated with the sum of `MB_ABORTRETRYIGNORE` and `MB_ICONEXCLAMATION`, because the dialog box should have Abort, Retry, and Ignore buttons, and an exclamation icon.

Once the variables `Message`, `DialogType`, and `Title` are updated, the `MsgBox()` function is executed, and its returned value is assigned to the variable `Response`:

```
Response = MsgBox(DialogMsg, DialogType, DialogTitle)
```

To determine which button the user clicked (that is, the Abort button, the Retry button, or the Ignore button), the value of the `Response` variable is examined with a `Select Case` statement:

```
Select Case Response
    Case IDABORT
      MsgBox "You clicked the Abort button!"
    Case IDRETRY
      MsgBox "You clicked the Retry button!"
```

```
     Case IDIGNORE
        MsgBox "You clicked the Ignore button!"
End Select
```

If, for example, the user clicked the Ignore button, the variable `Response` is equal to `IDIGNORE`, and the statement under `IDIGNORE Case` is executed. The constants `IDABORT`, `IDRETRY`, and `IDIGNORE` were declared in the general declarations section of the CONST.BAS module. (The values and meanings of these constants are listed in Table 6.4.)

The `MsgBox` statements under the `Select Case Response` statement specify only one parameter. For example, under the `Case IDABORT` line, the `MsgBox` statement is the following:

```
MsgBox "You clicked the Abort button!"
```

When the second and third parameters of the `MsgBox` statement are not specified, the dialog box is displayed with an OK button and without any icon. The title of the dialog box is set to the name of the program.

The rest of the procedures of the Dialogs program are similar to the procedure `mnuAbortRetryIgnore_Click()`. Just like the `mnuAbortRetryIgnore()` procedure, these procedures update the variables `DialogMsg`, `DialogType`, and `DialogTitle`, and then use the `MsgBox()` function to display a dialog box. The returned value of the `MsgBox()` function is used to determine which button the user clicked.

The *InputBox()* Function

You can use the `InputBox()` function to get information from the user. The `InputBox()` function displays to the user a dialog box with a message, a text box, an OK button, and a Cancel button. The user can type inside the text box and then close the dialog box by clicking the OK button.

The first parameter of the `InputBox()` function is the message of the dialog box. The second parameter is the title of the dialog box. The `InputBox()` function returns whatever the user typed inside the text box. For example, the following statement displays a dialog box that asks the user to enter a name:

```
Name = InputBox ("Enter your name:", "InputBox Demonstration")
```

This statement displays the dialog box shown in Figure 6.6. The user may type a name inside the text box and then close the dialog box by clicking the OK button. In this example, the returned value of the `InputBox()` function is assigned to the variable `Name`. After the user clicks the OK button, the variable `Name` is updated with the user's name.

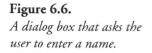

Figure 6.6.

A dialog box that asks the user to enter a name.

┌─────────────────────────────────┐
│ ▬   **InputBox Demonstration** │
│ Enter your name: ┌─────────┐ │
│   │   OK   │ │
│   └─────────┘ │
│   ┌─────────┐ │
│   │ Cancel │ │
│   └─────────┘ │
│   │
│ ┌──────────────────────────────┐ │
│ └──────────────────────────────┘ │
└─────────────────────────────────┘

Now enhance the Dialogs program. This enhancement illustrates how you can use the InputBox() function to get a string, a number, and a date from the user.

☐ Insert four new items to the menu of the Dialogs program with the following characteristics (insert them above the Exit menu item):

Caption	Name
Get A String	mnuGetString
Get A Number	mnuGetNumber
Get A Date	mnuGetDate
-	mnuSep2

After you insert these items, the menu table of the Dialogs program should look like the one shown in Table 6.7.

Table 6.7. The new menu table of the Dialogs program.

Caption	Name
Dialogs	mnuDialogs
...OK-Cancel dialog	mnuOkCancel
...Abort-Retry-Ignore dialog	mnuAbortRetryIgnore
...Yes-No-Cancel dialog	mnuYesNoCancel
...Yes-No dialog	mnuYesNo
...Retry-Cancel dialog	mnuRetryCancel
...-	mnuSep1
...Get A String .	mnuGetString
...Get A Number	mnuGetNumber
...Get A Date	mnuGetDate
...-	mnuSep2
...Exit	mnuExit

6

☐ Enter the following code inside the `mnuGetString_Click()` event procedure of the frmDialogs form:

```
Sub mnuGetString_Click ()

    Dim UserInput

    ' Get a string from the user.
    UserInput = InputBox("Type anything:", "InputBox Demo")

    ' If the user did not enter anything, or if the user
    ' pressed Cancel, exit the procedure.
    If UserInput = "" Then
        MsgBox "You did not type anything (or pressed
                              ➥ Cancel)."
        Exit Sub
    End If

    ' Display whatever the user typed.
    MsgBox "You typed: " + UserInput

End Sub
```

☐ Enter the following code inside the `mnuGetNumber_Click()` event procedure of the frmDialogs form:

```
Sub mnuGetNumber_Click ()

    Dim UserInput

    ' Get a number from the user.
    UserInput = InputBox("Enter a number:", "InputBox
                          ➥ Demo")

    ' If the user did not enter anything, or if the user
    ' pressed Cancel, exit the procedure.
    If UserInput = "" Then
        MsgBox "You did not type anything (or pressed
                              ➥ Cancel)."
        Exit Sub
    End If

    ' If the user did not enter a number, exit the
                          ➥ procedure.
    If Not IsNumeric(UserInput) Then
        MsgBox "Invalid number!"
        Exit Sub
    End If

    ' Display the number that the user entered.
    MsgBox "You entered the number: " + UserInput

End Sub
```

☐ Enter the following code inside the mnuGetDate_Click() event procedure of the frmDialogs form:

```
Sub mnuGetDate_Click ()

    Dim UserInput, DayOfWeek, Msg

    ' Get a date from the user.
    UserInput = InputBox("Enter a date:", "InputBox Demo")

    ' If the user did not enter anything, or if the user
    ' pressed Cancel, exit the procedure.
    If UserInput = "" Then
        MsgBox "You did not type anything (or pressed
                            ➡ Cancel)."
        Exit Sub
    End If

    ' If the user did not enter a date, exit the procedure.
    If Not IsDate(UserInput) Then
        MsgBox "Invalid date!"
        Exit Sub
    End If

    ' Calculate the day of week of the entered date.
    DayOfWeek = Format(UserInput, "dddd")

    ' Display the date that the user entered and the day
    ' of week of that date.
    Msg = "You entered the date: " + UserInput
    Msg = Msg + " The day of week of this date is: "+
                            ➡ DayOfWeek
    MsgBox Msg

End Sub
```

☐ Save your work!

Execute the Message program and experiment with the new menu items:

☐ Select Get A String from the menu.

The program responds by displaying the dialog box shown in Figure 6.7.

☐ Type anything inside the dialog box and click the OK button.

The program responds by displaying whatever you typed.

☐ Select Get A String again, but this time instead of clicking the OK button click the Cancel button.

The program responds by displaying a message telling you that you either typed nothing or pressed Cancel.

6

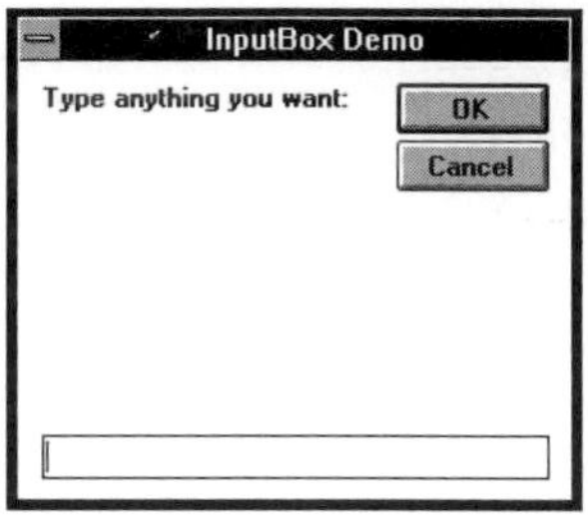

Figure 6.7.
The Get A String dialog box.

☐ Select Get A Number from the menu.

> *The program responds by displaying a dialog box that asks you to enter a number.*

☐ Enter any valid number (for example, 1234) and click the OK button.

> *The program responds by displaying a message with the number that you typed.*

☐ Select Get A Number again, but this time, instead of typing a valid number, type an invalid number (for example, ABCD).

> *The program responds by displaying a message that tells you that you entered an invalid number.*

☐ In a similar manner, experiment with the Get A Date menu item. That is, try to enter valid dates as well as invalid dates inside the Get A Date dialog box.

Examples of valid dates are the following:

> January, 1, 1994
> July 4, 1776
> 01/01/1994

Examples of invalid dates are the following:

> 1234
> ABCD
> 14/77/93

Notice that after you enter a valid date in the Get A Date dialog box, the program displays a message box with the date that you entered as well as the day of the week of that date. For example, if you enter the date July 4, 1776, the program responds by displaying this message:

```
You entered the date: July 4, 1776   The day of week of this date is: Thursday
```

The Code Inside the *mnuGetString_Click()* Procedure

Whenever the user selects Get A String from the menu, the mnuGetString_Click() procedure is executed. The code inside this procedure gets a string from the user.

The procedure begins by executing the InputBox() function:

```
UserInput = InputBox("Type anything:", "InputBox Demo")
```

This statement displays the dialog box that is shown in Figure 6.7. The returned value of the InputBox() function is assigned to the variable UserInput. If the user pressed the Cancel button, the returned value of the InputBox() function is null. If, however, the user typed something and clicked the OK button, the returned value of the InputBox() function is whatever the user typed.

To see if the user clicked the Cancel button, an If statement is used:

```
If UserInput = "" Then
    MsgBox "You did not type anything (or pressed Cancel)."
    Exit Sub
End If
```

If the user did not type anything or pressed the Cancel button, the condition UserInput="" is satisfied. As a result, the message You did not type anything (or pressed Cancel) is displayed, and the procedure is terminated with the Exit Sub statement.

If, however, the condition UserInput="" is not met, the last statement of the procedure is executed:

```
MsgBox "You typed: " + UserInput
```

This statement displays whatever the user entered.

The Code Inside the *mnuGetNumber_Click()* Procedure

Whenever the user selects Get A Number from the menu, the mnuGetNumber_Click() procedure is executed. The code inside this procedure asks the user to enter a number and then verifies that the user entered a valid number. The procedure begins by executing the InputBox() function:

```
UserInput = InputBox("Enter a number:", "InputBox Demo")
```

An If statement is used to determine if the user pressed Cancel:

```
If UserInput = "" Then
    MsgBox "You did not type anything (or pressed Cancel)."
    Exit Sub
End If
```

181

If the user did not type anything or if the user clicked the Cancel button, the condition UserInput="" is satisfied. As a result, the message You did not type anything (or pressed Cancel) is displayed, and the procedure is terminated with the Exit Sub statement.

After verifying that the user typed something (and did not press Cancel), the procedure determines if the user typed a valid number. This determination is made by using the IsNumeric() function:

```
If Not IsNumeric(UserInput) Then
    MsgBox "Invalid number!"
    Exit Sub
End If
```

If the variable UserInput is filled with characters such as ABC, the condition Not IsNumeric(UserInput) is satisfied. As a result, the user is prompted with the message Invalid number! and the procedure is terminated with the Exit Sub statement. If, however, the variable UserInput is filled with characters such as 123 the condition Not IsNumeric(UserInput) is not satisfied, and the last statement of the procedure is executed:

```
MsgBox "You entered the number: " + UserInput
```

This statement displays the number that the user entered.

The Code Inside the *mnuGetDate_Click()* Procedure

Whenever the user selects Get A Date from the menu, the mnuGetDate_Click() procedure is executed. The code inside this procedure asks the user to enter a date and then verifies that the user entered a valid date.

The procedure begins by executing the InputBox() function:

```
UserInput = InputBox("Enter a date:", "InputBox Demo")
```

An If statement is used to determine whether the user pressed Cancel:

```
If UserInput = "" Then
    MsgBox "You did not type anything (or pressed Cancel)."
    Exit Sub
End If
```

If the user did not type anything or if the user clicked the Cancel button, the condition UserInput="" is satisfied. As a result, the message You did not type anything (or pressed Cancel) is displayed, and the procedure is terminated with the Exit Sub statement.

After verifying that the user typed something (and did not press Cancel), the procedure determines if the user typed a valid date. This determination is made by using the IsDate() function:

```
If Not IsDate(UserInput) Then
    MsgBox "Invalid date!"
    Exit Sub
End If
```

If the variable `UserInput` is filled with characters such as `123` or `ABC`, the condition `Not IsDate(UserInput)` is satisfied. As a result, the user is prompted with the message `Invalid date!`, and the procedure is terminated with the `Exit Sub` statement. If, however, the variable `UserInput` is filled with characters such as `12/01/94`, the condition `Not IsDate(UserInput)` is not satisfied, and the last four statements of the procedure are executed:

```
DayOfWeek = Format(UserInput, "dddd")
Msg = "You entered the date: " + UserInput
Msg = Msg + " The day of week of this date is: "+ DayOfWeek
MsgBox Msg
```

These statements display the date that the user entered (that is, `UserInput`) as well as the day of week of that date (that is, `DayOfWeek`). The variable `DayOfWeek` is updated by utilizing the `Format()` function. If, for example, `UserInput` is equal to July 4, 1776, `Format(UserInput, "dddd")` returns `Thursday`.

The Other Parameters of the *InputBox()* Function

The Dialogs program uses the `InputBox()` function with only two parameters (the message to be displayed and the title of the dialog box). The `InputBox()` function has three more parameters (these parameters are optional). The third parameter of the `InputBox()` function specifies the default string that appears inside the text box of the dialog box. The fourth and fifth parameters of the dialog box specify the X and Y positions (in units of twips) at which the dialog box appears.

For example, to display a dialog box with the following characteristics:

- Message equals `Enter a number:`.
- Title equals `Demo`.
- The default string that appears in the text box of the dialog box is `7`.
- The left edge of the dialog box is 100 twips from the left edge of the screen.
- The upper edge of the dialog box is 200 twips from the top of the screen.

you should use the following statement:

```
MyNumber = InputBox("Enter a number:","Demo","7",100,200)
```

As a result, the dialog box appears at the screen coordinate `X=100`, `Y=200`, and the default value inside the text box is `7`.

Custom Dialog Boxes

As the name implies, *custom dialog boxes* are customized. That is, they are custom-made by you. Designing a custom dialog box is the same as designing a form. In fact, a custom dialog box is a regular form that is used to display information to the user and to get information from the user. The form is designed in such a way that it could be used by any application.

To illustrate how to design a custom dialog box and how to use it in a program, further enhance the Dialogs program. Design a custom dialog box called GetMonth.FRM that lets the user select a month. After you finish designing the GetMonth.Frm dialog box, add code to the Dialogs program that makes use of the GetMonth.Frm dialog box.

Designing a Custom Dialog Box

To design the GetMonth.Frm dialog box, use the following steps:

☐ Open the DIALOGS.MAK project.

☐ Select New Form from the File menu.

> *Visual Basic responds by displaying a new blank form.*

☐ Save the form as GetMonth.Frm (that is, select Save File As from the File menu and save the file as GetMonth.Frm).

☐ Build the GetMonth.Frm dialog box according to the specifications in Table 6.8.

The completed dialog box should look like the one shown in Figure 6.8.

☐ Save the project.

Table 6.8. The properties table of the GetMonth.Frm dialog box.

Object	Property	Value
Form	Name	frmGetMonth
	Caption	Select a month:
	BorderStyle	1-Fixed Single
	ControlBox	False
	MaxButton	False
	MinButton	False
	Height	2205
	Left	1380
	Top	2595
	Width	6720

Object	Property	Value
Command Button	**Name**	**cmdCancel**
	Caption	Cancel
	Cancel	True
	Height	495
	Left	5280
	Top	1080
	Width	1215
Command Button	**Name**	**cmdOK**
	Caption	OK
	Default	True
	Height	495
	Left	5280
	Top	360
	Width	1215
Option Button	**Name**	**optJan**
	Caption	January
	Height	255
	Left	120
	Top	240
	Width	1575
Option Button	**Name**	**optFeb**
	Caption	February
	Height	255
	Left	120
	Top	600
	Width	1575
Option Button	**Name**	**optMar**
	Caption	March
	Height	255
	Left	120

continues

Table 6.8. continued

Object	Property	Value
	Top	960
	Width	1575
Option Button	**Name**	**optApr**
	Caption	April
	Height	255
	Left	120
	Top	1320
	Width	1575
Option Button	**Name**	**optMay**
	Caption	May
	Height	255
	Left	1800
	Top	240
	Width	1575
Option Button	**Name**	**optJun**
	Caption	June
	Height	255
	Left	1800
	Top	600
	Width	1575
Option Button	**Name**	**optJul**
	Caption	July
	Height	255
	Left	1800
	Top	960
	Width	1575
Option Button	**Name**	**optAug**
	Caption	August
	Height	255
	Left	1800

Object	Property	Value
	Top	1320
	Width	1575
Option Button	**Name**	**optSep**
	Caption	September
	Height	255
	Left	3480
	Top	240
	Width	1575
Option Button	**Name**	**optOct**
	Caption	October
	Height	255
	Left	3480
	Top	600
	Width	1575
Option Button	**Name**	**optNov**
	Caption	November
	Height	255
	Left	3480
	Top	960
	Width	1575
Option Button	**Name**	**optDec**
	Caption	December
	Height	255
	Left	3480
	Top	1320
	Width	1575

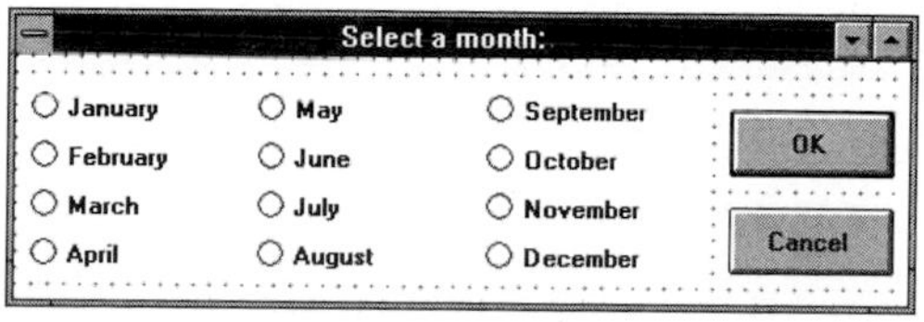

Figure 6.8.
The GetMonth.Frm dialog box.

Standard Dialog Box Properties

A typical dialog box is designed in such a way that the user is not able to change its appearance during runtime. As you can see from Table 6.8, the properties of the frmGetMonth dialog box are set in such a way that the user is not able to size, maximize, or minimize the frmGetMonth dialog box during runtime:

- The Border Style property of the frmGetMonth dialog box is set to Fixed Single. This prevents the user from changing the size of the dialog box during runtime.

- The Control Box property of the frmGetMonth dialog box is set to False. This causes the dialog box to display without the Control Menu box. The Control Menu box is the small minus icon (-) that appears in the top-left corner of a form.

- The Max Button property of the frmGetMonth dialog box is set to False. This prevents the user from maximizing the dialog box during runtime (that is, the dialog box is displayed without the Maximize button).

- The Min Button property of the frmGetMonth dialog box is set to False. This prevents the user from minimizing the dialog box during runtime (that is, the dialog box is displayed without the Minimize button).

The Cancel Property and Default Property of the Command Buttons

As you can see from Table 6.8, the Default property of the OK button is set to True, and the Cancel property of the Cancel button is set to True.

Setting the Default property of a command button to True makes this command button the Default button. The Default button is the button that is selected when the user presses Enter. Therefore, because the Default property of the OK button is set to True, during runtime, when the frmGetMonth dialog box is displayed, pressing Enter has the same effect as clicking the OK button.

Setting the Cancel property of a command button to True makes this command button the Cancel button. The Cancel button is the button that is selected when the user presses Esc. Therefore, because the Cancel property of the Cancel button is set to True, during runtime, when the frmGetMonth dialog box is displayed, pressing Esc has the same effect as clicking the Cancel button.

Displaying and Hiding a Custom Dialog Box

To display a custom dialog box, use the Show method. The dialog box should be displayed as modal (the user must respond to the dialog box before the program continues). To display the dialog box as modal, use the Show method with its argument equal to 1. For example, to display the dialog box frmMyDialog as modal, use the following statement:

```
frmMyDialog.Show 1
```

To hide a dialog box, use the Hide method. For example, if the dialog box frmMyDialog is displayed, the following statement hides it from view:

```
frmMyDialog.Hide
```

To see the Show method and Hide method in action, add code to the Dialogs program. This code displays the frmGetMonth dialog box whenever the user selects the menu item Get A Month and hides the dialog box whenever the user responds to the dialog box by clicking the OK button or Cancel button of the dialog box.

☐ Insert two new items to the menu of the frmDialogs form with the following characteristics (insert them above the Exit menu item):

Caption	Name
Get A Month (custom dialog)	mnuGetMonth
-	mnuSep3

After you insert these items, the menu table of the Dialogs program should look like the one shown in Table 6.9.

Table 6.9. The menu table of the Dialogs program after you add the Get Month item.

Caption	Name
Dialogs	mnuDialogs
...OK-Cancel dialog	mnuOkCancel
...Abort-Retry-Ignore dialog	mnuAbortRetryIgnore
...Yes-No-Cancel dialog	mnuYesNoCancel
...Yes-No dialog	mnuYesNo
...Retry-Cancel dialog	mnuRetryCancel
...-	mnuSep1

continues

Table 6.9. continued

Caption	Name
...Get A String	mnuGetString
...Get A Number	mnuGetNumber
...Get A Date	mnuGetDate
...-	mnuSep2
...Get A Month (custom dialog)	mnuGetMonth
...-	mnuSep3
...Exit	mnuExit

☐ Enter the following code inside the `mnuGetMonth_Click()` procedure of the frmDialogs form:

```
Sub mnuGetMonth_Click ()

    ' Display the frmGetMonth dialog box.
    frmGetMonth.Show 1

    ' Display the month that the user selected (if any).
    If frmGetMonth.Tag = "" Then
       MsgBox "You cancelled the dialog box!"
    Else
       MsgBox "You selected: " + frmGetMonth.Tag
    End If

End Sub
```

Whenever the user selects Get A Month from the Dialogs menu, the `mnuGetMonth_Click()` procedure is executed. The code of this procedure uses the Show method to display the frmGetMonth dialog box and displays the month that the user selected by displaying the Tag property of the frmGetMonth dialog box. As you will soon see, the code of the frmGetMonth dialog box uses frmGetMonth.Tag to store the name of the month that the user selected.

☐ Enter the following code inside the general declarations section of the frmGetMonth dialog box:

```
' All variables must be declared.
Option Explicit
```

☐ Enter the following code inside the `cmdOK_Click()` event procedure of the frmGetMonth dialog box:

```
Sub cmdOK_Click ()

    ' Update frmGetMonth.Tag with the month that the
    ' user selected. (frmGetMonth.Tag is used as the
```

```
' output of the form).
If optJan = True Then frmGetMonth.Tag = "January"
If optFeb = True Then frmGetMonth.Tag = "February"
If optMar = True Then frmGetMonth.Tag = "March"
If optApr = True Then frmGetMonth.Tag = "April"
If optMay = True Then frmGetMonth.Tag = "May"
If optJun = True Then frmGetMonth.Tag = "June"
If optJul = True Then frmGetMonth.Tag = "July"
If optAug = True Then frmGetMonth.Tag = "August"
If optSep = True Then frmGetMonth.Tag = "September"
If optOct = True Then frmGetMonth.Tag = "October"
If optNov = True Then frmGetMonth.Tag = "November"
If optDec = True Then frmGetMonth.Tag = "December"

' Hide the frmGetMonth form.
frmGetMonth.Hide
```

End Sub

Whenever the user clicks the OK button of the frmGetMonth dialog box, the cmdOK_Click()
procedure is executed. The code of this procedure uses a series of 12 If statements to see which
option button is currently selected and accordingly updates the Tag property of the dialog box
(frmGetMonth.Tag) with the name of the selected month. After the 12 If statements, the
procedure uses the Hide method to hide the frmGetMonth dialog box from view.

The Tag property of the frmGetMonth dialog box is used as the output of the dialog box. That
is, whoever displayed the frmGetMonth dialog box can use frmGetMonth.Tag to know which
month the user selected.

☐ Enter the following code inside the cmdCancel_Click() event procedure of the
   frmGetMonth dialog box:

Sub cmdCancel_Click ()

```
' Set frmGetMonth.Tag to null.
frmGetMonth.Tag = ""

' Hide the frmGetMonth form.
frmGetMonth.Hide
```

End Sub

Whenever the user clicks the Cancel button of the frmGetMonth dialog box, the
cmdCancel_Click() procedure is executed. The code of this procedure sets the Tag property of
the dialog box (frmGetMonth.Tag) to null and then uses the Hide method to hide the
frmGetMonth dialog box from view. Setting frmGetMonth.Tag to null serves as an indication
that the user clicked the Cancel button.

☐ Save the project:

☐ Execute the Dialogs program and experiment with the Get A Month custom dialog box.

6

The Common Dialog Custom Control

Starting with Visual Basic Version 3.0, you can use the common dialog custom control to display various common dialog boxes. You display these common dialog boxes during runtime by simply setting the properties of the common dialog custom control.

To illustrate how to use the common dialog custom control in a program, write the Common program. The Common program uses the common dialog custom control to display two common dialog boxes: the Color Selection dialog box and the Open File dialog box.

The Visual Implementation of the Common Program

☐ Start a new project.

☐ Save the form of the project as COMMON.FRM and save the make file of the project as COMMON.MAK.

Because the common dialog control is a custom control, before you can place it inside a form, you must first make sure that the .VBX file of this custom control is included in your project. The .VBX file of the common dialog custom control is CMDIALOG.VBX.

To see if the CMDIALOG.VBX file is included in the COMMON.MAK project:

☐ Select Project from the Window menu.

Visual Basic responds by displaying the project window.

☐ Look for CMDIALOG.VBX in the list of files of the project.

If CMDIALOG.VBX is not listed inside the project window, you need to add it. To add the CMDIALOG.VBX file to your project do the following:

☐ Select Add File from the File menu.

Visual Basic responds by displaying the Add File dialog box.

☐ Select the file CMDIALOG.VBX. This file resides in the SYSTEM subdirectory of the WINDOWS directory. For example, if your WINDOWS directory is C:\WINDOWS, you need to select the file C:\WINDOWS\SYSTEM\CMDIALOG.VBX.

Now that you are sure that the CMDIALOG.VBX custom control file is included in the project, you may place the common dialog custom control inside the COMMON.FRM form.

Use the following steps to place the common dialog custom control inside the COMMON.FRM form:

☐ Select Project from the Window menu.

Visual Basic responds by displaying the project window.

☐ Select COMMON.FRM in the project window and click the View Form button of the Project window.

Visual Basic responds by displaying the COMMON.FRM form.

☐ Double-click the icon of the common dialog custom control in the Toolbox. (The icon of the common dialog custom control is shown in Figure 6.9.)

Visual Basic responds by placing the common dialog custom control inside the COMMON.FRM form. The default name that Visual Basic assigns to this control is CMDialog1.

Figure 6.9.
The icon of the common dialog custom control.

☐ Build the COMMON.FRM form according to the specifications in Table 6.10.

The completed form should look like the one shown in Figure 6.10

Table 6.10. The properties table of the COMMON.FRM form.

Object	Property	Value
Form	**Name**	**frmCommon**
	Caption	The Common Program
Common Dialog	**Name**	**CMDialog1**
	CancelError	True
Menu	**(see Table 6.11)**	**(see Table 6.11)**

Table 6.11. The menu table of the frmCommon form.

Caption	Name
&File	mnuFile
...Color...	mnuColor
...Open...	mnuOpen
...-	mnuSep1
...E&xit	mnuExit

Figure 6.10.
The form of the Common program.

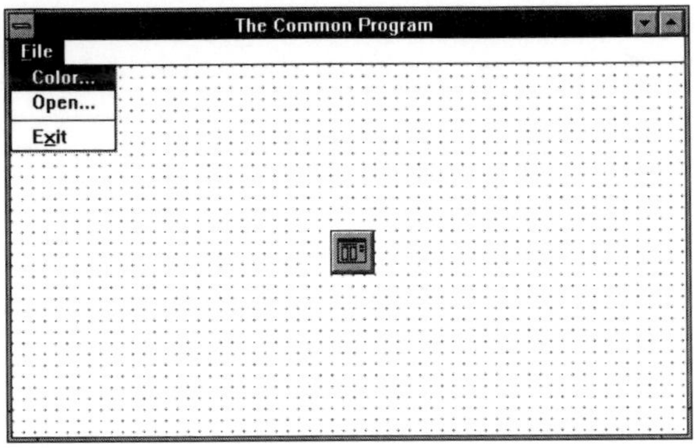

Entering the Code of the Common Program

☐ Enter the following code inside the general declarations area of the frmCommon form:

```
' All variables must be declared.
Option Explicit
```

☐ Enter the following code inside the mnuColor_Click() event procedure of the frmCommon form:

```
Sub mnuColor_Click ()

    ' Set an error trap to detect the pressing of the
    ' Cancel button of the Color dialog box.
    On Error GoTo ColorError

    ' Display the Color dialog box.
    CMDialog1.Action = 3

    ' Change the color of the form to the color that the
    ' user selected in the color dialog box.
    frmCommon.BackColor = CMDialog1.Color

    ' Exit the procedure.
    Exit Sub

ColorError:
    ' The user pressed the Cancel button of the Color
    ' dialog box.
    MsgBox "You cancelled the dialog box!"
    Exit Sub

End Sub
```

☐ Enter the following code inside the `mnuOpen_Click()` event procedure of the frmCommon form:

```
Sub mnuOpen_Click ()

    ' Set an error trap to detect the pressing of the
    ' Cancel key of the Open dialog box.
    On Error GoTo OpenError

    ' Fill the items of the File Type list box of
    ' the Open dialog box.
    CMDialog1.Filter = "All Files (*.*)¦*.* ¦
                    ➥ Text Files (*.txt)¦*.txt ¦
                    ➥ Batch Files (*.bat)¦*.bat"

    ' Set the default File Type to Text Files (*.txt).
    CMDialog1.FilterIndex = 2

    ' Display the Open dialog box.
    CMDialog1.Action = 1

    ' Display the name of the file that the user selected.
    MsgBox "You selected: " + CMDialog1.Filename

    ' Exit the procedure.
    Exit Sub

OpenError:
    ' The user pressed the Cancel key.
    MsgBox "You cancelled the dialog box!"
    Exit Sub

End Sub
```

☐ Enter the following code inside the `mnuExit_Click()` event procedure of the frmCommon form:

```
Sub mnuExit_Click ()

    End

End Sub
```

Executing the Common Program

Execute the Common program. Note that the common dialog custom control is invisible. The control comes to life as soon as you select Color or Open from the File menu.

☐ Select Color from the File menu.

The Common program responds by displaying the Color dialog box (see Figure 6.11).

Figure 6.11.
The Color dialog box.

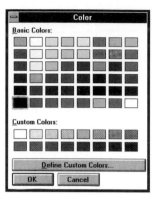

☐ Select a color from the Color dialog box by clicking the desired color and pressing the OK button.

> *The Common program responds by closing the Color dialog box and changing the color of the form to the selected color.*

☐ Select Open from the File menu.

> *The Common program responds by displaying the Open dialog box (see Figure 6.12).*

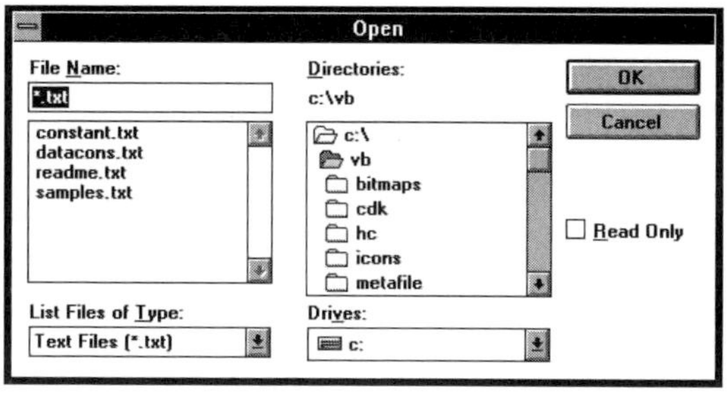

Figure 6.12.
The Open dialog box.

☐ Select a file from the Open dialog box.

> *The Common program responds by displaying the name of the selected file.*

How the Common Program Works

The Common program uses the common dialog custom control to display a Color dialog box and an Open dialog box. The Color dialog box lets the user select a color, and the Open dialog box lets the user select a file.

SAMS
Sams
Learning
Center
SAMS
PUBLISHING

The Color Dialog Box

Whenever the user selects Color from the File menu, the `mnuColor_Click()` event procedure is executed. The code inside this procedure uses the common dialog custom control to display a Color dialog box:

```
Sub mnuColor_Click ()

    ' Set an error trap to detect the pressing of the
    ' Cancel button of the Color dialog box.
    On Error GoTo ColorError

    ' Display the Color dialog box.
    CMDialog1.Action = 3

    ' Change the color of the form to the color that the
    ' user selected in the color dialog box.
    frmCommon.BackColor = CMDialog1.Color

    ' Exit the procedure.
    Exit Sub

ColorError:
    ' The user pressed the Cancel button of the Color
    ' dialog box.
    MsgBox "You cancelled the dialog box!"
    Exit Sub

End Sub
```

Before displaying the dialog box, the `mnuColor_Click()` procedure sets an error trap:

```
On Error GoTo ColorError
```

The purpose of this error trap is to detect an error during the display of the dialog box. Recall that during design time you set the CancelError property of the CMDialog1 common dialog control to True. Therefore, if the user presses the Cancel button while the dialog box is displayed, an error is generated, and as a result of the above error trap, the program branches to the ColorError label.

After setting the error trap, the procedure displays the Color dialog box by setting the Action property of the CMDialog common dialog control to 3:

```
CMDialog1.Action = 3
```

If the user presses the Cancel button while the dialog box is displayed, an error is generated, and as a result, the code under the ColorError label is executed. The code under the ColorError label displays a message and terminates the procedure:

```
ColorError:
    MsgBox "You cancelled the dialog box!"
    Exit Sub
```

6

If, however, the user does not press the Cancel button, but selects a color from the dialog box and presses the OK button, the procedure executes the following two statements:

```
frmCommon.BackColor = CMDialog1.Color
Exit Sub
```

The first statement changes the BackColor property of the form to the color that was selected by the user. The color that was selected by the user is contained in the Color property of the CMDialog1 control (CMDialog1.Color). The second statement terminates the procedure.

The Open Dialog Box

Whenever the user selects Open from the File menu, the mnuOpen_Click() event procedure is executed. The code inside this procedure uses the common dialog custom control to display an Open dialog box:

```
Sub mnuOpen_Click ()

    ' Set an error trap to detect the pressing of the
    ' Cancel key of the Open dialog box.
    On Error GoTo OpenError

    ' Fill the items of the File Type list box of
    ' the Open dialog box.
    CMDialog1.Filter = "All Files (*.*)¦*.* ¦
                   ➥ Text Files (*.txt)¦*.txt ¦
                   ➥ Batch Files (*.bat)¦*.bat"

    ' Set the default File Type to Text Files (*.txt).
    CMDialog1.FilterIndex = 2

    ' Display the Open dialog box.
    CMDialog1.Action = 1

    ' Display the name of the file that the user selected.
    MsgBox "You selected: " + CMDialog1.Filename

    ' Exit the procedure.
    Exit Sub

OpenError:
    ' The user pressed the Cancel key.
    MsgBox "You cancelled the dialog box!"
    Exit Sub

End Sub
```

The first statement of the procedure sets an error trap:

```
On Error GoTo OpenError
```

As a result of this error trap, if the user presses the Cancel button while the Open dialog box is displayed, the procedure branches to the OpenError label.

After setting the error trap, the procedure uses the Filter property of the CMDialog1 control to fill the items of the File Type list box of the Open dialog box. The File Type list box is filled with three file types:

```
CMDialog1.Filter = "All Files (*.*)¦*.* ¦
              ➡ Text Files (*.txt)¦*.txt ¦
              ➡ Batch Files (*.bat)¦*.bat"
```

Figure 6.13 shows the File Type list box that is created with this statement.

Figure 6.13.
A File Type list box.

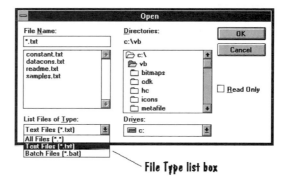

File Type list box

The Filter property is filled with a string that specifies the text of each of the items that appear in the File Type list box, as well as the skeleton of the files that are displayed.

For example, the first item that appears in the File Type list box is specified with the following string:

```
All Files (*.*)¦*.*
```

This string is made of two parts separated by the pipe symbol (¦). (The pipe character is typed by pressing Shift+\.) The first part indicates the text that appears in the list box:

```
All Files (*.*)
```

The second part indicates the skeleton of the files that are displayed when this item is selected:

```
*.*
```

That is, when the first item of the File Type list box is selected, the files with the skeleton *.* (that is, all the files) are displayed in the dialog box.

After the File Type list box of the dialog box is filled, the default File Type item that appears in the File Type list box is set to item number 2. This is done by setting the FilterIndex property of CMDialog1 to 2:

```
CMDialog1.FilterIndex = 2
```

6

Because item number 2 of the File Type list box is Text Files (*.txt), the default files that are listed in the Open dialog box are files with a .TXT extension.

The procedure displays the Open dialog box by setting the Action property of the CMDialog common dialog control to 1:

```
CMDialog1.Action = 1
```

If the user presses the Cancel button while the dialog box is displayed, an error is generated and, as a result, the code under the OpenError label is executed. The code under the OpenError label displays a message and terminates the procedure:

```
OpenError:
    MsgBox "You cancelled the dialog box!"
    Exit Sub
```

If, however, the user does not press the Cancel button, but selects a file from the dialog box, the name of the selected file is displayed and the procedure is terminated:

```
MsgBox "You selected: " + CMDialog1.Filename
Exit Sub
```

The file that was selected by the user is contained in the FileName property of the CMDialog1 control (CMDialog1.FileName).

Other Common Dialog Boxes

The Common program used the common dialog custom control to display a Color dialog box and an Open dialog box. You may use the common dialog control to display other common dialog boxes. Table 6.12 lists the common dialog boxes that may be displayed and the values that should be assigned to the Action property of the common dialog control to display a particular dialog box. For example, to display the Save As common dialog box, you should set the Action property of the common dialog control to 2:

```
CMDialog1.Action=2
```

Table 6.12. The common dialog boxes.

Displayed Common Dialog Box	Value of the Action Property
Open	1
Save As	2
Color	3
Font	4
Print	5

Like the Color and Open dialog boxes, the properties of the custom common dialog control may be used to determine the user's response to the dialog box.

Summary

This chapter discusses dialog boxes. You have learned how to display predefined dialog boxes with the MsgBox statement, the MsgBox() function, and the InputBox() function. These dialog boxes are ideal for cases in which you need to inform the user with short messages, get the user's response to yes/no types of questions, or solicit text data from the user (for example, get the user's name).

You have also learned how to design your own custom dialog boxes and how to use them in a program. When you design a custom dialog box there is no limit to the number of buttons or controls that you may have in the dialog box.

The last section of this chapter covers the common dialog custom control. This control is available starting with Visual Basic Version 3.0. You may use this control to display common dialog boxes such as Open, Save As, Print, Color, and Font.

Q&A

Q This chapter covers three types of dialog boxes (predefined, custom, and common). Which of these types of dialog box should I use?

A Whenever possible you should try to use the predefined dialog boxes or the common dialog boxes. However, in some cases, you will have to design your own custom dialog boxes. The advantage of designing your own custom dialog box is that there is no limit to the buttons or controls you can place inside the dialog box. For example, you may place any picture inside the custom dialog box. The disadvantage of designing your own custom control is that you need to spend some time designing it. Furthermore, if a predefined dialog box or a common dialog box can already do what your custom dialog box does, you are "reinventing the wheel."

6

Quiz

1. What is the difference between the MsgBox statement and the MsgBox() function?
2. What does the following statement do? (Assume that the constant MB_OK is defined according to Table 6.2.)

```
MsgBox "File is missing!", MB_OK, "ERROR"
```

3. What does the following code do? (Assume that the constants `MB_YESNO` and `ID_YES` are defined according to Tables 6.2 and 6.4.)

```
If MsgBox("Exit the program?", MB_YESNO, "DEMO")= ID_YES Then

    End

End If
```

4. What does the following code do?

```
UserName = InputBox ("Enter your name:", "Demo")
If UserName<>"" Then
    MsgBox "Hello "+Username
End If
```

5. Assume that you designed a custom dialog box called frmMyDialog. What does the following statement do?

```
frmMyDialog.Show 1
```

6. Assume that you designed a custom dialog box called frmMyDialog. What does the following statement do?

```
frmMyDialog.Hide
```

7. Assume that you have a common dialog custom control called CMDialog1. What does the following statement do? (Use Table 6.12 to answer this question.)

```
CMDialog1.Action = 2
```

Exercises

1. Write code that displays a dialog box with the title ERROR, the message `Disk error!`, an OK button, and an exclamation point icon.

2. Write code that displays a dialog box with the title QUESTION, the question message `Are you sure you want to quit?`, Yes and No buttons, and a question mark icon. If the user's response to the question is Yes, (the user clicked the Yes button), terminate the program.

3. Write code that displays a dialog box asking the user to enter a number between 1 and 10. If the user enters a number in the range 1 to 10, the code should display a dialog box with the selected number. If, however, the user enters a number that is not in the range 1 to 10 (or the user enters nonnumeric characters), the code should display an error message. If the user presses the Cancel button of the dialog box, the code should not display anything. (Hint: this code is similar to the code inside the `mnuGetNumber_Click()` procedure of the Dialogs program.)

Quiz Answers

1. The `MsgBox` statement and the `MsgBox()` function take the same parameters and display the same dialog boxes. The only difference between them is that the `MsgBox()` function returns a value that represents the button that the user selected in the dialog box. The `MsgBox` statement does not return any value.

2. This statement displays a dialog box with the title ERROR, the message `File is missing!`, and an OK button.

3. This code displays a message box with the title DEMO, the question message `Exit the program?`, and Yes and No buttons. If the user clicks the Yes button of the dialog box, the `MsgBox()` function returns the value `ID_YES`, in which case the condition of the `If` statement is satisfied and the program terminates with the `End` statement.

4. This code uses the `InputBox()` function to display a dialog box that prompts the user to enter a name. The returned value of the `InputBox` function is assigned to the variable `UserName`. If the user enters a name and does not press the Cancel button, the variable `UserName` is not null, in which case the condition of the `If` statement `If UserName<>""` is satisfied and the user is prompted with a Hello message that displays the user's name.

5. This statement uses the Show method to display the frmMyDialog dialog box as modal.

6. This statement uses the Hide method to hide the frmMyDialog dialog box from view. After this statement is executed, the frmMyDialog dialog box disappears. Typically, this statement is used in the code of the terminating buttons of the dialog box. For example, after the user responds to the dialog box by pressing the OK (or Cancel) button, use the Hide method to hide the dialog box from view.

7. This statement displays the Save As common dialog box.

Exercise Answers

1. To display such a dialog box, you may use the following code:

```
Const MB_OK = 0
Const MB_ICONEXCLAMATION = 48

MsgBox "Disk error!", MB_OK + MB_ICONEXCLAMATION, "ERROR"
```

2. To display such a dialog box, you may use the following code:

```
Const MB_YESNO = 4
Const MB_ICONQUESTION = 32
Const MB_IDYES = 6
```

```
If MsgBox ( "Are you sure you want to quit?",
           ➥ MB_YESNO + MB_ICONQUESTION",
           ➥ "QUESTION" ) = MB_IDYES Then

        End

End If
```

3. The following code is one possible solution:

```
Dim UserInput


' Get a number from the user.
UserInput = InputBox("Enter a number between 1 and 10",
                     ➥ "Demo")


' If the user did not enter anything, or if the user
' pressed Cancel, exit the procedure.
If UserInput = "" Then
   Exit Sub
End If


' If the user did not enter numeric characters, then display
' an error message and exit the procedure.

If Not IsNumeric(UserInput) Then
   MsgBox "Invalid number!"
   Exit Sub
End If


' If the number that the user entered is not in the range
' of 1 through 10, then display an error message and exit.
If UserInput<1 Or UserInput>10 Then
   MsgBox "You entered a number that is not between 1 and 10!"
   Exit Sub
End If


' Display the number that the user entered.
MsgBox "You entered the number: " + UserInput
```

Graphic Controls

One of the advantages of using Visual Basic for Windows is that it enables you to easily create programs that include graphics. In this chapter you'll learn how to write programs that include graphic controls.

The Twip

Visual Basic lets you display graphic objects such as lines, circles, and bitmap files. You need to specify the dimensions for these objects (for example, length of line, radius of circle). Although Visual Basic may use a variety of units for specifying the dimensions and locations of these graphic objects, the most commonly used unit is called a *twip*. There are 1440 twips in one inch.

Colors

An important characteristic of a graphic object is the color of the object. You may specify the color of objects by specifying the color with the RGB() function or with the QBColor() function.

Specifying Colors with the *RGB()* Function

The RGB() function enables you to specify colors. The three letters of the RGB() function stand for *red, green,* and *blue.* The reason for this name is that all the possible colors that a monitor and a color printer can display and print are generated by mixing these three basic colors (red, green, and blue). The RGB() function has three arguments: the value of the first argument represents the amount of red in the final color; the second argument represents the amount of green in the final color; and the third argument represents the amount of blue in the final color. For example, the following statement uses the RGB() function to return the color red:

```
RGB(255, 0, 0)
```

The maximum value of each argument in the RGB() function is 255, and the minimum value is 0. This explains why RGB(255,0,0) represents the color red. In a similar way, RGB(0,255,0) represents the color green, and RGB(0,0,255) represents the color blue.

To generate the color yellow, use RGB(255,255,0). How can you tell that this combination of numbers yields the color yellow? Well, if you have a Ph.D. in physics, you probably know the answer, and you probably can explain it in terms of wavelength and other light properties. Otherwise, you have to generate the color by trial and error. But there are two RGB() combinations that you should remember: The color white is represented as RGB(255,255,255), and the color black is represented as RGB(0,0,0).

For example, to change the BackColor property of the frmMyForm form to blue, use the following statement:

```
frmMyForm.BackColor = RGB(0,0,255)
```

Specifying Colors with the *QBColor()* Function

Another easy way to specify colors is by using the QBColor() function. The QBColor() function has one argument that may have any integer value between 0 and 15.

To change the BackColor property of the form frmMyForm to gray, use the following statement:

```
frmMyForm.BackColor = QBColor(8)
```

Table 4.3 in Chapter 4, "The Mouse," lists all the possible 16 colors and their corresponding values.

The QBColor() function is easier to use than the RGB() function, but it enables you to generate only 16 colors.

The Line Control

The line control is used for drawing lines. The Line program demonstrates how the line control is used in a program.

The Visual Implementation of the Line Program

Use the following steps to build the form of the Line program:

☐ Create a new project.

☐ Save the form of the project as LINE.FRM and save the make file of the project as LINE.MAK.

☐ Build the form of the Line program according to the specifications in Table 7.1.

The completed form should look like the one shown in Figure 7.1.

Table 7.1. The properties table of the Line program.

Object	Property	Setting
Form	**Name**	**frmLine**
	Caption	The Line Program
	Height	4425
	Left	1035

Table 7.1. continued

Object	Property	Setting
Form	**Name**	**frmLine**
	Top	1140
	Width	7485
Command Button	**Name**	**cmdExit**
	Caption	E&xit
	Height	495
	Left	3120
	Top	3360
	Width	1215
Command Button	**Name**	**cmdStart**
	Caption	&Start
	Height	975
	Left	480
	Top	2760
	Width	1215
Line	**Name**	**linLine**
	X1	3120
	X2	4320
	Y1	1800
	Y2	2280

Figure 7.1.
*The form of the Line
program.*

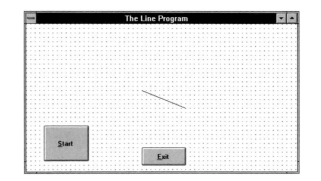

Entering the Code of the Line Program

☐ Enter the following code inside the general declarations section of the frmLine form:

```
' All variables MUST be declared.
Option Explicit
```

☐ Enter the following code inside the cmdExit_Click() procedure:

```
Sub cmdExit_Click ()

    End

End Sub
```

☐ Enter the following code inside the cmdStart_Click() procedure:

```
Sub cmdStart_Click ()

    ' Set the start and end points of the line
    ' control to random values.
    linLine.X1 = Int(frmLine.Width * Rnd)
    linLine.Y1 = Int(frmLine.Height * Rnd)
    linLine.X2 = Int(frmLine.Width * Rnd)
    linLine.Y2 = Int(frmLine.Height * Rnd)

End Sub
```

Executing the Line Program

☐ Execute the Line program.

Click the Start button several times, and notice that every time you click the button, the line control changes its location and its length.

How the Line Program Works

The Line program uses the cmdStart_Click() event procedure to display the line control at a different location every time you click the Start button.

The Code of the *cmdStart_Click()* Event Procedure

The cmdStart_Click() procedure is executed whenever you click the Start button:

```
Sub cmdStart_Click ()

    ' Set the start and end points of the line
    ' control to random values.
    linLine.X1 = Int(frmLine.Width * Rnd)
```

```
linLine.Y1 = Int(frmLine.Height * Rnd)
linLine.X2 = Int(frmLine.Width * Rnd)
linLine.Y2 = Int(frmLine.Height * Rnd)
```

End Sub

The Rnd function returns a random number between 0 and 1. The width of the frmLine form is given by the Width property. Therefore, the product:

```
frmLine.Width * Rnd
```

is equal to a number between 0 and the width of the form. For example, if the Rnd function returns 0, the product is equal to 0. If the Rnd function returns 1, the product is equal to the width of the form. If the Rnd function returns 0.75, the product is equal to three-quarters of the width of the form.

The Int() function converts its argument to an integer. For example, Int(3.5) returns 3, and Int(7.999) returns 7.

From the preceding discussion, it is clear that the product Int (frmLine.Width * Rnd) returns a random integer that is between 0 and the width of the form.

The first statement in the cmdStart_Click() procedure assigns an integer to the X1 property of the line control. This integer is between 0 and the width of the form:

```
linLine.X1 = Int(frmLine.Width * Rnd)
```

The X1 property of the line control is the horizontal coordinate of the point where the line begins. Because the line is drawn on the form, the coordinate system is referenced to the form. The default coordinate system that Visual Basic uses is defined so that the coordinate X1=0, Y1=0 specifies the top-left corner of the form.

In a similar manner, the second statement in the cmdStart_Click() procedure assigns a value to the Y1 property of the line control. The assigned value may be an integer between 0 and the height of the form:

```
linLine.Y1 = Int(frmLine.Height * Rnd)
```

The Y1 property of the line control is the vertical coordinate of the point where the line begins. In a similar manner, the last two statements of the cmdStart_Click() procedure assign values to the X2 and Y2 properties of the line control. The X2 and Y2 properties are the coordinates of the end points of the line control:

```
linLine.X2 = Int(frmLine.Width * Rnd)
linLine.Y2 = Int(frmLine.Height * Rnd)
```

In summary, whenever you click the Start button, the line moves to a new location. The new location depends on random numbers.

More About the Properties of the Line Control

Experiment with some of the properties of the line control at design time:

☐ Select the line control (at design time).

☐ Change the BorderColor property of the line control to red.

> *Visual Basic responds by changing the color of the line to red.*

☐ Change the BorderWidth property of the line control to 10.

> *Visual Basic responds by changing the width of the line to 10 twips.*

☐ Save the project (Select Save Project from the File menu).

☐ Execute the Line program.

> *The Line program now displays the line control as a red line that is 10 twips wide (see Figure 7.2).*

Figure 7.2.

Changing the BorderColor and BorderWidth properties of the line control.

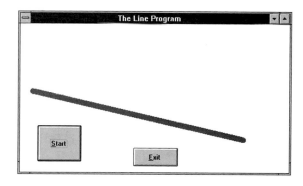

You may also change these properties at runtime:

☐ Insert the following statement at the beginning of the cmdStart_Click() procedure:

```
linLine.BorderColor=RGB(Int(255*Rnd),Int(255*Rnd),Int(255*Rnd))
linLine.BorderWidth = Int(100 * Rnd)
```

The first statement assigns a new value to the BorderColor property of the line control. The new value is the returned value from the RGB() function where all three arguments of the function are random numbers between 0 and 255. This means that the returned value from this RGB() function is a random color.

The second statement assigns a new value to the BorderWidth property of the line control. This new value is a random number between 0 and 100. This means that the width of the line is assigned a new width between 0 and 100 twips.

☐ Execute the program.

As you can see, the line changes its color and its width every time you click the Start button. (Of course, if the random color has the same color as the color of the form background, you will not see the line.)

The Shape Control

The Shape control is used for drawing several shapes: rectangle, square, rounded rectangle, rounded square, circle, and oval. The Shape program illustrates how to display these shapes.

The Visual Implementation of the Shape Program

Use the following steps to build the form of the Shape program:

☐ Create a new project.

☐ Save the form of the project as SHAPE.FRM and save the make file of the project as SHAPE.MAK.

☐ Build the form of the Shape program according to the specifications in Table 7.2.

The completed form should look like the one shown in Figure 7.3.

Table 7.2. The properties table of the Shape program.

Object	Property	Setting
Form	**Name**	**frmShape**
	Caption	The Shape Program
	Height	4425
	Left	1035
	Top	1140
	Width	7485
Shape	**Name**	**shpAllShapes**
	Height	1215
	Left	3120
	Top	960
	Width	2335

Object	Property	Setting
Command Button	**Name**	**cmdExit**
	Caption	&Exit
	Height	495
	Left	6000
	Top	3360
	Width	1215
Command Button	**Name**	**cmdRectangle**
	Caption	&Rectangle
	Height	495
	Left	360
	Top	120
	Width	2175
Command Button	**Name**	**cmdSquare**
	Caption	&Square
	Height	495
	Left	360
	Top	720
	Width	2175
Command Button	**Name**	**cmdOval**
	Caption	&Oval
	Height	495
	Left	360
	Top	1320
	Width	2175
Command Button	**Name**	**cmdCircle**
	Caption	&Circle
	Height	495
	Left	360
	Top	1920
	Width	2175

continues

Table 7.2. continued

Object	Property	Setting
Command Button	**Name**	**cmdRndRect**
	Caption	Rounded Rectan&gle
	Height	495
	Left	360
	Top	2520
	Width	2175
Command Button	**Name**	**cmdRndSqr**
	Caption	Rounded S&quare
	Height	495
	Left	360
	Top	3120
	Width	2175
Label	**Name**	**lblInfo**
	Caption	Change width:
	Height	255
	Left	3120
	Top	3120
	Width	1815
Horizontal Scroll Bar	**Name**	**hsbWidth**
	Min	1
	Max	10
	Height	255
	Left	3120
	Top	3480
	Width	2535

Figure 7.3.
The frmShape. form.

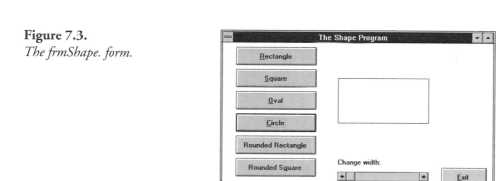

Entering the Code of the Shape Program

☐ Enter the following code inside the general declarations section of the frmShape form:

```
' All variables MUST be declared.
Option Explicit
```

☐ Enter the following code inside the cmdExit_Click() procedure:

```
Sub cmdExit_Click ()

    End

End Sub
```

☐ Enter the following code inside the cmdRectangle_Click() procedure:

```
Sub cmdRectangle_Click ()

    ' The user clicked the Rectangle button,
    ' so set the Shape property of shpAllShapes to
    ' rectangle (0).
    shpAllShapes.Shape = 0

End Sub
```

☐ Enter the following code inside the cmdSquare_Click() procedure:

```
Sub cmdSquare_Click ()

    ' The user clicked the Square button,
    ' so set the Shape property of shpAllShapes to
    ' square (1).
    shpAllShapes.Shape = 1

End Sub
```

☐ Enter the following code inside the cmdOval_Click() procedure:

```
Sub cmdOval_Click ()

    ' The user clicked the Oval button,
    ' so set the Shape property of shpAllShapes to
    ' oval (2).
    shpAllShapes.Shape = 2

End Sub
```

☐ Enter the following code inside the cmdCircle_Click() procedure:

```
Sub cmdCircle_Click ()

    ' The user clicked the Circle button,
    ' so set the Shape property of shpAllShapes to
    ' circle (3).
    shpAllShapes.Shape = 3

End Sub
```

☐ Enter the following code inside the cmdRndRect_Click() procedure:

```
Sub cmdRndRect_Click ()

    ' The user clicked the Rounded Rectangle button,
    ' so set the Shape property of shpAllShapes to
    ' rounded rectangle (4).
    shpAllShapes.Shape = 4

End Sub
```

☐ Enter the following code inside the cmdRndSqr() procedure:

```
Sub cmdRndSqr_Click ()

    ' The user clicked the Rounded Square button,
    ' so set the Shape property of shpAllShapes to
    ' rounded square (5).
    shpAllShapes.Shape = 5

End Sub
```

☐ Enter the following code inside the hsbWidth_Change() procedure:

```
Sub hsbWidth_Change ()

    ' The user changed the scroll bar position,
    ' so set the BorderWidth property of
    ' shpAllShapes to the new value of the scroll
    ' bar.
    shpAllShapes.BorderWidth = hsbWidth.Value

End Sub
```

Executing the Shape Program

Upon execution of the Shape program, the form shown in Figure 7.3 is displayed. When you click a button, the shape changes to the shape indicated by the button. For example, when you click the Circle button, the shape becomes a circle.

The width of the shape is changed whenever you change the scroll bar position. Figure 7.4 shows the shape after the Circle button was clicked (the scroll bar was set to its middle point).

Figure 7.4.
Changing the shape and width of the shape.

How the Shape Program Works

The code of the Shape program changes the shape and the width of the shpAllShapes control.

The Code Inside the *cmdRectangle_Click()* Event Procedure

The `cmdRectangle_Clck()` procedure is executed whenever you click the Rectangle button. The statement in this procedure sets the Shape property of shpAllShapes to 0:

```
shpAllShapes.Shape = 0
```

A value of 0 means a rectangle.

In a similar manner, the `cmdSquare_Click()` procedure is executed whenever you click the Square button. The statement inside the `cmdSquare_Click()` procedure sets the Shape property of shpAllShapes to 1. A value of 1 means a square.

Table 7.3 lists the possible values that the Shape property may have.

Table 7.3. Possible values for the Shape property of the Shape control.

Value	Meaning
0	Rectangle
1	Square
2	Oval
3	Circle
4	Rounded rectangle
5	Rounded square

The Code Inside the *hsbWidth_Change()* Event Procedure

The hsbWidth_Change() procedure is executed whenever you change the scroll bar position. As indicated in the properties table of the Shape program, the Min property of the scroll bar is 1, and the Max property of the scroll bar is 10. Therefore, the Value property of hsbWidth may be changed by the user to a value between 1 and 10. This value is assigned to the BorderWidth property of shpAllShapes in the hsbWidth_Change() procedure as follows:

```
shpAllShapes.BorderWidth = hsbWidth.Value
```

Therefore, shpAllShapes changes its width in accordance with the scroll bar position.

Other Properties of the Shape Control

The Shape program demonstrates only two properties of the Shape control. You may experiment with the other properties of the Shape control by placing a shape inside a form and changing the various properties of the shape. Here is an example:

☐ Place a Shape control inside the form.

Visual Basic responds by assigning the default rectangle shape.

☐ Change the Shape property of the shape to Circle.

Visual Basic responds by changing the shape from a rectangle to a circle.

☐ Change the FillColor property of the shape to red.

Visual Basic does not fill the circle with red because the default FillStyle property of the shape is Transparent.

☐ Change the FillStyle property of the shape to Solid.

As you can see, Visual Basic responds by filling the circle with solid red.

Pictures

The line control and the Shape control are capable of drawing simple geometric shapes such as lines, circles, and squares. To display more complex shapes, you need to use a picture file. You may place picture files on a form, inside an image control, or inside a picture control.

To place a picture file inside one of these objects, you have to change the Picture property of the object. For example, to place a picture file inside an image control, set the Picture property of the control to the desired picture file.

You may create a picture file by using Paintbrush to draw the picture. Then save your picture as a BMP file. Alternatively (if you don't think that you have the talent to draw pictures yourself), you may purchase professional pictures from a variety of vendors. These third-party picture products are called *clip art*.

Placing a Picture on a Form

You may place pictures on a form during design time and during runtime.

Placing a Picture on a Form During Design Time

Use the following steps to place a picture on a form at design time:

☐ Start Paintbrush.

☐ Select Image Attributes from the Options menu.

> *Paintbrush responds by displaying the Image Attributes dialog box.*

☐ Set the Width and Height fields inside the Image Attribute dialog box to 3 inches each. (These settings determine the size of the picture.)

☐ Use the Paintbrush tools to draw your picture.

☐ Save your work by saving the file as MyPic.BMP.

You now have a BMP picture file. Place this picture file on a form:

☐ Start a new Visual Basic project.

> *Visual Basic responds by displaying a blank form Form1.frm.*

☐ Highlight the Picture property of Form1.

> *Visual Basic responds by displaying three dots in the Setting box of the properties window.*

☐ Click the three dots, and select the BMP file that you created.

Figure 7.5 shows the form with the picture created with Paintbrush.

7

Figure 7.5.

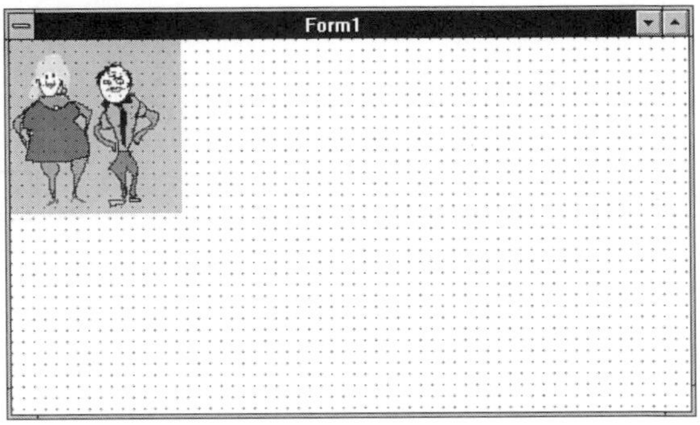

Placing a picture that was created with Paintbrush on a form.

As shown in Figure 7.5, the picture is displayed on the form with its upper-left corner at the 0,0 coordinate of the form. Visual Basic does not let you stretch the picture. The picture is shown with the same dimensions that you specified in the Image Attribute of Paintbrush.

The picture that is placed on the form serves as a background picture of the form. You may place command buttons and other controls directly on the picture of the form. Figure 7.6 shows the picture with a command button placed on the picture.

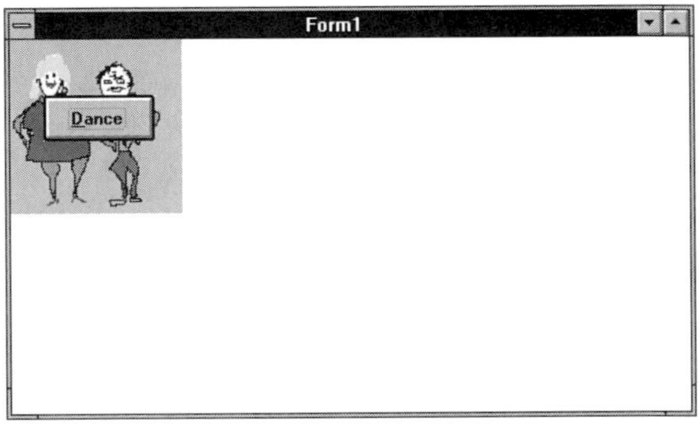

Figure 7.6.

Placing a button on the background picture of the form.

Because a picture that is placed on a form cannot be stretched, you may resize the form so that it will fit nicely around the picture, as shown in Figure 7.7. To prevent yourself from enlarging or shrinking the form at runtime, set the BorderStyle property of the form to either Fixed Double or Fixed Single. In both cases, you are prevented from sizing the form, and the border of the form is made of either double lines (Fixed Double) or a single line (Fixed Single).

There are several applications in which you may find it useful to place a background picture on the form. For example, some programs start by displaying a form with a picture in it. The picture may be the logo of the company that distributes the software.

Figure 7.7.
The form with its BorderStyle property set to Fixed Double.

Placing Pictures on a Form During Runtime

You may place pictures on a form during runtime. To load the picture c:\vb\bitmaps\assorted\balloon.bmp and place it on the frmMyForm form, use the following statement:

```
frmMyForm.Picture = LoadPicture("c:\vb\bitmaps\assorted\balloon.bmp")
```

Because only one picture may be placed on a form at any time, the LoadPicture() function replaces the current picture (if one exists on the form).

To clear a picture that exists on the form at runtime, use the following statement:

```
frmMyForm.Picture = LoadPicture("")
```

Image Control

You may also place picture files that were created with Paintbrush inside the image control. When using the image control, you may take advantage of the Stretch property that it supports. This property enables you to stretch the picture to any desired size. (The form and the picture controls do not support the Stretch property.)

To load the picture c:\vb\bitmaps\assorted\balloon.bmp and place it inside the imgMyImage image control, use the following statement:

```
imgMyImage.Picture = LoadPicture("c:\vb\bitmaps\assorted\balloon.bmp")
```

Because only one picture may be placed inside an image control at any time, the LoadPicture() function replaces the current picture (if one exists inside the image control).

To clear a picture that exists inside the image control at runtime, use the following statement:

```
imgMyImage.Picture = LoadPicture("")
```

To set the Stretch property of imgMyImage to True, use the following statement:

```
imgMyImage.Stretch = True
```

After you set the Stretch property to True, the picture file is automatically stretched so that the picture fills the entire area of the image control.

Picture Control

The picture control is very similar to the image control. The difference between the picture control and the image control is that the picture control supports more properties, more events, and more methods than the image control. However, the picture control does not support the Stretch property (only the image control supports the Stretch property).

The picture control supports the AutoSize property. If you set the AutoSize property of the picture control to True, Visual Basic adjusts the size of the picture control to the size of the picture file (that is, if the picture file is 3 inches by 2 inches, Visual Basic adjusts the size of the picture control to 3 inches by 2 inches. The form and the image control do not support the AutoSize property.)

The image control uses fewer resources that the picture control uses, and therefore is repainted faster than the picture control.

Standalone Applications

As stated, the `LoadPicture()` function may be used to load a picture into an image control and into a picture control at runtime. However, using the `LoadPicture()` function has a drawback: Your user must have the picture file in the directory specified by the argument of the `LoadPicture()` function. Therefore, your distribution disk (the disk that contains your complete program) must include the picture files that your program uses.

On the other hand, any picture file that was assigned to a picture holder control (form, picture control, image control) during design time becomes an integral part of the final EXE file, and you do not have to distribute the picture file as a separate file. An EXE file that can be executed without any other external files is called a *standalone* file.

The Different Types of Picture Files

The picture files that are supported by Visual Basic are bitmap files, icon files, and metafiles.

Bitmap Files

A bitmap file has either a .BMP or .DIB file extension. The bitmap file contains bytes that describe the pixel locations of the picture and the colors of the pixels.

Icon Files

An icon file has an .ICO file extension. Icon files are similar to BMP and DIB files. The only difference is that icon files may represent images that have a maximum size of 32 pixels by 32 pixels.

Metafiles

A metafile has a .WMF file extension. The metafiles contain a list of instructions that describe how to generate the picture.

Moving Controls

You may move a control at runtime by either changing its Left and Top properties, or by using the Move method.

Now write a program called MoveEye. This program illustrates how to move an object by changing its Left and Top properties.

The Visual Implementation of the MoveEye Program

☐ Create a new project.

☐ Save the form of the project as MoveEye.frm and save the make file of the project as MoveEye.mak.

☐ Build the form of the MoveEye program according to the specifications in Table 7.4.

The completed form should look like the one shown in Figure 7.8.

Table 7.4. The properties table of the MoveEye program.

Object	Property	Setting
Form	**Name**	**frmMoveEye**
	Caption	The MoveEye Program
	Height	4425
	Left	1035
	Top	1140
	Width	7485
Image	**Name**	**imgEye**
	Picture	c:\vb\icons\misc\eye.ico
	Stretch	True
	Height	480
	Left	3120

continues

Table 7.4. continued

Object	Property	Setting
Form	**Name**	**frmMoveEye**
	Top	1800
	Width	480
Command Button	**Name**	**cmdExit**
	Caption	&Exit
	Height	495
	Left	5760
	Top	3360
	Width	1215
Command Button	**Name**	**cmdMove**
	Caption	&Move
	Height	975
	Left	720
	Top	2880
	Width	1215

Figure 7.8.
The frmMoveEye form.

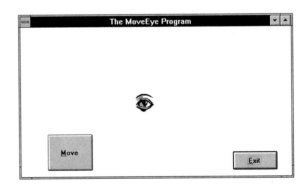

Entering the Code of the MoveEye Program

☐ Enter the following code inside the general declarations section of the frmMoveEye form:

```
' All variables MUST be declared.
Option Explicit
```

☐ Enter the following code inside the `cmdExit_Click()` procedure:

```
Sub cmdExit_Click ()

    End

End Sub
```

☐ Enter the following code inside the `cmdMove_Click()` procedure:

```
Sub cmdMove_Click ()

    ' Declare Counter as an integer.
    Dim Counter As Integer

    ' Execute the For loop 100 times.
    For Counter = 1 To 100 Step 1

        ' Raise the Top of the image 20 twips
        ' upward.
        imgEye.Top = imgEye.Top - 20

        ' Shift the Left edge of the image 20 twips
        ' to the left.
        imgEye.Left = imgEye.Left - 20

    Next Counter

End Sub
```

Executing the MoveEye Program

☐ Execute the MoveEye program.

As you click the Move button, the eye image is moved to a new location. You may keep clicking the Move button until the eye disappears from the form.

The Code of the MoveEye Program

The MoveEye program moves the image control by changing its Top and Left properties.

The *cmdMove_Click()* Event Procedure of the MoveEye Program

Whenever you click the Move button, the `cmdMove_Click()` procedure is executed:

```
Sub cmdMove_Click ()

    ' Declare Counter as an integer.
    Dim Counter As Integer

    ' Execute the For loop 100 times.
    For Counter = 1 To 100 Step 1
```

7

```
' Raise the Top of the image 20 twips
' upward.
imgEye.Top = imgEye.Top - 20

' Shift the Left edge of the image 20 twips
' to the left.
imgEye.Left = imgEye.Left - 20

    Next Counter

End Sub
```

The first statement inside the `For` loop of this procedure decreases the vertical coordinate of the top-left corner of the image by 20 twips:

```
imgEye.Top = imgEye.Top - 20
```

The second statement in the `For` loop of this procedure decreases the horizontal coordinate of the top-left corner of the image by 20 twips:

```
imgEye.Left = imgEye.Left - 20
```

Figure 7.9 shows the effect of these two statements.

Because the `For` loop is executed 100 times, the image is moved 100 times, giving the illusion of continuous motion.

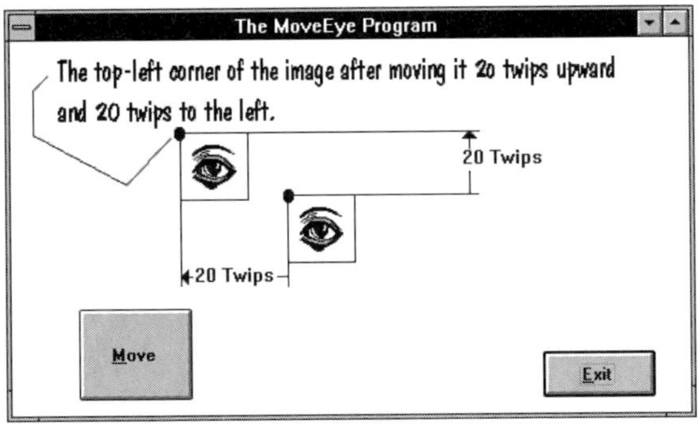

Figure 7.9.
Moving the image 20 twips upward and 20 twips to the left.

Moving a Control by Using the Move Method

The MoveEye program that was discussed in the previous section moves the image by changing its Top and Left properties. An alternate way to move the control is by using the Move method.

☐ Replace the code of the `cmdMove_Click()` procedure with the following code:

```
Sub cmdMove_Click ()

    ' Declare the variables.
    Dim Counter As Integer
```

```
Dim LeftEdge As Single
Dim TopEdge As Single

' Initialize the variables with the current
' location of the image.
LeftEdge = imgEye.Left
TopEdge = imgEye.Top

' Use the For loop to move the image 100
' times. In each Move, the image moves 20 twips
' upward and 20 twips to the left.
For Counter = 1 To 100 Step 1
    LeftEdge = LeftEdge - 20
    TopEdge = TopEdge - 20
    imgEye.Move LeftEdge, TopEdge
Next Counter
```

End Sub

The code in the procedure initializes the two variables, LeftEdge and TopEdge, to the current location of the top-left corner of the image, and the For loop is executed 100 times.

In each iteration of the For loop, the variables LeftEdge and TopEdge are decremented by 20. The Move method is used with the variable LeftEdge as the new horizontal coordinate, and the variable TopEdge as the new vertical coordinate.

More About the Move Method

The full syntax of the Move method is the following:

```
[Object name].Move. left, top, width, height
```

This means that you may also specify the new width and height that the object will have after the movement. Here is an example:

☐ Replace the cmdMove_Click() procedure of the MoveEye program with the following code:

Sub cmdMove_Click ()

```
Dim Counter As Integer
Dim LeftEdge As Single
Dim TopEdge As Single
Dim WidthOfImage As Single
Dim HeightOfImage As Single

imgEye.Stretch = True

LeftEdge = imgEye.Left
TopEdge = imgEye.Top
WidthOfImage = imgEye.Width
HeightOfImage = imgEye.Height

For Counter = 1 To 100 Step 1
    LeftEdge = LeftEdge - 20
    TopEdge = TopEdge - 20
```

7

```
    WidthOfImage = WidthOfImage + 10
    HeightOfImage = HeightOfImage + 10

    imgEye.Move LeftEdge, TopEdge, WidthOfImage, HeightOfImage
Next Counter
```

End Sub

☐ Execute the program and note how the eye moves and grows as it moves. After 100 moves, the form looks like the one shown in Figure 7.10.

Figure 7.10.
Using the Move method to move and enlarge the eye during its movement.

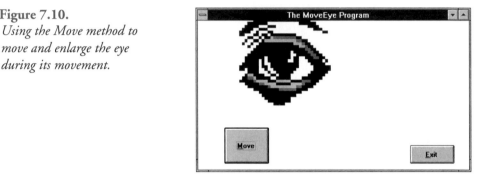

The first statement after the declaration statement is this:

```
imgEye.Stretch = True
```

This statement sets the Stretch property of imgEye to True, so that the program is able to stretch the image. (You may set the Stretch property during design time as well as during runtime.)

The variables `WidthOfImage` and `HeightOfImage` are initialized to the current width and height of the image:

```
WidthOfImage = imgEye.Width
HeightOfImage = imgEye.Height
```

Then the Move method is executed 100 times. In each iteration of the `For` loop, the `WidthOfImage` and `HeightOfImage` variables are increased by 10 twips.

The Move method specifies the new coordinates for the top-left corner of the image as well as the new width and height that the image should have after the movement:

```
imgEye.Move LeftEdge, TopEdge, WidthOfImage, HeightOfImage
```

Comparing the Moving Techniques

If you compare the performance of the MoveEye program when the Move method is used to the performance of the program when the Top and Left properties are changed, you might notice that the Move method is better. This is because the movement created by changing the Top and Left properties produces a jerky movement.

Moving a Picture Control

The previous program illustrates that using the Move method to move a control produces smoother motion than the motion produced by changing the Top and Left properties of the control. Yet even better results are obtained when you use a picture control instead of an image control. To prove it, change the frmMoveEye form as follows:

☐ Delete the imgEye image control from the form (select the imgEye control and press Delete).

☐ Create a picture control (double-click the picture control in the Toolbox).

Visual Basic responds by placing a picture control inside the form.

☐ Change the Name property of the picture control to picEye.

☐ Set the Picture property of picEye to c:\vb\icons\misc\eye.ico.

☐ Set the BorderStyle property of picEye to None (so that the picture will not be enclosed with a border).

☐ Replace the cmdMove_Click procedure with the following code:

```
Sub cmdMove_Click ()

    ' Declare the variables.
    Dim Counter As Integer
    Dim LeftEdge As Single
    Dim TopEdge As Single
    ' Initialize the variables with the current
    ' location of the picture.
    LeftEdge = picEye.Left
    TopEdge = picEye.Top

    ' Use the For loop to move the image 100
    ' times. In each Move, the picture moves 20
    ' twips upward and 20 twips to the left.
    For Counter = 1 To 100 Step 1
        LeftEdge = LeftEdge - 20
        TopEdge = TopEdge - 20
        picEye.Move LeftEdge, TopEdge
    Next Counter

End Sub
```

☐ Execute the program and notice that the eye does not flicker during the movement.

Control Arrays

A control array is an array that contains controls as its elements. For example, you may create an array where the elements of the array are image controls. Now write a program called Moon. The Moon program makes use of arrays of images.

The Visual Implementation of the Moon Program

☐ Create a new project.

☐ Save the form of the project as MOON.FRM and save the make file of the project as MOON.MAK.

☐ Place an image control inside the form by double-clicking the image control in the Toolbox.

Visual Basic responds by placing the image control inside the form.

☐ Drag the image control to the upper-left portion of the form (see Figure 7.11).

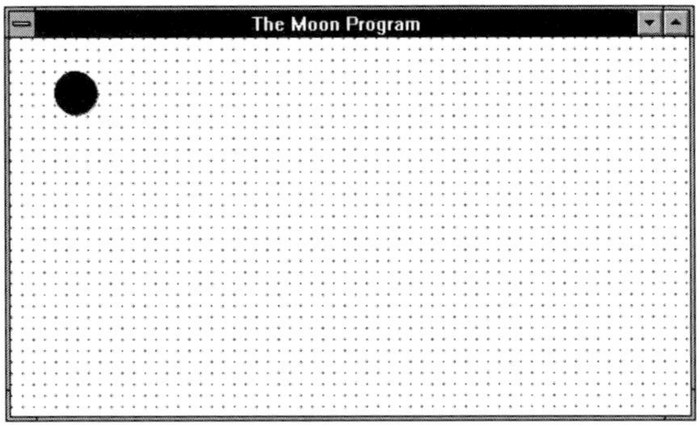

Figure 7.11.
The first element of the control array.

```
┌─────────────────────────────────────────────┐
│ ▄             The Moon Program          ▼ ▲ │
├─────────────────────────────────────────────┤
│   ●                                         │
│                                             │
│                                             │
│                                             │
│                                             │
│                                             │
│                                             │
│                                             │
└─────────────────────────────────────────────┘
```

☐ Change the Name property of the image to imgMoon.

☐ Change the Visible property of the image to False.

☐ Change the Stretch property of imgMoon to True.

☐ Set the Picture property of imgMoon to c:\vb\icons\elements\moon01.ico.

You have finished placing the image control inside the form. This image will soon serve as element number 0 of the array of images. Currently, the image that you placed is a "regular" (nonarray) control. You may verify this by examining the Index property of the image. It is blank.

Use the following steps to place the second element of the array:

☐ Double-click the image control of the Toolbox.

Visual Basic responds by placing the control inside the form.

☐ Drag the image to the right of the first image control (see Figure 7.12).

Figure 7.12.
The first and second elements of the control array.

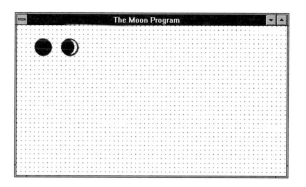

☐ Change the Visible property of the image to False.

☐ Change the Stretch property of the image to True.

☐ Set the Picture property of the image to c:\vb\icons\elements\moon2.ico.

☐ Change the Name property of the image to imgMoon.

Visual Basic responds by displaying the dialog box of Figure 7.13; that is, Visual Basic makes sure that you intend to name the second image with name identical to that of the first image.

Figure 7.13.
Creating a control array.

☐ Click the Yes button of the dialog box.

You are informing Visual Basic that you are creating a control array.

☐ Examine the Index property of the image.

The Index property of the image is 1.

Also examine the Index property of the first image. The Index property of the first image is 0.

This means that you now have a control array called imgMoon(). The first element of the array, imgMoon(0), is MOON01.ICO, which is the first image that you placed on the form. The second element of the array is the image MOON02.ICO.

☐ Now repeat this process and add six more elements to the control array. When you are finished, you should have a total of eight elements in the array, as shown in Figure 7.14 and Table 7.5. Don't forget to set the Name, Stretch, and Visible properties of the remaining six images.

Figure 7.14.
The eight moons of the control array.

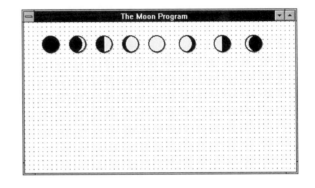

Table 7.5. The imgMoon() control array.

Element	Content of the Element
imgMoon(0)	c:\vb\icons\elements\moon01.ico
imgMoon(1)	c:\vb\icons\elements\moon02.ico
imgMoon(2)	c:\vb\icons\elements\moon03.ico
imgMoon(3)	c:\vb\icons\elements\moon04.ico
imgMoon(4)	c:\vb\icons\elements\moon05.ico
imgMoon(5)	c:\vb\icons\elements\moon06.ico
imgMoon(6)	c:\vb\icons\elements\moon07.ico
imgMoon(7)	c:\vb\icons\elements\moon08.ico

☐ Continue building the form according to the specifications in Table 7.6.

The completed form should look like the one shown in Figure 7.15.

Figure 7.15.
The frmMoon form.

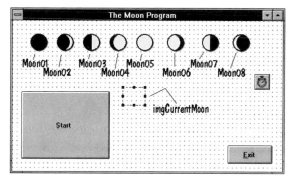

Table 7.7. The properties table of the Moon program.

Object	Property	Setting
Form	Name	frmMoon
	Caption	The Moon Program
	Height	4470
	Left	1035
	Top	1140
	Width	7485
Command Button	Name	cmdExit
	Caption	E&xit
	Height	495
	Left	5880
	Top	3360
	Width	1215
Command Button	Name	cmdStart
	Caption	&Start
	Height	1815
	Left	240
	Top	1920
	Width	2415
Image Control	Name	imgCurrentMoon
	Picture	(none)
	Stretch	True

continues

Table 7.7. continued

Object	Property	Setting
	Height	495
	Left	3000
	Top	1800
	Width	615
Timer	**Name**	**tmrTimer**
	Interval	250
Image Control Array	**(see Table 7.5)**	**(see Table 7.5)**

Note: Leave the Picture property of imgCurrentMoon at its default value (None). You'll assign a value to this property from within the code of the program. This image control is not part of the Image control array.

Entering the Code of the Moon Program

☐ Enter the following code inside the general declarations area of the Moon program:

```
' All variables MUST be declared.
Option Explicit

' Declaration of variables that are visible from any
' procedure in the form.
Dim RotateFlag As Integer
Dim CurrentMoon As Integer
```

☐ Enter the following code inside the cmdExit_Click() procedure:

```
Sub cmdExit_Click ()

    End

End Sub
```

☐ Enter the following code inside the cmdStart_Click() procedure:

```
Sub cmdStart_Click ()

    ' Toggle the RotateFlag, and toggle
    ' the caption of the Start/Stop button.
```

```
    If RotateFlag = 0 Then
        RotateFlag = 1
        cmdStart.Caption = "Stop"
    Else
        RotateFlag - 0
        cmdStart.Caption = "Start"
    End If

End Sub
```

☐ Enter the following code inside the `Form_Load()` procedure:

```
Sub Form_Load ()

    ' Initialize the flags.
    RotateFlag = 0
    CurrentMoon = 0

End Sub
```

☐ Enter the following code inside the `tmrTimer_Timer()` procedure:

```
Sub tmrTimer_Timer ()

    If RotateFlag = 1 Then
        imgCurrentMoon.Picture=imgMoon(CurrentMoon).Picture
    CurrentMoon = CurrentMoon + 1

        If CurrentMoon = 8 Then
            CurrentMoon = 0
        End If

    End If

End Sub
```

Executing the Moon Program

☐ Execute the Moon program.

As you can see, the image of the moon seems to rotate around its axis.

The Code of the Moon Program

The code of the Moon program uses a control array of images to display the elements (images) of the array one after the other, giving the illusion of a rotating moon.

The Code Inside the General Declarations Section of the Moon Program

The code inside the general declarations section declares two integers: `RotateFlag` and `CurrentMoon`. These variables are visible by all the procedures of the form.

The Code Inside the *Form_Load()* Event Procedure

The Form_Load() procedure is executed upon startup of the program, and it is a good place for performing various initializations. The two variables that were declared in the general declarations section are initialized to 0:

```
RotateFlag = 0
CurrentMoon = 0
```

> **Note:** Upon creation of these variables, Visual Basic initialized these variables to 0. However, including the redundant initialization in the Form_Load() procedure makes the program easier to read.

The Code Inside the *cmdStart_Click()* Event Procedure

The cmdStart_Click() procedure is executed whenever you click the Start button. This procedure executes an If…Else statement. The If statement checks the current value of the RotateFlag variable:

```
Sub cmdStart_Click ()

    ' Toggle the RotateFlag, and toggle
    ' the caption of the Start/Stop button.
    If RotateFlag = 0 Then
        RotateFlag = 1
        cmdStart.Caption = "Stop"
    Else
        RotateFlag = 0
        cmdStart.Caption = "Start"
    End If

End Sub
```

If the current value of RotateFlag is 0, it is changed to 1, and the caption of the cmdStart button changes to Stop. If, however, the current value of RotateFlag is 0, this procedure changes the value of RotateFlag to 1, and the caption of the cmdStart button is changed to Start.

The RotateFlag variable is used in the timer procedure that is discussed in the following section.

The Code Inside the *tmrTimer_Timer()* Event Procedure

Because you set the Interval property of the tmrTimer timer to 250, the `tmrTimer_Timer()` event procedure is executed every 250 milliseconds:

```
Sub tmrTimer_Timer ()

    If RotateFlag = 1 Then
       imgCurrentMoon.Picture=imgMoon(CurrentMoon).Picture
       CurrentMoon = CurrentMoon + 1

       If CurrentMoon = 8 Then
          CurrentMoon = 0
       End If

    End If

End Sub
```

If you did not yet click the Start button, `RotateFlag` is still equal to 0, and the statements inside the `If RotateFlag = 1` block are not executed. If you did click the Start button, `RotateFlag` is equal to 1, and the statements inside the `If RotateFlag = 1` block are executed.

The code inside the `If` statement assigns the Picture property of the control array of images to the Picture property of the imgCurrentMoon image:

```
imgCurrentMoon.Picture=imgMoon(CurrentMoon).Picture
```

For example, when the CurrentMoon variable is equal to 0, the Picture property of the 0th element of the control array is assigned to the Picture property of imgCurrentMoon. This causes the image MOON01.ICO to be displayed (because `imgMoon(0).Picture` contains the MOON01.ICO picture).

The next statement in the `If` block increases the variable `CurrentMoon`:

```
CurrentMoon = CurrentMoon + 1
```

The next time the `tmrTimer_Timer()` procedure is executed (that is, after 250 milliseconds), the variable `CurrentMoon` is already updated, pointing to the next element of the control array of images.

The next statements in the `tmrTimer_Timer()` procedure examine whether the value of `CurrentMoon` is equal to 8. If it is equal to 8, it means that the eighth element of the array was displayed already, so you need to reset `CurrentMoon` back to 0:

```
If CurrentMoon = 8 Then
    CurrentMoon = 0
End If
```

Animation

The Moon program illustrates how easy it is to write animation programs in Visual Basic. Enhance the Moon program so its animation performance is more impressive.

Enhancing the Moon Program

☐ Change the Interval property of the tmrTimer timer to 5.

☐ Change the general declarations section of the Moon program so that it looks like the following:

```
Option Explicit

Dim RotateFlag As Integer
Dim CurrentMoon As Integer
Dim Direction As Integer
Dim LeftCorner, TopCorner As Single
Dim WidthOfMoon, HeightOfMoon
Dim EnlargeShrink As Integer
```

☐ Change the Form_Load() procedure so that it looks like the following:

```
Sub Form_Load ()

    RotateFlag = 0
    CurrentMoon = 0
    Direction = 1
    LeftCorner = imgCurrentMoon.Left
    TopCorner = imgCurrentMoon.Top
    WidthOfMoon = 1
    HeightOfMoon = 1
    EnlargeShrink = 1

End Sub
```

☐ Change the tmrTimer_Timer() procedure so that it looks like the following:

```
Sub tmrTimer_Timer ()

    If RotateFlag = 1 Then
        imgCurrentMoon.Picture = imgMoon(CurrentMoon).Picture
        CurrentMoon = CurrentMoon + 1

        If CurrentMoon = 8 Then
            CurrentMoon = 0
        End If
    Else
        Exit Sub
    End If
```

```
' Use the Move method to move the image.
' After the movement, the image will have new
' width (=WidthOfMoon), and new Height
' (=HeightOfMoon).
imgCurrentMoon.Move LeftCorner, TopCorner, WidthOfMoon,HeightOfMoon

' Change the variables that the Move method uses
' for the next execution of this procedure,
LeftCorner = LeftCorner + 10 * Direction
TopCorner = TopCorner + 10 * Direction
WidthOfMoon = WidthOfMoon + 10 * EnlargeShrink
HeightOfMoon = HeightOfMoon + 10 * EnlargeShrink

' Is width of image too large?
If WidthOfMoon > 700 Then
   EnlargeShrink = -1
End If

' Is width of image too small?
If WidthOfMoon < 10 Then
   EnlargeShrink = 1
End If

' Image crosses bottom of frame?
If imgCurrentMoon.Top > frmMoon.ScaleHeight Then
   Direction = -1
End If

' Image crosses top of frame?
If imgCurrentMoon.Top < 10 Then
   Direction = 1
End If

End Sub
```

Executing the Enhanced Version of the Moon Program

☐ Execute the Moon program.

As you can see, the moon is rotating on its axis, and it also seems to move in three dimensions!

The Code Inside the General Declarations Section of the Program

The general declarations section of the program includes additional variable declarations of variables that are visible to all procedures in the form.

The Code Inside the *Form_Load()* Event Procedure

The code inside the `Form_Load()` procedure initializes the variables.

The variables `LeftCorner` and `TopCorner` are initialized to the initial position of the upper-left corner of the imgCurrentMoon image:

```
LeftCorner = imgCurrentMoon.Left
TopCorner = imgCurrentMoon.Top
```

The Code Inside the *tmrTimer_Timer()* Event Procedure

The first `If` block in the `tmrTimer_Timer()` procedure is not different from the earlier version, which displays one of the elements of the control array of images.

Once the image is displayed, the Move method is used to move the image. The image is moved so that the new location of the top-left corner of the image is at coordinate (X=LeftCorner, Y=TopCorner).

The Move method also uses the optional width and height arguments:

```
imgCurrentMoon.Move LeftCorner, TopCorner, WidthOfMoon,HeightOfMoon
```

After the movement, the image will have new width and new height.

The statements that follow the Move method statement prepare the variables for the next time the `tmrTimer_Timer()` procedure is executed:

```
LeftCorner = LeftCorner + 10 * Direction
TopCorner = TopCorner + 10 * Direction
WidthOfMoon = WidthOfMoon + 10 * EnlargeShrink
HeightOfMoon = HeightOfMoon + 10 * EnlargeShrink
```

Depending on the values of the variables `Direction` and `EnlargeShrink`, these variables would either increase or decrease (for example, if `Direction` is equal to 1, the value of `LeftCorner` is increased by 10 twips, and if `Direction` is equal to -1, the value of `LeftCorner` is decreased by 10 twips).

Next, the variable `WidthOfMoon` is examined to determine whether it is too large or too small.

```
If WidthOfMoon > 700 Then
   EnlargeShrink = -1
End If

If WidthOfMoon < 10 Then
   EnlargeShrink = 1
End If
```

In a similar manner, the current position of the top-left corner of the image is examined to determine whether the image crossed the bottom of the form or the top of the form:

```
If imgCurrentMoon.Top > FrmMoon.ScaleHeight Then
    Direction = -1
End If

If imgCurrentMoon.Top < 10 Then
    Direction = 1
End If
```

Summary

In this chapter you have learned how to use graphic controls: the Line control and the Shape control. You have also learned how to display picture files inside the image and picture controls and to create animation by displaying and moving pictures. As demonstrated, the control array is a useful technique often used in animation.

Q&A

Q **In this chapter I learned how to use the Move method to move an image control and a picture control. Can I use the same technique to move other controls such as buttons?**

A Yes. The Move method may be used to move any object except timers and menus.

Quiz

1. How many twips are in an inch?
   a. 1440
   b. 1
   c. There is no relationship between an inch and a twip.
2. The Min property of the horizontal scroll bar in the Shape program was set at design time to 1. Why not leave it at the default value 0?
3. What is the AutoSize property?
4. What is the difference between the Stretch property and the AutoSize property?

Exercise

Modify the MoveEye program so that it beeps whenever the imgEye image reaches the top of the form.

Quiz Answers

1. a

2. In the code of the `hsbWidth_Change()` event procedure of the Shape program you set the BorderWidth property of the Shape control to the current value of the scroll bar:

   ```
   shpAllShapes.BorderWidth = hsbWidth.Value
   ```

   If the minimum value that the scroll bar may have is 0, when the scroll bar is placed at its minimum position, the preceding statement assigns the value 0 to the BorderWidth property of the shpAllShapes control. However, a Shape control must have a minimum width of 1. Assigning 0 to the BorderWidth property of a Shape control causes a runtime error.

3. When the AutoSize property is set to True, the object sizes itself to the exact dimensions of the picture file.

4. The AutoSize property is supported by a picture control and by a label control. When this property is set to True, Visual Basic adjusts the size of the control so that the control fits its content.

   The Stretch property is supported by an image control. When this property is set to True, the size of the picture is stretched to fit the size of the image control.

Exercise Answer

The image reaches the top of the form whenever its Top property is equal to 0. You may detect it by inserting the following If statement inside the For loop of the `cmdMove_Click()` procedure:

```
If picEye.Top <= 0 Then
  Beep
  Exit Sub
End If
```

This If statement checks the value of the Top property. If the value is equal to or less than 0, the control reached the top of the form. In this case, the Beep statement is executed, and the Exit Sub statement terminates the procedure.

This technique is often used to write a bouncing program, wherein an object moves inside the form in straight lines. When the object hits the side of the form, the object changes direction. The code of such a program detects that the object reached the edge of the form by examining the values of the Top and Left properties of the form.

2

You've completed your first week, and you now know how to write simple Visual Basic programs. This week you'll learn how to use more powerful features of Visual Basic by writing more programs that illustrate many more new concepts.

Where You're Going

In Chapter 8, "Graphics Methods," you'll learn to use the powerful graphics methods, and in Chapter 9, "The Grid Control," you'll learn to use the powerful grid control. This week you'll also learn how to display and print data, how to interface with Windows, how to take advantage of Windows, and how to access files from within your Visual Basic programs.

Graphics Methods

This chapter focuses on graphics methods. Graphics methods are similar to the graphics controls discussed in Chapter 7, "Graphic Controls." Graphics methods are used because, in some cases, they are easier to use than graphics controls.

Drawing Points

The Points program, which draws points at random locations inside a form, illustrates how to draw points by using the Points method.

The Visual Implementation of the Points Program

☐ Open a new project, save the form of the project as POINTS.FRM, and save the make file of the project as POINTS.MAK.

☐ Build the frmPoints form according to the specifications in Table 8.1.

The completed form should look like the one shown in Figure 8.1.

Table 8.1. The properties table of frmPoints form.

Object	Property	Setting
Form	**Name**	**frmPoints**
	Caption	The Points Program
	Height	4710
	Left	1035
	Top	1140
	Width	7485
Timer ✓	**Name**	**tmrTimer1**
	Interval	60
Menu	**(see Table 8.2)**	**(see Table 8.2)**

Table 8.2. The menu table of the frmPoints form.

Caption	Name
&File	mnuFile
...&Exit	mnuExit
&Graphics	mnuGraphics

Caption	Name
...&Draw Points	mnuDrawPoints
...&Clear	mnuClear

Figure 8.1.
The frmPoints form.

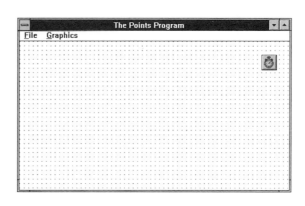

Entering the Code of the Points Program

☐ Enter the following code inside the general declarations section of the frmPoints form:

```
' All variables MUST be declared.
Option Explicit

' A flag that determines if points will be drawn.
Dim DrawPoints
```

☐ Enter the following code inside the Form_Load() procedure of the frmPoints form:

```
Sub Form_Load ()

    ' Disable drawing.
    DrawPoints = 0

End Sub
```

☐ Enter the following code inside the mnuClear_Click() procedure of the frmPoints form:

```
Sub mnuClear_Click ()

    ' Disable drawing.
    DrawPoints = 0

    ' Clear the form.
    frmPoints.Cls

End Sub
```

247

☐ Enter the following code inside the mnuDrawPoints_Click() procedure of the frmPoints form:

```
Sub mnuDrawPoints_Click ()

    ' Enable drawing.
    DrawPoints = 1

End Sub
```

☐ Enter the following code inside the mnuExit_Click() procedure of the frmPoints form:

```
Sub mnuExit_Click ()

    End

End Sub
```

☐ Enter the following code inside the tmrTimer1_Timer() procedure of the frmPoints form:

```
Sub tmrTimer1_Timer ()

    Dim R, G, B
    Dim X, Y
    Dim Counter

    ' Is it Ok to draw?
    If DrawPoints = 1 Then

        ' Draw 100 points.
        For Counter = 1 To 100 Step 1
            ' Get a random color.
            R = Rnd * 255
            G = Rnd * 255
            B = Rnd * 255

            ' Get a random (X,Y) coordinate.
            X = Rnd * frmPoints.ScaleWidth
            Y = Rnd * frmPoints.ScaleHeight

            ' Draw the point.
            frmPoints.PSet (X, Y), RGB(R, G, B)
        Next
    End If

End Sub
```

☐ Save the project.

Executing the Points Program

☐ Execute the Points program.

☐ Select Draw Points from the Graphics menu.

The program displays points with random colors at random locations inside the form (see Figure 8.2).

☐ Select Clear from the Graphics menu.

The program clears the form.

☐ Select Exit from the File menu to terminate the program.

Figure 8.2.
Drawing points inside a form.

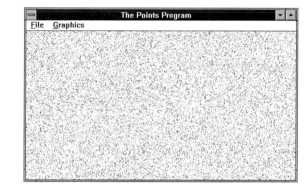

How the Points Program Works

The Points program uses the PSet graphics method to draw a point inside the form, and the Cls method to clear the form.

The Code Inside the General Declarations Area of the frmPoints Form

The general declarations area of the frmPoints form declares the DrawPoints variable. This variable serves as a flag: When it is equal to 1, drawing is enabled, and when it is equal to 0, drawing is disabled.

The Code Inside the *Form_Load()* Event Procedure of the frmPoints Form

The Form_Load() procedure is executed when the program is started:

```
Sub Form_Load ()

    ' Disable drawing.
    DrawPoints = 0

End Sub
```

This procedure initializes the DrawPoints flag to 0 to disable the drawing of the points.

The Code Inside the *mnuClear_Click()* Event Procedure of the frmPoints Form

The `mnuClear_Click()` procedure is executed whenever the user selects Clear from the Graphics menu:

```
Sub mnuClear_Click ()

    ' Disable drawing.
    DrawPoints = 0

    ' Clear the form.
    frmPoints.Cls

End Sub
```

This procedure disables the drawing by setting the `DrawPoints` variable to 0, and then uses the Cls method to clear the form.

DO	**DON'T**

> **DO** use the Cls method to clear an object. The Cls method clears graphics that were generated during runtime with the graphics methods. Here are two examples:
>
> - To clear the frmMyForm form, use `frmMyForm.Cls`.
> - To clear the picMyPicture picture, use `picMyPicture.Cls`.

The Code Inside the *mnuDrawPoints_Click()* Event Procedure of the frmPoints Form

The `mnuDrawPoints_Click()` procedure is executed whenever the user selects Draw Points from the Graphics menu:

```
Sub mnuDrawPoints_Click ()

    ' Enable drawing.
    DrawPoints = 1

End Sub
```

This procedure sets the `DrawPoints` flag to 1 to enable the drawing.

The Code Inside the *tmrTimer1_Timer()* Event Procedure of the frmPoints Form

Because you set the Interval property of the tmrTimer timer to 60, the `tmrTimer1_Timer()` procedure is executed every 60 milliseconds:

```
Sub tmrTimer1_Timer ()

    Dim R, G, B
    Dim X, Y
    Dim Counter

    ' Is it Ok to draw?
    If DrawPoints = 1 Then

        ' Draw 100 points.
        For Counter = 1 To 100 Step 1
            ' Get a random color.
            R = Rnd * 255
            G = Rnd * 255
            B = Rnd * 255

            ' Get a random (X,Y) coordinate.
            X = Rnd * frmPoints.ScaleWidth        A Form
            Y = Rnd * frmPoints.ScaleHeight

            ' Draw the point.
            frmPoints.PSet (X, Y), RGB(R, G, B)
        Next
    End If

End Sub
```

The If statement examines the value of the DrawPoints flag. If this flag is equal to 1, it means that the user selected Draw Points from the Graphics menu, and the code inside the If block is executed.

The For loop draws 100 points. Each point is drawn with a random color and at a random location. The PSet graphics method is used to draw each point:

```
frmPoints.PSet (X, Y), RGB(R, G, B)
```

DO	DON'T

DO use the PSet graphics method to draw a point inside an object.

The PSet Graphics Method

As demonstrated, the PSet method draws a point at the X,Y coordinate that is specified by its argument.

The PSet method has an optional argument called the Step. When you use the Step argument, the point is drawn relative to the CurrentX and CurrentY coordinate. For example, suppose that CurrentX is equal to 100 and CurrentY is equal to 50. Upon issuing the following statement:

```
frmPoints.PSet Step(10, 20), RGB(R, G, B)
```

a point is drawn at location 110,70. That is, the point is drawn 10 units to the right of CurrentX and 20 units below CurrentY. After the drawing, CurrentX and CurrentY are automatically updated—CurrentX is updated to 110, and CurrentY is updated to 70. (Recall from Chapter 4, "The Mouse," that CurrentX and CurrentY are automatically updated by Visual Basic to the endpoint of the last graphic that was drawn.)

☐ Replace the code inside tmrTimer1_Timer() procedure with the following code:

```
Sub tmrTimer1_Timer ()

    Dim R, G, B
    Dim X, Y
    Dim Counter

    If DrawPoints = 1 Then
        For Counter = 1 To 100 Step 1
            R = Rnd * 255
            G = Rnd * 255
            B = Rnd * 255

            frmPoints.PSet Step(1, 1), RGB(R, G, B)

            If CurrentX >= frmPoints.ScaleWidth Then
                CurrentX = Rnd * frmPoints.ScaleWidth
            End If

            If CurrentY >= frmPoints.ScaleHeight Then
                CurrentY = Rnd * frmPoints.ScaleHeight
            End If
        Next
    End If

End Sub
```

☐ Execute the Points program.

The program now draws lines as shown in Figure 8.3.

The code inside the tmrTimer1_Timer() procedure uses the PSet method with the Step option:

```
frmPoints.PSet Step(1, 1), RGB(R, G, B)
```

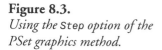

Figure 8.3.
Using the Step *option of the PSet graphics method.*

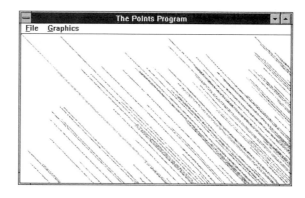

Each point is drawn one unit to the right and one unit below the previous point. This explains why the points are drawn as straight diagonal lines, as shown in Figure 8.3.

The two If statements in this procedure check that the points are drawn within the boundaries of the form.

The Point Method

The Point method returns the color of a particular pixel. For example, to find the color of the pixel at location (30,40), use the following statement:

```
PixelColor = Point (30,40)
```

Although the Points program did not use the Point method, you may find some use for this method in your future projects.

Drawing Lines

You may draw lines using the Line method. The syntax of the Line method is the following:

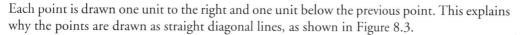

```
Line (x1,y1)-(x2,y2), color
```

where (x1,y1) is the coordinate of the starting point of the line, (x2,y2) is the coordinate of the ending point of the line, and color is the color of the line. If you omit the (x1,y1) argument, the line is drawn starting at coordinate CurrentX,CurrentY.

To see the Line method in action, add the Lines menu item to the menu system of the Points program. The new menu table of the Points program is shown in Table 8.3.

Table 8.3. The new menu table of the frmPoints form.

Caption	Name
&File	mnuFile
...&Exit	mnuExit
&Graphics	mnuGraphics
...&Draw Points	mnuDrawPoints
...&Clear	mnuClear
...&Lines	mnuLines

☐ Add the following code inside the `mnuLines_Click()` procedure of the frmPoints form:

```
Sub mnuLines_Click ()

 Line -(Rnd * frmPoints.ScaleWidth, Rnd*frmPoints.ScaleHeight), RGB(0, 0, 0)

End Sub
```

This procedure draws one line with random width, height, and color.

☐ Execute the Points program.

☐ Select Lines from the Graphics menu.

A line is drawn inside the form, as shown in Figure 8.4.

Figure 8.4.

Drawing a line with the Line method.

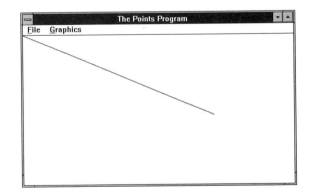

Because the (x1,y1) coordinate is omitted, the Line statement in the `mnuLines_Click()` procedure draws the line starting at coordinate CurrentX, CurrentY. The endpoint of the line is at a random location inside the form. Upon startup of the program, the initial values of CurrentX and CurrentY are 0—this explains why the line in Figure 8.4 starts at coordinate 0,0.

☐ Select Lines from the Graphics menu several times.

Each time you select Lines, a new line is drawn, starting from the endpoint of the previous line (see Figure 8.5)—the line starts from the endpoint of the last line.

☐ Select Exit from the File menu to terminate the program.

☐ Replace the code inside the mnuLines_Click() procedure with the following code:

```
Sub mnuLines_Click ()
   Dim Counter
For Counter = 1 To 100 Step 1
   Line -(Rnd * frmPoints.ScaleWidth, Rnd * frmPoints.ScaleHeight), RGB(0, 0, 0)
Next

End Sub
```

Figure 8.5.
Drawing connected lines.

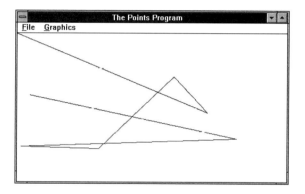

☐ Execute the program.

☐ Select Lines from the Graphics menu.

The program draws 100 connected lines, as shown in Figure 8.6.

Figure 8.6.
Drawing 100 connected lines.

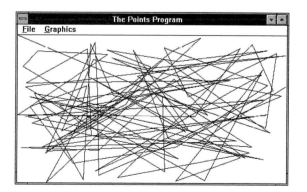

Using the *Step* Argument in the Line Method

The optional Step argument may be used with the Line method as follows:

```
Line (x1,y1)-Step (dX, dY), color
```

where (x1,y1) is the coordinate of the starting point, and Step (dX,dY) is an indication to Visual Basic that the endpoint of the line is at coordinate x1+dX,y1+dY. This statement:

```
Line (20,30)-Step(50,100), RGB(0,0,0)
```

draws a line with a starting point at 20,30, and an endpoint at 70,130.

The Step option may be used to draw a box. The following statements draw the box shown in Figure 8.7:

```
' Line from left top corner to right top corner.
Line (100, 20)-(400,20)

' Line from right top corner to right bottom corner.
Line -Step(0, 400)

' Line from right bottom corner to left bottom corner.
Line -Step (-300, 0)

' Line from left bottom corner to left top corner.
Line -Step (0, -400)
```

Figure 8.7.

Drawing a box with the Line method.

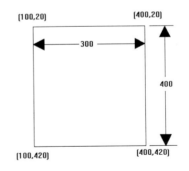

As you can see, four Line statements are needed to draw a single box! An easier way to draw a box is to use the Line method with the B option:

```
Line (100,20)- (400,420), RGB(0,0,0),B
```

The first coordinate—100,20—is the coordinate of the top-left corner of the box, and the second coordinate is the coordinate of the lower-right corner of the box. The B option instructs Visual Basic to draw a box with these two corners.

If you want to fill the box, use the F option:

```
Line (100,20)-(400,420),RGB(0,255,0),BF
```

This statement draws a box and fills the box with the color RGB(0,255,0), which is green. There is no comma between the B and the F options (because you can't use the F option without the B option).

Filling the Box with the FillStyle Property

An alternate way to fill the box is to set the FillColor and FillStyle properties of the form and use the Line method with the B option and without the F option:

```
frmMyForm.FillStyle = 2
frmMyForm.FillColor = RGB(255,0,0)
frmMyForm.Line(100,20)-(400,420),RGB(0,0,0),B
```

The first statement sets the FillStyle property of the form to 2. The eight possible values of FillStyle are shown in Table 8.4. As shown in Table 8.4, when the FillStyle property is equal to 2, the object is filled with horizontal lines. The second statement sets FillColor to RGB(255,0,0), which means that the box is filled with the color red.

So the three statements draw a box that is filled with horizontal lines, which are red.

Table 8.4. The eight possible values of the FillStyle property.

Value	Description
0	Solid
1	Transparent (this is the default setting)
2	Horizontal lines
3	Vertical lines
4	Upward diagonal lines
5	Downward diagonal lines
6	Crosshatch
7	Diagonal crosshatch

To see the meaning of each of the different FillStyles of Table 8.4 do the following:

☐ Add the Draw Box menu to the menu system of the frmPoints form. The new Menu table is shown in Table 8.5.

Table 8.5. Adding the Draw Box menu to the frmPoints form.

Caption	Name
&File	mnuFile
...&Exit	mnuExit
&Graphics	mnuGraphics
...&Draw Points	mnuDrawPoints
...&Clear	mnuClear
...&Lines	mnuLines
&Draw Box	mnuDrawBox ✓
...&Red	mnuRed
...&Green	mnuGreen
...&Blue	mnuBlue
...-	mnuSep1
...&Set Style...	mnuSetStyle

☐ Add the following code inside the `mnuRed_Click()` procedure of the frmPoints form:

```
Sub mnuRed_Click ()

    ' Set the FillColor property of the form.
    frmPoints.FillColor = RGB(255, 0, 0)
    ' Draw the box.
    frmPoints.Line(100,80)-Step(5000, 3000), RGB(0, 0, 0), B

End Sub
```

☐ Add the following code inside the `mnuBlue_Click()` procedure of the frmPoints form:

```
Sub mnuBlue_Click ()

    ' Set the FillColor property of the box.
    frmPoints.FillColor = RGB(0, 0, 255)

    ' Draw the box.
    frmPoints.Line(100,80)-Step(5000,3000), RGB(0, 0, 0), B

End Sub
```

☐ Add the following code inside the `mnuGreen_Click()` procedure of the frmPoints form:

```
Sub mnuGreen_Click ()

    ' Set the FillColor property of the Form.
    frmPoints.FillColor = RGB(0, 255, 0)

    ' Draw the box.
```

```
     frmPoints.Line(100,80)-Step(5000,3000), RGB(0, 0, 0), B

End Sub
```

☐ Add the following code inside the `mnuSetStyleClick()` procedure of the frmPoints form:

```
Sub mnuSetStyle_Click ()

    Dim FromUser
    Dim Instruction

    Instruction = "Enter a number between 0 and 7 for the FillStyle"

    ' Get from the user the desired FillStyle.
    FromUser = InputBox$(Instruction, "Setting the FillStyle")

    ' Clear the form.
    frmPoints.Cls

    ' Did the user enter a valid FillStyle?
    If Val(FromUser)>=0 And Val(FromUser)<= 7 Then
       frmPoints.FillStyle = Val(FromUser)
    Else
      Beep
      MsgBox ("Invalid FillStyle")
    End If

    ' Draw the box.
    frmPoints.Line(100,80)-Step(5000,3000), RGB(0, 0, 0), B

End Sub
```

Executing the Points Program

☐ Execute the Points program.

☐ Select Set Style from the Draw Box menu.

> *The program responds by displaying a message box, as shown in Figure 8.8.*

☐ Type a number between 0 and 7 and click the OK button. This number represents the FillStyle property.

> *The program displays the box and fills it with the FillStyle property entered. Figure 8.9 shows the box when the FillStyle is set to 2 (horizontal lines).*

☐ Select a color from the Draw Box menu.

> *The program draws the box with the selected color.*

Figure 8.8.
*Entering a value for the
FillStyle property.*

Figure 8.9.
*Experimenting with the
FillStyle property.*

The Code Inside the *mnuRed_Click()* Event Procedure of the frmPoints Form

The `mnuRed_Click()` procedure is executed when the user selects Red from the Draw Box menu:

```
Sub mnuRed_Click ()

    ' Set the FillColor property of the form.
    frmPoints.FillColor = RGB(255, 0, 0)

    ' Draw the box.
    frmPoints.Line(100,80)-Step(5000, 3000), RGB(0, 0, 0), B

End Sub
```

This procedure sets the value of the FillColor property to Red, and then the Line method with the B option is used to draw the box. The box is filled in accordance with the current setting of the FillStyle property of the form.

The `mnuBlue_Click()` and `mnuGreen_Click()` procedures of the frmPoints form work in a similar manner, but the FillColor property in these procedures is set to Blue and Green.

The Code Inside the *mnuSetStyleClick()* Event Procedure of the frmPoints Form

The mnuSetStyle_Click() procedure is executed whenever the user selects Set Style from the Draw Box menu:

```
Sub mnuSetStyle_Click ()

    Dim FromUser
    Dim Instruction

    Instruction = "Enter a number between 0 and 7 for the FillStyle"

    ' Get from the user the desired FillStyle.
    FromUser = InputBox$(Instruction, "Setting the FillStyle")

    ' Clear the form.
    frmPoints.Cls

    ' Did the user enter a valid FillStyle?
    If Val(FromUser)>=0 And Val(FromUser)<= 7 Then
       frmPoints.FillStyle = Val(FromUser)
    Else
       Beep
       MsgBox ("Invalid FillStyle")
    End If

    ' Draw the box.
    frmPoints.Line(100,80)-Step(5000,3000), RGB(0, 0, 0), B

End Sub
```

This procedure uses the InputBox$() function to get a number between 0 and 7 from the user. The form is cleared with the Cls method, and the user's input is checked with the If statement to determine whether the entered number is within the valid range.

If the entered number is between 0 and 7, the FillStyle property is updated with this number.

The last statement in the procedure draws a box using the Line method with the B option. The box is drawn with the current setting of the FillColor and FillStyle properties of the form.

Drawing Circles

An important graphics method is the Circle method. As implied by its name, this method draws circles. The Circles program illustrates how you can draw circles. Although you can use the Circle method to draw circles inside a form, the Circles program draws circles inside a picture control.

The Visual Implementation of the Circles Program

☐ Open a new project, save the form of the project as CIRCLES.FRM, and save the make file of the project as CIRCLES.MAK.

☐ Build the frmCircles form according to the specifications in Table 8.6.

The completed form should look like the one shown in Figure 8.10.

Table 8.6. The properties table of frmCircles form.

Object	Property	Setting
Form	**Name**	**frmCircles**
	BackColor	(black)
	Caption	The Circles Program
	Height	4425
	Left	1035
	Top	1140
	Width	7485
Horizontal Scroll Bar	**Name**	**hsbCircleWidth**
	Height	255
	Left	2280
	Max	10
	Min	1
	Top	600
	Value	1
	Width	4335
Vertical Scroll Bar	**Name**	**vsbRadius**
	Height	3495
	Left	960
	Max	100
	Min	1
	Top	360
	Value	1
	Width	255

Object	Property	Setting
Command Button	**Name**	**cmdExit**
	Caption	&Exit
	Height	495
	Left	6000
	Top	3360
	Width	1215
Picture Box	**Name**	**picCircles**
	Height	2655
	Left	2280
	Top	960
	Width	3615
Label	**Name**	**lblRadius**
	BackColor	(black)
	Caption	Radius:
	ForeColor	(white)
	Height	495
	Left	120
	Top	360
	Width	735
Label	**Name**	**lblWidth**
	BackColor	(black)
	Caption	Width:
	ForeColor	(white)
	Height	255
	Left	2400
	Top	240
	Width	1215

(handwritten margin note: x, y / x + width / y + height)

Figure 8.10.
The frmCircles form.

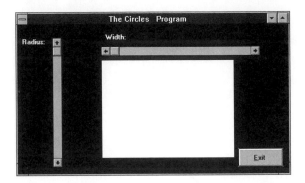

Entering the Code of the Circles Program

☐ Enter the following code inside the general declarations section of the frmCircles form:

```
' All variables MUST be declared.
Option Explicit
```

☐ Enter the following code inside the cmdExit_Click() procedure of the frmCircles form:

```
Sub cmdExit_Click ()

    End

End Sub
```

☐ Enter the following code inside the hsbCircleWidth_Change() procedure of the frmCircles form:

```
Sub hsbCircleWidth_Change ()

    ' Change the DrawWidth property of the picture
    ' control in accordance with the horizontal
    ' scroll bar.
    picCircles.DrawWidth = hsbCircleWidth.Value

End Sub
```

☐ Enter the following code inside the vsbRadius_Change() procedure of the frmCircles form:

```
Sub vsbRadius_Change ()

    Dim X, Y, Radius

    ' Calculate the coordinate of the center of the
    ' circle.
    X = picCircles.ScaleWidth / 2
    Y = picCircles.ScaleHeight / 2

    ' Clear the picture box.
    picCircles.Cls
```

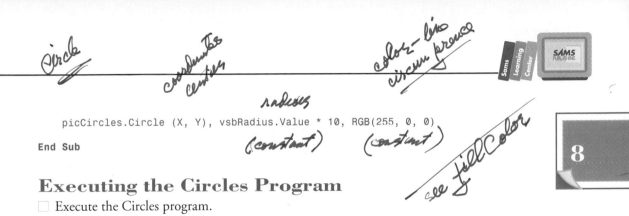

```
picCircles.Circle (X, Y), vsbRadius.Value * 10, RGB(255, 0, 0)
End Sub
```

8

Executing the Circles Program

☐ Execute the Circles program.

☐ Change the vertical scroll bar.

The radius of the circle that is displayed inside the picture control changes in accordance with the setting of the vertical scroll bar (see Figure 8.11).

☐ Change the horizontal scroll bar that sets a new value for the circle line width. The circle is now drawn with a different line width.

Figure 8.11.
Changing the radius with the vertical scroll bar.

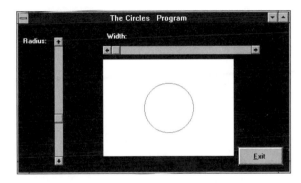

How the Circles Program Works

The Circles program uses the Circle method to draw the circle. The circle's radius is changed in accordance with the vertical scroll bar position, and the circle's width is changed in accordance with the horizontal scroll bar position.

The Code Inside the *hsbCircleWidth_Change()* Event Procedure of the frmCircles Form

The hsbCircleWidth_Change() procedure is executed whenever the user changes the position of the horizontal scroll bar's thumb tab:

```
Sub hsbCircleWidth_Change ()

    ' Change the DrawWidth property of the picture
    ' control in accordance with the horizontal
    ' scroll bar.
    picCircles.DrawWidth = hsbCircleWidth.Value

End Sub
```

This procedure changes the DrawWidth property of the picCircles control in accordance with the position of the horizontal scroll bar position. The value of the DrawWidth property of the picture control determines the width of the line of the circle that is drawn inside the picture control.

The Code Inside the *vsbRadius_Change()* Event Procedure of the frmCircles Form

The vsbRadius_Change() procedure is executed whenever the user changes the position of the vertical scroll bar's thumb tab:

```
Sub vsbRadius_Change ()

    Dim X, Y, Radius

    ' Calculate the coordinate of the center of the
    ' circle.
    X = picCircles.ScaleWidth / 2
    Y = picCircles.ScaleHeight / 2

    ' Clear the picture box.
    picCircles.Cls

    picCircles.Circle (X, Y), vsbRadius.Value * 10, RGB(255, 0, 0)

End Sub
```

This procedure calculates the coordinate of the center point by calculating the coordinate of the center of the picture control (that is, the center of the circle is placed at the center of the picture control).

Then the graphics content of the picture control is cleared with the Cls method (erasing the previous circle, if any), and finally, the circle is drawn with the Circle method:

```
picCircles.Circle (X, Y), vsbRadius.Value * 10, RGB(255, 0, 0)
```

The radius of the circle is 10 times larger than the current setting of the vertical scroll bar, and the circle is drawn in red.

DO	DON'T

DO draw a circle using the Circle method:

```
Object name.Circle (X coord. of center, Y coord. of center), Radius, Color
```

For example, to draw a blue circle inside the frmMyForm form with center at coordinate 1000,500 and radius equal to 75, use the following:

```
frmMyForm.Circle (1000,500), 75, RGB(0,0,255)
```

Enhancing the Circles Program

As you might expect, some impressive graphics effects may be created by adding several lines of code to the Circles program.

☐ Add the Draw Style button to the frmCircles form, as shown in Figure 8.12.

This button should have the following properties: The Name property should be cmdDrawStyle, and the Caption property should be &Draw Style.

Figure 8.12.
Adding the Draw Style button to the frmCircles form.

☐ Add the following code inside the cmdDrawStyle_Click() property of the frmCircles form:

```
Sub cmdDrawStyle_Click ()

    Dim TheStyle


    ' Get a number from the user.
    TheStyle = InputBox$("Enter DrawStyle:")

    ' Is the number between 0 and 6?
    If Val(TheStyle) < 0 Or Val(TheStyle) > 6 Then
        ' The entered number is not within the valid
        ' range.
        Beep
        MsgBox ("Invalid DrawStyle")
    Else
        ' The entered number is within the valid
        ' range, so change the DrawStyle property.
        picCircles.DrawStyle = Val(TheStyle)
    End If

End Sub
```

☐ Delete the horizontal scroll bar. (Make sure that the horizontal scroll bar is selected and press Delete.)

> **Note:** In the previous version of Circles, you wrote code inside the `hsbWidth_Change()` procedure. Now that you have deleted this control, Visual Basic placed the procedure inside the general declarations section. Therefore, after deleting the control, you also must remove its procedures.

☐ Delete the `hsbWidth_Change()` procedure. (You'll find this procedure inside the general declarations section. Highlight the whole procedure, including its first and last lines, and press Delete.)

☐ Delete the lblWidth label. (Make sure that the `lblWidth` label is selected and press Delete.)

When you finish removing these controls, the form should look like the one in Figure 8.12.

Executing the Circles Program

☐ Execute the Circles Program.

☐ Click the Draw Style button.

The program responds by displaying a message box that asks you to enter a number between 0 and 6.

☐ Enter a number between 0 and 6 and click the OK button.

This number represents the style in which the circle is drawn.

☐ Play with the vertical scroll bar and see the effects that the different styles and different radii have on the circle.

☐ Terminate the program by clicking the Exit button.

The DrawStyle Property

The `cmdDrawStyle_Click()` procedure is executed whenever the user clicks the Draw Style button. In this procedure, the user is asked to type a number between 0 and 6, and this number is assigned to the DrawStyle property of the picture control. Table 8.7 lists the seven possible values of the DrawStyle property and their meanings.

Table 8.7. The seven possible values of the DrawStyle property.

Value	Meaning
0	Solid (This is the default value)
1	Dash (- -)
2	Dot (...)
3	Dash-dot (-.-.)
4	Dash-dot-dot (-..-..-)
5	Invisible
6	Inside solid

If the DrawWidth property of the picture control is set to a value greater than 1, the DrawStyle property cannot be equal to 2, 3, or 4. This explains why you were instructed to remove the scroll bar that changes the DrawWidth property (that is, to experiment with the DrawStyle property, the DrawWidth property must be equal to 1).

Enhancing the Circles Program Again

Now make an additional enhancement to the Circles program:

☐ Replace the code inside the vsbRadius_Change() procedure with the following code:

```
Sub vsbRadius_Change ()

    Dim X, Y, Radius
    Static LastValue
    Dim R, G, B

    ' Generate random colors.
    R = Rnd * 255
    G = Rnd * 255
    B = Rnd * 255

    ' Calculate the coordinate of the center of the
    ' picture control.
    X = picCircles.ScaleWidth / 2
    Y = picCircles.ScaleHeight / 2

    ' If scroll bar was decremented, then clear the
    ' picture box.
    If LastValue > vsbRadius.Value Then
       picCircles.Cls
    End If

    ' Draw the circle.
    picCircles.Circle (X, Y), vsbRadius.Value * 10, RGB(R, G, B)
```

```
' Update LastValue for next time.
LastValue = vsbRadius.Value

End Sub
```

Executing the Enhanced Version of the Circles Program

☐ Execute the Circles program.

☐ Click the DrawStyle button.

> *The program responds by displaying the InputBox, which asks you to enter a number between 0 and 6.*

☐ Enter the number 2 and click the OK button.

☐ Increase the Radius scroll bar position by clicking several times on the down arrow that appears at the bottom of the scroll bar.

> *The program responds by drawing the circles shown in Figure 8.13.*

Figure 8.13.
Drawing circles with the enhanced version of the Circles program.

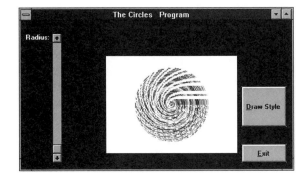

☐ Decrease the scroll bar position by clicking several times on the up arrow that appears at the top of the scroll bar.

> *The program responds by drawing successively smaller circles.*

☐ Terminate the program by clicking the Exit button.

The Code Inside the *vsbRadius_Change()* Event Procedure

The vsbRadius_Change() procedure is executed when the user changes the scroll bar position.

This procedure starts by declaring several variables. The second variable is defined as Static:

```
Static LastValue
```

This means that the value of the LastValue variable is not initialized to 0 every time this procedure is executed (that is, this variable retains its value).

The procedure then prepares the three variables R, G, and B, updating the values of these variables with numbers that represent random colors:

```
' Generate random colors.
R = Rnd * 255
G = Rnd * 255
B = Rnd * 255
```

The procedure then calculates the coordinate of the center of the picture box:

```
' Calculate the coordinate of the center of the
' picture control.
X = picCircles.ScaleWidth / 2
Y = picCircles.ScaleHeight / 2
```

This coordinate is used later in this procedure as the coordinate for the center of the circles.

The LastValue variable holds the Value property of the scroll bar before the user changed the scroll bar position. The If statement examines whether the current position of the scroll bar (which is given by the Value property) is smaller than the last position of the scroll bar:

```
' If scroll bar was decremented, then clear the
' picture box.
If LastValue > vsbRadius.Value Then
   picCircles.Cls
End If
```

If the current Value property of the scroll bar is smaller than LastValue, the user decremented the scroll bar. In this case, the Cls method is executed, which clears the picture box.

The procedure then draws the circle using the Circle method:

```
' Draw the circle.
picCircles.Circle (X, Y), vsbRadius.Value * 10, RGB(R, G, B)
```

The last thing this procedure does is update the LastValue variable. The next time this procedure is executed, the value of LastValue represents the Value property of the scroll bar before the change:

```
' Update LastValue for next time.
LastValue = vsbRadius.Value
```

When the scroll bar is incremented, the Cls method is not executed. Therefore, when incrementing the scroll bar, the already drawn circles remain onscreen.

Drawing Ellipses and Arcs

To draw ellipses and arcs, use the Circle method.

The complete syntax of the Circle method is the following:

```
[object.]Circle[Step](x,y), radius, [color], [start], [end], [aspect]
```

If you include the Step option, the x,y coordinate is referenced to the CurrentX,CurrentY point. For example, if CurrentX is 1000, and CurrentY is 3000, this statement:

```
frmMyForm.Circle Step(10,20),80
```

draws a circle with radius at 80 and the center at 1010,3020.

The *aspect* Argument

The aspect argument is a positive floating number that causes the Circle method to draw ellipses. For example, when the aspect ratio is equal to 1, the Circle method produces a perfect circle. When the aspect ratio is greater than 1, the Circle method produces an ellipse that is stretched along the vertical axis. When the aspect ratio is less than 1, the Circle method produces an ellipse that is stretched along the horizontal axis. Figures 8.14, 8.15, and 8.16 show three ellipses with three different aspects.

Figure 8.14.

The ellipse with the aspect *argument equal to 1.*

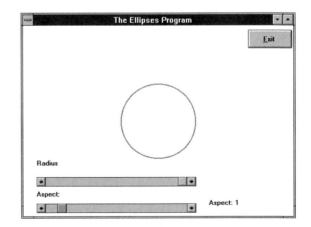

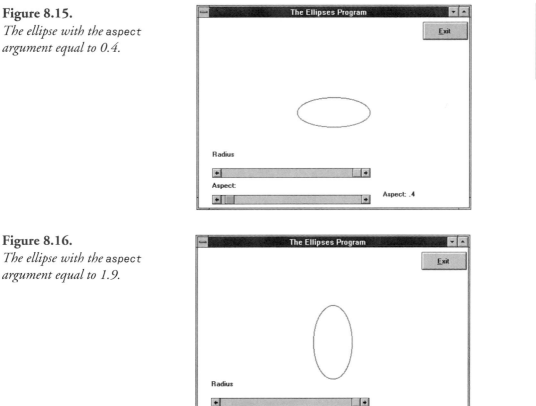

Figure 8.15.
The ellipse with the aspect *argument equal to 0.4.*

Figure 8.16.
The ellipse with the aspect *argument equal to 1.9.*

The Ellipses Program

The Ellipses program illustrates how to draw ellipses with different radii and aspects.

The Visual Implementation of the Ellipses Program

☐ Open a new project, save the form of the project as ELLIPSES.FRM, and save the make file of the project as ELLIPSES.MAK.

☐ Build the frmEllipses form according to the specifications in Table 8.8.

The completed form should look like the one shown in Figure 8.17.

Table 8.8. The properties table of frmEllipses form.

Object	Property	Setting
Form	**Name**	**frmEllipses**
	Caption	The Ellipses Program
	Height	5550
	Left	1035
	Top	1140
	Width	7485
Horizontal Scroll Bar	**Name**	**hsbRadius**
	Height	255
	Left	360
	Max	100
	Min	1
	Top	4080
	Width	4335
Horizontal Scroll Bar	**Name**	**hsbAspect**
	Height	255
	Left	360
	Max	100
	Min	1
	Top	4800
	Width	4335
Command Button	**Name**	**cmdExit**
	Caption	&Exit
	Height	495
	Left	6120
	Top	120
	Width	1215
Label	**Name**	**lblInfo**
	Caption	Aspect:
	Height	375
	Left	5040

Object	Property	Setting
	Top	4680
	Width	1215
Label	**Name**	**lblRadius**
	Caption	Radius:
	Height	375
	Left	360
	Top	3600
	Width	1215
Label	**Name**	**lblAspect**
	Caption	Aspect:
	Height	255
	Left	360
	Top	4440
	Width	1215

Figure 8.17.
The frmEllipses form.

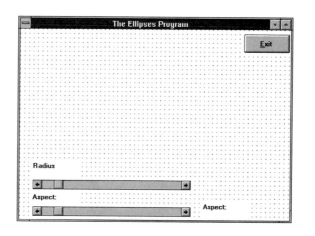

Entering the Code of the Ellipses Program

☐ Enter the following code inside the general declarations area of the frmEllipses form:

```
' All variables MUST be declared.
Option Explicit
```

Graphics Methods

☐ Enter the following code inside the cmdExit_Click() procedure of the frmEllipses form:

```
Sub cmdExit_Click ()

    End

End Sub
```

☐ Enter the following code inside the Form_Load() procedure of the frmEllipses form:

```
Sub Form_Load ()

    ' Initialize the radius and aspect scroll bars.
    hsbRadius.Value = 10
    hsbAspect.Value = 10

    ' Initialize the info label.
    lblInfo.Caption = "Aspect: 1"

    ' Set the DrawWidth property of the form.
    frmEllipses.DrawWidth = 2

End Sub
```

☐ Enter the following code inside the hsbAspect_Change() procedure of the frmEllipses form:

```
Sub hsbAspect_Change ()

    Dim X, Y
    Dim Info

    ' Calculate the center of the form.
    X = frmEllipses.ScaleWidth / 2
    Y = frmEllipses.ScaleHeight / 2

    ' Clear the form.
    frmEllipses.Cls
    ' Draw the ellipse.
    frmEllipses.Circle(X,Y),hsbRadius.Value*10,
            ➥ RGB(255,0,0), , , hsbAspect.Value/10

    ' Prepare the Info string.
    Info = "Aspect: " + hsbAspect.Value / 10

    ' Display the value of the aspect.
    frmEllipses.lblInfo.Caption = Info

End Sub
```

☐ Enter the following code inside the hsbRadius_Change() procedure of the frmEllipses form:

```
Sub hsbRadius_Change ()

    Dim X, Y
    Dim Info
```

```
X = frmEllipses.ScaleWidth / 2
Y = frmEllipses.ScaleHeight / 2

frmEllipses.Cls

frmEllipses.Circle(X,Y),hsbRadius.Value*10,
        ➥ RGB(255,0,0), , , hsbAspect.Value/10

Info = "Aspect: " + hsbAspect.Value / 10
frmEllipses.lblInfo.Caption - Info
```

End Sub

Executing the Ellipses Program

☐ Execute the Ellipses program.

☐ Change the position of the Radius scroll bar to draw circles and ellipses with different radii.

☐ Change the position of the Aspect scroll bar to draw ellipses with different aspects.

Note that the current aspect is displayed to the left of the Aspect scroll bar. When the aspect is equal to 1, the program draws a circle. When the aspect is less than 1, the program draws an ellipse stretched along the horizontal axis as shown in Figure 8.15. When the aspect is greater than 1, the program draws an ellipse stretched along its vertical axis, as shown in Figure 8.16.

How the Ellipses Program Works

The Ellipses program draws ellipses using the Circle method. The Value properties of the scroll bars are used as the arguments in the Circle method.

The Code Inside the *Form_Load()* Event Procedure of the frmEllipses Form

The Form_Load() procedure is executed when the frmEllipses form is loaded:

Sub Form_Load ()

```
    ' Initialize the radius and aspect scroll bars.
    hsbRadius.Value = 10
    hsbAspect.Value = 10

    ' Initialize the info label.
    lblInfo.Caption = "Aspect: 1"

    ' Set the DrawWidth property of the form.
    frmEllipses.DrawWidth = 2
```

End Sub

This procedure initializes the Value properties of the scroll bars to 10 and displays `Aspect: 1` in the lower-right label. As you will see later, the program uses one-tenth of the Value property of the Aspect scroll bar as the `aspect` argument in the Circle method. For example, when the Value property of the Aspect scroll bar is 20, the Circle method uses 2 as the `aspect` argument. This is why this procedure sets the lblInfo caption with `Aspect: 1` after initializing the Aspect scroll bar to 10.

The last statement in this procedure sets the DrawWidth property of the form to 2:

```
frmEllipses.DrawWidth = 2
```

This causes the graphics to be drawn with width of 2 units. So when you use the Circle method, the ellipses are drawn with a line that is 2 units wide. (Although the Ellipses program sets the DrawWidth of the form, the caption of the lblInfo label, and the Value properties of the scroll bars from within the code, you could have set these properties during design time.)

The Code Inside the *hsbAspect_Change()* Event Procedure of the frmEllipses Form

The `hsbAspect_Change()` procedure is executed when the user changes the Aspect scroll bar:

```
Sub hsbAspect_Change ()

    Dim X, Y
    Dim Info

    ' Calculate the center of the form.
    X = frmEllipses.ScaleWidth / 2
    Y = frmEllipses.ScaleHeight / 2

    ' Clear the form.
    frmEllipses.Cls

    ' Draw the ellipse.
    frmEllipses.Circle(X,Y),hsbRadius.Value*10,
                 ➥ RGB(255,0,0), , , hsbAspect.Value/10

    ' Prepare the Info string.
    Info = "Aspect: " + hsbAspect.Value / 10

    ' Display the value of the aspect.
    frmEllipses.lblInfo.Caption = Info

End Sub
```

This procedure calculates the coordinate of the center of the form and assigns the calculated values to X and Y.

The procedure clears any previously drawn ellipses using the Cls method and draws the ellipse:

```
frmEllipses.Circle(X,Y),hsbRadius.Value*10, RGB(255,0,0), , , hsbAspect.Value/10
```

The radius argument is set to the current value of the Radius scroll bar multiplied by 10, and the aspect argument is set as one-tenth the Value properties of the Aspect scroll bar.

Note that because the two optional arguments—start and end—of the Circle method are not used, two commas are typed between the color argument and the aspect argument. The two commas are an indication to Visual Basic that these two optional arguments are missing.

The Code Inside the *hsbRadius_Change()* Event Procedure of the frmEllipses Form

The hsbRadius_Change() procedure is executed when the user changes the Radius scroll bar. This procedure is identical to the hsbAspect_Change() procedure, displaying the ellipse and updating the lblInfo label.

The Arcs Program

Now you'll write a program called Arcs. This program illustrates how to use the Circle method for drawing arcs. The Arcs program lets you draw arcs at different starting points and endpoints.

As stated, the complete syntax of the Circle method is the following:

```
[object.]Circle[Step](x,y), radius, [color], [start], [end], [aspect]
```

The start and end arguments specify the starting point and endpoint of the circle. For example, if the starting point is at 0 degrees and the endpoint is at 45 degrees, only this section of the circle is drawn. Figure 8.18 shows a portion of a circle (arc) that was drawn with the Circle method with the start argument equal to 0 degree, and the end argument equal to 45 degrees. Similarly, Figure 8.19 shows an arc with the starting point at 23 degrees and the endpoint at 180 degrees.

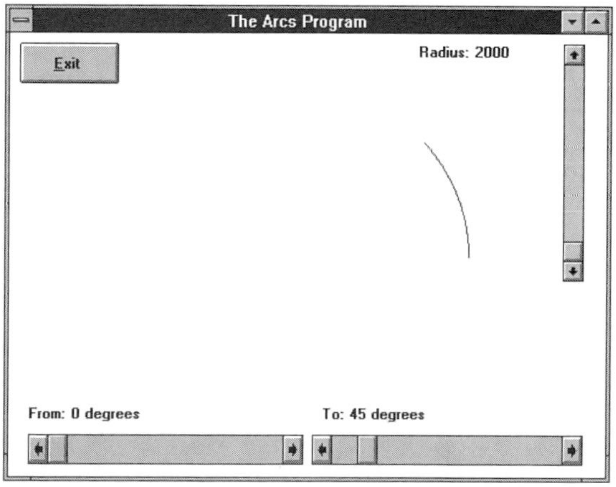

Figure 8.18.
Drawing a 45-degree arc.

Figure 8.19.
Drawing an arc from 23 degrees to 180 degrees.

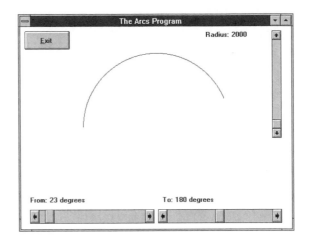

The Visual Implementation of the Arcs Program

☐ Open a new project, save the form of the project as ARCS.FRM, and save the make file of the project as ARCS.MAK.

☐ Build the frmArcs form according to the specifications in Table 8.9.

The completed form should look like the one shown in Figure 8.20.

Table 8.9. The properties table of frmArcs form.

Object	Property	Setting
Form	**Name**	**frmArcs**
	Caption	The Arcs Program
	Height	5850
	Left	1260
	Top	750
	Width	7485
Vertical Scroll Bar	**Name**	**vsbRadius**
	Height	2895
	Left	6840
	Max	100
	Min	1
	Top	120

Object	Property	Setting
	Value	10
	Width	255
Horizontal Scroll Bar	**Name**	**hsbTo**
	Height	375
	Left	3720
	Max	360
	Top	4920
	Width	3375
Horizontal Scroll Bar	**Name**	**hsbFrom**
	Height	375
	Left	240
	Max	360
	Top	4920
	Width	3375
Command Button	**Name**	**cmdExit**
	Caption	&Exit
	Height	495
	Left	120
	Top	120
	Width	1215
Label	**Name**	**lblRadius**
	Caption	Radius:
	Height	375
	Left	5040
	Top	120
	Width	1575
Label	**Name**	**lblTo**
	Caption	To:
	Height	255
	Left	3840
	Top	4560

continues

Table 8.9. continued

Object	Property	Setting
	Width	2175
Label	**Name**	**lblFrom**
	Caption	From:
	Height	255
	Left	240
	Top	4560
	Width	2775

Figure 8.20.
The frmArcs form.

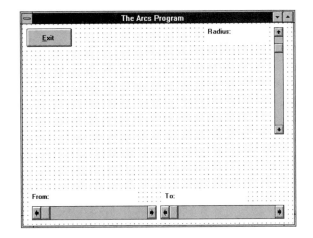

Entering the Code of the Arcs Program

☐ Enter the following code inside the general declarations section of the frmArcs form:

```
' All variables MUST be declared.
Option Explicit
```

☐ Create a new procedure called DrawArc() inside the general declarations section of the frmArcs form. (In the Project window, highlight the frmArcs form, click the View Code button, select New Procedure from the View menu, and type DrawArc in the Name field of the New Procedure dialog box.)

☐ Enter the following code inside the DrawArc() procedure you just created:

```
Sub DrawArc ()
     Dim X, Y
```

```
Const PI = 3.14159265

' Calculate the center of the form.
X = frmArcs.ScaleWidth / 2
Y = frmArcs.ScaleHeight / 2

' Clear the form.
frmArcs.Cls

' Draw an arc.
Circle (X, Y), vsbRadius.Value * 20, , hsbFrom* 2*PI/360, hsbTo*2*PI/360

' Update the lblFrom label.
lblFrom.Caption="From: "+hsbFrom.Value+" degrees"

' Update the lblTo label.
lblTo.Caption = "To: " + hsbTo.Value+" degrees"

' Update the lblRadius label.
lblRadius.Caption = "Radius: " +vsbRadius.Value * 20

End Sub
```

☐ Enter the following code inside the cmdExit_Click() procedure of the frmArcs form:

```
Sub cmdExit_Click ()

    End

End Sub
```

☐ Enter the following code inside the hsbFrom_Change() procedure of the frmArcs form:

```
Sub hsbFrom_Change ()

    ' Execute the DrawArc procedure to draw the arc.
    DrawArc

End Sub
```

☐ Enter the following code inside the hsbTo_Change() procedure of the frmArcs form:

```
Sub hsbTo_Change ()

    ' Execute the DrawArc procedure to draw the arc.
    DrawArc

End Sub
```

☐ Enter the following code inside the vsbRadius_Change() procedure of the frmArcs form:

```
Sub vsbRadius_Change ()

    ' Execute the DrawArc procedure to draw the arc.
    DrawArc

End Sub
```

Executing the Arcs Program

☐ Execute the Arcs program.

☐ Increase the radius by changing the Radius scroll bar (the vertical scroll bar).

☐ Increase the To scroll bar (the right horizontal scroll bar).

☐ Increase the From scroll bar (the left horizontal scroll bar).

As you can see, an arc is drawn starting at a point specified by the From scroll bar, and the arc ends at a point specified by the To scroll bar.

Note that the arc also can be drawn in the counterclockwise direction. For example, Figure 8.19 shows an arc that starts at 23 degrees and ends at 180 degrees. In Figure 8.21, an arc is drawn starting at 180 degrees and ending at 23 degrees.

☐ Click the Exit button to terminate the program.

Figure 8.21.
An arc from 180 degrees to 23 degrees.

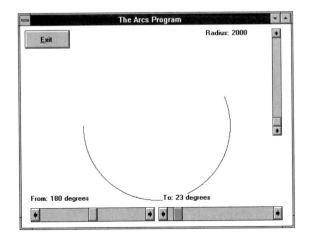

How the Arcs Program Works

The Arcs program uses the Circle method to draw the arcs. The Value properties of the Radius scroll bar, From scroll bar, and To scroll bar are used as the arguments for the Circle method.

The Code Inside the *DrawArc()* Procedure of the frmArcs Form

The DrawArc() procedure is executed whenever the user changes the Radius scroll bar, the From scroll bar, or the To scroll bar.

```
Sub DrawArc ()
```

This procedure defines the PI constant as the numeric equivalent of π:

```
Const PI = 3.14159265
```

The center of the form is calculated:

```
X = frmArcs.ScaleWidth / 2
Y = frmArcs.ScaleHeight / 2
```

The form is cleared with the Cls method:

```
frmArcs.Cls
```

The arc is drawn using the Circle method:

```
Circle (X, Y), vsbRadius.Value * 20, , hsbFrom* 2*PI/360, hsbTo*2*PI/360
```

Recall that the complete syntax of the Circle method is this:

```
[object.]Circle[Step](x,y), radius, [color], [start], [end], [aspect]
```

The center of the arc is given by the (x,y) argument, and the radius of the arc is given by the Value property of the vsbRadius scroll bar multiplied by 20.

At design time, the Min property of the vsbRadius scroll bar was set to 1, and its Max property was set to 100. This means that it takes 100 clicks to move the scroll bar position from its minimum position to its maximum position. Because the radius argument of the Circle method is obtained by multiplying the Value property by 20, the radius argument of the Circle method may have a value between 20 and 2000.

The Color property is not supplied, so just type a comma, indicating that the Circle method does not include the color argument. The program therefore uses the ForeColor property of the form (which by default is black).

The next two arguments of the Circle method are the start and end arguments. Visual Basic requires that you supply these arguments in radians. At design time, the Min properties of the From and To scroll bars were left at their default values of 1, and the Max properties of these scroll bars were set to 360. Therefore, each of these scroll bars is divided into 360 parts, each part represents 1 degree. To convert degrees to radians, use this formula:

```
Radians = Degrees * 2 * PI /360
```

For example, 360 degrees is equivalent to $2 \times \pi$ radians:

```
360*2*P/360=2*PI=2*3.14159265=  6.2831853
```

This explains why this procedure supplies the start and end properties of the Circle method as the Value properties of the From and To scroll bars multiplied by $2 \times \pi/360$.

The last argument of the Circle method is the optional aspect argument. This procedure does not specify this argument. Because the aspect argument is the very last argument, there is no need to type a comma after the end argument.

The last thing that this procedure does is display the Radius label, the From label, and the To label:

```
lblFrom.Caption="From: "+hsbFrom.Value+" degrees"

lblTo.Caption = "To: " + hsbTo.Value+" degrees"

lblRadius.Caption = "Radius: " +vsbRadius.Value * 20
```

This enables the user to see the current values of the scroll bars.

The Code Inside the *hsbFrom_Change()* Procedure of the frmArcs Form

The hsbFrom_Change() procedure is executed whenever the user changes the From scroll bar:

```
Sub hsbFrom_Change ()

    ' Execute the DrawArc procedure to draw the arc.
    DrawArc

End Sub
```

This procedure executes the DrawArc() procedure, which draws the arc in accordance with the new value of the hsbFrom scroll bar.

In a similar manner, the hsbTo_Change() and the vsbRadius_Change() procedures of the frmArcs form execute the DrawArc() procedure whenever the user changes these scroll bars.

More About the *start* and *end* Arguments of the Circle Method

You may also supply negative values for the start and end arguments of the Circle method. When the start argument is negative, Visual Basic draws a straight line from the center of the arc to the starting point of the arc. Similarly, when the endpoint is negative, Visual Basic draws a straight line from the center of the arc to the endpoint of the arc.

For example, Figure 8.22 shows an arc that was drawn with the following statement:

```
Circle(X,Y),1000, ,-25*2*PI/360,-45*2*PI/360
```

Figure 8.23 shows an arc that was drawn with the following statement:

```
Circle(X,Y),1000, ,-45*2*PI/360,-25*2*PI/360
```

Figure 8.24 shows an arc that was drawn with the following statement:

```
Circle(X,Y),1000, ,45*2*PI/360,-25*2*PI/360
```

Figure 8.25 shows an arc that was drawn with the following statement:

```
Circle(X,Y),1000, ,-45*2*PI/360,25*2*PI/360
```

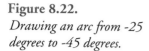
Figure 8.22.
Drawing an arc from -25 degrees to -45 degrees.

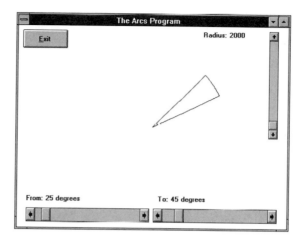

Figure 8.23.
Drawing an arc from -45 degrees to -25 degrees.

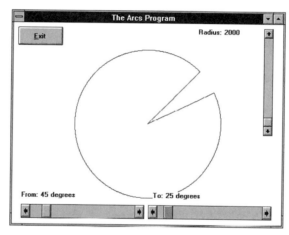

Figure 8.24.
Drawing an arc from 45 degrees to −25 degrees.

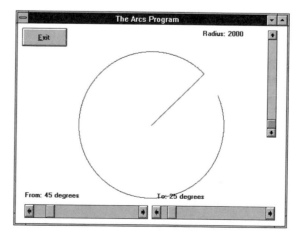

Figure 8.25.
Drawing an arc from –45 degrees to 25 degrees.

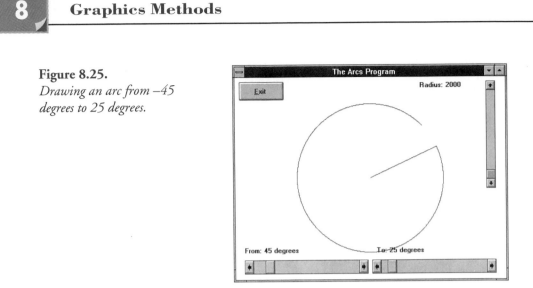

You can experiment with the start and end arguments of the Circle method in the DrawArc() procedure as follows:

☐ To draw arcs as shown in Figures 8.22 and 8.23, change the Circle method in the DrawArc() procedure to this:

```
Circle (X, Y), vsbRadius.Value * 20, , -hsbFrom* 2*PI/360, -hsbTo*2*PI/360
```

☐ To draw arcs as shown in Figure 8.24, change the Circle method in the DrawArc() procedure to this:

```
Circle (X, Y), vsbRadius.Value * 20, , -hsbFrom* 2*PI/360, hsbTo*2*PI/360
```

☐ To draw arcs as shown in Figure 8.25, change the Circle method in the DrawArc() procedure to this:

```
Circle (X, Y), vsbRadius.Value * 20, , hsbFrom* 2*PI/360, -hsbTo*2*PI/360
```

The AutoRedraw Property

The AutoRedraw property causes the graphics to be redrawn automatically whenever there is a need to do so. The default setting of the AutoRedraw property of the frmArcs is False. Use the following steps to see the effects of the AutoRedraw property:

☐ Execute the Arcs program.

☐ Draw an arc by changing the Radius, From, and To scroll bars.

☐ Minimize the Arcs program (by clicking the down arrow that appears on the top-right corner of the Arcs window).

> *The program responds by minimizing the window of the Arcs program and showing it as an icon.*

□ Restore the window of the Arcs program to its original size.

The Arcs window is displayed without the arc! This is because the Redraw property of the form is currently set to False.

□ Terminate the program and change the AutoRedraw property of the frmArcs form in the Properties window to True.

Now repeat this experiment (draw an arc, minimize the window, and restore the original size of the window). As you can see, this time the program automatically redraws the arc, because the AutoRedraw property of the form is set to True.

Drawing Graphics upon Loading the Form

Graphics methods may be used on an object only if the object is visible already. During the Form_Load() event, the form is not visible yet. This means that if you include graphics method statements inside the Form_Load() event, Visual Basic ignores these statements. For example, to draw five horizontal lines inside the frmMyForm form, you use the following statements:

```
frmMyForm.Line (100,100)-(1000,100)
frmMyForm.Line (100,200)-(1000,200)
frmMyForm.Line (100,300)-(1000,300)
frmMyForm.Line (100,400)-(1000,400)
frmMyForm.Line (100,500)-(1000,500)
```

However, if you put these statements inside the Form_Load() event procedure, Visual Basic does not display these five lines. If you want these five lines to be drawn upon startup of the program, you have to put the five statements inside the Form_Paint() event:

```
Sub Form_Paint()

    frmMyForm.Line (100,100)-(1000,100)
    frmMyForm.Line (100,200)-(1000,200)
    frmMyForm.Line (100,300)-(1000,300)
    frmMyForm.Line (100,400)-(1000,400)
    frmMyForm.Line (100,500)-(1000,500)

End Sub
```

The Form_Paint() event procedure is executed whenever Visual Basic needs to paint the form. Because Visual Basic paints the form when the form is made visible upon startup of the program, the Form_Paint() event procedure is executed.

289

In general, you may use the Form_Paint() procedure as a focal point in the program to perform the drawings. In this respect, Form_Paint() may serve the same role as the AutoRedraw property. The advantage of setting the AutoRedraw to True is that you do not have to insert code inside the Form_Paint() procedure that redraws your drawings (that is, AutoRedraw does the redrawing automatically). The disadvantage of setting the AutoRedraw property to True is that it consumes memory (to save current drawings), and on slow PCs the redrawing that occurs when AutoRedraw is set to True may cause noticeable delays in the execution of the program.

Summary

In this chapter you have learned how to use the graphics methods PSet, Cls, Point, Line, and Circle. You have also learned how to draw ellipses and arcs.

Q&A

Q What are the advantages and disadvantages of using graphics methods versus graphics controls?

A The advantage of using graphics methods is that these methods enable you to draw complicated graphics with a small amount of code. For example, the graphics shown in Figure 8.13 are easy to implement with graphics methods. The disadvantage of using graphics methods is that you may examine the results of these methods only during runtime. (When using the graphics controls, you can see how the form looks at design time.)

Quiz

1. The last graphics method that was used in a certain program was this:

   ```
   PSet (100,20) RGB(255,255,255)
   ```

   If the next statement executed in this program is this:

   ```
   PSet Step (-5,10) RGB(255,255,255)
   ```

   at what coordinate will the point be drawn?

2. BUG BUSTER. What is wrong with the following code?

   ```
   Line (100,20)-Step(300,400),RGB(0,255,0),F
   ```

3. For which of the following is the Point method used?

   a. Drawing a point
   b. There is no such thing as the Point method in Visual Basic
   c. Finding the color of a pixel

4. If you set the AutoRedraw property to True, what happens?

Exercise

Write a program using the Circle method that displays circles at random locations all over the form. These circles should be displayed upon startup of the program.

8

Quiz Answers

1. Because the last point was drawn at coordinate 100,20, after the drawing CurrentX is equal to 100, and CurrentY is equal to 20.

   Executing this statement:

   ```
   PSet Step (-5,10) RGB(255,255,255)
   ```

   causes the point to be drawn -5 units to the right of CurrentX, which means that the point is drawn +5 units to the left of Current X. In the Y direction, the point is drawn 10 units below CurrentY. Putting it all together, the point is drawn at coordinate 95,30.

2. You can't use the F option without the B option. The correct syntax is this:

   ```
   Line (100,20)-Step(300,400),RGB(0,255,0),BF
   ```

3. c

4. The form on which a graphics method is drawn is automatically redrawn whenever there is a need to redraw it.

Exercise Answer

Use the following steps:

☐ Open a new project, save the form of the project as CIRCLES2.FRM, and save the make file of the project as CIRCLES2.MAK.

☐ Build the frmCircles form according to the specifications in Table 8.10.

Table 8.10. The properties table of frmCircles form.

Object	Property	Setting
Form	Name	frmCircles
	Caption	The Circles2 Program
	Height	4425
	Left	1035
	Top	1140
	Width	7485

☐ Enter the following code inside the general declarations section of the frmCircles form:

```
'All variables MUST be declared.
Option Explicit
```

☐ Enter the following code inside the Form_Paint() procedure of the frmCircles form:

```
Sub Form_Paint ()

    Dim I

    For I = 1 To 100 Step 1
        frmCircles.DrawWidth = Int(Rnd * 10) +QBColor(Int(Rnd * 15))

        Circle (Rnd*frmCircles.ScaleWidth, Rnd*frmCircles.ScaleHeight),
    ➡        Rnd*frmCircles.ScaleHeight / 2
    Next

End Sub
```

The Form_Paint() procedure draws 100 circles with random width and at random locations.

If you insert the Circle method statement inside the Form_Load() procedure, Visual Basic ignores this statement because the form is not visible while the Form_Load() procedure is executed (that is, the graphics methods are executed only if the objects on which they are drawn are visible).

The Grid Control

In some applications it is necessary to display text in rows and columns (that is, in tables). You can accomplish such tasks by displaying the text line by line, calculating the required locations where the text should be displayed, and using the Print method to display the text. However, Visual Basic includes the grid control, a control that enables you to create tables easily. In this chapter you learn how to use the grid control.

The Custom Control GRID.VBX

To be able to use the grid control in your programs, you must include the custom grid control in your project. Figure 9.1 shows the project window of a typical project that uses the grid control. The project window contains the form TABLE.FRM and two custom controls: GRID.VBX and OLECLIEN.VBX. TABLE.FRM is the name of the form file as saved by the programmer. The GRID.VBX file is the grid custom control that must be included whenever the project uses the grid control. The OLECLIEN.VBX custom control must be included only if the program uses the OLE client control.

Figure 9.1.
The GRID.VBX custom control.

TABLE.MAK	
View Form	**View Code**
📄 TABLE.FRM	frmTable
🐾 GRID.VBX	
🐾 OLECLIEN.VBX	

If your program does not use the OLECLIEN.VBX custom control, you may remove it from the project with the following steps:

☐ Make sure that OLECLIEN.VBX is highlighted in the project window.

☐ Select Remove File from the File menu.

If for some reason your project window does not include the GRID.VBX file, you should add it in all the projects that are presented in this chapter. Use the following steps to add the GRID.VBX custom control file to your project:

☐ Make sure the project window is selected.

☐ Select Add File from the File menu.

Visual Basic responds by displaying the Add file dialog box.

☐ Select the file C:WINDOWS\SYSTEM\GRID.VBX and press the OK button.

Visual Basic responds by adding the GRID.VBX file to your project window and adding the icon of the grid control to the Toolbox (see Figure 9.2). Note that the file GRID.VBX was saved in your C:\WINDOWS\SYSTEM directory during the installation of Visual Basic.

The Table program illustrates how your program can utilize the grid control.

Figure 9.2.
The grid control in the Toolbox.

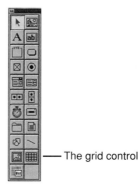

——— The grid control

The Visual Implementation of the Table Program

☐ Open a new project, save the form of the project as TABLE.FRM, and save the make file of the project as TABLE.MAK.

☐ Make sure that the GRID.VBX custom control is included in your project window. (If GRID.VBX is not included in your project, add it to the project as described previously.)

☐ Set the Name property of the form to frmTable and set the Caption property of the form to The Table Program.

Add the grid control to the frmTable form as follows:

☐ Double-click the grid control in the Toolbox.

   Visual Basic responds by placing the grid control inside your form (see Figure 9.3).

☐ Set the Name property of the grid to grdTable.

☐ Set the Rows property of grdTable to 13.

☐ Set the Cols property of grdTable to 5.

☐ Enlarge the grdTable vertically and horizontally by dragging its handles.

The enlarged grid control should look like the one shown in Figure 9.4.

Figure 9.3.
Placing the grid control inside a form.

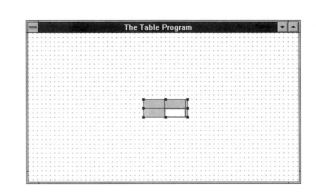

Figure 9.4.
The enlarged grid control.

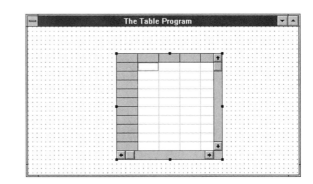

☐ Add the following code inside the Form_Load() event procedure of the frmTable form:

```
Sub Form_Load ()

    ' Set the current row to row #0.
    grdTable.Row = 0

    ' Write into Row #0, Col #1
    grdTable.Col = 1
    grdTable.Text = "Electricity"

    ' Write into Row #0, Col #2
    grdTable.Col = 2
    grdTable.Text = "Water"

    ' Write into Row #0, Col #3
    grdTable.Col = 3
    grdTable.Text = "Transportation"

    ' Write into Row #0, Col #4
    grdTable.Col = 4
    grdTable.Text = "Food"

    ' Set the current Column to column #0.
    grdTable.Col = 0
```

```
     ' Write into Row #1, Col #0
     grdTable.Row = 1
     grdTable.Text = "Jan."

     ' Write into Row #2, Col #0
     grdTable.Row = 2
     grdTable.Text = "Feb."

     ' Write into Row #3, Col #0
     grdTable.Row = 3
     grdTable.Text = "Mar."

     ' Write into Row #4, Col #0
     grdTable.Row = 4
     grdTable.Text = "Apr."

     ' Write into Row #5, Col #0
     grdTable.Row = 5
     grdTable.Text = "May."

     ' Write into Row #6, Col #0
     grdTable.Row = 6
     grdTable.Text = "Jun."

     ' Write into Row #7, Col #0
     grdTable.Row = 7
     grdTable.Text = "Jul."

     ' Write into Row #8, Col #0
     grdTable.Row = 8
     grdTable.Text = "Aug."

     ' Write into Row #9, Col #0
     grdTable.Row = 9
     grdTable.Text = "Sep."

     ' Write into Row #10, Col #0
     grdTable.Row = 10
     grdTable.Text = "Oct."

     ' Write into Row #11, Col #0
     grdTable.Row = 11
     grdTable.Text = "Nov."

     ' Write into Row #12, Col #0
     grdTable.Row = 12
     grdTable.Text = "Dec."
```

End Sub

Although you have not yet finished writing the Table program, execute it:

☐ Execute the Table program.

The program displays the grid control, as shown in Figure 9.5.

Figure 9.5.
Placing column and row headings.

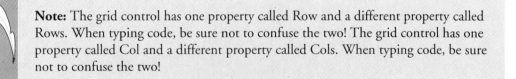

☐ Click the horizontal and vertical scroll bars of the grid control to see other cells of the grid control (alternatively, use the arrow keys to move from cell to cell).

As you can see, the grid control has a total of 13 rows (including the top heading row), and a total of 5 columns (including the left heading column). During design time you set the Rows property of grdTable to 13, and the Cols property of the grdTable to 5.

☐ Terminate the program by clicking the minus icon that appears on the top-left of the window of the Table program and selecting Close from the system menu that pops up.

The Code Inside the *Form_Load()* Procedure

The Form_Load() procedure is executed when the frmTable form is loaded at startup. The code inside this procedure sets the current row to 0:

```
' Set the current row to row #0.
grdTable.Row = 0
```

Note: The grid control has one property called Row and a different property called Rows. When typing code, be sure not to confuse the two! The grid control has one property called Col and a different property called Cols. When typing code, be sure not to confuse the two!

Once the active row is set to 0, the procedure writes into the cell Row #0, Col #1 as follows:

```
' Write into Row #0, Col #1
grdTable.Col = 1
grdTable.Text = "Electricity"
```

9

That is, the procedure makes row 0 the active row, it sets column 1 as the active column, and then it sets the Text property of the grid control to Electricity. Visual Basic places the text inside the cell at Row #0, Col #1.

In a similar manner, the procedure sets the Text properties of Row #0, Col #2; Row #0, Col #3; and Row #0, Col #4 to Water, Transportation, and Food. For example, to set the Text property of the cell Row #0, Col #4, the following statements are used:

```
' Write into Row #0, Col #4
grdTable.Col = 4
grdTable.Text = "Food"
```

There is no need to set the Row property to 0 again, because the property retains its value.

Once the four row headings are written, the procedure sets the Text property of the left column. For example, to set the Text property of the cell Row #1, Col #0, the following statements are used:

```
' Set the current Column to column #0.
grdTable.Col = 0

' Write into Row #1, Col #0
grdTable.Row = 1
grdTable.Text = "Jan."
```

In a similar manner, the rest of the cells in the left column are filled with the rest of the months.

Note: The grid control displays information in a tabular format. The user may move from cell to cell by using the arrow keys (or the scroll bars), but the user cannot enter information directly into the cells.

Changing the Cell Width

As you can see from Figure 9.5, the cells are not wide enough. For example, the word Electricity does not fit within its cell. You may widen the cell only during runtime. Use the following steps to add code that takes care of the column width:

☐ Add a procedure to the frmTable form (highlight the frmTable in the project window, click View Code in the project window, and select New procedure from the View menu).

☐ Name the new procedure SetColWidth.

Visual Basic creates a new procedure by the name of SetColWidth() *inside the general declarations section of the frmTable form.*

☐ Enter the following code inside the `SetColWidth()` procedure:

```
Sub SetColWidth ()

    Dim Counter

    For Counter = 0 To 4 Step 1
        grdTable.ColWidth(Counter) = 1300
    Next

End Sub
```

☐ Add the `SetColWidth` statement to the end of the `Form_Load()` procedure. The `Form_Load()` procedure should look like this:

```
Sub Form_Load ()

    ............................................
    ... No change to this section of the procedure ...
    ............................................
    SetColWidth

End Sub
```

☐ Execute the Table program.

The grdTable grid now looks like the one shown in Figure 9.6.

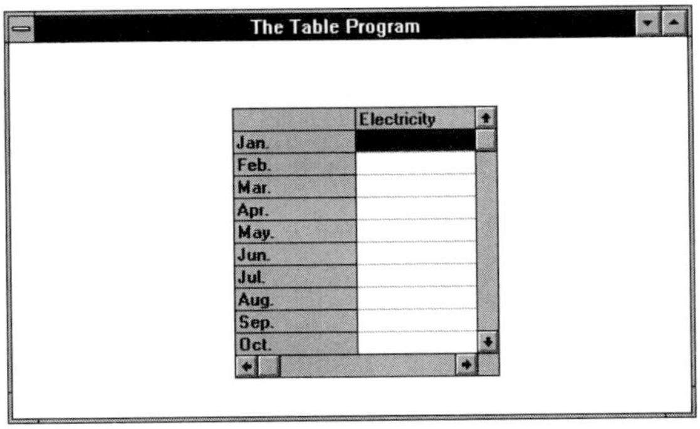

Figure 9.6.
Making the columns wider.

☐ Use the arrow keys (or the scroll bars) to move from cell to cell.

As you can see, all the columns changed their widths.

☐ Return to design mode and enlarge the grdTable grid by dragging its handle until it looks like the one shown in Figure 9.7.

As you can see, the total area of the grid control is larger, but the cell widths are still at their default widths. This is because you may widen the cell only during runtime.

☐ Execute the Table program.

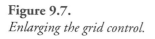

Figure 9.7.
Enlarging the grid control.

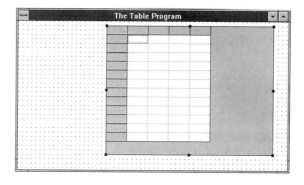

The grid control now looks like the one shown in Figure 9.8. As you can see, the total area of the grid control is larger, and the cells are wider.

Figure 9.8.
The enlarged grid control at runtime.

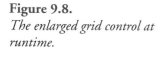

☐ Use the arrow keys (or the scroll bars) to move from cell to cell.

☐ Terminate the program.

Changing the Cell Height

You may change the height of the cells only during runtime. Use the following steps to change the height of the cells:

☐ Add a new procedure to the frmTable form (highlight frmTable in the project window, click View Code in the project window, and select New procedure from the View menu).

☐ Name the new procedure SetRowHeight.

Visual Basic creates the SetRowHeight() *procedure inside the general declarations section of the frmTable form.*

☐ Enter the following code inside the `SetRowHeight()` procedure:

```
Sub SetRowHeight ()

    Dim Counter

    For Counter = 0 To 12 Step 1
        grdTable.RowHeight(Counter) = 500
    Next

End Sub
```

The RowHeight property determines the height of the cell. The `SetRowHeight()` procedure sets the height of all the rows to 500 twips.

☐ Add the `SetRowHeight` statement to the end of the `Form_Load()` procedure.

The `Form_Load()` procedure should now look like this:

```
Sub Form_Load ()

    .................................................
    ... No change to this section of the procedure ...
    .................................................

    SetColWidth
    SetRowHeight

End Sub
```

☐ Execute the Table program.

The cells of the grid now look like the ones shown in Figure 9.9.

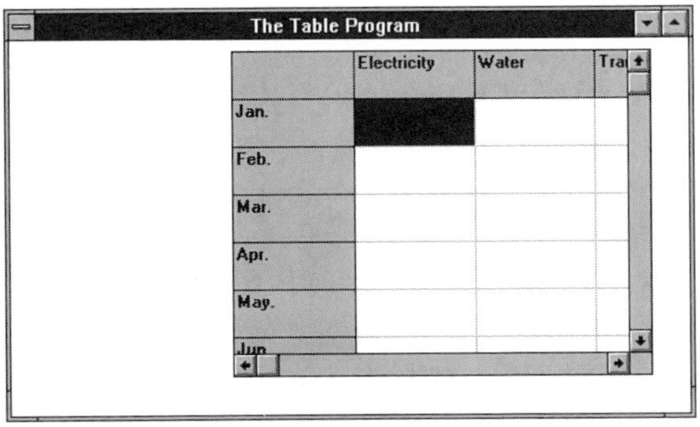

Figure 9.9.
Making rows with larger height.

The Scroll Bars of the Grid Control

As you have probably noticed by now, Visual Basic automatically adds scroll bars (horizontal and vertical) whenever the cells cannot fit within the area of the grid control. This is because you left the default value of the ScrollBars property of the grdTable grid control to 3-Both. If for some reason you do not want these scroll bars to appear, either set the ScrollBars property of the grid control to 0-None at design time, or issue the following statement from within the program:

```
grdTable.ScrollBars = 0
```

If you want the grid to have only a horizontal scroll bar, either set the ScrollBars property of the grid control to 1-Horizontal at design time or issue the following statement from within the program:

```
grdTable.ScrollBars = 1
```

If you want the grid control to have only a vertical scroll bar, set the ScrollBars property to 2-Vertical.

Note: No matter how you set the ScrollBars property of the grid control, the user is always able to move from cell to cell using the arrow keys.

Setting the Rows and Cols Properties During Runtime

During design time, you set the Rows property of the grid control to 13 and the Cols property to 5. This causes the grid control to have a total of 5 rows and 13 columns. Sometimes the number of rows and columns is known only during runtime. For example, you may write the Table program in such a way that it gives the user the option to display only the electric and the water bills for each month. If the user chooses to display only these two columns, your program has to change the number of columns to 3 (1 for the left column heading, 1 for the Electricity heading, and one for the Water heading).

To change the number of rows during runtime to 3, use the following statement:

```
grdTable.Rows = 3
```

If you need to change the number of rows during runtime, use the following statement:

```
grdTable.Rows = n
```

where n is the number of columns (including the top heading row).

Filling the Rest of the Cells of the Table Program

Use the following steps to fill the rest of the cells of the Table program:

☐ Add a new procedure to the general declarations section of the frmTable form.

☐ Name the new procedure FillCells.

☐ Add the FillCells statement to the end of the Form_Load() procedure.

The `Form_Load()` procedure should now look like this:

Sub Form_Load ()

```
.................................................
... No change to this section of the procedure ...
.................................................

SetColWidth
SetRowHeight
FillCells
```

End Sub

☐ Add the following code inside the `FillCells()` procedure:

Sub FillCells ()

```
Dim RowCounter, ColCounter

For ColCounter = 1 To 4 Step 1

    grdTable.Col = ColCounter
    For RowCounter = 1 To 12 Step 1
        grdTable.Row = RowCounter
        grdTable.Text = "Unknown"
    Next

Next
```

End Sub

The two `For` loops set the Text property of the grdTable grid to Unknown. The outer `For` loop counts from 1 to 4, and the inner `For` loop counts from 1 to 12. These two `For` loops set the Text property of all the cells in the grid (except the left heading column and the top heading row) to Unknown.

☐ Execute the Table program.

The cells of the grid controls are all filled with the text Unknown (see Figure 9.10).

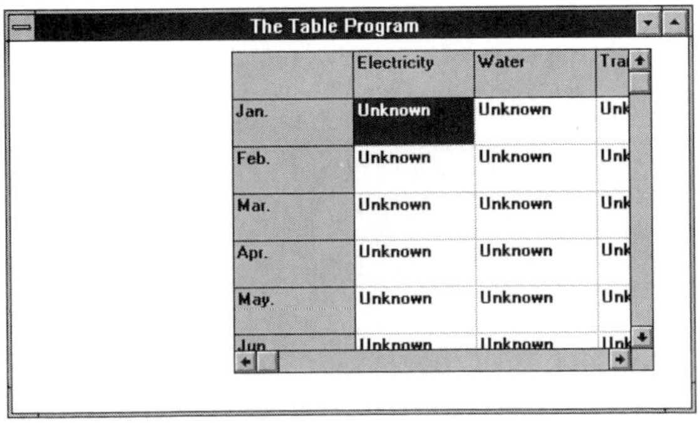

Figure 9.10.
Filling the text of the grid with text.

	Electricity	Water	Tra
Jan.	Unknown	Unknown	Unk
Feb.	Unknown	Unknown	Unk
Mar.	Unknown	Unknown	Unk
Apr.	Unknown	Unknown	Unk
May.	Unknown	Unknown	Unk
Jun.	Unknown	Unknown	Unk

The Table Program

☐ To fill a specific cell with specific data, add the following statements to the end of the
`FillCells()` procedure:

```
Sub FillCells ()

    ...............................................
    ... No change to this section of the procedure ...
    ...............................................

    ' Fill the Electricity bill for January.
    grdTable.Row = 1
    grdTable.Col = 1
    grdTable.Text = "$100.00"

    ' Fill the Electricity bill for February.
    grdTable.Row = 2
    grdTable.Col = 1
    grdTable.Text = "$50.00"

    ' Fill the Water bill for February.

    grdTable.Row = 2
    grdTable.Col = 2
    grdTable.Text = "$75.00"

End Sub
```

This procedure fills three cells in the grid control by setting the Row and Col properties with
the required row number and column number, and then sets the Text property of the cell with
the specific text.

☐ Execute the Table program.

As you can see, the three cells are filled with the text $100.00, $50.00, and $75.00 (see Fig-
ure 9.11).

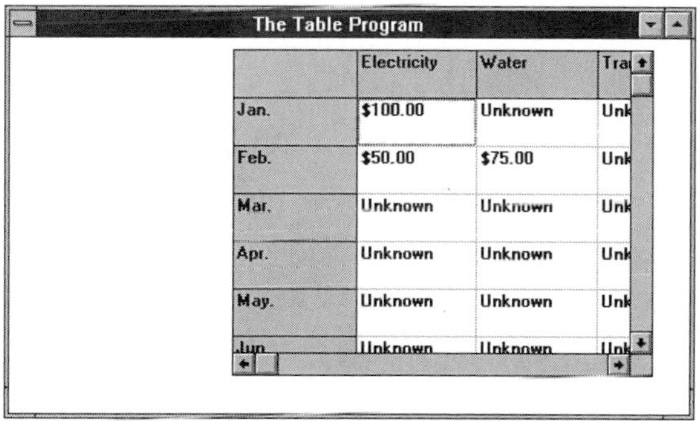

Figure 9.11.
Filling three cells in the grid.

The SetStartCol, SetStartRow, SetEndCol, and SetEndRow Properties

To select a range of cells, you may use the SetStartCol, SetStartRow, SetEndCol, and SetEndRow properties. Use the following steps to see these properties in action:

☐ Add a Clear button, as shown on Figure 9.12. This command button should have the following properties: The Name property should be cmdClear and the Caption property should be &Clear.

Figure 9.12.

Adding a Clear button.

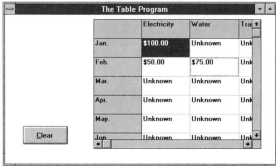

☐ Add the following code inside the cmdClear_Click() procedure of the frmTable form:

```
Sub cmdClear_Click ()

    ' Select from Row #1, Col #1.
    grdTable.SelStartCol = 1
    grdTable.SelStartRow = 1

    ' End selection at bottom right cell.
    grdTable.SelEndCol = grdTable.Cols - 1
    grdTable.SelEndRow = grdTable.Rows - 1

    ' Set FillStyle to 1 (fill them all).
    grdTable.FillStyle = 1

    ' Fill all the cells with null.
    grdTable.Text = ""

End Sub
```

☐ Execute the Table program.

☐ Click the Clear button.

> *The program responds by clearing all the cells inside the grid control.*

The Code Inside the *cmdClear_Click()* Procedure

The `cmdClear_Click()` procedure is executed whenever the user clicks the Clear button. The procedure sets a range of cells. The starting cell is declared with the following statements:

```
grdTable.SelStartCol = 1
grdTable.SelStartRow = 1
```

The ending cell is declared with the following statements:

```
grdTable.SelEndCol = grdTable.Cols - 1
grdTable.SelEndRow = grdTable.Rows - 1
```

The default value of the FillStyle property is 0-Single. The procedure sets the FillStyle property of the grdTable grid control to 1:

```
grdTable.FillStyle = 1
```

Once the FillStyle property is set to 1-Repeat, filling the Text property of a cell affects all the cells that are currently selected. Therefore, the following statement clears all the cells that are included in the selected range:

```
grdTable.Text = ""
```

If after clearing the cells you need to fill only a single cell, you have to unselect the selected cells. For example, to fill the cell at Row #2, Col #3, use the following statements:

```
' Set the selected cell to Row #2, Col #3.
grdTable.SelStartCol = 3
grdTable.SelStartRow = 2

grdTable.SelEndCol = 3
grdTable.SelEndRow = 2

' Fill the Text property of the cell.
grdTable.Text = "$34.00"
```

In other words, the selected range is the single cell Row #2, Col #3.

Note that the `cmdClear_Click()` procedure uses the Cols and Rows properties to determine the number of columns and rows. This means that these properties may serve two roles:

- Use the Cols and Rows properties to determine the number of columns and rows. For example, the following statement updates the variable NumOfColumns with the number of columns in the grid control:

  ```
  NumOfColumns = grdTable.Cols
  ```

  The following statement updates the variable NumOfRows with the number of rows in the grid control:

  ```
  NumOfRows = grdTable.Rows
  ```

- Use the Cols and Rows properties to set the number of columns and rows.

For example, to build a grid control with 10 columns, set the Cols property of the grid control to 10 at design time, or use the following statement in your program:

```
grdTable.Cols = 10
```

To build a grid control with 8 rows, set the Rows property of the grid control to 8 at design time, or use the following statement in your program:

```
grdTable.Rows = 8
```

Aligning Text Inside the Cells

The cells in the top row are used to store the headings of the columns, and the cells in the left column are used to store the heading of the rows. These cells are called fixed rows and fixed columns, because as you scroll inside the grid control, these cells are always fixed in their position. On the other hand, all the other cells in the grid control are able to scroll up and down, left and right. Appropriately, these cells are called non-fixed cells.

To align the non-fixed columns in a grid control, use the ColAlignment property. The possible values for the ColAlignment property are shown in Table 9.1.

Table 9.1. The possible settings of the ColAlignment property.

Setting for the ColAlignment Property	Description
0	Left Align (This is the default setting)
1	Right Align
2	Center

Use the following steps to see the ColAlignment property in action:

☐ Add the Align command button, as shown in Figure 9.13.

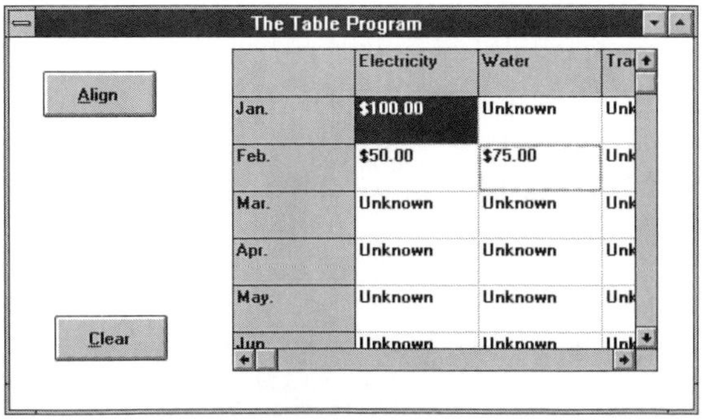

Figure 9.13.
Adding the Align button.

The Align button should have the following properties: The Name property should be cmdAlign and the Caption property should be &Align.

☐ Add the following code inside the cmdAlign_Click() procedure of the frmTable form:

```
Sub cmdAlign_Click ()

    Dim ColCounter
    ' Center the text inside the cells.
    For ColCounter = 1 To (grdTable.Cols - 2) Step 1
        grdTable.ColAlignment(ColCounter) = 2
    Next

End Sub
```

This procedure sets the text inside all the non-fixed columns except the extreme right column to 2-Center.

☐ Execute the Table program.

☐ Click the Align button.

As you can see, the text in the non-fixed cells except the extreme-right column are centered.

Note that the reason for not centering the text in the extreme-right column is to demonstrate that you may assign different ColAlignment properties to different columns. (That is, in this example, the non-fixed columns 1 to 11 have their Text property set to 2-Center, while the text alignment in column number 12 remains at its default alignment, which is 0-Left Align.)

To align the fixed columns and fixed rows, you have to use the FixedAlignment property. FixedAlignment may have the values listed in Table 9.2.

Table 9.2. The possible settings of the FixedAlignment property.

Setting for the FixedAlignment Property	Description
0	Left Align (This is the default setting)
1	Right Align
2	Center
3	Use the same alignment as used in the non-fixed column of this column

You may use the FixedAlignment property to align the text in a fixed column to a different alignment than the non-fixed cells below the heading. For example, if you set the FixedAlignment property of column number 1 to 1-Right Align, the text alignment of the cells below this heading may be set with the ColAlignment property to any of the values listed in Table 9.1.

As indicated in Table 9.2, if you set the FixedAlignment property to 3, the alignment of the text in the column heading is the same as the alignment of the text inside the non-fixed cells in that column.

To center the text in the extreme-left column (column 0), use the following statement:

```
grdTable.FixedAlignment(0) = 2
```

To center the Electricity and Water headings (Col #1 and Col #2), use the following statements:

```
grdTable.FixedAlignment(1) = 2
grdTable.FixedAlignment(2) = 2
```

The TV Program

The TV program illustrates how to present data in a tabular format with the grid control. The TV program further explores additional features and properties of the grid control.

The Visual Implementation of the TV Program

☐ Open a new project, save the form of the project as TV.FRM, and save the make file of the project as TV.MAK.

The TV program needs a BMP file called TV.BMP. Now you can use your artistic talent to draw the BMP picture, as shown in Figure 9.14:

☐ Start Paintbrush.

☐ Draw the picture shown in Figure 9.14 (use colors).

Figure 9.14.
The TV.bmp bitmap.

☐ Move the picture to the upper-left corner of the window of Paintbrush (see Figure 9.15).

☐ Select Cursor position from the View menu.

Paintbrush displays the current coordinate of the cursor in the upper-right corner of the window (see Figure 9.15). Use this coordinate in the following steps.

☐ Place the cursor at the lower-right corner of the picture and note the cursor coordinate—the first number of the cursor coordinate represents the width of the picture, and the second number represents the height of the picture.

☐ Copy the picture to the Clipboard (select the square scissors tool of Paintbrush, enclose the picture with the dashed square, and select Copy from the Edit menu).

Figure 9.15.

Moving the picture to the upper-left corner of the window.

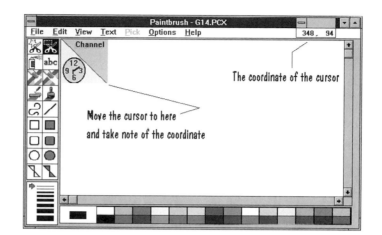

Your picture is now stored in the Clipboard.

☐ Select New from the File menu.

Note: It does not matter whether you save the current picture to the disk.

☐ Select Image Attribute from the Option menu.

☐ Select the Pels radio button (because you are about to enter new dimensions in pixels).

☐ In the Width text box, type the width of the picture.

☐ In the Height text box, type the height of the picture.

☐ Click the OK button.

> *Paintbrush responds by redimensioning the drawing area in accordance with the width and height that you supplied in the previous steps.*

☐ Select Paste from the Edit menu.

> *Your picture is copied from the Clipboard to Paintbrush.*

☐ Select Save As from the File menu and save the file as TV.BMP.

Why did you have to go through this exercise? You need the TV.BMP picture as a small file that contains only the picture you drew, not the whole drawing area of Paintbrush!

Now go back to Visual Basic.

☐ Build the frmTV form according to the specifications in Table 9.3.

The completed form should look like the one shown in Figure 9.16.

Table 9.3. The properties table of frmTV form.

Object	Property	Setting
Form	**Name**	**frmTV**
	Caption	The TV Program
	Height	4425
	Left	1035
	Top	1140
	Width	7485
Picture Box	**Name**	**picTV**
	Picture	TV.BMP
	Visible	0-False
Grid	**Name**	**grdTV**
	Cols	10
	Height	3375
	Left	2880
	Rows	24
	Top	360
	Width	4215
Command Button	**Name**	**cmdExit**
	Caption	&Exit
	Height	495
	Left	120
	Top	3360
	Width	1215

Figure 9.16.
The frmTV form.

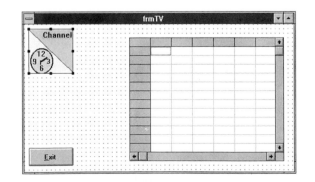

Entering the Code of the TV Program

☐ Enter the following code inside the general declarations area of the frmTV form:

```
' All variables MUST be declared.
Option Explicit
```

☐ Enter the following code inside the Form_Load() procedure of the frmTV form:

```
Sub Form_Load ()

    ' Make the upper left cell the active cell.
    grdTV.Row = 0
    grdTV.Col = 0

    ' Change the width and height of the cell to the
    ' width and height of the picTV picture.
    grdTV.ColWidth(0) = picTV.Width
    grdTV.RowHeight(0) = picTV.Height

    ' Place the picture into the cell.
    grdTV.Picture = picTV.Picture

End Sub
```

☐ Enter the following code inside the cmdExit_Click() procedure of the frmTV form:

```
Sub cmdExit_Click()

    End

End Sub
```

Executing the TV Program

☐ Execute the TV program.

The TV program contains a picture in its 0,0 cell, as shown in Figure 9.17.

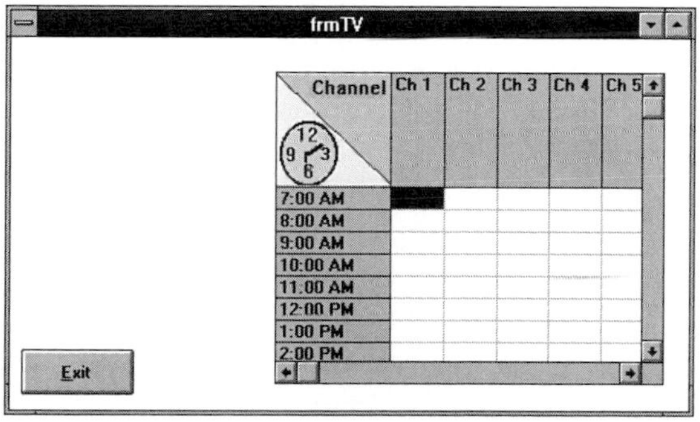

Figure 9.17.
The TV program with a picture in its 0,0 cell.

The Code Inside the *Form_Load()* Procedure of the frmTV Form

The Form_Load() procedure is executed when the form is loaded at startup. The procedure makes the 0,0 cell the active cell:

```
grdTV.Row = 0
grdTV.Col = 0
```

It also changes the width and height of the Picture property of the cell to the width and height of the TV.BMP picture:

```
grdTV.ColWidth(0) = picTV.Width
grdTV.RowHeight(0) = picTV.Height
```

The last thing this procedure does is place the picture inside the cell:

```
grdTV.Picture = picTV.Picture
```

Note that the Visible property of the TV.BMP picture was set to False during design time. This is why the picture is not shown on the left side of the form at runtime.

Updating the Fixed Rows and Columns

You may now add the TV schedule as follows:

☐ Create a new procedure and name it AddSchedule.

☐ Enter the following code inside the AddSchedule() procedure:

```
Sub AddSchdule ()

    grdTV.Row = 0

    grdTV.Col = 1
    grdTV.Text = "Ch 1"

    grdTV.Col = 2
    grdTV.Text = "Ch 2"

    grdTV.Col = 3
    grdTV.Text = "Ch 3"

    grdTV.Col = 4
    grdTV.Text = "Ch 4"

    grdTV.Col = 5
    grdTV.Text = "Ch 5"

    grdTV.Col = 6
    grdTV.Text = "Ch 6"

    grdTV.Col = 7
    grdTV.Text = "Ch 7"
```

```
grdTV.Col = 8
grdTV.Text = "Ch 8"

grdTV.Col = 9
grdTV.Text = "Ch 9"
grdTV.Col = 0

grdTV.Row = 1
grdTV.Text = "7:00 AM"

grdTV.Row = 2
grdTV.Text = "8:00 AM"

grdTV.Row = 3
grdTV.Text = "9:00 AM"

grdTV.Row = 4
grdTV.Text = "10:00 AM"

grdTV.Row = 5
grdTV.Text = "11:00 AM"

grdTV.Row = 6
grdTV.Text = "12:00 PM"

grdTV.Row = 7
grdTV.Text = "1:00 PM"

grdTV.Row = 8
grdTV.Text = "2:00 PM"

grdTV.Row = 9
grdTV.Text = "3:00 PM"

grdTV.Row = 10
grdTV.Text = "4:00 PM"
```

End Sub

☐ Add the statement AddSchedule to the Form_Load() procedure. The Form_Load() procedure should now look like this:

Sub Form_Load ()

```
.........................................
... No change to this section of the ...
... procedure.                        ...
.........................................
' Add the schedule
AddSchedule
```

End Sub

☐ Execute the TV program.

The fixed rows and columns are filled with the time and channel numbers.

315

The Clip Property

To fill each of the cells, you may set the active cell with the Row and Col properties, and then set the Text property to the required text. For example, to fill Row #1, Col #1 with Good morning, you can use the following:

```
grdTV.Row = 1
grdTV.Col = 1
grdTV.Text = "Good morning"
```

An alternate way to fill the cells is to use the Clip property. Use the following steps to see the Clip property in action:

☐ Add the Fill cells button to the form, as shown in Figure 9.18.

Figure 9.18.
Adding the Fill cells button.

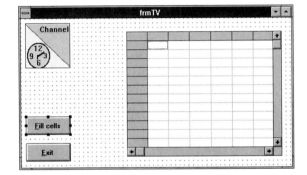

The command button should have the following properties: The Name property should be cmdFillCells and the Caption property should be &Fill Cells.

☐ Add the following code inside the cmdFillCells_Click() procedure of the frmTV form:

```
Sub cmdFillCells_Click ()

    Dim ColCounter
    Dim TextToSpread as String

    ' Set width of all non-fixed columns to 2,000
    ' twips.
    For ColCounter = 1 To grdTV.Cols - 1 Step 1
        grdTV.ColWidth(ColCounter) = 2000
    Next

    ' Define a selected area.
    grdTV.SelStartRow = 1
    grdTV.SelStartCol = 1
    grdTV.SelEndRow = 3
    grdTV.SelEndCol = 4
```

```
' Into Row #1, Col #1
TextToSpread = "Good morning"

' Into Row #1, Col #2.
TextToSpread = TextToSpread + Chr(9)

' Into Row #1, Col #3.
TextToSpread = TextToSpread + "News in the morning"

' Into Row #2, Col #3
TextToSpread = TextToSpread + Chr(13) + Chr(9) + Chr(9)

TextToSpread = TextToSpread + "Gone with the wind"

' Spread the text.
grdTV.Clip = TextToSpread

End Sub
```

Executing the TV Program

☐ Execute the TV program.

☐ Click the Fill Cells button.

The program responds by filling the following cells:

```
        Col #1           Col #2                Col #3
Row#1 [Good morning] [News in the morning] [      (blank)       ]
Row#2 [  (blank)   ] [         (blank)     ] [Gone with the wind]
```

The Code Inside the *cmdFillCells_Click()* Procedure

The cmdFillCells_Click() procedure is executed whenever the user clicks the FillCells procedure.

The procedure sets the width of all the non-fixed cells to 2000 twips:

```
For ColCounter = 1 To grdTV.Cols - 1 Step 1
    grdTV.ColWidth(ColCounter) = 2000
Next
```

Then the procedure defines a selected area:

```
grdTV.SelStartRow = 1
grdTV.SelStartCol = 1
grdTV.SelEndRow = 3
grdTV.SelEndCol = 4
```

The selected area is the following:

```
        Col #1 Col #2 Col #3 Col #4
Row #1  [ X  ] [ X  ] [ X  ] [ X  ]
Row #2  [ X  ] [ X  ] [ X  ] [ X  ]
Row #3  [ X  ] [ X  ] [ X  ] [ X  ]
```

The procedure prepares a string variable called `TextToSpread` that spreads its contents over the selected cells.

The string `Good morning` is placed in the cell Row #1, Col #1:

```
' Into Row #1, Col #1
TextToSpread = "Good morning"
```

The string `News in the morning` is placed in the cell Row #1, Col #2. Because this cell is to the right of the cell Row #1, Col #1, you need to include the tab character, which is Chr(9):

```
' Into Row #1, Col #2.
TextToSpread = TextToSpread + Chr(9)
TextToSpread = TextToSpread + "News in the morning"
```

The next cell to be filled is Row #2, Col #3. Because the current cell is Row #1, Col #2, you need to include the carriage return character Chr(13). This brings you to Row #2, Col #1. To place the text in Row #2, Col #3, two tab characters are needed:

```
' Into Row #2, Col #3
TextToSpread = TextToSpread + Chr(13) + Chr(9) + Chr(9)
TextToSpread = TextToSpread + "Gone with the wind"
```

Now that the string `TextToSpread` is ready, the Clip property is used to actually place the content of the string into the cells:

```
' Spread the text.
grdTV.Clip = TextToSpread
```

DO	DON'T

DO use the following steps to place text at various cells of a grid control:

☐ Select the area in the grid.

☐ Prepare a string.

☐ Use the tab character—Chr(9)—to move one cell to the right, and use the carriage return—Chr(13)—to move to the beginning of the next row.

☐ Use the Clip property to place the contents of the string inside the cells.

Adding Pictures to Non-Fixed Cells

Adding pictures to non-fixed cells is accomplished in the same way as adding pictures to the fixed cells. For example, suppose that at 8:00 a.m. there is a dog show on Channel 1. To add a picture of a dog to this cell, you can generate a picture of a dog (using Paintbrush or another program), save the picture as a BMP file, and place a picture control somewhere inside the form. Be sure that the Visible property of the picture control is set to False.

The following code places the dog picture inside the 8:00 AM, Ch1 cell:

```
grdTV.Row = 2
grdTV.Col = 1

grdTV.ColWidth(1) = picDog.Width
grdTV.RowHeight(2) = picDog.Height
grdTV.Picture = picDog.Picture
```

This code can be placed inside the cmdFillCells_Click() procedure.

Figure 9.19 shows the cell at Row #2, Col #1 with a picture of a dog.

Figure 9.19.
Placing the dog in the Row #2, Col #1 cell.

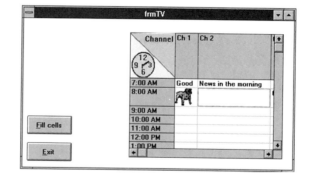

Of course, placing the dog picture inside the cell is not enough to tell what show is on. To place the text The Dog Show inside the cell, set the Text property of the cell. The following code places the dog picture and the name of the show inside the cell:

```
grdTV.Row = 2
grdTV.Col = 1

grdTV.ColWidth(1) = picDog.Width + 1000
grdTV.RowHeight(2) = picDog.Height
grdTV.Picture = picDog.Picture

grdTV.Text = "The Dog Show"
```

Note that the ColWidth property of the cell is set to this:

```
grdTV.ColWidth(1) = picDog.Width + 1000
```

which makes room for the added text.

The resultant cell is shown in Figure 9.20.

Figure 9.20.
Placing text and graphics inside a non-fixed cell.

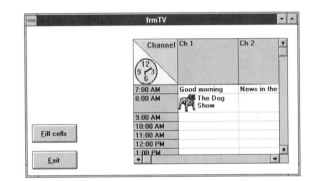

> **Note:** You may place graphics and text inside fixed and non-fixed cells.

Removing Pictures from Cells

To remove a picture from a cell, use the LoadPicture() function without any argument. For example, to remove the dog picture from the cell, use the following statements:

```
grdTV.Row = 2
grdTV.Col = 1

grdTV.Picture = LoadPicture()
```

Adding Rows During Runtime

You may insert rows to the grid control during runtime using the AddItem method. For example, the following statements insert a row at row 2:

```
ContentsOfCells = "7:30 AM" + Chr(9) + "gardening"
grdTV.AddItem ContentsOfCells, 2
```

The first argument of the AddItem method specifies the contents of the cells, and the second argument specifies the row number. The above statements fill two cells, and, therefore, the text to be inserted includes the tab character between the text contents of the cells. Figure 9.21 shows the resultant grid after the row is inserted.

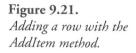

Figure 9.21.
*Adding a row with the
AddItem method.*

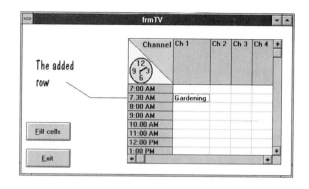

Removing Rows During Runtime

You may remove items from a grid control during runtime using the RemoveItem method. The
following statement removes row 2:

```
grdTV.RemoveItem 2
```

The argument of the RemoveItem method contains the row number to be removed.

Summary

In this chapter you have learned how to use the grid control, a powerful control that lets you
present data (text and graphics) in a professional and pleasing way. You have learned how to
insert text into the cells, how to align the text, how to insert pictures inside the cells, and how
to remove and add rows during runtime.

Q&A

Q Can I place more than one grid control in a form?

A Yes. You can place many grid controls in a form (just as you can place many Command buttons and other controls in a form).

**Q Figure 9.20 shows that the text The Dog Show that was added to the cell is Left
Aligned. Can I place the text in different text alignments?**

A Yes. The text can be centered and it can be aligned to the right. For example, the
following code places the dog picture and the text in the cell. The text is centered:

```
grdTV.Row = 2
grdTV.Col = 1

grdTV.ColWidth(1) = picDog.Width + 1000
grdTV.RowHeight(2) = picDog.Height
grdTV.Picture = picDog.Picture
```

```
grdTV.ColAlignment(1) = 2
grdTV.Text = "The Dog Show"
```

As discussed in this chapter, the ColAlignment property may align the text to any of the alignments shown in Table 9.1.

Q **The properties table of the grid control includes a property called GridLines. This property may be set to either True or False. What is this property?**

A The default setting of this property is True. This causes the grid control to appear with visible grid lines. If you set the value of this property to False, the grid control is shown without visible grid lines. Experiment with this property (as well as with the other properties of the grid control such as the ForeColor property) to see the effects.

Quiz

1. The height of the cells may be changed only during runtime.

    a. True

    b. False

2. The width of the cells may be changed only during runtime.

    a. True

    b. False

3. Which property should you set to change the height of a cell?

    a. RowHeight

    b. ColWidth

    c. Can't change the height of a cell

4. Which property should you set to change the width of a cell?

    a. RowHeight

    b. ColWidth

    c. Can't change the width of a cell

5. What code should be written to remove a picture from a cell?

Exercises

1. Suppose that the Clip property is used to place text in cells, as shown in the following table:

    ```
              Col#1   Col#2     Col#3
    Row #1      A    (blank)      C
    Row #2      D    (blank)   (blank)
    Row #3      E       F         G
    ```

9

What should be the contents of the string that places text in these cells?

2. Write a program that displays a multiplication table.

Quiz Answers

1. a

2. a

3. a

4. b

5. Make the cell from which you want to remove the picture of the currently active cell, and then use LoadPicture() with no argument. For example, to remove the picture from the cell at Row #4, Col #7, use the following:

```
grdTV.Row = 4
grdTV.Col = 7

grdTV.Picture = LoadPicture()
```

Exercise Answers

1. First select the area with the following statements:

```
Dim the Contents As String
' Select the area.
grdMyGrid.SelStartRow = 1
grdMyGrid.SelStartCol = 1
grdMyGrid.SelEndRow = 3
grdMyGrid.SelEndCol = 3
```

Then update a string variable as follows:

```
TheContents = "A" + Chr(9) + Chr(9) + "C" + Chr(13) +
    "D" + Chr(9) + Chr(9) + Chr(13) +
    "E" + Chr(9) + "F" + Chr(9) + "G"
```

Finally, issue the following statement:

```
grdMyGrid.Clip TheContents
```

2. There are several ways to build such a program. The grid control should look like this:

```
   0 1 2 3 ...
0  0 0 0 0 ...
1  0 1 2 3 ...
2  0 1 4 6 ...
3  0 3 6 9 ...
.  . . . . ...
.  . . . . ...
.  . . . . ...
```

Try to write the program yourself, and experiment with it by placing pictures inside the cells. (The Visual Basic package comes with plenty of icons.)

When implementing the program, calculate the Text property of the non-fixed cells by performing the multiplication. For example, the text that can be placed in the cell Row #2, Col #3 can be calculated as follows:

```
Dim X, Y

grdMultiply.Row = 2
grdMultiply.Col = 0
X = Val(grdMultiply.Text)

grdMultiply.Row = 0
grdMultiply.Col = 3
Y = Val(grdMultiply.Text)

grdMultiply.Row = 2
grdMultiply.Col = 3
grdMultiply.Text = X*Y
```

Try to implement a loop that goes through all the rows and columns and fills all the cells of the grid control.

Displaying and Printing

In this chapter you'll learn how to display and print information, how to display text in different fonts, how to format numbers, dates, and times, and how to send data (text and graphics) to the printer.

Fonts

There are two types of fonts: scaleable and nonscaleable. A scaleable font is created using mathematical formulas. For example, the basic B character is defined only once. All other sizes of the B character are produced from the basic character by enlarging or shrinking the basic B. A nonscaleable font is stored as a bitmap. Larger and smaller fonts of the same character are stored as different bitmaps.

Using Different Fonts in Your Programs

When you display text inside a form, you have to choose its font. Selecting the proper fonts is an important job. Will your user have this type of font on his/her system? If the user of your program does not have the font installed, Windows chooses a font that most closely resembles the required font. However, if your user does not have a large selection of fonts, Windows might choose a font that is larger than the font you intended to use. This of course may mess up your form by producing overlapped text.

The easiest way to overcome this problem is to use only the most common fonts, such as the fonts that are shipped with the original Windows package. Alternatively, your program can examine the file WIN.INI, which resides in the Windows directory. This file has a section that starts with the heading [fonts]. Under this heading, all the currently installed fonts are listed. Figure 10.1 shows the fonts section of the WIN.INI file in a typical system. Your program can examine this section and decide which font should be used.

The FontTransparent Property

The form and the picture control support the FontTransparent property. When the FontTransparent property is False (the default), the text is displayed with a background indicated by the BackColor property. For example, if the BackColor property is set to blue, the text is displayed with a blue background.

Figure 10.1.
The [fonts] section in
WIN.INI.

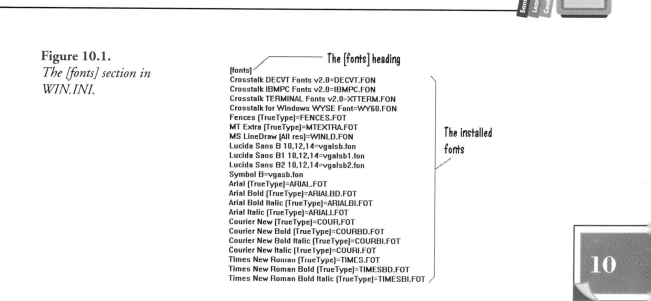

The code inside this procedure sets the FontTransparent property of the form to True and uses the Print method to display the text Testing.

The procedure then sets the FontTransparent property of the form to False and again displays the text Testing.

As shown in Figure 10.3, the first line in the form displays the text Testing, and the background of the text is the original background of the bitmap picture.

The second line of text in Figure 10.3 displays the text Testing with a white background. The background is white because the FontTransparent property of the form is set to False and the BackColor property of the form is set to White.

Figure 10.2 shows a form with a bitmap picture in it. You can display text inside the form by using the Print method. The following Form_Click() event procedure is executed whenever the user clicks the form:

```
Sub Form_Click ()

    ' Set the FontTransparent property to True.
    frmMyForm.FontTransparent = True
    ' Display text.
    frmMyForm.Print "Testing..."

    ' Set the FontTransparent property to False.
    frmMyForm.FontTransparent = False
    ' Display text.
    frmMyForm.Print "Testing..."

End Sub
```

Figure 10.2.
The frmMyForm form.

Figure 10.3.
*Displaying text with the
FontTransparent property
equal to True and False.*

The ShowFont Program

The ShowFont program illustrates the various font properties that are available in Visual Basic.

The Visual Implementation of the ShowFont Program

☐ Open a new project, save the form of the project as SHOWFONT.FRM, and save the make file of the project as SHOWFONT.MAK.

☐ Build the frmShowFont form according to the specifications in Table 10.1.

The completed form should look like the one shown in Figure 10.4.

Table 10.1. The properties table of the frmShowFont form.

Object	Property	Setting
Form	**Name**	**frmShowFont**
	Caption	The ShowFont Program
	Height	4425
	Left	1035

Object	Property	Setting
	Top	1140
	Width	7485
Check Box	**Name**	**chkFontUnderline**
	Caption	FontUnderline
	Height	495
	Left	2400
	Top	3120
	Width	1575
Check Box	**Name**	**chkFontStrike**
	Caption	FontStrikethru
	Height	495
	Left	2400
	Top	2640
	Width	1695
Check Box	**Name**	**chkFontItalic**
	Caption	FontItalic
	Height	495
	Left	240
	Top	3120
	Width	1215
Check Box	**Name**	**chkFontBold**
	Caption	FontBold
	Height	495
	Left	240
	Top	2640
	Width	1215
Command Button	**Name**	**cmdExit**
	Caption	&Exit
	Height	495
	Left	5880

continues

Table 10.1. continued

Object	Property	Setting
	Top	3360
	Width	1215
Text Box	**Name**	**txtTest**
	FontBold	0-False
	FontItalic	0-False
	FontName	MS Sans Serif
	FontSize	18
	FontStrikethru	0-False
Text Box	**Name**	**txtTest**
	FontUnderline	0-False
	Height	1935
	Left	360
	MultiLine	True
	ScrollBars	3-Both
	Text	(empty)
	Top	240
	Width	6375
Menu	**(see Table 10.2)**	**(see Table 10.2)**

Table 10.2. The menu table of the frmShowFont form.

Caption	Name
&Fonts	mnuFonts
...Courier	mnuCourier
...Script	mnuScript
...MS Sans Serif	mnuMSSansSerif
&Size	mnuSize
...10 Points	mnu10Points
...12 Points	mnu12Points
...16 Points	mnu16Points
...72 Points	mnu72Points

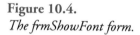

Figure 10.4.
The frmShowFont form.

Entering the Code of the ShowFont Program

☐ Enter the following code inside the general declarations section of the frmShowFont form:

```
' All variables MUST be declared.
Option Explicit
```

☐ Enter the following code inside the `chkFontBold_Click()` procedure of the frmShowFont form:

```
Sub chkFontBold_Click ()

    ' Update the FontBold property with the Value
    ' property of the chkFontBold.
    txtTest.FontBold = chkFontBold.Value

End Sub
```

☐ Enter the following code inside the `chkFontItalic_Click()` procedure of the frmShowFont form:

```
Sub chkFontItalic_Click ()

    ' Update the FontItalic property with the Value
    ' property of the chkFontItalic.
    txtTest.FontItalic = chkFontItalic.Value

End Sub
```

☐ Enter the following code inside the `chkStrike_Click()` procedure of the frmShowFont form:

```
Sub chkFontStrike_Click ()

    ' Update the FontStrikethru property with the
    ' Value property of the chkFontStrike.
    txtTest.FontStrikethru = chkFontStrike.Value

End Sub
```

☐ Enter the following code inside the `chkUnderline_Click()` procedure of the frmShowFont form:

```
Sub chkFontUnderline_Click ()

    ' Update the FontUnderline property with the
    ' Value property of the chkFontUnderline.
    txtTest.FontUnderline = chkFontUnderline.Value

End Sub
```

☐ Enter the following code inside the `cmdExit_Click()` procedure of the frmShowFont form:

```
Sub cmdExit_Click ()

    End

End Sub
```

☐ Enter the following code inside the `mnu10Points_Click()` procedure of the frmShowFont form:

```
Sub mnu10Points_Click ()

    ' Set the size of the font to 10 points.
    txtTest.FontSize = 10

End Sub
```

☐ Enter the following code inside the `mnu12Points_Click()` procedure of the frmShowFont form:

```
Sub mnu12Points_Click ()

    ' Set the size of the font to 12 points.
    txtTest.FontSize = 12

End Sub
```

☐ Enter the following code inside the `mnu16Points_Click()` procedure of the frmShowFont form:

```
Sub mnu16Points_Click ()

    ' Set the size of the font to 16 points.
    txtTest.FontSize = 16

End Sub
```

Enter the following code inside the `mnu72Points_Click()` procedure of the frmShowFont form:

```
Sub mnu72Points_Click ()

    ' Set the size of the font to 72 points.
    txtTest.FontSize = 72

End Sub
```

Enter the following code inside the `mnuCourier_Click()` procedure of the frmShowFont form:

```
Sub mnuCourier_Click ()

    ' Set the font name to Courier.
    txtTest.FontName = "Courier"

End Sub
```

Enter the following code inside the `mnuMSSansSerif_Click()` procedure of the frmShowFont form:

```
Sub mnuMSSansSerif_Click ()

    ' Set the font name to MS Sans Serif.
    txtTest.FontName = "MS Sans Serif"

End Sub
```

Enter the following code inside the `mnuScript_Click()` procedure of the frmShowFont form:

```
Sub mnuScript_Click ()

    ' Set the font name to Script.
    txtTest.FontName = "Script"

End Sub
```

Save the project.

Executing the ShowFont Program

Execute the ShowFont program.

Type something inside the text box (see Figure 10.5).

The text you typed appears with the default font (the font as it was set during design time).

Figure 10.5.
The default font of the ShowFont program.

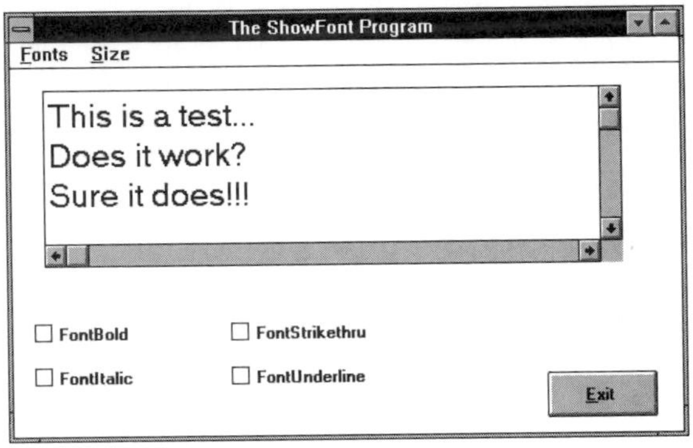

☐ Check the FontBold check box.

The program responds by changing the font inside the text box to bold (see Figure 10.6).

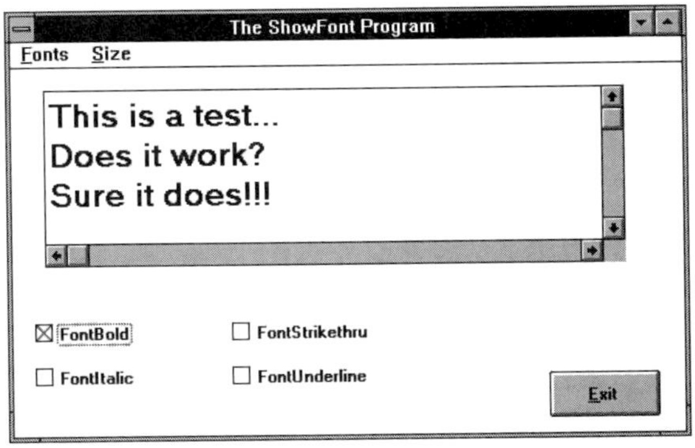

Figure 10.6.
Checking the FontBold check box.

☐ Check the FontItalic check box.

The program responds by changing the text inside the text box to italic. Because the FontBold is checked, the text is also bold (see Figure 10.7).

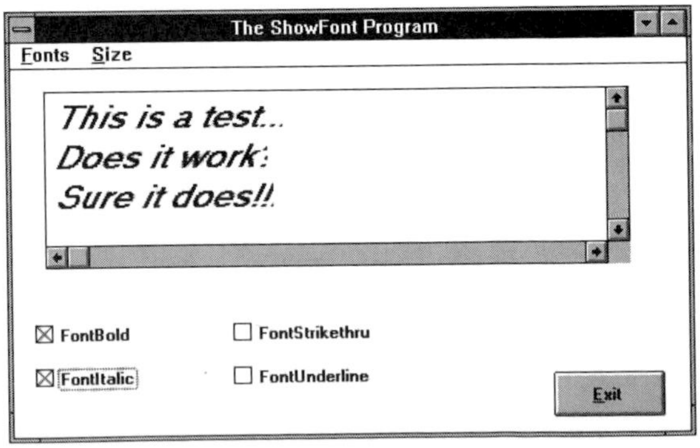

Figure 10.7.
Checking the FontBold and FontItalic check boxes.

☐ Click the FontBold and FontItalic check boxes to uncheck these check boxes.

The program responds by removing the bold and italic from the text in the text box.

☐ Check the FontStrikethru check box.

The program responds by displaying the text inside the text box as strikethrough text (see Figure 10.8).

Figure 10.8.
Checking the FontStrikethru check box.

~~This is a test...~~
~~Does it work?~~
~~Sure it does!!!~~

☐ FontBold ☒ FontStrikethru
☐ FontItalic ☐ FontUnderline

☐ Check the FontStrike check box to uncheck this box.

The program responds by removing the strikethru font from the text of the text box.

☐ Check the FontUnderline check box.

The program responds by underlining the text inside the text box (see Figure 10.9).

Figure 10.9.
Checking the Underline check box.

This is a test...
Does it work?
Sure it does!!!

☐ FontBold ☐ FontStrikethru
☐ FontItalic ☒ FontUnderline

☐ Change the font name by selecting a font from the Fonts menu.

The program responds by changing the text inside the text box to the font you selected.

☐ Change the font size by selecting a size from the Size menu.

The program responds by changing the text inside the text box to whichever size you selected. Figure 10.10 shows the text box after setting the size to 72 points.

☐ Click the Exit button to terminate the program.

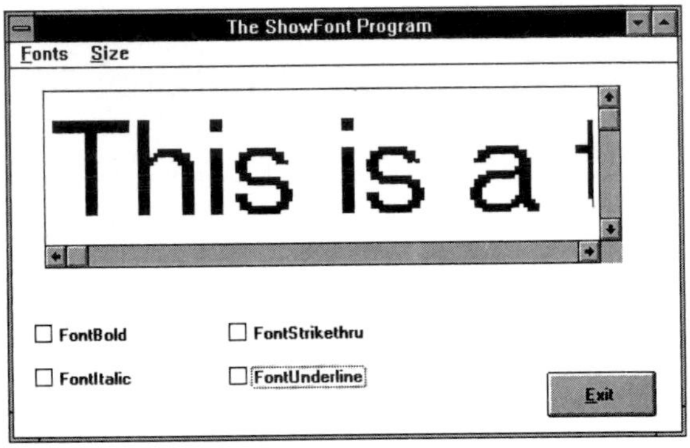

Figure 10.10.
Setting the FontSize property to 72 points.

```
                The ShowFont Program
Fonts   Size

 This is a t

 ☐ FontBold        ☐ FontStrikethru
 ☐ FontItalic      ☐ FontUnderline          Exit
```

How the ShowFont Program Works

The ShowFont program changes the font properties of the text box in accordance with the user selections.

The Code Inside the *chkFontBold_Click()* Event Procedure

The `chkFontBold_Click()` event procedure is executed whenever the user clicks on the chkFontBold check box:

```
Sub chkFontBold_Click ()

    ' Update the FontBold property with the Value
    ' property of the chkFontBold.
    txtTest.FontBold = chkFontBold.Value

End Sub
```

When the Value property of chkFontBold is True (that is, checked), the FontBold property is set to True, and when the Value property of chkFontBold is False (that is, unchecked), the FontBold property is set to False.

The `chkFontItalic_Click()`, `chkStrike_Click()`, and `chkUnderline_Click()` procedures work in a similar manner:

The `chkFontItalic_Click()` procedure sets the FontItalic property of the txtTest text box to True or False.

The chkFontStrike_Click() procedure sets the FontStrikethru property of the txtTest text box to True or False.

The chkUnderline_Click() procedure sets the FontUnderline property of the txtTest text box to True or False.

The Code Inside the *mnu10Points_Click()* Event Procedure of the frmShowFont Form

The mnu10Points_Click() procedure is executed whenever the user selects 10 Points from the Size menu:

```
Sub mnu10Points_Click ()

    ' Set the size of the font to 10 points.
    txtTest.FontSize = 10

End Sub
```

This procedure sets the FontSize property of the txtTest text box to 10.

In a similar manner, the mnu12Points_Click() procedure sets the FontSize property of the text box to 12, the mnu16Points_Click() procedure sets the FontSize property to 16, and the mnu72Points_Click() procedure sets the FontSize property to 72.

The Code Inside the *mnuCourier_Click()* Event Procedure of the frmShowFont Form

The mnuCourier_Click() procedure is executed whenever the user selects Courier from the Fonts menu:

```
Sub mnuCourier_Click ()

    ' Set the font name to Courier.
    txtTest.FontName = "Courier"

End Sub
```

This procedure sets the FontName property of the txtTest text box to Courier.

In a similar manner, the mnuMSSansSerif_Clicks() procedure sets the FontName property to MS Sans Serif, and the mnuScript_Click() procedure sets the FontName property to Script.

WYSIWYG

WYSIWYG is an abbreviation of "what you see is what you get." WYSIWYG refers to the capability of a program to produce hard copy on the printer that is an exact replica of the screen. Producing 100 percent WYSIWYG programs requires careful programming because users may have many types of printers, different monitors, different fonts, and so on.

The Fonts Program

The Fonts program illustrates how your program can make a decision regarding the available fonts in the system. The technique used by the Fonts program can be used to produce programs with WYSIWYG capability.

The Visual Implementation of the Fonts Program

☐ Open a new project, save the form of the program as FONTS.FRM, and save the make file of the project as FONTS.MAK.

☐ Build the frmFonts form according to the specifications in Table 10.3.

The completed form should look like the one shown in Figure 10.11.

Table 10.3. The properties table of frmFonts form.

Object	Property	Setting
Form	**Name**	**frmFonts**
	BorderStyle	1-Fixed Single
	Caption	The Fonts Program
	Height	4425
	Left	1035
	Top	1140
	Width	7485
Command Button	**Name**	**cmdNumberOfFonts**
	Caption	&Number of fonts
	Height	495
	Left	2400
	Top	2520
	Width	3255
Combo Box	**Name**	**cboFontsPrinter**
	Height	300
	Left	3240
	Sorted	True
	Style	2-Dropdown List
	Top	360
	Width	2775

Object	Property	Setting
ComboBox	**Name**	**cboFontsScreen**
	Height	300
	Left	360
	Sorted	True
	Style	2-Dropdown List
	Top	360
	Width	2775
Command Button	**Name**	**cmdExit**
	Caption	&Exit
	Height	495
	Left	6120
	Top	2040
	Width	1215
Label	**Name**	**lblSamplInfo**
	Caption	Sample:
	Height	375
	Left	480
	Top	2640
	Width	1695
Label	**Name**	**lblSample**
	Alignment	2-Center
	BorderStyle	1-Fixed Single
	Caption	AaBbCcDdEeFf
	FontSize	18
	Height	585
	Left	480
	Top	3120
	Width	6765
Label	**Name**	**lblPrinter**
	Caption	Available printer fonts:
	Height	255

continues

Table 10.3. continued

Object	Property	Setting
	Left	3240
	Top	120
	Width	2415
Label	**Name**	**lblScreen**
	Caption	Available screen fonts:
	Height	255
	Left	360
	Top	120
	Width	2535

Figure 10.11.

The frmFonts form.

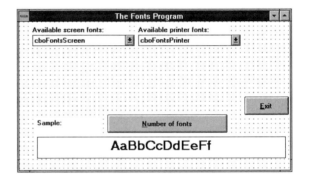

Entering the Code of the Fonts Program

☐ Enter the following code inside the general declarations section of the frmFonts form:

```
' All variables MUST be declared.
Option Explicit

Dim NumOfScreenFonts
Dim NumOfPrinterFonts
```

☐ Enter the following code inside the cboFontsScreen_Click() procedure of the frmFonts form:

```
Sub cboFontsScreen_Click ()

    ' User selected a new screen font. Change the
    ' font of the label in accordance with the user's font selection.
    lblSample.FontName = cboFontsScreen.Text

End Sub
```

☐ Enter the following code inside the cmdExit_Click() procedure of the frmFonts form:

```
Sub cmdExit_Click ()

    End

End Sub
```

☐ Enter the following code inside the cmdNumberOfFonts_Click() procedure of the frmFonts form:

```
Sub cmdNumberOfFonts_Click ()

    ' Display the number of screen fonts in the system.
    MsgBox "Number of Screen fonts: " + NumOfScreenFonts

    ' Display the number of printer fonts in the system.
    MsgBox "Number of Printer fonts: " + NumOfPrinterFonts

End Sub
```

☐ Enter the following code inside the Form_Load() procedure of the frmFonts form:

```
Sub Form_Load ()

    Dim I

    ' Calculate the number of screen fonts.
    NumOfScreenFonts = Screen.FontCount - 1

    ' Calculate the number of printer fonts.
    NumOfPrinterFonts = Printer.FontCount - 1

    ' Fill the items of the combo box with the screen fonts.
    For I = 0 To NumOfScreenFonts - 1 Step 1
        cboFontsScreen.AddItem Screen.Fonts(I)
    Next

    ' Fill the items of the combo box with the printer fonts.
    For I = 0 To NumOfPrinterFonts - 1 Step 1
        cboFontsPrinter.AddItem Printer.Fonts(I)
    Next

    ' initialize the text of the combo box to item #0.
    cboFontsScreen.ListIndex = 0

    ' Initialize the label font to value of the combo box.
    lblSample.FontName = cboFontsScreen.Text

End Sub
```

10

Executing the Fonts Program

☐ Execute the Fonts program.

☐ Click the Number of fonts button.

The program responds by displaying the number of available screen fonts and the number of available printer fonts.

☐ Click the right arrow of the left combo box.

As indicated by the label above this combo box, the list in the box includes all the available screen fonts on your system (see Figure 10.12).

The sample label at the bottom of the form changes its font in accordance with your selection.

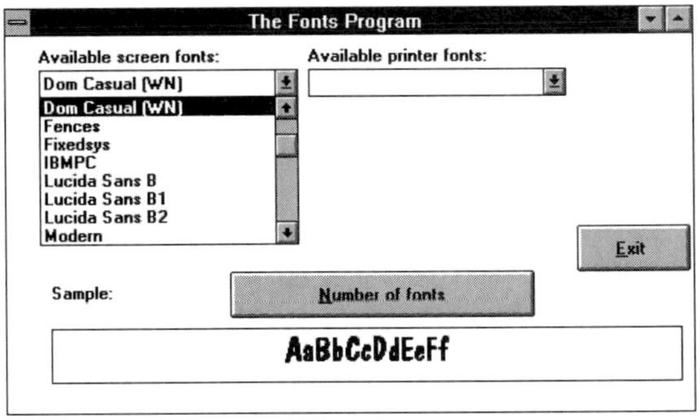

Figure 10.12.
Choosing the Dom Casual screen font.

The Fonts Program
Available screen fonts:	Available printer fonts:
Dom Casual (WN)	
Dom Casual (WN)	
Fences	
Fixedsys	
IBMPC	
Lucida Sans B	
Lucida Sans B1	
Lucida Sans B2	
Modern	Exit
Sample:	Number of fonts
AaBbCcDdEeFf	

☐ Select a font from the left combo box.

As indicated by the label above this combo box, the list in the box includes all the available printer fonts in your system.

The program responds by displaying all the available printer fonts (see Figure 10.13).

Note: The text in the Sample label is not changed as you select new fonts from the right combo box, because this combo box represents the fonts of the printer.

Figure 10.13.
Displaying the printer fonts.

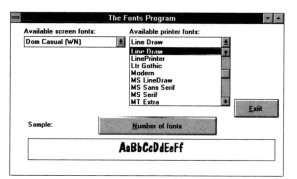

How the Fonts Program Works

The Fonts program extracts the available screen and printer fonts and displays them in combo boxes.

The Code Inside the General Declarations Section

The code inside the general declarations section of the program declares two variables:

```
Dim NumOfScreenFonts
Dim NumOfPrinterFonts
```

These variables represent the number of available screen fonts and printer fonts. Because these variables are declared in the general section, they are visible in all the procedures of the form.

The Code Inside the *Form_Load()* Procedure

The Form_Load() procedure is executed when the form is loaded:

```
Sub Form_Load ()

    Dim I

    ' Calculate the number of screen fonts.
    NumOfScreenFonts = Screen.FontCount

    ' Calculate the number of printer fonts.
    NumOfPrinterFonts = Printer.FontCount

    ' Fill the items of the combo box with the screen fonts.
    For I = 0 To NumOfScreenFonts - 1 Step 1
        cboFontsScreen.AddItem Screen.Fonts(I)
    Next

    ' Fill the items of the combo box with the printer fonts.
    For I = 0 To NumOfPrinterFonts - 1 Step 1
        cboFontsPrinter.AddItem Printer.Fonts(I)
    Next
```

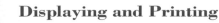

```
' initialize the text of the combo box to item #0.
cboFontsScreen.ListIndex = 0

' Initialize the label font to value of the combo box.
lblSample.FontName = cboFontsScreen.Text
```

End Sub

The number of screen fonts is obtained using the FontCount property of the screen:

```
' Calculate the number of screen fonts.
NumOfScreenFonts = Screen.FontCount
```

Similarly, the number of printer fonts is obtained using the FontCount property of the printer:

```
' Calculate the number of printer fonts.
NumOfPrinterFonts = Printer.FontCount
```

DO	**DON'T**

> **DO** find the number of available screen fonts by using the FontCount property. For example, to assign the number of screen fonts to the variable NumOfScreenFonts, use the following:
>
> ```
> NumOfScreenFonts = Screen.FontCount
> ```
>
> **DO** find the number of available printer fonts by using the FontCount property. For example, to assign the number of printer fonts to the variable NumOfPrinterFonts, use the following:
>
> ```
> NumOfPrinterFonts = Printer.FontCount
> ```

The Form_Load() procedure fills the item of the cboFontsScreen combo box with the screen fonts:

```
' Fill the items of the combo box with the screen fonts.
For I = 0 To NumOfScreenFonts - 1 Step 1
    cboFontsScreen.AddItem Screen.Fonts(I)
Next
```

Similarly, the procedure fills the items of the cboFontsPrinter combo box with the printer fonts:

```
' Fill the items of the combo box with the printer fonts.
For I = 0 To NumOfPrinterFonts - 1 Step 1
    cboFontsPrinter.AddItem Printer.Fonts(I)
Next
```

You extract the available fonts by using the Fonts property.

DO extract the fonts of the screen by using the Fonts property. For example, to assign the first font of the screen to a string variable called `CurrentScreenFont`, use the following:

```
CurrentScreenFont = Screen.Fonts(0)
```

DO extract the fonts of the printer by using the Fonts property. For example, to assign the ninth font of the printer to a string variable called `CurrentPrinterFont`, use the following:

```
CurrentPrinterFont = Printer.Fonts(8)
```

10

The procedure then initializes the cboFontScreen combo box to the first item:

```
cboFontsScreen.ListIndex = 0
```

Then the font of the text inside the `Sample` label is changed in accordance with the Text property of the combo box:

```
lblSample.FontName = cboFontsScreen.Text
```

The Code Inside the *cboFontsScreen_Click()* Procedure

The code inside the `cboFontsScreen_Click()` procedure is executed whenever the user selects a new screen font from the cboFontsScreen combo box:

```
Sub cboFontsScreen_Click ()

    ' User selected a new screen font. Change the
    ' font of the label in accordance with the user's font selection.
    lblSample.FontName = cboFontsScreen.Text

End Sub
```

The procedure changes the font of the `lblSample` label to the font that was selected.

The Code Inside the *cmdNumberOfFonts_Click()* Procedure

The `cmdNumberOfFonts_Click()` procedure is executed whenever the user clicks the Number of fonts button:

```
Sub cmdNumberOfFonts_Click ()

    ' Display the number of screen fonts in the system.
```

```
    MsgBox "Number of Screen fonts: " + NumOfScreenFonts

    ' Display the number of printer fonts in the system.
    MsgBox "Number of Printer fonts: " + NumOfPrinterFonts

End Sub
```

The procedure displays the number of available screen fonts and the number of available printer fonts using the `MsgBox` statements. The number of available fonts is stored in the variables `NumOfScreenFonts` and `NumOfPrinterFonts`. These variables were updated in the `Form_Load()` procedure.

The Print Method

The Print method may be used to print inside a form and inside a picture control. To display the text `Testing...` inside the frmMyForm form, use the following:

```
frmMyForm.Print "Testing..."
```

To display the text `Testing...` inside the picMyPicture picture control, use the following:

```
picMyPicture.Print "Testing..."
```

The semicolon (;) is used to instruct Visual Basic to place the text on the same line. For example, the following two statements:

```
frmMyForm.Print "This is line number 1 and ";
frmMyForm.Print "it continues..."
```

produce the following output:

```
This is line number 1 and it continues...
```

The following statement produces the same output:

```
frmMyForm.Print "This is line ";"number 1";"and it continues..."
```

Clearing Text

To clear text that was written inside a form or inside a picture control with the Print method, you can use the Cls method. For example, to clear the frmMyForm form, use the following:

```
frmMyForm.Cls
```

To clear the picMyPicture picture control, use the following:

```
picMyPicture.Cls
```

The Cls method clears text as well as graphics drawn with a graphics method.

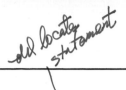
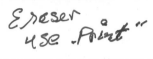

Placing Text at a Specified Location

To place text at a specified location, update the CurrentX and CurrentY properties. For example, to place the text Testing... inside the frmMyForm form at column 5, row 6, use the following:

```
frmMyForm.CurrentX = 5
frmMyForm.CurrentY = 6
frmMyForm.Print "Testing…"
```

Similarly, to place the text Testing... inside the picMyPicture picture control at column 11, row 10, use the following:

```
picMyPicture.CurrentX = 11
picMyPicture.CurrentY = 10
picMyPicture.Print "Testing…"
```

The TextWidth and TextHeight Methods

The TextWidth and TextHeight methods are used to determine the height and width of text. For example, the height of the text AaBbCc is assigned to the variable HeightOfabc as follows:

```
HeightOfabc = frmMyForm.TextHeight("AaBbCc")
```

The returned value of the TextHeight property is given in the same units as indicated by the ScaleMode property.

The TextHeight property is useful when you wish to calculate CurrentY for a certain line. For example, to calculate CurrentY for the tenth row, use the following:

```
CurrentY = frmMyForm.TextHeight("AaBbCc")*9
```

The TextWidth property returns the width of a text. For example, to calculate the width of the text Index, use this statement:

```
WidthOfIndex = frmMyForm.TextWidth("Index")
```

The TextHeight and TextWidth properties return the height and width of the text in accordance with the current value of the FontSize property.

The Index program illustrates how you can use the TextHeight and TextWidth properties to display text at any desired location.

The Visual Implementation of the Index Program

☐ Open a new project, save the form as INDEX.FRM, and save the make file of the project as INDEX.MAK.

☐ Build the frmIndex form according to the specifications in Table 10.4.

The completed form should look like the one shown in Figure 10.14.

Table 10.4. The properties table of frmIndex form.

Object	Property	Setting
Form	**Name**	**frmIndex**
	Caption	The Index Program
	Height	4710
	Left	1035
	Top	1140
	Width	7485
Menu	**(see Table 10.5)**	**(see Table 10.5)**

Table 10.5. The menu table of the frmIndex form.

Caption	Name
&File	mnuFile
...&Display Index	mnuDisplayIndex
...&Erase Chapter 2	mnuEraseCh2
...&Clear text	mnuClear
...E&xit	mnuExit

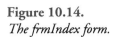

Figure 10.14.
The frmIndex form.

```
┌──────────────────────────────────────────────────┐
│ ▪       The Index Program                    ▼ ▲ │
├──────────────────────────────────────────────────┤
│ File                                             │
│ Display Index  · · · · · · · · · · · · · · · · · │
│ Erase Chapter 2· · · · · · · · · · · · · · · · · │
│ Clear text · · · · · · · · · · · · · · · · · · · │
│ Exit · · · · · · · · · · · · · · · · · · · · · · │
│ · · · · · · · · · · · · · · · · · · · · · · · · ·│
│ · · · · · · · · · · · · · · · · · · · · · · · · ·│
│ · · · · · · · · · · · · · · · · · · · · · · · · ·│
│ · · · · · · · · · · · · · · · · · · · · · · · · ·│
│ · · · · · · · · · · · · · · · · · · · · · · · · ·│
│ · · · · · · · · · · · · · · · · · · · · · · · · ·│
└──────────────────────────────────────────────────┘
```

Entering the Code of the Index Program

☐ Enter the following code inside the general declarations section of the frmIndex form:

```
' All variables MUST be declared.
Option Explicit

Dim Dots
```

☐ Enter the following code inside the `Form_Load()` procedure of the frmIndex form:

```
Sub Form_Load ()

    Dots = String$(84,".")

End Sub
```

☐ Enter the following code inside the `mnuClear_Click()` procedure of the frmIndex form:

```
Sub mnuClear_Click ()

    ' Clear the form.
    frmIndex.Cls

End Sub
```

☐ Enter the following code inside the `mnuDisplayIndex_Click()` procedure of the frmIndex form:

```
Sub mnuDisplayIndex_Click ()


    frmIndex.Cls

    ' Heading should be displayed 100 twips from the top.
    CurrentY = 100
    ' Place the heading at the center of the row.
```

```
    CurrentX = (frmIndex.ScaleWidth - frmIndex.TextWidth("Index")) / 2
    frmIndex.FontUnderline = True
    frmIndex.Print "Index"

    ' Display the chapters.
    frmIndex.FontUnderline = False
    CurrentY = frmIndex.TextHeight("VVV") * 2
    CurrentX = 100
    Print "Chapter 1" + Dots + "The world"

    CurrentY = frmIndex.TextHeight("VVV") * 3
    CurrentX = 100
    Print "Chapter 2" + Dots + "The chair"

    CurrentY = frmIndex.TextHeight("VVV") * 4
    CurrentX = 100
    Print "Chapter 3" + Dots + "The mouse"

    CurrentY = frmIndex.TextHeight("VVV") * 5
    CurrentX = 100
    Print "Chapter 4" + Dots + "The end"

End Sub
```

☐ Enter the following code inside the `mnuEraseCh2_Click()` procedure of the frmIndex form:

```
Sub mnuEraseCh2_Click ()

    Dim LengthOfLine
    Dim HeightOfLine

    ' Erase the line by placing a box with white background over the line.
    CurrentY = frmIndex.TextHeight("VVV") * 3
    CurrentX = 100
    LengthOfLine = frmIndex.TextWidth("Chapter 2" + Dots + "The chair")
    HeightOfLine = frmIndex.TextHeight("C")
    frmIndex.Line -Step(LengthOfLine, HeightOfLine), RGB(255, 255, 255), BF

End Sub
```

☐ Enter the following code inside the `mnuExit_Click()` procedure of the frmIndex form:

```
Sub mnuExit_Click ()

    End

End Sub
```

Executing the Index Program

☐ Execute the Index program.

☐ Select Display Index from the File menu.

The program responds by displaying text shown in Figure 10.15.

Figure 10.15.
Displaying the index.

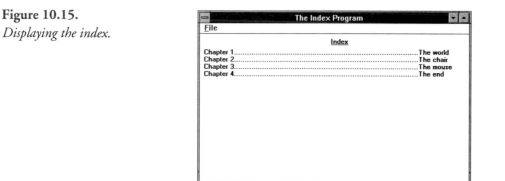

☐ Select Erase Chapter 2 from the File menu.

The program responds by erasing the Chapter 2 line (see Figure 10.16).

Figure 10.16.
Erasing the Chapter 2 line.

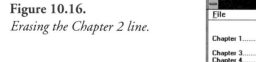

☐ Select Clear text from the File menu.

The program responds by erasing the text from the form.

How the Index Program Works

The Index program displays text with the Print method. You display the text at any desired location by updating the CurrentX and CurrentY properties.

The Code Inside the General Declarations Section of the frmIndex Form

The code inside the general declarations section of the frmIndex form declares the variable Dots. This variable, therefore, is visible in all the procedures of the frmIndex form.

The Code Inside the *Form_Load()* Procedure of the frmIndex Form

The Form_Load() procedure is executed when the frmIndex form is loaded:

```
Sub Form_Load ()

    Dots = String$(84,".")

End Sub
```

This procedure stores 84 dots inside the Dots variable.

The Code Inside the *mnuClear_Click()* Procedure of the frmIndex Form

The mnuClear_Click() procedure is executed whenever the user selects the Clear text from the File menu:

```
Sub mnuClear_Click ()

    ' Clear the form.
    frmIndex.Cls

End Sub
```

This procedure uses the Cls method to clear the form.

The Code Inside the *mnuDisplayIndex_Click()* Procedure of the frmIndex Form

The mnuDisplayIndex_Click() procedure is executed whenever the user selects Display Index from the File menu.

The procedure clears the text (if any) from the form and then updates CurrentY with 100. This causes text to be displayed 100 twips from the top:

SAMS
Sams
Learning
Center
SAMS
PUBLISHING

```
frmIndex.Cls
CurrentY = 100
```

Because the text Index should be displayed at the center of the form (see Figure 10.15), the CurrentX property is updated as follows:

```
CurrentX = (frmIndex.ScaleWidth - frmIndex.TextWidth("Index")) / 2
```

The procedure sets the FontUnderline property to True and uses the Print method to display the text Index:

```
frmIndex.FontUnderline = True
frmIndex.Print "Index"
```

The rest of the text is displayed as non-underlined text, so the FontUnderline property is set to False:

```
frmIndex.FontUnderline = False
```

The CurrentY property is updated for the Chapter 1 line as follows:

```
CurrentY = frmIndex.TextHeight("VVV") * 2
```

The CurrentX property is updated to 100 twips so that the line starts 100 twips from the left of the form:

```
CurrentX = 100
```

Now that CurrentX and CurrentY are updated, the Print method is used to display the text:

```
Print "Chapter 1" + Dots + "The world"
```

The rest of the lines are displayed in a similar manner.

Note that if you omit the name of the object before the Print method, the Print method displays text inside the currently active form. Therefore, this statement:

```
frmIndex.Print "Index"
```

produces the same result as does this statement:

```
Print "Index"
```

Similarly, in this procedure the CurrentX and CurrentY properties were updated without preceding these properties with the form name. When you omit the name of the object, Visual Basic updates the properties of the currently active form. For example, if the currently active form is frmIndex, the following two statements are identical:

```
frmIndex.CurrentY = 100
```

```
CurrentY = 100
```

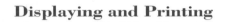
The Code Inside the *mnuEraseCh2_Click()* Procedure of the frmIndex Form

The mnuEraseCh2_Click() procedure is executed when the user selects Erase Chapter 2 from the File menu:

```
Sub mnuEraseCh2_Click ()

    Dim LengthOfLine
    Dim HeightOfLine

    ' Erase the line by placing a box with white
    ' background over the line.
    CurrentY = frmIndex.TextHeight("VVV") * 3
    CurrentX = 100
    LengthOfLine = frmIndex.TextWidth("Chapter 2" + Dots + "The chair")

    HeightOfLine = frmIndex.TextHeight("C")
    frmIndex.Line -Step(LengthOfLine, HeightOfLine), RGB(255, 255, 255), BF

End Sub
```

This procedure sets the CurrentX and CurrentY properties to the location where the Chapter 2 line starts and then draws a box with a white background. The width of the box is calculated using the TextWidth property.

Displaying Tables

You may use the Print method to display tables inside a form or inside a picture control. To see how this is accomplished do the following:

☐ Add the Table menu and Display Table menu item to the menu of the Index program. The new menu table is shown in Table 10.6

Table 10.6. The menu table of the frmIndex form.

Caption	Name
&File	mnuFile
...&Display Index	mnuDisplayIndex
...&Erase Chapter 2	mnuEraseCh2
...&Clear text	mnuClear
...&Exit	mnuExit
&Table	mnuTable
...&Display Table	mnuDisplayTable

☐ Add the following code inside the `mnuDisplayTable_Click()` menu of the frmIndex form:

```
Sub mnuDisplayTable_Click ()

    ' Clear the form.
    frmIndex.Cls

    ' Set the FontName and FontSize properties.
    frmIndex.FontName = "MS Sans Serif"
    frmIndex.FontSize = 10

    ' Display the heading.
    frmIndex.Print "Chapter", "Description", "Page"

    ' Display a blank line.
    frmIndex.Print

    ' Display the table.
    frmIndex.Print "1", "The world", "1"
    frmIndex.Print "2", "The chair", "12"
    frmIndex.Print "3", "The mouse", "42"
    frmIndex.Print "4", "The end", "100"

End Sub
```

Executing the Enhanced Version of the Index Program

☐ Execute the enhanced version of the Index program.

☐ Select Display Table from the table menu.

> *The program responds by displaying the table, as shown in Figure 10.17.*

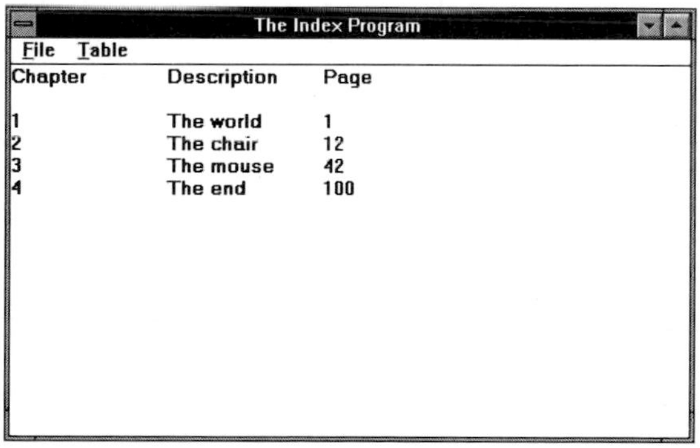

Figure 10.17.
The table of the Index program.

☐ Select Exit from the File menu to terminate the program.

The code inside the `mnuDisplayTable_Click()` procedure uses the Print method with commas:

```
frmIndex.Print "Chapter", "Description", "Page"
```

This causes the first string ("Chapter") to be displayed starting at column 0. The second string ("Description") is displayed starting at column 14, and the third string ("Page") is displayed starting at column 28. The commas are an indication to Visual Basic to change printing zones. (By default, Visual Basic defines each printing zone as 13 characters.)

Note: To print strings that start at different printing zones, use the Print method and type commas between the strings.

For example, the following statements:

```
Print "abc", "def", "ghj"
 Print "nop", "qrs", "tuv"
 Print "ABC", "DEF", "GHI"
```

produce the following output:

```
abc        def        ghj
nop        qrs        tuv
ABC        DEF        GHI
```

You may define new printing zones by using the Tab function.

☐ Replace the code inside the mnuDisplayTable_Click() procedure with the following code:

```
Sub mnuDisplayTable_Click ()

    ' Clear the form.
    frmIndex.Cls

    ' Set the FontName and FontSize properties.
    frmIndex.FontName = "MS Sans Serif"
    frmIndex.FontSize = 10

    frmIndex.Print Tab(5); "Chapter"; Tab(20); "Description"; Tab(50); "Page"

    ' Display a blank line.
    frmIndex.Print

    ' Display the table.
    frmIndex.Print Tab(5); "1"; Tab(20); "The world"; Tab(50); "1"
    frmIndex.Print Tab(5); "2"; Tab(20); "The chair"; Tab(50); "12"
    frmIndex.Print Tab(5); "3"; Tab(20); "The mouse"; Tab(50); "42"
    frmIndex.Print Tab(5); "4"; Tab(20); "The end"; Tab(50); "100"

End Sub
```

☐ Execute the Index program.

☐ Select Display Table from the Table menu.

The program responds by displaying the table, as shown in Figure 10.18.

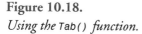

Figure 10.18.
Using the Tab() *function.*

```
┌─────────────────────────────────────────────────────┐
│ ▬              The Index Program              ▼ ▲ │
│ File  Table                                          │
│ ┌───────────────────────────────────────────────┐  │
│ │   Chapter        Description           Page    │  │
│ │                                                │  │
│ │   1              The world             1       │  │
│ │   2              The chair             12      │  │
│ │   3              The mouse             42      │  │
│ │   4              The end               100     │  │
│ │                                                │  │
│ │                                                │  │
│ │                                                │  │
│ │                                                │  │
│ │                                                │  │
│ │                                                │  │
│ │                                                │  │
│ │                                                │  │
│ └───────────────────────────────────────────────┘  │
└─────────────────────────────────────────────────────┘
```

The Tab() function causes the text to be displayed at the columns indicated by the argument of the Tab() function.

For example, the following statement displays the Chapter 1 line:

```
frmIndex.Print Tab(5); "1"; Tab(20); "The world"; Tab(50); "1"
```

The first argument of the Print method is Tab(5);. This sets CurrentX at column 5. The semicolon (;) instructs Visual Basic to stay on the current line.

The second argument of the Print method is 1. This causes the text 1 to be displayed at column 5.

The third argument of the Print method is Tab(20);. This sets CurrentX to column 20. The semicolon (;) instructs Visual Basic to stay on the same line. Therefore, the fourth argument (the string "The World") is displayed starting at column 20.

As you can see, the Tab() function enables you to display text at any desired column.

Formatting Numbers, Dates, and Times

The Format$() function is used to display numbers, dates, and times in different ways. This section discusses the Format$() function.

Formatting Numbers

You may have control over the way Visual Basic displays numbers by using the Format$() function. The Format$() function has two arguments: The first argument is the number to be displayed, and the second number serves as a format instruction. For example, to display the number 45.6 with leading and trailing zeros, use the following statement:

```
Print Format$(45.6, "000000.00")
```

The result is this:

```
000045.60
```

That is, the number 45.6 contains two digits to the left of the decimal point, and one digit to the right of the decimal point. The second argument contains `000000.00`. This means that there should be six digits to the left of the decimal point and two digits to the right of the decimal point. Because 45.6 has two digits before the decimal point, Visual Basic inserts four leading zeros. And because 45.6 has one digit to the right of the decimal point, Visual Basic inserts one trailing zero.

This feature is used to display numbers in a column where the decimal points are placed one under the other as in the following:

```
000324.45
000123.40
123546.67
000004.90
132123.76
```

To display numbers without leading and trailing zeros, use statements such as the following:

```
Print Format$(4.9, "######.##")
Print Format$(123.4, "######.##")
```

Visual Basic places 4.9 and 123.4 as follows:

```
  4.9
123.4
```

The decimal points are aligned, and because you specified # instead of 0 in the second argument of the `Format$()` function, no leading and trailing zeros are displayed.

Formatting Dates

You can use the following statement:

```
Print Format$(Now, "m/d/yy")
```

to display today's date. For example, if today's date is July 4, 1995, the preceding statement produces this output:

```
7/4/95
```

The `Now` function is used in the first argument of the `Format$()` function to supply the date, and the `m/d/yy` is supplied as the format indicator to format the date to month/day/year.

The following statement:

```
Print Format$(Now, "dddd, mmmm dd, yyyy")
```

produces this:

```
Monday, July 4, 1995
```

The following statement:

```
Print Format$(Now, "mmmm-yy")
```

produces this:

```
July-95
```

The Now function may also be used to display the current time. For example, this statement:

```
Print Format$(Now, "h:mm:ss a/p")
```

produces the following:

```
4:23:00 a
```

Using the Printer

The Print program demonstrates how easy it is to send data to the printer with the PrintForm method.

The Visual Implementation of the Print Program

☐ Open a new project, save the form of the project as PRINT.FRM, and save the make file of the project as PRINT.MAK.

☐ Build the frmPrint form according to the specifications in Table 10.7.

The complete form should look like the one shown in Figure 10.19.

Table 10.7. The properties table of frmPrint form.

Object	Property	Setting
Form	**Name**	**frmPrint**
	Caption	The Print Program
	Height	4425
	Left	1035
	Top	1140
	Width	7485
Command Button	**Name**	**cmdPrint**
	Caption	&Print
	Height	1335

Table 10.7. continued

Object	Property	Setting
	Left	240
	Top	2520
	Width	1455
Command Button	**Name**	**cmdExit**
	Caption	&Exit
	Height	495
	Left	6000
	Top	3240
	Width	1215

Figure 10.19.
The frmPrint form.

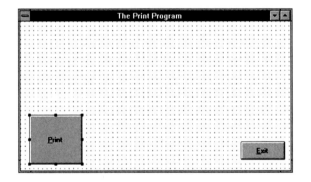

Entering the Code of the Print Program

☐ Enter the following code inside the general declarations section of the frmPrint form:

```
' All variables MUST be declared.
Option Explicit
```

☐ Enter the following code inside the cmdExit_Click() procedure of the frmPrint form:

```
Sub cmdExit_Click ()

    End

End Sub
```

☐ Enter the following code inside the cmdPrint_Click() procedure of the frmPrint form:

```
Sub cmdPrint_Click ()

    ' Print.
    Printer.Print "Testing... 1 2 3...Testing"
```

```
    Printer.EndDoc

End Sub
```

Executing the Print Program

☐ Make sure that your printer is ready to print.

☐ Execute the Print program.

☐ Click the Print button.

The program responds by printing text Testing… 1 2 3…Testing.

How the Print Program Works

The Print program uses the Print method to send data to the printer. The EndDoc method sends the "start printing" command to the printer device.

The Code Inside the *cmdPrint_Click()* Procedure of the Print Program

The cmdPrint_Click() procedure is executed whenever the user clicks the Print button:

```
Sub cmdPrint_Click ()

    ' Print.
    Printer.Print "Testing… 1 2 3…Testing"
    Printer.EndDoc

End Sub
```

The Print method is used with the Printer object. The argument of the Print method, "Testing… 1 2 3… Testing", is printed as soon as the EndDoc method is executed.

Enhancing the Print Program

The Print method sends the text that appears as its argument to the printer. Now enhance the Print program so that the printer prints the contents of the frmPrint form:

☐ Replace the cmdPrint_Click() procedure with the following code:

```
Sub cmdPrint_Click ()

    ' Display text inside the form.
    frmPrint.Print "Testing… 1 2 3…Testing"

    ' Print the form's contents.
    frmPrint.PrintForm
    Printer.EndDoc

End Sub
```

☐ It is very important that you set the AutoRedraw property of the frmPrint form to True.

Executing the Enhanced Version of the Print Program

☐ Execute the enhanced version of the Print program.

☐ Click the Print button.

The program responds by printing the contents of the form.

☐ Click the Exit button to terminate the program.

The Code Inside the Enhanced Version of the *cmdPrint_Click()* Procedure of the frmPrint Form

The cmdPrint_Click() procedure displays the text Testing... 1 2 3 Testing inside the form using the Print method on the form:

```
frmPrint.Print "Testing… 1 2 3…Testing"
```

Therefore, the form contains this text and two command buttons (Exit and Print).

The PrintForm method sends to the printer the content of the form, pixel by pixel:

```
' Print the contents of the form.
frmPrint.PrintForm
Printer.EndDoc
```

The last thing this procedure does is execute the EndDoc method, causing the printer to print the data it received.

DO	**DON'T**
DO use the PrintForm method to send the contents of the form to the printer.	

Note: The AutoRedraw property of the form must be set to True in order for PrintForm to work properly. For example, to send the contents of the frmMyForm form to the printer, use the following:

```
frmMyForm.PrintForm
```

Printing Several Pages

You may print several pages using the NewPage property. Visual Basic keeps track of the number of pages printed by updating the Page property. Use the following steps to print several pages:

☐ Replace the code inside the cmdPrint_Click() procedure with the following code:

```
Sub cmdPrint_Click ()

    Printer.Print "This is page number " + Printer.Page
    Printer.NewPage
    Printer.Print "This is page number " + Printer.Page
    Printer.EndDoc

End Sub
```

☐ Execute the Print program.

☐ Click the Print button.

> *The program responds by printing two pages. The first page is printed with* This is page number 1, *and the second page is printed with* This is page number 2.

☐ Click the Exit button to terminate the program.

The cmdPrint_Click() procedure prints the string This is page number + Printer.Page.

The Page property contains the current page number. Because this is the first printed page, Visual Basic automatically updates this property with 1.

The procedure then declares a new page by using the NewPage method:

```
Printer.NewPage
```

and sends to the printer this string:

```
This is page number + Printer.Page
```

Because the value of the Page property is currently 2, the printer prints the text This is page number 2.

Printing Images, Picture Controls, and Graphics

To print pictures, you may place bitmaps inside images and picture controls and then print the form with the PrintForm method.

Printing with Better Quality

The Print program illustrates how easy it is to send data to the printer with the Print method (text) and the PrintForm method (contents of the form). The best resolution that the hard copy that is produced by the PrintForm can have is determined by the resolution of the monitor. To obtain a better resolution, your program can use the PSet, Line, and Circle methods.

Generally speaking, you draw inside the Printer object just as you draw inside a form. Therefore you may set the CurrentX and CurrentY properties of the Printer object, as in the following:

```
Printer.CurrentX = 0
Printer.CurrentY = 0
```

You can use properties such as the following:

```
Printer.ScaleLeft
Printer.ScaleTop
Printer.Width
Printer.Height
```

To help you position text at specific locations, your program can use the TextHeight and TextWidth properties.

☐ Replace the code inside the cmdPrint_Click() procedure with the following code:

```
Sub cmdPrint_Click ()

    Printer.DrawWidth = 4
    Printer.Line (1000, 1000)-Step(1000, 1000)
    Printer.Circle (3000, 3000), 1000
    Printer.EndDoc

End Sub
```

The procedure sets the DrawWidth property of the printer to 4, draws a line and a circle, and then executes the EndDoc method. The output is shown in Figure 10.20.

As you can see, the preceding code is no different from the code that draws inside a form or inside a picture control.

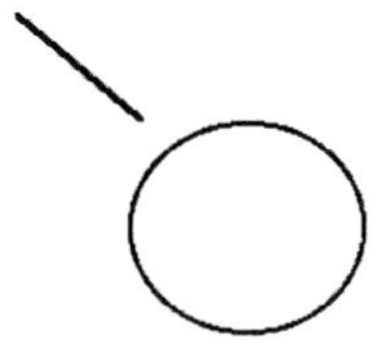

Figure 10.20.
Drawing a line and a circle
with the Printer object.

Summary

In this chapter you have learned how to set text to the desired font by changing the FontName, FontSize, FontBold, FontItalic, FontStrikethru, FontUnderline, and FontTransparent properties. You have learned how to extract the Screen and Printer fonts with the Fonts property, and how to extract the number of available fonts with the FontCount property. You have also learned how to use the TextWidth and TextHeight properties, and the Tab() function.

The chapter discusses how to send data (text and graphics) to the printer using two techniques:

- The PrintForm method. This method sends the content of the form, pixel by pixel, to the Printer.

- The Print and graphics methods, such as the following:

```
Printer.Print "Abc"
Printer.Line -(1000,1000)
Printer.Circle (400,500),800
Printer.EndDoc
```

Q&A

Q **I want to write a program that has WYSIWYG capability. How can I make sure the user chooses only the screen fonts that have corresponding printer fonts?**

A The Fonts program illustrates how you can extract the screen and printer fonts using the Fonts property. To achieve WYSIWYG, you must make sure that the screen fonts you use are available for the printer. This is easily accomplished by building a list that contains the screen fonts using the Fonts property of the screen. Then build another list that contains the printer fonts by using the Fonts property of the printer. Once you have the two lists, you can create a third list that contains only the fonts that appear in both lists. Your program should let the user choose a font from the third list only.

Quiz

1. When you set the FontTransparent property to True and then display text inside a form with the Print method, which of the following happens?

    a. The text will be drawn with white color.

    b. The text will not be visible.

    c. The text is displayed with the same background of the form.

2. The FontCount property is used to do which of the following:

    a. Assign a counting number to the fonts

    b. No such thing

    c. Extract the number of available fonts

3. The Fonts property is used to do which of the following:

    a. Extract the names of available fonts

    b. Assign a new font

    c. Remove a font

4. WYSIWYG is the capability to do which of the following:

    a. Speak a foreign language

    b. Print a hard copy that is an exact replica of the screen

    c. No meaning, just rubbish

5. What does the TextHeight property return?

6. What does the TextWidth property return?

7. To print the contents of a form, you'd use which of the following:

   a. The Print screen key

   b. The Print method

   c. The PrintForm method

Exercise

Write a program that asks the user to enter his/her date of birth. The program should respond by displaying the day of the week when this happy event occurred.

Quiz Answers

1. c

2. c

3. a

4. b

5. The height of the characters that are specified in the argument of the TextHeight property.

6. The width of the characters that are specified in the argument of the TextWidth property.

7. c

Exercise Answer

One possible solution is the following:

☐ Build a form with a command button called Enter Birthday and a command button called Find Day of Week.

The code inside the `cmdEnterBirthday_Click()` procedure should display an input box that asks the user to enter the data. For example, the following statement can be used:

```
UserDate = InputBox("Enter date")
```

The code inside the `cmdFindDayOfWeek` procedure may include this statement:

```
Print "Day of Week:", Format$(UserDate, "dddd")
```

Interfacing with Windows

The programs you write with Visual Basic are Windows programs. Therefore, you are entitled to use the various standard Windows features. In this chapter you'll learn to use two of these features: the Clipboard interface and idle loops.

The Clipboard Object

The Visual Basic programs that you write may use the Windows Clipboard. The Clipboard is used to transfer data, which may be text or picture files.

You will write a program called Clip, which enables you to type text inside a text box and perform the standard Windows edit manipulations. The program has a standard Edit menu that enables you to copy, cut, and paste text.

The Visual Implementation of the Clip Program

☐ Start a new project. Save the form of the project as CLIP.FRM and save the make file of the project as CLIP.MAK.

☐ Build the form of the Clip program according to the specifications in Table 11.1.

The completed form should look like the one shown in Figure 11.1.

Table 11.1. The properties table of the Clip program.

Object	Property	Setting
Form	**Name**	**frmClip**
	Caption	The Clip Program
	Height	4710
	Left	1035
	Top	1140
	Width	7485
Menu	**(see Table 11.2)**	**(see Table 11.2)**
Text Box	**Name**	**txtUserArea**
	Text	(empty)
	MultiLine	True
	ScrollBars	3-Both
	Height	2055
	Left	0

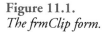

Object	Property	Setting
	Top	0
	Width	5055

Table 11.2. The menu table of the Clip program.

Caption	Name	Shortcut
&File	mnuFile	None
...&Exit	mnuExit	None
Edit	mnuEdit	None
...&Copy	mnuCopy	Ctrl+C
...C&ut	mnuCut	Ctrl+X
...&Paste	mnuPaste	Ctrl+V

Figure 11.1.
The frmClip form.

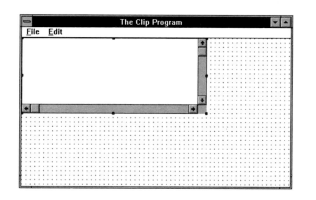

Entering the Code of the Clip Program

☐ Enter the following code inside the general declarations section of the frmClip form:

```
' All variables MUST be declared.
Option Explicit
```

☐ Enter the following code inside the Form_Resize() procedure:

```
Sub Form_Resize ()

    ' Make the text box cover the entire form area.
    txtUserArea.Width = frmClip.ScaleWidth
    txtUserArea.Height = frmClip.ScaleHeight

End Sub
```

☐ Enter the following code inside the mnuCopy_Click() procedure:

369

```
Sub mnuCopy_Click ()

    ' Clear the clipboard.
    Clipboard.Clear

    ' Transfer to the clipboard the currently selected text of the text box.
    Clipboard.SetText txtUserArea.SelText

End Sub
```

☐ Enter the following code inside the `mnuCut_Click()` procedure:

```
Sub mnuCut_Click ()

    ' Clear the clipboard.
    Clipboard.Clear

    ' Transfer to the clipboard the currently selected text of the text box.
    Clipboard.SetText txtUserArea.SelText

    ' Replace the currently selected text of the text box with null.
    txtUserArea.SelText = ""

End Sub
```

☐ Enter the following code inside the `mnuPaste_Click()` procedure:

```
Sub mnuPaste_Click ()

    ' Replace the currently selected area of the
    ' text box with the content of the clipboard.
    ' If nothing is selected in the text box,
    ' transfer the text of the clipboard to the text
    ' box at the current location of the cursor.
    txtUserArea.SelText = Clipboard.GetText()

End Sub
```

☐ Enter the following code inside the `mnuExit_Click()` procedure:

```
Sub mnuExit_Click ()

    End

End Sub
```

Executing the Clip Program

Execute the Clip program and note the many features it has (even though you have written only a small amount of code).

Experiment with the copy, cut, and paste operations of the program. Try to copy text from one part of the text box to another part of the text box. Try to copy text to and from another Windows program. For example, try to copy text to and from Word for Windows (if you do not have Word for Windows, copy text from Write, a word processing program that is shipped with Windows).

How the Clip Program Works

The Clip program uses the Form_Resize() procedure to fill the entire form with the text box and the mnuCopy_Click(), mnuCut_Clip(), and mnuPaste_Click() procedures to perform standard edit manipulations.

The Code Inside the *Form_Resize()* Event Procedure

The Form_Resize() procedure is executed whenever the form pops up and whenever the size of the form changes.

Throughout the program, the text box should fill the entire area of the form. Therefore, this is a good place to put the code that causes the text box to cover the entire area of the form. You accomplish this by changing the Width and Height properties of the text box to the ScaleWidth and ScaleHeight properties of the form:

```
Sub Form_Resize ()

    ' Make the text box cover the entire form area.
    txtUserArea.Width = frmClip.ScaleWidth
    txtUserArea.Height = frmClip.ScaleHeight

End Sub
```

The Code Inside the *mnuCopy_Click()* Event Procedure

The mnuCopy_Click() procedure is executed whenever you select Copy from the Edit menu:

```
Sub mnuCopy_Click ()

    ' Clear the clipboard.
    Clipboard.Clear

    ' Transfer the currently selected text of the text box to the clipboard.
    Clipboard.SetText txtUserArea.SelText

End Sub
```

Copy means copy the highlighted text of the text box into the Clipboard.

The first statement in this procedure clears the Clipboard:

```
Clipboard.Clear
```

Then the selected area inside the text box is copied to the Clipboard:

```
Clipboard.SetText txtUserArea.SelText
```

DO	DON'T

DO clear the Clipboard by using the Clear method:

```
Clipboard.Clear
```

DO copy selected text from a text box to the Clipboard by using the following:

```
Clipboard.SetText  Name of text box object.SelText
```

For example, to copy the highlighted (selected) text of the txtUserArea text box to the Clipboard, use the following:

```
Clipboard.SetText txtUserArea.SelText
```

The Code Inside the *mnuCutClick( )* Event Procedure

The mnuCut_Click() procedure is executed whenever you select Cut from the Edit menu:

```
Sub mnuCut_Click ()

    ' Clear the clipboard.
    Clipboard.Clear

    ' Transfer the currently selected text of the text box to the clipboard.
    Clipboard.SetText txtUserArea.SelText

    ' Replace the currently selected text of the text box with null.
    txtUserArea.SelText = ""

End Sub
```

Cut means copy the highlighted text to the Clipboard and delete the highlighted text.

The first statement in this procedure clears the Clipboard:

```
Clipboard.Clear
```

Then the highlighted (selected) text of the text box is copied to the Clipboard:

```
Clipboard.SetText txtUserArea.SelText
```

The last thing the procedure does is delete the currently highlighted (selected) text in the text box:

```
txtUserArea.SelText = ""
```

The Code Inside the *mnuPaste_Click()* Event Procedure

The mnuPaste_Click() procedure is executed whenever you select Paste from the Edit menu:

```
Sub mnuPaste_Click ()

    txtUserArea.SelText = Clipboard.GetText()

End Sub
```

Paste means replace the highlighted area of the text box with the contents of the Clipboard. If the text box does not currently have highlighted text in it, the contents of the Clipboard are inserted inside the text box at the current cursor location of the text box. This is accomplished with the following statement:

```
txtUserArea.SelText = Clipboard.GetText()
```

DO	DON'T

DO paste the contents of the Clipboard to a text box by using the following:

```
Name of text box.SelText = Clipboard.GetText()
```

For example, to paste the contents of the Clipboard to a text box called txtUserArea, use the following:

```
txtUserArea.SelText = Clipboard.GetText()
```

TheSelLength Property

The SelLength property is defined as a long variable, and it contains the number of characters that are currently highlighted (selected). Although the Clip program does not make use of this property, you may find a use for this property in your future Visual Basic projects.

For example, to determine the number of characters that are currently selected in txtMyTextBox, use the following:

```
NumberOfCharacters = txtMyTextBox.SelLength
```

Transferring Pictures to and from the Clipboard

The Clip program demonstrates how to transfer text between the Clipboard and a text box. The Clipboard is also capable of accepting pictures from picture holder controls. The AnyData program illustrates this capability.

The Visual Implementation of the AnyData Program

☐ Start a new project. Save the form of the project as AnyData.frm and save the make file of the project as AnyData.mak.

☐ Build the form according to the specifications in Table 11.3.

The completed form should look like the one shown in Figure 11.2.

Table 11.3. The properties table of the AnyData program.

Object	Property	Setting
Form	**Name**	**frmAnyData**
	Caption	The AnyData Program
	BackColor	(gray)
	Height	4710
	Left	1035
	Top	1140
	Width	7485
Text Box	**Name**	**txtUserArea**
	Text	(empty)
	MultiLine	True
	ScrollBars	3-Both
	Tag	The txtUserArea
	Height	975
	Left	3600
	Top	2880
	Width	3375
Combo Box	**Name**	**cboList**
	Text	(empty)
	Tag	The cboList
	Height	300
	Left	5160
	Top	1680
	Width	1215

Object	Property	Setting
List Box	**Name**	**lstList**
	Tag	The lstList
	Height	1005
	Left	3720
	Top	1680
	Width	1215
Picture Box	**Name**	**picMyPicture**
	Tag	The picMyPicture
	Height	3015
	Left	360
	Top	840
	Width	2655
Menu	**(see Table 11.4)**	**(see Table 11.4)**

Table 11.4. The menu table of the AnyData program.

Caption	Name
&File	mnuFile
...&Exit	mnuExit
Edit	mnuEdit
...&Copy	mnuCopy
...C&ut	mnuCut
...&Paste	mnuPaste

Figure 11.2.
The frmAnyData form.

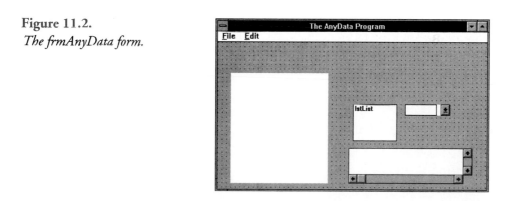

Entering the Code of the AnyData Program

☐ Enter the following code inside the general declarations section of the frmAnyData form:

```
' All variables must be declared.
Option Explicit
```

☐ Enter the following code inside the `Form_Load()` procedure:

```
Sub Form_Load ()

    ' Fill three items inside the combo box.
    cboList.AddItem "Clock"
    cboList.AddItem "Cup"
    cboList.AddItem "Bell"

    ' Fill three items inside the list control.
    lstList.AddItem "One"
    lstList.AddItem "Two"
    lstList.AddItem "Three"

End Sub
```

☐ Enter the following code inside the `picMyPicture_GotFocus()` procedure:

```
Sub picMyPicture_GotFocus ()

    ' Change the BorderStyle so that user will be
    ' able to tell that the picture control got the
    ' focus (that is, selected).
    picMyPicture.BorderStyle = 1

End Sub
```

☐ Enter the following code inside the `picMyPicture_LostFocus()` procedure:

```
Sub picMyPicture_LostFocus ()

    ' Change the BorderStyle so that user will be
    ' able to tell that the picture control lost the
    ' focus (that is, not selected).
    picMyPicture.BorderStyle = 0

End Sub
```

☐ Enter the following code inside the `mnuCopy_Click()` procedure:

```
Sub mnuCopy_Click ()

    ' Clear the clipboard.
    Clipboard.Clear

    ' Find which is the currently active control, and
    ' copy its highlighted content to the clipboard.
    If TypeOf Screen.ActiveControl Is TextBox Then
        Clipboard.SetText Screen.ActiveControl.SelText

    ElseIf TypeOf Screen.ActiveControl Is ComboBox Then
        Clipboard.SetText Screen.ActiveControl.Text
```

```
    ElseIf TypeOf Screen.ActiveControl Is PictureBox Then
        Clipboard.SetData Screen.ActiveControl.Picture

    ElseIf TypeOf Screen.ActiveControl Is ListBox Then
        Clipboard.SetText Screen.ActiveControl.Text

    Else
        ' Do nothing
    End If

End Sub
```

☐ Enter the following code inside the `mnuCut_Click()` procedure:

```
Sub mnuCut_Click ()

    'Execute the mnuCopy_Click() procedure
    mnuCopy_Click

    ' Find which is the currently highlighted control,
    ' and remove its highlighted content.
    If TypeOf Screen.ActiveControl Is TextBox Then
        Screen.ActiveControl.SelText = ""

    ElseIf TypeOf Screen.ActiveControl Is ComboBox Then
        Screen.ActiveControl.Text = ""

    ElseIf TypeOf Screen.ActiveControl Is PictureBox Then
        Screen.ActiveControl.Picture = LoadPicture()

    ElseIf TypeOf Screen.ActiveControl Is ListBox Then
        If Screen.ActiveControl.ListIndex >= 0 Then
            Screen.ActiveControl.RemoveItem Screen.ActiveControl.ListIndex
        End If
    Else
        ' Do nothing
    End If

End Sub
```

☐ Enter the following code inside the `mnuPaste_Click()` procedure:

```
Sub mnuPaste_Click ()

    ' Find which is the currently active control and
    ' paste the content of the clipboard to it.
    If TypeOf Screen.ActiveControl Is TextBox Then
        Screen.ActiveControl.SelText = Clipboard.GetText()

    ElseIf TypeOf Screen.ActiveControl Is ComboBox Then
        Screen.ActiveControl.Text = Clipboard.GetText()

    ElseIf TypeOf Screen.ActiveControl Is PictureBox Then
        Screen.ActiveControl.Picture = Clipboard.GetData()

    ElseIf TypeOf Screen.ActiveControl Is ListBox Then
        Screen.ActiveControl.AddItem Clipboard.GetText()
```

```
      Else
           ' Do nothing
      End If
```

End Sub

☐ Enter the following code inside the `mnuExit_Click()` procedure:

Sub mnuExit_Click ()

```
      End
```

End Sub

Executing the AnyData Program

☐ Execute the AnyData program.

The AnyData program lets you copy, cut, and paste data from and to the Clipboard. The data may be either text or pictures.

Use the following steps to copy a picture from Paintbrush to the picture box of the AnyData program:

☐ Start Paintbrush (while AnyData is still running).

☐ Draw something in Paintbrush.

☐ Copy a section of your drawing to the Clipboard by selecting a section and then selecting Copy from the Edit menu of Paintbrush. (For example, in Figure 11.3, the portion of the picture that includes the head of the man was copied to the Clipboard.)

Figure 11.3.
Using Paintbrush to draw a picture that will be copied to the AnyData program.

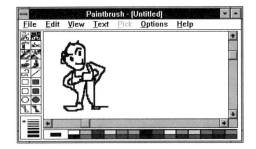

☐ Switch to the AnyData program.

☐ Make the picMyPicture picture control the active control. To make picMyPicture the active control, click inside it. You can tell that the picture box is selected by looking at its borders. If it has a border, it is selected.

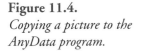

☐ Select Paste from the Edit menu.

> *The AnyData program responds by transferring the picture that is inside the Clipboard into picMyPicture (see Figure 11.4).*

Figure 11.4.
Copying a picture to the AnyData program.

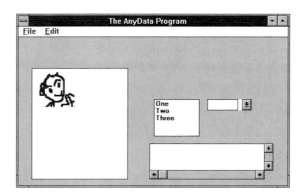

☐ The AnyData program also lets you copy, cut, and paste text to and from the text box, list box, and the combo box controls of the program. Experiment with these controls for a while. You can't paste pictures into the text box, list box, or the combo box, and you can't paste text into the picture box.

Before pasting data into an object, you must select the object by clicking inside it. You can tell which object is selected by doing the following:

- When a text box is selected, Visual Basic places a blinking cursor inside it.
- When a combo box is selected, Visual Basic places a blinking cursor on the currently selected item.
- When a list box is selected, Visual Basic places a rectangle around the selected item in the list box.

How the AnyData Program Works

The AnyData program uses the `mnuCopy_Click()`, `mnuCut_Click()`, and `mnuPaste_Click()` procedures to transfer text and pictures to and from the Clipboard.

The Code Inside the *Form_Load()* Event Procedure

The `Form_Load()` procedure is executed upon startup of the program:

```
Sub Form_Load ()

    ' Fill three items inside the combo box.
```

```
cboList.AddItem "Clock"
cboList.AddItem "Cup"
cboList.AddItem "Bell"

' Fill three items inside the list control.
lstList.AddItem "One"
lstList.AddItem "Two"
lstList.AddItem "Three"
```

End Sub

The code in this procedure fills three items in the combo box and three items in the list box.

The Code Inside the *picMyPicture_GotFocus()* Event Procedure

The `picMyPicture_GotFocus()` procedure is executed whenever the picture box gets the focus (that is, whenever you select the picture):

```
Sub picMyPicture_GotFocus ()

    ' Change the BorderStyle so that you will be
    ' able to tell that the picture control got the
    ' focus (that is, selected).
    picMyPicture.BorderStyle = 1
```

End Sub

Unlike the text box, combo box, and list box, when the picture box is selected, Visual Basic does not give any visible indication that the picture box is currently selected. This procedure changes the BorderStyle property of the picture box, so that you will realize that the picture box is selected. Setting the BorderStyle property of the picture box to 1 causes a border to appear around the picture control.

The Code Inside the *picMyPicture_LostFocus()* Event Procedure

The `picMyPicture_LostFocus()` procedure is executed whenever the picture box loses the focus:

```
Sub picMyPicture_LostFocus ()

    ' Change the BorderStyle so that you will be
    ' able to tell that the picture control lost the
    ' focus (that is, not selected).
    picMyPicture.BorderStyle = 0
```

End Sub

The code in this procedure removes the border around the picture control by setting its BorderStyle property to 0. This gives you a visual indication that the picture box is not selected.

The Code Inside the *mnuCopy_Click()* Event Procedure

The mnuCopy_Click() procedure is executed whenever you select Copy from the Edit menu. The code inside this procedure clears the Clipboard and copies the highlighted contents of the control to the Clipboard:

```
Sub mnuCopy_Click ()

    ' Clear the clipboard.
    Clipboard.Clear

    ' Find which is the currently active control and
    '  copy its highlighted content to the clipboard.
    If TypeOf Screen.ActiveControl Is TextBox Then
        Clipboard.SetText Screen.ActiveControl.SelText

    ElseIf TypeOf Screen.ActiveControl Is ComboBox Then
        Clipboard.SetText Screen.ActiveControl.Text

    ElseIf TypeOf Screen.ActiveControl Is PictureBox Then
        Clipboard.SetData Screen.ActiveControl.Picture

    ElseIf TypeOf Screen.ActiveControl Is ListBox Then
        Clipboard.SetText Screen.ActiveControl.Text

    Else
        ' Do nothing
    End If

End Sub
```

The Clipboard is cleared with the following statement:

```
' Clear the clipboard.
 Clipboard.Clear
```

To copy the contents of the control to the Clipboard, you must first decide which control is currently active. This is accomplished with a series of If TypeOf statements.

The first If TypeOf statement checks whether the currently active control is the text box. If this is the case, the contents of the highlighted text inside the text box are copied to the Clipboard:

```
Clipboard.SetText Screen.ActiveControl.SelText
```

If the currently active control is the combo box, the highlighted text in the combo box is copied to the Clipboard:

```
Clipboard.SetText Screen.ActiveControl.Text
```

If the currently active control is the picture box, the picture inside the picture box is copied to the Clipboard:

```
Clipboard.SetData Screen.ActiveControl.Picture
```

Finally, if the currently active control is the list box, the highlighted text in the list box is copied to the Clipboard:

```
Clipboard.SetText Screen.ActiveControl.Text
```

> **Note:** `Screen.ActiveControl` represents the currently active control. Visual Basic automatically updates this variable for you. As you can see, the value of `Screen.ActiveControl` is useful in situations in which you need to perform operations on the currently active control.

The Code Inside the *mnuCut_Click()* Event Procedure

The `mnuCut_Click()` procedure is executed whenever you select Cut from the Edit menu:

```
Sub mnuCut_Click ()

    'Execute the mnuCopy_Click() procedure
    mnuCopy_Click

    ' Find which is the currently highlighted control,
    ' and remove its highlighted content.
    If TypeOf Screen.ActiveControl Is TextBox Then
        Screen.ActiveControl.SelText = ""

    ElseIf TypeOf Screen.ActiveControl Is ComboBox Then
        Screen.ActiveControl.Text = ""

    ElseIf TypeOf Screen.ActiveControl Is PictureBox Then
        Screen.ActiveControl.Picture = LoadPicture()

    ElseIf TypeOf Screen.ActiveControl Is ListBox Then
        If Screen.ActiveControl.ListIndex >= 0 Then
            Screen.ActiveControl.RemoveItem Screen.ActiveControl.ListIndex
        End If
    Else
        ' Do nothing
    End If

End Sub
```

Cut is defined as copying the selected data to the Clipboard and deleting the data that was copied. Therefore, the first statement in this procedure executes the `mnuCopy_Click()` procedure:

```
'Execute the mnuCopy_Click() procedure
mnuCopy_Click
```

To delete the data, a series of `If TypeOf` statements is executed. Each `If TypeOf` statement determines which is the currently active control and clears the data that was copied.

If the currently active control is the text box, the text that was copied from this control is cleared with the following statement:

```
Screen.ActiveControl.SelText = ""
```

Similarly, the text that was copied from the combo box is cleared with the following statement:

```
Screen.ActiveControl.Text = ""
```

To clear the picture box, the `LoadPicture()` function is used:

```
Screen.ActiveControl.Picture = LoadPicture()
```

The `LoadPicture()` function loads a picture into a picture box. The argument of `LoadPicture()` specifies which picture file to load. Because the preceding statement did not specify the name of the picture file to be loaded, the `LoadPicture()` function clears the current picture from the picture box, which is exactly what you want it to do.

If the currently active control is the list box, the copied text (which is the highlighted item in the list) is cleared with the `RemoveItem` statement:

```
ElseIf TypeOf Screen.ActiveControl Is ListBox Then
     If Screen.ActiveControl.ListIndex >= 0 Then
        Screen.ActiveControl.RemoveItem Screen.ActiveControl.ListIndex
     End If
```

Before removing the item, the code checks that `ListIndex` is greater than or equal to 0. `ListIndex` is the currently selected item in the list, and you want to make sure that currently there is a selected item in the list box (that is, when `ListIndex` is equal to -1, no item is currently selected in the list box).

The Code of the *mnuPaste_Click()* Event Procedure

The `mnuPaste_Click()` event procedure is executed when you select Paste from the Edit menu:

```
Sub mnuPaste_Click ()

    ' Find which is the currently active control and
    ' paste the content of the clipboard to it.
    If TypeOf Screen.ActiveControl Is TextBox Then
       Screen.ActiveControl.SelText = Clipboard.GetText()

    ElseIf TypeOf Screen.ActiveControl Is ComboBox Then
       Screen.ActiveControl.Text = Clipboard.GetText()

    ElseIf TypeOf Screen.ActiveControl Is PictureBox Then
       Screen.ActiveControl.Picture = Clipboard.GetData()

    ElseIf TypeOf Screen.ActiveControl Is ListBox Then
       Screen.ActiveControl.AddItem Clipboard.GetText()

    Else
```

383

```
        ' Do nothing
    End If

End Sub
```

Like the `mnuCopy_Click()` and `mnuCut_Click()` procedures, this procedure determines which is the currently active control with a series of `If TypeOf` statements.

If the currently active control is the text box, the text of the Clipboard is copied into the text box:

```
Screen.ActiveControl.SelText = Clipboard.GetText()
```

If the currently active control is the combo box, the text of the Clipboard is copied into the combo box:

```
Screen.ActiveControl.Text = Clipboard.GetText()
```

If the currently active control is the picture box, the picture inside the Clipboard is copied to the picture box using `GetData()`:

```
Screen.ActiveControl.Picture = Clipboard.GetData()
```

Finally, if the currently active control is the list box, the text in the Clipboard is added as a new item to the list:

```
Screen.ActiveControl.AddItem Clipboard.GetText()
```

Using *GetFormat()* to Determine the Type of Data in the Clipboard

As demonstrated, the Clipboard is capable of holding text as well as pictures. To examine what type of data the Clipboard currently holds, you can use `GetFormat()`.

For example, the following statement determines whether the data inside the Clipboard holds text:

```
If Clipboard.GetFormat(CF_TEXT) Then
    ............................................
    ... GetFormat() returned True, so indeed ...
    ... the clipboard holds text.           ...
    ............................................
End If
```

If the Clipboard currently holds text, `GetFormat(CF_TEXT)` returns True. The constant `CF_TEXT` is declared as 1 in the file c:\vb\constant.txt.

To decide whether the Clipboard currently holds a bitmap, use the following:

```
If Clipboard.GetFormat(CF_BITMAP) Then
   ..............................................
   ... GetFormat() returned True, so indeed ...
   ... the clipboard holds bit map.         ...
   ..............................................
End If
```

GetFormat(CF_BITMAP) returns True if the Clipboard currently holds a bitmap. The constant CF_BITMAP is declared as 2 in the file c:\vb\constant.txt.

The Idle Time

During the execution of your Visual Basic program, there are many times when no code of your program is executed. These periods are called *idle time*. For example, suppose that you write a program that includes a button. When you click this button, the program beeps 100 times. Until you click the button, your program is sitting idle, not executing any of your code. This is idle time. Once you click the button, the corresponding event procedure is executed. During the execution of this procedure, your program is not in idle time any more. Upon completion of the execution of the event procedure, your program is again in idle time, waiting for you to press the button again.

During idle times, you are able to switch to other Windows programs. For example, in the beep program previously discussed, when the program is in the idle time, you can switch to another Windows program. But if you click the beep button, the program beeps 100 times, and during the beeping, you cannot switch to other Windows programs.

The Count Program

Now write the Count program, a program that counts numbers from 1 to 999. Several new topics are presented throughout the discussion of this program.

The Visual Implementation of the Count Program

☐ Start a new project. Save the form of the project as COUNT.FRM and save the make file of the project as COUNT.MAK.

☐ Build the form of the Count program according to the specifications in Table 11.5.

The completed form should look like the one shown in Figure 11.5.

Table 11.5. The properties table of the Count program.

Object	Property	Setting
Form	**Name**	**frmCount**
	Caption	The Count Program
	Height	4425
	Left	2100
	Top	1095
	Width	2985
Command Button	**Name**	**cmdStart**
	Caption	&Start
	Height	1215
	Left	120
	Top	1560
	Width	1215
Command Button	**Name**	**cmdPause**
	Caption	&Pause
	Height	1215
	Left	1440
	Top	1560
	Width	1215
Command Button	**Name**	**cmdExit**
	Caption	&Exit
	Height	1095
	Left	120
	Top	2880
	Width	2535
Label	**Name**	**lblResult**
	Caption	(empty)
	BorderStyle	Fixed Single
	Alignment	2-Center
	FontSize	13.5
	Height	1095
	Left	120

Object	Property	Setting
	Top	360
	Width	2535

Figure 11.5.
The frmCount form.

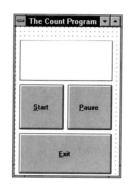

Entering the Code of the Count Program

☐ Enter the following code inside the general declarations section of the frmCount form:

```
' All variables MUST be declared.
Option Explicit
```

☐ Enter the following code inside the cmdExit_Click() procedure:

```
Sub cmdExit_Click ()

    End

End Sub
```

☐ Enter the following code inside the cmdStart_Click() procedure:

```
Sub cmdStart_Click ()

    Dim Counter As Integer

    Counter = 1
    ' Count from 1 to 999
    Do While Counter < 1000
       lblResult.Caption = Str$(Counter)
       Counter = Counter + 1
    Loop

End Sub
```

> **Note:** At this point, you are not instructed to attach any code to the
> cmdPause_Click() event procedure.

Executing the Count Program

☐ Execute the Count program.

☐ Click the Start button.

The program seems to do nothing for a while, and then the number 999 is displayed (depending on how fast your PC is, it may take several seconds until you see the number 999 displayed).

By reading the code inside the cmdStart_Click() procedure, you might expect to see the program display all the numbers from 1 to 999 during the counting.

To understand why the program does not display the numbers during the counting, look at the statements that are supposed to display the numbers:

```
Sub cmdStart_Click ()

    Dim Counter As Integer

    Counter = 1
    ' Count from 1 to 999
    Do While Counter < 1000
      lblResult.Caption = Str$(Counter)
      Counter = Counter + 1
    Loop

End Sub
```

The statement that is responsible for changing the caption of the label is this:

```
lblResult.Caption = Str$(Counter)
```

However, Visual Basic is able to refresh the screen only during idle time (that is, after the procedure is completed and the program returns to idle time). This is the reason the label does not display the numbers while counting is in progress.

An important point to note is that clicking the Exit button during the counting does not terminate the program. Again, the reason for this is that your program can recognize clicking only during idle times. Once the counting is complete, your program returns to idle time and responds to the clicking on the Exit button.

Modifying the Count Program

Use the following steps to modify the Count program so that the label displays the correct number on each count:

☐ Add the following statement inside the cmdStart_Click() procedure:

```
lblResult.Refresh
```

Now the cmdStart_Click() procedure looks like this:

```
Sub cmdStart_Click ()
```

```
Dim Counter As Integer

Counter = 1
' Count from 1 to 999
Do While Counter < 1000
  lblResult.Caption = Str$(Counter)

  lblResult.Refresh

  Counter = Counter + 1
Loop
```

End Sub

The Refresh method causes an immediate refreshing of the screen.

DO	DON'T
DO cause immediate paint refreshing of an object by using the Refresh method: `object.Refresh` For example, to refresh the lblResult object, use the following: `lblResult.Refresh`	

11

Executing the Modified Version of the Count Program

☐ Execute the modified version of the Count program.

Now the label displays all the numbers during the counting. During the counting, clicking the Exit button still does not terminate the program. Why? During the execution of the cmdStart_Click() procedure, your program is not in idle time.

Enhancing the Count Program

Now enhance the Count program so that it will respond to mouse clicking during the counting.

The enhanced Count program requires that you write a procedure called Main(), which will be the first procedure to be executed upon startup of the program.

Instruct Visual Basic to execute the Main() procedure upon startup as follows:

☐ Select Project from the Options menu.

Visual Basic responds by displaying the Project Options dialog box, as shown in Figure 11.6.

Figure 11.6.
Setting the startup form to
Sub Main.

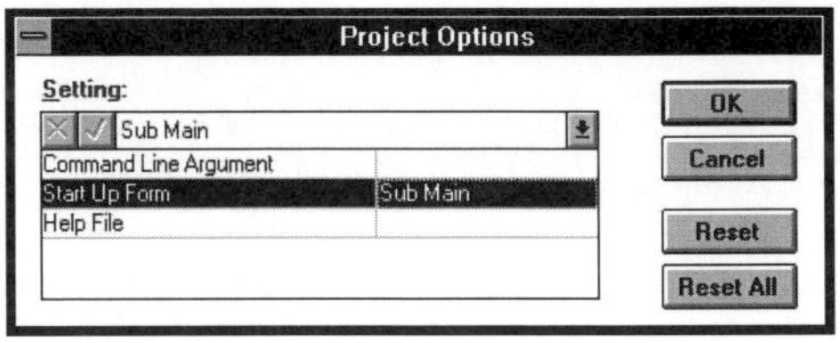

> **Project Options**
>
> Setting:
> ☒ ✓ Sub Main
> Command Line Argument
> Start Up Form   Sub Main
> Help File
>
> OK   Cancel   Reset   Reset All

☐ Highlight the Start Up Form field of the Project Options dialog box, click the arrow that appears on the right side of the Setting box, and select Sub Main.

Upon execution of the Count program, the first procedure that is executed is Main().

Now write the Main() procedure. Visual Basic requires that the procedure Main() resides in a separate module (that is, not inside the form module). So add a new module to the project:

☐ Select New Module from the File menu.

> *Visual Basic responds by adding a new module to the project window. The default name of the newly added module is Module1.bas. (Examine the project window.)*

Now save the newly added module as COUNTM.BAS:

☐ Make sure Module1.bas is highlighted in the project window and select Save File As from the File menu.

> *Visual Basic responds by displaying the Save File As dialog box.*

☐ Save the newly added module file as COUNTM.BAS.

> *Your project window should now contain COUNT.FRM, COUNTM.BAS, and the VBX files.*

Now add a procedure called Main() inside the module COUNTM.BAS:

☐ Make sure COUNTM.BAS is highlighted in the project window.

☐ Click the View Code button in the project window (because you are about to add a procedure into the code module COUNTM.BAS).

☐ Select New Procedure from the View menu.

> *Visual Basic responds by displaying the New Procedure dialog box (see Figure 11.7).*

Figure 11.7.
Adding the Main()
procedure to the
COUNTM.BAS module.

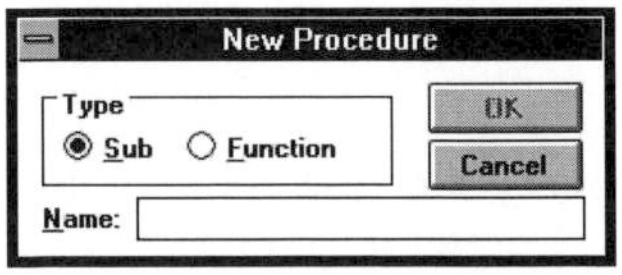

> **New Procedure**
>
> Type
> ◉ Sub   ○ Function
> Name:
>
> OK   Cancel

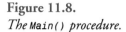

☐ Type Main in the Name field of the New Procedure dialog box.

Visual Basic responds by adding the Main() *procedure inside the COUNTM.BAS module. The* Main() *procedure is shown in Figure 11.8.*

Figure 11.8.
The Main() *procedure.*

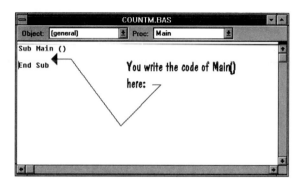

☐ Add the following code inside the general declarations area of the COUNTM.BAS module:

```
'  All variables MUST be declared.
Option Explicit
' Declare a global variable so that it is visible in
' all the procedures of all the modules and forms.
Global gFlag As Integer
```

☐ Add the following code inside the Main() procedure of the COUNTM.BAS module:

```
Sub Main ()

    Dim Counter As Integer

    ' Show the form.
    frmCount.Show

    ' Count from 1 to 999, then start counting all over again.
    Do While DoEvents()
       If gFlag = 1 Then
          Counter = Counter + 1
          frmCount.lblResult.Caption = Str$(Counter)
          If Counter = 999 Then
             Counter = 1
          End If
       End If
    Loop

End Sub
```

☐ Add the following code inside the general declarations section of the frmCount form:

```
' All variables MUST be declared.
Option Explicit
```

☐ Add the following code inside the `cmdExit_Click()` procedure of the frmCount form:

```
Sub cmdExit_Click ()

    End

End Sub
```

Note: This code already exists in the procedure from the earlier version of the Count program.

☐ Add the following code inside the `cmdPause_Click()` procedure of the frmCount form:

```
Sub cmdPause_Click ()

    ' Set the flag to 0 to disable counting.
    gFlag = 0

End Sub
```

☐ Change the code inside the `cmdStart_Click()` procedure of the COUNT.FRM form so that it looks like this:

```
Sub cmdStart_Click ()

    ' Set the flag to 1 to enable counting.
    gFlag = 1

End Sub
```

☐ Add the following code inside the `Form_Load()` procedure of the frmCount form:

```
Sub Form_Load ()

    ' Set the flag to 0 to disable counting.
    ' (You must click the Start button to start counting).
    gFlag = 0

End Sub
```

Executing the Count Program

☐ Execute the Count program.

The program counts from 1 to 999 and then starts counting again. The numbers inside the label are displayed during counting.

☐ Click the Pause button.

As you can see, you may click the Pause button to pause the counting!

☐ Click the Start button to continue counting.

☐ While the Count program is counting, start Paintbrush and manipulate and resize the windows of Paintbrush and the Count programs so that the Count form is shown together with the window of Paintbrush onscreen (as shown in Figure 11.9). As you can see, you can draw with Paintbrush while the Count program continues to count.

Figure 11.9.
Executing the Count program and Paintbrush together.

The *Main()* Procedure

The Main() procedure is the first procedure that is executed upon startup of the program. Therefore, the first statement in this procedure is responsible for showing the frmCount form:

```
' Show the form.
frmCount.Show
```

DO	**DON'T**

DO show the form by using the Show method as the first statement in the Main() procedure. Because the Main() procedure is the first procedure that is executed upon startup of the program, the form is not loaded automatically.

The Do While DoEvents() loop inside Main() is called the idle loop:

```
Do While DoEvents()
   If gFlag = 1 Then
      Counter = Counter + 1
      frmCount.lblResult.Caption = Str$(Counter)
      If Counter = 999 Then
         Counter = 1
      End If
   End If
Loop
```

The logic flow diagram of the Do While DoEvents() loop is shown in Figure 11.10. As shown in Figure 11.10, the program stays in an endless loop.

Figure 11.10.

The `Do While DoEvents()` *loop.*

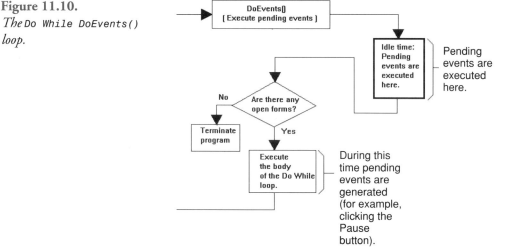

Terminating the Endless Loop

The top block in Figure 11.10 is the `DoEvents()` block. This function returns the number of currently open forms. If you close the frmCount form, there are no open forms in the program, and `DoEvents()` returns 0. The loop terminates, which terminates the program.

Executing the Body of the *Do While DoEvents()* Loop

As shown in Figure 11.10, if there is an open form, the body of the `Do While DoEvents()` loop is executed.

The first statement in the loop is an `If` statement that checks the value of `gFlag`. Assuming that you already clicked the Start button, which sets the value of this flag to 1, the statements of the `If` block are executed, increasing the `Counter` variable and updating the Caption property of the `lblResult` label.

During the execution of the body of the `Do While` loop, the program is not in idle time. This means that the program cannot act on certain events that occur during the execution of the body of the `Do While` loop. For example, if during the execution of the `Do While` loop you click the Pause button, the program cannot respond to this event. Events that occur while the program is not in idle time are called pending events. For example, clicking the Pause button while the program executes the body of the `Do While` loop causes a pending event.

The `Do While` loop contains the following statement:

```
frmCount.lblResult.Caption = Str$(Counter)
```

This statement causes a pending event because the Caption of the lblResult label may be refreshed only during idle time.

As shown in Figure 11.10, once the body of the Do While loop is executed, the program again executes the DoEvents() function.

The *DoEvents()* Function

In order to cause the program to act on the pending events, you must force the program to be in idle time. The DoEvents() function forces the program to be in idle time.

While a program is in idle time, Windows acts on any pending events. One pending event that is executed in idle time is the refreshing of the lblResult label (this pending event occurred while the program executed the body of the Do While loop). Also, if you click the Pause button during the execution of the Do While loop, the program acts on this pending event. Once Windows finishes acting on the pending events, it returns to the Do While loop and the whole process starts over.

> **Note:** The DoEvents() function in the Do While DoEvents() loop serves two purposes:
>
> - The returned value from DoEvents() is the number of the currently open forms. The loop is terminated when there are no more open forms.
> - The DoEvents() function forces the program to be in idle time (so that Windows can act on all pending events).

The Code Inside the General Declarations Area of the COUNTM.BAS Module

The code inside the general declarations area of the COUNTM.BAS includes the following statement:

```
' Declare a global variable that is visible in
' all procedures in all the modules and forms.
Global gFlag As Integer
```

This means that the variable gFlag is visible by all procedures in all modules and forms. Indeed, the gFlag variable is updated in the procedures Form_Load(), cmdStart_Click(), and cmdPause_Click() of the COUNT.FRM form, and it is used in the Main() procedure of the COUNTM.BAS module.

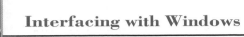
The Code Inside the *cmdPause_Click()* Procedure

The `cmdPause_Click()` procedure of the COUNT.FRM form is executed (during idle time) if you click the Pause button during the execution of the `Do While DoEvents()` loop. The code inside this procedure sets the global variable `gFlag` to 0 so that the counting process inside the `Main()` procedure is disabled:

```
Sub cmdPause_Click ()

    ' Set the flag to 0 to disable counting.
    gFlag = 0

End Sub
```

The Code Inside the *cmdStart_Click()* Event Procedure

The code inside the `cmdStart_Click()` procedure sets `gFlag` to 1 so that the counting process inside the `Main()` procedure is enabled.

Summary

In this chapter you have learned how your Visual Basic program can take advantage of the standard Windows features. You have learned how to copy, cut, and paste text and pictures to and from the Clipboard. You have learned how to request an immediate refreshing of objects using the Refresh method. You also have learned how to write code that is executed during idle time.

Q&A

Q I understand the functionality of copy, cut, and paste as implemented in this chapter. Can I implement copy, cut, and paste in a slightly different way?

A You can implement them in any way you like. However, the programs that you write with Visual Basic are designed to work in the Windows environment. As such, your users expect copy, cut, and paste to work in a certain known and acceptable manner (which is the manner described in this chapter).

Quiz

1. What does the value of `Screen.ActiveControl` represent?
2. `GetFormat()` is used to do which of the following:
    a. Find the type of data that the Clipboard currently holds.
    b. Format the hard drive.
    c. Format the disk (floppy and/or hard drive).
3. For what is the Refresh method responsible?

Exercise

As demonstrated in the AnyData program, if the Clipboard contains text, you can't paste the Clipboard contents to the picture box. Also, if the Clipboard contains a picture, you can't paste its content to the text box, list box, or combo box.

Enhance the AnyData program so that the Paste item in the Edit menu is disabled whenever the Paste operation does not make sense.

Quiz Answers

1. The currently active control
2. a
3. Causing an immediate refreshing of the screen

Exercise Answer

The code of the program needs to determine whether to enable or disable the Paste menu. A good focal point to insert such code is inside the `mnuEdit_Click()` procedure.

☐ The code you are about to insert uses constants from the c:\vb\constant.txt file. So add this file to the project (select Add File from the File menu and load the file c:\vb\constant.txt).

The following code enables or disables the Paste item in the Edit menu by comparing the data type of the Clipboard contents with the data type of the currently active control:

```
Sub mnuEdit_Click ()

    ' Start by enabling the Cut and Copy menus.
    mnuCut.Enabled = True
    mnuCopy.Enabled = True

    ' Initially, disable the Paste menu.
    mnuPaste.Enabled = False

    ' Is the currently active control a text box?
    If TypeOf Screen.ActiveControl Is TextBox Then
        ' Does the clipboard hold text?
        If Clipboard.GetFormat(CF_TEXT) Then
            ' It is Ok to paste.
            mnuPaste.Enabled = True
        End If

    ' Is the currently active control a combo box?
    ElseIf TypeOf Screen.ActiveControl Is ComboBox Then
        ' Does the clipboard hold text?
        If Clipboard.GetFormat(CF_TEXT) Then
            ' It is OK to paste.
            mnuPaste.Enabled = True
        End If

    ' Is the currently active control a list box?
    ElseIf TypeOf Screen.ActiveControl Is ListBox Then
        ' Does the clipboard hold text?
        If Clipboard.GetFormat(CF_TEXT) Then
            ' It is OK to paste.
            mnuPaste.Enabled = True
        End If

    ' Is the currently active control a picture box?
    ElseIf TypeOf Screen.ActiveControl Is PictureBox Then
        ' Does the clipboard hold bit map?
        If Clipboard.GetFormat(CF_BITMAP) Then
            ' It is OK to paste.
            mnuPaste.Enabled = True
        End If
    Else
        ' We checked all the valid possibilities!
        ' The user is trying to paste incompatible data types!
        ' Paste should be disabled!
        ' Do nothing (that is, leave the Paste menu gray.
    End If

End Sub
```

It is a good idea to include such code in your programs. For example, if you do not include such code in your programs, your user may try to paste text into a picture box and will not understand why the paste operation does not take place. Adding the preceding procedure prevents your user from trying to perform paste operations that do not make sense.

12

The Keyboard

This chapter shows how your program can respond to keyboard events, how to detect that a key was pressed or released, and how to manipulate the input data that comes from the keyboard.

The Keyboard Focus

The object that has the keyboard focus is the object that responds to keyboard inputs. When a control has the focus, its appearance changes in some way. For example, when a command button has the focus, a rectangle appears around its caption. When a scroll bar has the focus, its thumb tab blinks.

The Keyboard Events

Three keyboard events correspond to keyboard activities: KeyDown, KeyUp, and KeyPress.

The *KeyDown* Event   *Any Keys*

The KeyDown event occurs whenever the user presses any of the keys on the keyboard. For example, if the user presses a key while a command button called cmdPushMe has the focus, the cmdPushMe_KeyDown() procedure is executed.

The *KeyUp* Event

The KeyUp event occurs whenever the user releases any of the keys on the keyboard. For example, if the user releases a key while a command button called cmdPushMe has the focus, the cmdPushMe_KeyUp() procedure is executed.

The *KeyPress* Event   *ASCII only*

The KeyPress event occurs whenever the user presses a key that has a corresponding ASCII character. For example, if the user presses the A key while a command button called cmdPushMe has the focus, the cmdPushMe_KeyPress() procedure is executed. If the user presses F1, the KeyPress event does not occur, because the F1 key has no corresponding ASCII character.

The KEYS Program

The KEYS program illustrates how the three keyboard events are used in a program.

The Visual Implementation of the KEYS Program

☐ Open a new project, save the form of the project as KEYS.FRM, and save the make file of the project as KEYS.MAK.

☐ Build the form of the project according to the specifications in Table 12.1.

The completed form should look like the one shown in Figure 12.1.

Table 12.1. The properties table of the frmKeys form.

Object	Property	Setting
Form	**Name**	**frmKeys**
	Caption	The KEYS Program
	Height	4425
	Left	1035
	Top	1140
	Width	7485
Command Button	**Name**	**cmdPushMe**
	Caption	&Push Me
	Height	615
	Left	480
	Top	1320
	Width	1215
Command Button	**Name**	**cmdExit**
	Caption	&Exit
	Height	495
	Left	5520
	Top	3000
	Width	1215
Label	**Name**	**lblInfo**
	Alignment	2-Center
	BorderStyle	1-Fixed Single
	Height	495
	Left	1320

Table 12.1. continued

Object	Property	Setting
	Top	360
	Width	4815
	Caption	(empty)

Figure 12.1.
The frmKeys form.

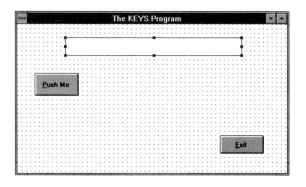

Entering the Code of the KEYS Program

☐ Enter the following code inside the general declarations section of the frmKeys form:

```
' All variables MUST be declared.
Option Explicit
```

☐ Enter the following code inside the cmdExit_Click() procedure of the frmKeys form:

```
Sub cmdExit_Click ()

    End

End Sub
```

☐ Enter the following code inside the cmdPushMe_KeyDown() procedure of the frmKeys form:

```
Sub cmdPushMe_KeyDown (KeyCode As Integer, Shift As Integer)

    lblInfo.Caption = "A key was pressed. KeyCode=" + Str
    ➡(KeyCode) + " Shift=" + Str(Shift)

End Sub
```

Executing the KEYS Program

☐ Execute the KEYS program.

☐ Click the Push Me button.

The KEYS program responds by placing a dashed rectangle around the caption of the Push Me button. This is an indication that the Push Me button now has the keyboard focus.

☐ Press the A key.

The KEYS program responds by displaying the ASCII code of the A key inside the lblInfo label, as shown in Figure 12.2.

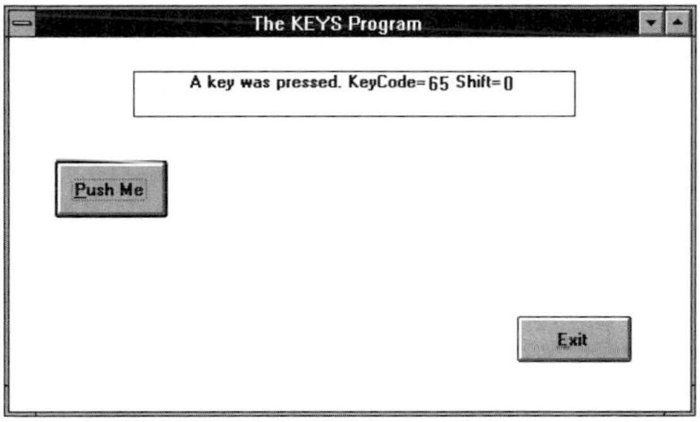

Figure 12.2.
Pressing the A key.

![The KEYS Program window showing "A key was pressed. KeyCode=65 Shift=0" with Push Me and Exit buttons]

☐ Press other keys on the keyboard and notice that the lblInfo label indicates which key was pressed.

☐ Press the Num Lock key and notice that the program reports that the key that corresponds to the value 144 was pressed. The correlation between the displayed numbers and the pressed keys is explained later in this chapter.

☐ Press the Shift key, press the Ctrl key (while holding down the Shift key), and then press the Alt key (while holding down the Shift and Ctrl keys).

The lblInfo label reports that Shift is equal to 1, 3, and then 7. The correlation between these numbers and the Shift, Ctrl, and Alt keys is explained later in this chapter.

☐ Click the Exit button to terminate the KEYS program.

How the KEYS Program Works

The KEYS program uses the KeyDown event to respond to keys that are pressed on the keyboard.

The Code Inside the *cmdPushMe_KeyDown()* Event Procedure of the frmKeys Form

The cmdPushMe_KeyDown() procedure is executed whenever the Push Me button has the focus and the user presses any key on the keyboard:

```
Sub cmdPushMe_KeyDown (KeyCode As Integer, Shift As Integer)

    lblInfo.Caption = "A key was pressed. KeyCode=" +
                    ➥ Str(KeyCode) + " Shift=" +Str(Shift)

End Sub
```

The `cmdPushMe_KeyDown()` procedure has two arguments: The first is an integer that represents the pressed key. The second represents the state of the Shift, Ctrl, and Alt keys.

The meanings of the values of the first argument are declared in the C:\VB\CONSTANT.TXT file. The declarations of the keys start with the characters KEY_. For example, the Num Lock key is declared in CONSTANT.TXT as this:

```
Global Const KEY_NUMLOCK = &H90
```

This means that whenever the user presses the Num Lock key, the first argument of the `cmdPushMe_KeyDown()` procedure is equal to the hexadecimal number 90, which is equivalent to the decimal number 144 ($9 \times 16 + 0$).

The F1 key is declared in CONSTANT.TXT as the following:

```
Global Const KEY_F1 = &H70
```

So whenever the user presses F1, the first argument of the `cmdPushMe_KeyDown()` procedure has the hexadecimal value 70, which is equivalent to the decimal number 112 ($7 \times 16 + 0$).

The meanings of the values of the second argument of the `cmdPushMe_KeyDown()` procedure are listed in Table 12.2. For example, when the value of the second argument is equal to 3, it means that both the Shift and the Ctrl keys are pressed and the Alt key is not pressed.

Table 12.2. The possible values of the second argument of the `cmdPushMe_KeyDown()` procedure.

Value of the Second Argument	Alt Status	Ctrl Status	Shift Status
0	Not pressed	Not pressed	Not pressed
1	Not pressed	Not pressed	Pressed
2	Not pressed	Pressed	Not pressed
3	Not pressed	Pressed	Pressed
4	Pressed	Not pressed	Not pressed
5	Pressed	Not pressed	Pressed
6	Pressed	Pressed	Not pressed
7	Pressed	Pressed	Pressed

The code inside the cmdPushMe_KeyDown() procedure assigns to the Caption property of the lblInfo label a string that represents the values of the two arguments:

```
lblInfo.Caption = "A key was pressed. KeyCode=" +
                ➡ Str(KeyCode) + " Shift=" + Str(Shift)
```

The Str() function is used because the Caption property is a string and the KeyCode and Shift variables are integers. Str(KeyCode) converts the integer KeyCode to a string, and Str(Shift) converts the integer Shift to a string.

Detecting a Released Key

As you have seen, the KeyUp and KeyDown events may be used to detect any pressed key. Another event that may be used to detect a pressed key is the KeyPress event. However, this event detects only ASCII keys. To see the KeyUp event in action, enter the following code inside the cmdPushMe_KeyUp() procedure of the frmKeys form:

```
Sub cmdPushMe_KeyUp (KeyCode As Integer, Shift As Integer)

lblInfo.Caption = "A key was released. KeyCode=" +
                ➡ Str(KeyCode) + " Shift=" + Str(Shift)

End Sub
```

☐ Execute the KEYS program.

☐ Click the Push Me button.

The KEYS program responds by displaying a dashed rectangle around the Push Me button, indicating that this button now has the keyboard focus.

☐ Press a key.

The KEYS program responds by displaying a number that corresponds to the key pressed.

☐ Release the key.

The KEYS program responds by displaying the value of the released key.

☐ Click the Exit button to terminate the KEYS program.

The cmdPushMe_KeyUp() procedure has arguments identical to those of the cmdPushMe_KeyDown() procedure. The difference is that the arguments of the cmdPushMe_KeyDown() procedure report which key was pressed, whereas the arguments of the cmdPushMe_KeyUp() procedure report which key was released.

Detecting the Pressing of an ASCII Key

To detect that the user pressed an ASCII key, you may use the KeyPress event. To see the KeyPress event in action, follow these steps:

☐ Enter the following code inside the `cmdPushMe_KeyPress()` procedure of the frmKeys form:

```
Sub cmdPushMe_KeyPress (KeyAscii As Integer)

    Dim Char

    Char = Chr(KeyAscii)
    lblInfo.Caption = "KeyAscii =" + Str(KeyAscii) +  " Char=" + Char

End Sub
```

☐ Comment out the code inside the `cmdPushMe_KeyDown()` procedure (that is, type an apostrophe at the beginning of the statement inside the `cmdPushMe_KeyDown()` procedure).

☐ Execute the KEYS program.

☐ Click the Push Me button.

The KEYS program responds by displaying a dashed rectangle around the Push Me button, indicating that this button now has the keyboard focus.

☐ Press the a key.

The KEYS program responds to the pressing of the a key by displaying the ASCII value of the key, which is 97.

☐ Press the A key.

The KEYS program responds to the pressing of the A key by displaying the ASCII value of the key, which is 65.

☐ Press F1.

The KEYS program does not display any value inside the lblInfo label because F1 does not have an ASCII code.

☐ Click the Exit button to terminate the KEYS program.

The Code Inside the *cmdPushMe_KeyPress()* Event Procedure of the frmKeys Form

The `cmdPushMe_KeyPress()` procedure is executed whenever the user presses an ASCII key. This procedure has one argument, which represents the ASCII value of the pressed key.

The `Chr()` function converts the integer `KeyAscii` to a character:

```
Char = Chr(KeyAscii)
```

The last statement in the `cmdPushMe_KeyPress()` procedure assigns a string to the Caption property of the lblInfo label:

```
lblInfo.Caption = "KeyAscii =" +  Str(KeyAscii) +   " Char=" + Char
```

Therefore, the user sees the character that was typed, as well as the ASCII value of the character.

Intercepting Keys with the *Form_KeyPress()* Procedure

A form may have the keyboard focus if there are no controls in it, or if the controls inside the form are disabled. However, in most programs a form has some enabled controls in it, so the `Form_KeyDown()`, `Form_KeyUp()`, and `Form_KeyPress()` procedures are not executed. To force the execution of these procedures even when the form does not have the keyboard focus, set the KeyPreview property of the form to True. To see the effect of the KeyPreview property, follow these steps:

☐ Set the KeyPreview property of the frmKeys form to True.

☐ Make sure that the code inside the `cmdPushMe_KeyDown()`, `cmdPushMe_KeyUp()` and `cmdPushMe_KeyPress()` procedures is commented out.

☐ Enter the following code inside the `Form_KeyPress ()` procedure:

```
Sub Form_KeyPress (KeyAscii As Integer)

    Dim Char
    Char = Chr(KeyAscii)
    lblInfo.Caption = "KeyAscii =" + Str(KeyAscii) + " Char=" + Char

End Sub
```

☐ Execute the KEYS program.

☐ Press any ASCII key and note that the lblInfo label displays the pressed key even if the Push Me button does not have the keyboard focus.

In a similar way, you may utilize the `Form_KeyDown()` and the `Form_KeyUp()` procedures to trap pressed keys, even if the form doesn't have the keyboard focus. However, don't forget to set the KeyPreview property of the form to True.

As implied by its name, the KeyPreview property enables the program to preview (or trap) the keyboard events. This enables you to write code that responds to key pressing regardless of which control has the keyboard focus.

The UPPER Program

The UPPER program illustrates how your program may trap ASCII keys.

The Visual Implementation of the UPPER Program

☐ Open a new project, save the form of the project as UPPER.FRM, and save the make file of the project as UPPER.MAK.

☐ Build the frmUpper form according to the specifications in Table 12.3.

The completed form should look like the one shown in Figure 12.3.

Table 12.3. The properties table of the frmUpper form.

Object	Property	Setting
Form	**Name**	**frmUpper**
	Caption	The UPPER Program
	Height	4425
	Left	1035
	Top	1140
	Width	7485
Command Button	**Name**	**cmdExit**
	Caption	&Exit
	Height	495
	Left	5760
	Top	3000
	Width	1215
Text Box	**Name**	**txtUserArea**
	Height	1095
	Left	600
	ScrollBars	3-Both
	Top	600
	Width	6375
	Text	(empty)

Figure 12.3.
The frmUpper form.

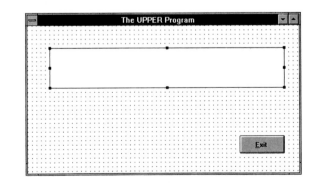

Entering the Code of the UPPER Program

☐ Enter the following code inside the general declarations section of the frmUpper form:

```
' All variables MUST be declared.
Option Explicit
```

☐ Enter the following code inside the cmdExit_Click() procedure of the frmUpper form:

```
Sub cmdExit_Click ()

    End

End Sub
```

Executing the UPPER Program

☐ Execute the UPPER program.

☐ Type something inside the text box.

☐ Try to press the Enter key to move to the next line.

> As you can see, the text box program refuses to move to the next line in the text box, because the MultiLine property of the txtUserArea text box is currently set to False. Note that every time you press Enter, the PC beeps, alerting you that you pressed an illegal key.

☐ Click the Exit button to exit the program.

Trapping the Enter Key

As demonstrated, the PC beeps whenever the user presses an illegal key. You may trap the event and fool the UPPER program as follows:

☐ Enter the following code inside the txtUserArea_KeyPress() procedure of the frmUpper form:

```
Sub txtUserArea_KeyPress (KeyAscii As Integer)

    If KeyAscii = 13 Then

        KeyAscii = 0
    End If

End Sub
```

☐ Execute the UPPER program.

☐ Type something inside the text box.

☐ Press Enter.

As you can see, the text box does not let you move to the next line, but the PC does not beep when you press Enter.

☐ Terminate the UPPER program by clicking the Exit button.

The Code Inside the *txtUserArea_KeyPress()* Event Procedure of the frmUpper Form

The `txtUserArea_KeyPress()` procedure is executed whenever the user presses an ASCII code. The code inside this procedure checks the value of `KeyAscii` (which was supplied as the argument to this procedure), and if the pressed key is equal to 13, it means that the user pressed Enter. The code inside this procedure changes the value of the `KeyAscii` argument to 0 (the null character). Therefore, when the UPPER program later processes the key of the txtUserArea text box, this text box does not know about the Enter key. From the point of view of the text box, the user pressed the 0 (null) key. This is why the PC does not beep when the user presses Enter.

The code inside the `txtUserArea_KeyPress()` procedure demonstrates that this procedure is executed before the text box has a chance to process the pressed key.

Modifying the UPPER Program

Modify the UPPER program as follows:

☐ Change the MultiLine property of the txtUserArea text box to True.

☐ Execute the UPPER program.

☐ Type something inside the text box and press Enter.

As you can see, the text box does not let you move to the next line because the Enter key is blocked by the code inside the `txtUserArea_KeyPress()` procedure.

☐ Click the Exit button to terminate the UPPER program.

Converting ASCII Characters to Uppercase

You will have situations in which you want the text that the user types to appear in uppercase only (or in lowercase only). To see how you may accomplish this, change the code inside the `txtUserArea_KeyPress()` procedure so that it looks like the following:

```
Sub txtUserArea_KeyPress (KeyAscii As Integer)

Dim Char

Char = Chr(KeyAscii)
KeyAscii = Asc(UCase(Char))

End Sub
```

☐ Execute the UPPER program.

☐ Type something inside the text box.

> *As you can see, whatever you type appears in uppercase letters regardless of the status of the Shift or Caps Lock keys.*

☐ Click the Exit button to terminate the UPPER program.

The code inside the `txtUserArea_KeyPress()` procedure uses the `Chr()` function to convert the pressed key to a character:

```
Char = Chr(KeyAscii)
```

Then the character is converted to uppercase using the `UCase()` function. The `UCase()` function returns the uppercase character of its argument. For example, the returned value of `UCase("a")` is A, and the returned value of `UCase("A")` is also A.

The `txtUserArea_KeyPress()` procedure converts the returned value of `UCase()` to an integer using the `Asc()` function:

```
KeyAscii = Asc( UCase(Char) )
```

The `Asc()` function returns an integer that represents the ASCII value of its argument.

So the argument of the `txtUserArea_KeyPress()` procedure contains an integer that represents the ASCII value of the pressed key. This integer is converted to a character, the character is converted to uppercase, and the ASCII value of the uppercase character is assigned to the `KeyAscii` argument. Therefore, the text box thinks that the user pressed an uppercase key.

The Cancel Property ✗ ESC

12

The Cancel property is used to provide response to the pressing of the Esc key. To see the Cancel property in action, follow these steps:

☐ Execute the UPPER program.

Cancel property : True

☐ Press Esc.

As you can see, no matter what has the keyboard focus, the UPPER program does not respond to the Esc key.

☐ Click the Exit button to exit the UPPER program.

☐ Change the Cancel property of the Exit button to True.

☐ Execute the UPPER program.

☐ Press Esc.

No matter which control has the focus, the program responds to the Esc key as if the Exit key were pressed. This is because you set the Cancel property of the Exit button to True.

In a similar manner, if you set the Default property of the Exit button to True, the program responds to the pressing of the Enter key in the same manner as it responds to the clicking of the Exit button (regardless of which control has the focus).

The Tab Order

Windows programs let the user move from control to control by pressing the Tab key (that is, moving the keyboard focus from control to control by pressing Tab). Pressing Shift+Tab moves the keyboard focus in the reverse order. The TAB program illustrates how the tab order works.

The TAB Program

☐ Open a new project, save the form of the project as TAB.FRM, and save the make file of the project as TAB.MAK.

☐ Implement the frmTab form according to the specifications in Table 12.4.

The completed form should look like the one shown in Figure 12.4.

Table 12.4. The properties table of the frmTab form.

Object	Property	Setting
Form	**Name**	**frmTab**
	Caption	The TAB Program
	Height	4425
	Left	1035
	Top	1140
	Width	7485
Command Button	**Name**	**Command1**
	Caption	Command1
	Height	495
	Left	240
	TabIndex	0
	Top	480
	Width	1215

Object	Property	Setting
Command Button	**Name**	**Command2**
	Caption	Command2
	Height	495
	Left	240
	TabIndex	1
	Top	1080
	Width	1215
Command Button	**Name**	**Command3**
	Caption	Command3
	Height	495
	Left	240
	TabIndex	2
	Top	1680
	Width	1215
Command Button	**Name**	**Command4**
	Caption	Command4
	Height	495
	Left	240
	TabIndex	3
	Top	2280
	Width	1215
Command Button	**Name**	**Command5**
	Caption	Command5
	Height	495
	Left	240
	TabIndex	4
	Top	2880
	Width	1215
Command Button	**Name**	**Command6**
	Caption	Command6
	Height	495

12

continues

Table 12.4. continued

Object	Property	Setting
	Left	1680
	TabIndex	5
	Top	480
	Width	1215
Command Button	**Name**	**Command7**
	Caption	Command7
	Height	495
	Left	1680
	TabIndex	6
	Top	1080
	Width	1215
Command Button	**Name**	**Command8**
	Caption	Command8
	Height	495
	Left	1680
	TabIndex	7
	Top	1680
	Width	1215
Command Button	**Name**	**Command9**
	Caption	Command9
	Height	495
	Left	1680
	TabIndex	8
	Top	2280
	Width	1215
Command Button	**Name**	**Command10**
	Caption	Command10
	Height	495
	Left	1680
	TabIndex	9
	Top	2880
	Width	1215

Object	Property	Setting
Command Button	Name	cmdExit
	Caption	&Exit
	Height	495
	Left	5880
	TabIndex	10
	Top	3360
	Width	1215
Check Box	Name	Check1
	Caption	Check1
	Height	495
	Left	3720
	TabIndex	11
	Top	360
	Width	1215
Check Box	Name	Check2
	Caption	Check2
	Height	495
	Left	3720
	TabIndex	12
	Top	960
	Width	1215
Check Box	Name	Check3
	Caption	Check3
	Height	495
	Left	3720
	TabIndex	13
	Top	1560
	Width	1215
Horizontal Scroll Bar	Height	255
	Left	3600
	Min	0
	Max	50

Table 12.4. continued

Object	Property	Setting
	TabIndex	14
	Top	2400
	Width	3015

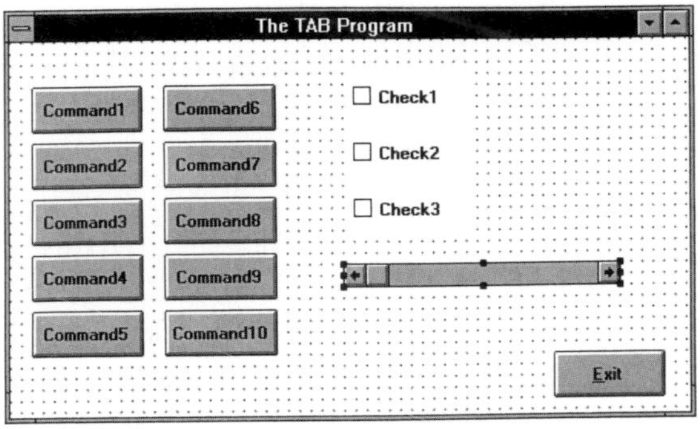

Figure 12.4.
The frmTab form.

Entering the Code of the TAB Program

☐ Enter the following code inside the general declarations section of the frmTab form:

```
' All variables MUST be declared.
Option Explicit
```

☐ Enter the following code inside the cmdExit_Click() procedure of the frmTab form:

```
Sub cmdExit_Click ()

    End

End Sub
```

Executing the TAB Program

☐ Execute the TAB program.

☐ Move the focus from one control to another by pressing the Tab key or the arrow keys. Notice that when the scroll bar has the focus the left and right arrow keys are used for changing the thumb tab position of the scroll bar.

☐ Click the Exit button to terminate the program.

The TabIndex Property

The TabIndex property determines the order in which controls receive the keyboard focus. For example, if the keyboard focus is currently on a control that has its TabIndex property set to 5, pressing Tab moves the keyboard focus to the control that has its TabIndex property set to 6. If the keyboard focus is currently on a control that has its TabIndex property set to 5, pressing Shift+Tab moves the keyboard focus back to the control that has its TabIndex property set to 4. The tab order works in a circular manner: If the control that currently has the keyboard focus is the control with the highest TabIndex value, pressing Tab moves the keyboard focus to the control that has its TabIndex property set to 0. Similarly, if the control that currently has the keyboard focus is the control that has its TabIndex property set to 0, pressing Shift+Tab moves the keyboard focus to the control with the highest TabIndex. Some controls cannot accept the keyboard focus. For example, a label control cannot accept the keyboard focus.

Visual Basic sets the TabIndex property with sequential numbers. That is, the TabIndex property of the first control placed in the form is set to 0, the TabProperty of the second control placed in the form is set to 1, and so on. However, you may change the value of the TabIndex property so that the Tab order is appropriate to your program.

The Focus Program

The Focus program demonstrates how your program can detect whenever a control gets or loses the focus.

The Visual Implementation of the Focus Program

☐ Open a new project, save the form of the project as FOCUS.FRM, and save the make file of the project as FOCUS.MAK.

☐ Build the frmFocus form according to the specifications in Table 12.5.

The completed form should look like the one shown in Figure 12.5.

Table 12.5. The properties table of the frmFocus form.

Object	Property	Setting
Form	**Name**	**frmFocus**
	Caption	The Focus Program
	Height	4425
	Left	1035

continues

Table 12.5. continued

Object	Property	Setting
	Top	1140
	Width	7485
Command Button	**Name**	**cmdSave**
	Caption	&Save
	Height	495
	Left	600
	Top	1080
	Width	1215
Command Button	**Name**	**cmdLoad**
	Caption	&Load
	Height	495
	Left	600
	Top	480
	Width	1215
Text Box	**Name**	**txtUserArea**
	Height	1695
	Left	2880
	MultiLine	True
	Top	600
	Width	3135
	Text	(empty)
Command Button	**Name**	**cmdExit**
	Caption	&Exit
	Height	495
	Left	5760
	Top	3120
	Width	1215
Label	**Name**	**lblTitle**
	Caption	Lost or got the focus?
	Height	255
	Left	840

Object	Property	Setting
	Top	2880
	Width	1935
Label	**Name**	**lblInfo**
	Caption	(empty)
	Alignment	2-Center
	BackColor	(black)
	BorderStyle	1-Fixed Single
	ForeColor	(white)
	Height	495
	Left	840
	Top	3240
	Width	3855

Figure 12.5.
The frmFocus form.

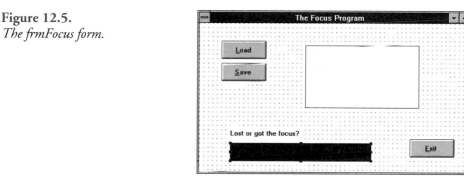

Entering the Code of the Focus Program

☐ Enter the following code inside the general declarations section of the frmFocus form:

```
' All variables must be declared.
Option Explicit
```

☐ Enter the following code inside the cmdExit_Click() procedure of the frmFocus form:

```
Sub cmdExit_Click ()

    End

End Sub
```

☐ Enter the following code inside the txtUserArea_GotFocus() procedure of the frmFocus form:

419

```
Sub txtUserArea_GotFocus ()

    lblInfo.Caption = "txtUserArea got the focus"

End Sub
```

☐ Enter the following code inside the `txtUserArea_LostFocus()` procedure of the frmFocus form:

```
Sub txtUserArea_LostFocus ()

    lblInfo.Caption = "txtUserArea lost the focus"

End Sub
```

Executing the Focus Program

☐ Execute the Focus program.

☐ Move the keyboard focus to the textUserArea text box by clicking inside the text box or using the Tab key (or the arrow keys).

When you move the focus to the text box, as in Figure 12.6, the lblInfo label displays the message `txtUserArea got the focus`.

☐ Move the focus away from the txtUserArea text box (by clicking the Save or Load buttons or using the Tab or arrow keys).

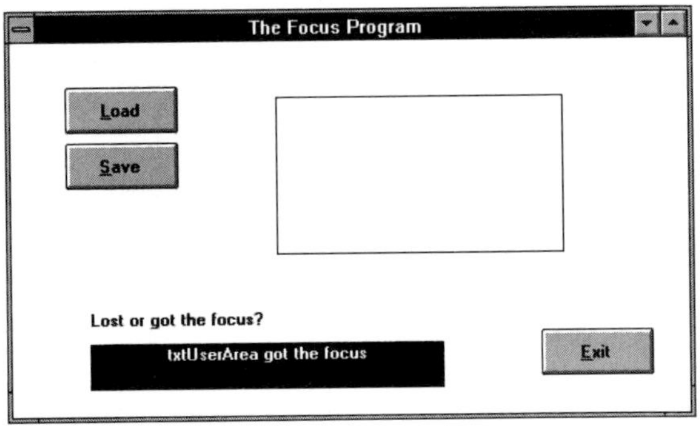

Figure 12.6.
The frmFocus form, with the focus on the text box.

When you move the focus away from the text box, the lblInfo label displays the message `txtUserArea lost the focus`.

☐ Exit the program by clicking the Exit button.

How the Focus Program Works

The Focus program utilizes the GotFocus and LostFocus events to detect whether the text box got or lost the focus.

The Code Inside the *txtUserArea_GotFocus()* Event Procedure of the frmFocus Form

The txtUserArea_GotFocus() procedure is executed whenever the user moves the focus to the text box:

```
Sub txtUserArea_GotFocus ()

    lblInfo.Caption = "txtUserArea got the focus"

End Sub
```

This procedure sets the Caption property of the lblInfo label to a string that indicates that the text box got the focus.

The Code Inside the *txtUserArea_LostFocus()* Event Procedure of the frmFocus Form

The txtUserArea_LostFocus() procedure is executed whenever the user moves the focus away from the text box:

```
Sub txtUserArea_LostFocus ()

    lblInfo.Caption = "txtUserArea lost the focus"

End Sub
```

This procedure sets the Caption property of the lblInfo label to a string indicating that the text box lost the focus.

Summary

In this chapter you have learned how to determine which key was pressed using the KeyDown, KeyUp, and KeyPress events. You have learned that when the KeyPreview property of a form is set to True, the Form_KeyDown(), Form_KeyUp(), and Form_KeyPress() procedures are executed.

You have also learned that the tab order is determined by the TabIndex property, and that the GotFocus and LostFocus events occur whenever a control loses or gets the keyboard focus.

Q&A

Q Which event should I use to trap key pressing: `KeyDown` or `KeyPress`?

A If your code is written to trap ASCII keys, you should use the `KeyPress` event, because this event occurs only when an ASCII key is pressed. If your code is written to trap any key (ASCII and non-ASCII), you need to use the `KeyDown` event.

Quiz

1. The `KeyPress` event occurs whenever the user does what?
2. The `KeyDown` event occurs whenever the user does what?
3. The `KeyUp` event occurs whenever the user does what?
4. What happens once the KeyPreview property of a form is set to True?

Exercises

1. Change the UPPER program so that whenever the user presses a or A on the keyboard the text box thinks that the user presses the b or B keys.
2. Add code to the TAB program so it is terminated whenever the user presses Shift+Alt+F1.

Quiz Answers

1. Whenever the user presses an ASCII key on the keyboard
2. Whenever the user presses any key on the keyboard
3. Whenever the user releases a key
4. Once the KeyPreview property of a form is set to True, the various keyboard event procedures are executed, such as `Form_KeyDown()`, `Form_KeyUp()`, and `Form_KeyPress()`.

Exercise Answers

1. The solution to this exercise is the following:

☐ Enter the following code inside the `txtUserArea_KeyPress()` procedure of the frmUpper form:

```
Sub txtUserArea_KeyPress (KeyAscii As Integer)

    If KeyAscii = 97 Then
        KeyAscii = 98
    End If

    If KeyAscii = 65 Then
```

```
        KeyAscii = 66
     End If
```

End Sub

☐ Save the project.

☐ Execute the UPPER program.

☐ Type the word Alabama inside the text box.

The text that you'll see inside the text box is Blbbbmb. (Each A is replaced with B, and each a is replaced with b.)

☐ Click the Exit button to terminate the program.

The first If statement checks whether the pressed key is the A key, and if so, it changes the KeyAscii value from 65 (A) to 66 (B). Similarly, the second If statement checks whether the pressed key is the a key. If it is a, the value of KeyAscii is changed from 97 (a) to 98 (b).

2. The solution to this exercise is the following:

☐ Set the KeyPreview property of the frmTab form to True.

☐ Enter the following code inside the Form_KeyDown() procedure:

```
Sub Form_KeyDown (KeyCode As Integer, Shift As Integer)

    Const KEY_F1 = &H70

    If Shift = 5 Then
        If KeyCode = KEY_F1 Then
            End
        End If
    End If

End Sub
```

☐ Save the project.

☐ Execute the TAB program.

☐ Press Shift+Alt+F1 to terminate the program.

The Form_KeyDown() procedure is executed whenever the user presses a key.

The KEY_F1 constant was extracted by searching for the string KEY_F1 in the file C:\CONSTANT.TXT.

The block of two nested If…End If statements checks whether the pressed keys are the Shift, Alt, or F1 keys.

When Shift is equal to 5, the Shift key and the Alt key are currently down (see Table 12.2).

File-System
Controls

This chapter focuses on using the file-system controls to write a program that lets you select a file from a drive. There are three file-system controls: the Drive list box, the Directory list box, and the File Name list box.

In a typical program that allows you to select files from drives, these three controls are used in combination. Whenever you need to select a file, a dialog box that has the three controls in it is displayed (see Figure 13.1). You can select the desired file by selecting a drive from the Drive list box, a directory from the Directory list box, and a file from the File Name list box.

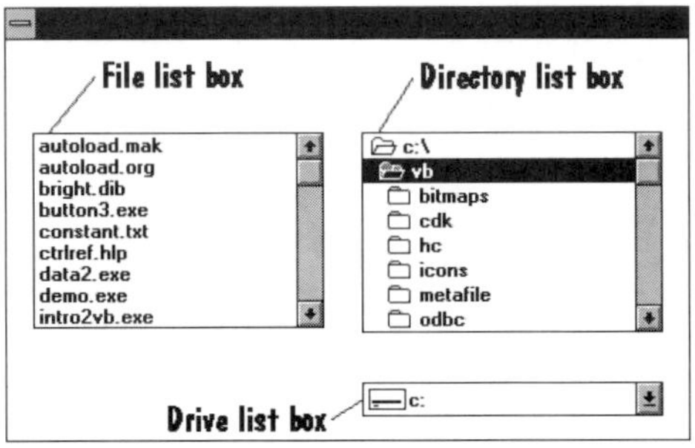

Figure 13.1.
The three file-system controls.

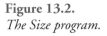

Writing a Program That Includes File-System Controls

Write a program that includes the three file-system controls. The program, called Size, lets you select a file from a drive and display the size of the selected file.

The Size program should do the following:

- Upon startup of the program, a file selection form is displayed on-screen, as shown in Figure 13.2. As you can also see in Figure 13.2, the form of the Size program also includes a combo box (below the File Name list box). This combo box lets you select a file type from a list.

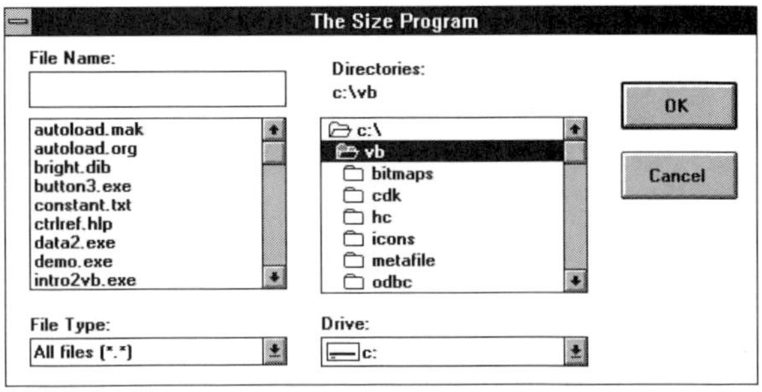

Figure 13.2.
The Size program.

- When you select a drive from the Drive list box, the Directory list box displays the directories of the selected drive.
- When you select a directory from the Directory list box, the files list box displays the files of the selected directory.
- When you select a file from the File Name list box, the selected filename is displayed in the File Name text box.
- When you push the OK button, the size of the selected file is displayed (see Figure 13.3).

Figure 13.3.
Displaying the size of the selected file.

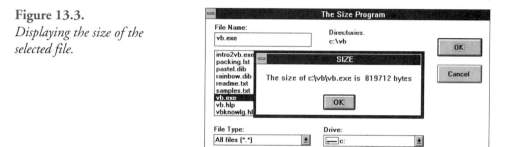

- When you push the Cancel button, the program terminates.
- When you select a file type from the File Type combo box, the File Name list box displays only files of the type that you selected. For example, if you select Text files (*.TXT) only files with the extension .TXT are displayed in the File Name list box.

The Visual Implementation of the Size Program

☐ Start a new project. Save the form of the project as SIZE.FRM and save the make file of the project as SIZE.MAK.

☐ Build the form according to the specifications in Table 13.1.

The completed form should look like the one shown in Figure 13.2.

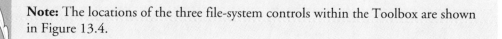

Note: The locations of the three file-system controls within the Toolbox are shown in Figure 13.4.

Table 13.1. The properties table of the Size program.

Object	Property	Value
Form	**Name**	**frmSize**
	Caption	The Size Program
	Height	4020
Form	**Name**	**frmSize**
	Left	1200
	Top	1740
	Width	7890
Label	**Name**	**lblFileName**
	Caption	File Name:
	Height	255
	Left	240
	Top	120
	Width	1095
Text Box	**Name**	**txtFileName**
	Text	(empty)
	Height	375
	Left	240
	Top	360
	Width	2655
File List Box	**Name**	**filFiles**
	Height	1785
	Left	240
	Top	840
	Width	2655
Label	**Name**	**lblFileType**
	Caption	File Type:
	Height	255
Label	**Name**	**lblFileType**
	Left	240
	Top	2880
	Width	1095

Object	Property	Value
Combo Box	**Name**	**cboFileType**
	Style	2-Dropdown List
	Height	300
	Left	240
	Top	3120
	Width	2655
Label	**Name**	**lblDirectories**
	Caption	Directories:
	Height	255
	Left	3360
	Top	240
	Width	1215
Label	**Name**	**lblDirName**
	Caption	(cmpty)
	Height	255
	Left	3360
	Top	480
	Width	1215
Directory List Box	**Name**	**dirDirectory**
	Height	1830
	Left	3240
	Top	840
	Width	2775
Command Button	**Name**	**cmdOK**
	Caption	OK
	Default	True
	Height	495
	Left	6360
	Top	480
	Width	1215

continues

Table 13.1. continued

Object	Property	Value
Label	**Name**	**lblDrive**
	Caption	Drive:
	Height	255
	Left	3240
	Top	2880
	Width	1095
Drive List Box	**Name**	**drvDrive**
	Height	315
	Left	3240
	Top	3120
	Width	2775
Command Button	**Name**	**cmdCancel**
	Caption	Cancel
	Cancel	True
	Height	495
	Left	6360
	Top	1200
	Width	1215

Figure 13.4.
*The locations of the
file-system controls within
the Toolbox.*

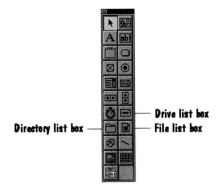

Directory list box ——

Drive list box
File list box

Entering the Code of the Size Program

> **Note:** The default property of a text box is Text. This means that `txtMyText.Text="Hello"` is the same as `txtMyText="Hello"`. That is, if you don't specify the property, the default property is assumed.

☐ Enter the following code inside the general declarations area of the frmSize form:

```
' All variables MUST be declared.
Option Explicit
```

☐ Enter the following code inside the `Form_Load()` event procedure:

```
Sub Form_Load ()

    ' Fill the cboFileType combo box.
    cboFileType.AddItem "All files (*.*)"
    cboFileType.AddItem "Text files (*.TXT)"
    cboFileType.AddItem "Doc files (*.DOC)"

    ' Initialize the cboFileType combo box to
    ' item #0. (i.e. All files *.*)
    cboFileType.ListIndex = 0

    ' Update the lblDirName label with the path.
    lblDirName.Caption = dirDirectory.Path

End Sub
```

☐ Enter the following code inside the `drvDrive_Change()` event procedure:

```
Sub drvDrive_Change ()

    ' The next statement may cause an error so we
    ' set error trap.
    On Error GoTo DriveError

    ' Change the path of the Directory list box to
    ' the new drive.
    dirDirectory.Path = drvDrive.Drive
    Exit Sub

DriveError:
    ' An error occurred! So tell the user and
    ' restore the original drive.
    MsgBox "Drive error!", 48, "Error"
    drvDrive.Drive = dirDirectory.Path
    Exit Sub

End Sub
```

☐ Enter the following code inside the `dirDirectory_Change()` event procedure:

```
Sub dirDirectory_Change ()
```

```
' A directory was just selected by the user so
' update the path of the File Name list box
' accordingly.
filFiles.Path = dirDirectory.Path

' Also update the lblDirName label.
lblDirName.Caption = dirDirectory.Path

End Sub
```

☐ Enter the following code inside the `cboFileType_Click()` event procedure:

```
Sub cboFileType_Click ()

    ' Change the Pattern of the File Name list box
    ' according to the File Type that the user
    ' selected.
    Select Case cboFileType.ListIndex
    Case 0
        filFiles.Pattern = "*.*"
    Case 1
        filFiles.Pattern = "*.TXT"
    Case 2
        filFiles.Pattern = "*.DOC"
    End Select

End Sub
```

☐ Enter the following code inside the `filFiles_Click()` event procedure:

```
Sub filFiles_Click ()

    ' Update the txtFileName text box with the file
    ' name that was just selected.
    txtFileName.Text = filFiles.FileName

End Sub
```

☐ Enter the following code inside the `cmdOK_Click()` event procedure:

```
Sub cmdOK_Click ()

    Dim PathAndName As String
    Dim FileSize As String
    Dim Path

    ' If no file is selected then tell the user and
    ' exit this procedure.
    If txtFileName.Text = "" Then
        MsgBox "You must first select a file!"
        Exit Sub
    End If

    'Make sure that Path ends with backslash (\).
    If Right$(filFiles.Path, 1) <> "\" Then
        Path = filFiles.Path + "\"
    Else
        Path = filFiles.Path
    End If
```

```
'Extract the Path and Name of the selected file.
If txtFileName.Text = filFiles.FileName Then
    PathAndName = Path + filFiles.FileName
Else
    PathAndName = txtFileName
End If

' The next statement may cause an error so we
' set an error trap.
On Error GoTo FileLenError

'Get the file size of the file.
FileSize = Str$(FileLen(PathAndName))

'Display the size of the file.
MsgBox "The size of "+PathAndName+" is "+FileSize+" bytes"

Exit Sub
FileLenError:
' There was an error, so display error message
' and exit.
MsgBox "Cannot find size of " + PathAndName, 48, "Error"

Exit Sub

End Sub
```

☐ Enter the following code inside the `filFiles_DblClick()` event procedure:

```
Sub filFiles_DblClick ()

' Update the txtFileName text box with the file
' name that was just double clicked.
txtFileName = filFiles.FileName

'Execute the cmdOK_Click() procedure.
cmdOK_Click

End Sub
```

☐ Enter the following code inside the `cmdCancel()` event procedure:

```
Sub cmdCancel_Click ()

End

End Sub
```

Executing the Size Program

☐ Execute the Size program and experiment with the controls that appear onscreen.

While you run the program, notice the following features:

- As soon as you select a drive from the Drive list box, the directories of the selected drive appear in the Directory list box.

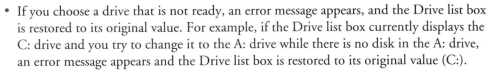
- If you choose a drive that is not ready, an error message appears, and the Drive list box is restored to its original value. For example, if the Drive list box currently displays the C: drive and you try to change it to the A: drive while there is no disk in the A: drive, an error message appears and the Drive list box is restored to its original value (C:).

- To select a directory from the Directory list box, you need to double-click the desired directory.

- As soon as you select a directory from the Directory list box, the files of the selected directory appear in the File Name list box, and the selected directory name appears above the Directory list box.

- As soon as you highlight a file in the File Name list box, the selected filename is displayed in the File Name text box.

- After you select a file type from the File Type combo box, the File Name list box displays only files of the type that you selected. You cannot type in the text area of the combo box, because at design time the Style property of the combo box was set to Dropdown list.

- When you push the OK button, a message appears that displays the file size of the selected file.

- Instead of selecting a file from the File Name list box, you may type the desired filename in the File Name text box.

- Pressing Enter is the same as pushing the OK button, because in design time, you set the Default property of the OK button to True.

- Pressing Esc is the same as pushing the Cancel button, because in design time you set the Cancel property of the Cancel button to True.

Terminate the Size program:

☐ Push the Cancel button.

How the Size Program Works

Like other controls, the file-system controls have event procedures. The code inside these procedures determines how the controls interact with each other.

The Code Inside the *Form_Load()* Procedure

Upon startup of the program, the `Form_Load()` procedure is executed. In this procedure the `cboFileType` combo box and the `lblDirName` label are initialized:

```
Sub Form_Load ()
```

```
' Fill the cboFileType combo box.
cboFileType.AddItem "All files (*.*)"
cboFileType.AddItem "Text files (*.TXT)"
cboFileType.AddItem "Doc files (*.DOC)"

' Initialize the cboFileType combo box to
' item #0 (i.e. All files *.*)
cboFileType.ListIndex = 0

' Update the lblDirName label with the path
' value of the Directory list box.
lblDirName.Caption = dirDirectory.Path

End Sub
```

The AddItem method is used three times to fill the cboFileType combo box with three items: All files (*.*), Text files (*.TXT), and Doc files (*.DOC).

Then the ListIndex property of the cboFileType combo box is set to 0. This sets the currently selected item of the combo box to item 0, or All files (*.*).

Finally, the caption of the lblDirName label is set to the Path property of the Directory list box. The initial value of the Path property of the Directory list box is the current directory. So upon startup of the program, lblDirName displays the name of the current directory.

The Code Inside the *drvDrive_Change()* Procedure

Whenever a drive is changed in the Drive list box, either by the user or by the program, the drvDrive_Change() procedure is executed. The code inside this procedure updates the Path property of the Directory list box with the new drive that was selected:

```
Sub drvDrive_Change ()

    ' The next statement may cause an error so we
    ' set error trap.
    On Error GoTo DriveError

    ' Change the path of the Directory list box to
    ' the new drive.
    dirDirectory.Path = drvDrive.Drive
    Exit Sub

DriveError:
    ' An error occurred! So tell the user and
    ' restore the original drive.
    MsgBox "Drive error!", 48, "Error"
    drvDrive.Drive = dirDirectory.Path
    Exit Sub

End Sub
```

13

File-System Controls

Before you execute the command that changes the Path property of the Directory list box, an error trap is set. The error trap is required because changing the path of the Directory list box may cause an error. For example, if the user changed the Drive list box to drive A:, and drive A: is not ready, changing the path of the Directory list box to A: causes an error. To avoid a runtime error, an error trap is set with the following statement:

```
On Error Goto DriveError
```

If an error occurs now during the execution of this statement:

```
dirDirectory.Path = drvDrive.Drive,
```

Visual Basic gives control to the code below the DriveError label. The code below the DriveError label displays an error message and restores the original value of the drive with the following statement:

```
drvDrive.Drive = dirDirectory.Path
```

Note that `dirDirectory.Path` still contains the original drive value because the statement that caused the error was not executed.

If the drive you selected is ready, an error does not occur. The path of the Directory list box is changed to the selected drive, and as a result, the Directory list box lists the directories of the selected drive.

The Code Inside the *dirDirectory_Change()* Event Procedure

Whenever a directory is changed in the Directory list box, either by the user or by the program, the `dirDirectory_Change()` procedure is executed. The code inside this procedure updates the Path property of the File Name list box and the Caption property of the lblDirName label with the new directory:

```
Sub dirDirectory_Change ()

    ' A directory was just selected by the user so
    ' update the Path of the File Name list box accordingly.
    filFiles.Path = dirDirectory.Path

    ' Also update the lblDirName label.
    lblDirName.Caption = dirDirectory.Path

End Sub
```

As a result of updating the Path property of the File Name list box with the selected directory, the File Name list box displays the files of the selected directory.

The Code Inside the *cboFileType_Click()* Procedure

Whenever the user makes a selection from the cboFileType combo box, the `cboFileType_Click()` event procedure is executed. The code inside this procedure updates the Pattern property of the File Name list box according to the file type that was selected by the user:

```
Sub cboFileType_Click ()

    ' Change the Pattern of the File Name list box
    ' according to the File Type that the user selected.
    Select Case cboFileType.ListIndex
    Case 0
      filFiles.Pattern = "*.*"
    Case 1
      filFiles.Pattern = "*.TXT"
    Case 2
      filFiles.Pattern = "*.DOC"
    End Select

End Sub
```

To determine which item in the cboFileType combo box the user selected, a `Select Case` is used. Recall that the `Form_Load()` procedure filled the cboFileType combo box with three items: All files (*.*), Text files (*.TXT), and Doc files (*.DOC). Depending on which item the user selects from the combo box, a different `Case` statement is executed. For example, if the user selects the second item from the combo box (that is, Text files (*.TXT)), the statement:

```
filFiles.Pattern = "*.TXT"
```

is executed. As a result, the File Name list box displays only files with .TXT extension.

The Code Inside the *filFiles_Click()* Procedure

13

Whenever the user highlights a file in the File Name list box, the `filFiles_Click()` event procedure is executed. The code inside this procedure updates the txtFileName text box with the name of the selected file:

```
Sub filFiles_Click ()

    ' Update the txtFileName text box with the file
    ' name that was just selected.
    txtFileName = filFiles.FileName

End Sub
```

The Code Inside the *cmdOK_Click()* Procedure

Whenever the user pushes the OK pushbutton, the cmdOK_Click() event procedure is executed. The code of this procedure displays the file size of the currently selected file:

```
Sub cmdOK_Click ()

    Dim PathAndName As String
    Dim FileSize As String
    Dim Path

    ' If no file is selected then tell the user and exit this procedure.
    If txtFileName.Text = "" Then
      MsgBox "You must first select a file!"
      Exit Sub
    End If

    'Make sure that Path ends with backslash (\).
    If Right$(filFiles.Path, 1) <> "\" Then
      Path = filFiles.Path + "\"
    Else
      Path = filFiles.Path
    End If

    'Extract the Path and Name of the selected file.
    If txtFileName.Text = filFiles.FileName Then
      PathAndName = Path + filFiles.FileName
    Else
      PathAndName = txtFileName
    End If

    ' The next statement may cause an error so we set an error trap.
    On Error GoTo FileLenError

    'Get the file size of the file.
    FileSize = Str$(FileLen(PathAndName))

    'Display the size of the file.
    MsgBox "The size of "+PathAndName+" is "+FileSize+" bytes"
    Exit Sub

FileLenError:
    ' There was an error, so display error message and exit.
    MsgBox "Cannot find size of " + PathAndName, 48, "Error"
    Exit Sub

End Sub
```

The first thing the procedure does is check whether the user selected a file. This is done by comparing the Text property of the txtFileName text box with null. If txtFileName.Text is null, a message is displayed and the procedure is terminated:

```
If txtFileName.Text = "" Then
    MsgBox "You must first select a file!"
```

```
    Exit Sub
End If
```

After making sure that the user selected a file, the `Path` variable is updated with the path of the selected file. The `Right$()` function is used to make sure that the extreme right character of the path of the selected file is the backslash character (\). If the extreme right character of the path is not the backslash, a backslash is added to the `Path` variable:

```
If Right$(filFiles.Path, 1) <> "\" Then
    Path = filFiles.Path + "\"
Else
    Path = filFiles.Path
End If
```

After the `Path` variable is ready, the `PathAndName` variable can be updated. As implied by its name, the `PathAndName` variable should contain the full name of the file (that is, Path and Name). The `PathAndName` variable is updated with an `If` statement:

```
If txtFileName.Text = filFiles.FileName Then
    PathAndName = Path + filFiles.FileName
Else
    PathAndName = txtFileName
End If
```

This `If` statement checks whether the currently highlighted file in the File Name list box is the same as the contents of the File Name text box. If the filename inside the text box is not the same as the currently highlighted file, the user manually typed the path and name of the file, in which case the `PathAndName` variable is updated with whatever the user typed. However, if the filename in the text box is the same as the currently highlighted file, the variable `PathAndName` is updated with the string `Path + filFiles.FileName`.

After the `PathAndName` variable is updated, the `FileLen()` function can be used to find the size of the file. But because the `FileLen()` function may cause a runtime error (for example, if the user typed the name of a file that does not exist), an error trap is set with the following statement:

```
On Error GoTo FileLenError
```

If an error now occurs during the execution of the following statement:

```
FileSize = Str$(FileLen(PathAndName))
```

Visual Basic gives control to the statement below the FileLenError label, which displays an error message and terminates the procedure:

```
FileLenError:
    MsgBox "Cannot find size of " + PathAndName, 48, "Error"
    Exit Sub
```

However, if the `FileLen()` function does not cause an error, the size of the file is displayed on-screen and the procedure is terminated:

```
MsgBox "The size of "+PathAndName+" is "+FileSize+" bytes"
Exit Sub
```

13

The Code Inside the *filFiles_DblClick()* Procedure

Whenever the user double-clicks on a file inside the File Name list box, the `filFiles_DblClick()` event procedure is executed. The code of this procedure updates the File Name text box with the name of the file that was doubled-clicked and executes the `cmdOK_Click()` procedure:

```
Sub filFiles_DblClick ()

    ' Update the txtFileName text box with the file
    ' name that was just double clicked.
    txtFileName = filFiles.FileName

    'Execute the cmdOK_Click() procedure.
    cmdOK_Click

End Sub
```

The Code Inside the *cmdCancel_Click()* Procedure

Whenever the user pushes the Cancel command button, the `cmdCancel_Click()` event procedure is executed. The code of this procedure terminates the program:

```
Sub cmdCancel_Click ()

    End

End Sub
```

The Attribute Properties of the File List Box

A file may have any of the following four attributes:

- Read-only. When the read-only attribute of a file is set, the file can only be read (that is, it cannot be erased or overwritten).
- Hidden. When the hidden attribute of a file is set, the DIR command of DOS does not display the file.
- System. DOS system files (files that are part of the operating system) have their system attribute set. A system file cannot be erased or overwritten.
- Archive. When the DOS BACKUP command (and other backup utilities) backs up a file, the archive attribute of the file is set. This attribute is used as a flag to indicate that the file was backed up. As soon as the file is modified, the archive attribute is automati-

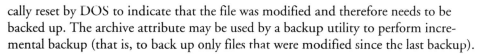

cally reset by DOS to indicate that the file was modified and therefore needs to be backed up. The archive attribute may be used by a backup utility to perform incremental backup (that is, to back up only files that were modified since the last backup).

The attribute properties of a File Name list box determine which files are displayed in the File Name list box, depending on the attributes of the files. The attribute properties of a File Name list box are ReadOnly, Archive, Normal, System, and Hidden. Each of these properties may be set to either True or False. For example, to display only the read-only files, you need to set the attribute properties of filMyFiles list box as follows:

```
filMyFiles.ReadOnly = True
filMyFiles.Archive  = False
filMyFiles.Normal   = False
filMyFiles.System   = False
filMyFiles.Hidden   = False
```

Creating a Get File Dialog Box

The Size program illustrates how to create a form that lets you select files from a drive. Because many programs need such a form, it is a good idea to create a general-purpose Get File dialog box form that could be used by many projects.

The Select program illustrates how to create and use a general-purpose Get File dialog box. Before you start writing the Select program, specify what it should do:

- Upon startup of the program, a menu bar with a File menu title appears (see Figure 13.5).

Figure 13.5.
The Select program.

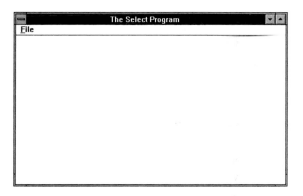

13

- The File menu has two items: Select file and Exit (see Figure 13.6).
- When you select Select file from the File menu, a Get File dialog box appears (see Figure 13.7).

Figure 13.6.
*The File menu of the
Select program.*

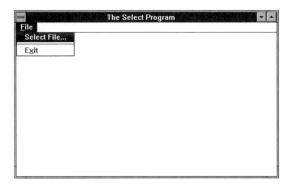

- After you select a file from the Get File dialog box, the dialog box closes and the name of the selected file is displayed.

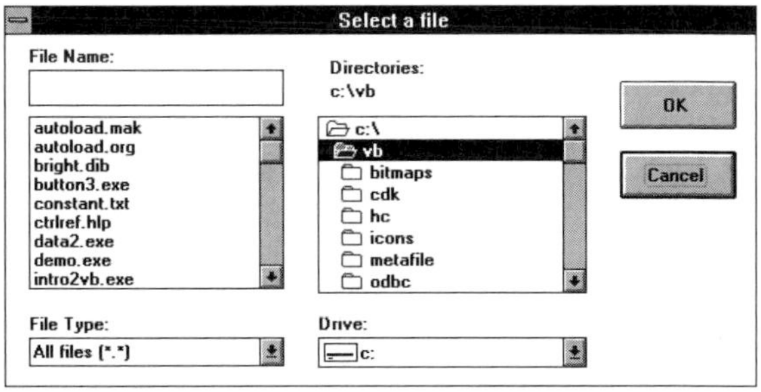

Figure 13.7.
The Get File dialog box.

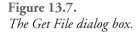

- When you select Exit from the File menu, the program terminates.

The Visual Implementation
of the Select Program

☐ Start a new project. Save the form of the project as SELECT.FRM and save the make file of the project as SELECT.MAK.

☐ Build the SELECT.FRM form according to the specifications in Table 13.2.

Table 13.2. The properties table of the SELECT.FRM form.

Object	Property	Value
Form	**Name**	**frmSelect**
	Caption	The Select Program
Menu	**(see Table 13.3)**	**(see Table 13.3)**

Table 13.3. The menu table of the SELECT.FRM form.

Caption	Name
&File	mnuFile
...&Select File...	mnuSelectFile
...-	mnuSep1
...E&xit	mnuExit

The completed form should look like the one shown in Figure 13.5.

☐ Add a new form to the project (select New Form from the File menu). Save the new form as GETFILE.FRM.

☐ Build the GETFILE.FRM form according to the specifications in Table 13.4.

The completed form should look like the one shown in Figure 13.7.

Table 13.4. The properties table of the GETFILE.FRM form.

Object	Property	Value
Form	**Name**	**frmGetFile**
	Caption	Select a file
	Height	4020
	Left	1200
	Top	1740
	Width	7890
Label	**Name**	**lblFileName**
	Caption	File Name:
	Height	255
	Left	240
	Top	120
	Width	1095
Text Box	**Name**	**txtFileName**
	Text	(empty)
	Height	375
	Left	240

continues

Table 13.4. continued

Object	Property	Value
	Top	360
	Width	2655
File List Box	**Name**	**filFiles**
	Height	1785
	Left	240
	Top	840
	Width	2655
Label	**Name**	**lblFileType**
	Caption	File Type:
	Height	255
	Left	240
	Top	2880
	Width	1095
Combo Box	**Name**	**cboFileType**
	Style	2-Dropdown List
	Height	300
	Left	240
	Top	3120
	Width	2655
Label	**Name**	**lblDirectories**
	Caption	Directories:
	Height	255
Label	**Name**	**lblDirectories**
	Left	3360
	Top	240
	Width	1215
Label	**Name**	**lblDirName**
	Caption	(empty)
	Height	255
	Left	3360
	Top	480

Object	Property	Value
	Width	1215
Directory List Box	**Name**	**dirDirectory**
	Height	1830
	Left	3240
	Top	840
	Width	2775
Command Button	**Name**	**cmdOK**
	Caption	OK
	Default	True
	Height	495
	Left	6360
	Top	480
	Width	1215
Label	**Name**	**lblDrive**
	Caption	Drive:
	Height	255
	Left	3240
	Top	2880
	Width	1095
Drive List Box	**Name**	**drvDrive**
	Height	315
	Left	3240
	Top	3120
	Width	2775
Command Button	**Name**	**cmdCancel**
	Caption	Cancel
	Cancel	True
	Height	495
	Left	6360
	Top	1200
	Width	1215

Entering the Code of the Select Program

The Select program has two forms: frmSelect and frmGetFile. The following sections list the procedures of these forms.

Entering the Code of the frmSelect Form

☐ Enter the following code inside the `Form_Load()` procedure of the frmSelect form:

```
Sub Form_Load ()

    ' Load the frmGetFile dialog box (without displaying it).
    Load frmGetFile

    ' Initialize the cboFileType combo box of the frmGetFile dialog box.
    frmGetFile.cboFileType.AddItem "All files (*.*)"
    frmGetFile.cboFileType.AddItem "Text files *.TXT)"
    frmGetFile.cboFileType.AddItem "Doc files  (*.DOC)"
    frmGetFile.cboFileType.ListIndex = 0

End Sub
```

☐ Enter the following code inside the `mnuSelectFile_Click()` procedure of the frmSelect form:

```
Sub mnuSelectFile_Click ()

    ' Set the Caption property of frmGetFile.
    frmGetFile.Caption = "Select a file"

    ' Display the frmGetFile form as a modal dialog box.
    frmGetFile.Show 1

    ' Display the name of the selected file on the screen.
    If frmGetFile.Tag = "" Then
        MsgBox "No file was selected!"
    Else
        MsgBox "You selected " + frmGetFile.Tag
    End If

End Sub
```

☐ Enter the following code inside the `mnuExit_Click()` event procedure of the frmSelect form:

```
Sub mnuExit_Click ()

    End

End Sub
```

Entering the Code of the frmGetFile Form

☐ Enter the following code in the `Form_Load()` procedure of the frmGetFile form:

```
Sub Form_Load ()

    ' Update the Directory lblDirName label with the
    ' path value of the Directory list box.
    lblDirName.Caption = dirDirectory.Path

End Sub
```

☐ Enter the following code inside the `drvDrive_Change()` procedure of the frmGetFile form:

```
Sub drvDrive_Change ()

    ' The next statement may cause an error so we set error trap.
    On Error GoTo DriveError

    ' Change the path of the Directory list box to the new drive.
    dirDirectory.Path = drvDrive.Drive
    Exit Sub

DriveError:
    ' An error occurred! So tell the user and restore the original drive.
    MsgBox "Drive error!", 48, "Error"
    drvDrive.Drive = dirDirectory.Path
    Exit Sub

End Sub
```

☐ Enter the following code in the `dirDirectory_Change()` procedure of the frmGetFile form:

```
Sub dirDirectory_Change ()

    ' A directory was just selected by the user so
    ' update the path of the File Name list box accordingly.
    filFiles.Path = dirDirectory.Path

    ' Also update the lblDirName label.
    lblDirName.Caption = dirDirectory.Path

End Sub
```

☐ Enter the following code inside the `cboFileType_Click()` procedure of the frmGetFile form:

```
Sub cboFileType_Click ()

    Dim PatternPos1 As Integer
    Dim PatternPos2 As Integer
    Dim PatternLen As Integer
```

```
Dim Pattern As String

' Find the start position of the pattern in the cboFileType combo box.
PatternPos1 = InStr(1, cboFileType.Text, "(") + 1

' Find the end position of the pattern in the cboFileType combo box.
PatternPos2 = InStr(1, cboFileType.Text, ")") - 1

' Calculate the length of the Pattern string.
PatternLen = PatternPos2 - PatternPos1 + 1

' Extract the Pattern portion of the cboFileType combo box.
Pattern=Mid$(cboFileType.Text,PatternPos1,PatternLen)

' Set the Pattern of the filFiles file listbox to the selected pattern.
filFiles.Pattern = Pattern

End Sub
```

☐ Enter the following code inside the `filFiles_Click()` procedure of the frmGetFile form:

```
Sub filFiles_Click ()

' Update the txtFileName text box with the file name that was just selected.
txtFileName = filFiles.FileName

End Sub
```

☐ Enter the following code inside the `cmdOK_Click()` procedure of the frmGetFile form:

```
Sub cmdOK_Click ()

Dim PathAndName As String
Dim Path

' If no file is selected then tell the user and exit this procedure.
If txtFileName.Text = "" Then
    MsgBox "No file is selected!", 48, "Error"
    Exit Sub
End If

' Make sure that Path ends with backslash (\).
If Right$(filFiles.Path, 1) <> "\" Then
    Path = filFiles.Path + "\"
Else
    Path = filFiles.Path
End If

' Extract the Path and Name of the selected file.
If txtFileName.Text = filFiles.FileName Then
    PathAndName = Path + filFiles.FileName
Else
    PathAndName = txtFileName
End If

' Set the tag property of the frmGetFile dialog
' box to the selected file path and name.
```

```
    frmGetFile.Tag = PathAndName

    ' Hide the frmGetFile dialog box.
    frmGetFile.Hide

End Sub
```

☐ Enter the following code inside the `filFiles_DblClick()` procedure of the frmGetFile form:

```
Sub filFiles_DblClick ()

    ' Update the txtFileName text box with the file
    ' name that was just double clicked.
    txtFileName = filFiles.FileName

    'Execute the cmdOK_Click() procedure.
    cmdOK_Click

End Sub
```

☐ Enter the following code inside the `cmdCancel()` event procedure of the frmGetFile form:

```
Sub cmdCancel_Click ()

    ' Set the tag property of the form to null.
    frmGetFile.Tag = ""
    ' Hide the frmGetFile dialog box.
    frmGetFile.Hide

End Sub
```

Executing the Select Program

☐ Execute the Select program.

After you select Select File from the File menu, the Get File dialog box appears onscreen as a modal form. This means that as long as the dialog box is open you cannot select other forms of the program. If you click the mouse inside the frmSelect form while the dialog box is displayed, you hear a beep.

13

☐ Experiment with the various controls of the Get File dialog box.

☐ Select Exit from the File menu.

How the Select Program Works

The Select program uses the frmGetFile form as a modal dialog box. Whenever there is a need to get a filename from the user, the code of the program displays the frmGetFile form.

The Code Inside the *Form_Load()* Procedure of the frmSelect Form

Upon startup of the program, the Form_Load() procedure of the frmSelect form is executed. In this procedure, the frmGetFile dialog box is loaded, and the cboFileType combo box of the dialog box is initialized:

```
Sub Form_Load ()

    ' Load the frmGetFile dialog box (without displaying it).
    Load frmGetFile

    ' Initialize the File Type combo box of the frmGetFile dialog box.
    frmGetFile.cboFileType.AddItem "All files (*.*)"
    frmGetFile.cboFileType.AddItem "Text files (*.TXT)"
    frmGetFile.cboFileType.AddItem "Doc files  (*.DOC)"
    frmGetFile.cboFileType.ListIndex = 0

End Sub
```

The frmGetFile dialog box is loaded into memory with the Load statement. Loading the form does not display it. The form is loaded into memory so that later other procedures can show the dialog box without delays. After the frmGetFile dialog box is loaded, the procedure initializes the cboFileType combo box of the dialog box.

The Code Inside the *mnuSelectFile_Click()* Procedure of the frmSelect Form

Whenever the user selects Select File from the File menu, the mnuSelectFile_Click() procedure is executed. The code inside this procedure displays the frmGetFile form as a modal dialog box, and then uses the output of the dialog box to determine which file the user selected from the dialog box. The output of the dialog box (that is, the name of the selected file) is provided in the Tag property of the frmGetFile form:

```
Sub mnuSelectFile_Click ()

    ' Set the Caption property of frmGetFile.
    frmGetFile.Caption = "Select a file"

    ' Display the frmGetFile form as a modal dialog box.
    frmGetFile.Show 1

    ' Display the name of the selected file on the screen.
    If frmGetFile.Tag = "" Then
      MsgBox "No file was selected!"
    Else
      MsgBox "You selected " + frmGetFile.Tag
    End If

End Sub
```

The first statement of the procedure sets the Caption property of the frmGetFile form to `Select a file`:

```
frmGetFile.Caption = "Select a file"
```

Then the frmGetFile form is displayed onscreen as a modal dialog box, by using the show method with style equal to 1:

```
frmGetFile.Show 1
```

The code inside the frmGetFile form updates the Tag property of frmGetFile with the name of the file the user selects. If the user does not select a file (for example, the user pushes the Cancel button), the code of frmGetFile sets the Tag property of frmGetFile to null.

After the user selects a file from the frmGetFile form, the name of the selected file (if any) is displayed onscreen:

```
If frmGetFile.Tag = "" Then
    MsgBox "No file was selected!"
Else
    MsgBox "You selected " + frmGetFile.Tag
End If
```

If frmGetFile.Tag is null, the user did not select any file, and the message `No file was selected!` is displayed. However, if frmGetFile.Tag is not null, the selected file (that is, frmGetFile.Tag) is displayed.

The Code Inside the *Form_Load()* Procedure of the frmGetFile Form

Whenever the frmGetFile form is loaded, the `Form_Load()` procedure is executed. The code of this procedure updates the `lblDirName` label with the path value of the Directory list box:

```
Sub Form_Load ()

    ' Update the lblDirName label with the path value of the Directory list box.
    lblDirName.Caption = dirDirectory.Path

End Sub
```

The Code Inside the *drvDrive_Change()* Procedure of the frmGetFile Form

The code of this procedure is the same as the code of the `drvDrive_Change()` procedure of the Size program.

The Code Inside the *dirDirectory_Change()* Procedure of the frmGetFile Form

The code of this procedure is the same as the code of the `drvDirectory_Change()` procedure of the Size program.

The Code Inside the *cboFileType_Click()* Procedure of the frmGetFile Form

Whenever the user makes a selection from the cboFileType combo box, the `cboFileType_Click()` event procedure is executed. The code inside this procedure updates the Pattern property of the File Name list box:

```
Sub cboFileType_Click ()

    Dim PatternPos1 As Integer
    Dim PatternPos2 As Integer
    Dim PatternLen As Integer
    Dim Pattern As String

    ' Find the start position of the pattern in the cbboFileType combo box.
    PatternPos1 = InStr(1, cboFileType.Text, "(") + 1

    ' Find the end position of the pattern in the cbboFileType combo box.
    PatternPos2 = InStr(1, cboFileType.Text, ")") - 1

    ' Calculate the length of the Pattern string.
    PatternLen = PatternPos2 - PatternPos1 + 1

    ' Extract the Pattern portion of the cboFileType combo box.
    Pattern=Mid$(cboFileType.Text,PatternPos1,PatternLen)

    ' Set the Pattern of the filFiles file listbox to the selected pattern.
    filFiles.Pattern = Pattern

End Sub
```

The Text property of the cboFileType combo box (cboFileType.Text) contains the file type that the user selected. To find the pattern of the selected file type, the procedure extracts the pattern portion from cboFileType.Text. For example, if cboFileType.Text is equal to Text files (*.TXT), the Pattern portion is *.TXT.

The procedure extracts the pattern portion from cboFileType.Text by finding the location of the first parenthesis and adding a 1 to it:

```
PatternPos1 = InStr(1, cboFileType.Text, "(" ) + 1
```

Similarly, the position of the last character of the pattern portion is found by locating the second parenthesis and subtracting 1 from it:

```
PatternPos2 = InStr(1, cboFileType.Text, ")") - 1
```

The length of the Pattern string is calculated by subtracting `PatternPos1` from `PatternPos2` and adding 1 to the result:

```
PatternLen = PatternPos2 - PatternPos1 + 1
```

Finally, the pattern portion is extracted by using the `Mid$()` function:

```
Pattern= Mid$(cboFileType.Text, PatternPos1, PatternLen)
```

The last statement of the procedure assigns the extracted pattern to the Pattern property of the filFiles File Name list box:

```
filFiles.Pattern = Pattern
```

So the File Name list box displays only files with the same pattern as the extracted pattern.

The Code Inside the *filFiles_Click()* Procedure of the frmGetFile Form

The code of this procedure is the same as the code of the `filFiles_Click()` procedure of the Size program.

The Code Inside the *cmdOK_Click()* Procedure of the frmGetFile Form

Whenever the user pushes the OK pushbutton, the `cmdOK_Click()` event procedure is executed:

```
Sub cmdOK_Click ()

    Dim PathAndName As String
    Dim Path

    ' If no file is selected, tell the user and exit this procedure.
    If txtFileName.Text = "" Then
       MsgBox "No file is selected!", 48, "Error"
       Exit Sub
    End If

    ' Make sure that Path ends with backslash (\).
    If Right$(filFiles.Path, 1) <> "\" Then
       Path = filFiles.Path + "\"
    Else
       Path = filFiles.Path
    End If

    ' Extract the Path and Name of the selected file.
    If txtFileName.Text = filFiles.FileName Then
       PathAndName = Path + filFiles.FileName
    Else
       PathAndName = txtFileName
    End If
```

```
' Set the tag property of the frmGetFile dialog
' box to the selected file path and name.
frmGetFile.Tag = PathAndName

' Hide the frmGetFile dialog box.
frmGetFile.Hide
```

End Sub

As you can see, this procedure is very similar to the cmdOK_Click() procedure of the Size program.

The first thing the procedure does is check whether the user selected a file. This is done by comparing the Text property of the txtFileName text box with null. If txtFileName.Text is null, a message is displayed and the procedure is terminated:

```
If txtFileName.Text = "" Then
    MsgBox "No file is selected!", 48, "Error"
    Exit Sub
End If
```

After making sure the user selected a file, the Path variable is updated with the path (directory name) of the selected file. The Right$() function is used to make sure that the extreme right character of the path of the selected file is the backslash character (\). If the extreme right character of the Path variable is not the backslash, a backslash is added to the Path variable:

```
If Right$(filFiles.Path, 1) <> "\" Then
    Path = filFiles.Path + "\"
Else
    Path = filFiles.Path
End If
```

After the Path variable is ready, the PathAndName variable can be updated. As implied by its name, the PathAndName variable should contain the full name of the file (that is, Path and Name). The PathAndName variable is updated with an If statement:

```
If txtFileName.Text = filFiles.FileName Then
    PathAndName = Path + filFiles.FileName
Else
    PathAndName = txtFileName
End If
```

This If statement checks whether the currently highlighted file in the File Name list box is the same as the contents of the File Name text box. If the filename inside the text box is not the same as the currently highlighted file, the user manually typed the path and name of the file, in which case the PathAndName variable is updated with whatever the user typed. However, if the filename in the text box is the same as the currently highlighted file, the variable PathAndName is updated with the string Path + filFiles.FileName.

Once the variable PathAndName is updated, its value is assigned to the Tag property of the frmGetFile form:

```
frmGetFile.Tag = PathAndName
```

The Tag property of the form is used to store the output of the frmGetFile form. The procedure that displayed the frmGetFile form "knows" which file the user selected by using frmGetFile.Tag.

The last statement in the procedure removes the frmGetFile form from the screen by using the Hide method:

```
frmGetFile.Hide
```

After this statement is executed, the frmGetFile is removed from the screen and control is given back to the procedure that displayed the frmGetFile form.

The Code Inside the *filFiles_DblClick()* Procedure of the frmGetFile Form

The code of this procedure is the same as the code of the filFiles_DblClick() procedure of the Size program.

The Code Inside the *cmdCancel_Click()* Procedure of the frmGetFile Form

When the user pushes the Cancel button, the cmdCancel_Click() event procedure is executed:

```
Sub cmdCancel_Click ()

    ' Set the tag property of the form to null.
    frmGetFile.Tag = ""

    ' Hide the frmGetFile dialog box.
    frmGetFile.Hide

End Sub
```

The Tag property of frmGetFile is used to store the path and name of the file that the user selected. Because the user pushed the Cancel button, this procedure assigns null to the Tag property:

```
frmGetFile.Tag = ""
```

The last statement in the procedure removes the frmGetFile form from the screen by using the Hide method:

```
frmGetFile.Hide
```

After executing this statement, the frmGetFile form is removed from the screen, and control is given back to the procedure that displayed the frmGetFile form.

13

Summary

In this chapter you have learned how to use the file-system controls to write programs that let you select files. You have also learned how to write a general-purpose GetFile form that can be used by any program that requires you to select files.

Q&A

Q How can I add the GETFILE.FRM form of the Select program to other projects?

A Let's say that you have a project called AnyProj. Use the following steps to add the GETFILE.FRM form to the AnyProj project:

☐ Open the AnyProj project.

☐ Select Project from the Window menu.

Visual Basic responds by displaying the project window.

☐ Select Add File from the File menu. Then select the GETFILE.FRM form.

Quiz

1. What is the purpose of the first line in the following code?

```
On Error GoTo DriveError
dirDirectory.Path = "A:"
Exit Sub
DriveError:
MsgBox "Drive error!", 48, "Error"
drvDrive.Drive = dirDirectory.Path
Exit Sub
```

2. What happens after the following statement is executed?

```
filFiles.Pattern = "*.BAT"
```

3. What happens after the following statement is executed?

```
filFiles.Path = dirDirectory.Path
```

4. What happens after the following statement is executed?

```
dirDirectory.Path = "D:"
```

Exercise

Enhance the Select program so that the File Type combo box of the GetFile dialog box will also include the file type Batch files (*.BAT).

Quiz Answers

1. The purpose of the first line of the code:

   ```
   On Error GoTo DriveError
   ```

   is to set an error trap so that if a runtime error occurs on the following line, the error will be trapped.

2. After this statement is executed:

   ```
   filFiles.Pattern = "*.BAT"
   ```

   the fillFiles File Name list box displays only files that have the .BAT extension.

3. After this statement is executed:

   ```
   filFiles.Path = dirDirectory.Path
   ```

   the Files list box displays the files of the directory that is currently selected in the Directory list box.

4. After this statement is executed:

   ```
   dirDirectory.Path = "D:"
   ```

   the dirDirectory Directory list box displays the directories of the D: drive.

Exercise Answer

To enhance the Select program so that the File Type combo box of the Get File dialog box includes the file type Batch files (*.BAT), you need to add the following statement to the Form_Load() procedure of the frmSelect form:

```
frmGetFile.cboFileType.AddItem "Batch files (*.BAT)"
```

After you add this statement, the Form_Load() procedure should look like this:

```
Sub Form_Load ()

    ' Load the frmGetFile dialog box
    '(without displaying it).
    Load frmGetFile

    ' Initialize the File Type combo box of the
    ' frmGetFile dialog box.
    frmGetFile.cboFileType.AddItem "All files (*.*)"
    frmGetFile.cboFileType.AddItem "Text files (*.TXT)"
    frmGetFile.cboFileType.AddItem "Doc files (*.DOC)"
```

13

```
frmGetFile.cboFileType.AddItem "Batch files (*.BAT)"
frmGetFile.cboFileType.ListIndex = 0
```

End Sub

Accessing Files

Many programs need to read and write data to disk files. In this chapter you'll learn how to create files, how to read data from files, and how to write data to files.

There are three file access techniques in Visual Basic:

- Random access
- Sequential access
- Binary access

This chapter teaches you how to use each of these file access techniques to manipulate files.

Random Access Files

A random access file is like a database. It is made up of records of identical size. Each record is made up of fields that store data. Figure 14.1 shows a random access file with two fields per record. The first field is a 5-byte string that corresponds to the name of a person. The second field is a 2-byte string that corresponds to the age of the person. The length of each record in this file is 7 bytes. The first sequence of 7 bytes belongs to the first record, the second sequence of 7 bytes belongs to the second record, and so on. Each record stores data about a specific person (that is, the name of the person and the person's age).

Figure 14.1.
A random access file.

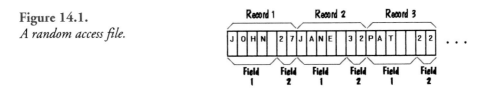

The PHONE program illustrates how to create and manipulate random access files. The program lets the user maintain a database file called PHONE.DAT that keeps records of people and their phone numbers.

The Visual Implementation of the PHONE Program

☐ Start a new project. Save the form of the project as PHONE.FRM and save the make file of the project as PHONE.MAK.

☐ Build the form according to the specifications in Table 14.1.

The completed form should look like the one shown in Figure 14.2

Table 14.1. The properties table of the PHONE program.

Object	Property	Value
Form	**Name**	**frmPhone**
	Caption	(empty)
	MaxButton	False
	Height	3555
	Left	1530
	Top	1875
	Width	6705
Text Box	**Name**	**txtName**
	Text	(empty)
	Height	285
	Left	840
	MaxLength	40
	Top	120
	Width	4335
Text Box	**Name**	**txtPhone**
	Text	(empty)
	Height	285
	Left	840
	MaxLength	40
	Top	720
	Width	4335
Text Box	**Name**	**txtComments**
	Text	(empty)
	Height	1455
	Left	120
	MaxLength	100
	MultiLine	True
	ScrollBars	2-Vertical
	Top	1560
	Width	5055

14

continues

Table 14.1. continued

Object	Property	Value
Command Button	**Name**	**cmdNew**
	Caption	New
	Height	495
	Left	5280
	Top	120
	Width	1215
Command Button	**Name**	**cmdNext**
	Caption	Next
	Height	495
	Left	5280
	Top	600
	Width	1215
Command Button	**Name**	**cmdPrevious**
	Caption	Previous
	Height	495
	Left	5280
	Top	1080
	Width	1215
Command Button	**Name**	**cmdExit**
	Caption	Exit
	Height	495
	Left	5280
	Top	2520
	Width	1215
Label	**Name**	**lblComments**
	Caption	Comments:
	Height	255
	Left	120
	Top	1320
	Width	975

Object	Property	Value
Label	Name	lblPhone
	Caption	Phone:
	Height	255
	Left	120
	Top	720
	Width	615
Label	Name	lblName
	Caption	Name:
	Height	255
	Left	120
	Top	120
	Width	615

Figure 14.2.
The form of the PHONE program.

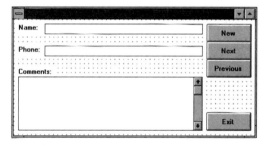

Entering the Code of the PHONE Program

☐ Create a new module and save it as PHONE.BAS (select Project from the Window menu, select New Module from the File menu, select Save File As from the File menu, and save the file as PHONE.BAS).

☐ Enter the following code inside the general declarations area of the module PHONE.BAS:

```
' All variables must be declared.
Option Explicit

' Declare a user-defined type that corresponds to a
' record in the file PHONE.DAT.
Type PersonInfo
    Name        As String * 40
    Phone       As String * 40
    Comments    As String * 100
End Type
```

☐ Enter the following code in the general declarations area of the frmPhone form:

```
' All variables must be declared.
Option Explicit

' Declare variables that should be visible in all
' the procedures of the form.
Dim Person As PersonInfo
Dim FileNum As Integer
Dim RecordLen As Long
Dim CurrentRecord As Long
Dim LastRecord As Long
```

☐ Create a new procedure inside the frmPhone form and name it SaveCurrentRecord.

☐ Enter the following code inside the procedure SaveCurrentRecord():

```
Sub SaveCurrentRecord ()

    ' Fill Person with the currently displayed data.
    Person.Name = txtName.Text
    Person.Phone = txtPhone.Text
    Person.Comments = txtComments.Text

    ' Save Person to the current record.
    Put #FileNum, CurrentRecord, Person

End Sub
```

☐ Create a new procedure inside the frmPhone form and name it ShowCurrentRecord.

☐ Enter the following code inside the procedure ShowCurrentRecord():

```
ShowCurrentRecord ()

    ' Fill Person with the data of the current
    ' record.
    Get #FileNum, CurrentRecord, Person

    ' Display Person.
    txtName.Text = Trim(Person.Name)
    txtPhone.Text = Trim(Person.Phone)
    txtComments.Text = Trim(Person.Comments)

    ' Display the current record number in the
    ' caption of the form.
    frmPhone.Caption="Record " + Str(CurrentRecord)+"/"+Str(LastRecord)

End Sub
```

☐ Enter the following code inside the Form_Load() event procedure:

```
Sub Form_Load ()

    ' Calculate the length of a record.
    RecordLen = Len(Person)
```

```
' Get the next available file number.
FileNum = FreeFile

' Open the file for random-access. If the file
' does not exist then it is created.
 Open "PHONE.DAT" For Random As FileNum Len = RecordLen

' Update CurrentRecord.
CurrentRecord = 1

' Find what is the last record number of
' the file.
LastRecord = FileLen("PHONE.DAT") / RecordLen

' If the file was just created
' (i.e. LastRecord=0) then update LastRecord
' to 1.
If LastRecord = 0 Then
    LastRecord = 1
End If

' Display the current record.
ShowCurrentRecord
```

End Sub

☐ Enter the following code inside the cmdNew_Click() event procedure:

Sub cmdNew_Click ()

```
' Save the current record.
SaveCurrentRecord

' Add a new blank record.
LastRecord = LastRecord + 1
Person.Name = ""
Person.Phone = ""
Person.Comments = ""
Put #FileNum, LastRecord, Person

' Update CurrentRecord.
CurrentRecord = LastRecord

' Display the record that was just created.
ShowCurrentRecord

' Give the focus to the txtName text box.
txtName.SetFocus
```

End Sub

☐ Enter the following code inside the cmdNext_Click() event procedure:

Sub cmdNext_Click ()

```
' If the current record is not the last record,
' then save the current record and skip to the
```

14

```
' next record.
If CurrentRecord = LastRecord Then
    Beep
    MsgBox "End of file encountered!", 48
Else
    SaveCurrentRecord
    CurrentRecord = CurrentRecord + 1
    ShowCurrentRecord
End If

' Give the focus to the txtName text box.
txtName.SetFocus
```

End Sub

☐ Enter the following code inside the cmdPrevious_Click() event procedure:

Sub cmdPrevious_Click ()

```
' If the current record is not the first record,
' then save the current record and skip one
' record backward.
If CurrentRecord = 1 Then
    Beep
    MsgBox "Beginning of file encountered!", 48
Else
    SaveCurrentRecord
    CurrentRecord = CurrentRecord - 1
    ShowCurrentRecord
End If

' Give the focus to the txtName text box.
txtName.SetFocus
```

End Sub

☐ Enter the following code inside the cmdExit_Click() event procedure:

Sub cmdExit_Click ()

```
' Save the current record.
SaveCurrentRecord

' End the program.
End
```

End Sub

Executing the PHONE Program

☐ Execute the PHONE program.

While you run the program, notice the following features:

- The first time you execute the program, the database is empty, and a blank record appears onscreen. The program lets you type the name of a person, the person's phone number, and comments about the person (see Figure 14.3). You can move from one field to another using the mouse or pressing Tab.

- To add a new record, push the New button. As soon as you press the New button, a new blank record appears. The caption of the form displays the record number of the displayed record and the total number of records (see Figure 14.4).

- Once you have a few records in the database, you can move from one record to another using the Next and Previous buttons. When you press the Next button, the next record is displayed. When you press the Previous button, the previous record is displayed.

Use the following step to terminate the PHONE program:

☐ Push the Exit button.

Figure 14.3.
Filling the first record in the PHONE program.

Record 1/ 1
Name: JOHN
Phone: 555-1234
Comments:
Returns from vacation on September 1.

New
Next
Previous
Exit

Figure 14.4.
The PHONE program after you add a new record.

Record 2/ 2
Name:
Phone:
Comments:

New
Next
Previous
Exit

All the records that you added to the database are stored in the file PHONE.DAT. If you execute the program again, you will see the records you entered.

As you can see, the PHONE program does not let you delete a record or search for a record. Later in this chapter, you will enhance the program so the user is able to delete records and search for records.

How the PHONE Program Works

The PHONE program opens the file PHONE.DAT as a random access file with the fields Name, Phone, and Comments. If the file does not exist, the program creates it.

Defining the Fields of the PHONE.DAT Records

The fields of the PHONE.DAT records are defined by declaring a user-defined type that corresponds to the fields of the records. The user-defined type is declared in the general declarations area of the module PHONE.BAS:

```
' Declare a user-defined type that corresponds to a
' record in the file PHONE.DAT.
Type PersonInfo
    Name      As String * 40
    Phone     As String * 40
    Comments  As String * 100
End Type
```

The declared type is called `PersonInfo`, and it is made up of three variables: `Name` (a 40-character string), `Phone` (a 40-character string), and `Comments` (a 100-character string). Each of these strings corresponds to a field in the PHONE.DAT file.

Later the PHONE program will use a variable of the type `PersonInfo` to write (and read) data to the PERSON.DAT file.

The reason `PersonInfo` is declared inside the general declarations area of the module PHONE.BAS, and not inside the general declarations area of the form, is that user-defined types are always global, and Visual Basic does not allow you to declare global declarations in a form.

The General Declarations Area of the Form

In the general declarations area of the frmPhone form all the variables that should be visible in all the form's procedures are declared:

```
' Declare variables that should be visible in all
' the procedures of the form.
Dim Person As PersonInfo
Dim FileNum As Integer
Dim RecordLen As Long
Dim CurrentRecord As Long
Dim LastRecord As Long
```

The variable `Person` is declared as type `PersonInfo`. Because the user-defined type `PersonInfo` is made of three variables (that is, `Name`, `Phone`, and `Comments`), the variable `Person` is also made of three variables: `Person.Name`, `Person.Phone`, and `Person.Comments`.

The variable `Person` is used to hold the data of a record.

Opening the PHONE.DAT File

Before data can be written to or read from a file, the file must be opened. The code that is responsible for opening the PHONE.DAT file resides in the `Form_Load()` procedure:

```
Sub Form_Load ()

    ' Calculate the length of a record.
    RecordLen = Len(Person)

    ' Get the next available file number.
    FileNum = FreeFile

    ' Open the file for random-access. If the file
    ' does not exist then it is created.
    Open "PHONE.DAT" For Random As FileNum Len = RecordLen

    ' Update CurrentRecord.
    CurrentRecord = 1

    ' Find what is the last record number of
    ' the file.
    LastRecord = FileLen("PHONE.DAT") / RecordLen

    ' If the file was just created
    ' (i.e. LastRecord=0) then update LastRecord
    ' to 1.
    If LastRecord = 0 Then
      LastRecord = 1
    End If

    ' Display the current record.
    ShowCurrentRecord

End Sub
```

When you open a file for random access, you need to specify the record size of the file and a file number. So before opening the file, the `Form_Load()` procedure extracts these values with the following two statements:

```
RecordLen = Len(Person)
FileNum = FreeFile
```

The first statement uses the `Len()` function to extract the length of the variable Person. Because the variable Person corresponds to the fields of the PHONE.DAT file, its length is the same as the length of a record.

The second statement uses the `FreeFile` function to get a file number that is not already in use. As stated previously, when you open a file you need to specify a file number. This number is used to identify the opened file. Subsequent statements that perform operations on this file need this file number to tell Visual Basic on which file to perform the operation.

Now that the variables `RecordLen` and `FileNum` are updated, the procedure opens the PHONE.DAT file for random access with the following statement:

```
Open "PHONE.DAT" For Random As FileNum Len = RecordLen
```

If the PHONE.DAT file does not exist, the `Open` statement creates it. So the very first time the user executes the PHONE program, the file PHONE.DAT is created. After the file PHONE.DAT is opened, the procedure updates the variables `CurrentRecord` and `LastRecord`.

The variable `CurrentRecord` is used to store the record number of the currently displayed record. Because initially record number 1 should be displayed, `CurrentRecord` is initialized to 1:

```
CurrentRecord = 1
```

The variable `LastRecord` is used to store the record number of the last record in the file (that is, the total number of records). This value is calculated by dividing the total file length by the length of a record:

```
LastRecord = FileLen("PHONE.DAT") / RecordLen
```

However, there is one special case for which this calculation does not work. If the file was just created, `FileLen()` returns 0, and the calculation yields a value of 0 for `LastRecord`. To make sure that `LastRecord` is not assigned a value of 0, an `If` statement is used:

```
If LastRecord = 0 Then
    LastRecord = 1
End If
```

This `If` statement checks whether `LastRecord` is 0. If it is, the `If` statement changes it to 1.

The last statement in the `Form_Load()` procedure executes the procedure `ShowCurrentRecord()`:

```
' Display the current record.
ShowCurrentRecord
```

The procedure `ShowCurrentRecord()` displays the data of the record that is specified by the variable `CurrentRecord`. Because `CurrentRecord` is now equal to 1, after executing the preceding statement, the data of record number 1 is displayed.

The Code of the *ShowCurrentRecord()* Procedure

The code of the `ShowCurrentRecord()` procedure displays the data of the record that is specified by the variable `CurrentRecord`:

```
Sub ShowCurrentRecord ()

    ' Fill Person with the data of the current
    ' record.
    Get #FileNum, CurrentRecord, Person

    ' Display Person.
    txtName.Text = Trim(Person.Name)
```

```
txtPhone.Text = Trim(Person.Phone)
txtComments.Text = Trim(Person.Comments)

' Display the current record number in the
' caption of the form.
frmPhone.Caption="Record " + Str(CurrentRecord)+"/"+Str(LastRecord)

End Sub
```

The first statement of the procedure uses the `Get` statement to fill the variable `Person` with the data of the current record:

```
Get #FileNum, CurrentRecord, Person
```

The `Get` statement takes three parameters: The first parameter specifies the file number of the file (this is the number that was specified when the file was opened), the second parameter specifies the record number of the record to be read, and the third parameter specifies the name of the variable that is filled with the data that is read from the record.

For example, if `CurrentRecord` is currently equal to 5, after the preceding statement is executed, the variable `Person` contains the data of record number 5. That is, `Person.Name`, `Person.Phone`, and `Person.Comments` contain the data that is stored in the fields Name, Phone, and Person of record number 5.

After the variable `Person` is filled with the data of the current record, its contents are displayed by updating the txtName, txtPhone, and txtComments text boxes:

```
txtName.Text = Trim(Person.Name)
txtPhone.Text = Trim(Person.Phone)
txtComments.Text = Trim(Person.Comments)
```

Note that the text boxes are assigned with the trimmed values of the `Person` variable. That's because the text boxes should not contain any trailing blanks. For example, if the current record in the database contains the name JOHN SMITH in the Name field, after executing the `Get` statement, the variable `Person.Name` contains these characters:

```
"JOHN SMITH..............................".
```

(that is, the name JOHN SMITH plus 30 blanks). The reason for the 30 trailing blanks is that the Name field was defined as 40 characters, and because JOHN SMITH is only 10 characters, when the record was stored, Visual Basic added to the field 30 trailing blanks. Because these trailing blanks should not appear in the text box, the `Trim` function was used.

The last statement of the procedure displays the current record number in the caption of the form:

```
frmPhone.Caption="Record " + Str(CurrentRecord)+"/"+Str(LastRecord)
```

For example, if the current value of `CurrentRecord` is 5 and the value of `LastRecord` is 15, the preceding statement sets the caption of the form to Record 15.

The Code Inside the *cmdNext_Click()* Procedure

Whenever the user pushes the Next button the `cmdNext_Click()` procedure is executed. The code inside this procedure is responsible for displaying the content of the next record:

```
Sub cmdNext_Click ()

    ' If the current record is not the last record,
    ' then save the current record and skip to the
    ' next record.
    If CurrentRecord = LastRecord Then
      Beep
      MsgBox "End of file encountered!", 48
    Else
      SaveCurrentRecord
      CurrentRecord = CurrentRecord + 1
      ShowCurrentRecord
    End If

    ' Give the focus to the txtName text box.
    txtName.SetFocus

End Sub
```

The first statement of the procedure is an `If` statement that checks whether `CurrentRecord` is equal to `LastRecord`. If `CurrentRecord` is equal to `LastRecord` (that is, there is no next record), the procedure beeps and displays a message informing the user that the current record is the end of the file:

```
Beep
MsgBox "End of file encountered!", 48
```

If, however, `CurrentRecord` is not equal to `LastRecord`, the following statements are executed:

```
SaveCurrentRecord
CurrentRecord = CurrentRecord + 1
ShowCurrentRecord
```

The first statement executes the `SaveCurrentRecord` procedure. This procedure saves the contents of the text boxes txtName, txtPhone, and txtComments into the file. The second statement increments the variable `CurrentRecord` by 1 so that it points to the next record. The third statement executes the procedure `ShowCurrentRecord()` so that the text boxes txtName, txtPhone, and txtComments display the record that is pointed to by the new value of `CurrentRecord`.

The last statement of the procedure uses the SetFocus method to set the keyboard focus to the txtName text box:

```
txtName.SetFocus
```

After this statement is executed, the cursor appears inside the txtName text box.

The Code of the *SaveCurrentRecord()* Procedure

The `SaveCurrentRecord()` procedure is responsible for saving the contents of the text boxes txtName, txtPhone, and txtComments into the record that is specified by `CurrentRecord`:

```
Sub SaveCurrentRecord ()

    ' Fill Person with the currently displayed data.
    Person.Name = txtName.Text
    Person.Phone = txtPhone.Text
    Person.Comments = txtComments.Text

    ' Save Person to the current record.
    Put #FileNum, CurrentRecord, Person

End Sub
```

The first three statements of the procedure fill the `Person` variable with the contents of the three text boxes:

```
Person.Name = txtName.Text
Person.Phone = txtPhone.Text
Person.Comments = txtComments.Text
```

After filling the `Person` variable, the procedure executes the `Put` statement to store the contents of the `Person` variable into record number `CurrentRecord` of the file:

```
Put #FileNum, CurrentRecord, Person
```

The `Put` statement takes three parameters: The first parameter specifies the file number of the file (this is the number that was specified when the file was opened), the second parameter specifies the record number that is being saved, and the third parameter specifies the name of the variable whose content will be saved into the record.

Adding a New Record to the PHONE.DAT File

The code that is responsible for adding a new record to the file is inside the `cmdNew_Click()` procedure. The `cmdNew_Click()` procedure is executed whenever the user pushes the New button:

```
Sub cmdNew_Click ()

    ' Save the current record.
    SaveCurrentRecord

    ' Add a new blank record.
    LastRecord = LastRecord + 1
    Person.Name = ""
    Person.Phone = ""
    Person.Comments = ""
    Put #FileNum, LastRecord, Person

    ' Update CurrentRecord.
```

```
    CurrentRecord = LastRecord

    ' Display the record that was just created.
    ShowCurrentRecord

    ' Give the focus to the txtName text box.
    txtName.SetFocus

End Sub
```

The first statement of the procedure executes the `SaveCurrentRecord()` procedure so that the current record (that is, the contents of the text boxes) is saved to the file.

After the current record is saved, the procedure adds a new blank record to the file with the following statements:

```
LastRecord = LastRecord + 1
Person.Name = ""
Person.Phone = ""
Person.Comments = ""
Put #FileNum, LastRecord, Person
```

The first statement increments `LastRecord` so that it points to the number of the new record, then the `Person` variable is set to null, and finally, the `Put` statement is used to create the new record. The number of the new record is `LastRecord`, and the content of the new record is the content of the `Person` variable (that is, null).

After the new blank record is created, the `CurrentRecord` variable is updated so that it points to the new record:

```
CurrentRecord = LastRecord
```

Then the `ShowCurrentRecord()` procedure is executed so that the record that was just created is displayed:

```
ShowCurrentRecord
```

The last statement of the procedure uses the SetFocus method to set the keyboard focus to the txtName text box:

```
txtName.SetFocus
```

After this statement is executed, the cursor appears inside the txtName text box.

The Code Inside the *cmdPrevious_Click()* Procedure

Whenever the user pushes the Previous button the `cmdPrevious_Click()` procedure is executed. The code inside this procedure is responsible for displaying the content of the previous record:

```
Sub cmdPrevious_Click ()

    ' If the current record is not the first record,
    ' then save the current record and skip one
    ' record backward.
    If CurrentRecord = 1 Then
      Beep
      MsgBox "Beginning of file encountered!", 48
    Else
      SaveCurrentRecord
      CurrentRecord = CurrentRecord - 1
      ShowCurrentRecord
    End If

    ' Give the focus to the txtName text box.
    txtName.SetFocus

End Sub
```

The first statement of the procedure is an `If` statement that checks whether `CurrentRecord` is equal to 1. If `CurrentRecord` is equal to 1 (that is, there is no previous record), the procedure beeps and displays a message informing the user that the current record is the beginning of the file:

```
Beep
MsgBox "Beginning of file encountered!", 48
```

If, however, `CurrentRecord` is not equal to 1, the following statements are executed:

```
SaveCurrentRecord
CurrentRecord = CurrentRecord - 1
ShowCurrentRecord
```

The first statement executes the `SaveCurrentRecord()` procedure to save the contents of the text boxes txtName, txtPhone, and txtComments into the file. The second statement decrements the variable `CurrentRecord` by 1 so that it points to the previous record. The third statement executes the procedure `ShowCurrentRecord` so that the text boxes txtName, txtPhone, and txtComments display the record that is pointed to by the new value of `CurrentRecord`.

The last statement of the procedure uses the SetFocus method to set the keyboard focus to the txtName text box:

```
txtName.SetFocus
```

After this statement is executed, the cursor appears inside the txtName text box.

The Code Inside the *cmdExit_Click()* Procedure

The `cmdExit_Click()` procedure is executed whenever the user pushes the Exit button. The code inside this procedure saves the current record to the file and terminates the program:

```
Sub cmdExit_Click ()

    ' Save the current record.
```

```
SaveCurrentRecord

' End the program.
End
```

End Sub

Enhancing the PHONE Program

Now enhance the PHONE program by adding a Search button and a Delete button to it. The Search button enables the user to search for a particular name, and the Delete button enables the user to delete records:

☐ Add a command button to the frmPhone form and set its properties as follows:

Command Button	Name	cmdSearch
	Caption	Search
	Height	495
	Left	5280
	Top	1560
	Width	1215

☐ Add another command button to the frmPhone form and set its properties as follows:

Command Button	Name	cmdDelete
	Caption	Delete
	Height	495
	Left	5280
	Top	2040
	Width	1215

When you finish setting the properties of the two new buttons, the frmPhone form should look like the one shown in Figure 14.5:

☐ Enter the following code inside the cmdSearch_Click() event procedure:

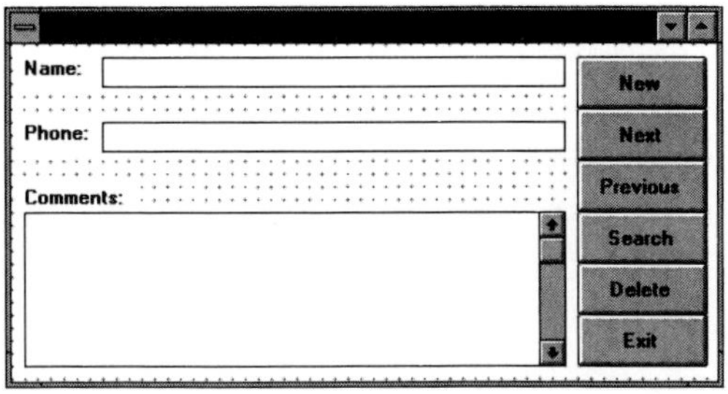

Figure 14.5.

The frmPhone form after you add the Search and Delete buttons.

```
Sub cmdSearch_Click ()

    Dim NameToSearch As String
    Dim Found As Integer
    Dim RecNum As Long
    Dim TmpPerson As PersonInfo

    ' Get the name to search from the user.
     NameToSearch = InputBox("Enter name to search:", "Search")
    ' If the user did not enter a name, then exit
    ' from this procedure.
    If NameToSearch = "" Then

        ' Give the focus to the txtName text box.
        txtName.SetFocus

        ' Exit this procedure.
        Exit Sub

    End If

    ' Convert the name to be searched to upper case.
    NameToSearch = UCase(NameTosearch)

    ' Initialize the Found flag to False.
    Found = False

    ' Search for the name that the user entered.
    For RecNum = 1 To LastRecord
        Get #FileNum, RecNum, TmpPerson
           If NameToSearch = UCase(Trim(TmpPerson.Name)) Then

               Found = True
               Exit For
           End If
    Next

    ' If the name was found then display the record
    ' of the found name.
    If Found = True Then
        SaveCurrentRecord
        CurrentRecord = RecNum
        ShowCurrentRecord
    Else
        MsgBox "Name " + NameToSearch + " not found!"
    End If

    ' Give the focus to the txtName field.
    txtName.SetFocus

End Sub
```

☐ Enter the following code inside the cmdDelete_Click() event procedure:

```
Sub cmdDelete_Click ()

    Dim DirResult
    Dim TmpFileNum
    Dim TmpPerson As PersonInfo
    Dim RecNum As Long
    Dim TmpRecNum As Long

    ' Before deleting get a confirmation from
    ' the user.
    If MsgBox("Delete this record?", 4) <> 6 Then

        ' Give the focus to the txtName field.
        txtName.SetFocus

        ' Exit the procedure without deleting.
        Exit Sub

    End If

    ' To physically delete the current record of PHONE.DAT,
    ' all the records of PHONE.DAT, except the
    ' current record, copied into a temporary file (PHONE.TMP),
    ' and then file PHONE.TMP is copied into PHONE.DAT:
    ' Make sure that PHONE.TMP does not exist.
    If Dir("PHONE.TMP") = "PHONE.TMP" Then
        Kill "PHONE.TMP"
    End If

    ' Create PHONE.TMP with the same format
    ' as PHONE.DAT.
    TmpFileNum = FreeFile
    Open "PHONE.TMP" For Random As TmpFileNum Len = RecordLen
    ' Copy all the records from PHONE.DAT
    ' to PHONE.TMP, except the current record.
    RecNum = 1
    TmpRecNum = 1
    Do While RecNum < LastRecord + 1
        If RecNum <> CurrentRecord Then
            Get #FileNum, RecNum, TmpPerson
            Put #TmpFileNum, TmpRecNum, TmpPerson
            TmpRecNum = TmpRecNum + 1
        End If
        RecNum = RecNum + 1
    Loop

    ' Delete PHONE.DAT.
    Close FileNum
    Kill "PHONE.DAT"

    ' Rename PHONE.TMP into PHONE.DAT.
    Close TmpFileNum
    Name "PHONE.TMP" As "PHONE.DAT"

    ' Re-open PHONE.DAT.
    FileNum = FreeFile
```

```
    Open "PHONE.DAT" For Random As FileNum Len = RecordLen

' Update the value of LastRecord.
LastRecord = LastRecord - 1

' Make sure that LastRecord is not 0.
If LastRecord = 0 Then LastRecord = 1

' Make sure that CurrentRecord is not out
' of range.
If CurrentRecord > LastRecord Then
    CurrentRecord = LastRecord
End If

' Show the current record.
ShowCurrentRecord

' Give the focus to the txtName text box.
txtName.SetFocus

End Sub
```

☐ Execute the PHONE program and experiment with the Search and Delete buttons.

Searching for a Record

Whenever the user pushes the Search button, the cmdSearch_Click() procedure is executed. This procedure lets the user search for a particular name.

The procedure begins by using the InputBox() function to get a name from the user. The name entered by the user is stored in the variable NameToSearch:

```
NameToSearch = InputBox("Enter name to search:", "Search")
```

The InputBox() function returns null if the user pushes the Cancel button. To take care of this case, an If statement is used. If the user presses the Cancel button, the procedure is terminated:

```
If NameToSearch = "" Then
    txtName.SetFocus
    Exit Sub
End If
```

After the variable NameToSearch is updated, the UCase() function is used to convert it to uppercase:

```
NameToSearch = UCase(NameTosearch)
```

This conversion is necessary because the search for the name should not be case sensitive (that is, even if the user types john, the record that contains the name JOHN should be found).

To search for the name the user entered, a For loop is used:

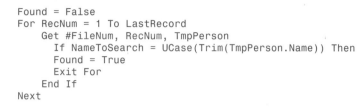

```
Found = False
For RecNum = 1 To LastRecord
    Get #FileNum, RecNum, TmpPerson
      If NameToSearch = UCase(Trim(TmpPerson.Name)) Then
      Found = True
      Exit For
    End If
Next
```

This `For` loop uses the `Get` statement to read the records of the file, record after record, into the variable `TmpPerson`. After each record is read, an `If` statement is used to see if the record that was just read contains the name that is being searched. The `If` statement compares the value of the variable `NameToSearch` with the value of `UCase(Trim(TmpPerson.Name))`. The `UCase()` function is used because the search should not be case sensitive. The `Trim()` function is used to get rid of leading and trailing blanks of the Name field.

If a record with its Name field equal to `NameToSearch` is found, the variable `Found` is set to True and the `For` loop is terminated. After the `For` loop ends, the procedure displays the results of the search:

```
If Found = True Then
    SaveCurrentRecord
    CurrentRecord = RecNum
    ShowCurrentRecord
Else
    MsgBox "Name " + NameToSearch + " not found!"
End If
```

If the search was successful, the current record is saved and the found record is displayed. If, however, the search failed, a `not found!` message is displayed.

Deleting a Record

Whenever the user pushes the Delete button, the `cmdDelete_Click()` procedure is executed. This procedure deletes the current record.

The following four steps are used by the `cmdDelete_Click()` procedure to delete the current record of PHONE.DAT:

1. Create an empty temporary file (PHONE.TMP).
2. Use a `For` loop to copy all the records of PHONE.DAT (record after record), except the current record, into the file PHONE.TMP.
3. Erase the file PHONE.DAT.
4. Rename the file PHONE.TMP as PHONE.DAT.

Sequential Access Files

Whereas random files are accessed record by record, sequential files are accessed line by line. That is, when you write data into a sequential file, you write lines of text into the file. When you read data from a sequential file, you read lines of text from the file. The fact that sequential files are accessed line by line makes them ideal for use in applications that manipulate text files.

You can open a sequential file in one of three ways: output, append, or input.

Opening a Sequential File for Output

To create a sequential file, you need to open the file for output. After the file is created, you can use output commands to write lines to the file. The following sample code creates the file TRY.TXT:

```
' Get a free file number.
FileNum = FreeFile

' Open the file TRY.TXT for output (i.e. create it).
Open "TRY.TXT" For Output As FileNum
```

If the file TRY.TXT does not exist, this code creates it. If the file does exist, this code erases the old file and creates a new one.

Note that in the preceding code, the file to be opened, TRY.TXT, was specified without a path. When a path is not specified, the file is opened in the current directory. For example, if the current directory is C:\PROGRAMS, the following two statements will do the same thing:

```
Open "TRY.TXT" For Output As FileNum

Open "C:\PROGRAMS\TRY.TXT" For Output As FileNum
```

Because opening a file for output creates the file, after the file is opened, it is empty. To write text into the file, you can use the Print # statement. The following example creates the file TRY.TXT and writes the content of the text box txtMyText into the file:

```
' Get a free file number.
FileNum = FreeFile

' Open TRY.TXT for output (i.e. create TRY.TXT).
Open "TRY.TXT" For Output As FileNum

' Write the contents of the text box txtMyText into the file TRY.TXT.
Print #FileNum, txtMyText.Text

' Close the file.
Close FileNum
```

The Print # statement takes two parameters: the first parameter is the file number and the second parameter is the string to be written into the file.

14

Opening a Sequential File for Append

Opening a sequential file for append is similar to opening it for output. The only difference is that when you open a file for append, if the file already exists, it is not erased. Rather, subsequent output commands append new lines to the opened file. For example, suppose that the file TRY.TXT already exists, and it contains the following two lines:

```
THIS IS LINE NUMBER 1
THIS IS LINE NUMBER 2
```

To append a new line to the file TRY.TXT, you can use the following code:

```
' Get a free file number.
FileNum = FreeFile

' Open TRY.TXT for append.
Open "TRY.TXT" For Append As FileNum

' Add new text to the file.
Print #FileNum, "THIS IS A NEW TEXT"

' Close the file.
Close FileNum
```

After you execute this code, the file TRY.TXT contains three lines:

```
THIS IS LINE NUMBER 1
THIS IS LINE NUMBER 2
THIS IS A NEW TEXT
```

If you execute the same code again, the file TRY.TXT contains four lines:

```
THIS IS LINE NUMBER 1
THIS IS LINE NUMBER 2
THIS IS A NEW TEXT
THIS IS A NEW TEXT
```

Opening a Sequential File for Input

To read the contents of a sequential file, you need to open the file for input. Once a file is opened for input, you can use the `Input$` function to read the entire content of the file into a text box (or into a string variable).

The following example opens the file TRY.TXT for input and uses the `Input$` function to read the content of the file into the text box txtMyText:

```
' Get a free file number.
FileNum = FreeFile

' Open TRY.TXT for input.
Open "TRY.TXT" For Input As FileNum

' Read all the contents of the file into the text
```

```
' box txtMyText.
txtMyText.Text = Input$(LOF(FileNum), FileNum)

' Close the file.
Close FileNum
```

The `Input$()` function takes two parameters: the first parameter specifies the number of bytes to be read from the file, and the second parameter specifies the file number of the file.

Because the purpose of the preceding code is to read the content of the file, the first parameter of the `Input$()` function was specified as `LOF(FileNum)`. The `LOF()` function returns the total length of the file in bytes.

The *Write #* and *Input #* Statements

In the preceding examples, the `Input$()` function and the `Print #` statement were used to read/write data from/to a sequential file. Another way to read and write data from/to a sequential file is to use the `Write #` and `Input #` statements.

The `Write #` statement lets you write a list of variables (strings or numeric) to a file. The following example creates the file TRY.TXT and stores the content of the string variable `MyString` and the content of the numeric variable `MyNumber` into the file:

```
' Get a free file number.
FileNum = FreeFile

' Create the file TRY.TXT.
Open "TRY.TXT" For Output As FileNum

' Write the contents of the variables MyString, and
' MyNumber into the file.
Write #FileNum MyString, MyNumber

' Close the file.
Close FileNum
```

The first parameter of the `Write #` statement is the file number of the file. The rest of the parameters are the variables that will be written into the file. Because in the preceding example only two variables are written into the file, there are only two parameters after the first parameter.

The `Input #` statement lets you read data from a file that contains the contents of a list of variables. The following code reads the content of the file that was created in the preceding example:

```
' Get a free file number.
FileNum = FreeFile

' Open the file TRY.TXT for input.
Open "TRY.TXT" For Input As FileNum

' Read the contents of the file into the variables
' MyString, and MyNumber.
```

14

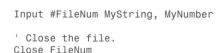

```
Input #FileNum MyString, MyNumber

' Close the file.
Close FileNum
```

The first parameter of the `Input #` statement is the file number of the file. The rest of the parameters are the variables that will be filled with the content of the file. The order in which the variables are placed in the `Input #` statement must match the order in which the variables were originally stored in the file.

Binary Access Files

Whereas random files are accessed record by record and sequential files are accessed line by line, binary files are accessed byte by byte. Once you open a file for binary access, you can read and write to any byte location in the file. This capability to access any desired byte in the file makes binary access the most flexible.

Opening a File for Binary Access

Before you can access a file in a binary mode (byte by byte), you must first open the file for binary access. The following sample code opens the file TRY.DAT for binary access:

```
' Get a free file number.
FileNum = FreeFile

' Open the file TRY.DAT for binary access.
Open "TRY.DAT" For Binary As FileNum
```

If the file TRY.DAT does not already exist, the preceding `Open` statement creates it.

Writing Bytes into a Binary File

After a file is opened for binary access, the `Put #` statement can be used to write bytes to any desired byte location in the file. The following sample code writes the string THIS IS A TEST into the file TRY.DAT, starting at byte location 100:

```
Dim MyString As String
' Fill the string variable MyString with the
' string "THIS IS A TEST".
MyString = "THIS IS A TEST"

' Get a free file number.
FileNum = FreeFile

' Open the file TRY.DAT for binary access.
Open "TRY.DAT" For Binary As FileNum
```

```
' Write the string variable MyString, starting at
' byte location 100.
Put #FileNum,100, MyString

' Close the file.
Close FileNum
```

The `Put #` statement takes three parameters: the first parameter is the file number, the second parameter is the byte location at which the writing starts, and the third parameter is the name of the variable whose content will be written to the file. In the preceding example, the variable whose content is written into the file is a string variable, but you could use other types of variables (for example, numeric).

After the `Put #` statement is executed, the position of the file is automatically set to the next byte after the last byte that was written. For example, in the preceding sample code, after the 14 characters of the string `THIS IS A TEST` are written into the file (starting at position 100), the position of the file is automatically set to 114. This means that if after the preceding `Put #` statement another `Put#` statement is executed without specification of the byte location, the writing of this new `Put #` statement starts at byte location 114. The following sample code illustrates how the file position is updated automatically after a `Put #` statement:

```
Dim MyString As String
' Get a free file number.
FileNum = FreeFile

' Open the file TRY.DAT for binary access.
Open "TRY.DAT" For Binary As FileNum

' Write the string "12345" starting at byte
' location 20 of the file.
MyString = "12345"
Put #FileNum, 20, MyString

' At this point the file position is set at byte
' location 25, so if the next Put # statement will
' not specify a byte location, then the writing of
' the next Put # statement will be performed at byte
' location 25.

' Write the string "67890" without specifying a byte
' location.
MyString = "67890"
Put #FileNum, , MyString

' Close the file.
Close FileNum
```

Note that the second `Put #` statement in the preceding code did not specify a byte location (that is, the second parameter is not specified—there is a blank between the first comma and the second comma).

14

Reading Bytes from a Binary File

After a file is opened for binary access, the `Get #` statement can be used to read bytes from any desired byte location in the file. The following sample code reads 15 characters, starting at byte location 40, of the file TRY.DAT:

```
' Get a free file number.
FileNum = FreeFile

' Open the file TRY.DAT for binary access.
Open "TRY.DAT" For Binary As FileNum

' Initialize the MyString string to 15 blanks. '
  MyString = String$(15, " ")

' Read 15 characters from the file, starting at byte
' location 40.
Get #FileNum, 40, MyString

' Close the file.
Close FileNum
```

As you can see, the `Get #` statement takes three parameters: the first parameter is the file number, the second parameter is the byte location from which the reading will start, and the third parameter is the name of the variable that will be filled with the data from the file. The number of bytes read from the file is determined by the size of the variable that is filled with the data. Because in the preceding code the variable `MyString` was initialized to 15 blanks, the `Get #` statement reads only 15 characters.

Summary

In this chapter you have learned how to create files, how to write data to files, and how to read data from files. You have learned that there are three types of files: random, sequential, and binary. Random files are accessed record by record and are useful in database applications. Sequential files are accessed line by line and are ideal for use with text files. Binary files are the most flexible because they are accessed byte by byte.

Q&A

Q Why are random files considered random?

A The word *random* in the name random file is used because once a file is opened for random access, the program can access any record in the file. In other words, the program can read and write records in a random order (first record 7, then record 3, then record 9, and so on).

Q In the PHONE program, the file PHONE.DAT was opened for random access
with the following statement:

```
Open "PHONE.DAT" For Random As FileNum Len = RecordLen
```

The name of the file (that is, PHONE.DAT) was specified without a path. In
which directory was the file opened?

A Because no path was specified, the file is opened in the current directory. The question is What is the current directory? Let's say that you create an .EXE file
PHONE.EXE from the PHONE program and save the file PHONE.EXE in the
C:\MyDir\ directory. Upon execution of the C:\MyDir\PHONE.EXE program, the
current directory is C:\MyDir by default. This means that the file PHONE.DAT is
opened in C:\MyDir.

Quiz

1. Assume that there is a user-defined data type that is defined as follows:

```
Type EmployeeInfo
   Name    As String * 40
   Age     As Integer
End Type
```

What does the following code do?

```
Dim FileNum As Integer
Dim Employee As EmployeeInfo

FileNum = FreeFile
Open "EMPLOYEE.DAT" For Random As FileNum Len = Len(Employee)
Employee.Name = "JOHN SMITH"
Employee.Age = 32
Put FileNum, 5, Employee
```

2. Assume that there is a user-defined data type that is defined as follows:

```
Type EmployeeInfo
   Name    As String * 40
   Age     As Integer
End Type
```

What does the following code do?

```
Dim FileNum As Integer
Dim Employee As EmployeeInfo

FileNum = FreeFile
Open "EMPLOYEE.DAT" For Random As FileNum Len = Len(Employee)
Get #FileNum, 10, Employee
MsgBox "The age of "+ Trim(Employee.Name)+ " is "+Str(Employee.Age)
```

14

3. What does the following code do?

```
FileNum = FreeFile
Open "TRY.TXT" For Output As FileNum
Print #FileNum, txtMyText.Text
Close FileNum
```

4. What do the following statements do?

```
FileNum = FreeFile

Open "C:\TRY\TRY.TXT" For Append As FileNum
```

5. What does the following code do?

```
FileNum = FreeFile
Open "INFO.TXT" For Append As FileNum
Print #FileNum, txtMyText.Text
Close FileNum
```

6. What does the following code do?

```
FileNum = FreeFile
Open "TRY.TXT" For Input As FileNum
txtMyText.Text = Input$(LOF(FileNum), FileNum)
Close FileNum
```

7. What does the following code do?

```
FileNum = FreeFile
Open "TRY.DAT" For Binary As FileNum
MyString = "THIS IS A TEST"
Put #FileNum, 75, MyString
Close FileNum
```

8. What does the following code do?

```
FileNum = FreeFile
Open "TRY.DAT" For Binary As FileNum
MyString = String$(20, " ")
Get #FileNum, 75, MyString
MsgBox "MyString="+MyString
Close FileNum
```

Exercises

1. Wave files (WAV files) are standard sound files that are used in Windows. The sampling rate of a WAV file is saved as an integer value starting at byte location 25 of the file. Write a program that displays the sampling rate of the file C:\WINDOWS\TADA.WAV. (The file TADA.WAV is included with Windows). (Hint: Use binary access.)

2. Write a program that displays the contents of the file C:\AUTOEXEC.BAT inside a text box. (Hint: Use sequential access.)

Quiz Answers

1. The code stores the name JOHN SMITH and his age (32) in record number 5 of the file EMPLOYEE.DAT:

```
' Declare variables.
Dim FileNum As Integer
Dim Employee As EmployeeInfo

' Get a free file number.
FileNum = FreeFile

' Open the file EMPLOYEE.DAT.
Open "EMPLOYEE.DAT" For Random As FileNum Len = Len(Employee)

' Fill the variable Employee.
Employee.Name = "JOHN SMITH"
Employee.Age = 32

' Store the contents of the variable Employee in
' record number 5 of the file.
Put FileNum, 5, Employee
```

2. The code displays the name of the person and his age from record number 10:

```
Dim FileNum As Integer
Dim Employee As EmployeeInfo

' Get a free file number.
FileNum = FreeFile

' Open the file EMPLOYEE.DAT.
Open "EMPLOYEE.DAT" For Random As FileNum Len = Len(Employee)

' Fill the variable Employee with the contents of
' record number 10 of the file.
Get #FileNum, 10, Employee

' Display the contents of the Employee variable.
MsgBox "The age of "+ Trim(Employee.Name)+ " is "+Str(Employee.Age)
```

3. These statements open the file C:\TRY\TRY.TXT for sequential output.

If the file does not exist, it is created. If it does exist, the current file is erased and a new one is created.

The code creates the file TRY.TXT and writes the contents of txtMyText text box into the file:

```
' Get a free file number.
FileNum = FreeFile

' Create the file TRY.TXT.

Open "C:\AUTOEXEC.BAT" For Output As FileNum
```

14

489

```
' Write the contents of the text box txtMyText into
' the file TRY.TXT.
Print #FileNum, txtMyText.Text

' Close the file.
Close FileNum
```

4. These statements open the file C:\TRY\TRY.TXT for sequential append.

   If the file does not exist, it is created. If it does exist, subsequent output statements append new data to the file.

5. The code appends the contents of the txtMyText text box to the file INFO.TXT:

```
' Get a free file number.
FileNum = FreeFile

' Open the file INFO.TXT for append.
Open "INFO.TXT" For Append As FileNum

' Add the contents of the text box txtMyText to the
' end of INFO.TXT.
Print #FileNum, txtMyText.Text

' Close the file.
Close FileNum
```

6. The code reads the contents of the file TRY.TXT into the txtMyText text box:

```
' Get a free file number.
FileNum = FreeFile

' Open the file TRY.TXT for input.
Open "TRY.TXT" For Input As FileNum

' Read all the contents of TRY.TXT into the text
' box txtMyText.
txtMyText.Text = Input$(LOF(FileNum), FileNum)

' Close the file.
Close FileNum
```

7. The code writes the string THIS IS A TEST into the file TRY.DAT, starting at byte location 75.

```
' Get a free file number.
FileNum = FreeFile

' Open the file TRY.DAT for binary access.
Open "TRY.DAT" For Binary As FileNum

' Fill the string variable MyString.
MyString = "THIS IS A TEST"

' Write the string variable MyString into the file,
' starting at byte location 75.
```

```
Put #FileNum, 75, MyString

' Close the file.
Close FileNum
```

8. The code reads 20 bytes from the file TRY.DAT, starting at byte location 75. The code then displays these 20 bytes:

```
' Get a free file number.
FileNum = FreeFile

' Open the file TRY.DAT for binary access.
Open "TRY.DAT" For Binary As FileNum

' Initialize the MyString string to 20 blanks.
MyString - String$(20, " ")

' Read 20 characters from the file, starting at byte
' location 75. Only 20 characters are read because the
' length of MyString is 20 characters.
Get #FileNum, 75, MyString

' Display MyString.
MsgBox "MyString="+MyString

' Close the file.
Close FileNum
```

Exercise Answers

1. One possible solution to this exercise is to open the file C:\WINDOWS\TADA.WAV for binary access and read an integer value starting at byte number 25 of the file. After the value is read into an integer variable, the value of the variable can be displayed using a message box. The following code does this:

```
Dim SamplingRate As Integer
Dim FileNum As Integer

' Get a free file number.
FileNum = FreeFile

' Open the file C:\WINDOWS\TADA.WAV for binary access.
Open "C:\WINDOWS\TADA.WAV" For Binary As FileNum

' Read the sampling rate into the integer variable
' SamplingRate, starting at byte location 25.
Get #FileNum, 25, SamplingRate

' Close the file.
Close FileNum

' Display the sampling rate.
MsgBox "The sampling rate of TADA.WAV is " +Str(SamplingRate)
```

14

You may place this code inside the `Click` event procedure of a command button. After you run the program and click the command button, the following message should be displayed:

```
The sampling rate of TADA.WAV is 22050
```

2. Because the file C:\AUTOEXEC.BAT is a text file, a good way to open it is with sequential access. The following code opens the file C:\AUTOEXEC.BAT for input and reads the content of the file into a text box. The code is placed inside the `Form_Load()` procedure of the program's form:

```
Sub Form_Load ()

Dim FileNum As Integer
    ' Get a free file number.
    FileNum = FreeFile

    ' Open the file C:\AUTOEXEC.BAT for input.
    Open "C:\AUTOEXEC.BAT" For Input As FileNum

    ' Read all the contents of AUTOEXEC.BAT into the
    ' text box txtMyText.
    txtMyText.Text = Input$(LOF(FileNum), FileNum)

    ' Close the file.
    Close FileNum

End Sub
```

3

You've made it to the third week! This week you'll learn about some of the most sophisticated features of Visual Basic—features that make it famous!

Where You're Going

This week you'll learn to create professional installation programs (similar to the SETUP.EXE program that you used to install Visual Basic), and you'll learn how to use the data control of Visual Basic that enables your Visual Basic programs to interface with databases such as Access, Paradox, FoxPro, and dBASE. You'll also learn how to write Visual Basic programs that utilize the dynamic data exchange capabilities that Windows offers, as well as dynamic linked libraries.

In Chapter 21, "Sound," you'll learn how to write programs that play sound through a sound card. If you or your users do not have a sound card installed, don't worry! You'll learn how to play real voice and real music through the PC speaker without any additional hardware.

WEEK
3

Other Topics

In this chapter you'll learn about miscellaneous topics in Visual Basic that have not been covered in previous chapters.

The AUTOLOAD.MAK File

The AUTOLOAD.MAK file resides in the C:\VB directory. This file determines which files are loaded when you open a new project in Visual Basic. For example, if you purchased the Professional Edition of Visual Basic, the project window of your new project contains the VBX files that are included in the Professional Edition. As stated in previous chapters, you can remove VBX files from the project window by highlighting the file to be removed and then selecting Remove File from the File menu. To add a file to the project window, you have to select Add File from the File menu and select the file to be added from the Add File dialog box that Visual Basic displays. The VBX files reside in the C:\WINDOWS\SYSTEM directory.

After working with Visual Basic for a while, you probably found out that having too many VBX files in the project window may be inconvenient, because loading a project that has many VBX files may take several seconds to load. Also, if you have many VBX files in your project, the Toolbox contains many control icons (each additional VBX file corresponds to an additional control icon in the Toolbox). Having too many icons in the Toolbox may slow down your visual implementation process, because it is difficult to locate the required control from the large collections of icons in the Toolbox.

Many programmers prefer to start a new project without any VBX flies and add the VBX files to the project only when there is a need for them. For example, you may start a project without any VBX files. As you develop your program, you may decide that you want to use the GRID.VBX file. To add the GRID.VBX file, simply select Add File from the File menu and select the file C:\WINDOWS\SYSTEM\GRID.VBX.

To cause the project that is loaded upon startup of a new project to be loaded without any VBX files, use the following steps:

☐ Double-click the MS-DOS icon (usually in the Main group of the Program Manager).

   Windows responds by taking the PC to a DOS shell.

☐ Log in to the directory C:\VB:

```
CD  C:\VB  {Enter}
```

☐ Copy the file AUTOLOAD.MAK:

```
COPY AUTOLOAD.MAK  AUTOLOAD.ORG  {Enter}
```

You now have the original AUTOLOAD.MAK file saved as AUTOLOAD.ORG. In the following steps, you'll make changes to the AUTOLOAD.MAK file. However, if in the future you decide that you want to use the original AUTOLOAD.MAK file, simply type the following at the DOS prompt:

```
COPY AUTOLOAD.ORG  AUTOLOAD.MAK {Enter}
```

☐ To return to Windows, type EXIT at the DOS prompt:

```
EXIT  {Enter}
```

☐ Start Visual Basic.

☐ Select New Project from the File menu.

Visual Basic responds by opening a new project. The Project window contains the form Form1.frm, as well as all the VBX files that are specified in the AUTOLOAD.MAK file.

☐ Remove all the VBX files that you don't want to be loaded automatically. For example, if you don't want any VBX file to be loaded when you start a new project, remove all the VBX files from the Project window. When you finish removing the VBX files, your Project window should contain only the file Form1.frm.

☐ If there is a certain module (BAS file) or another file that you want to be loaded whenever you start a new project, select Add File from the File menu and add the module or file to the project. For example, if you want your new projects to contain the file C:\CONSTANT.TXT, add this file to the project window now.

☐ Select Save Project As from the File menu.

Visual Basic responds by asking you if you want to save the Form1.frm (see Figure 15.1).

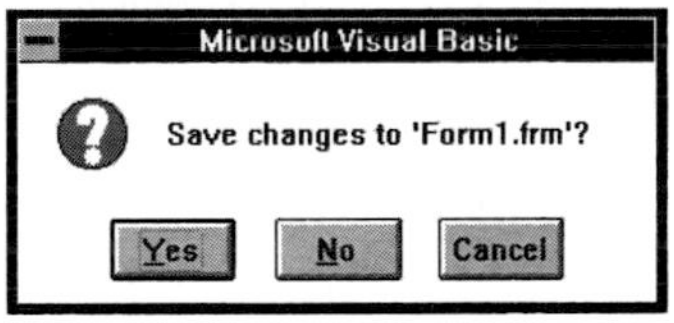

Figure 15.1.
The dialog box Visual Basic displays when you select Save Project As from the File menu.

☐ Click the No button (that is, there is no need to save the form).

Visual Basic responds by displaying the Save Project As dialog box (see Figure 15.2).

☐ Save the project as AUTOLOAD.MAK in the directory C:\VB.

From now on, any new project you start will contain the files that are specified in AUTOLOAD.MAK.

Figure 15.2.
The Save Project As dialog box.

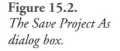

ASCII Files

As you develop your programs you may find it useful to print a hard copy of the properties table of the form and the code of the program. Visual Basic saves the properties table and the code of the form inside the form file. For example, the form file MYFORM.FRM contains the properties table and the code of the form. By default, the FRM files are binary files. However, you may instruct Visual Basic to save the FRM files as ASCII files instead of binary files.

Use the following steps to save an FRM file as an ASCII file:

☐ Start Visual Basic.

☐ Select Open Project from the File menu.

   Visual Basic responds by displaying the Open Project dialog box.

☐ Load an existing project. (For example, load the HELLO.MAK project that you wrote in Chapter 1, "Writing Your First Program.")

☐ Make sure that HELLO.FRM is highlighted in the Project window (because you are about to save this file to an ASCII file).

☐ Select Save File As from the File menu.

   Visual Basic responds by displaying the Save File As dialog box (see Figure 15.3).

☐ Check the Save as Text check box that appears on the right side of the dialog box (see Figure 15.3).

☐ Click the OK button of the Save File As dialog box.

   Visual Basic responds by displaying the confirmation box shown in Figure 15.4. (because the HELLO.FRM file exists already as a binary file).

☐ Click the Yes button of the confirmation box of Figure 15.4.

   Visual Basic responds by saving the HELLO.FRM file as an ASCII file.

Figure 15.3.
*The Save File As
dialog box.*

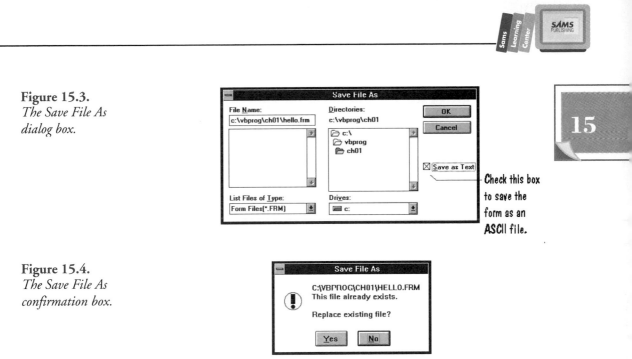

Check this box
to save the
form as an
ASCII file.

Figure 15.4.
*The Save File As
confirmation box.*

Now look at the HELLO.FRM file:

☐ Start Notepad (usually in the Accessories group of the Program Manager of Windows) or
any other word processor that is capable of loading ASCII files.

☐ Select Open from the File menu and load the file HELLO.FRM.

The HELLO.FRM file looks like the following:

```
VERSION X.00
Begin Form frmHello
    Caption         =    "The Hello Program"
    ClientHeight    -    4020
    ClientLeft      =    1740
    ClientTop       =    1440
    ClientWidth     =    7365
    Height          =    4425
    Left            =    1680
    LinkTopic       =    "Form1"
    ScaleHeight     =    4020
    ScaleWidth      =    7365
    Top             =    1095
    Width           =    7485
    Begin TextBox tbxDisplay
        Alignment       =    2    'Center
        FontBold        =    -1   'True
        FontItalic      =    0    'False
        FontName        =    "Times New Roman"
        FontSize        =    30
        FontStrikethru  =    0    'False
        FontUnderline   =    0    'False
        Height          =    1380
```

```
            Left            =    1200
            MultiLine       =    -1   'True
            TabIndex        =    3
            Top             =    120
            Width           =    4935
         End
         Begin CommandButton cmdClear
            Caption         =    "&Clear"
            FontBold        =    -1   'True
            FontItalic      =    0    'False
            FontName        =    "Times New Roman"
            FontSize        =    13.5
            FontStrikethru  =    0    'False
            FontUnderline   =    0    'False
            Height          =    1455
            Left            =    4320
            TabIndex        =    2
            Top             =    1560
            Width           =    1815
         End
         Begin CommandButton cmdHello
            Caption         =    "&Display Hello"
            FontBold        =    -1   'True
            FontItalic      =    0    'False
            FontName        =    "Times New Roman"
            FontSize        =    13.5
            FontStrikethru  =    0    'False
            FontUnderline   =    0    'False
            Height          =    1455
            Left            =    1200
            TabIndex        =    1
            Top             =    1560
            Width           =    1935
         End
         Begin CommandButton cmdExit
            Caption         =    "E&xit"
            FontBold        =    -1   'True
            FontItalic      =    0    'False
            FontName        =    "Times New Roman"
            FontSize        =    13.5
            FontStrikethru  =    0    'False
            FontUnderline   =    0    'False
            Height          =    495
            Left            =    3120
            TabIndex        =    0
            Top             =    3240
            Width           =    1215
         End
      End
   End
   Sub cmdClear_Click ()
       tbxDisplay.Text = ""
   End Sub
```

```
Sub cmdExit_Click ()
    Beep
    End
End Sub

Sub cmdHello_Click ()
    tbxDisplay.Text = "Hello World!"
End Sub
```

The first line of the ASCII file HELLO.FRM is a line that indicates which version of Visual Basic was used to generate the file. For example, if Visual Basic Version 2.0 was used to generate the file, the first line of the file is this:

```
VERSION 2.00
```

The next lines in the ASCII file describe the form and the controls inside the form (that is, the properties table). Only those properties that were changed from their default values are listed. The lines after the properties table are the code of the program. The ASCII file of the form may be useful for documenting programs.

Understanding the format of the ASCII files may be also useful for programmers who write programs that generate the ASCII files automatically (that is, you may write a program that asks the user several questions, and based on the user's answers, your program generates the ASCII file of the form file). Naturally, Visual Basic has no way of knowing who generated the ASCII file. However, the file must be in strict compliance with the format that Visual Basic expects.

Arrays

If your program uses arrays, your program must declare the arrays. The declaration of the array specifies the name of the array and the number of elements the array can hold.

Just like other variables, if you declare an array in the general declarations section of a form, the array is visible by all procedures and functions in the form. If you declare an array in a separate module and precede the declaration statement with the Global keyword, the array is visible by all the forms of the project.

Data Types

As you may have noticed by now, Visual Basic supports several data types. Table 15.1 lists the various data types and the range of values of the data that Visual Basic supports. For example, when you declare a variable as an integer, you may use the following statement:

```
Dim Counter As Integer
```

Table 15.1. The data types that Visual Basic supports.

Data Type	Number of Bytes	Shortcut Notation	Range
• Integer	2	%	-32,768 to 32,767
• Long	4	&	-2,147,483,648 to 2,147,483,647
Single positive	4	!	1.401298E-45 to 3.402823E38
Single negative	4	!	-3.402823E38 to -1.401298E-45
Double positive	8	#	4.94065645841247D-24 to 1.79769313486232D308
Double negative	8	#	1.79769313486232D308 to -4.94065645841247D-324
Currency	8	[064]	-922337203685477.5808 to 922337203685466.5807
• String	Depends on the number of characters in the string	$	A string may hold up to approximately 65,000 characters
Variant	Date, time, floating point, or string	(none)	Range of Date: from January 1, 0000 to December 31, 9999

The following statement yields identical results:

```
Dim Counter%
```

That is, the character % is a short notation for As Integer.

An integer variable has the range -32,768 to 32,768. Each integer occupies 2 bytes.

Similarly, you may declare the long variable Number as follows:

```
Dim Numbers As Long
```

The following statement is an alternate syntax notation of declaring the Number variable As Long:

```
Dim Numbers&
```

That is, the character & is a short notation for As Long.

A long variable has the range -2,147,483,648 to 2,147,483,647. Each long variable occupies 4 bytes.

The double variable MyVariable is declared as follows:

```
Dim MyVariable As Double
```

which is the same as this:

```
Dim MyVariable#
```

A double variable may be a positive number or a negative number. The ranges of positive and negative values are specified in Table 15.1.

The Arrays Program

The Arrays program illustrates how you declare arrays in Visual Basic.

The Visual Implementation of the Arrays Program

☐ Open a new project, save the form of the project as ARRAYS.FRM, and save the make file of the project as ARRAYS.MAK.

☐ Build the frmArrays form according to the specifications in Table 15.2.

The completed form should look like the one shown in Figure 15.5.

Table 15.2. The properties table of the frmArrays form.

Object	Property	Setting
Form	**Name**	**frmArrays**
	Caption	The Arrays Program
	Height	4425
	Left	1035
	Top	1140
	Width	7485
Command Button	**Name**	**cmdArray2**
	Caption	Array&2
	Height	495

continues

Table 15.2. continued

Object	Property	Setting
	Left	3360
	Top	1320
	Width	1215
Command Button	**Name**	**cmdArray1**
	Caption	Array&1
	Height	495
	Left	3360
	Top	720
	Width	1215
Command Button	**Name**	**cmdExit**
	Caption	&Exit
	Height	495
	Left	5880
	Top	3360
	Width	1215

Figure 15.5.
The frmArrays form.

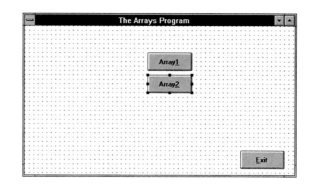

Entering the Code of the Arrays Program

☐ Enter the following code inside the general declarations section of the frmArrays form:

```
' All variables MUST be declared.
Option Explicit

' Declare  the array.
' The first element of the array is Array2(10).
' The last element of the array is Array2(20).
Dim Array2(10 To 20)  As Integer
```

☐ Enter the following code inside the `cmdArray1_Click()` procedure of the frmArrays form:

```
Sub cmdArray1_Click ()

    Dim Counter

    ' Declare the array.
    ' The first element of the array is Array1(1).
    ' The last element of the array is Array(10).
    Static Array1(1 To 10)  As String

    ' Fill 3 elements of the array.
    Array1(1) = "ABC"
    Array1(2) = "DEF"
    Array1(3) = "GHI"

    ' Clear the form.
    frmArrays.Cls

    ' Display 3 elements of the array.
    Print "Here are the elements of Array1[]:"
    For Counter = 1 To 3 Step 1
        Print "Array1(" + Str(Counter) + ") =" + Array1(Counter)
    Next

End Sub
```

☐ Enter the following code inside the `cmdArray2_Click()` procedure of the frmArrays form:

```
Sub cmdArray2_Click ()

    Dim Counter

    ' Fill 3 elements of the array.
    Array2(11) = 234
    Array2(12) = 567
    Array2(13) = 890

    ' Clear the form.
    frmArrays.Cls

    ' Display 3 elements of the array.
    Print "Here are the elements of Array2[]:"
    For Counter = 11 To 13 Step 1
        Print "Array2(" + Str(Counter) + ") = " + Str(Array2(Counter))
    Next

End Sub
```

☐ Enter the following code inside the `cmdExit_Click()` procedure of the frmArrays form:

```
Sub cmdExit_Click ()

    End

End Sub
```

Executing the Arrays Program

☐ Execute the Arrays program.

☐ Click the Array1 button.

The Arrays program responds by displaying the elements of Array1 *(see Figure 15.6).*

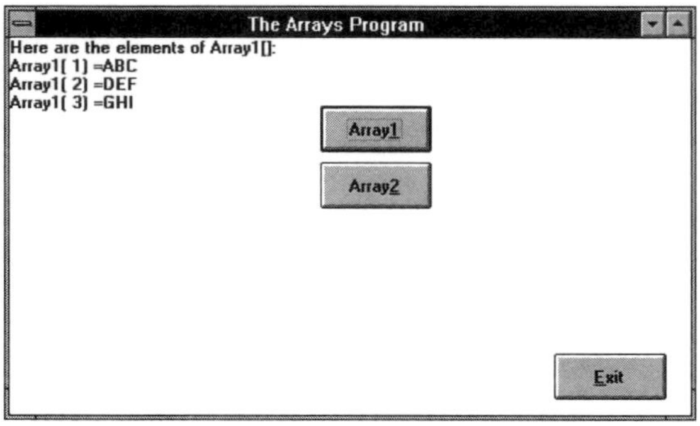

Figure 15.6.
Displaying the elements
of Array1().

☐ Click the Array2 button.

The Arrays program responds by displaying the elements of Array2 *(see Figure 15.7).*

☐ Click the Exit button to exit the Arrays program.

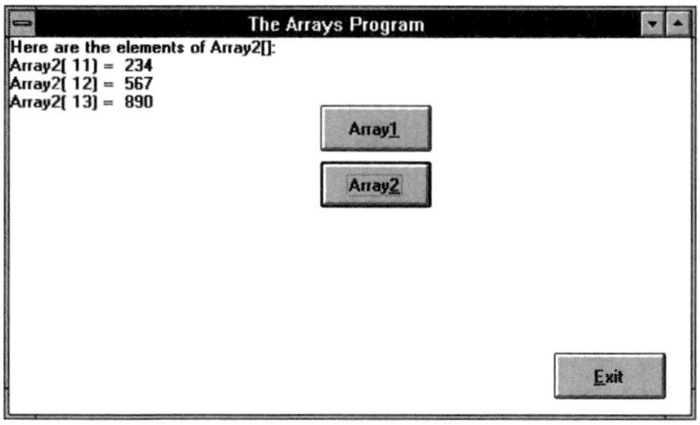

Figure 15.7.
Displaying the elements
of Array2.

How the Arrays Program Works

The Arrays program declares the arrays Array1 and Array2. When you click the Array1 button, the program fills three elements of the array and displays them. Similarly, when you click the Array2 button, the program fills three elements in the array and displays them.

The General Declarations Section of the Arrays Program

The code inside the general declarations section declares the `Array2` array:

```
Dim Array2(10 To 20)  As Integer
```

The array is declared `As Integer`. This means that the elements of the array are integers. The words inside the parentheses indicate that the first element of the array is `Array(10)`, the second element of the array is `Array(11)`, and so on. The last element of the array is `Array(20)`.

Because the `Array2` array is declared inside the general declarations section of the form, it is visible in all procedures and functions of the form.

The Code Inside the *cmdArray1_Click()* Procedure of the frmArrays Form

The `cmdArray1_Click()` procedure is executed whenever the user clicks the Array1 button:

```
Sub cmdArray1_Click ()

    Dim Counter

    ' Declare the array.
    ' The first element of the array is Array1(1).
    ' The last element of the array is Array(10).
    Static Array1(1 To 10)  As String

    ' Fill 3 elements of the array.
    Array1(1) = "ABC"
    Array1(2) = "DEF"
    Array1(3) = "GHI"

    ' Clear the form.
    frmArrays.Cls

    ' Display 3 elements of the array.
    Print "Here are the elements of Array1[]:"
    For Counter = 1 To 3 Step 1
        Print "Array1(" + Str(Counter) + ") =" + Array1(Counter)
    Next

End Sub
```

This procedure declares the `Array1` array as follows:

```
Static Array1(1 To 10) As String
```

Note that because `Array1` is declared inside the procedure, you must declare it as `Static`. The first element of the array is `Array1(1)`, the second element of the array is `Array1(2)`, and so on. The last element of the array is `Array1(10)`.

The procedure then fills three elements in the array and clears the form with the Cls method:

```
Array1(1) = "ABC"
Array1(2) = "DEF"
Array1(3) = "GHI"

frmArrays.Cls
```

Finally, the procedure displays the first three elements of the array with a For loop:

```
Print "Here are the elements of Array1[]:"
For Counter = 1 To 3 Step 1
    Print "Array1(" + Str(Counter) + ") =" + Array1(Counter)
Next
```

The Code Inside the *cmdArray2_Click()* Procedure of the frmArrays Form

The `cmdArray2_Click()` procedure is executed whenever the user clicks the Array2 button:

```
Sub cmdArray2_Click ()

    Dim Counter

    ' Fill 3 elements of the array.
    Array2(11) = 234
    Array2(12) = 567
    Array2(13) = 890

    ' Clear the form.
    frmArrays.Cls

    ' Display 3 elements of the array.
    Print "Here are the elements of Array2[]:"
    For Counter = 11 To 13 Step 1
        Print "Array2(" + Str(Counter) + ") = " + Str(Array2(Counter))
    Next

End Sub
```

This procedure is similar to the `cmdArray1_Click()` procedure. Because the `Array2` array is declared in the general declarations section of the form, this array is visible in this procedure.

The Upper and Lower Bounds of Arrays

As illustrated in the Arrays program, the first and last elements of the array are specified in the declaration of the array. For example, this declaration:

```
Dim MyArray (0 to 35) As Long
```

declares an array of long numbers. The first element (the lower bound) is `MyArray(0)`, and the last (the upper bound) is `MyArray(35)`. As a short cut, you can also declare arrays as follows:

```
Dim MyArray(5) As long
```

The preceding notations are interpreted by Visual Basic as follows: The first element of the array is MyArray(0); the second element of the array is MyArray(1); and so on. The last element of the array is MyArray(5). The disadvantage of using this shortcut notation for the declaration is that the lower bound of the array must be 0.

Multidimensional Arrays

The Arrays program utilizes a one-dimensional array. In Visual Basic you can declare multidimensional arrays. For example, the following declares a two-dimensional array:

```
Static MyArray (0 To 3, 1 To 4 )
```

The elements of the preceding array are the following:

```
MyArray(0,1) MyArray(0,2) MyArray(0,3) MyArray(0,4)

MyArray(1,1) MyArray(1,2) MyArray(1,3) MyArray(1,4)

MyArray(2,1) MyArray(2,2) MyArray(2,3) MyArray(2,4)

MyArray(3,1) MyArray(3,2) MyArray(3,3) MyArray(3,4)
```

In a similar way, you can declare a three-dimensional array. Here's an example:

```
Dim MyArray ( 1 To 3, 1 To 7, 1 To 5)
```

In Visual Basic you can declare arrays with up to 60 dimensions!

The following code uses two For loops to fill all the elements of a two-dimensional array with the value 3:

```
Static MyArray (1 To 10, 1 To 10) As Integer
Dim Counter1, Counter2

For Counter1 = 1 To 10
    For Counter2 = 1 To 10
      MyArray(Counter1, Counter2) = 3
    Next Counter2
Next Counter3
```

Dynamic Arrays

When declaring arrays, you have to be careful not to consume too much memory. For example, this declaration:

```
Static MyArray (10000) As long
```

declares an array with 10001 elements. Because each element is defined as Long, and according to Table 15.1 a long variable occupies 4 bytes of memory, the MyArray() array requires 40004 (10001 × 4) bytes. 40004 bytes of memory might not sound like a lot of memory, but if you have 10 such arrays in your program, these arrays consume 400040 (40004 × 10) bytes of memory! Therefore, always try to set the size of your arrays to the minimum size that your program requires. Sometimes, however, the size of the arrays can be determined only during runtime. In these cases, you may use the `ReDim` (redimensioning) statement that Visual Basic supports. An array that changes its size during runtime is called a dynamic array.

The following code illustrates how to redimension an array:

```
Sub cmdArray1_Click ()

    Dim Counter
    ' Declare Array1 as a dynamic array.
    Dim Array1()As Integer

    ' Assign the size of the dynamic array.
    ReDim Array1(1 To 15)  As Integer

    For Counter = 1 To 15 Step 1
        Array1(Counter) = Counter
    Next Counter

    ' Assign a new size to the dynamic array.
    ReDim Array1(1 To 5)  As Integer

End Sub
```

The procedure declares `Array1` as a dynamic array. Note that the declaration of a fixed array is different from the declaration of a dynamic array. That is, when you declare a dynamic array, the size of the array is not specified in the declaration.

The next statement in the preceding code assigns a size to the array by using the `ReDim` statement:

```
ReDim Array1(1 To 15) As Integer
```

This `ReDim` statement assigns 15 elements to the array. The elements of the arrays are defined as integers.

The `For` loop fills the 15 elements of the array, and then the `ReDim` statement is used again to redimension the array:

```
ReDim Array1(1 To 5)  As Integer
```

After the second `ReDim` statement is executed, the `Array1` array has only 5 elements. Therefore, you may use this technique to change the size of your arrays during runtime and conserve memory. In the preceding code, `Array1` required 30 (15 × 2) bytes. However, after the execution of the second `ReDim` statement, the size of `Array1` was changed to 5 elements, and from that point on, `Array1` occupied only 10 (5 × 2) bytes.

It is important to understand that once the `ReDim` statement is executed, the values that were stored in the array are lost forever! If you want to preserve the values of the array, you must use the `Preserve` keyword. The Arrays2 program illustrates how you can accomplish this.

The Arrays2 Program

☐ Open a new project, save the new form of the project as ARRAYS2.FRM, and save the make file of the project as ARRAYS2.MAK.

☐ Build the frmArrays form according to the specifications in Table 15.3.

The completed form should look like the one shown in Figure 15.8.

Table 15.3. The properties table of the frmArrays form.

Object	Property	Setting
Form	Name	frmArrays
	Caption	The Arrays2 Program
	Height	4425
	Left	1035
	Top	1140
	Width	7485
Command Button	Name	cmdFill10
	Caption	Fill &10 Elements
	Height	495
	Left	3240
	Top	1320
	Width	3855
Command Button	Name	cmdOnly5
	Caption	Cut to &5 Elements
	Height	495
	Left	3240
	Top	1920
	Width	3855
Combo Box	Name	cboElements
	Height	300
	Left	1080
	Text	(empty)
	Top	1320
	Width	1215

Table 15.3. continued

Object	Property	Setting
Command Button	**Name**	**cmdExit**
	Caption	&Exit
	Height	495
	Left	5880
	Top	3240
	Width	1215

Figure 15.8.
The frmArrays form.

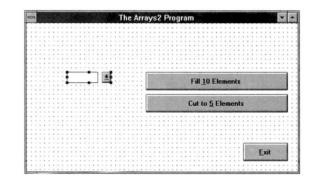

Entering the Code of the Arrays2 Program

☐ Enter the following code inside the general declarations section of the frmArray form:

```
' All variables MUST be declared.
Option Explicit

' Declare a dynamic array.
Dim TheArray() As Integer
```

☐ Enter the following code inside the cmdExit_Click() procedures of the frmArrays form:

```
Sub cmdExit_Click ()

    End

End Sub
```

☐ Enter the following code inside the cmdFill10_Click() procedures of the frmArrays form:

```
Sub cmdFill10_Click ()

    ' Set the size of the array.
    ReDim TheArray(1 To 10) As Integer
    Dim Counter

    ' Fill the elements of the array.
```

```
For Counter = 1 To 10 Step 1
    TheArray(Counter) = Counter
Next Counter

' Clear the combo box.
cboElements.Clear

' Fill the items of the combo box.
For Counter = 0 To 9 Step 1
    cboElements.AddItem Str(TheArray(Counter + 1))
Next Counter
```

End Sub

☐ Enter the following code inside the cmdOnly5_Click() procedures of the frmArrays form:

Sub cmdOnly5_Click ()

```
' Set the size of the array.
ReDim Preserve TheArray(1 To 5) As Integer

Dim Counter

' Clear the combo box.
cboElements.Clear

' Fill the items of the combo box.
For Counter = 0 To 4 Step 1
    cboElements.AddItem Str(TheArray(Counter + 1))
Next Counter
```

End Sub

Executing the Arrays2 Program

☐ Execute the Arrays2 program.

☐ Click the Fill 10 Elements button.

> *The Arrays2 program responds by filling the combo box with 10 elements. You can see these 10 elements by clicking the right arrow of the combo box to drop down the list (see Figure 15.9).*

☐ Click the Cut to 5 Elements button.

> *The Arrays2 program responds by eliminating 5 elements from the combo box. You can see the 5 elements that are left in the combo box by clicking the right arrow of the combo box to drop down the list (see Figure 15.10).*

☐ Click the Exit button to exit the program.

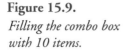

Figure 15.9.

Filling the combo box with 10 items.

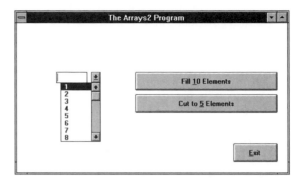

Figure 15.10.

Preserving 5 elements of the array.

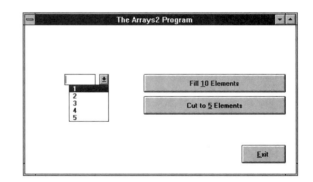

How the Arrays2 Program Works

The Arrays2 program fills an array and then fills the items of the combo box with the elements of the array. The array is then redimensioned with the Preserve keyword. This causes the elements of the array to retain their values.

The Code Inside the General Declarations Section of the frmArrays Form

The code inside the general declarations section of the frmArrays form declares a dynamic array:

```
Dim TheArray() As Integer
```

Visual Basic interprets it as a declaration of a dynamic array, because the parentheses that follow the name of the array are empty.

The Code Inside the *cmdFill10_Click()* Procedure of the frmArrays Form

The cmdFill10_Click() procedure is executed whenever the user clicks the Fill 10 Elements button:

```
Sub cmdFill10_Click ()

    ' Set the size of the array.
    ReDim TheArray(1 To 10) As Integer

    Dim Counter

    ' Fill the elements of the array.
    For Counter = 1 To 10 Step 1
       TheArray(Counter) = Counter
    Next Counter

    ' Clear the combo box.
    cboElements.Clear

    ' Fill the items of the combo box.
    For Counter = 0 To 9 Step 1
       cboElements.AddItem Str(TheArray(Counter + 1))
    Next Counter

End Sub
```

The procedure uses the ReDim statement to set the size of the array to 10 elements:

```
ReDim TheArray(1 To 10) As Integer
```

The elements of the array are filled using a For loop:

```
For Counter = 1 To 10 Step 1
    TheArray(Counter) = Counter
Next Counter
```

The elements of the combo box are cleared, and then a For loop is used to fill 10 items in the combo box. The items in the combo box correspond to the elements of the array:

```
cboElements.Clear
For Counter = 0 To 9 Step 1
    cboElements.AddItem Str(TheArray(Counter + 1))
Next Counter
```

Note that the first item in the combo box is item number 0, and the first element of the array is element number 1. Also, the last item of the combo box is item number 9, and the last element of the array is element number 10.

The Code Inside the *cmdOnly5_Click()* Procedures of the *frmArrays* Form

The cmdOnly5_Click() procedure is executed whenever the user clicks the Cut to 5 Elements button:

```
Sub cmdOnly5_Click ()

    ' Set the size of the array.
    ReDim Preserve TheArray(1 To 5) As Integer

    Dim Counter
```

```
' Clear the combo box.
cboElements.Clear

' Fill the items of the combo box.
For Counter = 0 To 4 Step 1
   cboElements.AddItem Str(TheArray(Counter + 1))
Next Counter
```

End Sub

The procedure uses the ReDim statement to change the size of the array to 5 elements:

```
ReDim Preserve TheArray(1 To 5) As Integer
```

The Preserve keyword causes the first 5 elements of the array to retain their original values. The procedure then clears the items of the combo box and fills 5 elements in the combo box:

```
cboElements.Clear
For Counter = 0 To 4 Step 1
    cboElements.AddItem Str(TheArray(Counter + 1))
Next Counter
```

Use the following steps to see the effect of the Preserve keyword:

☐ Remove the Preserve keyword from the ReDim statement (that is, change the ReDim statement in the cmdOnly5_Click()) procedure so that it looks like this:

```
ReDim TheArray(1 To 5) As Integer
```

☐ Execute the Arrays2 program.

☐ Click the Fill 10 Elements button.

☐ Open the combo list and verify that the list is filled with 10 items (each item corresponds to an element of the array).

☐ Click the Cut to 5 Elements.

☐ Open the combo list and verify that the list is filled with 5 items (each item corresponds to an element of the array). Because you removed the Preserve keyword, the elements of the array are all zeros.

☐ Click the Exit button to terminate the Arrays2 program.

Arrays that Exceed 64KB

The size of the arrays may exceed 64KB. An array that exceeds 64KB is called a *huge array*. You do not have to use any special declaration for huge arrays. Generally, huge arrays are handled in the same way as non-huge arrays—the only exception is that if the huge array is declared as a string, all the elements of the array must have the same number of characters in each element of the array.

The Windows operating system may be set to work in enhanced mode and in standard mode. In enhanced mode, huge arrays may have a maximum size of 64MB, and in the standard mode, huge arrays may have a maximum size of 1MB.

Passing Arguments by Values and by Reference

In Visual Basic you may pass arguments to a function by one of two methods: by reference or by value. The difference between these two methods is illustrated with the VARY program.

The Visual Implementation of the VARY Program

☐ Open a new project, save the form of the project as VARY.FRM, and save the make file of the project as VARY.MAK.

☐ Build the frmVary form according to the specifications in Table 15.4.

The completed form should look like the one shown in Figure 15.11.

Table 15.4. The properties table of the frmVary form.

Object	Property	Setting
Form	**Name**	**frmVary**
	Caption	The VARY Program
	Height	4425
	Left	1035
	Top	1140
	Width	7485
Command Button	**Name**	**cmdDoIt**
	Caption	&Do It
	Height	1335
	Left	1920
	Top	1680
	Width	1575

continues

Table 15.4. continued

Object	Property	Setting
Command Button	**Name**	**cmdExit**
	Caption	&Exit
	Height	495
	Left	6000
	Top	3240
	Width	1215
Label	**Name**	**lblInfo**
	Alignment	2-Center
	BorderStyle	1-Fixed Single
	Caption	(empty)
	Height	495
	Left	1560
	Top	720
	Width	2415

Figure 15.11.
The frmVary form.

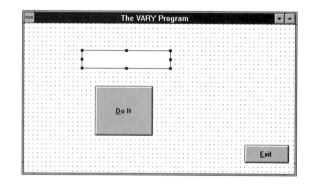

Entering the Code of the VARY Program

☐ Enter the following code inside the general declarations section of the frmVary form:

```
' All variables MUST be declared.
Option Explicit
```

☐ Enter the following code inside the cmdDoIt_Click() procedure of the frmVary form:

```
Sub cmdDoIt_Click ()

    Dim V As Integer
```

```
Dim Result As Integer

V = 3

Result = VSquare(V)

lblInfo.Caption = "V=" + Str(V) + "   4*4=" + Str(Result)
```

End Sub

☐ Enter the following code inside the cmdExit_Click() procedure of the frmVary form:

Sub cmdExit_Click ()

```
End
```

End Sub

☐ Create a new function in the frmArray form and name it VSquare.

☐ Enter the following code inside the VSquare() function:

Function VSquare (ByVal V As Integer)

```
V = 4

VSquare = V * V
```

End Function

Executing the VARY Program

☐ Execute the VARY program.

☐ Click the Do It button.

> *The VARY program responds by displaying the values in the lblInfo label, as shown in Figure 15.12.*

☐ Click the Exit button to exit the VARY program.

Figure 15.12.
The VARY program when passing the V variable to the function ByVal.

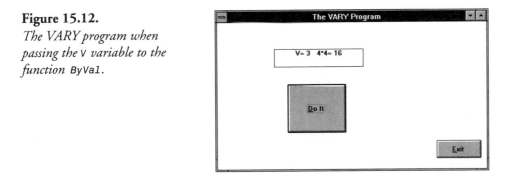

How the VARY Program Works

The VARY program passes a variable to a function by value (ByVal). The meaning of passing the function ByVal is explained in the following sections.

The Code Inside the *cmdDoIt_Click()* Procedure of the frmVary Form

The cmdDoIt_Click() procedure is executed whenever the user clicks the Do It button:

```
Sub cmdDoIt_Click ()

    Dim V As Integer
    Dim Result As Integer

    V = 3

    Result = VSquare(V)

    lblInfo.Caption = "V=" + Str(V) + "    4*4=" + Str(Result)

End Sub
```

The procedure sets the value of the V variable to 3, and then executes the VSquare() function. VSquare() returns the result of 4×4.

The procedure then displays the value of V and the returned value from VSquare() inside the lblInfo label.

The Code Inside the *VSquare()* Function

The VSquare() function is called by the cmdDoIt_Click() procedure:

```
Function VSquare (ByVal V As Integer)

    V = 4

    VSquare = V * V

End Function
```

This function sets the value of V to 4, and then sets the value of VSquare to $V \times V$.

The important thing to note is that the V variable is passed to the function ByVal. This means that this procedure creates a new copy of a variable called V. There are no connections between the variable V in the calling procedure (cmdDoIt_Click()) and the variable V in the VSquare() function. This explains why the value of V that was displayed in the lblInfo label is 3 and not 4 (see Figure 15.12). To summarize, when you pass a variable to a function ByVal, the value of the passed variable does not change within the calling procedure.

Modifying the VARY Program

☐ Change the VSquare() function so that it looks like this:

```
Function VSquare (V As Integer)

    V = 4

    VSquare = V * V

End Function
```

☐ Execute the VARY program.

☐ Click the Do It button.

The VARY program responds by displaying values in the lblInfo label, as shown in Figure 15.13.

Figure 15.13.
The VARY program when passing V *by reference.*

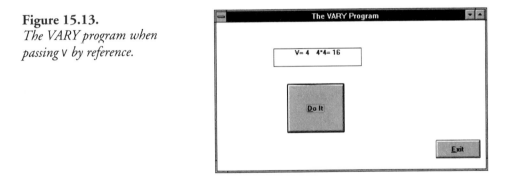

Note that now the variable is not passed ByVal. When a variable is not passed ByVal, it is passed by reference. Passing an argument by reference means that the passed variable is the same variable in the calling procedure and the called function. Therefore, when you pass V by reference, the V variable in the cmdDoIt_Click() procedure is the same V variable that is used in the VSquare() function. This is why the value of V is displayed in the lblInfo label as 4 (see Figure 15.13).

Readers familiar with the C programming language may recognize that passing an argument by reference is the equivalent of passing the address of the variable in C. If you are not familiar with C and find the concept a little confusing, just note the differences between the two methods of passing arguments:

When passing an argument by value (ByVal), the called function is not able to change the value of the passed variable in the calling procedure. For example, in the VARY program, even though the VSquare() function sets the value of V to 4, the value of V in the cmdDoIt_Click() procedure remains 3.

- When passing an argument by reference, the called function and the calling function are using the same variable. For example, in the modified version of the VARY program, the VSquare() function sets the value of V to 4, and this value is displayed in the lblInfo label by the cmdDoIt_Click() procedure.

Modifying the VARY Program Again

☐ Change the VSquare() function so that it looks like this:

```
Function VSquare (VV As Integer)

    VV = 4

    VSquare = VV * VV

End Function
```

☐ Execute the VARY program.

☐ Click the DoIt button.

The VARY program again responds, as shown in Figure 15.13.

☐ Terminate the program by clicking the Exit button.

As you can see, you changed the name of the variable in the VSquare() function from V to VV. However, this did not affect the way the program works! This is because the variable V was passed by reference. So, although inside the VSquare() function the variable is called VV, it is the same variable that was passed by the calling procedure (that is, V and VV are the same variable).

As you can see, passing variables by reference can be tricky.

OLE

Object linking and embedding (OLE) is an important Windows topic that is available in Visual Basic. (The topic of OLE actually deserves a whole book.) OLE is so powerful that you may think of it as a different software package that is included with your Visual Basic package. The rest of this chapter serves as a brief introduction to OLE.

Note: To see the OLE operation in action, you have to see it working with another Windows application that supports OLE, such as Word for Windows or Excel. The rest of this chapter demonstrates the concept of OLE by using the Word for Windows program. If you do not own the Word for Windows program, feel free to skip the material or just browse through it.

What Is OLE?

OLE is the abbreviation of object linking and embedding. A program that includes an OLE capability is able to communicate data (text and graphics) with other Windows applications that are OLE based.

Suppose that your Visual Basic program requires the user to enter text. One way to accomplish this task is to include a text box inside the form of the program. However, a text box is not equipped with a spell checker, and it does not have the capabilities to format paragraphs and pages. In short, a text box cannot substitute for a full-blown professional word processor. The solution is to link a word processing program to the Visual Basic program. Similarly, if your Visual Basic application requires the user to generate a pie graph, it is better to link a professional graphics program to the Visual Basic program than to write a pie generator program yourself. By including OLE capabilities in your program, you use existing professional OLE-based programs that the user has and knows how to operate.

The Front Program

The Front program illustrates how an OLE-based Visual Basic program may be used as a front-end application. A *front-end application* is an application that is used in front of all the other applications. That is, upon startup of the front-end application, the user sees menus and icons that enable him/her to perform word processing, spreadsheet work, and other common tasks. When the user clicks the word processor icon, a word processor program starts just as if the word processor's icon were clicked from the Program Manager of Windows.

So why not use the Program Manager? In a typical Windows system, the Program Manager might include many groups—the Visual Basic group, the communication group, the word processor group, and so on. The Program Manager is suitable for a developing environment. If, in a certain working environment, the PC is dedicated to performing a particular job, a front-end program is more user-friendly and more elegant than the Program Manager of Windows. In other words, the front-end program serves as a focal point to all the Windows applications that the user is likely to use every day.

The Visual Implementation of the Front Program

☐ Open a new project, save the form of the project as FRONT.FRM, and save the make file of the project as FRONT.MAK.

The Front program uses the custom control MSOLE2.VBX (see Figure 15.14). Therefore, make sure that the Project window contains the custom control MSOLE2. This control is available only in Visual Basic 3.0 and above. If you are currently working with an older version of Visual Basic, you will not be able to implement the Front program.

Figure 15.14.
The MSOLE2 control.

The **MS OLE 2** control

If for some reason your project window does not include the MSOLE2.VBX file, you may add it to the project as follows:

☐ Select Add File from the File menu.

Visual Basic responds by displaying the Add File dialog box.

☐ Select the file C:\WINDOWS\SYSTEM\MSOLE2.VBX.

Visual Basic responds by adding the MSOLE2.VBX file to your project. Note that the file MSOLE2.VBX was stored in the C:\WINDOWS\SYSTEM directory during the installation of the Visual Basic product.

Now that your project includes the MSOLE2.VBX file, take a look at the Toolbox. It contains the OLE 2.0 icon, as shown in Figure 15.14.

☐ Change the properties of the form as follows: The Name property should be frmFront, the Caption property should be The Front Program, and the WindowState property should be 2-Maximized.

Adding the MSOLE2 Control to the frmFront Form

Now add the MSOLE2 control:

☐ Double-click the MSOLE2 icon in the Toolbox.

Visual Basic responds by placing the MSOLE2 control inside the form and displaying the Insert Object dialog box (see Figure 15.15).

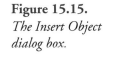

Figure 15.15.
The Insert Object dialog box.

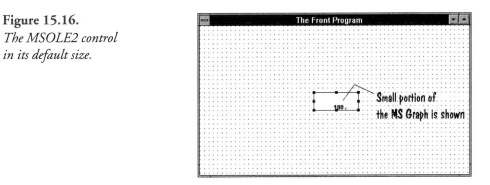

15

As you can see, the Insert Object dialog box displays a list of Windows applications that may be used as objects in the Front program. Now select the Microsoft Graph application as the object to be inserted into the Front program. If you have the program Word for Windows Version 2.0 installed in your PC, you also have the MS Graph program installed (MS Graph comes with Word for Windows).

☐ Select the item Microsoft Graph from the list of the Insert Object dialog box and then select OK.

> *Visual Basic responds by inserting the MS Graph application inside the MSOLE2 control (see Figure 15.16).*

Figure 15.16.
The MSOLE2 control in its default size.

The Front Program

Small portion of
the MS Graph is shown

☐ Set the SizeMode property of the MSOLE2 control to 2-Auto Size.

> *Visual Basic responds by enlarging the MSOLE2 control so it fits the graph of MS Graph (see Figure 15.17).*

525

Figure 15.17.
Setting the SizeMode of the MSOLE2 control to Auto Size.

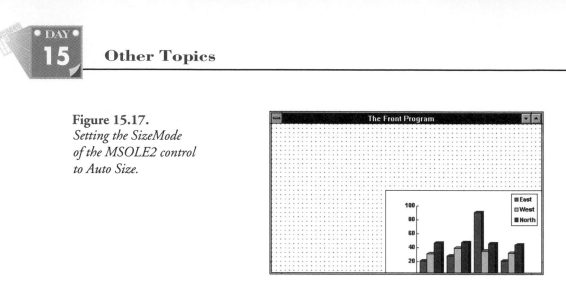

☐ Add a menu to the frmFront form according to the specifications in Table 15.5.

Table 15.5. The menu table of the frmFront form.

Caption	Name
&File	mnuFile
...&Exit	mnuExit

☐ Add the following code inside the `mnuExit_Click()` procedure of the frmFront form:

```
Sub mnuExit_Click ()

    End

End Sub
```

☐ Save the project.

Executing the Front Program

☐ Execute the Front program.

The window of the Front program appears, as shown in Figure 15.18.

☐ Double-click the MSOLE2 control (the MSOLE2 control contains the graph).

The program responds by displaying the MS Graph program (see Figure 15.19).

Figure 15.18.
The Front program.

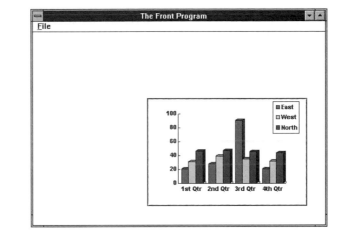

Figure 15.19.
Executing the MS Graph program by double-clicking the MSOLE2 control.

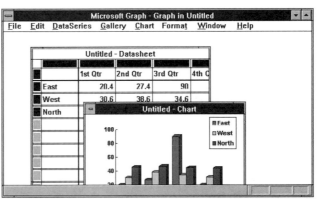

You may now change the values in the table of MS Graph and the format of the graph:

☐ Select Pie from the Gallery menu.

> *The MS Graph responds by displaying the Chart Gallery dialog box (see Figure 15.20 and Figure 15.21).*

☐ Select Pie number 4 from the Chart Gallery dialog box and push the OK button.

> *MS Graph responds by changing the graph in accordance with the pie number 4 format (see Figure 15.22).*

Figure 15.20.
Selecting Pie from the
Gallery menu.

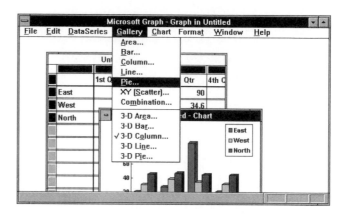

Figure 15.21.
The Chart Gallery dialog
box of MS Graph.

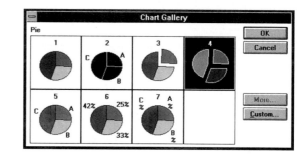

Figure 15.22.
Changing the graph in
accordance with pie
number 4.

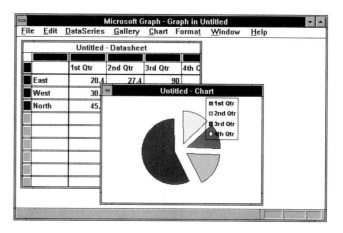

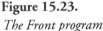

☐ Close the MS Graph program (double-click the minus icon that appears in the upper-left corner of the window of the MS Graph window).

> *The MS Graph program responds by displaying a dialog box that asks you if you want to update the data.*

☐ Click the Yes button.

> *The program responds by closing the MS Graph program and returning to the Visual Basic Front program. As you can see, the graph shown in the window of the Front program is the updated pie graph (see Figure 15.23).*

Figure 15.23.

The Front program with its new graph.

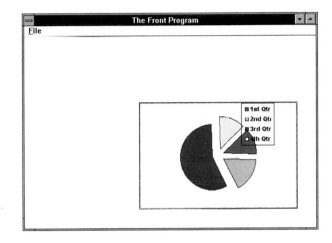

☐ Terminate the Front program by selecting Exit from the File menu.

The Front program illustrates how easy it is to link an object (the MS Graph) into the MSOLE2 control. In a similar manner, you may link other Windows applications that support OLE to your Visual Basic programs.

Summary

In this chapter you have learned how to modify the AUTOLOAD.MAK file, how to save your forms in binary and ASCII formats, how to declare and use arrays, and how to pass arguments by reference and ByVal. This chapter also introduces the OLE topic.

Q&A

Q Should I save the forms as binary files or as ASCII files?

A It does not matter in which format you save the forms. However, the advantage of saving the FRM files as ASCII files is that they may serve as complete documentation of the visual implementations and code of your forms.

Q Should I pass arguments `ByVal` or by reference?

A As you'll learn in Chapter 20, "Dynamic Linked Libraries," sometimes it is not up to you to decide whether a variable should be passed `ByVal` or by reference. DLLs are functions written by others, and, therefore, you must pass the arguments as specified by the authors of the DLL functions.

When you write your own functions, you may design them in such a way that it is required to pass the variables `ByVal` or by reference. Generally, the easiest and safest way to pass arguments to a function is by value (`ByVal`). However, there are applications in which it might be more convenient to pass arguments by reference.

Quiz

1. The file that determines what files will be loaded into a project whenever you open a new project is which of the following:

   a. AUTOLOAD.MAK

   b. AUTOLOAD.TXT

   c. CONSTANT.TXT

2. A file with FRM file extension is which of the following:

   a. A file that describes the form and its procedures in an ASCII format.

   b. A file that describes the form and its procedures in a binary format.

   c. A file that describes the form and its procedures either in a binary format or in an ASCII format. The format depends on how you saved the file.

3. The following declaration is used to declare an array:

   ```
   Dim OurArray (7) As integer
   ```

   Is the following statement correct?

   ```
   OurArray(12) = 32
   ```

4. Is the variable `MyVariable` in the following statement passed `ByVal` or by reference?

   ```
   Result = Calculate( MyVariable)
   ```

   a. `ByVal`

   b. By reference

   c. There is no way to answer this question just by looking at this statement.

5. Is the variable `MyVariable` in the following function passed `ByVal` or by reference?

```
Function Calculate (MyVariable)
        . . . . . . . . . .
        . . . . . . . . .
        . . . . . . . . .


End Function
```

    a. By reference

    b. `ByVal`

    c. There is no way to answer this question just by looking at this statement.

6. Is the variable `MyVariable` in the following function passed `ByVal` or by reference?

```
Function Calculate (ByVal MyVariable)


        . . . . . . . . . .
        . . . . . . . . . .
        . . . . . . . . .


End Function
```

    a. By reference

    b. `ByVal`

    c. There is no way to answer this question just by looking at this statement.

Exercise

Write a loop that declares a two-dimensional array. The loop should fill the elements of the array with an integer that represents the multiplication of its two indexes. For example, the element 3,5 should contain the value $3 \times 5 = 15$.

Quiz Answers

    1. a

    2. c

    3. No, the subscript of the array may be any value between 0 and 7.

    4. c

    5. a

    6. b

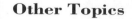

Exercise Answer

The following loop declares a two-dimensional array, the elements of which are filled with an integer that represents the multiplication of its two indexes:

```
Static TheArray (1 To 5, 1 To 5 )As Integer

Dim I, J

For I = 1 To 5 Step 1
    For J = 1 To 5 Step 1
      TheArray(I,J) = I*J
    Next J
Next I
```

16

The Data Control

This chapter shows how to use the data control. The data control is a powerful control that is supplied with the standard Visual Basic package starting with Version 3.0. Data controls enable you to write programs that access databases such as Access, dBASE, Btrieve, Paradox, and FoxPro.

The DATA Program

The DATA program illustrates how easy it is to access data from within your Visual Basic programs using the data control. Figure 16.1 shows the data control as it appears in the Toolbox.

Figure 16.1.
The data control.

Building a Database

The DATA program communicates with a database. Therefore, in order to see the data control in action, you must first create a database. In this chapter, the Microsoft Access database manager program is used as the database manager program for creating the database. If you do not own Access, use another database manager (for example, dBASE, Paradox, FoxPro, or Btrieve).

The Specifications of the Database

The database you'll create with Access (or another database manager program) is called TEST.MDB, and it has one table called Parts.

The structure of the Parts table is shown in Table 16.1.

Table 16.1. The structure of the Parts table.

Field Name	Data Type
PartNum	Text
Description	Text
VendorID	Number

The data inside the records of the Parts table is listed in Table 16.2.

Table 16.2. The records of the Parts table.

PartNum	Description	VendorID
CPU-486-66DX	486 CPU 66MHz	3433
CT-132	Case (Tower)	4434
DT-565	Case (Desktop)	4434
K-656	Keyboard	5655
K-657	Keyboard	1311
M-898	Monitor 15"	4545
RAM-989-70	70ns RAM	5457

If you do not own the Access program, build the Parts table according to the specifications in Tables 16.1 and 16.2 using either FoxPro Version 2.0, FoxPro Version 2.5, dBASE III, dBASE IV, Btrieve, Paradox, or another program that is capable of producing a database file that is compatible with FoxPro 2.0 or 2.5, dBASE III or IV, Paradox, or Btrieve. When you finish the Parts table, skip to the section "The Visual Implementation of the DATA Program," later in this chapter.

If you own the Microsoft Access program, use the following steps to create the Parts table:

☐ Click the Microsoft Access icon from the Microsoft Access group of programs (see Figure 16.2).

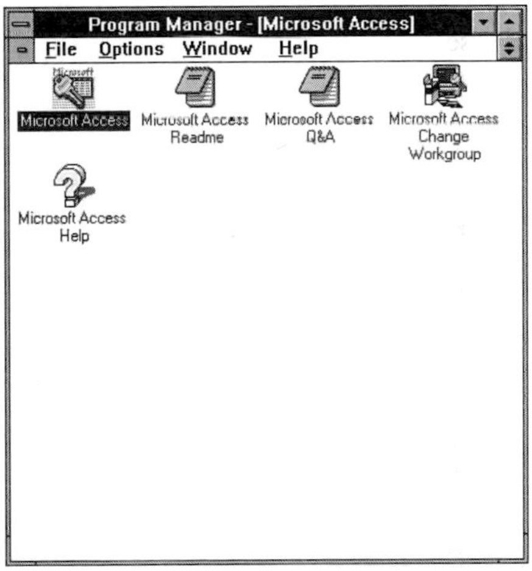

Figure 16.2.
The Microsoft Access group of programs.

Access responds by displaying an opening window, and then the Microsoft Access window is displayed, as shown in Figure 16.3.

Figure 16.3.

The Microsoft Access window.

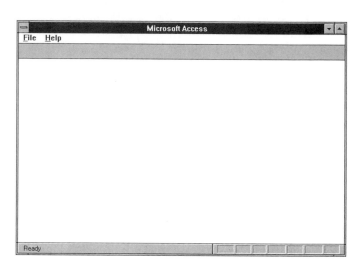

☐ Select New Database from the File menu.

Access responds by displaying the New Database dialog box (see Figure 16.4).

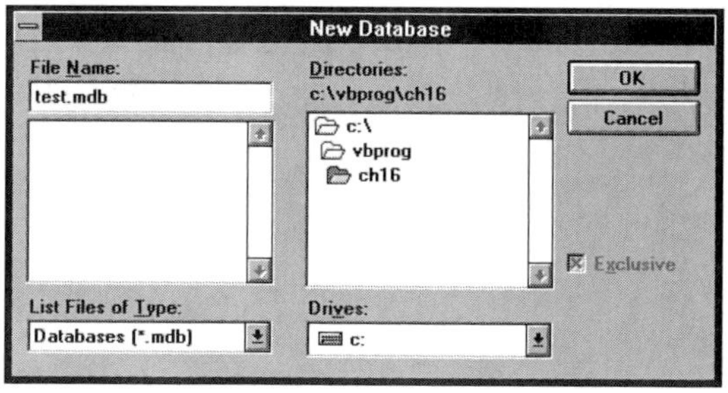

Figure 16.4.

The New Database dialog box.

☐ Save the new database (that you are about to build) as TEST.MDB.

Access responds by displaying the Database:TEST window (see Figure 16.5). This window will contain all the tables of the database TEST.MDB. In this example, there will be only one table in the TEST.MDB database: the Parts table.

Figure 16.5.
The Database:TEST
window.

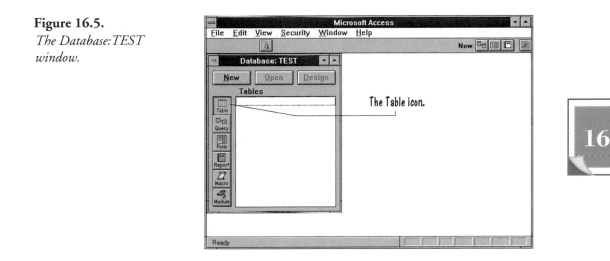

As shown in Figure 16.5, the Database:TEST window has several icons on its left side.

☐ Make sure that the Table icon is selected, and then click the New button in the Database:TEST window.

> *Access responds by displaying an empty table. The title of the empty table is Table:Table1 (see Figure 16.6).*

Figure 16.6.
The Table:Table1 window.

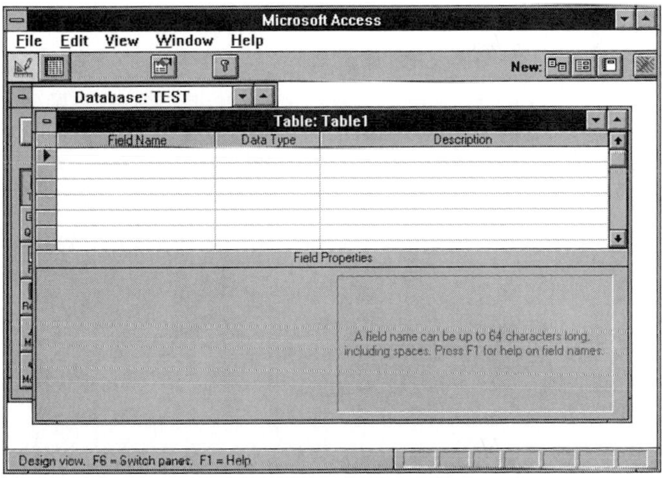

The left icon on the toolbar (the icon that has a picture of a designer in it) is highlighted. This means that Access is in design mode (that is, ready for you to design your table).

☐ Build the table according to the specifications in Table 16.1.

The completed table should look like the one shown in Figure 16.7.

Figure 16.7.
Constructing the database.

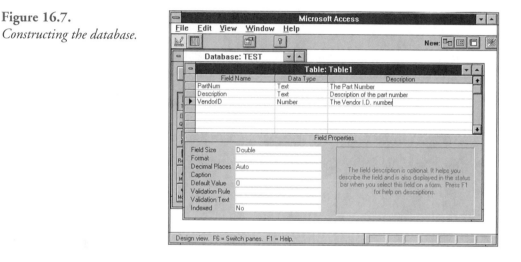

☐ Make sure that the cursor is in the PartNum field (or in any of the fields in the first row), and then click the Key icon on the toolbar.

Access responds by placing a small Key icon to the left of this row (see Figure 16.8). The small Key icon that is placed to the left of the PartNum row is an indication that the PartNum field is the key field.

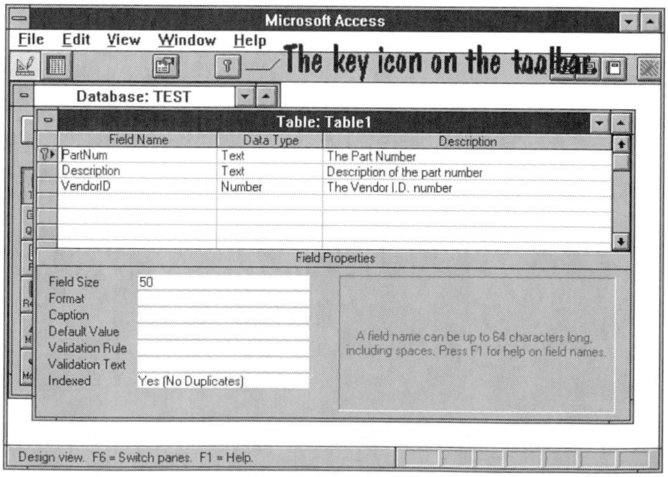

Figure 16.8.
Making the PartNum field the key field.

☐ Select Save As from the File menu.

Access responds by displaying the Save As dialog box (see Figure 16.9).

☐ Type Parts in the Table Name text box and click the OK button (see Figure 16.9). Access responds by saving the table as Parts. (Note that the title of the window is now Table:Parts.)

Your Parts table of the TEST.MDB database is now complete.

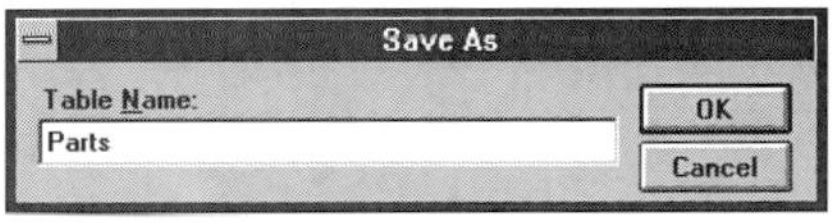

Figure 16.9.
The Save As dialog box.

Entering Data into the Parts Table

Now enter data into the Parts table.

☐ Click the icon that appears to the right of the triangle icon on the toolbar. Access responds by displaying the Parts table, which is ready to receive data (see Figure 16.10).

Figure 16.10.
Entering data into the Parts table.

☐ Enter the data into the Parts table according to the specifications in Table 16.2. When you finish entering the data, the Table:Parts window should look like the one shown in Figure 16.11.

☐ Close the database by selecting Close Database from the File menu.

Figure 16.11.
The Parts table with data in it.

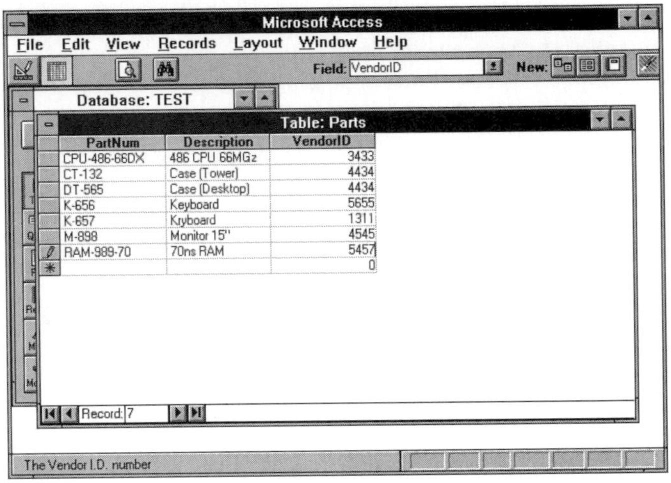

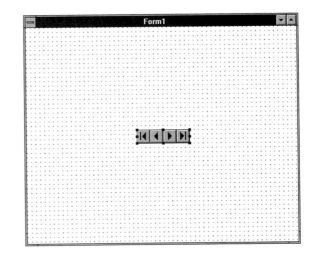

The Visual Implementation of the DATA Program

☐ Open a new project, save the form of the project as DATA.FRM, and save the make file of the project as DATA.MAK.

☐ Place the data control inside the form, as shown in Figure 16.12.

Figure 16.12.
Placing the data control inside the form.

You can move, enlarge, and shrink the data control just as you would any other control.

☐ Move the data control to the lower part of the form, and then enlarge the data control by dragging its handles. The enlarged data control is shown in Figure 16.13.

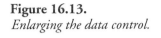

Figure 16.13.
Enlarging the data control.

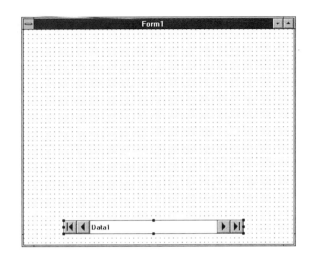

The default name that Visual Basic assigns to the control is Data1.

☐ Change the properties of the form as follows: The Name property should be frmData and the Caption property should be The DATA program.

Now enter the name and path of the database file that will communicate with the Data1 data control. Specifying an Access database is a little different from specifying a non-Access database (for example, a DBF file).

Specifying an Access Database

Use the following steps to enter the name and path of an Access database:

☐ Make sure that the data control is selected and select Properties from the Window menu.

Visual Basic responds by displaying the properties window of the data control.

☐ Double-click the DatabaseName property in the properties table of the data control.

Visual Basic responds by displaying the DatabaseName dialog box shown in Figure 16.14.

Figure 16.14.
The DatabaseName dialog box.

☐ Select the TEST.MDB file that you created with Access and click the OK button.

☐ Double-click the RecordSource property in the properties table of the data control.

Visual Basic responds by letting you select a table from a list box that contains all the tables in the TEST.MDB database.

☐ Click the right arrow of the list box (see Figure 16.15).

Visual Basic responds by displaying the RecordSource drop-down list shown in Figure 16.15.

Because the TEST database has only one table (the Parts table) in it, this is the only table that appears in the drop-down list. However, if the TEST database contained several tables, the drop-down list would list all the tables in the database, and you would have to select a table from the list.

Figure 16.15.
The RecordSource drop-down list.

Specifying a Non-Access Database

Use the following steps to enter the name and path of a non-Access database (for example, a DBF file):

☐ Make sure that the data control is selected, and select Properties from the Window menu.

Visual Basic responds by displaying the properties window of the data control.

☐ Set the DatabaseName property of the data control to the directory name at which the database is located. For example, if the full path name of the database is C:\TRY\TEST.DBF, you should set the DatabaseName property to C:\TRY.

☐ Set the RecordSource property of the data control to the name of the database without its path and without its file extension. For example, if the full pathname of the database is C:\TRY\TEST.DBF, you should set the RecordSource property to TEST.

☐ Set the Connect property of the data control according to the specifications in Table 16.3. For example, if you are using a FoxPro 2.0 database, set the Connect property to FoxPro 2.5;.

Table 16.3. The Connect property of the data control.

Database	Value of the Connect Property
Microsoft Access	(empty)
FoxPro Version 2.0	FoxPro 2.0;
FoxPro Version 2.5	FoxPro 2.5;
dBASE III	dBASE III;
dBASE IV	dBASE IV;
Paradox	Paradox 3.X;
Btrieve	btrieve;

Placing a Text Box to Hold the Data

Now place a text box inside the frmData form. This text box serves as a placeholder for the PartNum field from the Parts table.

☐ Place a text box control inside the frmData form, as shown in Figure 16.16.

Figure 16.16.

Placing a text box, a label, and a command button inside the frmData form.

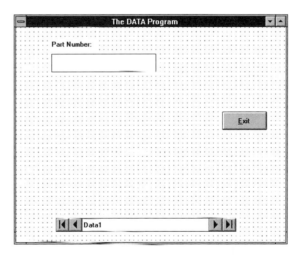

Set the properties of the text box as follows: Set the Name property to txtPartNumber and leave the Text property empty.

□ Place a label control inside the frmData form, as shown in Figure 16.16.

Set the properties of the text box as follows: The Name property should be lblPartNumber and the Caption property should be Part Number:.

□ Add the Exit command button to the frmData form, as shown in Figure 16.16.

□ Add the following code inside the cmdExit_Click() procedure of the frmData form:

```
Sub cmdExit_Click ()

    End

End Sub
```

As stated, the txtPartNumber text box that you placed inside the form will be used to display the contents of the PartNum field of the Parts table, as well as to edit the contents of the PartNum field.

Now tell Visual Basic which data control is associated with this text box:

□ Set the DataSource property of the txtPartNumber text box in the properties window to Data1 by double-clicking the DataSource property.

Visual Basic responds by displaying a drop-down list that contains all the data controls that exist in the form (you have to click the right arrow of the drop-down list to see the items in the list).

□ Click the right arrow of the drop-down list box to see the items in the list box (see Figure 16.17).

Figure 16.17.

The drop-down list of data controls in the form.

Because you have only one data control in the form (Data1), the drop-down list contains only one item: Data1.

☐ Select Data1 from the list.

Now tell Visual Basic that this text box should hold the contents of the PartNum field:

☐ Set the DataField property of the txtPartNumber text box to PartNum by double-clicking the DataField property of the txtPartNumber text box.

Visual Basic responds by displaying a drop-down list that contains a list of all the fields in the table. To see the items in the list, click the right arrow of the drop-down list (see Figure 16.18).

☐ Select the PartNum item from the list.

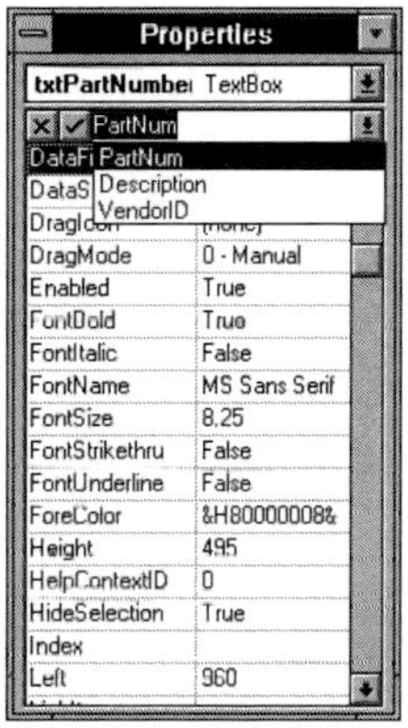

16

Figure 16.18.
The drop-down list of the fields in the table.

☐ Save the project.

Executing the DATA Program

Note: Before you execute the DATA program, you must first make sure that the DOS program SHARE.EXE is loaded:

☐ Exit Windows.

☐ At the DOS command line type the following:

```
C:\DOS\SHARE.EXE {Enter}
```

(The preceding statement assumes that your SHARE.EXE file resides in C:\ DOS.)

Note that many users prefer to add the following line to their AUTOEXEC.BAT file:

```
C:\DOS\SHARE.EXE {Enter}
```

☐ Execute the DATA program.

The DATA program responds by displaying the form shown in Figure 16.19.

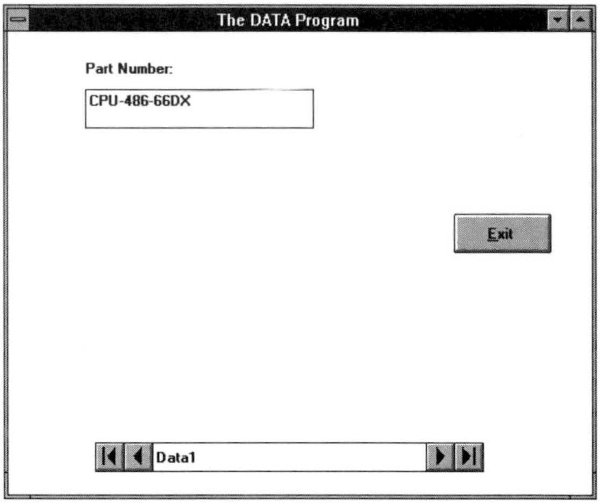

Figure 16.19.
The DATA program.

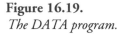

☐ Click the arrows of the Data1 data control and notice that the content of the text box changes in accordance with the content of the PartNum field of the Parts table. Each click of the inner-right arrow of the Data1 data control causes the record in the table to advance one record, and each click of the inner-left arrow of the Data1 data control causes the record to retreat one record. Clicking the extreme-right arrow of the Data1 control causes the text box to display the contents of the PartNum field of the very last record, and clicking the extreme-left arrow of the Data1 control causes the text box to display the content of the PartNum field of the very first record.

☐ Click the Exit button to terminate the DATA program.

As shown in Figure 16.19, the text inside the Data1 data control displays the text Data1. This is the default content of the Caption property of Data1 (that is, the default Caption property is the default Name property, which is Data1). You may set the Caption property of Data1 at design time to TEST.MDB, or to any other text that is appropriate to your application. Alternatively, you can change the Caption property of Data1 during runtime.

Enhancing the DATA Program

Now enhance the DATA program by adding additional text boxes to the frmData form. Each text box will contain the content of a different field of the record:

☐ Add a label to the frmData form with the following properties (see Figure 16.20): The Name property should be lblDescription and the Caption property should be Part Description:.

☐ Add a text box to the frmData form with the following properties (see Figure 16.20): The Name property should be txtDescription and the Text property should be left empty.

Figure 16.20.
Adding text boxes that correspond to fields.

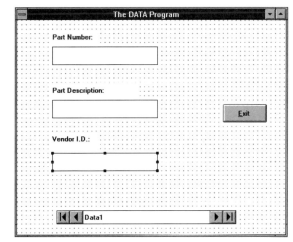

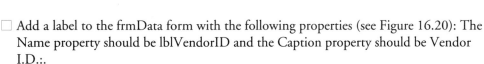

☐ Add a label to the frmData form with the following properties (see Figure 16.20): The Name property should be lblVendorID and the Caption property should be Vendor I.D.:.

☐ Add a text box to the frmData form with the following properties (see Figure 16.20): The Name property should be txtVendorID and the Text property should be left empty.

☐ Set the DataSource property of the txtDescription text box to Data1.

☐ Set the DataField property of the txtDescription text box to Description.

☐ Set the DataSource property of the txtVendorID text box to Data1.

☐ Set the DataField property of the txtVendorID text box to VendorID.

☐ Save the project.

Executing the Enhanced DATA Program

☐ Execute the DATA program.

The DATA program appears, as shown in Figure 16.21.

☐ Click the arrows of the Data1 data control to move from record to record.

As you can see, the contents of the three text boxes correspond to the contents of the three fields in the Parts table.

☐ Click the Exit button to terminate the program.

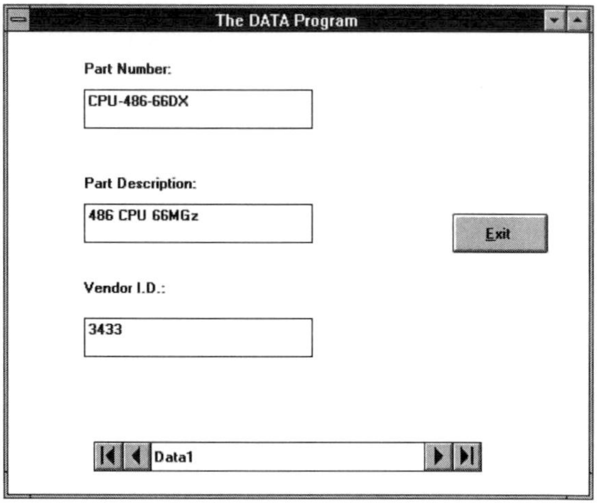

Figure 16.21.
The DATA program with three text boxes that correspond to three fields.

Adding a Field to the Table of the Database

In the following discussion, you are instructed to add a Boolean field (logical field) to the TEST table with the Access program. If your database is a non-Access database (for example, a DBF file), use the appropriate software package to add the logical field.

Now add a Boolean field called InStock to the Parts table of the TEST database:

☐ Start Access.

☐ Select Open from the File menu.

Access responds by displaying the Open Database dialog box.

☐ Select the TEST.MDB file and click the OK button.

Access responds by displaying the Database:TEST window shown in Figure 16.22.

Figure 16.22.

The TEST database with the Parts table.

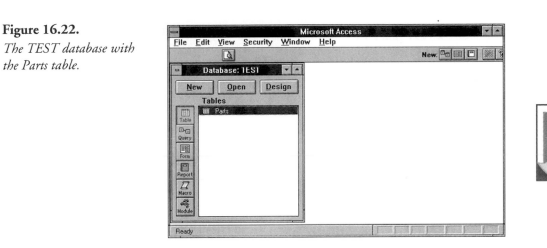

Now modify the structure of the Parts table:

☐ Click the Design button that appears at the top-right area of the Database:TEST window.

> *Access responds by displaying the Table:Parts window, which is ready for modification to the table (see Figure 16.23).*

Figure 16.23.

The Table:Parts window in design mode.

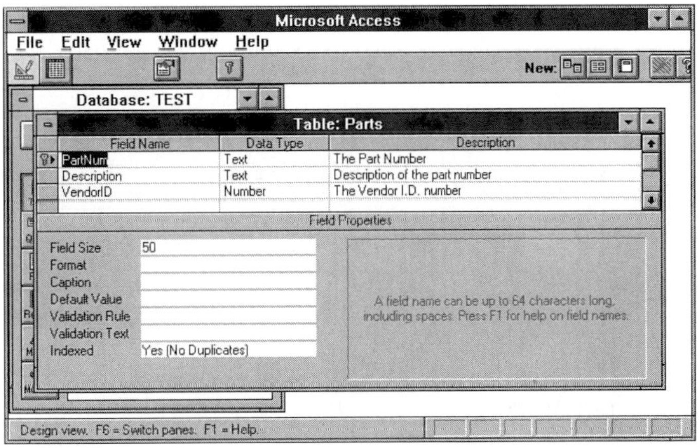

☐ Add a new field to the Parts table as follows (see Figure 16.24): The Field Name property should be InStock, the DataType property should be Yes/No, and the Description property should be Currently in Stock?.

Figure 16.24.
Adding the InStock field to the Parts table.

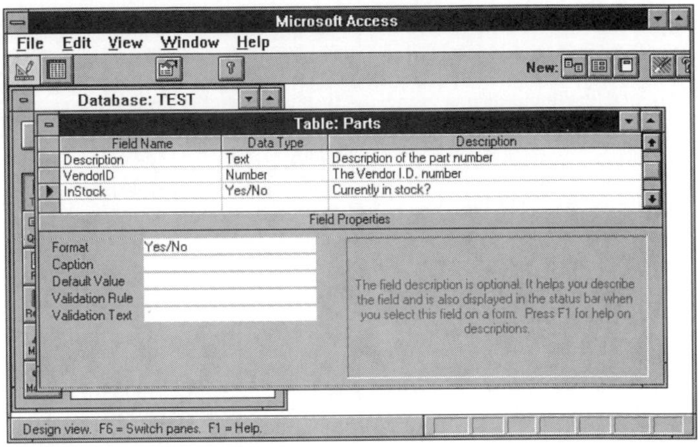

☐ Select Save from the File menu to save the changes to the table structure.

Now update the InStock field of the Parts table:

☐ Change to Enter Data mode (select the icon that appears to the right of the triangle icon on the toolbar).

> *Access responds by displaying the Table:Parts, which is ready to receive data (see Figure 16.25). Note that the default value of the InStock field for all the records is No.*

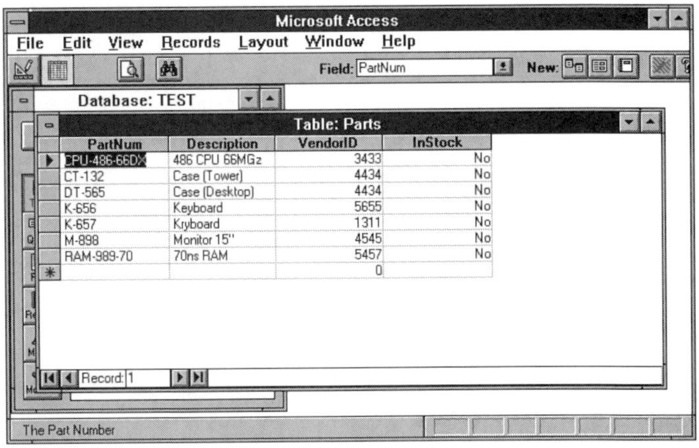

Figure 16.25.
The Table:Parts window.

☐ Update the InStock field of the Parts table by entering Yes and No in the InStock field, as shown in Figure 16.26.

550

Figure 16.26.
Updating the InStock fields of the Parts table.

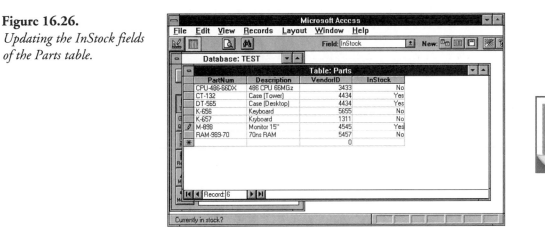

☐ Close the database.

☐ Switch back to Visual Basic.

☐ Add the chkInStock check box to the frmData form, as shown in Figure 16.27.

The check box should have the following properties: The Name property should be chkInStock and the Caption property should be In Stock?.

Figure 16.27.
Adding the chkInStock check box to the frmData form.

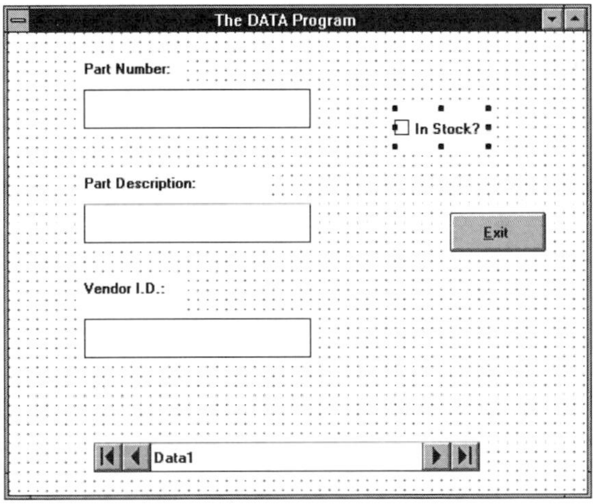

☐ Set the DataSource property of the chkInStock check box to Data1.

☐ Set the DataField property of the chkInStock check box to InStock.

☐ Save the project.

Executing the DATA Program Again

☐ Execute the DATA program.

☐ Click the arrows of the Data1 data control.

As you can see, the chkInStock check box is empty for each record that has its InStock field equal to No, and it is filled with an × for each record that has its InStock field equal to Yes (see Figure 16.28).

☐ Terminate the DATA program by clicking the Exit button.

Figure 16.28.

The chkInStock check box corresponds to the InStock field of the Parts table.

```
┌──────────────────────── The DATA Program ──────────────────┐
│                                                              │
│   Part Number:                                               │
│   ┌─────────────────────────┐                                │
│   │ CT-132                  │            ☒ In Stock?         │
│   └─────────────────────────┘                                │
│                                                              │
│                                                              │
│   Part Description:                                          │
│   ┌─────────────────────────┐         ┌───────────┐          │
│   │ Case (Tower)            │         │   Exit    │          │
│   └─────────────────────────┘         └───────────┘          │
│                                                              │
│                                                              │
│   Vendor I.D.:                                               │
│   ┌─────────────────────────┐                                │
│   │ 4434                    │                                │
│   └─────────────────────────┘                                │
│                                                              │
│                                                              │
│   ┌──┬──┬──────────────────────────────────────┬──┬──┐       │
│   │|◄│◄ │ Data1                                │ ►│►|│       │
│   └──┴──┴──────────────────────────────────────┴──┴──┘       │
└──────────────────────────────────────────────────────────────┘
```

Bound Controls

The DATA program illustrates how a text box and a check box are used to bind the data of a table. A control that is used for the purpose of displaying the contents of a field is called a bound control.

Therefore, a text box control and a check box control may be used in a program as bound controls. In a similar manner, you may add a field to the Parts table that contains a BMP file, and then add a picture control or an image control to the frmData form that corresponds to the picture field in the Parts table. That is, a picture control and an image control may also serve as bound controls.

In the Standard Edition of Visual Basic Version 3.0, the controls mentioned are the only controls that may be used as bound controls. Other bound controls are available in the Professional Edition of Visual Basic, as well as from other third-party vendors that sell custom controls (VBX files) for Visual Basic.

Properties and Methods of the Data Control

The DATA program illustrates how your Visual Basic program can display the contents of the fields of a table. As you might expect, the data control has many more properties and methods that enable you to manipulate the database in almost any conceivable way. The following sections discuss some of these properties and methods in detail.

The Refresh Method

You may use the Refresh method to update the bound controls with the most updated values of the fields in the table. For example, if the database resides on a file server that is connected to your PC through a LAN, and another user on a different station changed the values of a field in the table, the current values displayed on-screen are not the most updated values. To update the screen with the most updated values, use the following statement:

```
Data1.Refresh
```

The Exclusive Property

If you want your program to be the only program that can access the database, you have to set the Exclusive property to True, as shown in the following statement:

```
Data1.Exlusive = True
```

Setting the Exclusive property to True prevents all other programs from accessing the database.

The default value of the Exclusive property is False. To return the Exclusive property to its default value, use the following statement:

```
Data1.Exlusive = False
```

If the database is already open and you change the Exclusive property, you must execute the Refresh method to make the change effective:

```
Data1.Exlusive = False
Data1.Refresh
```

Working with a database with the Exclusive property set to True makes access to the database much faster (at the inconvenience of other users, who have to wait until you are kind enough to set the Exclusive property back to False).

The ReadOnly Property

Once you modify the contents of a field, you can click the arrows of the Data1 data control to move to the next record. The changes you made to the previous record are automatically saved. To see the automatic saving in action, perform the following experiment:

☐ Execute the DATA program.

☐ Click the InStock check box (that is, put an × in the check box) of the first record.

☐ Click the inner-right arrow of the Data1 data control to move to the next record.

☐ Click the Exit button to terminate the DATA program.

☐ Start the DATA program again.

As you can see, the first record appears with its InStock field equal to Yes (it has an × in it). This means that the changes you made to the database in the previous execution of the DATA program were saved to the database.

If you want your program to only read records, set the ReadOnly property of the data control to True. For example, modify the Form_Load() procedure so that it looks like this:

```
Sub Form_Load ()

    Data1.ReadOnly = True
    Data1.Refresh

End Sub:
```

☐ Execute the DATA program.

☐ Change the InStock property of the first record.

> *The program responds by changing the status of the check box, but as you'll see in the next step, it does not change the value in the table.*

☐ Click the inner-right arrow of the Data1 data control to move to the next record.

☐ Click the inner-left arrow of the Data1 data control to return to the previous record.

As you can see, the InStock field was not changed because the ReadOnly property was set to True.

To set the ReadOnly property back to its default value of False, change the Form_Load() procedure so that it looks like this:

```
Sub Form_Load ()

    Data1.ReadOnly = False
    Data1.Refresh

End Sub:
```

☐ Perform the previous experiment and notice that now you are able to change the contents of the fields in the table.

Again, if you change properties (such as the ReadOnly property) after the database is open already, you must use the Refresh property to make the change to the property effective.

> **Note:** You must set the ReadOnly property of Data1 to False (as indicated above) to be able to perform the experiments with the properties and methods that are described in the next sections.

Using *SQL* Statements

Your program may utilize Structured Query Language (SQL) statements to select only a set of records that comply with a certain condition. To see an SQL statement in action do the following:

☐ Add the Select command button, as shown in Figure 16.29.

Figure 16.29.
Adding the Select button.

![The DATA Program window showing Part Number, In Stock?, Part Description, Vendor I.D. fields, and Exit and Select buttons with Data1 navigation control]

The Select button should have the following properties: The Name property should be cmdSelect and the Caption property should be &Select.

☐ Add the following code inside the `cmdSelect_Click()` procedure of the frmData form:

```
Sub cmdSelect_Click ()

    Data1.RecordSource = "Select * from Parts where PartNum = 'CT-132' "
    Data1.Refresh

End Sub
```

The preceding procedure uses the standard SQL `Select` statement to select all the records from the Parts table that satisfy the condition `PartNum = 'CT-132'`. To make the SQL request effective, the Refresh method is executed.

☐ Execute the DATA program.

☐ Click the arrows of the Data1 data control to browse from record to record.

As you can see, you are able to browse through all the records.

☐ Click the Select button.

Because there is only one record that satisfies the SQL statement, the DATA program displays this record, as shown in Figure 16.30.

Figure 16.30.
Clicking the Select button to select the CT-132 record.

```
┌─────────────────────────────────────────────────┐
│ ═                    The DATA Program      ▼ ▲  │
│ ┌─────────────────────────────────────────────┐ │
│   Part Number:                                  │
│   ┌──────────────────┐                          │
│   │CT-132            │           ☒ In Stock?    │
│   └──────────────────┘                          │
│                                                 │
│                                                 │
│   Part Description:                             │
│   ┌──────────────────┐        ┌──────────┐     │
│   │Case (Tower)      │        │   Exit   │     │
│   └──────────────────┘        └──────────┘     │
│                                                 │
│   Vendor I.D.:                                  │
│   ┌──────────────────┐        ┌──────────┐     │
│   │4434              │        │  Select  │     │
│   └──────────────────┘        └──────────┘     │
│                                                 │
│          ┌──┬──┬─────────────┬──┬──┐           │
│          │I◀│ ◀│ Data1       │ ▶│▶I│           │
│          └──┴──┴─────────────┴──┴──┘           │
└─────────────────────────────────────────────────┘
```

Clicking the arrow of the Data1 data control does not display any other records, because there is only a single record that satisfies the SQL selection. The SQL statement filtered out all the records that do not satisfy the SQL requirement.

☐ Exit the DATA program by clicking the Exit button.

You may use SQL statements to select any group of records. For example, change the cmdSelect_Click() procedure so that it looks like this:

```
Sub cmdSelect_Click ()

    Data1.RecordSource = "Select * from Parts where InStock = True "
    Data1.Refresh

End Sub
```

☐ Execute the DATA program.

☐ Click the arrows of the Data1 data control.

As you can see, the only records that are displayed are the records that have their InStock field equal to Yes.

☐ Terminate the DATA program by clicking the Exit button.

Generally, the syntax of the SQL statements is simple, but this book does not teach SQL syntax.

Adding a New Record at Runtime

You may add a new record by using the AddNew method. To see the AddNew method in action do the following:

☐ Add the New Record button, as shown in Figure 16.31. The New Record should have the following properties: The Name property should be cmdAddRecord and the Caption property should be &AddRecord.

Figure 16.31.
Adding the Add Record button to the frmData form.

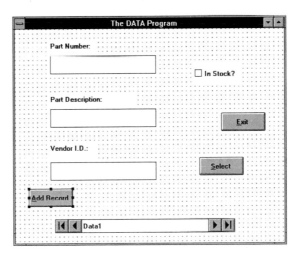

557

☐ Add the following code inside the `cmdAddRecord_Click()` procedure of the frmData form:

```
Sub cmdAddRecord_Click ()

    Data1.RecordSet.AddNew

End Sub
```

The AddNew method is applied to the RecordSet property of Data1. (The RecordSet property is discussed later in this chapter.)

☐ Execute the DATA program.

☐ Click the Add Record button.

> *The DATA program responds by displaying a blank record (that is, all the bound controls are empty).*

☐ Fill the contents of the bound controls with new values.

Because the PartNum field is a key field, you can't add a part number that already exists in the table.

The data control saves the new record once you move the record pointer (that is, click the inner-left arrow of the Data1 data control to the next or previous record).

☐ Exit the program by clicking the Exit button.

The Delete Method

To delete a record, you may use the Delete method. To see the Delete method in action do the following:

☐ Add the Delete button, as shown in Figure 16.32.

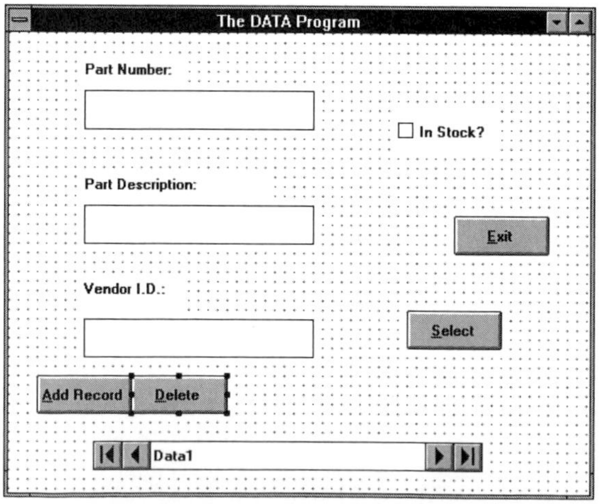

Figure 16.32.
Adding the Delete button to the frmData form.

The Delete button should have the following properties: The Name property should be cmdDelete and the Caption property should be &Delete.

☐ Add the following code inside the cmdDelete_Click() procedure of the frmData form:

```
Sub cmdDelete_Click ()

    Data1.RecordSet.Delete
    Data1.RecordSet.MoveNext

End Sub
```

☐ Execute the DATA program.

Use the arrow keys of the Data1 data control to move the record pointer to the record you want to delete.

☐ Click the Delete button.

The DATA program responds by deleting the record.

☐ Practice with the Delete and Add Record buttons for a while, and then click the Exit button to terminate the DATA program.

Like the AddNew method, the Delete method is used on the RecordSet property of the Data1 data control.

The MoveNext Method

In the cmdDelete_Click() procedure, the MoveNext method was executed after the Delete method:

```
Data1.RecordSet.MoveNext
```

The MoveNext method moves the record pointer to the next record. Using the MoveNext method has the same effect as clicking the inner-right arrow of the data control.

The MovePrevious Method

The MovePrevious method moves the record pointer to the previous record. You may use the MovePrevious method as follows:

```
Data1.RecordSet.MovePrevious
```

Using the MovePrevious method has the same effect as clicking the inner-left arrow of the data control.

The MoveLast Method

The MoveLast method moves the record pointer to the very last record. You may use the MoveLast method as follows:

```
Data1.RecordSet.MoveLast
```

The MoveLast method has the same effect as clicking the outer-right arrow of the data control.

The MoveFirst Method

The MoveFirst method moves the record pointer to the very first record. You may use the MoveFirst method as follows:

```
Data1.RecordSet.MoveFirst
```

The MoveFirst method has the same effect as clicking the outer-left arrow of the data control.

The RecordSet Property

You may think of the RecordSet property of the data control as the current records your program may access. For example, if you do not set any filter by issuing an SQL statement, the RecordSet property represents all the records in the Parts table. Because the data control may represent a database that includes several tables, you may use SQL statements to create a RecordSet property that represent records from several tables.

As demonstrated in the previous sections, many of the methods are applied to the RecordSet property (for example, Data1.RecordSet.Delete, Data1.RecordSet.ASddNew, and Data1.RecordSet.MoveNext).

The following steps illustrate how your program may determine the number of records in the RecordSet property:

☐ Add the Count Records button, as shown in Figure 16.33.

The Count Records button should have the following properties: The Name property should be cmdCountRecords and the Caption property should be &Count Records.

☐ Add the following code inside the cmdCountRecords_Click() procedure:

```
Sub cmdCountRecords_Click ()

    Data1.RecordSet.MoveLast
    MsgBox Data1.RecordSet.RecordCount

End Sub
```

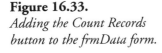

Figure 16.33.
Adding the Count Records button to the frmData form.

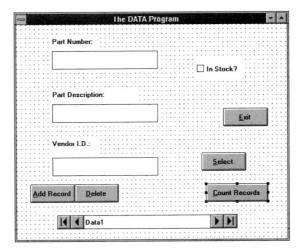

The cmdCountRecords_Click() procedure moves the record pointer to the last record of the RecordSet property, and then the RecordCount method counts all the records up to the current record. Because the MoveLast method moved the record pointer to the last record of the RecordSet property and the RecordSet represents the Parts table, the RecordCount method returns the total number of records in the Parts table.

☐ Execute the DATA program.

☐ Click the Count Records button.

> *The DATA program responds by displaying the total number of records in the RecordSet property (which represents the total number of records in the Parts table).*

☐ Delete and add new records by clicking the Add Record and Delete buttons, and then click the Count Records to see that indeed the number of total records in the table increases/decreases.

☐ Terminate the DATA program by clicking the Exit button.

The Value Property

The contents of the fields may be extracted by examining the corresponding properties of the bound controls. For example, you may determine the contents of the PartNum field of the current record by examining the Text property of the txtPartNumber text box. The following code illustrates how to display the contents of the PartNum field of the current record whenever the user clicks the form:

☐ Add the following code inside the `Form_Click()` procedure of the frmData form:

```
Sub Form_Click ()

    MsgBox "Part number: " + txtPartNumber.Text

End Sub
```

☐ Execute the DATA program.

☐ Click the form.

   The DATA program responds by displaying the contents of the PartNum field of the current record.

☐ Click the Exit button to terminate the program.

Sometimes you might want to know the contents of a field that does not have a corresponding bound control in the form. In these cases, you may use the Value property. To see how the Value property works do the following:

☐ Change the code inside the `Form_Click()` procedure so that it looks like this:

```
Sub Form_Click ()

    Dim MyString As String

    MyString = Data1.RecordSet.Fields("PartNum").Value

    MsgBox MyString

End Sub
```

☐ Execute the DATA program.

☐ Click the form.

   The DATA program responds by displaying a message box with the contents of the PartNum field of the current record.

☐ Click the Exit button to terminate the program.

The code inside the `Form_Click()` procedure assigns the Value property of the PartNum field of the current record to the `MyString` variable, and then this string is displayed by using the `MsgBox` statement.

In a similar manner, you may extract the Value property of the other fields of the database. For example, to assign the Value property of the Description field of the current record to the `MyString` variable, you can use the following statement:

```
MyString = Data1.RecordSet.Fields("Description").Value
```

The EOF and BOF Properties of the RecordSet Property

Your program may utilize the EOF property (End of File) and BOF (Beginning of File) property to determine whether the current record is valid. For example, your program might display a particular record, and while the record is being displayed, another station deletes that record. In this case, the record pointer points to an invalid record. Your program may determine the validity of the pointer as follows:

```
If Data1.RecordSet.EOF = False AND Data1.RecordSet.BOF-False Then
    ..................................
    ... The record pointer points ...
    ... to a valid record.         ...
    ..................................
End If
```

This `If…End If` block of statements checks that the record pointer points to a valid record by verifying that both the EOF and the BOF properties are False.

As shown in Table 16.5, any other combination of values for the EOF and BOF properties means that the record pointer points to an invalid record. For example, when both EOF and BOF are True, the current record points to an invalid record.

Table 16.5. The BOF and EOF properties.

BOF	EOF	Comment
False	False	Valid record
False	True	Invalid record
True	False	Invalid record
True	True	Invalid record

What Else Can the Data Control Do?

The properties and methods that have been introduced in this chapter are the basic properties and methods of the data control, and you can use them to display the contents of the fields of tables as well as to modify the contents of the fields. However, the data control supports many more features that enable your Visual Basic to manipulate databases in almost any conceivable way (for example, building a database, modifying the constructions of tables). In fact, the data control of Visual Basic is so powerful that you may think of it as a separate programming package that is included with the Visual Basic package. Although the data control can handle databases other than the Access database, it uses the same software engine that powers the Access program, and it therefore makes sense to assume that for faster, bug-free operations, the Access database is the easiest database platform to use.

Summary

In this chapter you have been introduced to the data control that is supplied with the Visual Basic package starting with Version 3.0. You have learned how to assign properties to the data control and how to assign properties to the bound controls that display the contents of the fields in the tables.

You have also learned how to refresh the data, how to issue SQL statements, and how to delete and add new records to the tables.

Q&A

Q Is it possible to place more than one data control inside a form?

A Yes. You may place several data controls inside a form. Make sure to set the DatabaseName property and the RecordSource property of each of the data controls to the corresponding database and tables that each of them represents.

Quiz

1. When using an Access database, the DatabaseName property of a data control is a string that specifies which of the following:

    a. The name of the required table

    b. The name of the required database

    c. The name of the bound control

2. When using an Access database, the RecordSource property of a data control is a string that specifies which of the following:

    a. The name of the required table in the database

    b. The content of the SQL statement

    c. The name of the field

3. A scroll bar may be a bound control.

    a. False

    b. True

4. The ReadOnly property is used for what?

5. The AddNew method is used for what?

6. The Delete method is used for what?

7. The MoveNext method is used for what?

Exercise

Change the SQL statement of the DATA program so that the Data1 control accesses only those records that have their InStock fields equal to No.

Quiz Answers

1. b
2. Both a and b
3. a
4. Preventing your program from changing the contents of the field in the table from within your Visual Basic program
5. Adding a record
6. Deleting a record
7. Moving the record pointer to the next record

Exercise Answer

Change the code inside the cmdSelect_Click() procedure so it looks like this:

```
Sub cmdSelect_Click ()

    Data1.RecordSource = "Select * from Parts where InStock = False"
    Data1.Refresh

End Sub
```

☐ Execute the DATA program.

☐ Click the Select button.

☐ Click the arrows of the Data1 data control.

As you can see, only those records that have their InStock field equal to No are displayed.

Multiple-
Document
Interface

This chapter focuses on developing multiple-document interface (MDI) programs. An MDI program is a program that contains several documents. Each document has its own window, and all the documents are contained within a single parent form. Some well-known MDI applications are programs such as the Program Manager (shipped with Windows), the File Manager program (shipped with Windows), and a variety of professional Windows programs such as Microsoft Word for Windows and Microsoft Excel.

Your First MDI Program

The Pictures program illustrates how to create an MDI program. The key to designing impressive MDI programs with Visual Basic is to understand how to manipulate the various forms of the program.

Creating the Pictures Project

Build an MDI project called Pictures.MAK that consists of a parent form called Pictures.FRM and three child forms: Picture1.frm, Picture2.frm, and Picture3.frm.

To create the Pictures project, follow these steps:

☐ Create a new project by selecting New Project from the File menu.

Visual Basic responds by opening a new project and displaying a blank form. The default name of the form file is Form1.frm and the default name of the make file is Project1.mak. This step is not different from the step of creating a new regular (standard non-MDI) project.

Every MDI program has one parent form. Use the following step to create the parent form:

☐ Select New MDI Form from the File menu.

Visual Basic responds by displaying a blank form with the default name MDIForm1 (see Figure 17.1). This blank form is the parent form.

Figure 17.1.
The blank MDIForm1 form.

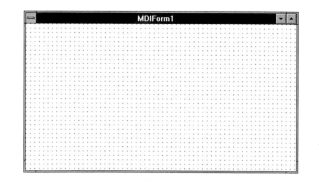

See how the project window looks at this point:

☐ Select Project from the Window menu.

Visual Basic responds by displaying the project window shown in Figure 17.2. As shown, the project window contains the following:

- *Form1.frm, a standard (non-MDI) blank form.*
- *MDIForm1.frm, the blank parent form.*
- *VBX files. (These are the custom controls files. If you are using the Professional Edition of Visual Basic, your project window contains more VBX files.)*

Figure 17.2.
The project window with default filenames.

Note the little icons that appear to the left of each file in the project window. These icons serve as indicators of the type of file. The standard form (Form1.frm) has an icon that looks like a form standing on its edge. The parent form (MDIForm1.frm) has an icon that looks like a form standing on its edge with a little form standing next to it.

Your Visual Basic program can have only one parent form. Use the following steps to see for yourself:

☐ Open the File menu.

As you can see, the New MDI Form item is gray (not available). This item is not available now because you already have a parent MDI window in the project.

So what do you have so far? As indicated by the project window, you have one parent form (MDIForm1.frm) and one standard form (Form1.frm). Use the following steps to convert the standard form Form1.frm from a standard form into a child form:

☐ Highlight Form1.frm in the project window.

☐ Click the View Form button in the project window.

☐ Change the MDIChild property of Form1 to True.

Now take a look at the project window. Form1.frm now appears as a child form (it has the MDI icon next to its name in the project window). You can tell which is the parent form and which is the child form by observing that the icon of the parent form (MDIForm1.frm) and the icon of the child form (Form1.frm) are different (that is, the little form of the parent icon is dimmed).

The MDI program that you are currently building is called Pictures. Therefore, a more appropriate name for the child form is Picture1.frm.

Use the following steps to change the name of the child form from Form1.frm to Picture1.frm:

☐ Highlight Form1.frm in the project window.

☐ Select Save File As from the File menu.

> *Visual Basic responds by displaying the Save File As dialog box.*

☐ Save the file as Picture1.frm.

Now that Visual Basic has saved the child form, take a look at the project window. The child form Form1.frm has been replaced with the child form Picture1.frm.

Currently, the name of the parent form is MDIForm1.frm. Use the following steps to change its name to Pictures.frm:

☐ Highlight MDIForm1.frm in the project window.

☐ Select Save File As from the File menu.

> *Visual Basic responds by displaying the Save File As dialog box.*

☐ Save the parent form as Pictures.frm.

Take a look at the project window. The parent form MDIForm1.frm was replaced with the file Pictures.frm.

Currently, the project name is Project1.mak (as shown by the title of the project window in Figure 17.2). Use the following steps to change the name of the project from Project1.mak to Pictures.mak:

☐ Select Save Project As from the File menu.

> *Visual Basic responds by displaying the Save Project As dialog box.*

☐ Save the project as Pictures.mak.

> *The project window now has the title Pictures.mak.*

MDI programs usually have more than one child form. Use the following steps to add two more child windows:

☐ Select New Form from the File menu.

> *Visual Basic responds by adding a standard form called Form2.frm to the project window.*

☐ Select New Form from the File menu again.

> *Visual Basic responds by adding a standard form called Form3.frm to the project window.*

The project window now has two new standard forms. Of course, you need these two new forms to be child forms, not standard forms, so change Form2.frm and Form3.frm from standard forms to child forms:

☐ Highlight Form2.frm in the project window and click the View Form button in the project window (so that you'll have access to the properties window of Form2.frm).

☐ Change the MDIChild property of Form2.frm to True.

☐ Highlight Form3.frm in the project window and click the View Form button in the project window (so that you'll have access to the properties window of Form3.frm).

☐ Change the MDIChild property of Form3.frm to True.

Currently, the two newly added child forms are called Form2.frm and Form3.frm (the default names that Visual Basic assigned to these forms). Use the following steps to change the filenames of these child forms:

☐ Highlight Form2.frm in the project window.

☐ Select Save File As from the File menu and save the form as Picture2.frm.

☐ Highlight Form3.frm in the project window.

☐ Select Save File As from the File menu and save the form as Picture3.frm.

You now have a project called Pictures.mak with a parent form called Pictures.frm and three child forms: Picture1.frm, Picture2.frm, and Picture3.frm. The complete project window is shown in Figure 17.3.

Figure 17.3.
The complete project window of the Pictures project.

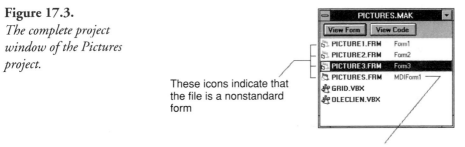

These icons indicate that the file is a nonstandard form

This is the parent form

Use the following step to save the project:

☐ Select Save Project from the File menu.

Changing the Properties of the Child Forms

Now change several properties of the forms. Use the following steps to change the properties of the child form Picture1.frm:

☐ Select the Picture1 form. (To select the form, click anywhere inside the form, or highlight Picture1.frm in the project window, then click the View Form button.)

☐ Select Properties from the Window menu and change the properties of Picture1.frm as follows: Change the Caption property of Picture1 to The Picture 1 Child. Change the Name property of the Picture1 to frmPicture1.

Now change the properties of the other child windows:

☐ Change the Caption property of Picture2 to The Picture 2 Child.

☐ Change the Name property of Picture2 to frmPicture2.

☐ Change the Caption property of Picture3 to The Picture 3 Child.

☐ Change the Name property of Picture3 to frmPicture3.

Changing the Properties of the Parent Form

To change the properties of Pictures.frm (the parent form), highlight Pictures.frm in the project window and click the View Form button. (This gives you access to the properties window of Pictures.frm.)

☐ Change the Caption property of Pictures.frm to I am the parent window.

☐ Change the Name property of Pictures.frm to frmPictures.

☐ To save the work that you've done so far, select Save Project from the File menu.

The Visual Implementation of the Pictures Program

An MDI program has several properties tables: a properties table for the parent form and a properties table for each of the child forms.

The Visual Implementation of the Parent Form

☐ Build the frmPictures form according to the specifications in Table 17.1.

The completed form should look like the one shown in Figure 17.4.

Table 17.1. The properties table of the parent form Pictures.frm.

Object	Property	Setting
Form	Name	frmPictures
	Caption	I am the parent window
	Height	4710
	Left	820
	Top	915
	Width	7485
Menu	(see Table 17.2)	(see Table 17.2)

17

Note: You already set the properties of the parent form according to the specifications in Table 17.1 in the previous steps. So just build the menu of the parent form according to the specifications in Table 17.2. Make sure to attach the menu of Table 17.2 to the Pictures form—that is, select the Pictures form, then select Menu Design from the Window menu.

Table 17.2. The menu table of the parent form Pictures.frm.

Caption	Name
&File	mnuFile
...&Exit	mnuExit
&Show Pictures	mnuShow
...Show Picture &1	mnuShowPicture1
...Show Picture &2	mnuShowPicture2
...Show Picture &3	mnuShowPicture3
...- (separator)	mnuSep1
...Show &All Pictures	mnuShowAll
...&Clear All Pictures	mnuClearAll

sub routines created for each menu action, (clicked on in menus)

The Visual Implementation of the Child Forms

Because the Pictures project contains three child forms, the visual implementations of the children involve three separate properties tables.

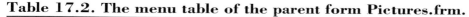

Figure 17.4.
*The parent form
frmPictures.*

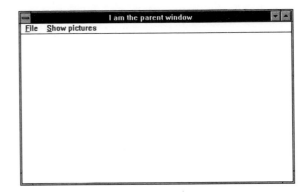

The Visual Implementation of Picture1

☐ Build the form of Picture1 according to the specifications in Table 17.3.

The completed form should look like the one shown in Figure 17.5.

Note: You already set some of the properties that are listed in Table 17.3 in the previous steps.

Table 17.3. The properties table of Picture1.

Object	Property	Setting
Form	**Name**	**frmPicture1**
	MDIChild	True
	Caption	The Picture 1 Child
	BackColor	(yellow)
	Height	2670
	Left	1800
	Top	1485
	Width	3225
Image	**Name**	**imgClock**
	Picture	c:\vb\bitmaps\assorted\clock.bmp
	Stretch	True
	Height	735

Object	Property	Setting
	Left	960
	Top	240
	Width	855
Command Button	**Name**	**cmdClose**
	Caption	&Close
	Height	495
	Left	1560
	Top	1320
	Width	1215
Menu	**(see Table 17.4)**	**(see Table 17.4)**

Table 17.4. The menu table of Picture1.frm.

Caption	Name
&File	mnuFile
...&Close	mnuClose
&Beep	mnuBeep
...Beep &Once	mnuBeepOnce
...Beep &Twice	mnuBeepTwice

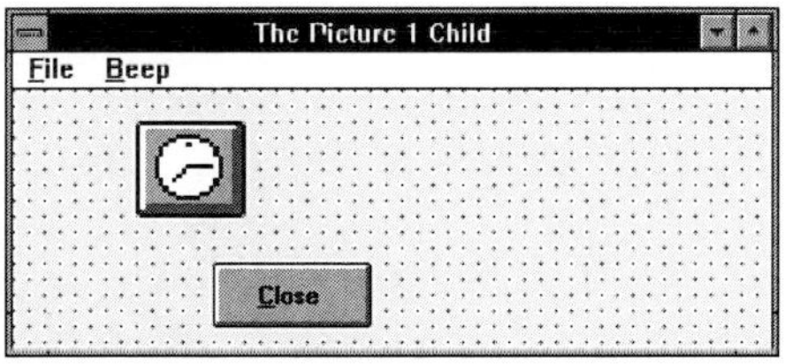

Figure 17.5.
The Picture1 form.

The Visual Implementation of Picture2

☐ Build the form of Picture2 according to the specifications in Table 17.5.

The completed form should look like the one shown in Figure 17.6.

Note: The form of Picture2 does not have a menu.

Table 17.5. The properties table of Picture2.

Object	Property	Setting
Form	**Name**	**frmPicture2**
	MDIChild	True
	Caption	The Picture 2 Child
	BackColor	(yellow)
	Height	1935
	Left	1920
	Top	3675
	Width	3420
Image	**Name**	**imgCup**
	Picture	c:\vb\bitmaps\assorted\cup.bmp
	Stretch	True
	Height	855
	Left	600
	Top	240
	Width	975
Command Button	**Name**	**cmdClose**
	Caption	&Close
	Height	495
	Left	1800
	Top	840
	Width	1215

Figure 17.6.
The Picture2 form.

The Visual Implementation of Picture3

☐ Build the form of Picture3 according to the specifications in Table 17.6.

The completed form should look like the one shown in Figure 17.7.

> **Note:** The form of Picture3 does not have a menu.

17

Table 17.6. The properties table of Picture3.

Object	Property	Setting
Form	**Name**	**frmPicture3**
	MDIChild	True
	Caption	The Picture 3 Child
	BackColor	(yellow)
	Height	2310
	Left	2385
	Top	1920
	Width	4230
Image	**Name**	**imgBell**
	Picture	c:\vb\bitmaps\assorted\bell.bmp
	Stretch	True
	Height	855
	Left	720
	Top	240
	Width	975
Command Button	**Name**	**cmdClose**
	Caption	&Close
	Height	495
	Left	2280
	Top	960
	Width	1215

Figure 17.7.
The Picture3 form.

Entering the Code of the Pictures Program

You enter the code of the Pictures program inside the various forms that are included in the program. Therefore, the code of the parent form is typed inside the procedures of Pictures.frm, the code of the child Picture1 is typed inside the procedures of Picture1.frm, and so on.

Entering the Code of the Parent Form Pictures.frm

☐ Enter the following code inside the general declarations section of the Pictures form:

```
' Each variable MUST be declared.
Option Explicit
```

☐ Enter the following code inside the MDIForm_Load() procedure of the Pictures form:

✔ **Sub MDIForm_Load ()**

```
    ' Upon startup of the program, show the three
    ' children.
    frmPicture1.Show
    frmPicture2.Show
    frmPicture3.Show
```

End Sub

☐ Enter the following code inside the mnuExit_Click() procedure of the Pictures form:

Sub mnuExit_Click ()

```
    ' The user selected Exit from the menu,
    ' so terminate the program.
    End
```

End Sub

☐ Enter the following code inside the mnuShowAll_Click() procedure of the Pictures form:

Sub mnuShowAll_Click ()

```
    ' The user selected Show All from the menu,
    ' so show all the children.
    frmPicture1.Show
    frmPicture2.Show
    frmPicture3.Show
```

End Sub

Enter the following code inside the `mnuShowPicture1_Click()` procedure of the Pictures form:

```
Sub mnuShowPicture1_Click()

    ' The user selected Show Picture 1 from the
    ' menu, so show Picture1.
    frmPicture1.Show

End Sub
```

Enter the following code inside the `mnuShowPicture2_Click()` procedure of the Pictures form:

```
Sub mnuShowPicture2_Click ()

    ' The user selected Show Picture 2 from
    ' the menu, so show Picture2.
    frmPicture2.Show

End Sub
```

Enter the following code inside the `mnuShowPicture3_Click()` procedure of the Pictures form:

```
Sub mnuShowPicture3_Click ()

    ' The user selected Show Picture 3 from the
    ' menu, so show Picture3.
    frmPicture3.Show

End Sub
```

Enter the following code inside the `mnuClearAll_Click()` procedure of the Pictures form:

```
Sub mnuClearAll_Click ()

    ' The user selected Clear All from the Show
    ' Picture menu, so unload the children.
    Unload frmPicture1
    Unload frmPicture2
    Unload frmPicture3

End Sub
```

Entering the Code of the Picture1 Form

Enter the following code inside the general declarations section of the Picture1 form:

```
' Each variable MUST be declared.
Option Explicit
```

☐ Enter the following code inside the `cmdClose_Click()` procedure of Picture1:

```
Sub cmdClose_Click ()

    ' The user clicked the Close button of Picture1,
    ' so unload Picture1.
    Unload frmPicture1

End Sub
```

☐ Enter the following code inside the `mnuBeepOnce_Click()` procedure of Picture1:

```
Sub mnuBeepOnce_Click ()

    ' The user selected Beep Once from the menu,
    ' so beep once.
    Beep

End Sub
```

☐ Enter the following code inside the `mnuBeepTwice_Click()` procedure of Picture1:

```
Sub mnuBeepTwice_Click ()

    ' Declare the variable as a long variable.
    Dim Counter As Long

    ' First beep.
    Beep

    ' A delay loop in between the first and
    ' second beep.
    For Counter = 0 To 10000
    Next Counter

    ' Second beep.
    Beep

End Sub
```

Entering the Code of the Picture2 Form

☐ Enter the following code inside the general declarations section of the Picture2 form:

```
' Each variable MUST be declared.
Option Explicit
```

☐ Enter the following code inside the `cmdClose_Click()` procedure of Picture2:

```
Sub cmdClose_Click ()

    ' The user clicked the Close button,
    ' so unload Picture2.
    Unload frmPicture2

End Sub
```

Entering the Code of the Picture3 Form

☐ Enter the following code inside the general declarations section of the Picture3 form:

```
' Each variable MUST be declared.
Option Explicit
```

☐ Enter the following code inside the cmdClose_Click() procedure of Picture3:

```
Sub cmdClose_Click ()

    ' The user clicked the Close button,
    ' so unload Picture3.
    Unload frmPicture3

End Sub
```

Executing the Pictures Program

☐ Execute the Pictures program.

Upon execution of the Pictures program, the parent form pops up, as shown in Figure 17.8. The child forms are contained within the parent form.

Figure 17.8.
The Pictures program.

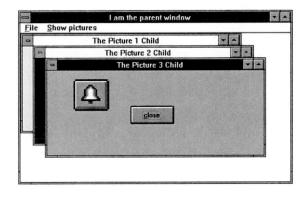

☐ Drag the child forms by dragging the titles of the forms.

As you can see, the child forms may be dragged anywhere inside the parent form, but they cannot be dragged outside the parent form.

You can minimize each child form as you would any standard form (by clicking the minus icon that appears on the top-left of each child form and selecting Minimize from the system menu that pops up). Figure 17.9 shows the Pictures program after two child forms, Picture1 and Picture2, have been minimized. As shown, the minimized forms appear as icons at the bottom of the parent form.

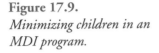
Figure 17.9.
Minimizing children in an MDI program.

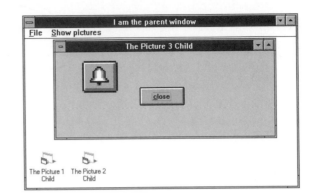

The Menus of the Parent and Child Forms

Experiment with the Pictures program and note that the menu bar of the parent form is displayed and is available as long as the currently active child form does not have a menu:

☐ Make Picture2 the active form by clicking inside its form, or by selecting Show Picture 2 from the Show Pictures menu. Because Picture2 does not have a menu, the menu bar that appears in the parent form is the menu bar of the parent form.

☐ Make Picture3 the active form by clicking inside its form or by selecting Show Picture 3 from the Show Pictures menu. Because Picture3 does not have a menu, the menu bar that appears in the parent form is the menu bar of the parent form.

However, if the currently active child form has a menu, the menu bar of the parent form contains the menu of the child form.

☐ Make Picture1 the active form by clicking inside its form or by selecting Show Picture 1 from the Show Picture menu. Because Picture1 has a menu, the menu bar that appears in the parent form is the menu of Picture1 (see Figure 17.10).

Figure 17.10.
The menu of the parent form when Picture1 is the active form.

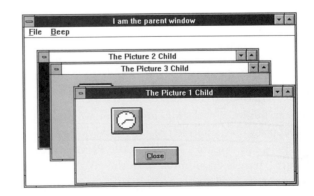

☐ Play with the Pictures program and study its features and behavior (for example, minimize and maximize the child forms, select items from the various menus).

The Code of the Parent Form

The code inside the procedures of the parent form contains the code that corresponds to events that are related to the parent form. For example, selecting Show All Pictures from the Show Pictures menu of the parent form causes the execution of the mnuShowAll_Click() procedure.

The Code of the *MDIForm_Load()* Event Procedure

The Pictures program consists of an MDI parent form and three child forms. Upon startup of the program, the form that is loaded is the parent MDI form Pictures.frm. The event procedure that corresponds to loading the parent form is called MDIForm_Load():

```
Sub MDIForm_Load ()

    ' Upon startup of the program, show the three
    ' children.
    frmPicture1.Show
    frmPicture2.Show
    frmPicture3.Show

End Sub
```

Because the Pictures program is an MDI program, the MDI parent form is loaded upon startup of the program. You may take advantage of this and perform various initializations and startup tasks inside the MDIForm_Load() procedure.

The code inside the MDIForm_Load() procedure of the Pictures program displays the three child forms by using the Show method.

For example, to display Picture1 child form, the MDIForm_Load() procedure uses the following statement:

```
frmPicture1.Show
```

The Code of the *mnuClearAll_Click()* Event Procedure

The mnuClearAll_Click() procedure of the Pictures parent form is executed whenever you select Clear All from the Show Pictures menu:

```
Sub mnuClearAll_Click ()

    ' You selected Clear All from the Show
    ' Pictures menu, so unload the children.
    Unload frmPicture1
    Unload frmPicture2
    Unload frmPicture3

End Sub
```

To remove a child form, use the Unload statement. For example, to remove the frmPicture1 child form, the mnuClearAll_Click() procedure uses the following statement:

```
Unload frmPicture1
```

The Code of the *mnuExit_Click()* Event Procedure

The mnuExit_Click() procedure of the Pictures parent form is executed whenever you select Exit from the File menu. This procedure terminates the program by executing the End statement.

The Code of the *mnuShowAll_Click()* Event Procedure

The mnuShowAll_Click() procedure of the Pictures parent form is executed whenever you select Show All from the Show Pictures menu:

```
Sub mnuShowAll_Click ()

    ' The user selected Show All from the menu,
    ' so show all the children.
    frmPicture1.Show
    frmPicture2.Show
    frmPicture3.Show

End Sub
```

This procedure uses the Show method for each of the child forms.

The Code of the *mnuShowPicture1_Click()* Event Procedure

The mnuShowPicture1_Click() procedure of the Pictures parent form is executed whenever you select Show Picture 1 from the Show Pictures menu:

```
Sub mnuShowPicture1_Click ()

    'You selected the Show Picture 1 from the
    ' menu, so show Picture1.
    frmPicture1.Show

End Sub
```

This procedure uses the Show method to display the child form frmPicture.

In a similar manner, the mnuShowPicture2_Click() and mnuShowPicture3_Click() event procedures are executed whenever you select Show Picture2 and Show Picture3 from the Show Pictures menu. Again, these procedures use the Show method for displaying the corresponding child form.

The Code of the Child Form Picture1

The procedures of the child form frmPicture1 contain the code that corresponds to events that are related to the Picture1 form. For example, clicking the Close button (cmdClose) of Picture1 causes the execution of the cmdClose_Click() procedure.

The Code of the *mnuBeepOnce_Click()* Event Procedure

The `mnuBeepOnce_Click()` procedure is executed whenever you select Beep Once from the Beep menu of the Picture1 form. Therefore, this procedure contains the `Beep` statement:

```
Sub mnuBeepOnce_Click ()

    ' You selected Beep Once from the menu,
    ' so beep once.
    Beep

End Sub
```

The Code of the *mnuBeepTwice_Click()* Event Procedure

The `mnuBeepTwice_Click()` procedure is executed whenever you select Beep Twice from the Beep menu of the Picture1 form. Therefore, this procedure contains two `Beep` statements. A delay code is inserted between the beeps. The delay is implemented by counting from 0 to 10000:

```
Sub mnuBeepTwice_Click ()

    ' Declare the variable as a long variable.
    Dim Counter As Long

    ' First beep.
    Beep
    ' A delay loop in between the first and
    ' second beep.
    For Counter = 0 To 10000
    Next Counter

    ' Second beep.
    Beep

End Sub
```

The Code of the *cmdClose_Click()* Event Procedure

The `cmdClose_Click()` procedure is executed whenever you click the Close button in the Picture1 form:

```
Sub mnuClose_Click ()

    ' You selected Close from the menu,
    ' so unload Picture1
    Unload frmPicture1

End Sub
```

The form is unloaded with the following statement:

```
Unload frmPicture1
```

The Code of the Child Forms Picture2 and Picture3

Child forms Picture2 and Picture3 each have a Close button. Whenever you click the Close button in the Picture2 form, the cmdClose_Click() procedure of Picture2 is executed. Likewise, whenever you click the Close button in the Picture3 form, the cmdClose_Click() procedure of Picture3 is executed.

To close the Picture2 form, the cmdClose_Click() procedure of the Picture2 form uses the Unload statement:

```
Unload frmPicture2
```

To close the Picture3 form, the cmdClose_Click() procedure of the Picture3 form uses the Unload statement:

```
Unload frmPicture3
```

Which Form Is Loaded First?

The Pictures program is comprised of an MDI parent form and its child forms. As previously stated, a Visual Basic program can contain only one MDI form. However, it is possible to design a program that has one MDI form and several standard forms. Now add a standard form to the Pictures program:

☐ Select New Form from the File menu.

   Visual Basic responds by adding a standard form to the project window. The default name that Visual Basic assigned to the form is Form4.frm.

Use the following steps to save the newly added standard form:

☐ Make sure that Form4 is highlighted in the project window.

☐ Select Save File As from the File menu.

   Visual Basic responds by displaying the Save File As dialog box.

☐ Save the newly added form as Standard.frm.

☐ Build the Standard.frm form according to the specifications in Table 17.7.

The completed form should look like the one shown in Figure 17.11.

☐ Save the project (select Save Project from the File menu).

Table 17.7. The properties table of Standard.frm.

Object	Property	Setting
Form	**Name**	**frmStandard**
	Caption	I am a standard form
	BackColor	(gray)
	Height	4425
	Left	1035
	Top	1140
	Width	7485
Command Button	**Name**	**cmdExit**
	Caption	E&xit
	Height	495
	Left	3000
	Top	3120
	Width	1215
Command Button	**Name**	**cmdSwitch**
	Caption	&Switch to the MDI form
	Height	855
	Left	1560
	Top	1320
	Width	4215

Figure 17.11.
The Standard.frm form.

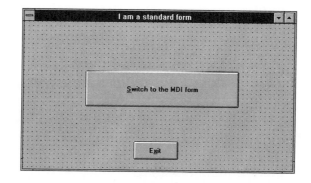

☐ Add the following code to the `cmdSwitch_Click()` procedure of the Standard.frm form:

```
Sub cmdSwitch_Click()

    ' Show the parent form.
    frmPictures.Show

End Sub
```

☐ Add the following code to the `cmdExit_Click()` procedure of the Standard.frm form:

```
Sub cmdExit_Click()

    End

End Sub
```

The Pictures project now contains the following forms:

- An MDI parent form and its child forms
- The Standard.frm form

Which form is loaded upon startup of the program: the MDI parent form or the standard form? At design time you decide which form is to be loaded by updating the Project Options window.

Use the following step to update the Project Options window:

☐ Select Projects... from the Options menu.

> *Visual Basic responds by displaying the Project Options dialog box (see Figure 17.12). As shown in Figure 17.12, the content of the Start Up Form field is frmPicture1. This means that the form that is loaded upon startup of the program is the child form frmPicture1. But because frmPicture1 is a child of picPictures, the forms that are loaded upon startup of the program are both the parent form frmPictures and the child form frmPicture1.*

Figure 17.12.
The Project Options window.

Highlight the Start Up Form field and then click this arrow to select a form.

Project Options	
Setting:	
☒ ☑ frmPicture1	⬇
Command Line Argument	
Start Up Form	frmPicture1
Help File	

OK
Cancel
Reset
Reset All

Use the following steps to change which form is loaded upon startup of the program:

☐ Change the content of the Start Up Form field of the Project Options window to Standard.frm. (Click the Start Up Form field and click the right arrow that appears in the setting box to select the desired form from the list of forms.)

☐ Now execute the Pictures program. As you can see, Standard.frm is loaded upon startup of the program.

Switching Between Forms at Runtime

At runtime you can switch between the Standard.frm and the Pictures.frm by clicking the cmdSwitch button in the Standard.frm form. The code inside the cmdSwitch_Click() procedure is executed whenever this button is clicked:

```
Sub cmdSwitch_Click()

    ' Show the parent form.
    frmPictures.Show

End Sub
```

The statement frmPictures.Show causes the MDI parent form to be displayed.

☐ Execute the program.

As you can see, the loaded form is the Standard.frm form.

☐ Switch to the MDI form by clicking the Switch to the MDI form button.

The program responds by displaying the MDI form.

In a similar way, you can add code to the MDI parent form or to any of the child forms that would cause the program to switch from the MDI form to the standard form. For example, you can add a command button with the caption Switch to the standard form to the Picture1 form, and insert the following statement inside the Click procedure of this button:

```
frmStandard.Show
```

The Window List Menu

Many professional MDI programs include a Window menu. Look at the Program Manager program that is shipped with Windows. It includes a Window menu (see Figure 17.13). The Window menu contains a list of all the child forms that the parent form currently contains.

Figure 17.13.
The Window menu of the Program Manager.

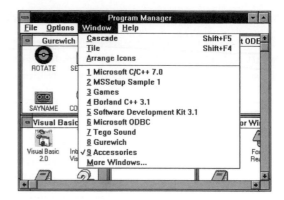

Adding a Window List Menu to the Parent Window

Now add a Window list menu to the parent window Pictures.frm. Use the following steps to implement the Window list:

☐ Select the Pictures form and add a menu item called Window. (Make sure the frmPicture form is selected. Select Menu Design from the Window menu and add the Window item, as shown in Figure 17.14.)

☐ Check the Window List box that appears in the Menu Design Window, as shown in Figure 17.14.

That's all! The Pictures form now has a Window menu.

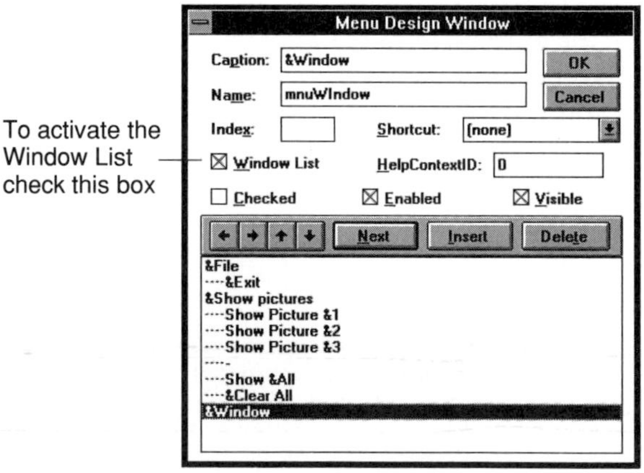

Figure 17.14.
Adding a Window list.

To activate the
Window List
check this box

☐ Execute the Pictures program and select the Window menu. The Window menu should list the three child forms (see Figure 17.15).

☐ Experiment with the Window menu. For example, close the Picture1 child and note that the list in the Window menu is updated.

Also note that in the Window menu, a check mark appears next to the child form that is currently active. For example, in Figure 17.15, Picture3 is active, and therefore this item has a check mark in the window list.

Figure 17.15.
The Window menu of the Pictures program.

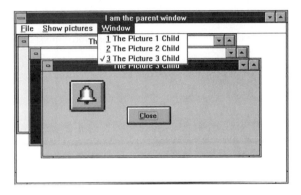

Adding a Window List Menu to a Child Form

A Window list menu may also be added to a child form. Use the following steps to add a Window list menu to the Picture1 child form:

☐ Select the Picture1 form and add a menu item called Window. (Select the Picture1 form, select Menu Design from the Window menu, and add the Window item to the menu of Picture1.)

☐ Check the Window List box that appears in the Menu Design window.

In many applications it is convenient to have the Window menu in the parent form as well as in the child forms.

Adding Cascade, Tile, and Arrange Icons Items to the Window Menu

As shown in Figure 17.13, the Window menu of the Program Manager program also contains the items Cascade, Tile, and Arrange Icons. These items are helpful when you want to arrange the child forms in the MDI parent form.

The Visual Implementation of the Window Menu

☐ Add the Cascade, Tile, and Arrange Icons items to the Window menu of the Pictures form, as shown in Figure 17.16.

☐ Type mnuCascade in the Name field of the Cascade item.

☐ Type mnuTile in the Name field of the Tile item.

☐ Type mnuArrangeIcons in the Name field of the Arrange Icons item.

The complete Window menu of the program is shown in Figure 17.17.

Figure 17.16.
Adding items to the Window menu.

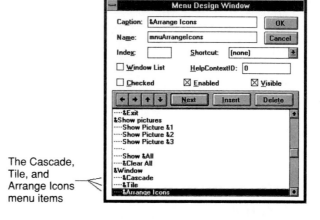

The Cascade, Tile, and Arrange Icons menu items

Figure 17.17.
The complete Window menu of the Pictures program.

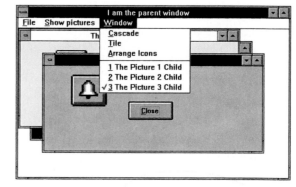

Adding the File Constant.txt to the Project

Before writing the code inside the mnuCascade_Click(), mnuTile_Click(), and mnuArrangeIcons_Click() procedures of Pictures.FRM, you need to add the Constant.txt file to the project. (The text file Constant.txt is in the directory C:\VB.)

Use the following steps to add the Constant.txt file to the project:

☐ Select Add File from the File menu.

Visual Basic responds by displaying the Add file dialog box.

☐ Load the file C:\VB\Constant.txt.

Take a look at the project window. It now includes the file Constant.txt (see Figure 17.18).

Figure 17.18.
*Adding the file
Constant.txt to the
project.*

Attaching Code to the Cascade, Tile, and Arrange Icons Menu Items

☐ Add the following code to the mnuCascade_Click() procedure of the Pictures form:

```
Sub mnuCascade_Click()

   ' The user selected Cascade from the Window menu.
   frmPictures.Arrange CASCADE

End Sub
```

☐ Add the following code to the mnuTile_Click() procedure of the Pictures form:

```
Sub mnuTile_Click()

   ' The user selected Tile from the Window menu.
   frmPictures.Arrange TILE_HORIZONTAL

End Sub
```

☐ Add the following code to the mnuArrangeIcons_Click() procedure of the Pictures form:

```
Sub mnuArrangeIcons_Click()

   ' The user selected Arrange Icons from the
   ' Window menu.
   frmPictures.Arrange ARRANGE_ICONS

End Sub
```

The *mnuCascade_Click()* Event Procedure

The mnuCascade_Click() procedure is executed whenever you select Cascade from the Window menu of the Pictures program.

The code inside this procedure consists of this statement:

```
frmPictures.Arrange CASCADE
```

which uses the Arrange method to cascade the child forms.

Note that the CASCADE constant is defined in C:\VB\Constant.txt as this:

```
Global Const CASCADE = 0
```

Because you included the file Constant.txt in the project, CASCADE is defined as 0.

If you did not include the file Constant.txt in the project, the code inside the mnuCascade_Click() procedure should be the following:

```
frmPictures.Arrange 0
```

By including the file Constant.txt in the project and using the constant CASCADE instead of 0, your program is easier to read.

Figure 17.19 shows how the child forms are arranged after you select Cascade from the Window menu.

Figure 17.19.
The child forms after selecting Cascade from the Window menu.

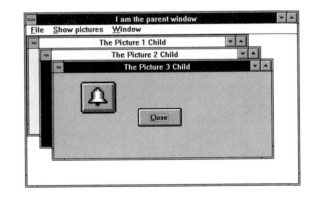

The *mnuTile_Click()* Event Procedure

The mnuTile_Click() procedure is executed whenever you select Tile from the Window menu of the Pictures program.

The code inside the mnuTile_Click() procedure contains the following statement:

```
frmPictures.Arrange TILE_HORIZONTAL
```

`TILE_HORIZONTAL` is declared in Constant.txt as the following:

```
Global Const TILE_HORIZONTAL = 1
```

When the Arrange method is used with 1 (`TILE_HORIZONTAL`), the child forms are arranged in the parent window, as shown in Figure 17.20.

Figure 17.20.
The child forms after selecting Tile from the Window menu.

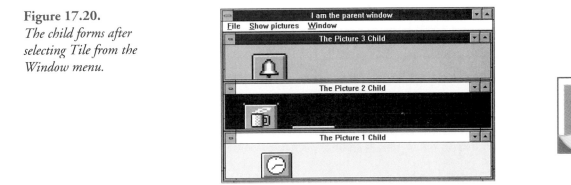

The *mnuArrangeIcons_Click( )* Event Procedure

The `mnuArrangeIcons_Click()` procedure is executed whenever you select Arrange Icons from the Window menu of the Pictures program.

The code inside the `mnuArrangeIcons_Click()` procedure contains the following statement:

```
frmPictures.Arrange ARRANGE_ICONS
```

`ARRANGE_ICONS` is declared in Constant.txt as the following:

```
Global Const ARRANGE_ICONS = 3
```

During the execution of the Pictures program, you can minimize the child forms and drag them, as shown in Figure 17.21. After you select Arrange Icons from the Window menu, the icons are rearranged, as shown in Figure 17.22.

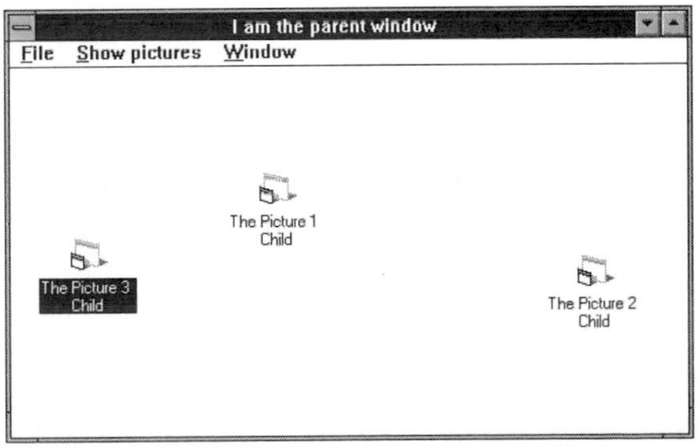

Figure 17.21.
The icons of the child forms before you select Arrange Icons from the Window menu.

Figure 17.22.
The icons of the child forms after you select Arrange Icons from the Window menu.

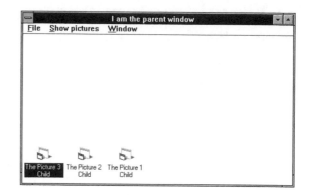

The *TILE_VERTICAL* Constant

You may examine the file Constant.txt and see that next to the constants CASCADE, TILE_HORIZONTAL, and ARRANGE_ICONS there is another related constant, the TILE_VERTICAL constant:

```
Global Const TILE_VERTICAL = 2
```

When the Arrange method is used with the TILE_VERTICAL constant, the child forms are arranged, as shown in Figure 17.23.

Figure 17.23.
Arranging the child forms vertically.

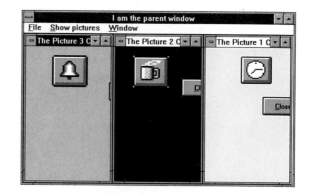

Designing a Text Editor Program

Now build an MDI program called TextEd. This program illustrates how a text editor program may be designed as an MDI program wherein each child form represents a new document.

The Visual Implementation of the TextEd Program

☐ Open a new project (select New Project from the File menu).

☐ Create an MDI parent form (select New MDI Form from the File menu).

Your project window should now contain a standard form, Form1.frm, and an MDI parent form, MDIForm1.frm.

☐ Save the standard form, Form1.frm, as Template.frm (highlight Form1.frm in the Project menu, select Save File As from the File menu, and save the file as Template.frm).

☐ Save the MDI parent form, MDIForm1.frm, as TextEd.frm (highlight MDIForm1.frm in the Project menu, select Save File As from the File menu, and save the file as TextEd.frm).

☐ Save the make file of the project as TextEd.mak (select Save Project As from the File menu and save the project as TextEd.mak).

Your Project Window should now contain the following items:

- A standard form Template.frm.
- An MDI parent form TextEd.frm.
- Custom control files (VBX files).

Now convert the non-MDI form Template.frm to an MDI child form and change its properties:

☐ Build the Template.frm form according to the specifications in Table 17.8.

The completed form should look like the one shown in Figure 17.24.

Note that once you change the MDIChild property of Template.frm to True (as specified in Table 17.8), the icon that appears in the project window on the left side of Template.frm indicates that this form is a child form.

Table 17.8. The properties table of the Template.frm child form.

Object	Property	Setting
Form	**Name**	**frmTemplate**
	Caption	Untitled
	MDIChild	True
	Height	4425

continues

597

Table 17.8. continued

Object	Property	Setting
	Left	1035
	Top	1149
	Width	7485
Text Box	**Name**	**txtUserArea**
	Text	(empty)
	MultiLine	True
	ScrollBars	3-Both
	Height	1935
	Left	0
	Top	0
	Width	2895

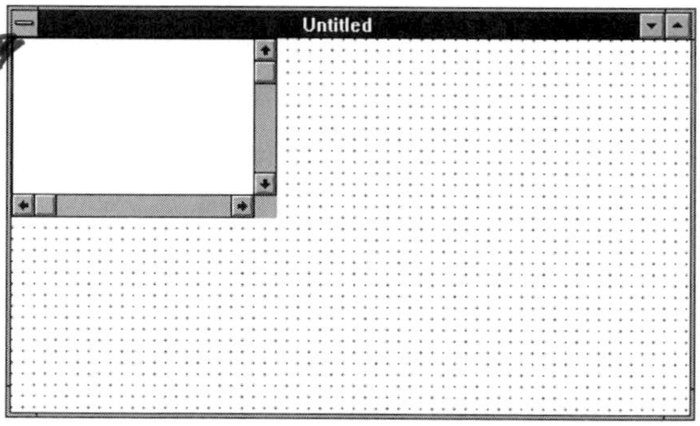

Figure 17.24.
The Template.frm form.

Now build the parent form of the project:

☐ Build the MDI parent form according to the specifications in Table 17.9.

The completed form should look like the one shown in Figure 17.25.

Table 17.9. The properties table of the MDI parent form TextEd.frm.

Object	Property	Setting
Form	Name	frmTextEd
	Caption	My Text Editor
	Height	4710
	Left	1035
	Top	1140
	Width	7486
Menu	(see Table 17.10)	(see Table 17.10)

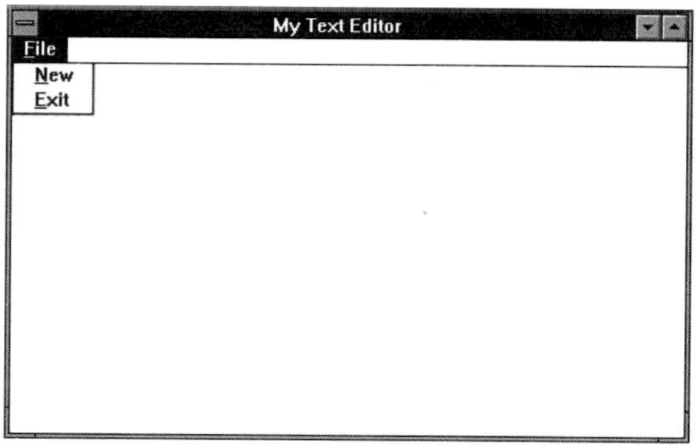

Figure 17.25.
The frmTextEd form.

Table 17.10. The menu table of the MDI parent form TextEd.frm.

Caption	Procedure Name
&File	mnuFile
...&New	mnuNew
...&Exit	mnuExit

Subroutines

☐ Select Project from the Options menu.

☐ Set the Start Up Form field of the Project Option dialog box to frmTextEd.

☐ Save the project (select Save Project from the File menu).

Entering the Code of the TextEd Program

☐ Enter the following code inside the general declarations section of the TextEd form:

```
' Variables MUST be declared.
Option Explicit
```

☐ Enter the following code inside the `mnuNew_Click()` procedure of the TextEd form:

```
Sub mnuNew_Click ()

    ' Declare a variable for the instance form
    ' as a copy of the form frmTemplate.
    Dim frmNewForm As New frmTemplate

    ' Show the instance form.
    frmNewForm.Show

End Sub
```

☐ Enter the following code inside the `mnuExit_Click()` procedure of the TextEd form:

```
Sub mnuExit_Click ()

    End

End Sub
```

☐ Save the project (select Save Project from the File menu).

Executing the TextEd Program

The TextEd program is not completed yet, but look at what you have accomplished so far.

☐ Execute the TextEd program.

The parent form frmTextEd pops up.

☐ Select New from the File menu.

A new child form pops up (see Figure 17.26). You may now type text inside the text box. As you can see, the text box area is not big enough! But don't worry about it, you'll fix this problem soon.

☐ Select New from the File menu several more times.

The program displays the child forms, as shown in Figure 17.27.

☐ Terminate the program by selecting Exit from the File menu.

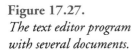

Figure 17.26.
The text editor program with one document.

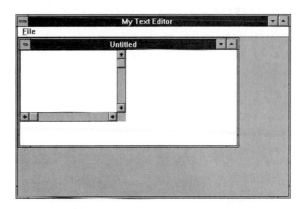

Figure 17.27.
The text editor program with several documents.

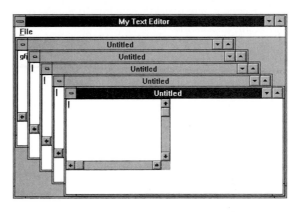

The Code of the *mnuNew_Click()* Event Procedure

The mnuNew_Click() procedure is executed whenever you select New from the File menu:

```
Sub mnuNew_Click ()

    ' Declare a variable for the instance form
    ' as a copy of the form frmTemplate.
    Dim frmNewForm As New frmTemplate

    ' Show the instance form.
    frmNewForm.Show

End Sub
```

The first statement in this procedure is this:

```
Dim frmNewForm As New frmTemplate
```

This statement declares a variable called frmNewForm as a new instance of the form frmTemplate. This means that for all purposes, you may refer to frmNewForm as a regular form that has the same properties as the frmTemplate form that you designed. In other words, you create a copy of the Template form. Once the frmNewForm form is created, you may use it in the program just as you would any other form.

For example, the second statement of the mnuNew_Click() procedure causes the newly created form to pop up using the following statement:

```
frmNewForm.Show
```

Every time you select New from the File menu, a new instance is created that is an identical copy of the Template form.

DO	DON'T

DO declare a new form variable that is a copy of an existing form by using the following statement:
 	
`Dim Name Of the new variable As New Name of existing form`
 	
For example, to declare the variable frmNewForm that is a copy of the frmTemplate form use the following:
 	
`Dim frmNewForm As New frmTemplate`	

Adjusting the Text Box Size in Accordance with the Form Size

Here is how the problem of the text box size is solved: The size of the text box should fill the entire child form area. Therefore, no matter how big or small the child form is, the text box should always cover the whole form. This can be achieved using the Resize event.

The Resize Event

The resize event occurs whenever the form pops up and whenever the size of the form is changed. Therefore, the Form_Resize() procedure is a focal point that is executed whenever the form size changes. This is a good place to resize the text box in accordance with the form size.

☐ Enter the following code inside the Form_Resize() procedure of the frmTemplate form:

```
Sub Form_Resize ()

    Me.txtUserArea.Height = Me.ScaleHeight
    Me.txtUserArea.Width  = Me.ScaleWidth

End Sub
```

The first statement of the Form_Resize() procedure assigns the ScaleHeight property of the current form to the Height property of the text box. In a similar way, the second statement of the `Form_Resize()` procedure assigns the ScaleWidth property of the current form to the Width property of the text box. Therefore, the text box has the size of the current form.

The Me reserved word that is used in the two statements of `Form_Resize()`, is a Visual Basic reserved word. It means the form where code is currently being executed.

The *Me* Reserved Word

The Me reserved word is a very useful feature in Visual Basic. Me is a variable that contains the name of the form where code is currently executed.

For example, in the TextEd program, there may be several instances (copies) of the Template form inside the parent form. When the size of one of these forms is changed, Visual Basic executes the `Form_Resize()` procedure and automatically updates the Me variable with the name of the instance that was resized. It is the responsibility of Visual Basic to maintain and update the value of the Me variable with the instance where code is currently executed.

Interestingly, if you omit the Me word in the statements of the `Form_Resize()` procedure, the program still works, because when you omit the name of the form, it has the same effect as substituting Me for the name of the form.

Changing the Caption Property of a Form

Another useful feature that exists in Visual Basic is the ActiveForm property. This property specifies the form that is currently active. If there currently is no active child form, the ActiveForm property specifies the last active child form.

To illustrate how useful the ActiveForm property is, enhance the TextEd program so that it allows you to change the Caption property of the child forms at runtime.

☐ Add the Assign Name menu to the parent form, as shown in Figure 17.28.

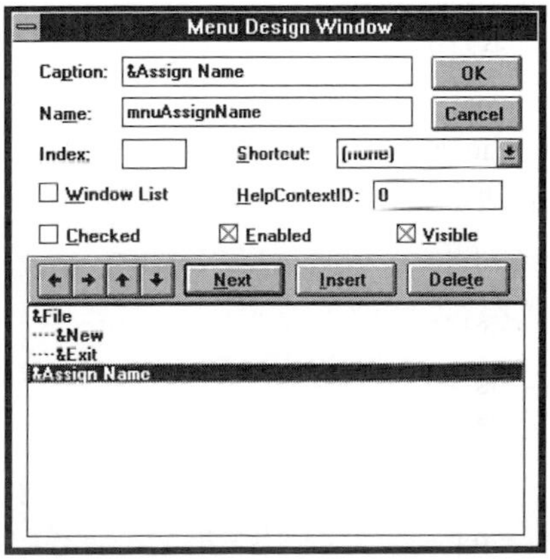

Figure 17.28.
Adding the Assign Name menu to the parent form.

17

603

Entering the Code Inside the *mnuAssignName_Click()* Event Procedure

☐ Enter the following code inside the mnuAssignName_Click() procedure of the TextEd parent form:

```
Sub mnuAssignName_Click ()

    ' Declare a string variable
    Dim DocumentName As String

    ' Get from the user the name of the document
    DocumentName = InputBox("Document name:", "Assign Name")

    ' Change the Caption property of the currently
    ' active (or last active)form.
    frmTextEd.ActiveForm.Caption = DocumentName

End Sub
```

Executing the TextEd Program

☐ Execute the TextEd program.

☐ Select New from the File menu.

A new child document appears.

☐ Select the Assign Name menu.

The program responds by displaying the input box, as shown in Figure 17.29.

☐ Type Document Number 1 in the input box and click the OK button.

The program responds by changing the Caption property of the currently active child form from Untitled to Document Number 1.

☐ Add several more new documents by selecting New from the File menu.

☐ You may switch to other child documents and change their names by selecting the Assign Name menu.

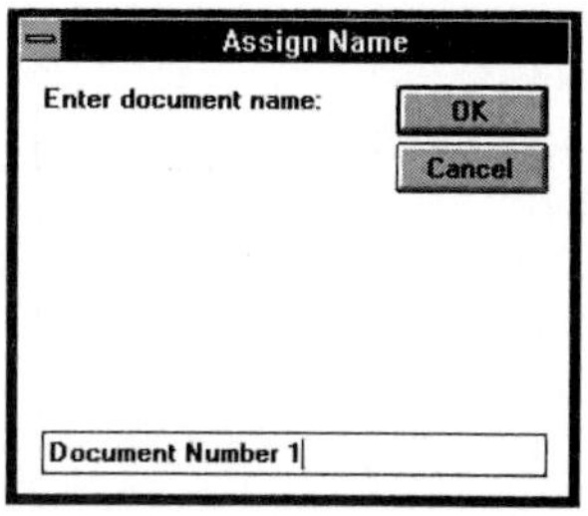

Figure 17.29.
Entering the document name by using an input box.

Assign Name
Enter document name:
OK
Cancel
Document Number 1

The Code of the *mnuAssignName_Click()* Event Procedure

The `mnuAssignName_Click()` procedure is executed whenever you select the Assign Name menu:

```
Sub mnuAssignName_Click ()

    ' Declare a string variable
    Dim DocumentName As String

    ' Get from the user the name of the document
    DocumentName = InputBox("Document name:", "Assign Name")

    ' Change the Caption property of the currently
    ' active (or last active)form.
    frmTextEd.ActiveForm.Caption = DocumentName

End Sub
```

The first statement in this procedure declares `DocumentName` as a string variable.

The second statement in the procedure displays the input box of Figure 17.29. The user's input is assigned to the `DocumentName` string variable:

```
DocumentName = InputBox("Enter Document name:", "Assign Name")
```

The last statement in the procedure assigns the content of the `DocumentName` variable to the Caption property of the currently active child form:

```
frmTextEd.ActiveForm.Caption = DocumentName
```

Visual Basic automatically maintains and updates the `ActiveForm` variable. So when the `mnuAssignName_Click()` procedure is executed, ActiveForm is already updated with the value of the currently active form (which is the form to which the user is assigning a new name).

> **Note:** The properties of the currently active or the last active child form can be changed by using the ActiveForm property as follows:
>
> ```
> ParentForm.ActiveForm.Property to be changed = Value
> ```
>
> For example, to change the Caption property of the currently active child form of the frmTextEd parent form to DocumentName, use the following:
>
> ```
> frmTextEd.ActiveForm.Caption = DocumentName
> ```

Creating a Toolbar

Many Windows programs include toolbars. A toolbar is an area that contains controls the user may select. Figure 17.30 shows the toolbar of the Microsoft Word for Windows program. Typically, these controls are included in programs to provide quick access for the most commonly used operations of the program. The controls on the toolbar may be images, push buttons, scroll bars, and so on. For example, clicking the disk image on the toolbar of Word for Windows has the same effect as selecting Save from the File menu of the Word program.

Figure 17.30.
The toolbar of Microsoft Word for Windows.

This icon is the save icon on the toolbar.

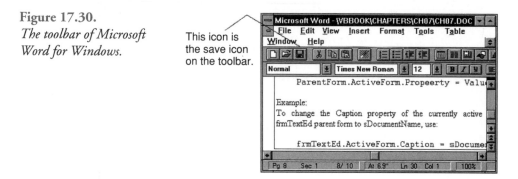

Note: In some Windows literature, the toolbar is called a ribbon bar or a control bar.

The Visual Implementation of the Toolbar and the Status Bar

Now add a toolbar and a status bar to the TextEd program. The complete form of the TextEd form with its toolbar is shown in Figure 17.31.

☐ Select the MDI parent form.

☐ Double-click the image icon of the Toolbox.

Visual Basic responds by displaying an error box (see Figure 17.32). Why is Visual Basic unhappy with your action? You tried to place in the MDI parent form a control that does not support the Align property. (If you examine the Properties window of the image control, you'll see that this control does not support the Align property.)

The only control that supports the Align property is the picture control.

☐ Double-click the picture icon of the Toolbox.

Visual Basic responds by placing the picture control on the MDI form, as shown in Figure 17.33. The icons of the toolbar are placed inside the area of this picture area that you just placed. If you try to drag the picture control to another location inside the MDI parent form, Visual Basic refuses to honor your request.

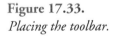

Figure 17.31.
The toolbar and the status bar in the TextEd program.

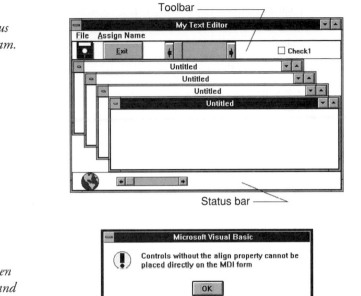

Figure 17.32.
The error message that Visual Basic displays when you try to place a command button inside the MDI parent form.

Now prepare the area where the icons of the status bar are located.

☐ Double-click the picture icon of the Toolbox again.

Visual Basic responds by placing the picture control below the first picture control that you placed in the previous step.

Figure 17.33.
Placing the toolbar.

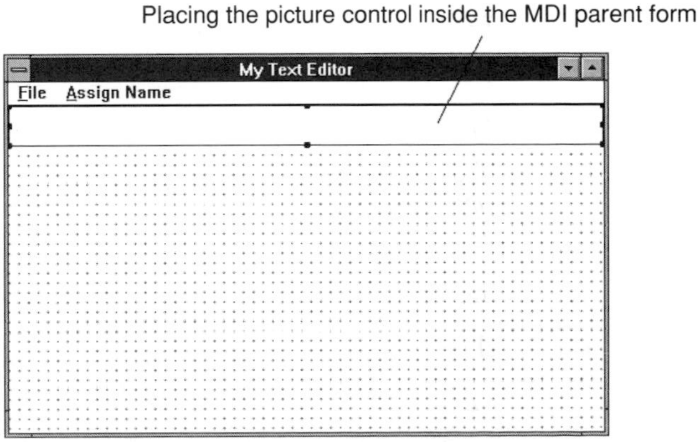

As shown in Figure 17.31, the status bar is located at the bottom of the form, so you need to reposition this picture control:

☐ Make sure the second picture control that you placed is selected and change its Align property to 2-Align Bottom.

Visual Basic responds by positioning the picture control at the bottom of the form (see Figure 17.34).

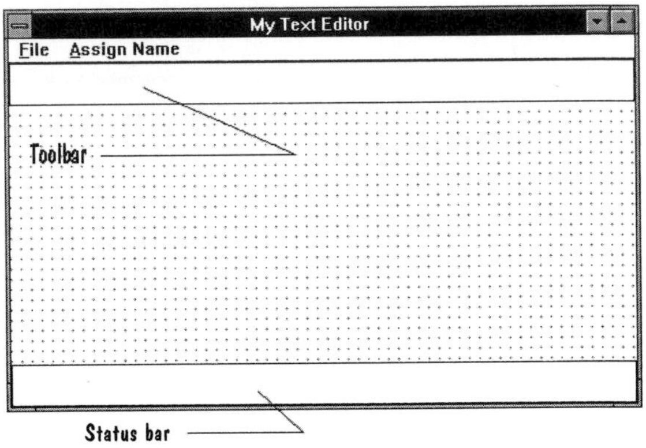

Figure 17.34.

Placing the status bar.

Now place controls on the toolbar and on the status bar, as shown in Figure 17.31.

Use the following steps to place the disk image on the toolbar:

☐ Click (do not double-click) the image icon in the Toolbox.

Visual Basic responds by highlighting the image icon in the Toolbox.

☐ Place the mouse cursor inside the toolbar area, press the left mouse button, and, while pressing the button, move the mouse.

Visual Basic responds by placing the image control inside the toolbar area.

☐ Change the Picture property of the image control to C:\VB\ICONS\COMPUTER\DISK03.ICO.

☐ Change the Stretch property of the image control to True. This enables you to stretch the image to any desired size (as long as it fits inside the toolbar area).

☐ Change the Name property of the image to imgSave.

In a similar manner, you may now place the other controls shown in Figure 17.31 in the toolbar area and in the status bar area. (The globe shown on the status bar in Figure 17.31 is an image control with its Picture property set to C:\VB\ICONS\ELEMENTS\EARTH.ICO.)

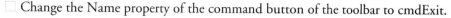

☐ Change the Name property of the command button of the toolbar to cmdExit.

☐ Change the Caption property of the cmdExit button to &Exit.

This concludes the visual implementation of the toolbar and status bar. Now attach code to the controls of these bars.

> **Note:** You have not been instructed to change the properties of the other controls that you placed on the toolbar and status bar.

Entering the Code of the Toolbar Icons

Attaching code to the icons and controls of the toolbar and status bar is done in the same way as attaching code to other controls.

Entering Code Inside the *imgSave_Click()* Procedure

The `imgSave_Click()` procedure is executed whenever you click the disk icon on the toolbar.

Use the following steps to enter code inside the `imgSave_Click()` procedure:

☐ Make sure that the parent form is selected.

☐ Click the disk image.

> *Visual Basic responds by displaying the `imgSave_Click()` procedure. Enter the `Beep` statement inside this procedure:*

```
Sub imgSave_Click ()

    Beep

End Sub
```

Saving files is the subject of another chapter, so for simplicity, the concept is demonstrated by inserting the `Beep` statement instead of statements that save files. In other words, during the execution of the program, whenever you click the disk icon, you'll hear a beep instead of actually saving the file.

Executing the TextEd Program

☐ Execute the TextEd program.

> *The TextEd form pops up, as shown in Figure 17.31.*

☐ Click the disk icon on the toolbar.

The program beeps whenever you click this icon.

Attaching Code to the Other Controls of the Toolbar and Status Bar

You may now attach code to the other controls that appear on the toolbar and status bar. For example, type the following code inside the cmdExit_Click() event procedure of the Exit button:

```
Sub cmdExit_Click()

    End

End Sub
```

Summary

In this chapter you have learned how to use MDI programs. MDI programs include one parent form and at least one child form. You have learned how to display (show) the child forms, how to unload child forms, and how to use the powerful Window List feature that helps you maneuver and arrange child forms inside the parent form.

You have also learned how to create instances (copies) of a child form at runtime, how to change the properties of the instances at runtime, how to build a toolbar and status bar, and how to attach code to the controls of these bars.

Q&A

Q I want to design an MDI program that does not load any of its child forms upon startup. Is it possible?

A Yes. By default, Visual Basic initializes the Start Up Form field of the Project Options window with the name of the first child form. For example, in the Pictures program, the default startup form is frmPicture1.frm. This means that upon startup of the program, the loaded forms are the MDI parent form and the child form frmPicture1. If you want only the parent MDI form to be loaded upon startup, set the Start Up Form to the parent MDI form.

You can try this by making the following changes to the Pictures program:

☐ Set the Start Up Form field of the Pictures project to frmPictures.frm.

☐ Remove the statements inside the MDIForm_Load() procedure. (These statements cause all the child forms to be displayed.)

Upon startup of the Pictures program, the parent form is shown without any of its child forms.

Q **If the currently active child form has a menu, the menu of the parent form changes to the menu of the child form. Is it possible to design the program so that the menu of the parent form remains unchanged, and the menu of the child form appears on the child form?**

A No. That's how MDI programs work! Generally, it is best to accept the rules and standards of the MDI, because your users expect the MDI program to work in a certain, acceptable, known way. After all, one of the main advantages of using Windows programs is that the user interface aspect of all Windows programs is well known and accepted by millions of happy users.

Quiz

1. How many MDI parent forms can a Visual Basic program have?

    a. 255

    b. No limit

    c. 1

    d. Depends on the number of child forms

2. The `BeepTwice_Click()` event procedure that is discussed in the Pictures program implements a delay. This code is machine dependent. Explain.

3. A program contains the following forms:

    - An MDI parent form and its child forms

    - Two standard forms

    Which form is loaded upon execution of the program?

    a. The MDI parent form

    b. The form mentioned in the startup form of the Project Option window

    c. Depends on the code inside the `Form_Load()` procedure

4. The difference between a toolbar and a status bar is which of the following:

    a. They're the same thing—it's just different terminology.

    b. The toolbar is located on top of the MDI parent form, the status bar is located at the bottom of the MDI parent form.

    c. Status bars are not supported in Visual Basic.

17

Exercises

1. Enhance the Window menu of the Pictures program by adding the Tile Vertical item to the Window menu.

2. Enhance the TextEd program as follows:

   ☐ Add a new menu to the TextEd parent form called Color. This menu should have two items in it: Green and Gray.

   ☐ When Green or Gray is selected from the Color menu, the currently active document should change its background color to the selected color.

Quiz Answers

1. c

2. The delay is implemented as follows:

```
For Counter = 0 To 10000
Next Counter
```

A fast computer would execute the loop in less time than it would take a slow computer to execute the same loop. This means that the performance of the code depends on the type of computer on which the program runs. In general, try to avoid writing code that depends on the type of computer that your users have.

3. b

4. b

Exercise Answers

1. To enhance the program, complete the following steps:

   ☐ Highlight the Pictures form and select Menu Design from the Window menu.

   ☐ Add the menu item Tile Vertical to the Window menu of the Pictures form.

   ☐ Add the following code inside the `mnuTileVertical_Click()` procedure of frmPictures.frm:

```
Sub mnuTileVertical_Click ()
        frmPictures.Arrange TILE_VERTICAL

End Sub
```

The constant `TILE_VERTICAL` is declared in Constant.txt as:

```
Global Const TILE_VERTICAL = 2
```

The `mnuVertical_Click()` procedure causes the child forms to be arranged vertically, as shown in Figure 17.23.

2. To enhance the program, complete the following steps:

☐ Add the following items to the menu of the TextEd parent form:

Caption	Procedure Name
&Color	mnuColor
...&Green	mnuGreen
...G&ray	mnuGray

☐ Enter the following code inside the mnuGray_Click() procedure:

```
Sub mnuGray_Click ()

    frmTextEd.ActiveForm.txtUserArea.BackColor = QBColor(8)

End Sub
```

☐ Enter the following code inside the mnuGreen_Color() procedure:

```
Sub mnuGreen_Click ()

    frmTextEd.ActiveForm.txtUserArea.BackColor = QBColor(2)

End Sub
```

☐ Enter the following code inside the mnuGreen_Click() procedure:

```
Sub mnuGreen_Click ()

    frmTextEd.ActiveForm.txtUserArea.BackColor = QBColor(8)

End Sub
```

(Note that the Active property is used as a substitute for the form name in the preceding two procedures.)

Dynamic Data Exchange

In this chapter you'll learn how to implement dynamic data exchange–based programs. Dynamic data exchange (DDE) is a sophisticated feature of Windows. As implied by its name, DDE provides you with the capability of exchanging data between programs. If you have never worked with DDE-based programs and you are not familiar with the concept, don't worry. This chapter does not assume any prior knowledge of DDE, but it explains what DDE is, as well as how to implement Visual Basic programs that support this feature.

Writing Your First DDE Program

The concept of DDE is best explained as follows: A DDE program exchanges data with another DDE program. This means that to illustrate the DDE operation you need two programs. The programs you are about to write are called SOURCE and DEST.

In DDE programs, data is flowing from one DDE program to another DDE program. The program that supplies the data is called the *source application*, and the program that initiates the request for data and receives the data is called the *destination application*.

Descriptions of the SOURCE and DEST Programs

Figure 18.1 shows the SOURCE and DEST programs. The objective is to write the SOURCE and the DEST programs in such a way that when you type text in the text box of the SOURCE program, the text automatically appears in the text box of the DEST program. That's what DDE is all about!

The SOURCE and DEST programs exchange text. However, other types of data exchange are possible as well (for example, bitmaps, icons, metafiles).

The Visual Implementation of the DEST Program

☐ Open a new project, save the form of the project as DEST.FRM, and save the make file of the project as DEST.MAK.

☐ Build the frmDest form according to the specifications in Table 18.1.

The completed form should look like the right form shown in Figure 18.1.

Table 18.1. The properties table of frmDest form.

Object	Property	Setting
Form	**Name**	**frmDEST**
	Caption	The DEST Program
	Height	4305
	Left	4890
	Top	1305
	Width	2925
Command Button	**Name**	**cmdLink**
	Caption	&Link
	Height	495
	Left	240
	Top	2640
	Width	2295
Text Box	**Name**	**txtFromSource**
	Height	1215
	Left	240
	MultiLine	True
	Text	(empty)
	Top	1320
	Width	2295
Command Button	**Name**	**cmdExit**
	Caption	&Exit
	Height	495
	Left	1320
	Top	3240
	Width	1215
Label	**Name**	**lblInfo**
	Caption	The following data came from SOURCE:
	FontSize	13.5
	ForeColor	(blue)
	Height	1095

Table 18.1. continued

Object	Property	Setting
	Left	240
	Top	120
	Width	2295

Figure 18.1.
Exchanging data from SOURCE to DEST.

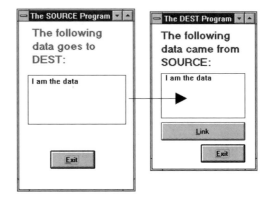

Entering the Code of the DEST Program

☐ Enter the following code inside the general declarations section of frmDest:

```
' All variables MUST be declared.
Option Explicit
```

☐ Enter the following code inside the cmdExit_Click() procedure of frmDest:

```
Sub cmdExit_Click ()

    End

End Sub
```

☐ Enter the following code inside the cmdLink_Click() procedure of frmDest:

```
Sub cmdLink_Click ()

    ' Set the topic.
    txtFromSource.LinkTopic = "SOURCE|Dummy"

    ' Set the Item.
    txtFromSource.LinkItem = "txtToDest"

    ' Establish DDE.
    txtFromSource.LinkMode = 1

End Sub
```

Creating an EXE File for the DEST Program

☐ Save the project (select Save Project from the File menu).

☐ Save the project as an EXE file by selecting Make EXE File from the File menu, and save the file as DEST.EXE.

Now the DEST program is completed, and data (text) will flow from the SOURCE program to the DEST program.

Because you haven't created the SOURCE program yet, you can't test the DDE operation. Nevertheless, look at what happens when you try to execute the DEST program. Execute the DEST.EXE program using the following steps:

☐ Switch to the File Manager. Select Run from the File menu, select Browse, and select DEST.EXE.

☐ Click the Link button.

> *The program responds by displaying the dialog box shown in Figure 18.2.*

As expected, the destination program is complaining that no foreign application responded to a DDE request (that is, the DEST program tried to initialize a DDE connection with the SOURCE program and received no response). This, of course, makes sense, because you haven't started writing the SOURCE program.

☐ Push the OK button of the warning dialog box shown in Figure 18.2.

Figure 18.2.
The warning message that pops up when the source application is not running.

DEST
⊘ No foreign application responded to a DDE initiate
OK

The Visual Implementation of the SOURCE Program

☐ Open a new project, save the form of the project as SOURCE.FRM, and save the make file of the program as SOURCE.MAK.

☐ Build the frmSource form according to the specifications in Table 18.2.

The completed form should look like the left form shown in Figure 18.1.

Table 18.2. The properties table of frmSource form.

Object	Property	Setting
Form	**Name**	**frmSource**
	Caption	The SOURCE Program
	Height	4935
	Left	1035
	LinkMode	1-Source
	ScaleHeight	4530
	ScaleWidth	3090
	Top	1140
	Width	3210
Text Box	**Name**	**txtToDest**
	Height	1335
	Left	240
	MultiLine	True
	Text	(empty)
	Top	1440
	Width	2655
Command Button	**Name**	**cmdExit**
	Caption	&Exit
	Height	495
	Left	840
	Top	3480
	Width	1215
Label	**Name**	**lblInfo**
	Caption	The following data goes to DEST:
	FontSize	13.5
	ForeColor	(red)
	Height	1095
	Left	360
	Top	120
	Width	2295

Entering the Code of the SOURCE Program

☐ Enter the following code inside the general declarations section of the frmSource form:

```
' All variables MUST be declared.
Option Explicit
```

☐ Enter the following code inside the cmdExit_Click() procedure of the frmSource form:

```
Sub cmdExit_Click ()

    End

End Sub
```

☐ Enter the following code inside the Form_Load() procedure of the frmSource form:

```
Sub Form_Load ()

    ' Set the topic of the DDE.
    frmSource.LinkTopic = "Dummy"

End Sub
```

Creating an EXE file for the SOURCE Program

☐ Save the program by selecting Save Project from the File menu.

☐ Create an EXE file for the SOURCE program (select Make EXE File from the File menu and save the file in the directory as SOURCE.EXE).

Testing the SOURCE and DEST Programs

To clearly see what is going on during the testing of the DDE program, close and/or minimize Visual Basic and all other running applications.

☐ Execute the SOURCE program (switch to the Program Manager, select Run from the File menu, select Browse, and then select SOURCE.EXE).

The SOURCE program should be displayed, as shown on the left side of Figure 18.1.

☐ Execute the DEST program (while SOURCE is running).

The DEST program is displayed, as shown on the right side of Figure 18.1.

Now test the DDE link between the SOURCE and the DEST programs:

☐ Type something inside the SOURCE program.

☐ Push the Link button of the DEST program.

If the DDE link is implemented successfully, the text inside the text box of the SOURCE form is transferred to the text box of the DEST form.

☐ Keep typing inside the text box of the SOURCE program.

Because the DDE link is already established, everything that you type inside the text box of SOURCE is automatically transferred to the DEST program.

How the SOURCE and DEST Programs Work

The following sections describe how the SOURCE and DEST programs work.

The *Form_Load()* Event Procedure of the SOURCE Program

The Form_Load() procedure is executed when the frmSource form is first loaded:

```
Sub Form_Load ()

    ' Set the topic of the DDE.
    frmSource.LinkTopic = "Dummy"

End Sub
```

The statement in this procedure sets the LinkTopic property of the form. The LinkTopic property defines the topic of the communication. In the SOURCE/DEST application, you really don't have a specific topic, so supply Dummy as the topic of the communication. The LinkTopic property is covered in greater detail later in this chapter.

The *cmdLink_Click()* Event Procedure of the DEST Program

The cmdLink_Click() procedure is executed whenever you click the Link button in the DEST program:

```
Sub cmdLink_Click ()

    ' Set the topic.
    txtFromSource.LinkTopic = "SOURCE¦Dummy"

    ' Set the Item.
    txtFromSource.LinkItem = "txtToDest"

    ' Establish DDE.
    txtFromSource.LinkMode = 1

End Sub
```

To establish the DDE link, the LinkTopic property and the LinkItem property of the text box in the DEST program must be set. The LinkTopic property of the text box is set with the following statement:

```
txtFromSource.LinkTopic = "SOURCE|Dummy"
```

As you can see, the LinkTopic property is a string that is made of two parts separated by the pipestem character (|).

The first part, SOURCE, is the name of the source application. Because the data will come from the SOURCE program, the first half of the LinkTopic property is SOURCE.

The second half of the LinkTopic property is the topic of the communication as specified by the LinkTopic property in the SOURCE application. Recall that in the SOURCE program you set the LinkTopic property of the form of the source application to Dummy (see the `Form_Load()` procedure of SOURCE). So the LinkProperty of the control that receives the data is the topic Dummy from the program SOURCE.

Now that the LinkTopic property of the control that will receive the data is updated, the destination application will know who supplies the data. But which control in the source application supplies the data? The text box? The label? That's why you need to specify the LinkItem property:

18

```
txtFromSource.LinkItem = "txtToDest"
```

This statement specifies that the data should come from a control called txtToDest (which is the name of the text box in the SOURCE program).

Now that everything is prepared for the link, the last statement in the `cmdLink_Click()` procedure actually establishes the link by setting the LinkMode property of the text box to 1-Automatic Mode:

```
txtFromSource.LinkMode = 1
```

After this statement is executed, the txtToDest text box in the SOURCE program is linked to the txtFromSource text box in the DEST program. Anything that is typed in the text box of the SOURCE program is transferred to the text box of the DEST program.

Topics and Items

The SOURCE and DEST programs illustrate how to establish DDE communication between two Visual Basic programs. However, you may establish a DDE communication between your Visual Basic program and any Windows program that supports DDE. Examples of some well-known Windows programs that support DDE include Word for Windows, Excel, FoxPro for Windows, and Access. These programs can serve as the source and/or as the destination applications.

To establish DDE communication between your Visual Basic program and any of these DDE programs, you have to read the corresponding documentation of these programs and find the syntax for the Topic and the syntax for the Item. For example, to transfer data from an Excel spreadsheet called BUDGET.XLS that resides in the directory C:\EXCEL\PROJECT into a text box called txtGotItFromExcel in your Visual Basic program, your destination Visual Basic program has to specify the topic as follows:

```
txtGotItFromExcel.LinkTopic = EXCEL¦C:\EXCEL\PROJECT\BUDGET.XLS
```

The LinkItem property in your Visual Basic destination application may be this:

```
txtGotItFromExcel.LinkItem = R1C1
```

where R1C1 is the cell (row 1, column 1) in the spreadsheet that you want to import from Excel.

You may include a button in your Visual Basic program that causes your Visual Basic program to import several cells from the spreadsheet. For example, if you name the button cmdStartImport, the event procedure that corresponds to clicking this button is cmdStartImport_Click(). To import the cells in column 4 from row 12 to row 52 do the following:

```
Sub cmdStartImport_Click()

    'Set the mode to automatic (=1).
    txtGotItFromExecl.LinkMode = 1

    RowNumber = 12
    Do While RowNumber <=  52
        txtGotItFromExcel.LinkTopic= EXCEL¦C:\EXCEL\PROJECT\BUDGET.XLS
        txtGotItFromExcel.LinkItem = "R"+RowNumber+"C4"
    Loop

End Sub
```

The Manual and Notify Modes

As previously stated, setting the LinkMode property of the control that receives the data to 1 means that DDE mode is automatic, and data is therefore automatically flowing to the destination control whenever the data changes in the source application.

Two other possible modes are the manual mode (LinkMode = 2) and the notify mode (LinkMode = 3).

Manual Link

If you set the LinkMode property of the control that receives the data to 2, the data does not come in automatically; rather, your program has to request the data.

Use the following steps to see the manual link mode in action:

☐ Change the cmdLink_Click() procedure of the frmDest form so it looks like this:

```
Sub cmdLink_Click ()
```

```
' Set the topic.
txtFromSource.LinkTopic = "Source¦Dummy"

' Set the Item.
txtFromSource.LinkItem = "txtToDest"

' Establish the DDE mode as Manual mode (=2).
txtFromSource.LinkMode = 2
```

```
End Sub
```

☐ Add the Request button, as shown in Figure 18.3.

The button should have the following properties: The Name property should be cmdRequest and the Caption property should be &Request.

Figure 18.3.
Adding the Request button to the DEST program.

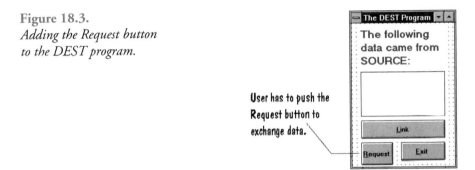

User has to push the Request button to exchange data.

☐ Add the following code inside the cmdRequest_Click() procedure of the frmDest form:

```
Sub cmdRequest_Click()

    ' Request data from the source application.
    txtFromSource.LinkRequest

End Sub
```

☐ Save the project (select Save Project from the File menu).

☐ Make an EXE file for the DEST program (select Make EXE File from the File menu and save the file as DEST.EXE).

Executing the SOURCE and DEST Programs with Manual LinkMode

☐ Start the SOURCE program.

☐ Start the DEST program.

☐ For easy windows manipulation, close and/or minimize all running windows (except the SOURCE and DEST programs).

☐ Type something inside the text box of the SOURCE program.

☐ Click the Link button of the DEST program to establish a DDE communication.

As you can see, the data is not transferred to the DEST program.

☐ Click the Request button of the DEST program.

The programs respond by exchanging the data.

☐ Type something again in the text box of the SOURCE program.

As you can see, the new text that you typed is not transferred.

Use the following step to transfer the data to the DEST program:

☐ Click the Request button again.

The LinkRequest Method

In the previous experiment, you set the LinkMode property of txtFromSource to 2, which means that the DDE mode is manual. Therefore, whenever you change the data in the text box of the SOURCE program, data is not flowing automatically to the DEST program. Rather, you have to manually push the Request button, which causes the execution of the LinkRequest method in the `cmdRequest_Click()` procedure.

DO	**DON'T**
DO set the LinkMode property of the control that will receive the data to 2-Manual Mode and use the LinkRequest method to retrieve data from the source application to establish manual DDE mode.	
The source application responds to the LinkRequest method by transferring data (if it has any new data to transfer).	

Notify Link

When you set the LinkMode property of the control that receives the data to 3, the DDE is in Notify mode. In this mode, the destination application is notified whenever there is new data in the source application. When in Notify mode, the LinkNotify event is generated for the control that receives the data. For example, if the data control that receives the data in the destination application is a picture box called picFromSource, whenever the picture box in the source application changes, the `picFromSource_LinkNotify()` event procedure is executed in the destination application. This is illustrated in the SPICTURE and DPICTURE programs.

The SPICTURE and DPICTURE Programs

The SPICTURE program serves as the source application, and the DPICTURE program serves as the destination application. These programs are involved in a DDE communication, and the exchanged data is a picture.

The Visual Implementation of the SPICTURE Program

Use the following steps to implement the source application SPICTURE:

☐ Open a new project, save the form of the project as SPICTURE.FRM, and save the make file of the project as SPICTURE.MAK.

☐ Build the frmSPicture form according to the specifications in Table 18.3.

The completed form should look like the one shown in Figure 18.4.

Table 18.3. The properties table of frmSPicture form.

Object	Property	Setting
Form	**Name**	**frmSPicture**
	Caption	The SPICTURE Program
	Height	4050
	Left	1035
	LinkMode	1-Source
Form	**Name**	**frmSPicture**
	ScaleHeight	3645
	ScaleWidth	3375
	Top	1140
	Width	3495
Option Button	**Name**	**optClear**
	Caption	&Clear picture
	Height	495
	Left	240
	Top	1080
	Value	True
	Width	1695

continues

627

Table 18.3. continued

Object	Property	Setting
Option Button	**Name**	**optDisk3**
	Caption	&3.5" diskette
	Height	495
	Left	240
	Top	600
	Width	1575
Option Button	**Name**	**optDisk5**
	Caption	&5.25" diskette
	Height	495
	Left	240
	Top	120
	Width	1575
Picture Box	**Name**	**picUserChoice**
	AutoSize	True
	Height	510
	Left	240
	Top	1680
	Width	510
Command Button	**Name**	**cmdExit**
	Caption	&Exit
	Height	975
	Left	1080
	Top	2400
	Width	1215

Entering the Code of the SPICTURE Program

☐ Enter the following code inside the general declarations section of the frmSPicture form:

```
' All variables MUST be declared.
Option Explicit
```

Figure 18.4.
The frmSPicture form.

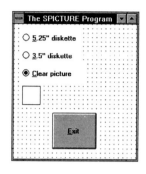

☐ Enter the following code inside the cmdExit_Click() procedure of the frmSPicture form:

```
Sub cmdExit_Click ()

    End

End Sub
```

☐ Enter the following code inside the Form_Load() procedure of the frmSPicture form:

```
Sub Form_Load ()

    ' Define the topic.
    frmSPicture.LinkTopic = "C:\"

End Sub
```

☐ Enter the following code inside the optClear_Click() procedure of the frmSPicture form:

```
Sub optClear_Click ()

    ' Picture box will have a border when there is
    ' no picture in it.
    picUserChoice.BorderStyle = 1

    ' Clear the content of the picture box.
    picUserChoice.Picture = LoadPicture()

End Sub
```

☐ Enter the following code inside the optDisk3_Click() procedure of the frmSPicture form:

```
Sub optDisk3_Click ()

    ' Picture box will not have a border when the
    ' diskette icon appears in it (for cosmetic
    ' reasons).
    picUserChoice.BorderStyle = 0

    ' Load the 3.5" diskette picture.
    picUserChoice.Picture =
        ➥ LoadPicture("c:\vb\icons\computer\disk04.ico")

End Sub
```

☐ Enter the following code inside the `optDisk5_Click()` procedure of the frmSPicture form:

```
Sub optDisk5_Click ()

    ' Picture box will not have a border when the
    ' diskette icon appears in it (for cosmetic
    ' reasons).
    picUserChoice.BorderStyle = 0

    ' Load the 5.25" diskette picture.
    picUserChoice.Picture =
        ➥ LoadPicture("c:\vb\icons\computer\disk05.ico")

End Sub
```

☐ Save the project.

☐ Select Make EXE File from the File menu and save the program as SPICTURE.EXE.

Executing the SPICTURE Program

Even though you have not written the DPICTURE program yet, execute SPICTURE now:

☐ Execute the SPICTURE program.

☐ Select the 5.25" disk button to display the 5.25" disk, and select the 3.5" disk to display the 3.5" disk icon (see Figure 18.5).

☐ Select the Clear button to clear the picture.

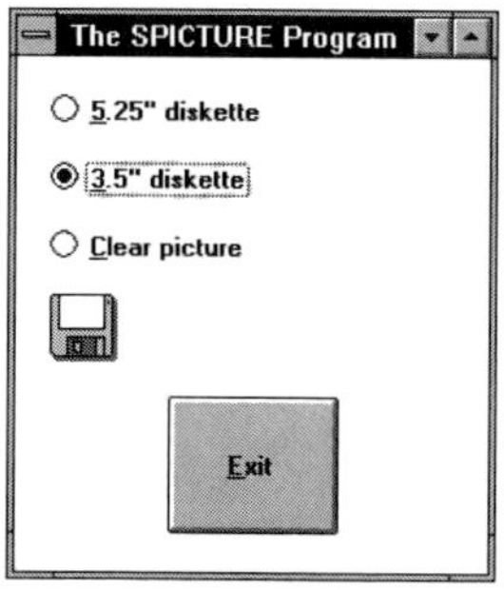

Figure 18.5.
Changing the picture in the SPICTURE program.

Now that you understand what the SPICTURE picture does, build the DPICTURE program.

The Visual Implementation of the DPICTURE Program

Use the following steps to implement the destination application DPICTURE:

☐ Open a new project, save the form of the project as DPICTURE.FRM, and save the make file of the project as DPICTURE.MAK.

☐ Build the form frmDPicture according to the specifications in Table 18.4.

The completed form should look like the form shown in Figure 18.6.

Table 18.4. The properties table of frmDPicture form.

Object	Property	Setting
Form	**Name**	**frmDPicture**
	Caption	The DPICTURE Program
	Height	4425
	Left	4485
	ScaleHeight	4020
	ScaleWidth	3600
	Top	1380
	Width	3720
Command Button	**Name**	**cmdRequest**
	Caption	&Request
	FontSize	18
	Height	1095
	Left	240
	Top	120
	Width	3135
Picture Box	**Name**	**picFromSource**
	AutoSize	True
	BorderStyle	0-None
	Height	480
	Left	1440
	ScaleHeight	480
	ScaleWidth	480
	Top	1680
	Width	480
Command Button	**Name**	**cmdExit**
	Caption	&Exit
	Height	495
	Left	1200

18

Table 18.4. continued

Object	Property	Setting
	Top	3360
	Width	1215
Label	**Name**	**lblInfo**
	Alignment	2-Center
	BorderStyle	1-Fixed Single
	Caption	(empty)
	FontName	Dom Casual (US)
	FontSize	13.5
	Height	855
	Left	210
	Top	2400
	Width	3285

Figure 18.6.
The frmDPicture form.

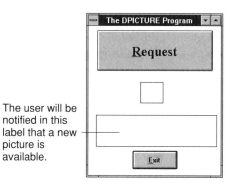

The user will be
notified in this
label that a new
picture is
available.

Entering the Code of the DPICTURE Program

☐ Enter the following code inside the general declarations area of the frmDPicture form:

```
' All variables MUST be declared.
Option Explicit
```

☐ Enter the following code inside the cmdExit_Click() procedure of the frmDPicture form:

```
Sub cmdExit_Click ()

    End

End Sub
```

☐ Enter the following code inside the cmdRequest_Click() procedure of the frmDPicture form:

```
Sub cmdRequest_Click ()

    ' Clear the label.
    lblInfo.Caption = ""

    ' Disable the Request button.
    cmdRequest.Enabled = False

    ' Request the new picture.
    picFromSource.LinkRequest

End Sub
```

☐ Enter the following code inside the Form_Load() procedure of the frmDPicture form:

```
Sub Form_Load ()

    ' Define the topic.
    picFromSource.LinkTopic = "SPICTURE¦C:\"

    ' Define the item.
    picFromSource.LinkItem = "picUserChoice"

    ' Set the LinkMode to Notify (=3).
    picFromSource.LinkMode = 3

End Sub
```

☐ Enter the following code inside the picFormSource_LinkNotify() procedure of the frmDPicture form:

```
Sub picFromSource_LinkNotify ()

    ' Beep (so that the user will notice that a new
    ' picture is available).
    Beep

    ' Enable the Request button (so that the user
    ' will be able to push it).
    cmdRequest.Enabled = True

    ' Display a note to the user inside the label
    ' (in case the user didn't hear the beep).
    lblInfo.Caption = "New picture is available..."

End Sub
```

☐ Save the project.

☐ Select Make EXE File from the File menu and save the program as DPICTURE.EXE.

Executing the SPICTURE and DPICTURE Programs

☐ Make sure that the SPICTURE program is running.

☐ Execute the DPICTURE program.

☐ To see what's going on, close and/or minimize all windows except the SPICTURE and DPICTURE programs.

☐ Click the 3.5" disk radio button in the SPICTURE program.

> *The SPICTURE program responds by displaying the 3.5" disk icon. The DPICTURE program responds by beeping and changing the caption of the label, which tells you that new data is ready.*

☐ Click the Request button of the DPICTURE program.

☐ The picture from the SPICTURE program is transferred to the DPICTURE program.

☐ Change the picture of SPICTURE again, and when DPICTURE tells you (by beeping and displaying a message) that a new picture is ready, click the Request button (see Figure 18.7).

Figure 18.7.
A new picture in the DPICTURE program.

How the SPICTURE and DPICTURE Programs Work

The SPICTURE and DPICTURE programs are communicating via DDE in mode 3-Notify Mode. The `picFromSource_LinkNotify()` event procedure is executed whenever the source program notifies the destination program that new data is available.

The Code Inside the *Form_Load()* Event Procedure of the SPICTURE Program

The Form_Load() procedure of the SPICTURE program is executed whenever you start the SPICTURE program. The statement inside this procedure sets the LinkTopic property of the form:

```
Sub Form_Load ()

    ' Define the topic.
    frmSPicture.LinkTopic = "C:\"

End Sub
```

The Code Inside the *optDisk5_Click()* Event Procedure of the SPICTURE Program

The optDisk5_Click() procedure of the SPICTURE program is executed whenever you click the 5.25" disk option button:

```
Sub optDisk5_Click ()

    ' Picture box will not have a border when the
    ' diskette icon appears in it (for cosmetic
    ' reasons).
    picUserChoice.BorderStyle = 0

    ' Load the 5.25" diskette picture.
    picUserChoice.Picture = LoadPicture("c:\vb\icons\computer\disk05.ico")

End Sub
```

The first statement in this procedure removes the border of the picture box (for cosmetic reasons). The second statement in this procedure loads the picture into the picture box. In a similar manner, the optDisk3_Click() procedure is executed whenever you click the 3.5" disk option button. The statement in the optDisk3_Click() procedures loads the 3.5" disk picture.

The Code Inside the *optClear_Click()* Event Procedure of the SPICTURE Form

The optClear_Click() procedure of the SPICTURE program is executed whenever you click the Clear option button of the SPICTURE form:

```
Sub optClear_Click ()

    ' Picture box will have a border when there is
    ' no picture in it.
    picUserChoice.BorderStyle = 1

    ' Clear the content of the picture box.
    picUserChoice.Picture = LoadPicture()
```

```
End Sub
```

This procedure sets the BorderStyle property of the picture box to 1:

```
picUserChoice.BorderStyle = 1
```

This way it will be obvious that the picture box is empty. The second statement in the `optClear_Click()` procedure clears the picture box by loading nothing (no argument) with the `LoadPicture()` function:

```
picUserChoice.Picture = LoadPicture()
```

The Code Inside the *Form_Load()* Event Procedure of the frmDPicture Form

The `Form_Load()` procedure of the DPICTURE program is executed when the frmDPicture form is loaded:

```
Sub Form_Load ()

    ' Define the topic.
    picFromSource.LinkTopic = "SPICTURE¦C:\"

    ' Define the item.
    picFromSource.LinkItem = "picUserChoice"

    ' Set the LinkMode to Notify (=3).
    picFromSource.LinkMode = 3

End Sub
```

This procedure is a good place to insert initialization statements. The first statement sets the LinkTopic property of the control that will receive the picture to the same topic that was set to the LinkTopic of the frmSPicture form (see the `Form_Load()` procedure of the SPICTURE program). Because the LinkTopic property of frmSPicture was set to C:\, the corresponding LinkTopic of picFromSource is set to SPICTURE|C:\.

The second statement in this procedure sets the LinkItem property of the control that will receive the data. This property is set to picUserChoice, which is the name of the control in the SPICTURE program that holds the new data.

The last statement in this procedure sets the LinkMode property of the control that will receive the data to 3-Notify Mode.

The Code Inside the *picFormSource_LinkNotify()* Event Procedure of the frmDPicture Form

The `picFromSource_LinkNotify()` procedure of the DPICTURE program is executed whenever the SPICTURE program has new data to send:

```
Sub picFromSource_LinkNotify ()
```

```
' Beep (so that the user will notice that a new
' picture is available).
Beep

' Enable the Request button (so that the user
' will be able to push it).
cmdRequest.Enabled = True

' Display inside the label a note to the user
' (in case the user didn't hear the beep).
lblInfo.Caption = "New picture is available..."
```

End Sub

The code beeps in this procedure to attract the user's attention, and it enables the Request button so that the user can push it. Finally, the caption of the label is changed to New Picture Is Available.

The Code Inside the *cmdRequest_Click()* Event Procedure of the DPICTURE Program

The cmdRequest_Click() procedure of the DPICTURE program is executed whenever the user clicks the Request button of the DPICTURE program:

Sub cmdRequest_Click ()

```
' Clear the label.
lblInfo.Caption = ""

' Disable the Request button.
cmdRequest.Enabled = False

' Request the new picture.
picFromSource.LinkRequest
```

End Sub

This procedure clears the caption of the lblInfo label and disables the Request button.

The last statement in this procedure executes the LinkRequest method, requesting the new data.

The LinkTimeout Property

The time that it takes to transfer data from one application to another depends on several factors: the amount of data to be transferred, the speed of the PC, and the resources (free memory) of the PC. Although the DPICTURE programs did not change the default value of the LinkTimeout property, you may set the LinkTimeout property of the control that receives the data in the destination application to the desired time-out value. For example, if you set the time-out to 15 seconds, and for some reason the data does not arrive within 15 seconds, the program generates a runtime error. Your program may trap the error by recognizing error number 286.

The LinkTimeout property is specified in tenths of seconds. For example, Visual Basic assigns the default value of 50 to the LinkTimeout property. This means that the time-out is 5 seconds.

You may set the LinkTimeout of the control that receives the data at design time (by setting a new value to this property from the Properties window of the control), or from within your code.

The LinkTimeout property may be set for a label, a picture box, and a text box (these are the controls that are capable of receiving data in DDE programs). To set the LinkTimeout property of a text box called txtFromSource to 60 seconds, use the following:

```
txtFromSource.LinkTimeout = 600
```

The LinkTimeout property is an integer, so the maximum value you can assign to this property is 65535 (65535/10=6553.5 seconds).

Setting the LinkTimeout property to -1 has the identical effect, setting the value of this property to 65535.

> **Note:** The default value of the LinkTimeout property (5 seconds) is appropriate in most cases. So unless you are developing a special application that requires a new setting for this property, leave the LinkTimeout property at its default value.
>
> No matter what value is assigned to the LinkTimeout property, the user may always interrupt a DDE by pressing Esc.

The S and D Programs

The previous programs demonstrated that the source application must be executed before the destination program. However, in practice it would be much more convenient to eliminate this limitation. The S and D programs illustrate how you can accomplish that.

The Visual Implementation of the S Program

As implied by its name, the S program serves as the source application.

☐ Build the frmS form of the S program according to the specifications in Table 18.5.

The completed form should look like the one shown in Figure 18.8.

Table 18.5. The properties table of the frmS form.

Object	Property	Setting
Form	**Name**	**frmS**
	Caption	The S Program
	Height	2235
	Left	1560
	LinkMode	1-Source
	Top	1020
	Width	6765
Text Box	**Name**	**txtS**
	Height	1095
	Left	0
	MultiLine	True
	ScrollBars	3-Both
	Top	0
	Width	3135
Menu	**(see Table 8.6)**	**(see Table 18.6)**

Table 18.6. The menu table of the frmS program.

Caption	Name
&File	mnuFilc
...&Exit	mnuExit
End	

Figure 18.8.
The frmS form.

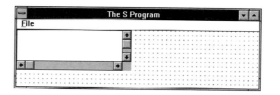

Entering the Code of the S Program

☐ Enter the following code inside the general declarations area of the frmS form:

```
' All variables MUST be declared.
Option Explicit
```

☐ Enter the following code inside the `Form_Load()` procedures of the frmS form:

```
Sub Form_Load ()

    ' Set the topic of the DDE communication.
    frmS.LinkTopic = "C:\"

End Sub
```

☐ Enter the following code inside the `Form_Resize()` procedure of the frmS form:

```
Sub Form_Resize ()

    ' Make the text box fill the entire area of the
    ' form.
    txtS.Width = frmS.ScaleWidth
    txtS.Height = frmS.ScaleHeight

End Sub
```

☐ Enter the following code inside the `mnuExit_Click()` procedure of the frmS form:

```
Sub mnuExit_Click ()

    End

End Sub
```

Executing the S Program

☐ Execute the S program.

The S program displays a text box that fills the entire area of the S form.

☐ Select Exit from the File menu to terminate the program.

The Visual Implementation of the D Program

As implied by its name, the D program serves as the destination application of the S and D programs.

☐ Build the frmD form according to the specifications in Table 18.7.

The completed form should look like the one shown in Figure 18.9.

Table 18.7. The properties table of the frmD form.

Object	Property	Setting
Form	**Name**	**frmD**
	Caption	The D Program
	Height	2190
	Left	1035
	Top	1140
	Width	7485
Text Box	**Name**	**txtD**
	Height	1095
	Left	0
	MultiLine	True
	ScrollBars	3-Both
	Text	(empty)
	Top	0
	Width	3015
Menu	**(see Table 18.8)**	**(see Table 18.8)**

Table 18.8. The menu table of the frmD form.

Caption	Name
&File	mnuFile
...&Exit	mnuExit
&Get Data	mnuGetData
...&Request	mnuRequest

Figure 18.9.
The frmD form.

Entering the Code of the D Program

☐ Enter the following code inside the general declarations section of the frmD from:

```
' All variables MUST be declared.
Option explicit
```

☐ Enter the following code inside the `Form_Load()` procedure of the frmD form:

```
Sub Form_Load ()

    Dim ID

    ' If an error will occur, then execute the
    ' code starting at the line: HandleError.
    On Error GoTo HandleError

    ' Set the Topic, Item, and Mode of the DDE
    ' communication.
    txtD.LinkMode = 0
    txtD.LinkTopic = "S¦C:\"
    txtD.LinkItem = "txtS"
    txtD.LinkMode = 2
    Exit Sub

HandleError:
    ' Error occurred. Is it error 282?
    ' (error 282 is generated if DDE cannot be
    '  established).
    If Err = 282 Then
        ' Load the source application.
        ' The following statement assumes that the
        ' S.EXE program resides in c:\vbprog\ch18.
        ID = Shell("C:\VBPROG\CH18\S.EXE")
        Resume
    Else
        MsgBox ("Error")
        Stop
    End If

End Sub
```

☐ Enter the following code inside the `Form_Resize()` procedure of the frmD form:

```
Sub Form_Resize ()

    ' Make the text box fill the entire area of the
    ' form.
    txtD.Width = frmD.ScaleWidth
    txtD.Height = frmD.ScaleHeight

End Sub
```

☐ Enter the following code inside the `mnuRequest_Click()` procedure of the frmD form:

```
Sub mnuRequest_Click ()
```

```
' User selected Request from the Get Data menu.
txtD.LinkRequest
```

End Sub

☐ Enter the following code inside the `mnuExit_Click()` procedure of the frmD form:

Sub mnuExit_Click ()

```
    End
```

End Sub

Executing the D and S Programs

☐ Make sure that the S program is not running.

☐ Execute the D program.

The D program detects that the S program is not running and executes it.

Once the S program is running, the DDE is established. To see how the DDE works:

☐ Type something inside the text box of the S program.

☐ Switch to the D program and select Request from the Get Data menu.

The program responds by transferring the text from the S program to the text box of the D program.

How the S and D Programs Work

The S and D programs communicate with each other via DDE. The D program tries to establish the DDE, and if an error occurred, the program assumes that the error occurred because the S program is not running, and it executes the S program.

The Code Inside the *Form_Load()* Event Procedure of the frmS Form

The `Form_Load()` procedure of the frmS form is executed when the frmS form is loaded:

Sub Form_Load ()

```
    ' Set the topic of the DDE communication.
    frmS.LinkTopic = "C:\"
```

End Sub

The code inside this procedure sets the LinkTopic of the DDE communication.

The Code Inside the *Form_Resize()* Event Procedure of the frmS Form

The Form_Resize() procedure is executed whenever the frmS form pops up or is resized:

```
Sub Form_Resize ()

    ' Make the text box fill the entire area of the
    ' form.
    txtS.Width = frmS.ScaleWidth
    txtS.Height = frmS.ScaleHeight

End Sub
```

The code inside this procedure sets the Width and Height properties of the txtS text box so that it fills the entire area of the frmS form.

The Code Inside the *Form_Load()* Event Procedure of the frmD Form

The Form_Load() procedure is executed when the frmD form is loaded:

```
Sub Form_Load ()

    Dim ID

    ' If an error will occur, then execute the
    ' code starting at the line: HandleError.
    On Error GoTo HandleError

    ' Set the Topic, Item, and Mode of the DDE
    ' communication.
    txtD.LinkMode = 0
    txtD.LinkTopic = "S|Dummy"
    txtD.LinkItem = "txtS"
    txtD.LinkMode = 2
    Exit Sub

HandleError:
    ' Error occurred. Is it error 282?
    ' (error 282 is generated if DDE cannot be
    ' established).
    If Err = 282 Then
        ' Load the source application.
        ' The following statement assumes that the
        ' S.EXE program resides in c:\vbprog\ch18.
        ID = Shell("C:\VBPROG\CH18\S.EXE")
        Resume
    Else
        MsgBox ("Error")
        Stop
    End If
End Sub
```

This procedure sets the LinkTopic, LinkItem, and LinkMode properties of the txtD text box. Before setting these DDE-related properties, the procedure sets an error trap:

```
On Error GoTo HandleError
```

which means that if a runtime error occurs, the next statement to be executed is at the line where the HandleError label is located.

The code starting at the HandleError label checks whether the runtime error occurred due to error number 282. Error number 282 is generated whenever the destination application fails to establish a DDE communication with the source application. Of course, there may be numerous reasons a DDE link fails, but in most cases the reason for the failure is that the source application is not running. So once the code under the HandleError label verifies that the error number is 282, it loads the source application by using the Shell() function:

```
ID = Shell("C:\VBPROG\CH18\S.EXE")
```

(The Shell() function returns a task identification number, but this returned value is not used in the D program.)

If the runtime error occurred due to other reasons, the Stop statement is executed.

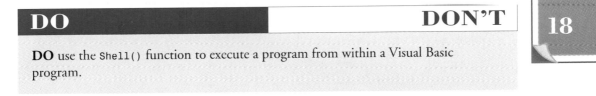

DO   **DON'T**

DO use the Shell() function to execute a program from within a Visual Basic program.

The Code Inside the *Form_Resize()* Event Procedure of the frmD Form

The Form_Resize() procedure of the frmD form is executed whenever the form pops up and whenever the form is resized:

```
Sub Form_Resize ()

    ' Make the text box fill the entire area of the
    ' form.
    txtD.Width = frmD.ScaleWidth
    txtD.Height = frmD.ScaleHeight

End Sub
```

This procedure sets the Width and Height properties of the txtD text form so that it fills the entire area of the form.

The Code Inside the *mnuRequest_Click()* Event Procedure of the frmD Form

The mnuRequest_Click() procedure is executed whenever the user selects Request from the Get Data menu:

```
Sub mnuRequest_Click ()

    ' User selected Request from the Get Data menu.
    txtD.LinkRequest

End Sub
```

This procedure uses the LinkRequest method to request a data transfer. Recall that the LinkMode property of the text box was set to 2-Manual Mode in the Form_Load() procedure of the frmD form, which means that the data is not transferred automatically.

Poking Data

So far all the examples in this chapter have included a pair of programs: a source program that supplies the data and a destination program that requests and receives the data. However, it is also possible to cause the destination application to send data to the source application. This is accomplished using the LinkPoke method.

Enhancing the D Program

Now enhance the D program so it sends data to the source program.

☐ Add the Send Data menu title and the Poke item to the menu system of the D program. The new menu table is shown in Table 18.9.

Table 18.9. The menu table of the enhanced version of frmD form.

Caption	Name
&File	mnuFile
...&Exit	mnuExit
&Get Data	mnuGetData
...&Request	mnuRequest
&Send Data	mnuSendData
...&Poke	mnuPoke

Entering the Code of the Enhanced Version of the D Program

☐ Add the following code to the mnuPoke_Click() procedure of the frmD form:

```
Sub mnuPoke_Click ()

    ' Transfer the content of the text box to the
    ' source application.
```

```
    txtD.LinkPoke
```

```
End Sub
```

Executing the Enhanced Version of the D Program

☐ Execute the D program.

To clearly see what's going on, minimize and/or close all applications except the S and D programs.

☐ Type something inside the text box of the S program, switch to the D program, and select Request from the Get Data menu.

The D program responds by transferring the text from the S program to the D program.

☐ Type something inside the text box of the D program, and select Poke from the Send Data menu.

The program responds by transferring the text from the D program to the S program. (Switch to the S program and observe that its text box is filled with the contents of the text box of the D program.)

The Code Inside the *mnuPoke_Click()* Event Procedure

The mnuPoke_Click() procedure is executed whenever the user selects Poke from the Send Data menu:

```
Sub mnuPoke_Click ()

    ' Transfer the content of the text box to the
    ' source application.
    txtD.LinkPoke

End Sub
```

The LinkPoke method is used to cause the text of the txtD text box to be transferred to the txtS text box of the S program.

Trapping DDE-Related Runtime Errors

The S and D programs illustrate how you may trap the runtime error 282. However, during a DDE session, there may be other reasons for runtime errors. To trap the error, you may use the LinkError event procedure. For example, in the D program, whenever there is a runtime error that is DDE-related, the txtD_LinkError() event procedure is executed:

```
Sub txtD_LinkError (LinkErr As Integer)

    ...............................
    ... Here you insert the code ...
    ... that corresponds to the  ...
    ... error.                   ...
    ...............................
```

End Sub

The argument of this procedure is an integer that represents the nature of the error. The possible values that LinkErr can have are 1, 6, 7, 8, and 11:

- Error number 1 means that the format of the data to be transferred is not the same in the source and the destination applications. It is normal to receive several successive errors of this type because when establishing the DDE session, several data formats are tried until the source and destination applications agree on the format.

- Error number 6 means that the LinkMode of the source application was changed to 0 (turn off DDE), but the destination application is still involved in DDE activities.

- Error number 7 means that the source application is already involved in 128 separate DDE links. Because the maximum number of links that the source application may establish is 128, this error is generated.

- Error number 8 means that during automatic link mode, or during the execution of the LinkRequest method, there was a failure to update the data of the receiving control.

- Error number 11 means that there is not enough memory to carry out the DDE operation.

In a similar manner, the DDE-related runtime error that occurs in the source application causes the Form_LinkError() event procedures to be executed:

Sub Form_LinkError (LinkErr As Integer)

```
    ...............................
    ... Here you insert the code ...
    ... that corresponds to this ...
    ... error.                   ...
    ...............................
```

End Sub

The meanings of the error numbers are the same for the destination application and the source application, except for error number 8. In the Form_LinkErr() procedure, error number 8 means that the destination application attempted to poke data into a control of the source application and the operation failed.

Emulating Keystrokes

As discussed, in order to establish DDE communication between two programs, the programs must be written in a way that supports DDE. However, it is also possible to establish some communication with any Windows program (even non-DDE programs). Non-DDE communication consists of sending keystrokes from one program to another program.

Now write a program called NONDDE1. This program illustrates how keystrokes are sent from a non-DDE Visual Basic program to the Notepad program that is shipped with Windows.

The Visual Implementation of the NONDDE1 Program

☐ Open a new project, save the form of the project as NONDDE1.FRM, and save the make file of the project as NONDDE1.MAK.

☐ Build the frmNonDDE1 form according to the specifications in Table 18.10.

The completed form should look like the one shown in Figure 18.10.

18

Table 18.10. The properties table of the frmNonDDE1 form.

Object	Property	Setting
Form	**Name**	**frmNonDDE1**
	Caption	The NonDDE1 Program
	Height	3495
	Left	1020
	Top	1410
	Width	7380
Command Button	**Name**	**cmdSend**
	Caption	&Send
	Height	495
	Left	1920
	Top	2520
	Width	1215
Text Box	**Name**	**txtUserArea**
	Height	1935
	Left	360

continues

Table 18.10. continued

Object	Property	Setting
	MultiLine	True
	ScrollBars	3-Both
	Text	(empty)
	Top	360
	Width	6615
Command Button	**Name**	**cmdExit**
	Caption	&Exit
	Height	495
	Left	4560
	Top	2520
	Width	1215

Figure 18.10.
The frmNonDDE1 form.

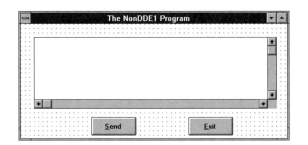

Entering the Code of the NONDDE1 Program

☐ Enter the following code inside the general declarations section of the frmNonDDE1 form:

```
' All variables MUST be declared.
Option Explicit
```

☐ Enter the following code inside the Form_Load() procedure of the frmNonDDE1 form:

```
Sub Form_Load ()

    Dim ID

    ' Execute the Notepad program.
    ID = Shell("Notepad.exe", 1)

End Sub
```

☐ Enter the following code inside the `cmdSend_Click()` procedure of the frmNonDDE1 form:

```
Sub cmdSend_Click ()

    ' Make the Notepad program the active program.
    AppActivate "Notepad - (Untitled)"

    ' Send characters to the Notepad program.
    SendKeys txtUserArea.Text, True

End Sub
```

☐ Enter the following code inside the `cmdExit_Click()` procedure of the frmNonDDE1 form:

```
Sub cmdExit_Click ()

    End

End Sub
```

☐ Save the project.

☐ Create the NONDDE1.EXE file (select Make EXE File from the File menu and save the file as NONDDE1.EXE).

Executing the NONDDE1 Program

To be able to see what's going on during the execution of the NONDDE1 program, close/minimize all other windows.

☐ Execute the NONDDE1 program.

The Notepad program pops up.

☐ Type something inside the text box of the NONDDE1 program, then click the Send button.

The text you typed is transferred to the Notepad program (see Figure 18.11).

How the NONDDE1 Program Works

The code of the NONDDE1 program executes the Notepad program by using the `Shell()` function and the `SendKeys` statement to send characters to the Notepad program.

Figure 18.11.
The Notepad program.

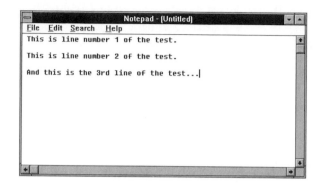

The Code Inside the *Form_Load()* Event Procedure of the frmNonDDE1 Form

The Form_Load() procedure is executed whenever the frmNonDDE1 form is loaded:

```
Sub Form_Load ()

    Dim ID

    ' Execute the Notepad program.
    ID = Shell("Notepad.exe", 1)

End Sub
```

This procedure uses the Shell() function to load the Notepad program. The first argument of the Shell() function is a string that contains the name of the program to be executed. The second argument is an optional argument that specifies the window style of the program to be executed. A value of 1 means that the program to be executed will be shown with a normal window.

The Code Inside the *cmdSend_Click()* Event Procedure of the frmNonDDE1 Form

The cmdSend_Click() procedure is executed whenever you click the Send button:

```
Sub cmdSend_Click ()

    ' Make the Notepad program the active program.
    AppActivate "Notepad - (Untitled)"

    ' Send characters to the Notepad program.
    SendKeys txtUserArea.Text, True

End Sub
```

This procedure makes the Notepad program the active application with the AppActivate statement:

```
AppActivate "Notepad - (Untitled)"
```

The argument of the `AppActivate` statement is the title of the program to be activated. It is important to supply this argument exactly as it appears in the window title of the program to be activated. Upon startup of the Notepad program, the window title that appears is the following:

```
Notepad - (Untitled)
```

For example, if you supply this:

```
Notepad- (Untitled)
```

as the argument of the `AppActivate` statement, you get a runtime error, because there should be space between the word `Notepad` and the `-`.

The `AppActivate` argument is not case sensitive. The following statement is valid for activating the Notepad program:

```
NoTePaD - (UnTITled)
```

The second statement in the `cmdSend_Click()` procedure sends characters to the currently active application with the `SendKeys` statement:

```
SendKeys txtUserArea.Text, True
```

The characters that are sent are the contents of the `txtUserArea`.

It is important to understand that these characters are transferred to the currently active application. This explains why you activated the Notepad program before issuing the `SendKeys` statement.

After you send the keys to Notepad, the active program is still the Notepad program. To make the NONDDE1 program the active program you have to open the system menu (by clicking the minus icon that appears on the upper-left corner of the Notepad window), selecting the Switch to item, and selecting the NONDDE1 program.

Alternatively, you can add the following statement after the `SendKeys` statement in the `cmdSend_Click()` procedure:

```
AppActivate "The NONDDE1 Program"
```

This statement makes NONDDE1 the active program.

The *SendKeys* Statement

As demonstrated in the NONDDE1 program, the `SendKeys` statement is used to send characters to the currently active program. The True argument causes these keys to be processed before the program returns to the `cmdSend_Click()` procedure. This means that the NONDDE1 program yields to the program that receives the characters, letting it execute its code. If you supply False as the second argument of the `SendKeys` statement, control is returned to the NONDDE1 program immediately after the characters are sent. (In the case of the Notepad program, the second argument of the SendKeys statement can be True or False because Notepad does not have to execute any code.)

You can send the special keys using the codes specified in Table 18.11. For example, to send the Alt+S key, use the following:

```
%{S}
```

When you press Alt+S in Notepad, the Search menu is opened.

Table 18.11. The code of the special keys when used with the SendKeys statement.

Key	Use in SendKeys
Shift	+
Ctrl	^ (above the 6 key)
Alt	%
Backspace	{BACKSPACE}
Break	{BREAK}
CapsLock	{CAPLOCKS}
Clear	{CLEAR}
Del	{DELETE}
Down arrow	{DOWN}
End	{END}
Enter	{ENTER}
Esc	{ESCAPE}
Help	{HELP}
Home	{HOME}
Ins	{INSERT}
Left arrow	{LEFT}
Num Lock	{NUMLOCK}
Page Down	{PGDN}
Page Up	{PGUP}
Print Screen	{PRTSC}
Right Arrow	{RIGHT}
Scroll Lock	{SCROLLLOCK}
Tab	{TAB}

Key	Use in SendKeys
Up Arrow	{UP}
F1	{F1}
...	...
...	...
...	...
F16	{F16}

To send Alt+S from the NONDDE1 program to the Notepad program do the following:

☐ Type %{S} in the text box of the NONDDE1 program and then click the Send button.

The Notepad program responds by opening its Search menu (see Figure 18.12).

Figure 18.12.
Opening the Search menu of Notepad.

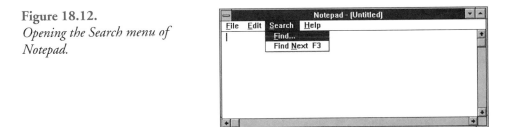

To select Find from the Search menu of Notepad, the user has to press Alt+S and then press the F key. To accomplish this from the NONDDE1 program do the following:

☐ Type %{S}F in the text box of the NONDDE1 program and click the Send button.

Sending Keystrokes to Yourself

As stated, the SendKeys statement sends the keys to the currently active program. What happens when the currently active program is the NONDDE1 program? As expected, the keys are sent to themselves!

Does sending keystrokes to your program have any practical uses? Sure. For example, you may build a demo program or a tutorial program that demonstrates what happens when a sequence of keystrokes is pressed. The NONDDE2 program demonstrates how a Visual Basic program can send keystrokes to itself.

The Visual Implementation of the NONDDE2 Program

☐ Open a new project, save the form of the project as NONDDE2.FRM, and save the make file of the project as NONDDE2.MAK.

☐ Build the frmNonDDE2 form according to the specifications in Table 18.12.

The completed form should look like the one shown in Figure 18.13.

Table 18.12. The properties table of the frmNonDDE2 form.

Object	Property	Setting
Form	Name	frmNonDDE2
	Caption	The NonDDE2 program
	Height	2205
	Left	1035
	Top	1140
	Width	7485
Command Button	Name	cmdBeep
	Caption	&Beep
	Height	495
	Left	1080
	Top	1080
	Width	1215
Command Button	Name	cmdSend
	Caption	&Send
	Height	495
	Left	3000
	Top	1080
	Width	1215
Text Box	Name	txtUserArea
	Height	495
	Left	240
	MultiLine	True
	Text	(empty)

Object	Property	Setting
	Top	360
	Width	6855
Command Button	**Name**	**cmdExit**
	Caption	&Exit
	Height	495
	Left	4800
	Top	1080
	Width	1215

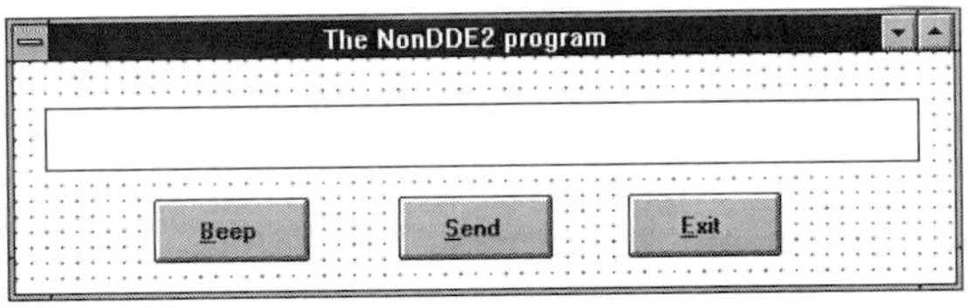

Figure 18.13.
The frmNonDDE2 form.

Entering the Code of the NONDDE2 Program

☐ Enter the following code inside the general declarations section of the frmNonDDE2 form:

```
' All variables MUST be declared.
Option Explicit
```

☐ Enter the following code inside the cmdSend_Click() procedure of the frmNonDDE2 form:

```
Sub cmdSend_Click ()

    ' Make sure this program is the active program.
    AppActivate "The NonDDE2 Program"

    ' Send the text to this program that is
    ' currently inside the text box.
    SendKeys txtUserArea.Text, True

End Sub
```

☐ Enter the following code inside the cmdBeep_Click() procedure of the frmNonDDE2 form:

```
Sub cmdBeep_Click ()

    Beep

End Sub
```

☐ Enter the following code inside the `cmdExit_Click()` procedure of the frmNonDDE2 form:

```
Sub cmdExit_Click ()

    End

End Sub
```

Executing the NONDDE2 Program

☐ Execute the NONDDE2 program.

☐ Click the Beep button.

The PC beeps.

☐ Press Alt+B.

The PC beeps (because the caption of the Beep button is &Beep).

☐ Type the following in the text box of the NONDDE2 program and click the Send button:

```
%{B}
```

The PC beeps!

The Code Inside the *cmdSend_Click()* Event Procedure

The `cmdSend_Click` procedure is executed whenever you click the Send button:

```
Sub cmdSend_Click ()

    ' Make sure this program is the active program.
    AppActivate "The NonDDE2 Program"

    ' Send the text to this program that is
    ' currently inside the text box.
    SendKeys txtUserArea.Text, True

End Sub
```

The first statement in this procedure makes sure that the currently active program is the NONDDE2 program. (This statement is really not necessary because even if you omit this statement, the currently active program is the NONDDE2 program. Nevertheless, we included this statement just to emphasize that we are sending keystrokes to ourselves.)

The second statement in this procedure executes the `SendKeys` statement to send whatever characters are inside the text box.

If you type %{B} in the text box, this text is translated into Alt+B (see Table 18.12), which is the same as pressing the Beep button.

The code inside the cmdBeep_Click() event procedure contains the Beep statement, which causes the PC to beep.

Summary

In this chapter you have learned about the DDE features that are available in Visual Basic. You have learned how to accept and transfer data from and to other DDE programs. The data may be text, bitmaps, icons, or metafiles.

You have also learned how to use the Shell() function to execute the source application from within the destination application; how to send data from the destination application to the source application by using the LinkPoke method; how to trap DDE-related runtime errors; and how to emulate keystrokes.

Q&A

18

Q When should I use the DDE Manual mode, and when should I use the DDE Automatic mode?

A The Automatic mode causes the data to be exchanged automatically at the moment the data changes in the source application. This is OK for text, because text is transferred rather quickly.

Now suppose that your user works with a program that enables him or her to change a picture, and that this picture is copied via DDE communication to another program. If the picture is large, every time the user changes a pixel in the source application the whole picture is transferred to the destination program. This might take a long time (especially if the picture is large) and might be very annoying to the user. In such applications, it is better to use the Manual mode and to write the destination program in such a way that when the user returns to the destination program, a message is waiting, indicating that a new picture is ready.

Quiz

1. DDE communication is possible between which of the following:
   a. Word for Windows and Excel
   b. Word for Windows and a Visual Basic program
   c. Excel and a Visual Basic program
   d. Two Visual Basic programs

     e. All of the above

2. The `Shell()` function provides which of the following:

     a. A good seafood dinner

     b. A means to execute any program from within a Visual Basic program

Exercise

What should you type inside the text box of the NONDDE2 program so that clicking the Send button terminates the program?

Quiz Answers

    1. e

    2. b

Exercise Answer

To terminate the program do the following:

☐ Type `&{E}` inside the text box

☐ Click the Send button

The sequence %{E} is translated to Alt+E (see Table 18.11). The caption of the Exit button is &Exit, and pressing Alt+E terminates the program. Typing %{E} inside the text box and clicking the Send button causes the program to send the Alt+E keystrokes to itself, which has the same effect as clicking the Exit button.

19

Installing Your Applications

In this chapter you'll learn how to distribute and install your applications into your user's machine. One way to do that is simply to copy all your files into a disk and instruct your user to copy the files from your disk into the PC. You also have to instruct your user to create a program group for your application in the Program Manager of Windows. Alternatively, you can write a program that does the installation automatically. Such a program should let the user choose the drive and directory in which the application should be installed, copy the files from your disk into the selected directory, check whether the user's hard drive has sufficient space, create the program group in the Program Manager of Windows, update the user WIN.INI file, and complete a variety of other tasks.

As you may realize, writing such a program involves a lot of details. Luckily, the Visual Basic package (starting with Version 3.0) includes the programs that perform all these tasks for you.

The Installation Programs

To create your distribution disk, you have to copy to it various files. One of these files is an EXE file that was written with Visual Basic. The name of the Visual Basic project is SETUP1.MAK, and it resides in the directory C:\VB\SETUPKIT\SETUP1. To create the SETUP1.EXE file, you have to load the SETUP1.MAK project with Visual Basic and make several changes to the SETUP1.FRM file (you have to customize the file). Once you finish customizing the SETUP1.FRM file, you have to create an EXE file by selecting Create EXE File from the File menu. You may save the EXE file by any name except SETUP.EXE. This chapter assumes that you'll save the file as SETUP1.EXE.

As stated, besides copying SETUP1.EXE to your disk, you need to copy to the disk other files. The following sections examine each of these files.

Preparing the Distribution Disk

☐ Format a disk.

☐ Insert the disk into your A: or B: drive. (This disk serves as the distribution disk. In the following sections, you'll be instructed to copy files onto this disk.)

Preparing the Application to Be Distributed

Assume that the application you are distributing is the MOON program from Chapter 7, "Graphic Controls." Also assume that the MOON project resides in the directory C:\VBPROG\CH07.

☐ Start Visual Basic.

☐ Load the MOON.MAK project.

☐ Make sure that the project window of MOON contains only the file MOON.FRM, because the MOON program uses only the MOON.FRM file. It makes no sense to distribute files that are not used by the program.

If the project window of MOON.MAK contains VBX files or any other files, remove them. To remove files from the project window, highlight the file to be removed in the project window and select Remove File from the File menu.

Repeat removing files from the project window until the project window contains only the MOON.FRM file, as shown in Figure 19.1.

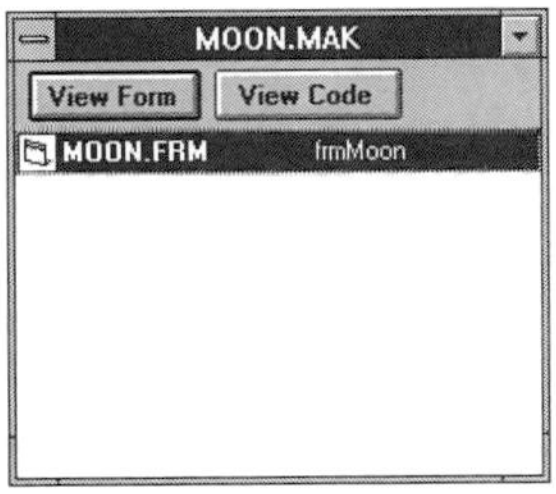

Figure 19.1.
The project window of the MOON program.

MOON.MAK	
View Form	View Code
MOON.FRM	frmMoon

☐ Run the MOON program and make sure that it works properly.

☐ Terminate the program by clicking the Exit button.

Create an icon for the MOON program as follows:

☐ Highlight MOON.FRM in the project window and click the View Form button.

Visual Basic responds by displaying the MOON.FRM form.

☐ Select Properties from the Window menu.

Visual Basic responds by displaying the properties window of the form.

☐ Double-click the Icon property in the properties windows.

Visual Basic responds by displaying the Load Icon dialog box shown in Figure 19.2.

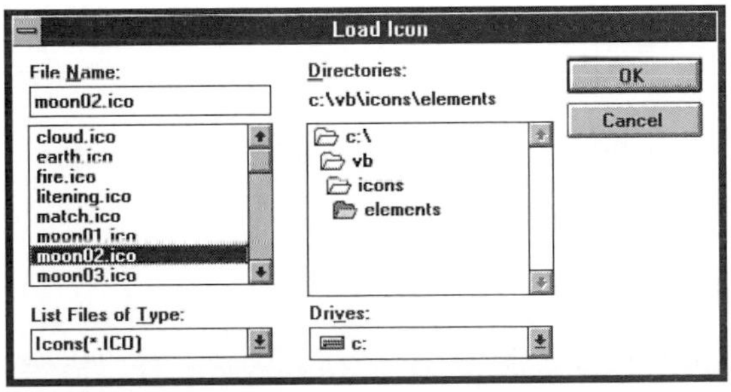

19

Figure 19.2.
The Load Icon dialog box.

Load Icon

File Name:
moon02.ico

cloud.ico
earth.ico
fire.ico
litening.ico
match.ico
moon01.ico
moon02.ico
moon03.ico

List Files of Type:
Icons(*.ICO)

Directories:
c:\vb\icons\elements

c:\
vb
icons
elements

Drives:
c:

OK
Cancel

☐ Select the icon MOON02.ICO that resides in the C:\VB\ICONS\ELEMENTS directory and then click the OK button.

☐ Save the project (select Save Project from the File menu).

☐ Run the MOON program again.

When you click the down arrow icon that appears in the top-right corner of the MOON window, the MOON window should be minimized to the MOON02.ICO icon, as shown in Figure 19.3.

Figure 19.3.
Minimizing the MOON program.

The icon of the Moon program

☐ Terminate the MOON program.

☐ Create an EXE file for the MOON program by selecting Make EXE File from the File menu.

Visual Basic responds by displaying the Make EXE File dialog box shown in Figure 19.4.

Note that the right side of the Make EXE File dialog box shows the icon of the application (which is the MOON02.ICO icon that you selected in the previous step).

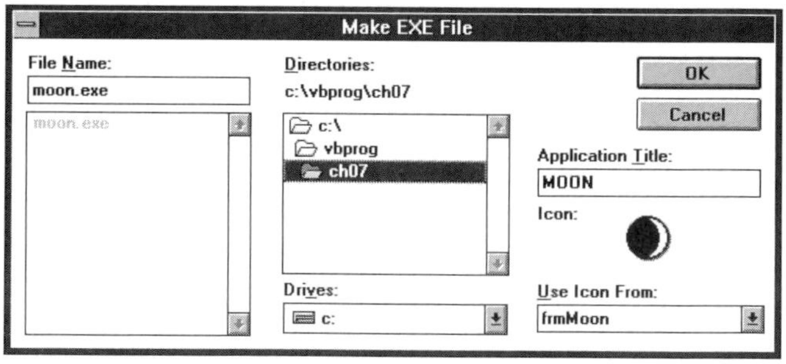

Figure 19.4.
The Make EXE File dialog box.

☐ Save the EXE file as MOON.EXE in the directory C:\VBPROG\CH07.

☐ Exit Visual Basic.

☐ Select Run from the File menu of the Program Manager of Windows.

Windows responds by displaying the Run dialog box.

- [ ] Select Browse and then select the MOON.EXE file.

- [ ] Click the OK button.

- [ ] Make sure that the MOON.EXE program operates properly.

- [ ] Terminate the MOON.EXE program by clicking the Exit button.

The SETUP.LST File

You must include the SETUP.LST file in your distribution disk. The SETUP.LST file is a text file that contains a list of all the files that should be copied from the disk to your user's \WINDOWS and \WINDOWS\SYSTEM directories.

The files in the list are listed line after line—each file is in a separate line. The very first line must contain the name of the Visual Basic installation program. For example, if the name of the installation program is SETUP1.EXE, the first line in the SETUP.LST file must be SETUP1.EX_.

Use the following steps to create the SETUP.LST file:

- [ ] Start Notepad (which usually resides in the Accessories group) or any other word processor that is capable of saving text files.

- [ ] Type the following lines:

```
SETUP1.EX_
VER.DL_
VBRUN300.DL_
SETUPKIT.DL_
```

- [ ] Save the file as SETUP.LST into your distribution disk. (The files that appear in the SETUP.LST file are discussed later in this chapter.)

The order of the files in the SETUP.LST is not important, except that the first line of the file must be SETUP1.EX_.

The SETUP.EXE File

The SETUP.EXE program is the program your user executes in order to install your application. This preinstallation program is called the *bootstrap program*.

DO	DON'T

DON'T get confused! There is a file (which you have to customize) called SETUP1.EXE that is written in Visual Basic, and there is another file, SETUP.EXE, that comes with the Visual Basic package. The SETUP.EXE file resides in the C:\VB\SETUPKIT\KITFILES directory.

☐ Copy the file SETUP.EXE from the C:\VB\SETUPKIT\KITFILES directory to your distribution disk.

To install your application, your user executes the SETUP.EXE program. The SETUP.EXE program copies all the overhead files from your distribution disk to your user's hard drive and then automatically executes the SETUP1.EXE program.

Compressing Files

In order to fit as many bytes as possible on the distribution disk, you have to compress the files. To compress files, you have to use the COMPRESS.EXE utility that comes with Visual Basic Version 3.0. This utility resides in the C:\VB\SETUPKIT\KITFILES directory.

To use the COMPRESS utility, your PC must be at the DOS command line:

☐ Double-click the MS-DOS prompt icon that appears in the Main group of the Program Manager.

> *Windows responds by taking the PC to a DOS shell (you'll see the DOS command line).*

☐ Log in to the C:\VBPROG\CH07 directory by typing the following at the DOS prompt:

```
CD C:\VBPROG\CH07   {Enter}
```

Compress the MOON.EXE file as follows:

☐ At the DOS prompt type this:

```
C:\VB\SETUPKIT\KITFILES\COMPRESS -r MOON.EXE {Enter}
```

The COMPRESS.EXE utility compresses the MOON.EXE to a file called MOON.EX_ (see Figure 19.5).

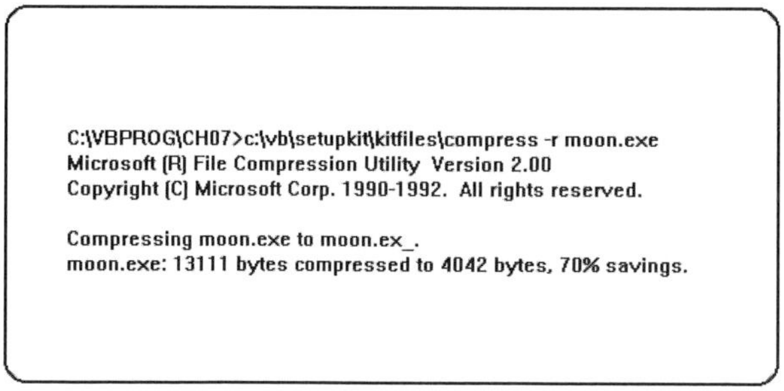

Figure 19.5.
Using the COMPRESS.EXE utility.

```
C:\VBPROG\CH07>c:\vb\setupkit\kitfiles\compress -r moon.exe
Microsoft (R) File Compression Utility  Version 2.00
Copyright (C) Microsoft Corp. 1990-1992.  All rights reserved.

Compressing moon.exe to moon.ex_.
moon.exe: 13111 bytes compressed to 4042 bytes, 70% savings.
```

☐ Copy the MOON.EX_ file to the distribution disk:

```
Copy MOON.EX_   a:\   {Enter}
```

or

```
Copy MOON.EX_   b:\   {Enter}
```

You now need to compress two more files.

The first file to be compressed is the file VBRUN300.DLL that resides in the C:\WINDOWS\SYSTEM directory. Use the following steps to compress this file:

☐ Log in to the directory C:\WINDOWS\SYSTEM by typing the following at the DOS prompt:

```
CD C:\WINDOWS\SYSTEM   {Enter}
```

To compress the VBRUN300.DLL file, at the DOS prompt type this:

```
C:\VB\SETUPKIT\KITFILES\COMPRESS -r VBRUN300.DLL {Enter}
```

The COMPRESS.EXE utility compresses the VBRUN300.DLL to a file called VBRUN300.DL_.

☐ Copy the VBRUN300.DL_ file to the distribution disk:

```
Copy VBRUN300.DL_   a:\   {Enter}
```

or

```
Copy VBRUN300.DL_   b:\   {Enter}
```

The second file to be compressed is the file SETUPKIT.DLL that resides in the C:\VB\SETUPKIT\KITFILES directory. Use the following steps to compress this file:

☐ Log in to the C:\VB\SETUPKIT\KITFILES directory by typing the following at the DOS prompt:

```
CD C:\VB\SETUPKIT\KITFILES   {Enter}
```

To compress the SETUPKIT.DLL file, at the DOS prompt type this:

```
COMPRESS -r SETUPKIT.DLL {Enter}
```

The COMPRESS.EXE utility compresses the SETUPKIT.DLL to a file called SETUPKIT.DL_.

☐ Copy the SETUPKIT.DL_ file to the distribution disk:

```
Copy SETUPKIT.DL_   a:\   {Enter}
```

or

```
Copy SETUPKIT.DL_   b:\   {Enter}
```

19

> **Note:** The files SETUP.LST and SETUP.EXE that you already copied to the
> distribution disk are not compressed. These files must not be compressed.

As you can see from the list of files in the SETUP.LST file, you also need to copy the file
VER.DL_ to the distribution disk. The name of the file is VER.DL_. However, this file should
not be compressed (even though the file extension is DL_). You may find the file VER.DLL in
the C:\WINDOWS\SYSTEM directory.

☐ Log in to the C:\WINDOWS\SYSTEM directory by typing the following at the DOS
prompt:

```
CD C:\WINDOWS\SYSTEM  {Enter}
```

☐ Copy the file VER.DLL to the distribution disk as VER.DL_ by typing the following at
the DOS prompt:

```
COPY VER.DLL  a:\VER.DL_  {Enter}
```

or

```
COPY VER.DLL  b:\VER.DL_  {Enter}
```

☐ To return to Windows, at the DOS prompt type this:

```
EXIT {Enter}
```

Customizing the SETUP1 Project

You have finished copying all the necessary files into the distribution disk, except the file
SETUP1.EX_. Now customize this file.

Use the following steps to customize the SETUP1.MAK project:

☐ Start Visual Basic.

☐ Load the SETUP1.MAK file by selecting Open Project from the File menu.

Visual Basic responds by displaying the Open Project dialog box.

☐ Select the file C:\VB\SETUPKIT\SETUP1\SETUP1.MAK and click the OK button.

Visual Basic responds by loading the SETUP1.MAK file.

Now customize the SETUP1.FRM file:

☐ Highlight SETUP1.FRM in the project window.

☐ Click the View Code button that appears at the top-right corner of the project window.

Visual Basic responds by displaying the code window of the SETUP1.FRM file.

☐ Display the general declarations section of the SETUP1.FRM and note the following constants that appear in the general declarations section of the SETUP1.FRM:

```
Const APPNAME = "Loan Application"
Const APPDIR = "C:\LOAN"  ' The default install directory
Const fDataAccess% = False
Const fODBC% = False
Const fBtrieve% = False
Const fOLE2% = False
' Set the total uncompressed file sizes
' by adding the sizes of the files
' Files that go into WINDOWS and SYSTEM directory
Const WINSYSNEEDED = 40896
' Files that don't go into the WINDOWS or SYSTEM directory
Const OTHERNEEDED = 12555
```

Customizing the Constants

The first constant is this:

```
Const APPNAME = "Loan Application"
```

You have to change the constant as follows:

☐ Change the APPNAME constant to this:

```
Const APPNAME = "The MOON Application"
```

☐ Change the second constant to this:

```
Const APPDIR = "C:\MOON"  ' The default install directory
```

The SETUP program suggests to the user the C:\MOON directory as the default directory in which the MOON program will be installed.

☐ The last two constants represent the number of bytes of the uncompressed files that will be copied from the distribution disk to the hard drive.

The first constant, WINSYSNEEDED, contains the number of bytes in the uncompressed files that will be copied into the \WINDOWS directory and the \WINDOWS\SYSTEM directory (that is, some of the files in the distribution disk are copied to the \WINDOWS and \WINDOWS\SYSTEM directories).

The second constant, OTHERNEEDED, contains the number of bytes in the files that will copied to the directory where the MOON program will be installed (that is, the size of the uncompressed MOON.EXE file).

Based on these two constants, the SETUP program makes a determination of whether the user has sufficient hard drive space to install the program.

☐ Leave the values of the WINSYSNEEDED and OTHERNEEDED constants at their current values (these values are good for the MOON program).

Customizing the *Form_Load()* Procedure

☐ Display the Form_Load() procedure of the SETUP1.FRM file.

☐ Select Find from the Edit menu, search for the string PromptForNextDisk, and then change the argument of the PromptForNextDisk() function as follows:

```
If Not PromptForNextDisk(1, SourcePath$ + "MOON.EX_") Then GoTo ErrorSetup
```

During the installation, the preceding statement checks whether the file MOON.EXE exists on the disk. If the file does not exist, the user has the wrong disk in the drive and the installation program prompts the user to insert the correct disk.

Now customize the argument of the CopyFile() function that appears several lines below the PromptForDisk() function:

☐ Change the argument of the CopyFile() function as follows:

```
If Not CopyFile(SourcePath$, destPath$,
        ➡ "MOON.EX_", "MOON.EXE") Then GoTo ErrorSetup
```

The preceding statement copies the MOON.EX_ file to the directory that the user chooses during the installation process.

In the case of the MOON program, the MOON.EX_ file is the only file that has to be copied into this directory. However, if there is a need to copy more files, include more CopyFile() statements. For example, if your application needs to copy the file ABC.BMP to the same directory where MOON.EXE resides, add the following statement:

```
If Not CopyFile(SourcePath$, destPath$, "ABC.BM_",  "ABC.BMP") Then GoTo ErrorSetup
```

Don't forget to compress the file ABC.BMP to the file ABC.BM_ with the COMPRESS.EXE utility, and, of course, to copy ABC.BM_ to the distribution disk.

You may repeat the process, adding more CopyFile() statements as necessary. For example, the following three statements copy the files MOON.EX_, ABC.BM_, and DEF.IC_ to the directory where the user selected to install the application:

```
If Not CopyFile(SourcePath$, destPath$, "MOON.EX_",
        ➡ "MOON.EXE") Then GoTo ErrorSetup

If Not CopyFile(SourcePath$, destPath$, "ABC.BM_", "ABC.BMP") Then GoTo ErrorSetup

If Not CopyFile(SourcePath$, destPath$, "DEF.IC_",  "DEF.ICO") Then GoTo ErrorSetup
```

Again, don't forget to compress these files (MOON.EXE to MOON.EX_, ABC.BMP to ABC.BM_, and DEF.ICO to DEF.IC_) and copy these files to the distribution disk.

The last argument in the CopyFile() function contains the name of the file after the installation program expands the file. Therefore, MOON.EX_ will be expanded back to MOON.EXE, ABC.BM_ will be expanded back to ABC.BMP, and DEF.IC_ will be expanded back to DEF.ICO.

As stated, the distribution disk of the MOON program does not need any BMP file, ICO file, or any other file.

The distribution disk of the MOON program may be saved on a single disk. However, some applications require more than one disk. In these cases, you have to create more PromptForNextDisk() statements and CopyFile() statements. For example, suppose that the MOON program requires three distribution disks. Assume that the three disks include the files as listed in Table 19.1.

Table 19.1. An example of an application that requires three distribution disks.

Disk Number 1	Comment
SETUP.EXE	Must reside in Disk #1
SETUP.LST	Must reside in Disk #1
VBRUN300.DL_	Must reside in Disk #1
SETUPKIT.DL_	Must reside in Disk #1
VER.DL_	Must reside in Disk #1
SETUP1.EX_	Must reside in Disk #1
MOON.EX_	Part of the application
FILE1.BM_	Part of the application
FILE2.DA_	Part of the application
Disk Number 2	**Comment**
FILE3.BM_	Part of the application
FILE4.BM_	Part of the application
Disk Number 3	**Comment**
FILE5.BM_	Part of the application
FILE6.BM_	Part of the application

The corresponding code in Form_Load() is the following:

```
' Is Disk #1 in the drive?
If Not PromptForNextDisk(1, SourcePath$ + "MOON.EX_") Then
                                ➥ GoTo ErrorSetup

' Copy the file MOON.EX_ from disk #1 to the directory where
' the user wants to install the program.
If Not CopyFile(SourcePath$, destPath$, "MOON.EX_",
                                ➥ "MOON.EXE") Then GoTo ErrorSetup

' Copy the file FILE1.BM_ from disk #1 to the directory where
' the user wants to install the program.
If Not CopyFile(SourcePath$, destPath$, "FILE1.BM_",
                                ➥ "FILE1.BMP") Then GoTo ErrorSetup

' Copy the file FILE2.DA_ from disk #1 to the directory where
' the user wants to install the program.
If Not CopyFile(SourcePath$, destPath$, "FILE2.DA_",
                                ➥ "FILE2.DAT") Then GoTo ErrorSetup

' Is Disk #2 in the drive?
If Not PromptForNextDisk(2, SourcePath$ + "FILE3.BM_") Then
                                ➥ GoTo ErrorSetup

' Copy the file FILE3.BM_ from disk #2 to the directory where
' the user wants to install the program.
If Not CopyFile(SourcePath$, destPath$, "FILE3.BM_",
                                ➥ "FILE3.BMP") Then GoTo ErrorSetup

' Copy file FILE4.BM_from disk #2 to the directory where the
' user wants to install the program.
If Not CopyFile(SourcePath$, destPath$, "FILE4.BM_",
                                ➥ "FILE4.BMP") Then GoTo ErrorSetup

' Is Disk #3 in the drive?
If Not PromptForNextDisk(3, SourcePath$ + "FILE5.BM_") Then
                                ➥ GoTo ErrorSetup

' Copy the file FILE5.BM_ from disk #3 to the directory where
' the user wants to install the program.
If Not CopyFile(SourcePath$, destPath$, "FILE5.BM_",
                                ➥ "FILE5.BMP") Then GoTo ErrorSetup

' Copy the file FILE6.BM_ from disk #3 to the directory where
' the user wants to install the program.
If Not CopyFile(SourcePath$, destPath$, "FILE6.BM_",
                                ➥ "FILE6.BMP") Then GoTo ErrorSetup
```

The preceding code causes the installation program to install the three disks. During the installation, the installation program prompts the user to insert the proper disk. The correct disk is recognized by using the PromptForNextDisk() function. The first argument of this function is the disk number (so the user will see the prompts Insert disk #1, Insert disk #2, and so on), and the second argument contains a name of one of the files that is included on the disk. For example, the second argument of the PromptForNextDisk() function of Disk #2 is FILE3.BM_. Therefore, the installation program makes a determination whether the user inserted the correct disk by looking for the file FILE3.BM_ in the disk. If this file exists on the disk, the program assumes that Disk #2 is in the drive. If the program does not find FILE3.BM_ on the disk, it prompts the user: Insert disk #2.

It is important to understand that all the overhead files (SETUP.LST, SETUP.EXE, SETUP1.EXE, VBRUN300.DL_, VER.DL_, SETUPKIT.DL_) must be included in Disk #1. You should not use the CopyFile() function to copy these files, because the SETUP.EXE program is responsible for copying these files.

The MOON program does not require any VBX file. However, if your application requires VBX file(s), add a CopyFile() statement for each of the files. For example, if your application uses the GRID.VBX file, use the following statement:

```
If Not CopyFile(SourcePath$, WinSysDir$,
    ➡ "GRID.VB_", "GRID.VBX") Then GoTo ErrorSetup
```

The second argument of the CopyFile() function in this case is WinSysDir$. This causes the installation program to copy the file GRID.VB_ from the distribution disk to the /WINDOWS/SYSTEM directory. As specified by the third argument of the CopyFile() function, this file will be expanded as GRID.DLL.

Note: Because the MOON program does not need the GRID.VBX file, be sure to comment out the following statement:

```
If Not CopyFile(SourcePath$, WinSysDir$,
    ➡ "GRID.VB_", "GRID.VBX") Then GoTo ErrorSetup
```

(That is, insert an apostrophe at the beginning of the line.)

Complying with the Software License Agreement

Of course, before distributing DLLs, VBX files, and other files, you must make sure that you are complying with the software license agreement of the copyright owner of these files. (DLL files are discussed later in this book.)

Creating a Program Group in the Program Manager

The last thing you have to do in the customization process is to change the statements that are responsible for creating the program group in the Program Manager of Windows. You'll see the `CreateProgManGroup()` function and the `CreateProgManItem()` function in the SETUP1.FRM file several lines below the `CopyFile()` statements.

Change these statements as follows:

```
CreateProgManGroup Setup1, "The Moon Application", "MOON.GRP"

CreateProgManItem Setup1, destPath$ + "MOON.EXE", "The MOON Application"
```

These two statements determine the title of the group and the title of the icon of the application that will appear in the group.

Making SETUP1.EXE and Copying It to the Distribution Disk

☐ Save the project (select Save Project from the File menu).

☐ Save the SETUP1 file as EXE file by selecting Make EXE File from the File menu.

Visual Basic responds by displaying the Make EXE File dialog box shown in Figure 19.6.

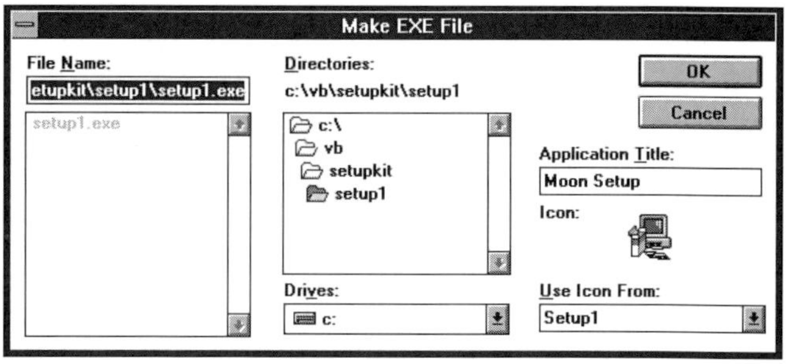

Figure 19.6.
Making SETUP1.EXE.

☐ Type Moon Setup in the Application Title text box of the Make EXE dialog box (see Figure 19.6).

☐ Save the file as SETUP1.EXE in the C:\VB\SETUPKIT\SETUP1 directory.

Now compress the file SETUP1.EXE:

☐ Double-click the MS-DOS prompt icon in the Main group of the Program Manager.

Windows responds by displaying the DOS command line.

- Log into the C:\VB\SETUPKIT\SETUP1 directory by typing the following at the DOS command line:

```
CD C:\VB\SETUPKIT\SETUP1  {Enter}
```

- Compress the SETUP1.EXE by typing the following at the DOS prompt:

```
C:\VB\SETUPKIT\KITFILES\COMPRESS -r SETUP1.EXE {Enter}
```

The COMPRESS.EXE utility compresses the file SETUP1.EXE to the file SETUP1.EX_.

- Copy the file SETUP1.EX_ to the distribution disk by typing the following at the DOS prompt:

```
COPY SETUP1.EX_  a:\ {Enter}
```

or

```
COPY SETUP1.EX_ b:\ {Enter}
```

- To return to Windows, type EXIT at the DOS prompt:

```
EXIT  {Enter}
```

Installing the MOON Program

You are now ready to install the MOON program.

Make sure that your distribution disk contains the following files: SETUP.EXE, SETUP.LST, MOON.EX_, VBRUN300.DL_, SETUPKIT.DL_, VER.DL_, and SETUP1.EX_.

The following steps are the steps that your user has to complete to perform the installation:

- Select Run from the File menu of the Program Manager.
- Click the Browse button.

    Windows responds by displaying the Browse dialog box (see Figure 19.7).

- Select the A: or B: drive from the Drive dialog box.
- Select the SETUP.EXE file and click the OK button.

    Windows responds by displaying the Run dialog box (see Figure 19.8).

- Click the OK button of the Run dialog box.

    Windows responds by executing SETUP.EXE program.

An initialization window displays the text Initializing Setup..., and after several seconds the dialog box shown in Figure 19.9 appears.

19

Figure 19.7.
The Browse dialog box.

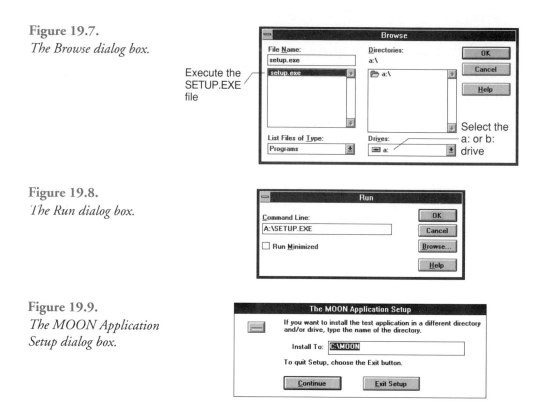

Execute the
SETUP.EXE
file

Select the
a: or b:
drive

Figure 19.8.
The Run dialog box.

Figure 19.9.
*The MOON Application
Setup dialog box.*

The MOON Application Setup dialog box lets the user change the default drive and directory in which the MOON program will be installed, and it also gives the user an opportunity to abort the installation.

☐ Click the Continue button.

The SETUP program responds by installing the application and creating a program group.

The installation is complete. To execute the MOON.EXE program, double-click the MOON icon.

Use the following steps if you wish to remove the MOON group from the Program Manager of Windows:

☐ Make sure the MOON icon is selected.

☐ Press Delete.

Windows responds by displaying a dialog box that asks you to confirm the deletion.

☐ Click OK to confirm the deletion.

☐ Now that there are no more icons in the MOON group, make sure that the group is selected.

☐ Press Delete.

> *Windows displays a dialog box, asking you to confirm the deletion.*

☐ Click the OK button to confirm the deletion.

To actually remove the MOON.EXE file from your hard drive, log into the C:\MOON directory (or whichever directory in which you installed the MOON.EXE program) and erase the MOON.EXE file.

Summary

In this chapter you have learned how to create an installation program that installs your Visual Basic program and creates a program group and a program item in the Program Manager of Windows.

Preparing such an installation program is a matter of following simple steps that involve compressing files, copying files to the distribution disk, and customizing several lines of code in the SETUP1.FRM file.

Q&A

Q What is the advantage of using the SETUP1.EXE program rather than writing my own program?

A You can write your own installation program. However, the supplied setup program is easy to use, it includes a lot of features (for example, it checks whether the user has enough disk space, it expands files), and many Windows users are used to this type of professional installation program. To summarize, say "thank you" to Microsoft for providing this feature, and then use it.

Q Can I change the name of the customized program from SETUP1.EXE to another name?

A Yes. In fact it is recommended that you do that, because when the user selects the EXE file to run, he/she will see two EXE files: SETUP.EXE and SETUP1.EXE. As stated in this chapter, the user has to select and execute the SETUP.EXE file (not the SETUP1.EXE file). The authors of this book prefer to name the file with an un-friendly name that discourages users from selecting this file. (for example, S__01.EXE). Don't forget to change the name of the file in line number 1 of the SETUP.LST file from SETUP1.EX_ to whichever name you decide to name the file.

19

Quiz

1. What should be the contents of the first line in the SETUP.LST file?

    a. It doesn't matter

    b. SETUP1.EX_

    c. The Windows version

2. One of the files that you should copy into the distribution disk is the VER.DL_ file. Is this file in a compressed form?

Exercise

Create a distribution disk to the TV program that you wrote in Chapter 9, "The Grid Control."

Quiz Answers

1. b

2. The VER.DL_ file is not in a compressed form. You generate the VER.DL_ file by copying VER.DLL to the distribution disk as VER.DL_. The rest of the files that have DL_ extension were compressed using the COMPRESS.EXE utility.

Exercise Answer

The TV program that was introduced in Chapter 9 uses the GRID.VBX control. Your distribution disk should include the file GRID.VB_. When you customize the SETUP1.EXE file, be sure to include the following statement:

```
If Not CopyFile(SourcePath$, winSysDir$,
    ➥ "GRID.VB_", "GRID.VBX") Then GoTo ErrorSetup
```

Follow the steps that were outlined in this chapter to create the distribution disk.

Dynamic Linked
Libraries

Dynamic linked libraries (DLLs) are files that contain powerful functions and procedures that may be used by your program. This chapter shows you how to incorporate DLL functions into your programs.

What Is a DLL?

DLLs are files that contain functions and procedures that may be used by your program. There are two types of DLL files: Windows API DLLs and third-party DLLs.

Windows API DLLs

Windows API DLLs are shipped with the Windows package, and therefore your program may safely assume that your user has these DLLs installed on the PC.

The Windows API DLLs contain powerful functions and procedures that extend the capabilities of the Visual Basic package.

Third-Party DLLs

In addition to the standard Windows API DLLs, your program can use third-party DLLs (DLLs that are distributed by companies other than Microsoft). These DLLs contain functions and procedures that further extend the capabilities of Visual Basic. Unlike with the Windows API DLLs, you cannot assume that your user has the third-party DLLs installed on the PC. Therefore, if your program makes use of third-party DLLs, your distribution disk must include these DLLs, and your installation program must copy these DLL files from the distribution disk into the user's hard drive. Of course, you must comply with the software license agreement of the third-party vendor.

You can also create DLL files yourself. Usually you do this using the C programming language.

The DLLs Covered in This Chapter

This chapter shows you how to use the Windows API DLLs. Because there are so many API DLLs, this chapter can't cover all of them. However, once you practice and use the DLLs that are presented in this chapter, you'll get the idea of how to use DLLs.

Declaring a DLL

To be able to use a DLL from within your Visual Basic program, you must declare the DLL. If you declare the DLL in the general declarations section of a form, this DLL may be used only from within the form. If you declare the DLL in a separate module (BAS file), the DLL can be called from any form or module.

DLLs are very similar to the procedures and functions that you write in Visual Basic. Therefore, a DLL may or may not return a value. If the DLL does not return a value, you have to declare the DLL as a Sub. If the DLL returns a value, you have to declare it as a function.

The CPU Program

The advantage of using DLL functions is that you are able to use Windows API functions that perform tasks that are not available in Visual Basic. The CPU program demonstrates how to use the GetWinFlags() DLL function.

The Visual Implementation of the CPU Program

☐ Open a new project, save the form of the project as CPU.FRM, and save the make file of the project as CPU.MAK.

☐ Build the frmCPU form according to the specifications in Table 20.1.

The completed form should look like the one shown in Figure 20.1.

Table 20.1. The properties table of frmCPU form.

Object	Property	Setting
Form	Name	frmCPU
	Caption	The CPU Program
	Height	4425
	Left	1035
	Top	1140
	Width	7485
Command Button	Name	cmd486
	Caption	Is it &486?
	Height	495
	Left	360
	Top	1680
	Width	2535

continues

Table 20.1. continued

Object	Property	Setting
Command Button	**Name**	**cmd386**
	Caption	Is it &386?
	Height	495
	Left	360
	Top	1080
	Width	2535
Command Button	**Name**	**cmd286**
	Caption	Is it &286?
	Height	495
	Left	360
	Top	480
	Width	2535
Command Button	**Name**	**cmdExit**
	Caption	&Exit
	Height	495
	Left	5760
	Top	3240
	Width	1215

Figure 20.1.
The frmCPU form.

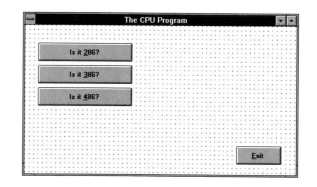

Entering the Code of the CPU Program

☐ Enter the following code inside the general declarations section of the frmCPU form:

```
' All variables MUST be declared.
Option Explicit

' Declare constants.
Const WF_CPU286 = &H2
Const WF_CPU386 = &H4
Const WF_CPU486 = &H8

' Declare the GetWinFlags() DLL function.
Declare Function GetWinFlags Lib "Kernel" () As Long
```

☐ Enter the following code inside the `cmd286_Click()` procedure of the frmCPU form:

```
Sub cmd286_Click ()

    Dim Result

    Result = GetWinFlags()
    If Result And WF_CPU286 Then
        MsgBox "80286 processor"
    Else
        MsgBox "Not 80286 processor"
    End If

End Sub
```

☐ Enter the following code inside the `cmd386_Click()` procedure of the frmCPU form:

```
Sub cmd386_Click ()

    Dim Result

    Result = GetWinFlags()

    If Result And WF_CPU386 Then
        MsgBox "80386 processor"
    Else
        MsgBox "Not 80386 processor"
    End If

End Sub
```

☐ Enter the following code inside the `cmd486_Click()` procedure of the frmCPU form:

```
Sub cmd486_Click ()

    Dim Result

    Result = GetWinFlags()

    If Result And WF_CPU486 Then
        MsgBox "80486 processor"
    Else
        MsgBox "Not 80486 processor"
    End If

End Sub
```

20

683

☐ Enter the following code inside the `cmdExit_Click()` procedure of the frmCPU form:

```
Sub cmdExit_Click ()

    End

End Sub
```

Executing the CPU Program

☐ Execute the CPU program.

☐ Click the Is it 286? button.

   The program responds by displaying a message box telling whether the PC has an 80286 CPU.

☐ Click the other buttons to find out whether your PC has an 80386 CPU or an 80486 CPU.

☐ Click the Exit button to terminate the program.

How the CPU Program Works

The CPU program utilizes the `GetWinFlags()` DLL function to find which CPU is installed in the PC.

The Code Inside the General Declarations Section of the frmCPU Form

The general declarations section of the frmCPU form includes the constant declaration of `WF_CPU286`, `WF_CPU386`, and `WF_CPU486`:

```
' Declare constants.
Const WF_CPU286 = &H2
Const WF_CPU386 = &H4
Const WF_CPU486 = &H8
```

These constants are defined in the file C:\VB\WINAPI\WIN30API.TXT. Note that C:\VB\WINAPI\WIN30API.TXT is too large, and therefore Notepad is not able to load this file. To load the WIN30API.TXT, use another word processing program (such as Write, which is shipped with Windows). Use the Search or Find feature of your word processing program to search for the required string. For example, to search for the declaration of the `GetWinFlags()` DLL function, search for the string `GetWinFlags`.

The general declarations section also includes the declaration of the `GetWinFlags()` DLL function:

```
Declare Function GetWinFlags Lib "Kernel" () As Long
```

You may find this declaration in the file C:\VB\WINAPI\WIN30API.TXT.

Lib "Kernel" means that the GetWinFlags() function resides in the kernel file of Windows (that is, one of the DLL files that is shipped with Windows).

Because the GetWinFlags() DLL function does not take any arguments, its declaration includes the empty parentheses.

The declaration of the GetWinFlags() DLL function ends with As Long, because this DLL function returns a long number.

You may find the complete description of the GetWinFlags() DLL function in a book that describes the Windows API functions, such as *Microsoft's Programmer's Reference, Volume 2: Functions*. This book is part of the Microsoft Windows Software Development Kit (SDK).

The GetWinFlags() DLL function returns a long number that represents which CPU is installed in the system.

The Code Inside the *cmd286_Click()* Procedure of the frmCPU Form

The code in the cmd286_Click() procedure is executed when the user clicks the cmd286 button:

```
Sub cmd286_Click ()

    Dim Result

    Result = GetWinFlags()

    If Result And WF_CPU286 Then
      MsgBox "80286 processor"
    Else
      MsgBox "Not 80286 processor"
    End If

End Sub
```

This procedure executes the GetWinFlags() DLL function. The returned value of GetWinFlags() is stored in the variable Result.

The procedure then performs an AND operation; if Result And WF_CPU286 is True, the CPU is 80286. In a similar way, the cmd386_Click() procedure performs an AND operation between the returned value of GetWinFlags() and WF_CPU386, and the cmd486_Click() procedure performs an AND operation between the returned value of GetWinFlags() and WF_CPU486.

The CPU program uses the GetWinFlags() procedure to determine the type of CPU. However, the returned value of GetWinFlags() may indicate other Windows-related status, such as whether the CPU is in protected mode.

20

Exiting Windows from Within Visual Basic

The End statement causes your Visual Basic program to terminate. You may use the ExitWindows() DLL function to terminate Windows.

☐ Add the following code inside the general declarations section of the frmCPU form:

```
Declare Function ExitWindows Lib "User" (ByVal dwReserved As Long,
                          ➥ ByVal wReturnCode As Integer) As Integer
```

☐ Add the Exit Windows command button to the frmCPU form, as shown in Figure 20.2.

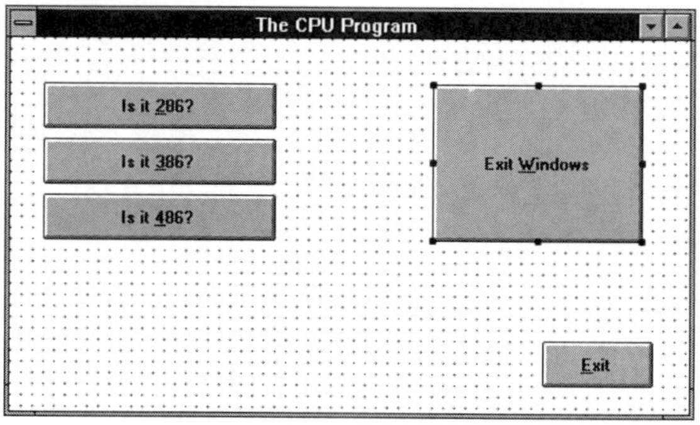

Figure 20.2.
Adding the Exit Windows button.

The Exit Windows button should have the following properties: The Name property should be cmdExitWindows and the Caption property should be Exit &Windows.

☐ Add the following code inside the cmdExitWindows() procedure of the frmCPU form:

```
Sub cmdExitWindows_Click ()

    Dim Result

    Result = ExitWindows(0, 0)

End Sub
```

☐ Save the project.

Executing the CPU Program

☐ Execute the CPU program.

☐ Click the Exit Windows button.

If there is no other Windows application that objects to the closing of Windows, Windows terminates and the PC returns to the DOS prompt.

- ☐ Start Windows.

- ☐ Start Visual Basic and execute the CPU program.

- ☐ Switch to the Program Manager and start Notepad (the icon of Notepad resides in the Accessories group).

- ☐ Write some text inside the window of Notepad. Do not save the document.

- ☐ Execute the CPU program.

- ☐ Click the Exit Windows button of the CPU program.

The program does not cause the termination of Windows because Notepad objects (because the document in Notepad had not been saved).

Declaring the *ExitWindows()* DLL Function

You declared the ExitWindows() DLL function inside the general declarations section of frmCPU:

```
Declare Function ExitWindows Lib "User" (ByVal dwReserved As Long,
                ➥ ByVal wReturnCode As Integer) As Integer
```

Lib "User" means that the ExitWindows() DLL function resides inside the DLL library file USER.EXE. (The file USER.EXE exists in every PC that has Windows installed in it. Usually, USER.EXE resides in the directory C:\WINDOWS\SYSTEM.) The declaration of ExitWindows() was copied from the file C:\VB\WINAPI\WIN30API.TXT.

The ExitWindows() DLL function has two arguments. When these two arguments are set to 0, the ExitWindows() function causes the termination of Windows and takes the PC back to the DOS command line.

The ExitWindows() DLL function returns an integer. This integer indicates whether all other running applications agree to the termination of Windows. If the returned value of ExitWindows() is True, no other application objects to the termination. If the returned value from ExitWindows() is False, one of the applications that is currently running objects to the termination of Windows.

The Code Inside the *cmdExitWindows_Click()* Procedure

The cmdExitWindows_Click() procedure is executed whenever the user clicks the Exit Windows button:

```
Sub cmdExitWindows_Click ()

    Dim Result

    Result = ExitWindows(0, 0)

End Sub
```

The procedure executes the ExitWindows() DLL function. Note that the returned value of ExitWindows() is stored in the variable Result. However, the procedure does not make use of the returned value.

The *GetFreeSpace()* DLL Function

You may use the GetFreeSpace() DLL function to find the current free space in the PC.

☐ Add the Get Free Space button to the frmCPU form, as shown in Figure 20.3.

The Get Free Space button should have the following properties: The Name property should be cmdGetFreeSpace and the Caption property should be Get &Free Space.

☐ Add the following code inside the general declarations section of the CPU program:

```
Declare Function GetFreeSpace Lib "Kernel" (ByVal wFlags As Integer) As Long
```

☐ Add the following code inside the cmdGetFreeSpace() procedure of the frmCPU form:

```
Sub cmdGetFreeSpace_Click ()

    Dim Result

    Result = GetFreeSpace(0)

    MsgBox "Free space:" + Result

End Sub
```

Executing the CPU Program

☐ Execute the CPU program.

☐ Click the Get Free Space button.

The program responds by displaying the total amount of free space in the system.

☐ While the CPU is still running, start a new Windows program (such as Paintbrush).

☐ Switch back to the CPU program and click the Get Free Space button again.

The program responds by displaying the amount of free space. Because you started a new application, the amount of free space should decrease.

Declaring the *GetFreeSpace()* DLL Function

The declaration of the GetFreeSpace() DLL function was copied from the file C:\VB\WINAPI\WIN30API.TXT:

Figure 20.3.
Adding the Get Free Space button.

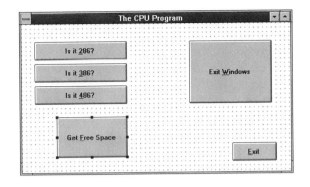

```
Declare Function GetFreeSpace Lib "Kernel" (ByVal wFlags As Integer) As Long
```

The GetFreeSpace() DLL function resides in the kernel file of Windows, and it returns a long number. The function has one integer argument.

The Code Inside the *cmdGetFreeSpace_Click()* Procedure

☐ The cmdGetFreeSpace_Click() procedure is executed whenever the user clicks the Get Free Space button:

```
Sub cmdGetFreeSpace_Click ()

    Dim Result

    Result = GetFreeSpace(0)

    MsgBox "Free space:" + Result

End Sub
```

This procedure executes the GetFreeSpace() DLL function. The returned number from the GetFreeSpace() DLL function represents the number of free bytes in the system. This number is displayed using the MsgBox function.

The WhereIs Program

Now write the WhereIs program. This program determines in which directory and drive the Windows program is installed. Finding the Windows drive and directory is important for programs that copy DLLs and VBX files into the user Windows directory.

The Visual Implementation of the WhereIs Program

☐ Open a new project, save the form of the project as WHEREIS.FRM, and save the make file of the project as WHEREIS.MAK.

☐ Build the frmWhereIs form according to the specifications in Table 20.2.

The completed form should look like the one shown in Figure 20.4.

Table 20.2. The properties table of the frmWhereIs form.

Object	Property	Setting
Form	**Name**	**frmWhereIs**
	Caption	The WhereIs Program
	Height	4425
	Left	1035
	Top	1140
	Width	7485
Command Button	**Name**	**cmdSys**
	Caption	Where Is &System?
	Height	1455
	Left	3480
	Top	960
	Width	1935
Command Button	**Name**	**cmdWin**
	Caption	Where Is &Windows?
	Height	1455
	Left	960
	Top	960
	Width	1935
Command Button	**Name**	**cmdExit**
	Caption	&Exit
	Height	495
	Left	5400
	Top	3120
	Width	1215

Object	Property	Setting
Label	**Name**	**lblInfo**
	Alignment	2-Center
	BorderStyle	1-Fixed Single
	Caption	(empty)
	Height	495
	Left	360
	Top	240
	Width	6495

Figure 20.4.
The frmWhereIs form.

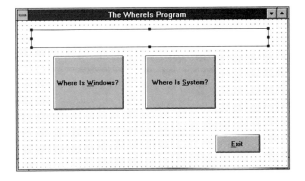

Entering the Code of the WhereIs Program

☐ Enter the following code inside the general declarations section of the frmWhereIs form:

```
' All variables MUST be declared.
Option Explicit

' Declare the GetWindowsDirectory() DLL function.
Declare Function GetWindowsDirectory Lib "Kernel"
        ➥ (ByVal lpBuffer As String, ByVal nSize As Integer) As Integer

' Declare the GetSystemDirectory() DLL function.
Declare Function GetSystemDirectory Lib "Kernel"
        ➥ (ByVal lpBuffer As String, ByVal nSize As Integer) As Integer
```

☐ Enter the following code inside the cmdExit_Click() procedure of the frmWhereIs form:

```
Sub cmdExit_Click ()

    End

End Sub
```

☐ Enter the following code inside the cmdSys_Click() procedure of the frmWhereIs form:

```
Sub cmdSys_Click ()

    Dim DirOfSys As String
    Dim Result

    ' Fill 144 spaces in the DirOfSys variable.
    DirOfSys = Space(144)

    ' Get the directory of System.
    Result = GetSystemDirectory(DirOfSys, 144)

    If Result = 0 Then
       lblInfo.Caption = "Can't find the System directory"
    Else

       DirOfSys = Trim(DirOfSys)
       lblInfo.Caption = "System directory: " + DirOfSys

    End If

End Sub
```

☐ Enter the following code inside the cmdWin_Click() procedure of the frmWhereIs form:

```
Sub cmdWin_Click ()

    Dim DirOfWin As String
    Dim Result

    ' Fill 144 spaces in the DirOfWin variable.
    DirOfWin = Space(144)

    ' Get the directory of Windows.
    Result = GetWindowsDirectory(DirOfWin, 144)

    If Result = 0 Then
       lblInfo.Caption = "Can't find the Windows directory"
    Else
       DirOfWin = Trim(DirOfWin)
       lblInfo.Caption = "Windows directory: " + DirOfWin

    End If

End Sub
```

Executing the WhereIs Program

☐ Execute the WhereIs program.

☐ Click the Where Is Windows? button.

> *The program responds by displaying the directory in which Windows is installed (see Figure 20.5).*

Figure 20.5.
*Pushing the Where Is
Windows? button.*

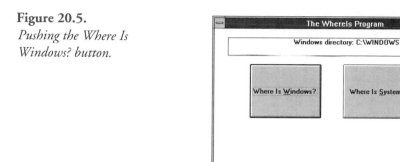

☐ Click the Where Is System? button.

The program responds by displaying the directory in which the System directory of Windows is installed (see Figure 20.6).

Figure 20.6.
*Pushing the Where Is
System? button.*

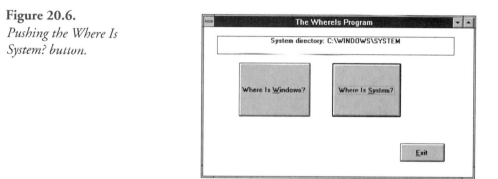

How the WhereIs Program Works

The WhereIs program utilizes the `GetWindowsDirectory()` DLL function and the `GetSystemDirectory()` DLL function to get the directories of Windows and SYSTEM.

The Code Inside the General Declarations Section of the frmWhereIs Form

The code inside the general declarations section of the frmWhereIs form declares the two DLL functions:

```
' Declare the GetWindowsDirectory() DLL function.
Declare Function GetWindowsDirectory Lib "Kernel"
                  ➥ (ByVal lpBuffer As String,
                  ➥ ByVal nSize As Integer) As Integer
```

Dynamic Linked Libraries

```
' Declare the GetSystemDirectory() DLL function.
Declare Function GetSystemDirectory Lib "Kernel"
                         ➥ (ByVal lpBuffer As String,
                         ➥ ByVal nSize As Integer) As Integer
```

These two DLL declarations were copied from the file C:\VB\WINAPI\WIN30API.TXT.

The first DLL function declaration declares the GetWindowsDirectory() DLL function. This function resides in the kernel DLL of Windows.

The first argument of GetWindowsDirectory() is the string that contains the directory of Windows. Note that the argument serves as the variable that contains the output of the DLL function. This technique of using the argument of a DLL as the variable that contains the output is common in DLL functions.

The second argument in GetWindowsDirectory() specifies the length of the first argument. Therefore, Windows will know that the variable that holds the directory where Windows is installed (the first argument) can have a maximum number of characters, as specified by the second argument of the GetWindowsDirectory() DLL function.

The function returns an integer that specifies the number of characters that were stored in the first argument.

The second DLL declaration is similar to the first declaration. The only difference is that the GetSystemDirectory() DLL function returns (in its first argument) the System directory.

The Code Inside the *cmdWin_Click()* Procedure of the frmWhereIs Form

The cmdWin_Click() procedure is executed whenever the user clicks the cmdWin button:

```
Sub cmdWin_Click ()

    Dim DirOfWin As String
    Dim Result

    ' Fill 144 spaces in the DirOfSys variable.
    DirOfWin = Space(144)

    ' Get the directory of System.
    Result = GetWindowsDirectory(DirOfWin, 144)

    If Result = 0 Then
       lblInfo.Caption = "Can't find the Windows directory"
    Else
       DirOfWin = Trim(DirOfWin)
       lblInfo.Caption = "Windows directory: " + DirOfWin
    End If

End Sub
```

The code in this procedure fills the DirOfWin string with 144 spaces:

```
DirOfWin = Space(144)
```

Why 144 spaces? This is the maximum number of characters that the path of DOS can have.

The procedure then executes the GetWindowsDirectory() DLL function:

```
Result = GetWindowsDirectory(DirOfWin, 144)
```

The returned value is stored in the variable Result. If GetWindowsDirectory() is successful in determining the directory of Windows, Result contains the number of characters the path of this directory has. For example, if Windows is installed in C:\WINDOWS, the returned value is 10, and the variable DirOfWin contains the string C:\WINDOWS.

The procedure then examined the value of Result with an If statement. If Result is 0, GetWindowsDirectory() could not determine the Windows directory. If the value of Result is not 0, the string DirOfWin is assigned to the Caption property of the lblInfo label.

The cmdSys_Click() procedure works similarly to the cmdWin_Click() procedure.

Summary

In this chapter you have learned that because the programs you write with Visual Basic are true Windows programs, your programs may utilize DLLs. The DLL may be any of the standard DLLs that are included in every PC that can run Windows, or they may be custom DLLs written by you or a third-party vendor.

Q&A

Q Can I write DLLs with Visual Basic?

A No. You can use DLLs from within your Visual Basic program, but you can't write them using Visual Basic.

Q How can I write DLLs?

A Most programmers write DLLs using the C programming language. You can use the C compiler by Microsoft, the C compiler by Borland, or a C compiler from another vendor. Be sure that the compiler package includes the SDK for Windows (that is, that the C compiler package includes all the documentation and software that enable you to develop DLLs for Windows). Of course, you have to learn how to write programs with the C programming language.

Q I understand the DLL material this chapter covers. Are there more DLLs I should know about?

A Yes. This chapter covers only a few DLLs. There are hundreds of standard Windows API DLLs that you may use. To be able to use these DLLs, you have to know the Windows API (you have to know what each DLL function accomplishes and what arguments each DLL function takes).

You can find complete descriptions of all the Windows API DLL functions in a book that describes them—for example, *Microsoft's Programmer's Reference, Volume 2: Functions*. This book is part of the Microsoft Windows Software Development Kit.

Q The **WhereIs** program uses the **GetWindowsDirectory()** DLL function to determine the Windows directory. I looked inside the Windows directory and saw many files there. What makes this directory the Windows directory?

A The Windows directory is where the files WIN.COM and WIN.INI reside.

Quiz

The declarations of the DLL functions and the various constants that the DLL function use may be found in which of the following:

a. The file C:\VB\WINAPI\WIN30API.TXT or the file C:\VB\WINAPI\WIN31.TXT.

b. You have to guess the declarations.

Exercises

1. When the argument of the GetKeyboardType() DLL function is 1, this DLL function returns the type of keyboard in the PC. Enhance the CPU program so that when the user clicks the form, a message box displays the type of keyboard. The returned values from the GetKeyboardType() DLL function are the following:

Returned Value from GetKeyboardType(1)	Type of Keyboard
1	IBM PC/XT
2	Olivetti M24
3	IBM AT
4	IBM Enhanced
5	Nokia 1050
6	Nokia 9140

2. When the argument of the GetKeyboardType() DLL function is 2, the function returns the number of function keys on the keyboard. Enhance the program of Exercise 1 so that when the user clicks the form the number of function keys is displayed.

Quiz Answer

a

Exercise Answers

1. You can enhance the CPU program so that when the user clicks the form a message box displays the type of keyboard by doing the following:

☐ Search for the string `GetKeyboardType` in the file C:\VB\WINAPI\WIN30API.TXT.

☐ Copy the string that you found in the previous step to the general declarations section of the frmCPU form:

```
Declare Function GetKeyboardType Lib "Keyboard"
        ➥    (ByVal nTypeFlag As Integer) As Integer
```

☐ Add the following code inside the `Form_Click()` procedure of the frmCPU form:

```
Sub Form_Click ()

    Dim Result

    Result = GetKeyboardType(0)

    Select Case Result
            Case 1
                MsgBox "IBM PC/XT"
            Case 2
                MsgBox "Olivetti M24"
            Case 3
                MsgBox "IBM AT"
            Case 4
                MsgBox "IBM Enhanced"
            Case 5
                MsgBox "Nokia 1050"
            Case 6
                MsgBox "Nokia 9140"
    End Select

End Sub
```

☐ Save the project.

You can now execute the CPU program. Whenever you click inside the form, a message box appears. The message box displays the type of keyboard on your system.

2. You can enhance the program of Exercise 1 so that whenever the user clicks the form the number of function keys is displayed by doing the following:

☐ Add code to the `Form_Click()` procedure so that it looks like the following:

```
Sub Form_Click ()

    Dim Result

    Result = GetKeyboardType(0)

    Select Case Result
        Case 1
            MsgBox "IBM PC/XT"
        Case 2
            MsgBox "Olivetti M24"
        Case 3
            MsgBox "IBM AT"
        Case 4
            MsgBox "IBM Enhanced"
        Case 5
            MsgBox "Nokia 1050"
        Case 6
            MsgBox "Nokia 9140"
      End Select

      Result = GetKeyboardType(2)
      MsgBox "Number of function keys:" + Result

End Sub
```

The last two statements in the `Form_Click()` procedure execute the `GetKeyboardType()` DLL function with arguments equal to 2, and then displays the returned value by using a `MsgBox` statement.

21

Sound

In this chapter you'll learn how to write Visual Basic programs that play WAV sound files. You'll learn how to play WAV files through a sound card, and you'll also learn how to play them through the PC speaker without any additional hardware or any drivers. You'll also learn how to detect whether the PC has a sound card in it and play the sound through the sound card, or if the PC does not have a sound card in it, play the WAV file through the PC speaker.

What Is a WAV File?

A WAV file is a file that contains recording. Basically, the concept of a WAV file is similar to that of the recording you perform with a tape recorder. However, when you use a tape recorder, the recording is saved into the cassette, and when you are recording WAV files, the recording is saved into a file (for example, MySong.WAV).

You can purchase disks or CDs that contain WAV files recorded by others or you can record your own WAV files by using a sound card. Inexpensive sound cards can cost less than $100.

DO	DON'T

DO read the software license agreement to see whether you are allowed to distribute the WAV files together with your applications when you purchase a CD or a disk that contains WAV files.

Figure 21.1 shows a schematic of a sound card installed in a PC. As shown, a microphone is attached to the sound card. Also, a set of speakers is attached to the sound card. When you play WAV files, the sound is played through the speakers.

Figure 21.1.

A sound card.

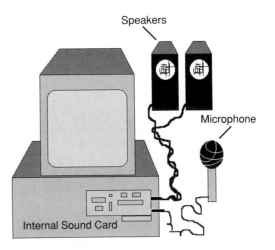

The Process of Recording

Here is how the WAV file is constructed by the sound card: When you speak into the microphone, an electronic circuit on the sound card converts the incoming air waves to a continuous electrical signal. This signal is called an analog signal. An example of an analog recording signal is shown in Figure 21.2.

Figure 21.2.

An analog recording signal.

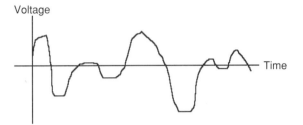

So if you store the analog signal shown in Figure 21.2 and at a later time apply this exact analog signal to a speaker, the speaker will play the same sound that was recorded. This technology of recording and playing is used, for example, in the record playing industry. That is, the analog signal is etched by the manufacturer of the records to the record. The etched groove on the record has the same shape as the analog signal that is produced by the recording.

When you play a record, the record player moves a needle over the etched grooves of the record, the needle movement generates the original analog signal, and this analog signal is fed to a speaker that plays the sound.

A PC is a digital machine, and as such, it cannot deal with analog signals (that is, the PC cannot directly read or save analog signals). So there is a need to convert the analog recording to a digital recording. Therefore, the sound card converts the analog signal to a digital signal as shown in Figure 21.3.

As shown in Figure 21.3, the sound card samples the incoming analog signal at various times. For example, at time 0, the sound card senses the incoming analog signal and discovers that at time 0 the amplitude of the analog signal is 0. Then the sound card senses the incoming analog signal again and discovers that at the time of the second sampling, the amplitude of the analog signal is 25. The value of the sampled signal at the next sampling is -50. So from the point of view of the sound card, the incoming signal is the following:

```
0
25
-50
-1
. . .
. . .
. . .
```

21

Figure 21.3.

Converting an analog signal to a digital signal.

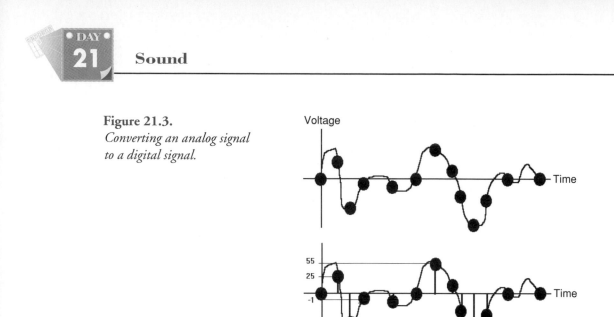

The sound card then converts the samples as follows:

```
A sample of value 0 is converted to a byte with a value of 128.
A sample of value 1 is converted to a byte with a value of 129.
A sample of value 2 is converted to a byte with a value of 130.
A sample of value 3 is converted to a byte with a value of 131.
 . . . . . . . . . . . . . . . . . . . .
 . . . . . . . . . . . . . . . . . . . .
 . . . . . . . . . . . . . . . . . . . .
A sample of value -1 is converted to a byte with a value of 127.
A sample of value -2 is converted to a byte with a value of 126.
A sample of value -3 is converted to a byte with a value of 125.
 . . . . . . . . . . . . . . . . . . . .
 . . . . . . . . . . . . . . . . . . . .
 . . . . . . . . . . . . . . . . . . . .
```

So, for example, if the sound card samples the following samples:

```
0
-1
0
1
2
```

the sound card creates a WAV file with the following values in it:

```
128,127,128,129,130
```

Before the values of the samples are written into the WAV file, various overhead bytes are written at the beginning of the WAV file. These overhead bytes are later used by the sound card as instructions for how to play the WAV file. For example, at the beginning of the WAV file, some of the bytes indicate the sampling rate at which the recording was performed.

Sampling Rate

In the previous section you learned the principle of recording a WAV file. Recall that the sound card samples the incoming analog signal at regular time intervals. What is this time interval? Say, for example, that the sound card samples the incoming analog signal every minute. As you can imagine, a recording that was sampled at 1-minute intervals is not worth much. That is, the sound card missed a lot of sound information between the samples! So what sampling rate should the sound card use? There are several "standard" sampling rates at which sound cards record WAV files. The sampling rate is expressed in units of hertz. For example, if the sound card samples every 60 seconds, the sampling rate in hertz is calculated as follows:

```
Sampling Rate = 1/60 = 0.0166 hertz
```

As previously stated, this is a very low sampling rate, and in almost all cases the recording it produces is useless.

If the sound card samples every 1 millisecond (0.001 second), the sampling rate is calculated as follows:

```
Sampling Rate = 1/0.001 = 1000 hertz.
```

As it turns out, a sampling rate of 1000 hertz is also too low. When recording WAV files, the sampling rates used are the following:

- `8000 hertz (8 kilohertz)`
- `11025 hertz (11 kilohertz)`
- `22050 hertz (22 kilohertz)`
- `44100 hertz (44 Kilohertz)`

Note that 11,025 hertz is commonly known as 11 kilohertz, not as 11.025 kilohertz.

As you might have guessed, the higher the sampling rate (the more samplings the sound card takes each second), the better the quality of the recording. An 8 khertz (8000 hertz) recording produces a telephone-like quality, an 11 khertz recording produces a tape recorder quality, a 22 khertz recording produces a fairly good recording for speech and music, and a 44 khertz recording produces a CD-like quality.

So which sampling rate should you use? It depends on the particular application you are developing. Naturally, if the application you are writing is to demonstrate your singing ability, you want the recording to be as good as possible, and hence you want to record with 44 khertz sampling rate.

Note that when you are recording at 44 khertz, the WAV file contains 44100 bytes for each second of recording. So when you record at 44 Khertz, 2 seconds of recording requires

$44100 \times 2 = 88200$ bytes, and so on. On the other hand, when you record at a sampling rate of 22 khertz, 1 second of recording requires 22050 bytes; 2 seconds of recording requires 22050 $\times 2 = 44100$ bytes; and so on. In other words, as you increase the sampling rate, the recording quality is better, but the size of the resultant WAV file increases.

Mono and Stereo Recording

So far in this chapter, only mono WAV files have been discussed.

Some sound cards have the ability to record stereo WAV files. A stereo recording records two separate recordings. For example, during a stereo recording, the sound that is picked up from the left side of the room is recorded as one recording, and the sound that is picked up from the right side of the room is recorded as a second recording.

The WAV file of a stereo recording is constructed as follows: Suppose that the samples picked up from the left side of the room are 127, 128, 126, and the samples picked up from the right side of the room are 127, 126, 125. The resultant bytes in the WAV file are the following:

```
LEFT   RIGHT   LEFT   RIGHT   LEFT   RIGHT
 127    127    128    126    126    125
```

In other words, the samples are written one after another, one sample from the left channel, followed by one sample from the right channel.

Of course the quality of a stereo recording is better than a mono recording, but the size of the stereo WAV file is double the size of the mono WAV file. If you record a mono WAV file with a 44 Khertz sampling rate for 1 second, the resultant WAV file needs 44100 bytes for the mono recording. For a stereo recording, the WAV file needs 88200 bytes for this recording (44100 bytes for the left channel and 44100 bytes for the right channel).

8-bit and 16-bit Recording

So far in this chapter you have read about mono and stereo recording. But there is another factor to consider when recording WAV files. As previously stated, the sound card samples the analog incoming signal and assigns a value to the sample. The range of the sample can be from 0 to 255, with 128 representing the middle point. This means that each sample can be expressed as a byte. A byte consists of 8 bits, hence the expression 8-bit recording.

Some sound cards have the capability of recording so that each sample is composed of 2 bytes. Because each byte is composed of 8 bits, and each sample occupies 2 bytes, such recording is called 16-bit recording. The 16-bit recording produces a better quality. Why? The samples have better resolution. For example, suppose the sound card senses that the amplitude of the incoming analog signal is 32.5 units. Because the sound card must assign an integer to the resultant sample, the sound card rounds the amplitude. So an incoming analog signal with an amplitude of 32.5 produces the same sample as an analog signal with an amplitude of 32.4. If, however, the sound card can record with 16-bit technique, a better resolution can be achieved than the resolution achieved with 8-bit recording. When performing 8-bit recording, the range of the incoming analog signal is broken into 256 distinct parts. When performing a 16-bit recording, the range of the incoming analog signal is broken into about 64000 parts.

So should you use the 8-bit recording technique or the 16-bit recording technique? As you can imagine, the WAV file for a 16-bit recording is larger than that for an 8-bit recording.

In a 16-bit recording each sample occupies 2 bytes, So here are the first three samples (3 bytes) of a mono 8-bit recording:

```
BYTE1 = Represents sample #1
BYTE2 = Represents sample #2
BYTE3 = Represents sample #3
```

Here are the first three samples (6 bytes) of a 16-bit recording (each sample occupies 2 bytes):

```
BYTE1 = Represents sample #1
BYTE2 = Represents sample #1

BYTE3 = Represents sample #2
BYTE4 = Represents sample #2

BYTE5 = Represents sample #3
BYTE6 = Represents sample #3
```

The MyWAV Program

You'll now write a program called MyWAV. This program lets the user load a WAV file, record into the WAV file, and play the WAV file. Before writing the MyWAV program yourself, review its specifications.

Upon startup of the MyWAV program, the window shown in Figure 21.4 appears.

Figure 21.4.
The MyWAV program.

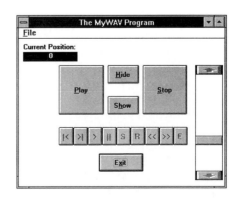

The user can now select Open from the File menu (see Figure 21.5) to load a WAV file. The Open dialog box is shown in Figure 21.6.

Figure 21.5.
The File menu of the MyWAV program.

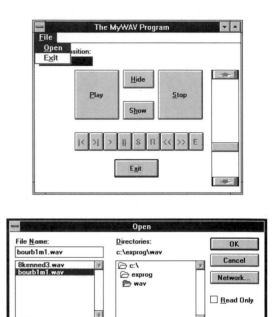

Figure 21.6.
Loading a WAV file.

Once the user selects a WAV file, the caption of the program's window indicates the name of the WAV file that was opened (see Figure 21.7).

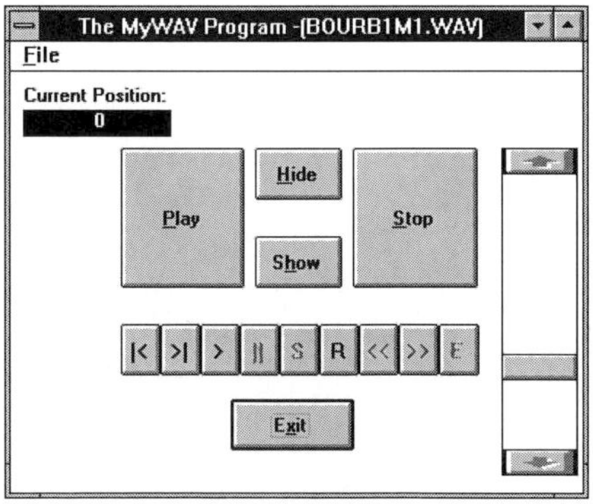

Figure 21.7.
The caption of the MyWAV window indicates which WAV file was selected.

The user can now use the various buttons of the multimedia control. Figure 21.8 shows the multimedia control and its buttons.

Figure 21.8.
The TegoMM.VBX
multimedia control.

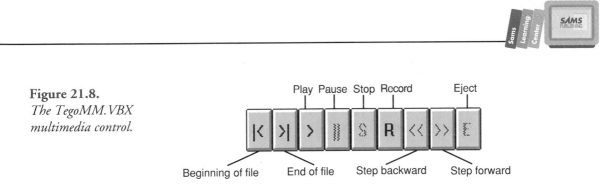

As shown in Figure 21.8, the multimedia control has nine buttons. This multimedia control can play a variety of multimedia devices. In Bonus Day 1, "Multimedia," you'll learn that the same control is utilized for playing MIDI files (synthesized music files), CD audio, and movie AVI files. Therefore, some of the buttons of the multimedia control have different meanings when using the multimedia control on different multimedia devices. When the multimedia device is used for playing WAV files (as is the case of the MyWAV program), the first button from the left is the Beginning of File button. This button rewinds the WAV file to the beginning of the file. The second button from the left places the current position of the WAV file at the end of the file. The third button from the left is the Play button, the fourth button from the left is the Pause button, the fifth button from the left is the Stop button, and the sixth button from the left is the Record button.

The first three buttons from the right on the multimedia control are not applicable when using the multimedia control for playing WAV files. Take a look at the extreme right button of the multimedia control (the Eject button). This button is applicable, for example, when you play CD audio. Clicking the Eject button causes the CD-ROM drive to eject the CD-ROM. However, the Eject button has no meaning when you play WAV files, and hence the Eject button is dimmed when you play WAV files. Similarly, the Step Backward and Step Forward buttons are used when you play movie AVI files (as you'll learn in Bonus Day 1). These buttons let the user step forward and backward to different frames of a movie.

The user can now play the WAV file through the sound card by clicking the Play button of the multimedia control. The user can stop and pause the playback, and even record sound by clicking the Record button and speaking into the microphone.

Providing the User with Custom Multimedia Buttons

In many cases you will want to provide the user with buttons more friendly than the buttons of the multimedia control. For example, instead of letting the user play the WAV file by clicking the third button form the left of the multimedia control, you can place your own Play button inside the form. Whenever the user clicks the Play button, the WAV file will be played. Similarly, you can place other buttons that perform the same tasks as the buttons of the multimedia control. The MyWAV program has two such buttons: the Play button and the Stop button. So once the user loads a WAV file, he or she can play the WAV file either by using the buttons of the multimedia devices or by using your Play and Stop buttons.

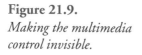
The Hide and Show buttons of the MyWAV program let the user hide and show the multimedia control. For example, after the user clicks the Hide button, the multimedia control becomes invisible, as shown in Figure 21.9.

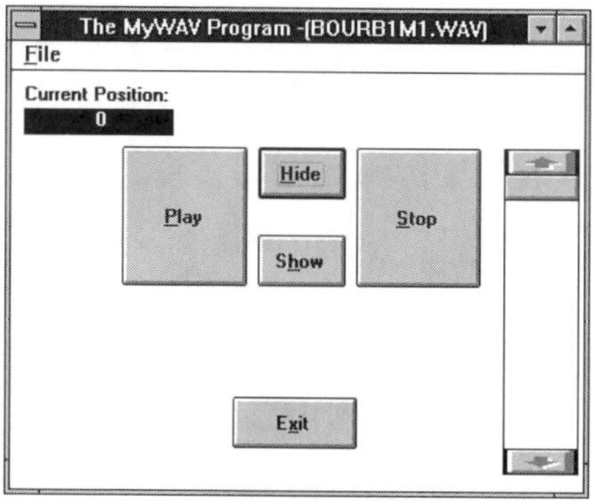

Figure 21.9.
Making the multimedia control invisible.

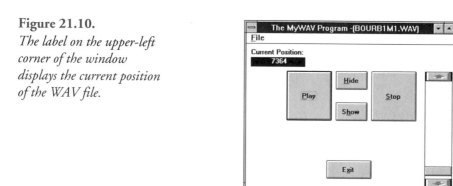

The only reason for using the Hide and Show buttons in the MyWAV program is to illustrate that the MyWAV program does not have to display the multimedia control during runtime.

The MyWAV program has a label control on its upper-left corner. This label displays the current position of the playback. For example, in Figure 21.9, the current position of the WAV file is 0, which means that the WAV file is at the beginning of the file. Once the user plays the WAV file, the label displays the current position of the WAV file during the playback. In Figure 21.10, the current position is at 7364 milliseconds from the beginning of the file.

Figure 21.10.
The label on the upper-left corner of the window displays the current position of the WAV file.

The MyWAV program also displays a vertical scroll bar, which changes its position randomly. The purpose of including this scroll bar is cosmetic, and to illustrate the important concept of the StatusUpdate event of the multimedia control (as you'll see later in this chapter).

Now that you know what the MyWAV program is supposed to do you can implement it.

The Visual Implementation of the MyWAV Program

You'll now visually implement the frmMyWAV form of the MyWAV program.

☐ Select New Project from the File menu and save the new project as follows: Save the new form as MyWAV.frm inside the C:\EXPROG\CH21 directory and save the new project file as MyWAV.mak inside the C:\EXPROG\CH21 directory.

The MyWAV program utilizes the TegoMM.VBX multimedia control. Therefore, you need to add this control to your project.

> **Note:** You can purchase the TegoMM.VBX multimedia control directly from TegoSoft, Inc. (See disk offer at the end of this book.) Even if you do not have the TegoMM.VBX multimedia control, it is recommended that you read the material of this chapter to learn how WAV files are played through an installed sound card or through the PC speaker that every PC has.

If you have a copy of the TegoMM.VBX control, make sure that this file resides inside the \Windows\System directory, and add the file to your project as follows:

☐ Select Add File from the File menu, and select the C:\Windows\System\TegoMM.VBX file.

Visual Basic responds by adding the TegoMM.VBX control to your project. The icon of the TegoMM.VBX multimedia control is shown in Figure 21.11.

Figure 21.11.
The icon of the TegoMM.VBX control inside the Toolbox.

☐ Implement the frmMyWAV form according to the specifications in Table 21.1. When you finish implementing the from, it should look like the one shown in Figure 21.12.

Table 21.1. The properties table of the frmMyWAV form.

Object	Property	Setting
Form	**Name**	**frmMyWAV**
	Caption	The MyWAV Program
	Height	4710
	Icon	C:\VB\Icons\Industry\ SINEWAVE.ICO
	Left	1020
	Top	1140
	Width	5700
Vertical Scroll Bar	**Name**	**vsbNothing**
	Enabled	0-False
	Height	3135
	Left	4800
	Max	100
	Top	720
	Width	735
Command Button	**Name**	**cmdShow**
	Caption	S&how
	Height	495
	Left	2400
	Top	1560
	Width	855
Command Button	**Name**	**cmdHide**
	Caption	&Hide
	Height	495
	Left	2400
	Top	720
	Width	855
Command Button	**Name**	**cmdStop**
	Caption	&Stop

Object	Property	Setting
	Height	1335
	Left	3360
	Top	720
	Width	1215
Command Button	**Name**	**cmdPlay**
	Caption	&Play
	Height	1335
	Left	1080
	Top	720
	Width	1215
Common Dialog Box	**Name**	**CMDialog1**
	CancelError	True
	Left	1440
	Top	3240
TegoMM.VBX	**Name**	**Tegomm1**
	Height	495
	Left	1080
	Top	2400
	Width	3510
Command Button	**Name**	**cmdExit**
	Caption	E&xit
	Height	495
	Left	2160
	Top	3120
	Width	1215
Label	**Name**	**lblPosition**
	Alignment	2-Center
	BackColor	(black)
	ForeColor	(white)
	Height	255
	Left	120

continues

Table 21.1. continued

Object	Property	Setting
Label	**Name**	**lblPosition**
	Top	360
	Width	1455
Label	**Name**	**lblCurrentPosition**
	Caption	Current Position:
	Height	255
	Left	120
	Top	120
	Width	1575
Menu	**(see Table 21.2)**	**(see Table 21.2)**

Table 21.2. The menu table of the frmMyWAV form.

Caption	Name
&File	mnuFile
...&Open	mnuOpen
...E&xit	mnuExit

Figure 21.12.

The frmMyWAV form (in design mode).

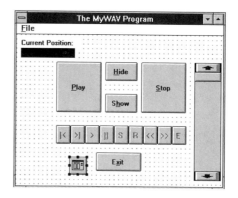

Attaching Code to the *Click* Event of the Exit Button

You'll now attach code to the Click event of the Exit button.

☐ Type the following code inside the cmdExit_Click() procedure of the frmMyWAV form:

```
Sub cmdExit_Click ()

    End

End Sub
```

So whenever the user clicks the Exit button, the MyWAV program terminates.

Attaching Code to the *Click* Event of the Exit Menu Item

☐ Type the following code inside the mnuExit_Click() procedure of the frmMyWAV form:

```
Sub mnuExit_Click ()

    End

End Sub
```

The code you typed terminates the MyWAV program whenever the user selects Exit from the File menu.

Attaching Code to the *Click* Event of the Hide Button

You'll now attach code to the Click event of the Hide button.

☐ Type the following code inside the cmdHide_Click() procedure of the frmMyWAV form:

```
Sub cmdHide_Click ()

    Tegomm1.Visible = False

End Sub
```

The code you typed sets the Visible property of the multimedia control to False. Therefore, whenever the user clicks the Hide button, the multimedia control becomes invisible.

Attaching Code to the *Click* Event of the Show Button

You'll now attach code to the Click event of the Show button.

☐ Type the following code inside the cmdShow_Click() procedure of the frmMyWAV form:

```
Sub cmdShow_Click ()

    Tegomm1.Visible = True

End Sub
```

The code you typed sets the Visible property of the multimedia control to True. Therefore, whenever the user clicks the Show button, the multimedia control becomes visible.

Attaching Code to the *Click* Event of the Open Menu Item

You'll now attach code to the Click event of the Open menu. Recall that when the user selects Open from the File menu, the MyWAV program displays an Open dialog box that lets the user select a WAV file. The code that you'll now attach to the Open item of the File menu will be used frequently in the rest of the chapters of this book.

☐ Type the following code inside the mnuOpen_Click() procedure:

```
Sub mnuOpen_Click ()

    ' Selecting a file (with the common dialog box)

    ' Set an error trap
    On Error GoTo OpenError

    ' Set the items of the File Type list box
    CMDialog1.Filter =
        ➥ "All Files (*.*) ¦ *.* ¦WAV Files (*.wav)¦*.wav"

    ' Set the default File Type
    CMDialog1.FilterIndex = 2

    ' Display the common dialog box
    CMDialog1.Action = 1

    ' Remove the error trap
    On Error GoTo 0

    ' Open the selected file
    Tegomm1.DeviceType = "WaveAudio"
    Tegomm1.FileName = CMDialog1.Filename
    Tegomm1.Command = "Open"
    If Tegomm1.Error > 0 Then
```

```
        cmdPlay.Enabled = False
        cmdStop.Enabled = False
        frmMyWAV.Caption =
           ➥ "The MyWAV Program - (No file is loaded)"

        MsgBox "Can't open " + CMDialog1.Filename, 16, "Error"

    Else
        cmdPlay.Enabled = True
        cmdStop.Enabled = True
        frmMyWAV.Caption =
           ➥ "The MyWAV Program -(" + CMDialog1.Filetitle + ")"
    End If

    ' Exit this procedure
    Exit Sub

OpenError:
    ' The user pressed the Cancel key of the common dialog
    ' box or an error occurred
    ' Exit this procedure
    Exit Sub

End Sub
```

The code you typed sets an error trap:

```
On Error GoTo OpenError
```

So if an error occurred during the process of selecting a file, the program immediately jumps to the OpenError line of this procedure:

```
OpenError:
    Exit Sub
```

Recall that during design time you set the CancelError property of the common dialog control to True. This means that if the user clicks the Cancel button of the Open dialog, an error occurs (and because you set the error trap, the program will immediately jump to the OpenError line).

The common dialog box is then prepared:

```
CMDialog1.Filter = "All Files (*.*) ¦ *.* ¦WAV Files (*.wav)¦*.wav"
```

```
CMDialog1.FilterIndex = 2
```

Then the Open dialog box is displayed:

```
CMDialog1.Action = 1
```

When the user selects a file, the program proceeds with the statement following the CMDialog1.Action = 1 statement. Because there is no need to trap errors anymore, the error trap is removed:

```
On Error GoTo 0
```

The DeviceType property of the multimedia control determines which medium is played. When playing WAV files through the sound card, you have to set the DeviceType property to WaveAudio:

```
Tegomm1.DeviceType = "WaveAudio"
```

Then the FileName property of the multimedia control is set:

```
Tegomm1.FileName = CMDialog1.Filename
```

Recall that the user selected the WAV file by using the Open dialog box, and the selected file is saved as the Filename property of the CMDialog1 control.

Finally, the `Open` command is issued, as follows:

```
Tegomm1.Command = "Open"
```

An `If…Else` statement is then executed to examine whether the `Open` command was executed successfully:

```
If Tegomm1.Error > 0 Then
    ........................................
    ... An error occurred during
    ... the execution of the last command
    ........................................
Else
    ........................................
    ... No error occurred during
    ... the execution of the last command
    ........................................
End If
```

The code under the `If` is executed if an error occurred during the last execution of a command by the multimedia control. Because the last command that was executed by the multimedia control was the `Open` command, the `If` statement indicates whether there was an error during the execution of the `Open` command. An error could occur if the FileName property of the multimedia control was set with an invalid WAV file, because the sound card is missing, or because one of the drivers of the sound card is missing.

The code under the `If` statement disables the Play and Stop buttons:

```
cmdPlay.Enabled = False
cmdStop.Enabled = False
```

The Caption property of the program's window is set to indicate that no WAV file is loaded:

```
frmMyWAV.Caption = "The MyWAV Program - (No file is loaded)"
```

A message box is then displayed to indicate that the selected file cannot be opened:

```
MsgBox "Can't open " + CMDialog1.Filename, 16, "Error"
```

> **Note:** The preceding code disables the Play and Stop buttons that you placed inside the form. But what about the Play and Stop buttons of the multimedia control? You don't have to disable or enable the buttons of the multimedia control because the multimedia control takes care of this automatically. For example, if the WAV file was not opened successfully, the multimedia control does not enable its Play and Stop buttons.

The code under the `Else` statement is executed provided that the `Open` command was executed successfully. This code enables the Play and Stop button that you placed inside the form:

```
cmdPlay.Enabled = True
cmdStop.Enabled = True
```

The Caption property of the form is changed so that the user can see which WAV file is open:

```
frmMyWAV.Caption = "The MyWAV Program -(" + CMDialog1.Filetitle + ")"
```
Finally, the procedure is terminated:

```
Exit Sub
```

Attaching Code to the *Click* Event of the cmdPlay Button

You'll now attach code to the `Click` event of the cmdPlay button.

☐ Type the following code inside the `cmdPlay_Click()` procedure:

```
Sub cmdPlay_Click ()

    Tegomm1.Command = "Play"

End Sub
```

The code you typed starts the playback by issuing the `Play` command to the multimedia control.

Attaching Code to the *Click* Event of the cmdStop Button

You'll now attach code to the `Click` event of the cmdStop button.

☐ Type the following code inside the `cmdStop_Click()` procedure:

```
Sub cmdStop_Click ()

    Tegomm1.Command = "Stop"

End Sub
```

The code you typed stops the playback by issuing the Stop command to the multimedia control.

Attaching Code to the *Load* Event of the Form

You'll now attach code to the Load event of the Form.

☐ Type the following code inside the Form_Load() procedure:

```
Sub Form_Load ()

    Tegomm1.UpdateInterval = 250

End Sub
```

The code you typed sets the UpdateInterval property of the multimedia control to 250. This means that from now on the Tegomm1_StatusUpdate() procedure will be executed automatically every 250 milliseconds. Later in this chapter you'll write the code of the Tegomm1_StatusUpdate() procedure.

Attaching Code to the *Done* Event of the Multimedia Control

You'll now attach code to the Done event of the multimedia control.

☐ Type the following code inside the Tegomm1_Done() procedure:

```
Sub Tegomm1_Done ()

    If Tegomm1.Position = Tegomm1.Length Then
        Tegomm1.Command = "Prev"
    End If

End Sub
```

The Position property of the multimedia control indicates the current position of the WAV file. The Length property of the multimedia control indicates the length of the WAV file. So if the Position property is equal to the Length property, you know that the Done event occurred because the WAV file was played in its entirety. The code under the If statement is therefore executed whenever the WAV file is played in its entirety. In other words, the Done event occurs whenever the multimedia control finishes executing commands. The If statement you typed inside the Tegomm1_Done() procedure checks whether the Done event occurred because the Play command was executed and the playback position reached the end of the WAV file.

The code under the `If` statement issues the `Prev` command:

```
Tegomm1.Command = "Prev"
```

This causes the WAV file to rewind itself to the beginning of the file. Therefore, the WAV file is ready for the next time the user clicks the Play button.

Attaching Code to the *StatusUpdate* Event of the Multimedia Control

Inside the `Form_Load()` procedure you set the UpdateInterval property of the multimedia control to 250. This means that the `Tegomm1_StatusUpdate()` procedure is executed automatically every 250 milliseconds.

☐ Type the following code inside the `Tegomm1_StatusUpdate()` procedure:

```
Sub Tegomm1_StatusUpdate ()

    lblPosition.Caption = Str(Tegomm1.Position)

    vsbNothing.Value = Int(Rnd * 100)

End Sub
```

The code you typed updates the Caption property of the lblPosition label with the value of the Position property of the multimedia control:

```
lblPosition.Caption = Str(Tegomm1.Position)
```

So every 250 milliseconds the lblPosition label displays the current position of the WAV file. (The default units are milliseconds. That is, the Position property and other properties such as the Length property are in units of milliseconds. However, you can set the TimeFormat property of the multimedia control to other units, such as samples. When the TimeFormat property is set to Samples, the units of the Position and Length properties are samples.)

The second statement inside the `Tegomm1_StatusUpdate()` procedure is this:

```
vsbNothing.Value = Int(Rnd * 100)
```

The preceding statement sets the Value property of the vsbNothing scroll bar to a random number between 0 and 99. The only reason this statement is included is to show that indeed the `Tegomm1_StatusUpdate()` procedure is executed automatically every 250 milliseconds. That is, during the execution of the MyWAV program, you'll see the scroll bar position change to random values.

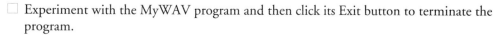

☐ Experiment with the MyWAV program and then click its Exit button to terminate the program.

Playing WAV Files Through the Internal PC Speaker

Playing through the internal speaker of the PC is very easy when using the TegoMM.VBX multimedia control. In fact, the MyWAV program that you developed in this chapter can also play through the PC speaker. All you have to do is change a single statement inside the `mnuOpen_Click()` procedure.

Inside the `mnuOpen_Click()` procedure you set the DeviceType property of the multimedia control to play through the sound card as follows:

```
Tegomm1.DeviceType = "WaveAudio"
```

To play through the PC speaker, change the preceding statement as follows:

```
Tegomm1.DeviceType = "PCSpeaker"
```

Now the MyWAV program plays WAV files through the PC speaker.

Note: To play WAV files through the PC speaker, set the DeviceType property of the multimedia control as follows:

```
Tegomm1.DeviceType = "PCSpeaker"
```

Note that the multimedia control can play WAV files through the PC speaker without any additional hardware, and no drivers are required.

Note: When you issue the Play command to the sound card, the sound card is on its own. That is, the PC can continue performing other tasks. When you play WAV files through the PC speaker, the PC is occupied with playing the WAV file through the PC speaker. However, the TegoMM.VBX multimedia control includes properties that enable you to write programs that play through the PC speaker, and simultaneously, the user can perform other tasks. For example, while the WAV file is played through the PC speaker, the user can use the mouse to click buttons, and the program will respond to the clicking. You can also set the multimedia control properties so that you can play WAV files through the PC speaker and simultaneously move graphic objects and text on the screen. For a more detailed description, see Sams Publishing's *Master Visual Basic 3* by Gurewich and Gurewich.

Determining the Existence of a Sound Card

Generally, you will want to play the WAV files through an installed sound card. However, not all PCs have a sound card installed in them. For such PCs, your program should direct the playback to the internal speaker of the PC. To determine whether the PC has a sound card installed in it, you can use the following code:

```
Tegomm1.DeviceType = "WaveAudio"
Tegomm1.FileName = CMDialog1.Filename
Tegomm1.Command = "Open"
If Tegomm1.Error > 0 Then
    Tegomm1.DeviceType = "PCSpeaker"
    Tegomm1.Command = "Open"
End If
```

That is, you try to open the WAV file with DeviceType equal to WaveAudio (playing through the sound card). If the Open command will not execute successfully, it means that the sound card is not installed, and therefore the code under the If statement sets the DeviceType property to PCSpeaker, and the Open command is issued again. Now when the Play command is issued (or when the user clicks the Play button of the multimedia control), the WAV file is played through the PC speaker.

Summary

In this chapter you have learned how to play WAV files both through the sound card and how to play WAV files through the internal speaker of the PC. You have also learned how to determine whether the PC has a sound card installed in it, and accordingly, to direct the sound to the sound card or to the PC speaker. When playing WAV files through the PC speaker, you do not need any additional hardware, and you do not need any drivers.

Q&A

Q What other tasks can I perform with the TegoMM.VBX multimedia control?

A Practically every sound trick you can think of. For example, you can cut, copy, and paste sections of the WAV file; you can record and then save your recording as a new WAV file; you can record your own voice and then change the WAV file so that it will sound like a different person; you can add echo; you can increase/decrease the volume; and so on. *Master Visual Basic 3* explains in great detail how to design a complete WAV editor program that accomplishes a lot of sound manipulations.

Quiz

1. What code should you write to disable the Play button of the multimedia control when the WAV file is not opened successfully?

2. There are two properties that must be set before issuing the `Play` command to the multimedia control. What are they?

Exercise

Enhance the MyWAV program so that the scroll bar position moves randomly only if playback is in progress. Also, make the multimedia control always invisible.

Quiz Answer

1. You don't have to write any such code. The multimedia control automatically disables/enables its own buttons.

2. The DeviceType property and the FileName property

Exercise Answer

To make the multimedia control always invisible, set the Visible property of the multimedia control to False at design time.

Because the multimedia control is always invisible, you don't need the Hide and Show buttons anymore, so remove the Hide and Show buttons from the form.

Inside the general declarations section declare a variable as follows:

```
Option Explicit

Dim gPlayInProgress
```

The gPlayInProgress variable is declared inside the general declarations section; therefore, this variable is accessible from all procedures of the form.

Inside the `Form_Load()` procedure add the following statement:

```
gPlayInProgress = 0
```

That is, the `gPlayInProgress` variable serves as a flag that indicates whether the playback is in progress. A value of 0 means that the playback is not in progress. A value of 1 means that the playback is in progress.

Inside the `cmdPlay_Click()` procedure add the following statement:

`gPlayInProgress = 1`

That is, because the user clicked the Play button, the playback will start, and you set the gPlayInProgess flag to 1.

Inside the `cmdStop_Click()` procedure add the following statement:

`gPlayInProgress = 0`

That is, because the user clicked the Stop button, the playback will stop, and so you set the gPlayInProgess flag to 0.

Change the `Tegomm1_StatusUpdate()` procedure so that it looks like this:

```
Sub Tegomm1_StatusUpdate ()

    lblPosition.Caption = Str(Tegomm1.Position)

    If gPlayInProgress = 1 Then
        vsbNothing.Value = Int(Rnd * 100)
    End IF

End Sub
```

The code you added uses an `If` statement to examine whether a playback is in progress. If the playback is in progress, the Value property of the scroll bar is changed.

> **Note:** Another way to determine whether playback is in progress is to use the Mode property of the multimedia control. When the Mode property of the multimedia control is equal to 526, playback is in progress.

21

BD1

BD2

BD3

BD4

BD5

BD6

BD7

The first 21 chapters of this book cover the essentials of Visual Basic. You have learned how to design Windows applications by using the Visual Basic package. As you have seen, you can extend the power of Visual Basic by utilizing third-party software.

Typically, you extend the power of Visual Basic by incorporating VBX controls. The Professional Edition of Visual Basic contains several VBX controls that are not supplied with the Standard Edition of Visual Basic. Another source of VBX controls is the Borland Visual Solutions Pack.

Where You're Going

This part of the book contains seven bonus chapters. These chapters concentrate on very specific programming areas. As you'll soon see, the programs that you'll design in the seven bonus chapters make extensive use of third-party VBX controls, and some of these chapters also require special hardware (for example, sound card, CD-ROM drive, network).

Bonus Day 1+

Multimedia

In this chapter you'll learn about the interesting topic of multimedia.

What Is Multimedia?

As the name implies, multimedia programs use various media that are installed in the PC. For example, the sound card is used to play sound, the monitor is used to display movies, and the CD-ROM drive is used to play CD audio.

Multimedia technology is becoming very popular, and many PC vendors are now shipping their PCs with multimedia hardware already installed.

Typically, a multimedia set includes a sound card, a microphone, speakers, a CD-ROM drive that is capable of playing CD audio, and a monitor that is capable of displaying movies (for example, a VGA monitor).

Multimedia technology is used in a wide range of applications, including those for business, education, and games. In this chapter you'll learn how to write Visual Basic programs that utilize various multimedia devices.

DOS Versus Windows: Device Independence

One of the main advantages of Windows over DOS is that Windows is device independent. That is, the multimedia Windows programs you write should work on any multimedia device, regardless of the manufacturer of the device. For example, it does not matter who manufactured your sound card—if Windows accepted the sound card, any multimedia program you write should be able to use this sound card.

Determining Your Multimedia Capabilities

Before you start to write the multimedia programs of this chapter, you need to examine the multimedia capabilities of your PC. That is, you installed the multimedia hardware, and you installed the associated multimedia software (drivers) that come with the multimedia hardware. The question is Did Windows accept your installation?

There is a very easy way to determine the multimedia capabilities of your PC:

☐ Start the Media Player program. Media Player usually resides inside the Accessories group (see Figure BD1.1).

Windows responds by displaying the Media Player window shown in Figure BD1.2.

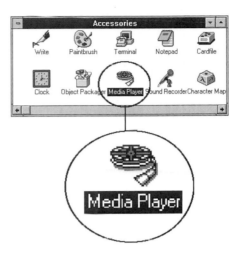
Figure BD1.1.

The program icon of Media Player (usually inside the Accessories group).

Figure BD1.2.

The Media Player program.

☐ Open the Device menu of Media Player.

The Device menu of Media Player displays the names of devices that are installed on your system (see Figure BD1.3).

Figure BD1.3.

The Device menu of the Media Player program.

Now examine the various items that appear inside the Device menu of Media Player (see Figure BD1.3). The Sound item is an indication that the PC is capable of playing WAV files. The CD Audio item is an indication that the PC is capable of playing CD audio. The MIDI Sequencer item is an indication that the PC can play MIDI files. The Video for Windows item is an indication that the PC is capable of playing movie AVI files. If you don't see any of these devices in the Device menu, something is wrong with the hardware or software installation of the devices that are missing from the Device menu.

Note: You might encounter a situation in which a certain proprietary program is capable of playing a certain device, but that device does not appear inside the Device menu of Media Player. It means that that application uses some special proprietary drivers. And even though you can play the device with that particular application, other "normal" applications will not be able to play the device.

So the bottom line is this: Insist on seeing the multimedia device you are installing among the items of the Device menu. This will ensure that every Windows application that needs to utilize the device will be able to do so.

MIDI Files

The PlayMIDI program that you'll write in this chapter demonstrates how you can play MIDI files. MIDI files are synthesized music files. You can consider the MIDI file to be a file that contains instructions to the sound card. These instructions consist of information such as the music notes, the type of instruments to play, the tempo (the playback speed), and other information that the sound card needs to know in order to play the music. How does the sound card play the music? The sound card has special MIDI electronic hardware on it that enables the playback of musical instruments. For example, the sound card can generate piano music, violin music, drum music, and music of a variety of other instruments.

The MIDI file cannot emulate human voice, nor can it emulate sounds that are not the sound of musical instruments. For example, a MIDI file cannot play the sound of breaking glass.

Typically, the MIDI file instructs the sound card to play several musical instruments simultaneously. In fact, you can play a MIDI file that produces music that is otherwise generated by a whole orchestra. Naturally, the more expensive the sound card, the more impressive the MIDI capabilities of the sound card.

Note: Most sound cards include the electronic circuit that enables them to play MIDI files.

Unlike WAV files (which contain the actual samples of recording), MIDI files contain only the instructions that tell the sound card how to play the music. Therefore, MIDI files are very short.

So how do you obtain MIDI files? A typical programmer purchases the MIDI files. Alternatively, you can generate the MIDI files by using special hardware that lets you "record" the MIDI file. The hardware includes a keyboard that is connected to the PC. As you play the keyboard, the music is stored as a MIDI file. Special MIDI software lets you manipulate the music (mixing several instruments, selecting an instrument and making its volume higher/lower, and so on). As you can see, "recording" MIDI files is not as easy as recording WAV files. To begin with, you need special software and hardware, but more importantly, you need musical talent. Professional MIDI equipment is typically purchased in stores that specialize in selling musical instruments. Lately, computer stores have begun carrying inexpensive MIDI equipment that lets you interface the MIDI hardware to the sound card for the purpose of "recording" MIDI files.

DO	DON'T

DO make sure that the sound card you are purchasing is capable of interfacing to MIDI equipment if you plan to "record" MIDI files yourself using a sound card. Typically, the sound card lets you interface to MIDI equipment through the joystick port of the sound card. That is, most sound cards include a joystick port (where you can connect a joystick). When recording MIDI files, you'll connect the MIDI hardware to the joystick port of the sound card (provided that the MIDI equipment and the sound card were designed to interface with each other this way).

Note: When a sound card plays a MIDI file, the music is played through the speakers that are attached to the sound card (just like when you play WAV files).

Most sound cards let you play a WAV file and a MIDI file simultaneously. Typically, MIDI files are used as background music. For example, you can announce "Happy birthday, Jean" with a WAV file while a MIDI file of the song "Happy Birthday" is played in the background.

The PlayMIDI Program

In the following sections you'll write the PlayMIDI program. The PlayMIDI program is an example of a program that lets the user play MIDI files.

Before writing the PlayMIDI program yourself, review its specifications.

Upon startup of the PlayMIDI program, the window shown in Figure BD1.4 appears.

As shown in Figure BD1.4, a picture of a guitar appears (this is an appropriate picture because the subject of the PlayMIDI program is playing musical instruments).

The Current Position scroll bar does not indicate any position, because no MIDI file is open.

Figure BD1.4.
The window of the
PlayMIDI program.

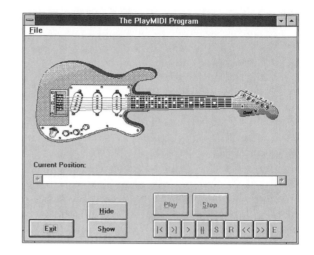

The PlayMIDI program has a menu, as shown in Figure BD1.5.

Figure BD1.5.
The File menu of the
playMIDI program.

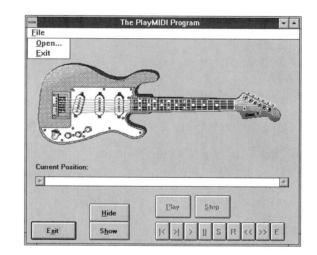

☐ To load a MIDI file, select Open from the File menu.

The PlayMIDI program responds by displaying the Open dialog box, as shown in
Figure BD1.6.

As shown in Figure BD1.6, the Open dialog box lets you load a MIDI file (a file with the .MID
file extension).

The user can now load a MIDI file.

Figure BD1.6.
The Open dialog box that appears after you select Open from the File menu.

Open

File Name:
*.mid

Directories:
c:\vb

- c:\
- vb
  - bitmaps
  - cdk
  - hc
  - icons
  - metafile

List Files of Type:
Midi Files (*.mid)

Drives:
c:

OK
Cancel
Network...
☐ Read Only

Note: Windows is shipped with a MIDI file called Canyon.MID. This file usually resides inside the \Windows directory.

Figure BD1.7 shows the main window of the PlayMIDI program after the user loads the Canyon.MID file.

Figure BD1.7.
The title of the PlayMIDI program indicates that the Canyon.MID file is loaded.

The PlayMIDI Program -[CANYON.MID]
File

Current Position:

Hide   Play   Stop
Exit   Show |< >| > || S R << >> E

Note the Show and Hide buttons that appear inside the window of the PlayMIDI program. These buttons are implemented for the sole purpose of demonstrating that you can make the TegoMM.VBX multimedia control visible or invisible.

When the user clicks the Hide button, PlayMIDI responds by making the TegoMM multimedia control invisible (see Figure BD1.8).

When the user clicks the Show button, PlayMIDI responds by making the TegoMM multimedia control visible.

Figure BD1.8.
*Making the TegoMM
multimedia control
invisible.*

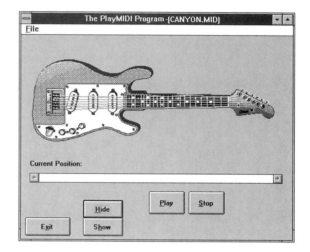

Note: Why would you want to make the TegoMM multimedia control invisible? You might want to make your program visually more fancy. Instead of using the standard multimedia control buttons of the TegoMM control, you could make your own buttons. For example, the PlayMIDI program implements the Play and Stop buttons.

Also, sometimes you might want the MIDI file to be played without the need to click any button. In such a case, you would make the multimedia control invisible, and you would not implement the Stop and Play buttons. For example, you might want to implement a program in which, upon startup of the program a section of a MIDI file is played automatically, without requiring the user to click any button.

The user can now play the MIDI file by clicking the Play button you placed inside the form or by clicking the Play button of the multimedia control (the third button from the left on the multimedia control).

To stop the playback, the user has to click the Stop button you placed inside the form or click the Stop button of the multimedia control (the fifth button from the left on the multimedia control), or click the Pause button of the multimedia control (the fourth button from the left on the multimedia control).

During the playback, the scroll bar indicates the current position of the playback. For example, Figure BD1.9 shows the window of the PlayMIDI program after you play approximately half of the file.

Figure BD1.9.
The scroll bar indicates that approximately half of the MIDI file has been played.

Note: In the PlayMIDI program the scroll bar is disabled so the user will not be able to manually scroll to any desired position. Nevertheless, it is very easy to enable the scroll bar, and to enable the user to start playing from any desired position.

The Visual Implementation of the PlayMIDI Program

Now that you know what the PlayMIDI program is supposed to do, you can implement it.

☐ Select New Project from the File menu, and save the new project as follows: Save the new form as C:\EXPROG\BD1\PlayMIDI.FRM and save the new project file as C:\EXPROG\BD1\PlayMIDI.MAK.

The PlayMIDI program uses the TegoMM.VBX control. Therefore, you have to add this VBX control to your project:

☐ Select Add File from the Project menu, and add the C:\Windows\System\TegoMM.VBX control.

DO	DON'T

DO incorporate multimedia into your Windows applications. Nowadays many people have multimedia capabilities in their PCs, and most users expect to be able to utilize the multimedia devices.

☐ Implement the frmPlayMIDI form according to the specifications in Table BD1.1. When you finish implementing the form, it should look like the one shown in Figure BD1.10.

Table BD1.1. The properties table of the frmPlayMIDI form.

Object	Property	Setting
Form	Name	frmPlayMIDI
	BackColor	(light gray)
	Caption	The PlayMIDI Program
	Height	6195
	Icon	\VB\Icons\Misc\Misc21.ICO
	Left	1035
	Top	525
	Width	7485
Horizontal Scroll Bar	Name	hsbPosition
	Enabled	0-False
	Height	255
	Left	240
	Top	3720
	Width	6855
Common Dialog Box	Name	CMDialog1
	CancelError	-1-True
	Left	2880
	Top	4560
Command Button	Name	cmdShow
	Caption	S&how
	Height	495
	Left	1680

Object	Property	Setting
	Top	4920
	Width	1095
Command Button	**Name**	**cmdHide**
	Caption	&Hide
	Height	495
	Left	1680
	Top	4440
	Width	1095
Command Button	**Name**	**cmdStop**
	Caption	&Stop
	Enabled	0-False
	Height	615
	Left	4560
	Top	4200
	Width	975
Command Button	**Name**	**cmdPlay**
	Caption	&Play
	Enabled	0-False
	Height	615
	Left	3480
	Top	4200
	Width	975
TegoMM.VBX	**Name**	**Tegomm1**
	Height	495
	Left	3480
	Top	4920
	Width	3510
Command Button	**Name**	**cmdExit**
	Caption	E&xit
	Height	495
	Left	120

continues

Table BD1.1. continued

Object	Property	Setting
	Top	4920
	Width	1215
Label	**Name**	**lblNowPlaying**
	BackColor	(light gray)
	Caption	Current Position:
	Height	255
	Left	240
	Top	3360
	Width	2055
Image	**Name**	**imgMusic**
	Height	3090
	Left	120
	Picture	C:\EXPROG\Gallery\Midi.BMP (a BMP picture that is appropriate for the subject of this program)
	Top	120
	Width	6900
Menu	**(see Table BD1.2)**	**(see Figure BD1.5)**

Table BD1.2. The menu table of the frmPlayMIDI form.

Caption	Name
&File	mnuFile
...&Open	mnuOpen
...&Exit	mnuExit

Figure BD1.10.
*The frmPlayMIDI form
(in design mode).*

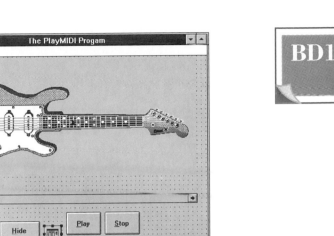

Attaching Code to the *Click* Event of the Exit Button

☐ Type the following code inside the cmdExit_Click() procedure of the frmPlayMIDI form:

```
Sub cmdExit_Click ()

    End

End Sub
```

Attaching Code to the *Click* Event of the Exit Menu Item

☐ Type the following code inside the mnuExit_Click() procedure of the frmPlayMIDI form:

```
Sub mnuExit_Click ()

    cmdExit_Click

End Sub
```

The code you typed executes the cmdExit_Click() procedure. Therefore, selecting the Exit item from the File menu has the same results as clicking the Exit button.

Attaching Code to the *Click* Event of the Hide Button

Whenever the user clicks the Hide button, the multimedia control is made invisible.

☐ Type the following code inside the cmdHide_Click() procedure of the frmPlayMIDI form:

```
Sub cmdHide_Click ()

    Tegomm1.Visible = False

End Sub
```

> **Note:** The only reason you were instructed to implement the Show and Hide buttons is to demonstrate that you can make your own multimedia buttons and make the multimedia control invisible.

Attaching Code to the *Click* Event of the Show Button

Whenever the user clicks the Show button, the multimedia control is made visible.

☐ Type the following code inside the cmdShow_Click() procedure of the frmPlayMIDI form:

```
Sub cmdShow_Click ()

    Tegomm1.Visible = True

End Sub
```

The code you typed sets the Visible property of the multimedia control to True.

Attaching Code to the *Load* Event of the Form

You'll now attach code to the Load event of the frmPlayMIDI form. The Form_Load() procedure is executed whenever the program starts.

☐ Type the following code inside the Form_Load() procedure of the frmPlayMIDI form:

```
Sub Form_Load ()

    Tegomm1.UpdateInterval = 250

End Sub
```

The code you typed sets the UpdateInterval property of the multimedia control to 250. This means that the `Tegomm1_StatusUpdate()` procedure is automatically executed every 250 milliseconds. Later in this chapter you'll write the code of the `Tegomm1_StatusUpdate()` procedure.

Opening a MIDI File

During design time, you placed the common dialog control inside the frmPlayMIDI file. This control is used to select a MIDI file. Whenever the user clicks the Open item from the File menu, the `mnuOpen_Click()` procedure is executed, which uses the common dialog control for selecting a file.

☐ Type the following code inside the `mnuOpen_Click()` procedure:

```
Sub mnuOpen_Click ()

    ' Selecting a file (with the common dialog box)

    ' Set an error trap
    On Error GoTo OpenError

    ' Set the items of the File Type list box
    CMDialog1.Filter = "All Files (*.*) ¦ *.* ¦Midi Files (*.mid)¦*.mid"

    ' Set the default File Type
    CMDialog1.FilterIndex = 2

    ' Display the common dialog box
    CMDialog1.Action = 1

    ' Remove the error trap
    On Error GoTo 0

    ' Open the selected file
    Tegomm1.DeviceType = "Sequencer"
    Tegomm1.Filename = CMDialog1.Filename
    Tegomm1.Command = "Open"
    If Tegomm1.Error > 0 Then
        cmdPlay.Enabled = False
        cmdStop.Enabled = False
        frmPlayMIDI.Caption = "The PlayMIDI Program - (No file is loaded)"
        MsgBox "Can't open " + CMDialog1.Filename, 16, "Error"
    Else
        cmdPlay.Enabled = True
        cmdStop.Enabled = True
        frmPlayMIDI.Caption = "The PlayMIDI Program -(" + CMDialog1.Filetitle + ")"

        hsbPosition.Min = 0
        hsbPosition.Max = Tegomm1.Length
        hsbPosition.Enabled = False
    End If

    ' Exit this procedure
    Exit Sub
```

```
OpenError:
    ' The user pressed the Cancel key of the common dialog
    'box or an error occurred.
    ' Exit this procedure
    Exit Sub
```

End Sub

The code you typed lets your user select a file.

An error trap is set:

```
On Error GoTo OpenError
```

This means that if during the execution of the mnuOpen_Click() procedure an error occurs, the procedure jumps to the OpenError line:

```
OpenError:

    ' Exit this procedure
    Exit Sub
```

So if an error occurred, the procedure terminates.

The Filter property of the common dialog control is set:

```
CMDialog1.Filter = "All Files (*.*) ¦ *.* ¦Midi Files (*.mid)¦*.mid"
```

This means that the user will be able to examine all the files (*.*) or just the files with the .MID file extension.

The default setting of the common dialog box is set so the user will see the files with the .MID file extension:

```
CMDialog1.FilterIndex = 2
```

Now that the settings of the common dialog control have been set, you can display the common dialog box as an Open dialog box:

```
CMDialog1.Action = 1
```

When the common dialog box is displayed, the user can type a name of a file that does not exist, or the user can select a file that resides on a drive that is not ready (for example, the user can select a file from the A: drive and there is no disk inside the A: drive). The common dialog box responds by generating an error, which cause the procedure to immediately branch to the OpenError line.

Recall that during design time you set the CancelError property of the common dialog box to True. This means that if the user clicks the Cancel button of the Open dialog box an error is generated, and again, the procedure immediately jumps to the OpenError line.

However, if the user selects a legal file, no error is generated. So after displaying the common dialog box by setting its Action property to 1, the procedure will not jump to the OpenError line if an error did not occur. Instead, if no error occurred, the mnuOpen_Click() procedure continues with its normal execution. Because there is no need to trap errors anymore, the error trapping is canceled:

```
On Error GoTo 0
```

Next, the DeviceType property of the multimedia control is set to play MIDI files:

```
Tegomm1.DeviceType = "Sequencer"
```

> **Note:** Before playing MIDI files with the multimedia control, you have to set the DeviceType property of the multimedia control to Sequencer.
>
> Before playing MIDI files with the multimedia control, you have to set the Filename property of the multimedia control to the name of the MIDI file.

The user selects a file with the common dialog box, and the selected file is stored in the Filename property of the common dialog box. The Filename property of the multimedia control is assigned with the filename and path that the user selected with the common dialog box:

```
Tegomm1.Filename = CMDialog1.Filename
```

Next, the Open command is issued:

```
    Tegomm1.Command = "Open"
```

An If…Else statement is executed to determine whether the Open command was carried out successfully:

```
If Tegomm1.Error > 0 Then
   cmdPlay.Enabled = False
   cmdStop.Enabled = False
   frmPlayMIDI.Caption = "The PlayMIDI Program - (No file is loaded)"
   MsgBox "Can't open " + CMDialog1.Filename, 16, "Error"
Else
   cmdPlay.Enabled = True
   cmdStop.Enabled = True
   frmPlayMIDI.Caption = "The PlayMIDI Program -(" + CMDialog1.Filetitle + ")"

   hsbPosition.Min = 0
   hsbPosition.Max = Tegomm1.Length
   hsbPosition.Enabled = False
End If
```

If the Error property of the multimedia control is greater than 0, it means that an error occurred during the execution of the last command of the multimedia control. The last command that was executed by the multimedia control was the Open command, so the preceding If…Else statement examines whether the Open command was successfully executed.

If an error occurred during the execution of the Open command, the Play and Stop buttons that you placed inside the frmPlayMIDI form are disabled:

```
cmdPlay.Enabled = False
cmdStop.Enabled = False
```

and the Caption property of the frmPlayMIDI form is set as follows:

```
frmPlayMIDI.Caption = "The PlayMIDI Program - (No file is loaded)"
```

Finally, a message box is displayed, telling the user that the file can't be opened:

```
MsgBox "Can't open " + CMDialog1.Filename, 16, "Error"
```

If no error occurred during the execution of the Open command, the code under the Else is executed.

The Play and Stop buttons you placed inside the form are enabled:

```
cmdPlay.Enabled = True
cmdStop.Enabled = True
```

The Caption property of the form is set to indicate which MIDI file is open:

```
frmPlayMIDI.Caption = "The PlayMIDI Program -(" + CMDialog1.Filetitle + ")"
```

The Min property of the scroll bar is set to 0:

```
hsbPosition.Min = 0
```

The Max property of the scroll bar is set to the Length property of the MIDI file:

```
hsbPosition.Max = Tegomm1.Length
```

So the range of the scroll bar represents the entire range of the MIDI file. Later in this chapter you'll type code that changes the scroll bar position according to the position of the played MIDI file.

Note: The length of the MIDI file is stored as the Length property of the multimedia control.

The Enabled property of the scroll bar is set to False (so that the user will not be able to manually change the position of the scroll bar):

```
hsbPosition.Enabled = False
```

Then the Exit Sub statement is executed to terminate the procedure.

Note: The PlayMIDI program does not let the user change the position of the MIDI file. However, you can implement your own programs that do let the user set the position of the MIDI file to any desired position by changing the scroll bar position.

Attaching Code to the *Click* Event of the Play Button

Whenever the user clicks the Play button, the MIDI file is played.

☐ Type the following code inside the cmdPlay_Click() procedure:

```
Sub cmdPlay_Click ()

    Tegomm1.Command = "Play"

End Sub
```

The code you typed issues the Play command to the multimedia control.

Attaching Code to the *Click* Event of the Stop Button

Whenever the user clicks the Stop button the MIDI file stops playing.

☐ Type the following code inside the cmdStop_Click() procedure:

```
Sub cmdStop_Click ()

    Tegomm1.Command = "Stop"

End Sub
```

The code you typed issues the Stop command to the multimedia control.

Attaching Code to the *StatusUpdate* Event of the Multimedia Control

Recall that during design time you set the UpdateInterval property of the multimedia control to 250. This means that the Tegomm1_StatusUpdate() procedure is executed automatically every 250 milliseconds.

☐ Type the following code inside the `Tegomm1_StatusUpdate()` procedure:

```
Sub Tegomm1_StatusUpdate ()

    hsbPosition.Value = Tegomm1.Position

End Sub
```

The code you type sets the Value property of the scroll bar to the Position property of the multimedia control:

```
hsbPosition.Value = Tegomm1.Position
```

As the MIDI file is played, the multimedia control automatically updates the Position property of the multimedia control. Because the `Tegomm1_StatusUpdate()` procedure is executed every 250 milliseconds, the scroll bar changes its position every 250 milliseconds.

Attaching Code to the *Done* Event of the Multimedia Control

You'll now attach code to the `Done` event of the multimedia control.

☐ Type the following code inside the `Tegomm1_Done()` procedure:

```
Sub Tegomm1_Done ()

    If Tegomm1.Position = Tegomm1.Length Then
        Tegomm1.Command = "Prev"
    End If

End Sub
```

The `Done` event occurs whenever the multimedia control finishes playing. An `If` statement is executed to examine the reason for the occurrence of the `Done` event. After the `Play` command is issued, the MIDI file is played. Eventually the entire MIDI file will be played, and this will generate a `Done` event. The `If` statement checks whether the current position of the MIDI file is equal to the Length property of the multimedia control:

```
If Tegomm1.Position = Tegomm1.Length Then

    Tegomm1.Command = "Prev"

End If
```

If the Position property is equal to the Length property, it means that the current position (the Position property) of the MIDI file is at the end of the file, and the entire MIDI file was played.

The `Prev` command is issued to rewind the MIDI file, so the next time the user clicks the Play button, the MIDI file is ready to be played from its beginning.

☐ Execute the PlayMIDI program and experiment with it.

The PlayAVI Program

The PlayAVI program that you'll now write demonstrates how you can play movie AVI files. What is a movie AVI file? It is a file that contains a movie (video and audio). Your PC then acts as a TV that plays movies. To play a movie AVI file, you need a PC with an 80386 processor or better, and a VGA monitor or better. You do not need any other hardware.

As stated at the beginning of this chapter, the Media Player program can be used to determine whether your PC is capable of playing movie AVI files.

> **Note:** If your PC has an 80386 or better CPU and a VGA monitor or better, you'll be able to play movie AVI files, provided that you installed the movie AVI drivers (just like you have to install the appropriate drivers for playing WAV and MIDI files).

Generating Movie AVI Files

There are two ways you can obtain movie AVI files: purchase a CD with movie AVI files in it or generate the AVI files with a camcorder and a video capture card.

When purchasing a CD that has in it movie AVI files, make sure to read the software license agreement of the CD to make sure that you are allowed to distribute the movie AVI files with your programs.

If you want to generate the AVI files yourself, you have to install a video capture card into your PC (which costs about $500 to $800), and you have to use a camcorder. Figure BD1.11 is a schematic diagram showing a camcorder connected to a video capture card inside the PC. Typically, the manufacturer of the video capture card supplies the software that converts the captured video into an AVI file (for example, you record something, and your recordings are saved as the MyFilm.AVI file).

Figure BD1.11.
Generating a movie AVI file using a camcorder.

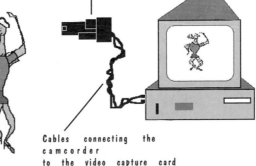

Using the PlayAVI Program to Play Movie AVI Files

You'll now write a Visual Basic program called PlayAVI that plays movie AVI files.

Upon startup of the PlayAVI program, the window shown in Figure BD1.12 appears.

Figure BD1.12.
The window of the PlayAVI program.

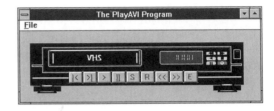

As shown in Figure BD1.12, the TegoMM.VBX multimedia control is used for playing the AVI file.

Note: The PlayAVI program uses the buttons of the TegoMM.VBX control as the buttons of the VCR. However, just like the PlayMIDI program that uses your Play and Stop buttons, you can make the multimedia control invisible and use your own buttons for the buttons that manipulate the playback of the AVI file.

Figure BD1.13.
The File menu of the PlayAVI program.

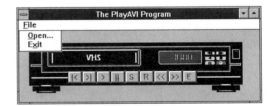

Figure BD1.13 shows the menu of the PlayAVI program.

Here is how the PlayAVI program operates:

☐ The user selects Open item from the File menu and loads an AVI file.

PlayAVI responds by loading the AVI file, and the title of the PlayAVI window indicates which AVI file is loaded.

☐ The user clicks the Play button of the multimedia control (the third button from the left to play the AVI file).

PlayAVI responds by playing the movie of the AVI file that was loaded (see FigureBD1.14). The sound of the movie is played through the sound card.

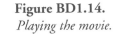

Figure BD1.14.
Playing the movie.

BD1

After writing the PlayAVI program, experiment with the buttons of the multimedia control. In particular, click the Stop button to stop the playback, and then click the Step button (second button from the right) and the Back button (third button from the right). As you click the Step and Back buttons, you can view individual frames of the movie.

The Visual Implementation of the frmPlayAVI Form

You'll now visually design the frmPlayAVI form of the PlayAVI form.

☐ Select New Project from the File menu, and save the new project as follows: Save the new form as PlayAVI.frm inside the C:\EXPROG\BD1 directory and save the new project file as PlayAVI.mak inside the C:\EXPROG\BD1 directory.

If the TegoMM.VBX control does not appear inside your Toolbox, add it to your project:

☐ Select Add File from the File menu, and add the file C:\Windows\System\TegoMM.VBX.

☐ Implement the frmPlayAVI form according to the specifications in Table BD1.3. When you finish implementing the form, it should look like the one shown in Figure BD1.15.

Table BD1.3. The properties table of the frmPlayAVI form.

Object	Property	Setting
Form	Name	frmPlayAVI
	BackColor	(light gray)
	Caption	The PlayAVI Program
	Height	2595
	Icon	C:\VB\Icons\Misc\Misc42.ICO
	Left	1020
	Top	1140
	Width	6645
Common Dialog Box	Name	CMDialog1
	CancelError	-1-True

continues 749

Table BD1.3. continued

Object	Property	Setting
	Left	6000
	Top	1320
TegoMM.VBX	**Name**	**Tegomm1**
	Height	330
	Left	1320
	Top	1080
	Width	3510
Image	**Name**	**imgMovie**
	Height	1665
	Left	120
	Picture	C:\EXPROG\Gallery\AVI.BMP
	Top	120
	Width	6060
Menu	**(see Table BD1.4)**	**(see Figure BD1.13)**

Table BD1.4. The menu table of frmPlayAVI.

Caption	Name
&File	mnuFile
...&Open...	mnuOpen
...E&xit	mnuExit

Figure BD1.15.
The frmPlayAVI form (in design mode).

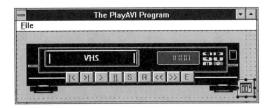

Attaching Code to the *Click* Event of the Exit Menu Item

You'll now attach code to the Exit item of the File menu.

☐ Type the following code inside the mnuExit_Click() procedure:

```
Sub mnuExit_Click ()

    End

End Sub
```

Attaching Code to the *Click* Event of the Open Menu Item

You'll now attach code to the Click event of the Open menu item.

☐ Type the following code inside the mnuOpen_Click() procedure of the frmPlayAVI form:

```
Sub mnuOpen_Click ()

    ' Selecting a file (with the common dialog box)

    ' Set an error trap
    On Error GoTo OpenError

    ' Set the items of the File Type list box
    CMDialog1.Filter = "All Files (*.*) ¦ *.* ¦Movie AVI Files (*.avi)¦*.avi"

    ' Set the default File Type
    CMDialog1.FilterIndex = 2

    ' Display the common dialog box
    CMDialog1.Action = 1

    ' Remove the error trap
    On Error GoTo 0

    ' Open the selected file
    Tegomm1.DeviceType = "AVIVideo"
    Tegomm1.FileName = CMDialog1.Filename
    Tegomm1.Command = "Open"
    If Tegomm1.Error > 0 Then
        frmPlayAVI.Caption = "The PlayAVI Program - (No file is loaded)"
        MsgBox "Can't open " + CMDialog1.Filename, 16, "Error"
    Else
        frmPlayAVI.Caption = "The PlayAVI Program -(" + CMDialog1.Filetitle + ")"

    End If

    ' Exit this procedure
    Exit Sub

OpenError:
    ' The user pressed the Cancel key of the common dialog box or an error occured

    ' Exit this procedure
    Exit Sub

End Sub
```

The code you typed is very similar to the code you typed inside the `mnuOpen_Click()` procedure of the frmPlayMIDI form of the PlayMIDI program. Of course, now you are opening an AVI file. Therefore, the Filter property of the common dialog box is set as follows:

```
CMDialog1.Filter = "All Files (*.*) ¦ *.* ¦Movie AVI Files (*.avi)¦*.avi"
```

When opening the AVI file, you set the Device type to AVIVideo:

```
Tegomm1.DeviceType = "AVIVideo"
```

The selected AVI file is assigned to the FileName property of the multimedia control:

```
Tegomm1.FileName = CMDialog1.Filename
```

Then the Open command is issued:

```
Tegomm1.Command = "Open"
If Tegomm1.Error > 0 Then
    frmPlayAVI.Caption = "The PlayAVI Program - (No file is loaded)"
    MsgBox "Can't open " + CMDialog1.Filename, 16, "Error"
Else
    frmPlayAVI.Caption = "The PlayAVI Program -(" + CMDialog1.Filetitle + ")"
End If
```

☐ Execute the PlayAVI program and experiment with it.

Data CDs and Audio CDs

Many PCs have CD-ROM drives. Typically, you can use the CD-ROM drive for using data CDs as well as for using audio CDs.

A *data CD* is a CD that stores data. It is a standard data storage device like the hard drive, a 5.25" disk, or a 3.5" disk, but a data CD has the following special characteristics:

- Your CD-ROM drive cannot write into the data CD. You can only read the data of the data CD.

- The data CD can store about 700 MB.

Most PC users do not have the machinery to generate data CDs by themselves.

Once a CD-ROM drive is installed into your PC, it is treated like any other drives. (However, you can only read data from the CD. You cannot write data into the CD.)

You can access the CD-ROM drive just as you would other drives. For example, if your CD-ROM drive is installed as a D: drive, then from the DOS prompt you can examine the directories of the data CD that was inserted into the CD-ROM drive as follows:

```
DIR D:\  {Enter}
```

Similarly, you can use the File Manager of Windows to read the contents of a data CD that was inserted into the CD-ROM drive.

You can also copy files from the data CD to your hard drive. However, the data CD is a read-only device. This means that you cannot copy files to the data CD.

Note: Once you copy a file from the data CD to your hard drive, the file on your hard drive has the read-only attribute (the r attribute). This means that you cannot modify the file.

Nevertheless, you can change the attribute of the file on your hard drive by using the Properties item of the File menu in File Manager. In File Manager select the file that was copied from the data CD, select Properties from the File menu of File Manager, and remove the × of the Read-Only check box. Now that the r attribute has been removed from the file, you can modify the file.

Note: There are many types of CD-ROM drives. Basically, the faster the CD-ROM drive, the more expensive it is. Usually, the CD-ROM drive is categorized as double speed (2X), triple speed (3X), and nowadays, some companies manufacture the 4X CD-ROM drive.

You should be aware that the operating system known as Windows NT does not recognize all CD-ROM drives. Windows NT requires that the CD-ROM drive be an SCSI CD-ROM drive. SCSI is a special interface protocol. So, for example, you can have a CD-ROM drive that is recognized by Windows, but if that CD-ROM drive is not an SCSI drive, Windows NT 3.5 will report that you do not have a CD-ROM drive in your system.

A data CD looks just like an audio CD sold in a music stores. An audio CD contains recording, and you can play the audio only if your CD-ROM drive is capable of playing CD audio. Most CD-ROM drives are capable of using both data CDs and audio CDs.

There are several ways to listen to an audio CD:

- Typically, the CD-ROM drive has a jack that lets you plug in earphones (see Figure BD1.16).
- Many sound card vendors sell their sound cards as a multimedia package that includes a CD-ROM drive and a sound card. The CD-ROM drive can serve as both a data CD-ROM drive and as an audio CD-ROM drive. When installing the CD-ROM drive, you have to internally connect the CD-ROM drive to the sound card. So when you play CD audio, the sound is played through the sound card (see Figure BD1.17).

Figure BD1.16.
Connecting earphones to a CD-ROM drive that is capable of playing CD audio. Typically, a volume control lets you adjust the volume.

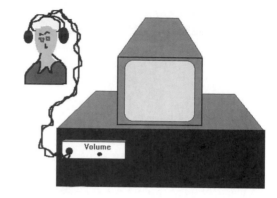

DO   DON'T

DO consider your selection of a CD-ROM drive based on the following factors:

- You should consider the speed of the CD-ROM drive. Ideally, you want the fastest CD-ROM drive so that you can read data CDs as fast as possible. For example, if the data CD that you insert into the CD-ROM drive is an encyclopedia program, you want to be able to extract information from the encyclopedia as fast as possible. Also, many programs are now sold on data CDs. When you install the program, the installation (copying files from the CD to your hard drive) will be performed faster on a fast CD-ROM drive than on a slow one. And yes, a faster CD-ROM drive costs more!

- Most CD-ROM drives can use both data CDs and audio CDs. Make sure that the CD-ROM drive you are planning to purchase can use both types of CDs.

- Most CD-ROM drives let you connect the CD to the sound card so that you can hear the CD audio through the sound card.

- There are other features that may or may not be important to you. For example, some CD-ROM drives require that you use a cartridge. That is, you cannot simply insert the CD (a data CD or an audio CD) into your CD-ROM drive. Instead, you have to insert the CD into a cartridge, and then insert the cartridge into the CD-ROM drive. (This makes the process of inserting CDs into the CD-ROM drive a little bit longer, but most users get used to it.)

- A consideration with some CD-ROM drives is the mechanical robotics capabilities. For example, in some CD-ROM drives, you have to manually open and close the door of the CD-ROM to insert or eject a CD. Other CD-ROM drives let the software eject the CD. So instead of pressing a button on the CD-ROM drive, the software has an Eject button, and when you click the Eject button, the door of the CD-ROM drive opens.

- You need to decide whether you want to purchase an SCSI-type CD-ROM drive. If you plan to use the PC for Windows NT, you must purchase a CD-ROM drive that has an SCSI connection.

As you can see, there are many things to consider when purchasing a CD-ROM drive.

Figure BD1.17.
An internal connection between a CD-ROM drive that is capable of playing CD audio and the sound card. The sound is played through the speakers of the sound card.

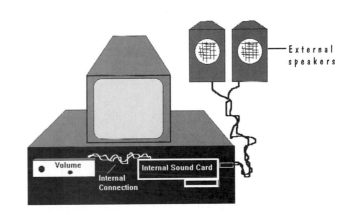

Note: As previously stated, the data CD is treated like a regular storage device. For example, you can execute the DIR DOS command to examine the directory of the data CD, you can use the COPY DOS command to copy files from the data CD, and so on.

However, when you insert an audio CD into your CD-ROM drive, you cannot execute the DIR, COPY, or any other command. When a CD audio is inserted into your CD-ROM drive, your CD-ROM drive simply serves as a CD audio player machine that can be remotely operated by software to play, stop, and so on.

The PlayCD Program

You'll now write the PlayCD program, which demonstrates how easy it is to write a Visual Basic program that plays CD audio.

Before writing the PlayCD program yourself, review its specifications.

☐ Upon startup of the PlayCD program, the window shown in Figure BD1.18 appears.

The user can now insert an audio CD into the CD-ROM drive and play the CD audio.

Figure BD1.18.

The PlayCD program.

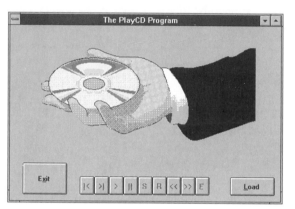

To play the audio CD the user has to do the following:

☐ Click the Load button to load the CD.

☐ Click the Play button of the multimedia control (the third button from the left on the multimedia control).

After you write the PlayCD program, experiment with it. Click the Play button to play. Click the Stop and Pause buttons to stop and pause the playback. Click the Next button (second button from the left on the multimedia control) to advance to the next track. Click the Prev button (first button from the left on the multimedia control) to go back to the previous track.

Now that you know what the PlayCD program is supposed to do you can write the program.

The Visual Implementation of the frmPlayCD Form

☐ Select New Project from the File menu and save the new project as follows: Save the new form as PlayCD.frm inside the C:\EXPROG\BD1 directory and save the new project file as PlayCD.mak inside the C:\EXPROG\BD1 directory.

The PlayCD program uses the TegoMM.VBX control. Therefore, you have to add this control to your project:

☐ Select Add File from the File menu and select the C:\Windows\System\TegoMM.VBX file.

☐ Implement the frmPlayCD form according to the specifications in Table BD1.5. When you finish implementing the form, it should look like the one shown in Figure BD1.19.

Table BD1.5. The properties table of the frmPlayCD form.

Object	Property	Setting
Form	**Name**	**frmPlayCD**
	BackColor	(light gray)
	Caption	The PlayCD Program
	Height	5145
	Icon	C:\VB\Icons\Misc\EAR.ICO
	Left	1035
	Top	1140
	Width	7485
Command Button	**Name**	**cmdLoad**
	Caption	&Load
	Height	495
	Left	6000
	Top	4080
	Width	1215
Command Button	**Name**	**cmdExit**
	Caption	E&xit
	Height	855
	Left	360
	Top	3720
	Width	1215
TegoMM.VBX	**Name**	**Tegomm1**
	Height	495
	Left	1920

continues

Table BD1.5. continued

Object	Property	Setting
Command Button	**Name**	**cmdLoad**
	Top	4080
	Width	3510
Image	**Name**	**imgCD**
	Height	3135
	Left	720
	Picture	C:\EXPROG\Gallery\CD.BMP (a picture that is appropriate for the subject of the program)
	Top	120
	Width	6075

Attaching Code to the *Click* Event of the Exit Button

You'll now attach code to the Click event of the Exit button of the frmPlayCD form.

☐ Type the following code inside the cmdExit_Click() procedure of the frmPlayCD form:

```
Sub cmdExit_Click ()

    End

End Sub
```

Figure BD1.19.
The frmPlayCD form (in design mode).

Attaching Code to the *Click* Event of the Load Button

You'll now attach code to the `Click` event of the Load button.

☐ Type the following code inside the `cmdLoad_Click()` procedure of the frmPlayCD form:

```
Sub cmdLoad_Click ()

    Tegomm1.DeviceType = "CDAudio"
    Tegomm1.Command = "Open"

End Sub
```

The code you typed sets the DeviceType property of the multimedia control to CDAudio:

```
Tegomm1.DeviceType = "CDAudio"
```

Then the `Open` command is issued:

```
Tegomm1.Command = "Open"
```

That's it! the PlayCD program is complete.

☐ Execute the PlayCD program and experiment with it. Note that in order to see the PlayCD program in action you have to insert an audio CD into the CD-ROM drive, click the Load button, and then click the Play button.

Summary

In this chapter you have written simple multimedia programs that play various multi-media devices. The PlayMIDI program illustrates how to play MIDI files, the PlayAVI program illustrates how to play movie AVI files, and the PlayCD program illustrates how to play audio CDs.

Q&A

Q I would like to perform additional multimedia-related tasks. For example, in the PlayMIDI program, I want to display the total length of the MIDI file in seconds, and as the MIDI file is played, I want to display the elapsed time. Also, I want to be able to cut, paste, and copy sections of WAV files; I want to be able to increase/decrease the volume; I want to create echo; I want to be able to record my own voice and then play it so it will sound like a different person; and I have millions of other ideas that I want to implement. Help!

A   In this chapter you just touched the surface of multimedia programming. The multimedia control is capable of performing all the tasks you mentioned in your question, but we can't cover all these topics in this book, because every book has a limited finite thickness. You might want to consult the Sams Publishing book *Master Visual Basic 3* by Gurewich and Gurewich, which elaborates on multimedia programming (as well as other powerful programming topics in Visual Basic).

Q   **I purchased a sound card, installed it according to the manufacturer's instructions, and later checked the Device menu of Media Player. Guess what? The Sound item does not appear inside the Device menu. Nevertheless, the sound card comes with software, which plays WAV files without any problems! Should I insist on seeing Sound inside the Device menu of Media Player?**

A   Yes. This way other Windows application will also be able to play WAV files on your PC. That's what Windows is all about—if Windows accepts the device (and the acceptance can be tested by examining the Device menu), every Windows application should be able to use the device.

Quiz

1. The current position of the played file is given by the _____ property of the multimedia control.

2. The length of the played file is given by the _____ property of the multimedia control.

3. The DeviceType property of the TegoMM.VBX control determines various media. Give some examples of values you can assign to the DeviceType property.

Exercise

Modify the PlayMIDI program so that when the file has been played in its entirety the playback starts all over again.

Quiz Answers

1. Position

2. Length

3. To play WAV files through the sound card, set the DeviceType property as follows:

   ```
   MyTegoMM.DeviceType = "WaveAudio"
   ```

   To play WAV files through the PC speaker, set the DeviceType property as follows:

   ```
   MyTegoMM.DeviceType = "PCSpeaker"
   ```

   To play MIDI files through the sound card, set the DeviceType property as follows:

```
MyTegoMM.DeviceType = "Sequencer"
```

To play AVI files, set the DeviceType property as follows:

```
MyTegoMM.DeviceType = "AVIVideo"
```

Exercise Answer

Here is the `Tegomm1_Done()` procedure of the PlayMIDI program:

```
Sub Tegomm1_Done ()

    If Tegomm1.Position = Tegomm1.Length Then
        Tegomm1.Command = "Prev"
    End If

End Sub
```

When the file has been played in its entirety, the `Prev` command is issued. The next time the user plays the file, the MIDI file starts playing from the beginning.

To cause the MIDI file to automatically start playing all over again when the entire file is played modify the `Tegomm1_Done()` procedure as follows:

```
Sub Tegomm1_Done ()

    If Tegomm1.Position = Tegomm1.Length Then

        Tegomm1.Command = "Prev"
        Tegomm1.Command = "Play"

    End If

End Sub
```

When the file has been played in its entirety, you issue the Prev command to rewind the file, and then you issue the Play command to start the file playing again.

Bonus Day 2+

Animation

In this chapter you'll learn how to write animation programs with Visual Basic.

What Is Animation?

Animation is the process of displaying pictures one after the other, thereby creating the illusion that the objects shown in the pictures are moving. So in effect, creating animation amounts to creating a movie or a show on your PC.

Animation is used in education applications, game applications, and for adding cosmetic value to your programs. For example, you can incorporate animation into your Visual Basic programs so that upon startup of your programs your users will see an animated welcome show.

As you'll see in this chapter, creating animation shows with Visual Basic is a lot of fun!

The HelpMe Program

The HelpMe program that you'll now write is an example of a Visual Basic program that provides help to your user via animation.

Before writing the HelpMe program, review its specifications.

Upon startup of the program, the window shown in Figure BD2.1 appears.

Figure BD2.1.
The HelpMe program.

The user can now click the Start button to display a small animation show that teaches how to place a command button inside a Visual Basic form.

When the user clicks the Start button, a sequence of pictures is displayed. Each picture remains on the screen for a few seconds.

The first picture is shown in Figure BD2.2. This picture remains on the screen for 2 seconds. As you can see, the HelpMe program displays an empty Visual Basic form and the Toolbox of Visual Basic. The user also sees the message Double click this icon.

Figure BD2.2.
Telling the user to double-click the icon of the command button inside the Toolbox.

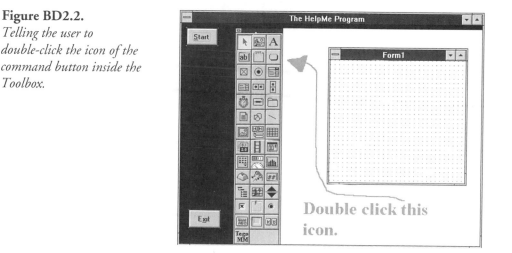

BD2

The next picture the user sees is the picture shown in Figure BD2.3. As shown, the command icon button inside the Toolbox is emphasized, and the user sees a message that says that Visual Basic will place the button inside the form.

The picture shown in Figure BD2.3 remains on the screen for 2 seconds, and then the picture shown in Figure BD2.4 is displayed.

Figure BD2.3.
Showing the command button icon inside the Toolbox, and telling the user that Visual Basic will place the button inside the form.

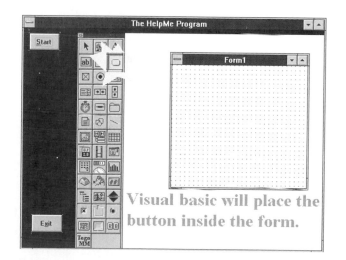

Figure BD2.4.

Showing the button inside the form.

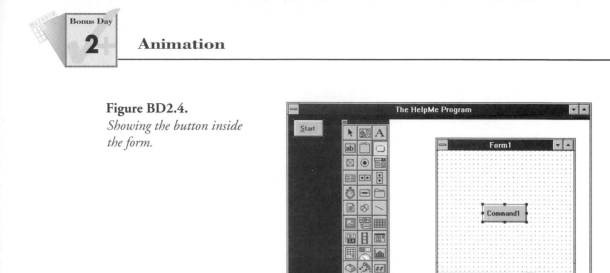

The picture shown in Figure BD2.4 shows the button inside the form. Also, a message is displayed, telling the user that the button is now inside the form.

The picture shown in Figure BD2.4 remains on the screen for 2 seconds, and then the picture shown in Figure BD2.5 is displayed.

Figure BD2.5.

Telling the user that the button can now be enlarged.

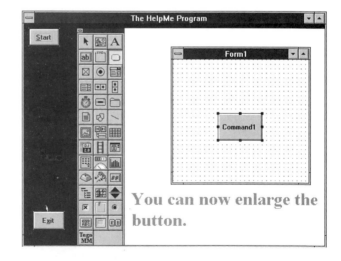

Note that the button in Figure BD2.5 is now wider. The picture shown in Figure BD2.5 remains on the screen for 2 seconds, and then the picture shown in Figure BD2.6 is displayed. As shown in Figure BD2.6, the button inside the form is enlarged again.

Figure BD2.6.
Additional enlargement of the command button.

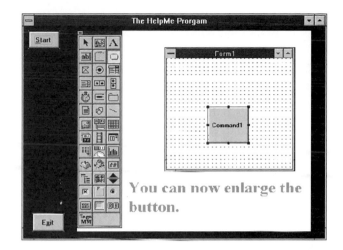

Now take a look at the whole process from the time the user clicks the Start button. The objective of the HelpMe program is to teach the user how to place a command button inside a Visual Basic form. The user will see the following sequence of figures:

Figure BD2.2
Figure BD2.3
Figure BD2.4
Figure BD2.5
Figure BD2.6

If you look at these figures, you'll see that the pictures explain how to place a button inside the form.

> **Note:** As the first animation program in this chapter, the HelpMe program demonstrates a very simple animation. Later in this chapter, you'll learn how to create an animation show with non-synchronized sound, and an animation show with synchronized sound.

Preparing the Pictures for the Animation

Typically, you'll use the Paintbrush program that comes with Windows to create your animation pictures.

Here is how you can prepare the animation pictures of the HelpMe program.

☐ Start Paintbrush (the program icon of Paintbrush is usually inside the Accessories group of icons).

☐ Select Image Attributes from the Options menu of Paintbrush.

   Paintbrush responds by displaying the Image Attributes dialog box.

☐ Set the Units option to Pels (pixels), because you want to indicate the size of the new picture in pixels.

☐ Set the Width of the picture to 455.

☐ Set the Height of the picture to 400.

☐ Click the OK button of the Image Attributes dialog box.

   Paintbrush responds by displaying an empty picture with a size of 455 by 400 pixels, ready to be painted by you.

You can now draw your own pictures, or, as is the case with the HelpMe program, paste pictures from the Clipboard to Paintbrush.

☐ Start a new project with Visual Basic, make the Toolbox the active window, and then press Alt+Print Screen.

   Windows responds by copying the Toolbox to the Clipboard.

☐ Switch to Paintbrush, and select Paste from the Edit menu.

   Paintbrush responds by pasting the contents of the Clipboard (which currently contains the picture of the Toolbox) into Paintbrush.

☐ In a similar manner, you can now return to Visual Basic, make Form1 form smaller, make Form1 the active form, press Alt+Print Screen, switch back to Paintbrush, and finally select Paste from the Edit menu of Paintbrush.

   Paintbrush responds by pasting the contents of the Clipboard (which currently contains the picture of Form1) to Paintbrush.

☐ Now drag the pasted picture to the right. Your Paintbrush picture now should look similar to the picture shown in Figure BD2.2.

☐ Use the tools of Paintbrush to add the message shown in Figure BD2.2. That is, use the text tool of Paintbrush to type `Double click this icon`. Then use the free-hand tool to draw a sloppy arrow pointing to the command icon.

☐ Save the picture as Help00.BMP (a BMP file) inside the C:\EXPROG\BMP directory.

The trick is to now generate the second BMP file, which is shown in Figure BD2.3. In order to provide the user with the illusion that the animation continues, the objects of the second BMP file must be placed at exactly the same coordinates as the objects of the previous picture. You can achieve this by selecting Cursor Location from the View menu of Paintbrush, and noticing the coordinates of the mouse. So to place Form1 at the same coordinates in all the BMP pictures, you can place the mouse cursor on the upper-left corner of Form1 inside the first BMP picture and note the coordinates. Then you can load the second BMP file, mark the point where the upper-left corner of Form1 should be, and then use the tools of Paintbrush to move Form1 to the same coordinates. This sounds like a lot of work, but after a little practice, you'll be able to manipulate pictures very easily.

Note: The HelpMe program uses the five BMP files shown in Figures BD2.7 through BD2.11.

If you prefer, you can invest time preparing the pictures of the animation at a later time. For now, so that you will be able to quickly continue with this tutorial, using Paintbrush to create simple small BMP pictures that do not take a long time to prepare. That is, use Paintbrush to create five BMP files similar to the pictures shown in Figures BD2.12 through BD2.16, which show a man lifting weights. As you can see, it does not take much work to create the five pictures of this animation show. Make sure to save the BMP files as Help00.BMP, Help01.BMP, Help02.BMP, Help03.BMP, and Help04.BMP inside the C:\EXPROG\BMP directory. Don't forget to use the Image Attributes item of the Options menu of Paintbrush to set the sizes of the BMP pictures before you draw the pictures.

Figure BD2.7.
*The Help00.BMP file
(frame 1 of 5).*

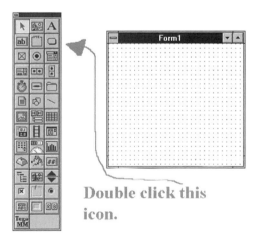

**Double click this
icon.**

Figure BD2.8.
The Help01.BMP file (frame 2 of 5).

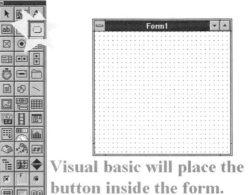

Visual basic will place the button inside the form.

Figure BD2.9.
The Help02.BMP file (frame 3 of 5).

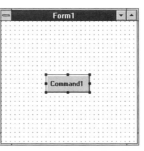

As you can see, the button is inside the form.

Figure BD2.10.
The Help03.BMP file (frame 4 of 5).

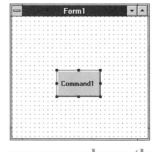

You can now enlarge the button.

Figure BD2.11.
The Help04.BMP file (frame 5 of 5).

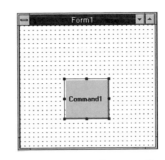

You can now enlarge the button.

Figure BD2.12.
The Help00.BMP file (frame 1 of 5). A simplified version.

Figure BD2.13.
The Help01.BMP file (frame 2 of 5). A simplified version.

Figure BD2.14.
*The Help02.BMP file
(frame 3 of 5). A simplified
version.*

Figure BD2.15.
*The Help03.BMP file
(frame 4 of 5). A simplified
version.*

Figure BD2.16.
*The Help04.BMP file
(frame 5 of 5). A simplified
version.*

The Visual Implementation of the frmHelpMe Form

You'll now visually implement the frmHelpMe form of the HelpMe program.

☐ Select New Project from the File menu, and save the project as follows: Save the new form file as HelpMe.frm inside the C:\EXPROG\BD2 directory and save the new project file as HelpMe.MAK inside the C:\EXPROG\BD2 directory.

☐ Implement the frmHelpMe form according to the specifications in Table BD2.1. When you finish implementing the form, it should look like the one shown in Figure BD2.17.

BD2

Table BD2.1. The properties table of the frmHelpMe form.

Object	Property	Setting
Form	**Name**	**frmHelpMe**
	BackColor	(black)
	Caption	The HelpMe Program
	Height	6690
	Icon	C:\VB\Icons\Arrows\Point01.ICO
	Left	825
	Top	180
	Width	8310
Timer	**Name**	**tmrAnimation**
	Interval	2000
	Left	480
	Top	3960
Command Button	**Name**	**cmdStart**
	Caption	&Start
	Height	495
	Left	120
	Top	120
	Width	855
Command Button	**Name**	**cmdExit**
	Caption	E&xit
	Height	495
	Left	240

continued

Table BD2.1. continued

Object	Property	Setting
	Top	5040
	Width	855
Image	**Name**	**imgHelp**
	Height	6000
	Left	1440
	Picture	C:\EXPROG\BMP\Help00.BMP
	Top	120
	Visible	0-False
	Width	6825

Figure BD2.17.
*The frmHelpMe form (in
design mode).*

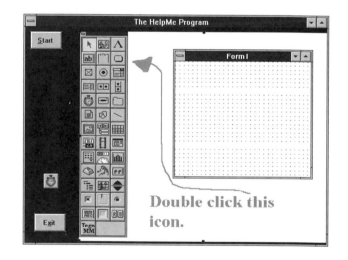

Entering the Code of the General Declarations Section of the frmHelpMe Form

☐ Type the following code inside the general declarations section of the form:

```
Option Explicit

Dim gAnimationInProgress
```

As you'll soon see, gAnimationInProgress serves as a flag that indicates whether the animation
is in progress.

Attaching Code to the *Click* Event of the Exit Button

You'll now attach code to the Click event of the Exit button.

☐ Type the following code inside the cmdExit_Click() procedure:

```
Sub cmdExit_Click ()

    End

End Sub
```

Attaching Code to the *Load* Event of the Form

You'll now attach code to the Load event of the from.

☐ Type the following code inside the Form_Load() procedure:

```
Sub Form_Load ()

    gAnimationInProgress = 0

End Sub
```

The code you typed is executed whenever the program starts. You set the gAnimationInProgress variable to 0. The gAnimationInProgress was declared inside the general declarations section, and it is therefore accessible from any procedure of the form.

The gAnimationInProgress variable serves as a flag: When gAnimationInProgress is equal to 1, animation is in progress; when gAnimationInProgress is equal to 0, the animation is not in progress. Because you do not want the animation to start unless the user clicks the Start button, the code inside the Form_Load() procedure sets the value of this flag to 0.

Attaching Code to the *Click* Event of the Start Button

You'll now attach code to the Click event of the Start button.

☐ Type the following code inside the cmdStart_Click() procedure:

```
Sub cmdStart_Click ()

    gAnimationInProgress = 1
    imgHelp.Visible = True

End Sub
```

The code you typed sets the gAnimationInProgress variable to 1. As you'll soon see, this causes the animation to start.

The code you typed also sets the Visible property of the imgHelp control to True. This means that the first picture of the help session is displayed. At design time, you set the Picture property of the imgHelp control to Help00.BMP. So upon clicking the Start button, the first picture that will be displayed is the Help00.BMP picture.

Attaching Code to the *Timer* Event of the tmrAnimation Timer

You'll now attach code to the Timer event of the tmrAnimation timer. As you'll see, this code is responsible for displaying the animation. During design time, you set the Interval property of the timer to 2000. This means that every 2000 milliseconds (2 seconds) the tmrAnimation_Timer() procedure is executed automatically.

☐ Type the following code inside the tmrAnimation_Timer() procedure:

```
Sub tmrAnimation_Timer ()

    Static FrameIndex

    If gAnimationInProgress = 0 Then Exit Sub

    FrameIndex = FrameIndex + 1
    If FrameIndex = 5 Then
       FrameIndex = 0
       gAnimationInProgress = 0
       imgHelp.Picture = LoadPicture("C:\EXPROG\BMP\Help00.BMP")
       imgHelp.Visible = False
       Exit Sub
    End If

    Select Case FrameIndex
        Case 1
        imgHelp.Picture = LoadPicture("C:\EXPROG\BMP\Help01.BMP")

        Case 2
        imgHelp.Picture = LoadPicture("C:\EXPROG\BMP\Help02.BMP")

        Case 3
        imgHelp.Picture = LoadPicture("C:\EXPROG\BMP\Help03.BMP")

        Case 4
        imgHelp.Picture = LoadPicture("C:\EXPROG\BMP\Help04.BMP")

    End Select

End Sub
```

The code you typed declares a static variable:

```
Static FrameIndex
```

A static variable does not lose its value when the procedure terminates. Upon the first execution of the tmrAnimation_Timer() procedure, FrameIndex is equal to 0. During the execution of the tmrAnimation_Timer() procedure, the FrameIndex variable is increased. The next time the

tmrAnimation_Timer() procedure is executed, FrameIndex is not equal to 0, but to the value that existed after the last execution of the tmrAnimation_Timer() procedure.

An If statement is then executed to determine if the gAnimationInProgress is equal to 0:

```
If gAnimationInProgress = 0 Then Exit Sub
```

So if gAnimationInProgress is equal to 0, the procedure is terminated, and the animation is not displayed.

If the If condition is not satisfied, the rest of the statements inside the tmrAnimation_Timer() procedure are executed. As you know, these statements are responsible for displaying the animation.

The static variable FrameIndex is increased by 1:

```
FrameIndex = FrameIndex + 1
```

FrameIndex serves as a counter that determines which BMP picture will be displayed. If FrameIndex is equal to 1, Help01.BMP will be displayed, if FrameIndex is equal to 2, Help02.BMP will be displayed, and so on.

The animation consists of five frames. This means that when FrameIndex is equal to 4, the Help04.BMP picture (the last frame) is displayed. Therefore, you need to make sure that FrameIndex does not exceed 4. You do that by using an If statement:

```
If FrameIndex = 5 Then
    FrameIndex = 0
    gAnimationInProgress = 0
    imgHelp.Picture = LoadPicture("C:\EXPROG\BMP\Help00.BMP")
    imgHelp.Visible = False
    Exit Sub
End If
```

If FrameIndex is equal to 5, all the five frames have already been displayed, and the statements under the If statements initialize the variables and properties for the next animation show. That is, FrameIndex is set back to 0, the gAnimationInProgress flag is set to 0, the imgHelp image is filled with the first frame, and finally, the Visible property of the imgHelp control is set to False.

If FrameIndex is not equal to 5, a Select Case statement is executed to determine which BMP picture file to display next:

```
Select Case FrameIndex
        Case 1
        imgHelp.Picture = LoadPicture("C:\FXPROG\BMP\Help01.BMP")

        Case 2
        imgHelp.Picture = LoadPicture("C:\EXPROG\BMP\Help02.BMP")

        Case 3
        imgHelp.Picture = LoadPicture("C:\EXPROG\BMP\Help03.BMP")

        Case 4
        imgHelp.Picture = LoadPicture("C:\EXPROG\BMP\Help04.BMP")

    End Select
```

Now review the process of displaying the BMP pictures. Upon startup of the show (when the user clicks the Start button), the HELP00.BMP picture is displayed (because the Visible property of imgHelp is set to True inside the `cmdStart_Click()` procedure). The first time the `tmrAnimation_Timer()` procedure is executed, `FrameIndex` is equal to 0, its value is increased by 1, and the `Select Case` statements load the Help01.BMP file. After 2 seconds, the `tmrAnimation_Timer()` procedure is executed again. Because `FrameIndex` is a static variable, `FrameIndex` is equal to 1 (its value from the last execution of the procedure). `FrameIndex` is increased by 1. So now the value of `FrameIndex` is 1+1=2. This causes the `Select Case` statement to load the Help02.BMP file. This process continues until `FrameIndex` is equal to 5, and `gAnimationInProgress` is set to 0.

☐ Experiment with the HelpMe program. In particular, note that the Interval property of the tmrAnimation timer determines how fast the animation help session runs.

A Nonsynchronized Animation Program: The Dance Program

The HelpMe program illustrates the principle of animation. However, the HelpMe program is like a silent movie (it does not have sound). The next program you'll write in this chapter is the Dance program. The Dance program combines animation with sound. As you'll soon see, the Dance program is an example of nonsynchronized animation. That is, you'll see a couple dancing. While the couple is dancing, you'll hear music. However, there is no connection between the music and the dance.

Before writing the Dance program, review its specifications.

Upon startup of the Dance program, the window shown in Figure BD2.18 is displayed.

Figure BD2.18.
The Dance program
(frame 1 of 5).

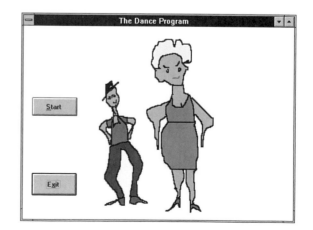

The user can now click the Start button to start the show. Once the Start button is clicked, its caption changes to Stop. During the show, the user can click the Stop button to stop the show.

The show consists of five frames. Figures BD2.18 through BD2.22 show the window of the Dance program with the five frames.

Figure BD2.19.
*The Dance program
(frame 2 of 5).*

Figure BD2.20.
*The Dance program
(frame 3 of 5).*

As previously stated, music is played during the show. The program plays the music and the animation, which are in an endless loop. Once the WAV file is played in its entirety, the WAV file is played all over again. The user can stop the show by clicking the Stop button.

To terminate the program, the user has to click the Exit button.

Now that you know what the Dance program is supposed to do, you can implement it.

Figure BD2.21.
The Dance program (frame 4 of 5).

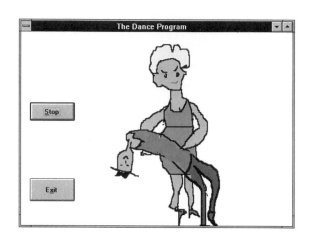

Figure BD2.22.
The Dance program (frame 5 of 5).

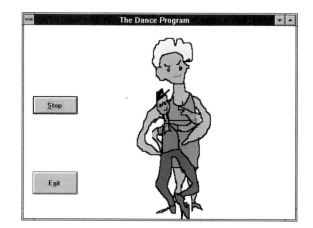

The Visual Implementation of the frmDance Form

You'll now visually implement the frmDance form of the Dance program.

☐ Select New Project from the File menu and save the new project as follows: Save the new form as Dance.FRM inside the C:\EXPROG\BD2 directory and save the new project file as Dance.MAK inside the C:\EXPROG\BD2 directory.

The Dance program uses the TegoMM.VBX multimedia control. If the TegoMM.VBX control does not appear in the Toolbox, add it as follows:

☐ Select Add File from the File menu and select the C:\Windows\System\TegoMM.VBX file.

☐ Implement the frmDance form according to the specifications in Table BD2.2. When you finish implementing the form, it should look like the one shown in Figure BD2.23. The Dance program uses five BMP pictures. These five BMP pictures are shown in Figures BD2.24 through BD2.28.

Note: Even if you don't have a copy of the TegoMM.VBX multimedia control, it is recommended that you read the material of this chapter, because you'll learn how to simultaneously display animation and play sound.

Table BD2.2. The properties table of the frmDance form.

Object	Property	Setting
Form	Name	frmDance
	Caption	The Dance Program
	Height	5625
	Icon	C:\VB\Icon\Misc\Misc34.ICO
	Left	1035
	Top	525
	Width	7485
Command Button	Name	cmdStartStop
	Caption	&Start
	Height	495
	Left	240
	Top	1920
	Width	1215
TegoMM.VBX	Name	Tegomm1
	Height	375
	Left	120
	Top	120
	UpdateInterval	400
	Visible	0-False
	Width	3510
Command Button	Name	cmdExit
	Caption	E&xit
	Height	615
	Left	240

continues

Table BD2.2. continued

Object	Property	Setting
	Top	3960
	Width	1215
Image	**Name**	**imgDance**
	Height	5850
	Left	1800
	Picture	C:\EXPROG\BMP\Dance00.BMP
	Top	120
	Width	3750

Figure BD2.23.
The frmDance form
(in design mode).

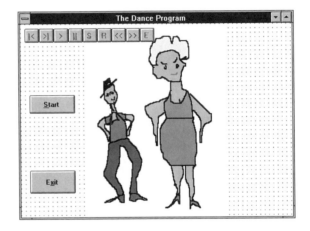

Figure BD2.24.
The Dance00.BMP picture.

Figure BD2.25.
The Dance01.BMP picture.

Figure BD2.26.
The Dance02.BMP picture.

Figure BD2.27.
The Dance03.BMP picture.

Figure BD2.28.
The Dance04.BMP picture.

Entering the Code of the General Declarations Section of the frmDance Form

☐ Type the following code inside the general declarations section of the frmDance form:

```
Option Explicit

Dim gDanceInProgress
```

The code you typed declares the `gDanceInProgress` variable. Because this variable is declared inside the general declarations section of the from, this variable is accessible from any procedure of the form.

Attaching Code to the *Click* Event of the Exit Button

☐ Type the following code inside the `cmdExit_Click()` procedure of the frmDance form:

```
Sub cmdExit_Click ()

    End

End Sub
```

Attaching Code to the *Load* Event of the Form

You'll now attach code to the `Load` event of the form.

☐ Type the following code inside the `Form_Load()` procedure of the frmDance form:

```
Sub Form_Load ()

    gDanceInProgress = 0
    Tegomm1.DeviceType = "WaveAudio"
    Tegomm1.FileName = "C:\EXPROG\WAV\BOURB1M1.WAV"
    Tegomm1.Command = "Open"

End Sub
```

The code you typed sets the gDanceInProgress variable to 0:

```
gDanceInProgress = 0
```

gDanceInProgress serves as a flag that indicates whether currently the dance is in progress. Upon startup of the Dance program, you don't want the dance to start, so you set gDanceInProgress to 0.

The rest of the statements inside the Form_Load() procedure open the WAV file for playback through the sound card:

```
Tegomm1.DeviceType = "WaveAudio"
Tegomm1.FileName = "C:\EXPROG\WAV\BOURB1M1.WAV"
Tegomm1.Command = "Open"
```

Note that for proper execution of the Dance program you must save a WAV file in the C:\EXPROG\WAV directory, and name the WAV file BOURB1M1.WAV. (Use any WAV file that plays music, but rename your WAV file as BOURB1M1.WAV, and make sure that the WAV file resides inside the C:\EXPROG\WAV directory.)

Attaching Code to the *Click* Event of the cmdStartStop Button

You'll now attach code to the Click event of the cmdStartStop button. The cmdStartStop button serves both as the Start button and as the Stop button. When the dance is not in progress, the caption of the cmdStartStop button is Start, so the user is able to start the dance. When the dance is in progress, the caption of the button is Stop, so the user is able to stop the dance.

☐ Type the following code inside the Click event of the cmdStartStop button:

```
Sub cmdStartStop_Click ()

    If cmdStartStop.Caption = "&Start" Then
        cmdStartStop.Caption = "&Stop"
        gDanceInProgress = 1
        Tegomm1.Command = "Prev"
        Tegomm1.Command = "Play"
    Else
        cmdStartStop.Caption = "&Start"
        gDanceInProgress = 0
        imgDance.Picture = LoadPicture("C:\EXPROG\BMP\Dance00.BMP")
        Tegomm1.Command = "Stop"
    End If

End Sub
```

The code you typed uses an If...Else statement to determine the current value of the Caption property:

```
If cmdStartStop.Caption = "&Start" Then
    ....................
    ... Currently the button serves
    ... as the Start button
```

```
. . . . . . . . . . . . . . . . . .
Else
      . . . . . . . . . . . . . . . . . .
      ... Currently the button serves
      ... as the Stop button
      . . . . . . . . . . . . . . . . . .
End If
```

The code under the `If` starts the dance. The Caption property of the button is changed to &Stop:

```
cmdStartStop.Caption = "&Stop"
```

The `gDanceInProgress` variable is set to 1:

```
gDanceInProgress - 1
```

As you'll soon see, setting `gDanceInProgress` to 1 starts the dance.

The WAV file is then rewound, and the playback is started:

```
    Tegomm1.Command = "Prev"
    Tegomm1.Command = "Play"
```

The code under the `Else` stops the dance. The Caption property of the cmdStartStop button is changed back to &Start:

```
cmdStartStop.Caption = "&Start"
```

The `gDanceInProgress` flag is set to 0 (to stop the dance):

```
gDanceInProgress = 0
```

The Picture property of the imgDance image control is set so that the image displays the first frame of the animation:

```
imgDance.Picture = LoadPicture("C:\EXPROG\BMP\Dance00.BMP")
```

Finally, the playback is stopped:

```
Tegomm1.Command = "Stop"
```

Attaching Code to the *Done* Event of the Multimedia Control

Once the user starts the animation, the show displaying the couple dancing continues in an endless loop. As stated, the WAV file is played during the animation. When the WAV file is played in its entirety, the WAV file is rewound and the playback starts all over again (for as long as the animation is in progress). The code inside the `Tegomm1_Done()` procedure checks whether the WAV file was played in its entirety, and if this is the case, the WAV file is rewound, and the playback starts all over.

Type the following code inside the `Tegomm1_Done()` procedure:

```
Sub Tegomm1_Done ()

    If Tegomm1.Position = Tegomm1.Length Then
        Tegomm1.Command = "Prev"
        Tegomm1.Command = "Play"
    End If

End Sub
```

Attaching Code to the *StatusUpdate* Event of the Multimedia Control

Recall that during design time you set the UpdateInterval property of the multimedia control to 400. This means that the `Tegomm1_StatusUpdate()` procedure is executed automatically every 400 milliseconds (0.4 seconds). Therefore, you can perform various tasks every 400 milliseconds. The code you'll type inside the `Tegomm1_StatusUpdate()` procedure changes pictures. So every 400 milliseconds, the user will see a new picture.

> **Note:** The UpdateInterval property of the multimedia control was set to 400 during design time. You can set the `UpdateInterval` property of the multimedia control during runtime with the following statement:
>
> `Tegomm1.UpdateInterval = 400`
>
> For example, you can add the preceding statement inside the `Form_Load()` procedure.

Type the following code inside the `Tegomm1_StatusUpdate()` procedure:

```
Sub Tegomm1_StatusUpdate ()

    Static DanceFrame

    If gDanceInProgress = 0 Then Exit Sub

    DanceFrame = DanceFrame + 1
    If DanceFrame = 5 Then
        DanceFrame = 0
    End If

    Select Case DanceFrame
        Case 0
        imgDance.Picture = LoadPicture("C:\EXPROG\BMP\Dance00.BMP")
        Case 1
        imgDance.Picture = LoadPicture("C:\EXPROG\BMP\Dance01.BMP")
        Case 2
        imgDance.Picture = LoadPicture("C:\EXPROG\BMP\Dance02.BMP")
        Case 3
        imgDance.Picture = LoadPicture("C:\EXPROG\BMP\Dance03.BMP")
```

787

```
                    Case 4
                    imgDance.Picture = LoadPicture("C:\EXPROG\BMP\Dance04.BMP")

            End Select

    End Sub
```

The code you typed declares a static variable:

```
Static DanceFrame
```

This means that upon the first execution of the `Tegomm1_StatusUpdate()` procedure, `DanceFrame` is equal to 0. The next time the `Tegomm1_StatusUpdate()` procedure is executed, the `DanceFrame` variable is equal to the value it had from the last execution of the `Tegomm1_StatusUpdate()` procedure.

An `If` statement is used to determine whether the dance is in progress:

```
If gDanceInProgress = 0 Then Exit Sub
```

That is, if the dance is currently not is progress, the rest of the statements of the `Tegomm1_StatusUpdate()` procedure are not executed.

If `gDanceInProgress` is not equal to 0, the rest of the statements inside the `Tegomm1_StatusUpdate()` are executed. These statements display the animation.

The static variable is increased by 1:

```
DanceFrame = DanceFrame + 1
```

Then an `If` statement makes sure that `DanceFrame` does not exceed 4:

```
        If DanceFrame = 5 Then
            DanceFrame = 0
        End If
```

So every 400 milliseconds, the value of `DanceFrame` changes. If you look at the value of `DanceFrame` after the execution of the preceding `If` statement, you'll see that `DanceFrame` has the following values:

```
0
1
2
3
4
0
1
2
3
4
...
...
...
```

A `Select Case` statement is then executed:

```
Select Case DanceFrame
      Case 0
      imgDance.Picture = LoadPicture("C:\EXPROG\BMP\Dance00.BMP")
      Case 1
      imgDance.Picture = LoadPicture("C:\EXPROG\BMP\Dance01.BMP")
      Case 2
      imgDance.Picture = LoadPicture("C:\EXPROG\BMP\Dance02.BMP")
      Case 3
      imgDance.Picture = LoadPicture("C:\EXPROG\BMP\Dance03.BMP")
      Case 4
      imgDance.Picture = LoadPicture("C:\EXPROG\BMP\Dance04.BMP")
End Select
```

As you can see from the preceding `Select Case` statement, the imgDance image control is assigned with different pictures. That is, depending on the current value of `DanceFrame`, the appropriate BMP file is loaded. So the imgDance image control changes picture very 400 milliseconds. Here is the sequence of pictures that the imgDance image control displays:

DanceFrame	BMP Picture
0	Dance00.BMP
1	Dance01.BMP
2	Dancc02.BMP
3	Dance03.BMP
4	Dance04.BMP
1	Dance01.BMP
2	Dance02.BMP
3	Dance03.BMP
4	Dance04.BMP
...	....
...	....
...	....

☐ Experiment with the Dance program, and then click its Exit button to terminate the program.

A Synchronized Animation Program: The Kennedy Program

The Dance program illustrated how you can play sound through the sound card simultaneously with the displaying of animation. As you noticed, the animation of the Dance program has no connection with the played WAV file. That is, the dancers are not dancing according to the played music!

The Kennedy program that you'll now write demonstrates how to write a synchronized animation program. That is, the WAV file is synchronized with the animation.

Before writing the Kennedy program, review it specifications.

Upon startup of the Kennedy program, the window shown in Figure BD2.29 appears.

Figure BD2.29.
The Kennedy program.

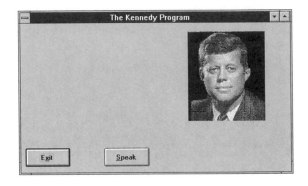

The user can now click the Speak button to listen to and view a speech by President Kennedy.

When you click the Speak button, the window shown in Figure BD2.30 appears and the phrase So my fellow Americans is played. In other words, there is a synchronization between the text being displayed and the sound being played.

Figure BD2.30.
The Kennedy program,
displaying and playing the
phrase So my fellow
Americans.

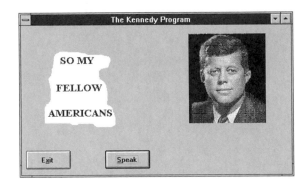

When the program finishes playing So my fellow Americans the window shown in Figure BD2.31 appears. As shown in Figure BD2.31, the phrase Ask not what your country can do for you is displayed. At the same time, the phrase is played through the sound card.

Then the Kennedy program displays the window shown in Figure BD2.32, and the phrase Ask what you can do for your country is played.

Figure BD2.31.
The Kennedy program, displaying and playing the phrase Ask not what your country can do for you.

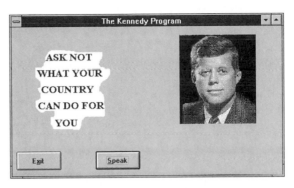

Figure BD2.32.
The Kennedy program displaying and playing the phrase Ask what you can do for your country.

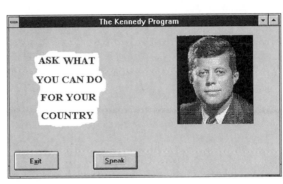

After the phrase Ask what you can do for your country is played, the Kennedy program displays the window shown in Figure BD2.29. The user can now start the show all over again by clicking the Speak button again.

Now that you know what the Kennedy program is supposed to do, you can write it.

The Visual Implementation of the frmKennedy Form

You'll now visually implement the frmKennedy form.

☐ Select New Project from the File menu of Visual Basic and save the new project as follows: Save the new form as Kennedy.FRM inside the C:\EXPROG\BD2 directory and save the new project file as Kennedy.MAK inside the C:\EXPROG\BD2 directory.

The Kennedy program uses the TegoMM.VBX multimedia control. If your Toolbox does not contain the TegoMM.VBX control add it as follows:

☐ Select Add File from the File menu and add the C:\Windows\System\TegoMM.VBX file.

☐ Implement the frmKennedy form according to the specifications in Table BD2.3. When you finish implementing the form, it should look like the one shown in Figure BD2.33.

Figure BD2.33.
*The frmKennedy form
(in design mode).*

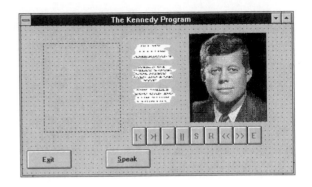

Table BD2.3 instructs you to place four image controls inside the frmKennedy form. When you place the four image controls, set the Name property of the first image control that you place to imgSpeech. Then place a second image control inside the form and set its Name property to imgSpeech. Because you already have an image control by that name, Visual Basic prompts you with a dialog box, asking you if you want to create an array of images. Click the Yes button of the dialog box. So the first image control that you placed is imgSpeech(0) (the index is 0). The second image control is imgSpeech(1) (the index is 1). The third image control is imgSpeech(2) (the index is 2). The fourth image control is imgSpeech(3) (the index is 3). During design time you set the `Visible` property of imgSpeech(0) to True and you set the Visible properties of imgSpeech(1), imgSpeech(2), and imgSpeech(3) to False.

During the implementation of Table BD2.3 you'll set the Picture property of imgSpeech(1) to Ken1.BMP, the Picture property of imgSpeech(2) to Ken2.BMP, and the Picture property of imgSpeech(3) to Ken3.BMP. Figures BD2.34 through BD2.36 show the Ken1.BMP, Ken2.BMP, and Ken3.BMP pictures. You can draw these BMP files by using Paintbrush.

Figure BD2.34.
The Ken1.BMP picture.

SO MY

FELLOW

AMERICANS

Figure BD2.35.
The Ken2.BMP picture.

ASK NOT
WHAT YOUR
COUNTRY
CAN DO FOR
YOU

Figure BD2.36.
The Ken3.BMP picture.

The Picture property of the imgKennedy control is set to Kennedy.BMP. The Kennedy.BMP picture is shown in Figure BD2.37. If you don't have a BMP picture of Kennedy, create a BMP picture of size 139 by 159 pixels, and use the text tool of Paintbrush to write Kennedy Picture here.

Table BD2.3. The properties table of the frmKennedy form.

Object	Property	Setting
Form	**Name**	**frmKennedy**
	BackColor	(light gray)
	Caption	The Kennedy Program
	Height	4425
	Icon	C:\VB\Icons\Flags\CTRUSA.ICO
	Left	1035
	Top	1140
	Width	7485
Command Button	**Name**	**cmdSpeak**
	Caption	&Speak
	Height	495
	Left	2280
	Top	3360
	Width	1215
TegoMM.VBX	**Name**	**Tegomm1**
	Height	495
	Left	3000
	Top	2760
	Visible	0-False
	Width	3510

continues

Table BD2.3. continued

Object	Property	Setting
Command Button	**Name**	**cmdExit**
	Caption	E&xit
	Height	495
	Left	120
	Top	3360
	Width	1215
Image	**Name**	**imgSpeech**
	Stretch	False
	Height	2400
	Index	0
	Left	600
	Top	480
	Width	2100
Image	**Name**	**imgSpeech**
	Stretch	-1-True
	Height	495
	Index	1
	Left	3000
	Picture	C:\EXPROG\BMP\KEN1.BMP
	Top	480
	Visible	0-False
	Width	1215
Image	**Name**	**imgSpeech**
	Stretch	-1-True
	Height	495
	Index	2
	Left	3000
	Picture	C:\EXPROG\BMP\KEN2.BMP
	Top	1080
	Visible	0-False
	Width	1215

Object	Property	Setting
Image	**Name**	**imgSpeech**
	Stretch	-1-True
	Height	495
	Index	3
	Left	3000
	Picture	C:\EXPROG\BMP\KEN3.BMP
	Top	1680
	Visible	0-False
	Width	1215
Image	**Name**	**imgKennedy**
	Height	2400
	Left	4560
	Picture	C:\EXPROG\BMP\KENNEDY.BMP
	Top	240
	Width	2100

Figure BD2.37.
The Kennedy.BMP picture.

Entering the Code of the General Declarations Section of the frmKennedy Form

☐ Type the following code inside the general declarations section:

```
Option Explicit

Dim gSpeechInProgress
```

As you'll soon see, the `gSpeechInProgress` variable serves as a flag that indicates whether Kennedy's speech is in progress.

Attaching Code to the *Click* Event of the Exit Button

☐ Type the following code inside the cmdExit_Click() procedure of the frmKennedy form:

```
Sub cmdExit_Click ()

    End

End Sub
```

Attaching Code to the *Load* Event of the Form

☐ Type the following code inside the Form_Load() procedure of the frmKennedy form:

```
Sub Form_Load ()

    Tegomm1.UpdateInterval = 100
    gSpeechInProgress = 0

    Tegomm1.FileName = "C:\EXPROG\WAV\8Kenned3.WAV"
    Tegomm1.DeviceType = "WaveAudio"
    Tegomm1.Command = "Open"

End Sub
```

The code you typed sets the UpdateInterval property of the multimedia control to 100:

```
Tegomm1.UpdateInterval = 100
```

This means that the Tegomm1_StatusUpdate() procedure will be executed automatically every 100 milliseconds (0.1 second).

The gSpeechInProgress variable is set to 0:

```
gSpeechInProgress = 0
```

gSpeechInProgress serves as flag that indicates whether the speech is in progress.

The 8Kenned3.WAV file is then opened:

```
    Tegomm1.FileName = "C:\EXPROG\WAV\8Kenned3.WAV"
    Tegomm1.DeviceType = "WaveAudio"
    Tegomm1.Command = "Open"
```

8Kenned3.WAV is the WAV file that contains Kennedy's speech. (If you do not have the 8Kenned3.WAV file, use a different WAV file. For example, record the speech by yourself, name your recording 8Kenned3.WAV, and save the file inside the C:\EXPROG\WAV directory.)

Attaching Code to the *Click* Event of the *Speak* Command

Whenever the user clicks the Speak button, the Kennedy's speech and the animation show starts.

☐ Type the following code inside the cmdSpeak_Click() procedure:

```
Sub cmdSpeak_Click ()

    gSpeechInProgress = 1

    Tegomm1.Command = "Play"

End Sub
```

The code you typed sets the gSpeechInProgress variable to 1 (because from now on the speech is in progress):

```
gSpeechInProgress = 1
```

Then the Play command is issued:

```
Tegomm1.Command = "Play"
```

Attaching Code to the *Done* Event of the Multimedia Control

Whenever the multimedia control finishes playing, the Done event occurs. This is your opportunity to perform various operations at the end of the playback.

☐ Type the following code inside the Tegomm1_Done() procedure:

```
Sub Tegomm1_Done ()

    If Tegomm1.Position = Tegomm1.Length Then

        Tegomm1.Command = "Prev"
        imgSpeech(0).Picture = LoadPicture("")

    End If

End Sub
```

An If statement is executed to verify that the Done event occurred due to the fact that the multimedia control completed playing the entire WAV file:

```
If Tegomm1.Position = Tegomm1.Length Then

    Tegomm1.Command = "Prev"
    imgSpeech(0).Picture = LoadPicture("")

End If
```

If the Position property of the multimedia control is equal to the Length property of the multimedia control, the WAV file was played in its entirety. Therefore, the Prev command is executed to rewind the WAV file (preparing the WAV file for the next time the user clicks the Speak button):

```
Tegomm1.Command = "Prev"
```

and the Picture property of the `imgSpeech(0)` image control is set to null:

```
imgSpeech(0).Picture = LoadPicture("")
```

Recall that during design time you set the Visible property of `imgSpeech(0)` to True, and you set the Visible property of all the other images to False. This means that during runtime the `imgSpeech(0)` image control is the only visible control. When the WAV file is played in its entirety, the picture of `imgSpeech(0)` is "erased" from the screen by loading "nothing" into the image.

The Code Inside the *StatusUpdate* Event of the Multimedia Control

Recall that during design time you set the UpdateInterval property of the multimedia control to 100. This means that the `Tegomm1_StatusUpdate()` procedure is executed every 100 milliseconds.

☐ Type the following code inside the `Tegomm1_StatusUpdate()` procedure of the frmKennedy form:

```
Sub Tegomm1_StatusUpdate ()

    If gSpeechInProgress = 0 Then Exit Sub

    If Tegomm1.Position > 0 And Tegomm1.Position < 3001 Then
       imgSpeech(0).Picture = imgSpeech(1).Picture
    End If

    If Tegomm1.Position > 3000 And Tegomm1.Position < 7001 Then
       imgSpeech(0).Picture = imgSpeech(2).Picture
    End If

    If Tegomm1.Position > 7000 And
                [ic:ccc] Tegomm1.Position < Tegomm1.Length Then

       imgSpeech(0).Picture = imgSpeech(3).Picture

    End If

End Sub
```

The code you typed uses an `If` statement to examine the value of `gSpeechInProgress`:

```
If gSpeechInProgress = 0 Then Exit Sub
```

If `gSpeechInProgress` is equal to 0, the speech is not is progress, and the procedure terminates. If the speech is in progress, the rest of the statements of the `Tegomm1_StatusUpdate()` procedure are executed. An `If` statement is executed to check whether the Position property of the multimedia control is between 0 and 3000 milliseconds:

```
If Tegomm1.Position > 0 And Tegomm1.Position < 3001 Then
   imgSpeech(0).Picture = imgSpeech(1).Picture
End If
```

That is, the phrase So my fellow Americans is played during the first 3000 milliseconds of the speech. So during the first 3000 milliseconds of the speech, the Picture property of the imgSpeech(0) image control is set to the Picture property of imgSpeech(1) (which contains the Ken1.BMP picture):

```
imgSpeech(0).Picture = imgSpeech(1).Picture
```

Another If statement is executed to examine whether the Position property of the multimedia control is between 3000 and 7000 milliseconds:

```
If Tegomm1.Position > 3000 And Tegomm1.Position < 7001 Then
   imgSpeech(0).Picture = imgSpeech(2)
End If
```

The phrase Ask not what your country can do for you is played between the 3001th millisecond and the 7000th milliseconds. Therefore, during this time, the Ken2.BMP picture is displayed:

```
imgSpeech(0).Picture = imgSpeech(2)
```

The last If statement examines whether the Position property of the multimedia control is between the 7000th millisecond and the end of the file:

```
If Tegomm1.Position > 7000 And Tegomm1.Position < Tegomm1.Length Then
   imgSpeech(0).Picture = imgSpeech(3)
End If
```

That is, now the Ken3.BMP picture is displayed, because during this time the multimedia control plays the phrase that the Ken3.BMP picture displays.

☐ Execute the Kennedy program and verify its proper operations.

Note: The Kennedy program assumes that the WAV file is composed of the following sections:

From	To	Phrase
0	3000	So my fellow Americans
3001	7000	Ask not what your country can do for you
7001	end	Ask what you can do for your country

Naturally, if for the sake of implementing this tutorial you use your own WAV file, you have to match the three If statements inside the Tegomm1_StatusUpdate() procedure according to the WAV file you are using.

Icon Animation: The MyIcon Program

You can apply the same technique that you applied in the animation programs of this chapter to create programs that display animated icons.

The MyIcon program illustrates how to design a program that displays an animated icon.

Before writing the MyIcon program, review its specifications.

Upon startup of the MyIcon program, the window shown in Figure BD2.38 appears.

Figure BD2.38.
The MyIcon program.

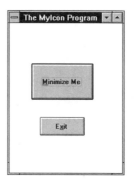

When you click the Minimize Me button, the MyIcon program minimizes itself, and the icon of the program keeps changing. Figures BD2.39 through BD2.41 show three icons of the MyIcon

Figure BD2.39.
An icon of the MyIcon program (MOON03.ICO).

Figure BD2.40.
An icon of the MyIcon program (MOON01.ICO).

Figure BD2.41.
An icon of the MyIcon program (MOON08.ICO).

program.

The icon animation consists of eight icons. The eight icons are the following:

```
C:\VB\Icons\Elements\Moon01.ICO
C:\VB\Icons\Elements\Moon02.ICO
C:\VB\Icons\Elements\Moon03.ICO
C:\VB\Icons\Elements\Moon04.ICO
C:\VB\Icons\Elements\Moon05.ICO
C:\VB\Icons\Elements\Moon06.ICO
C:\VB\Icons\Elements\Moon07.ICO
```

```
C:\VB\Icons\Elements\Moon08.ICO
```

So once the user clicks the Minimize Me button, the MyIcon program minimizes itself, and the icon of the program keeps changing. The icon animation program shows the moon in eight different positions, and then the animation show starts over.

Now that you know what the MyIcon program should do, you can write it.

The Visual Implementation of the MyIcon Program

You'll now visually implement the frmMyIcon form of the MyIcon program.

☐ Implement the frmMyIcon form according to the specifications in Table BD2.4. When you finish implementing the form, it should look alike the one shown in Figure BD2.42.

Table BD2.4. The properties table of the frmMyIcon form.

Object	Property	Setting
Form	**Name**	**frmMyIcon**
	Caption	The MyIcon Program
	Height	4425
	Icon	C:\VB\Icons\Elements\Moon01.ICO
	Left	1035
	Top	1140
	Width	3195
Timer	**Name**	**tmrMyIcon**
	Interval	250
	Left	1320
	Top	3240
Command Button	**Name**	**cmdMinimizeMe**
	Caption	&Minimize Me
	Height	975
	Left	600
	Top	1080
	Width	1695

continues

Table BD2.4. continued

Object	Property	Setting
Command Button	**Name**	**cmdExit**
	Caption	E&xit
	Height	495
	Left	840
	Top	2520
	Width	1215

Figure BD2.42.
*The frmMyIcon form
(in design mode).*

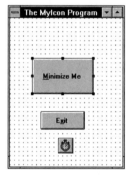

Attaching Code to the *Click* Event of the Exit Button

☐ Type the following code inside the cmdExit_Click() procedure of the frmMyIcon form:

```
Sub cmdExit_Click ()

    End

End Sub
```

Attaching Code to the *Click* Event of the Minimize Me Button

Whenever the user clicks the Minimize Me button, the MyIcon program minimizes itself.

☐ Type the following code inside the cmdMinimizeMe_Click() procedure:

```
Sub cmdMinimizeMe_Click ()

    frmMyIcon.WindowState = 1

End Sub
```

The code you typed sets the WindowState property of the form to 1. This causes the window of the frmMyIcon form to be minimized.

Attaching Code to the *Timer* Event of the tmrMyIcon Timer

The user can minimize the window of the program either by clicking the Minimize Me button or by clicking the minimize icon of the program's window. The code inside the tmrMyIcon_Timer() procedure is executed every 250 milliseconds (because you set the Interval property of the timer to 250 during design time). The tmrMyIcon_Timer() procedure is responsible for displaying the animated icon.

☐ Type the following code inside the tmrMyIcon_Timer() procedure:

```
Sub tmrMyIcon_Timer ()

    Dim MoonFileName
    Static MoonPosition

    If frmMyIcon.WindowState <> 1 Then Exit Sub

    MoonPosition = MoonPosition + 1
    If MoonPosition = 9 Then MoonPosition = 1

    MoonFileName = "Moon0" + Format(MoonPosition) + ".ICO"

    MoonFileName = "C:\VB\Icons\Elements\" + MoonFileName


    frmMyIcon.Icon = LoadPicture(MoonFileName)

End Sub
```

The code you typed declares a local variable MoonFileName and a static variable:

```
Dim MoonFileName
Static MoonPosition
```

An If statement is then executed to examine whether currently the window of the program is minimized:

```
If frmMyIcon.WindowState <> 1 Then Exit Sub
```

If the WindowState property of the form is not equal to 1, the window is not minimized, and the procedure terminates. If the window is minimized, the rest of the statements inside the tmrMyIcon_Timer() procedure are executed.

The static variable `MoonPosition` is increased by 1:

```
MoonPosition = MoonPosition + 1
```

Then an `If` statement is executed to make sure that `MoonPosition` does not exceed 8:

```
If MoonPosition = 9 Then MoonPosition = 1
```

As you'll soon see, the icon animation consists of eight icons. `MoonPosition` determines which icon is displayed.

The filename of the icon is then constructed:

```
MoonFileName = "Moon0" + Format(MoonPosition) + ".ICO"
```

On the first execution of the `tmrMyIcon_Timer()` procedure, `MoonPosition` is equal to 0. Because this static variable is increased by 1, the value of `MoonPosition` is equal to 0+1=1. The preceding statement sets the value of `MoonFileName` to Moon01.ICO (because currently `MoonPosition` is equal to 1).

On the next execution of the `tmrMyIcon_Timer()` procedure, `MoonPosition` is equal to 1 (because a static variable retains its value from the last execution of the procedure). So on the next execution of the `tmrMyIcon_Timer()` procedure `MoonFileName` is set to Moon02.ICO. This process repeats itself every 250 milliseconds o the values of `MoonFileName` are the following:

```
Moon01.ICO
Moon02.ICO
Moon03.ICO
Moon04.ICO
Moon05.ICO
Moon06.ICO
Moon07.ICO
Moon08.ICO
Moon01.ICO
Moon02.ICO
....
....
....
```

The next statement attaches the full pathname of the icons:

```
MoonFileName = "C:\VB\Icons\Elements\" + MoonFileName
```

So the values of `MoonFileName` are the following:

```
C:\VB\Icons\Elements\Moon01.ICO
C:\VB\Icons\Elements\Moon02.ICO
C:\VB\Icons\Elements\Moon03.ICO
C:\VB\Icons\Elements\Moon04.ICO
C:\VB\Icons\Elements\Moon05.ICO
C:\VB\Icons\Elements\Moon06.ICO
C:\VB\Icons\Elements\Moon07.ICO
C:\VB\Icons\Elements\Moon08.ICO
```

```
C:\VB\Icons\Elements\Moon01.ICO
C:\VB\Icons\Elements\Moon01.ICO
.....
.....
.....
```

Finally, the Icon property of the form is set:

```
frmMyIcon.Icon = LoadPicture(MoonFileName)
```

So the icon of the frmMyIcon changes every 250 milliseconds.

☐ Execute the MyIcon program and verify its proper operation.

Summary

In this chapter you have learned how to write animation programs. You have learned how to write synchronized and nonsynchronized animation programs, and you have also learned how to write an icon animation program.

Q&A

Q Does icon animation have any practical use?

A Yes. For example, you can design a program that works in the background. An example is the Print Manager program of Windows, which shows the status of the print buffer. Typically the window of the Print Manager program appears minimized, because while the PC uses the printer you can perform other operations. You can design your own Print Manager program that has an animated icon. The animated icon can show an animated printer printing. You can design the new Print Manager program so that when the PC does not have any more documents to print (the print buffer is empty) the icon animation stops. So while printing, the user can observe the icon of your new Print Manager program, and determine whether printing is in progress. Similarly, icon animation is applicable in other background-based programs such as fax programs. You can design a fax program that receives/sends faxes. While the fax program sends/receives faxes, the icon of the program displays animation of a fax machine that receives/sends faxes.

Quiz

1. The Dance program that you wrote in this chapter is an example of a synchronized animation.

a. True. The people dance according to the music (they synchronize their dance steps according to the tempo of the music).

b. False. The Dance program is an example of a nonsynchronized animation program.

2. The Kennedy program that you wrote in this chapter is an example of which of the following:

a. Synchronized animation

b. Nonsynchronized animation

Exercise

Enhance the HelpMe program so that the user has a mechanism to control the speed of the animation.

Quiz Answers

1. b

2. a

Exercise Answer

There are, of course, many ways to implement this enhancement.

Here is one way of doing it:

☐ Place a scroll bar inside the form.

☐ Set the Min property of the scroll bar to 1.

☐ Set the Max property of the scroll bar to 5.

The scroll bar position represents the amount of time that each frame remains on the screen.

Attach code to the Change event of the scroll bar. For example, if the name of the scroll bar is hsbSpeed, type the following code inside the hsbSpeed_Change() procedure:

```
hsbSpeed_Change()

    tmrAnimation.Interval= hsbSpeed.Value * 1000

End Sub
```

So if, for example, the scroll bar position is changed so that its Value property is equal to 4, the Interval property of the timer control is set to 4×1000=4000 milliseconds = 4 seconds. This way the user can control the speed at which the animation help session runs.

Bonus Day

3+

Networks

In this chapter you'll learn about networks and how you can write interesting network-based programs with Visual Basic.

What Is a Network?

In the PC industry *network* refers to the capability of connecting several PCs via cables for the purpose of transferring data between the PCs.

Figure BD3.1 shows two PCs connected by a cable. Therefore, PC A can send data to PC B, and PC B can send data to PC A. Furthermore, PC A can execute programs that reside in PC B, and PC B can execute programs that reside in PC A.

Figure BD3.1.

Connecting two PCs.

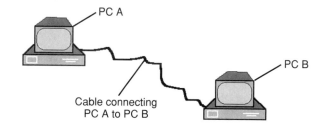

At this point in the discussion, we don't care how the PCs are connected. That is, you can imagine that PC A is connected to PC B by connecting the serial ports of the two PCs, or if you prefer, you can imagine that the two PCs in Figure BD3.1 are connected via their parallel ports. The actual physical connection—the type of cable and the type of cards that are used to connect the two PCs—is discussed later in this chapter.

Network Techniques

Figure BD3.1 shows a network that consists of only two PCs. But what if you want to connect three PCs? Again, assume that the PCs are connected via their parallel ports. One (bad) way to implement a network that connects three PCs together is shown in Figure BD3.2. As shown, each PC has two parallel ports, and each PC has two dedicated cables that connect it to the other two PCs. This method of connecting PCs to each other by having dedicated cables and cards for each PC connection is called space division multiplexing (because space is divided by cables). To see how bad the space division multiplexing technique is, see Figures BD3.2 through BD3.4, which show several PCs connected in space-multiplexing networks.

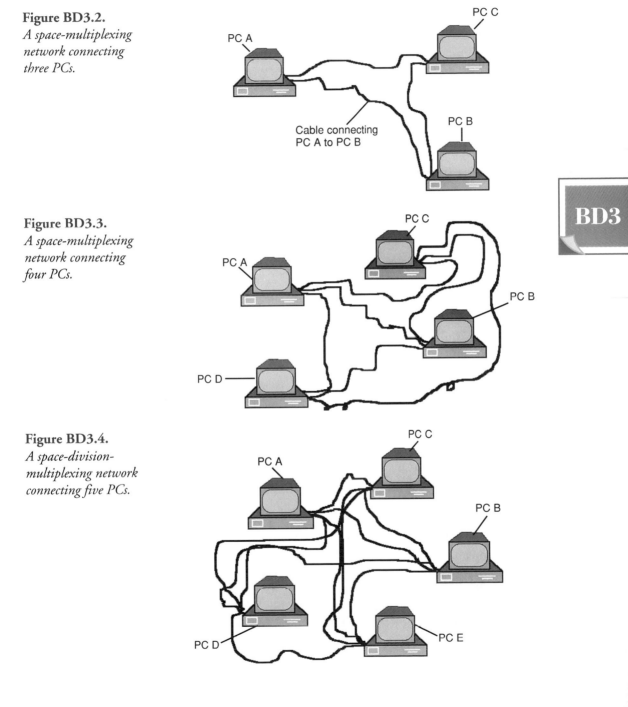

Figure BD3.2.
A space-multiplexing network connecting three PCs.

PC C

PC A

Cable connecting
PC A to PC B

PC B

Figure BD3.3.
A space-multiplexing network connecting four PCs.

PC C

PC A

PC B

PC D

Figure BD3.4.
A space-division-multiplexing network connecting five PCs.

PC C

PC A

PC B

PC D

PC E

The space-division-multiplexing technique is not a practical way to connect PCs, because it simply requires too much hardware! In Figure BD3.4, the network connects only five PCs. Assuming that each PC-to-PC connection is accomplished via a dedicated cable and a dedicated parallel port, you need a total of 10 cables.

If you connect 10 PCs this way, you need a total of 10×(10-1)/2=45 cables.

If you connect 100 PCs this way, you need a total of 100×(100-1)/2=4,950 cables.

As you can see, the space-multiplexing technique is impractical because it requires too many cables. It will be almost impossible to repair such a network if one of the cables is broken —go search for the broken cable among hundreds of cables!— and this technique also requires the use of too many parallel port cards.

A better technique than space multiplexing is required. The solution is to compromise between network performance and hardware requirements. That is, you can make the network hardware less expensive and less complex, but this means that the network will not be able to perform as well as the space-multiplexing network.

Consider for example the network shown in Figure BD3.5.

Figure BD3.5.
Connecting five PCs
with a single cable.

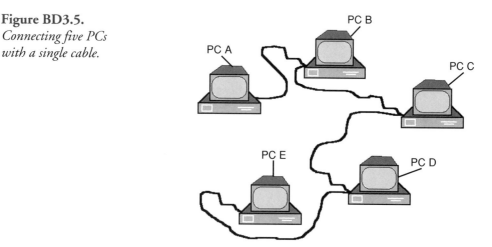

The network of Figure BD3.5 connects the PCs as follows: The cable starts at PC A; this cable is connected to a card inside PC B; then a cable is also connected from the card of PC B to a card in PC C; another cable connects PC C to PC D; and another cable connects PC D to PC E. The card that connects each PC to the cables is called a *network card.*

The advantage of the network shown in Figure BD3.5 is evident (that is, you use many fewer cables than in the network shown in Figure BD3.4). However, the network of Figure BD3.5

has the disadvantage that at any given time only one "conversation" can be transferred over the network. Look at Figure BD3.4. In Figure BD3.4 it is possible to have PC A "talk" to PC B while PC C is "talking" to PC D. This is possible because the "conversations" are accomplished over separate cables.

Consider what happens when PC A is sending data to PC D in the network shown in Figure BD3.5. The data is transferred over the A–B cable. PC B "senses" that the data does not belong to it, so it simply ignores the incoming data. PC B "knows" that the data does not belong to it because the data that PC A sends includes an address. This address is a unique identification number that is included in the transferred data. PC C also receives the incoming data over the B–C cable, but it too ignores the incoming data because it realizes that the address that is attached to the data does not belong to it. PC D receives the data via the C–D cable. Because the transferred data contains the address of PC D, PC D receives the incoming data. In a similar manner, the data also reaches PC E, but PC E ignores the incoming data because the data does not contain its address.

From the preceding discussion, it is obvious that when PC A sends data the data appears all over the cables. Hence, no other PC is allowed to send data while data is being transferred over the cables. If PC B wants to send data, its card must first investigate whether there is any incoming data, and if there is no incoming data, only then can PC B start sending data over the cables.

The objective of the preceding discussion is to illustrate how complex the network software and the network card can be.

Due to the complexity of the network implementation, networks are conceptually implemented in layers. Typically, a network is composed of seven layers. The first layer is the physical layer. This layer is responsible for establishing the physical connection. So when implementing the first layer of a network, you have to consider factors such as the length of the cable, the type of connectors used, and other factors of a physical nature.

The second layer is that part of the software that is implemented on the network card itself. This software is responsible for sensing whether there is incoming data, and accordingly sending a signal to the PC to indicate that it is okay to send data now (or that there is incoming data, and the PC must wait before transmitting its data). This software layer is also responsible, for example, for examining the incoming data and determining if the incoming data belongs to the PC, based on the address that is being transferred with the data.

It will be very impractical for you, the programmer, to deal with every layer of the network. You have to accept and use certain parts of the network as given. This is not much different from the way you use the hard drive of the PC. To copy a file from the floppy disk to the hard drive, you use the DOS COPY command. As a PC user and as a programmer, you don't concern yourself with the cables that connect the floppy drive to the hard drive, and you are not concerned with the details of who is responsible for turning the mechanical motors of the floppy and hard drives. All that you want is the data to be copied once you issue the DOS COPY command.

In a similar manner, you must separate yourself from the lower layers of the network. As stated, you can make full use of the floppy drive and the hard drive without getting into their lower-layers details. But you have to understand what hardware to purchase when purchasing floppy and hard drives. For example, when purchasing floppy drives, you have to indicate whether you need a 3.5" or 5.25" drive, and when purchasing a hard drive, you need to indicate the hard drive capacity (for example, 500 MB, 2 GB) and how fast the hard drive performances should be. In a similar way, there are certain things you have to know about PC networks.

One important thing that you should know about networks is that there are several available network topologies. For example, the topology shown in Figure BD3.5 is known as *bus topology*. Another possible topology is shown in Figure BD3.6, and is called a *star topology*. Note that this network topology requires additional hardware called the *hub hardware*. Another topology, for example, is the ring topology. If in Figure BD3.5 you also connect PC A to PC E, you have a ring topology.

Figure BD3.6.
Five PCs connected with a star topology.

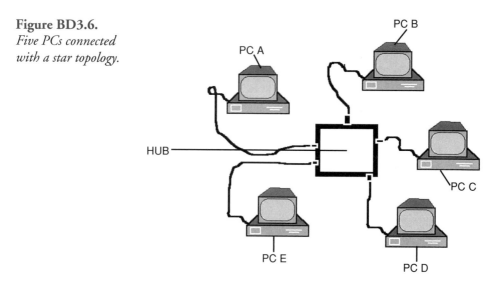

In Figure BD3.6 all the PCs are connected to the hub. The hub is responsible for switching the data to the appropriate PC. For example, if PC A is currently transmitting data, the hub receives the data, and based on the address that is attached to the data, the hub transmits the incoming data to the appropriate PC that is connected to it.

Just like the bus topology, the star topology can have only one "conversation" at any given time.

The Ethernet Network

One of the most popular ways to connect PCs in a network is called Ethernet. The Ethernet network is a bus network like the one shown in Figure BD3.5. In Ethernet, each PC has a network card that looks like the one shown in Figure BD3.7. That is, each network card can have a connection to two cables. The connector itself is called a *BNC connector*. This connector enables you to connect two cables to the card. The cable itself is called a *shielded cable*, and it is a cable similar in appearance to the cables used by the cable television companies to connect your television to the cable service.

Figure BD3.7.
A schematic Ethernet network card.

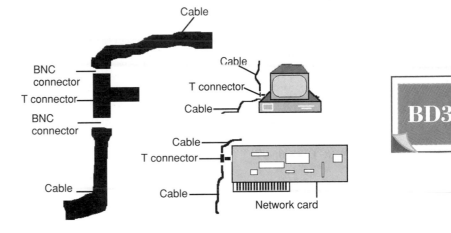

When connecting PCs in an Ethernet network, you'll have PCs that have two cables connected to them. For example, in Figure BD3.5, PC B, PC C, and PC D each have two cables connected to them. A close-up schematic diagram of the cables is shown in Figure BD3.7.

However, in Ethernet there will always be two PCs with only one cable connected to them (see PC A and PC E in Figure BD3.5).

In Ethernet, you must use a terminator for the two PCs that have only one cable connected to them (see Figure BD3.8).

Figure BD3.8.
Attaching a terminator to the PC that has only one cable connected to it.

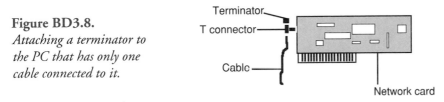

Therefore, in Figure BD3.9 for example, PC A and PC D have terminators. Note that if your Ethernet network consists of only two PCs, these two PCs have terminators (see Figure BD3.10).

Figure BD3.9.
An Ethernet network with only four PCs in the network. PC A and PC D have terminators.

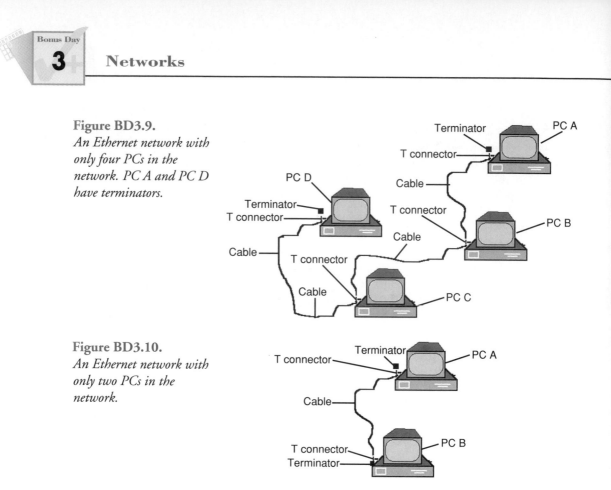

Figure BD3.10.
An Ethernet network with only two PCs in the network.

If you haven't dealt with network components before, you should know that a terminator costs about $1.50, a 50-foot Ethernet cable costs about $15.00, and each network card costs about $100.00.

Windows for Workgroups 3.11

Most PC vendors ship their PCs with either Windows 3.1 installed or with Windows for Workgroups 3.11 installed.

Windows for Workgroups is very similar to Windows 3.1. In fact, while working in Windows for Workgroups you will not be able to tell whether you are working in Windows 3.1 or in Windows for Workgroups 3.11. The only difference is that Windows for Workgroups comes with additional basic software network utilities.

To use the software utilities of Windows for Workgroups, you need to connect the PCs with network hardware as described earlier in this chapter.

Note: In a corporate environment, a network is a necessity! That is, the PCs are connected in a network, and users can communicate with each other via the network. For example, one user can send files to any other user on the network, and users can send each other e-mail messages.

Even if you are a programmer working at home, you might find that having a network is a lot of fun, and it can add significantly to your productivity. As it turns out, PC technology changes very rapidly, and as you may know already, after a couple years of using one PC, you find yourself purchasing a better PC. So what should you do with the old PC? Some try to sell their old PCs, and some try to salvage as much as possible from their old PCs. For example, one can salvage RAM chips, monitors, and so on.

Alternatively, you can consider connecting the old PC to the new PC via an Ethernet network, as shown in Figure BD3.10.

This can add a lot to your productivity. For example, you can let the old computer send data to the printer while you keep working with the new PC. Because the PCs are connected via a network, you don't transfer files from one PC to the other via diskettes, but rather via the network.

Again, Windows for Workgroups is almost identical to Windows 3.1. However, Windows for Workgroups includes various network-related software. For example, the File Manager of Windows for Workgroups lets you add a new hard drive to the list of accessible hard drives. The new hard drive is the hard drive of another PC in the network. So on your PC you'll see the File Manager with the local drives of your PC, and you'll also see the hard drives of other PCs in the network. And just as you use the File Manager to copy files from your local hard drive, you can use the File Manager to copy files from remote hard drives that reside inside PCs on the network. Also, just as you use the File Manager program to double-click an EXE file on your local hard drive to execute the program file, you can use File Manager to double-click a file that resides on a remote hard drive. Of course, Windows for Workgroups includes a security mechanism, which means that you can execute programs of other PCs, provided that the other PCs gave you permission to do so. Similarly, you can copy and delete files on other people's PCs, provided that these PCs gave you access to their PCs.

Microsoft Mail Post Office Upgrade for Windows

One of the software network utilities included with Windows for Workgroups 3.11 is a program called Mail. As implied by its name, this program lets you send mail to other users on the network.

Later in this chapter you'll write a Visual Basic program that is network based. As you'll see, you'll utilize the MSMAPI.VBX control in your Visual Basic network-based program. The MSMAPI.VBX control comes with the Professional Edition of Visual Basic 3.0. As it turns out, to use the MSMAPI.VBX control from within your Visual Basic programs, it is not enough to have Windows for Workgroups 3.11 installed on your network, but you also must install the MAPI server. You can install the MAPI server, for example, by purchasing yet another Microsoft product called Mail Post Office Upgrade for Windows. This program is the upgrade program to the Mail program that comes with Windows for Workgroups.

So to be able to write network e-mail–based programs with Visual Basic you need the following:

- The necessary hardware to connect at least two PCs in a network
- Windows for Workgroups 3.11
- The MSMAPI.VBX control that comes with the Professional Edition of Visual Basic
- The MAPI server software (for example, the Microsoft Mail Post Office Upgrade for Windows program installs this server)

If you have all of this hardware and software, you can design some very impressive Visual Basic network e-mail–based programs.

The MyNet Program

Before writing the MyNet program yourself, review its specifications.

Upon startup of the MyNET program, the window shown in Figure BD3.11 appears.

Figure BD3.11.
The MyNET program.

The objective of the MyNET program is to enable the user to send mail via the Microsoft Mail program. Again, note that the MyNET program uses the MSMAPI.VBX control. Therefore, you need to install MAPI software. Such software is included, for example, with the Microsoft Mail Post Office Upgrade for Windows program. (The Mail program that comes with Windows for Workgroups 3.11 is the limited version of the Mail program.)

The first thing the user has to do is to log on to Mail by clicking the Log ON button.

MyNET responds by displaying the Mail Sign In dialog box shown in Figure BD3.12. As shown in Figure BD3.12, the user has to type the mailbox name and the password. The mailbox name and the password are assumed to be established already. (The mailbox name and the password were established after the Mail Post Office Upgrade for Windows program was installed.)

Figure BD3.12.
The Mail Sign In dialog box.

If the user types a valid mailbox name and password, the logon is successful, and the caption of the Log ON button becomes Log OFF (see Figure BD3.13). If the user did not type the correct mailbox name and password, an error message appears.

Figure BD3.13.
The MyNET program after a successful logon.

Another indication that the logon was successful is the presence of the Mail program icon on the desktop of Windows (see Figure BD3.14). Once the MyNET program performs a successful log on, the icon shown in Figure BD3.14 appears. (You may have to minimize the windows of the desktop to be able to see this icon.)

Figure BD3.14.
The Mail icon that appears after a successful logon.

The user can now type text inside the text box. Figure BD3.15 shows the MyNET program, with text inside the text box.

Figure BD3.15.
The text inside the text box will be sent via Mail.

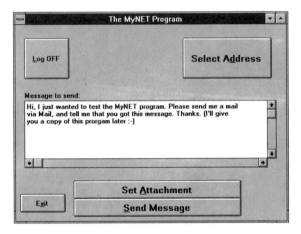

The user can now click the Select Address button to select the address to which the text will be sent.

In Figure BD3.16 you can see that currently there are three PCs connected to the network. (One of these PCs is the PC on which the MyNET program is executed.)

The user can now highlight the address of the destination PC, click the Add button, and then click the OK button.

The message is now ready for transmission!

If the user clicks the Send button, the message will be sent to the address the user selected. However, the user can also send an attachment with the mail. An attachment can be a text file or any other file that Mail accepts.

Once the user clicks the Set Attachment button, MyNET responds by displaying the Attach a File to your message dialog box (see Figure BD3.17). In Figure BD3.17, a WAV file is selected. This file will be sent as an attachment to the text that the user typed inside the text box.

Figure BD3.16.
Selecting an address.

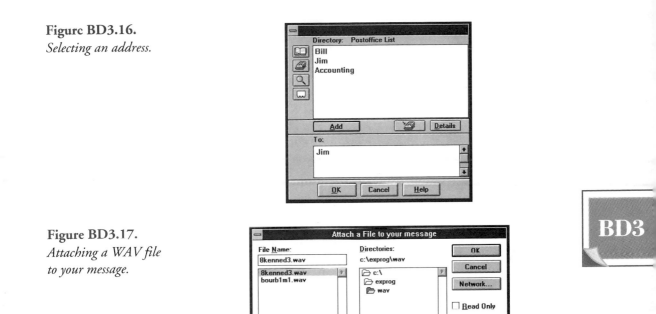

Figure BD3.17.
*Attaching a WAV file
to your message.*

Once the user clicks the OK button of the Attach a File to Your Message dialog box, the text and the attachment are ready for delivery.

To send the mail, the user has to click the Send Message button.

The user can verify that the MyNET program sent the message:

☐ Click the Exit button of the MyNET program to terminate the program.

☐ Start the Mail program by clicking its program icon (see Figure BD3.18).

Mail responds by displaying the Mail Sign In dialog box (see Figure BD3.12).

☐ Type the mailbox name and the password of the mailbox to which the message was sent, and click the OK button.

Mail responds by displaying its desktop.

☐ Select Inbox from the Window menu of Mail to display the received mail.

Mail responds by displaying the Inbox window (see Figure BD3.19).

Figure BD3.18.
The Mail program icon.

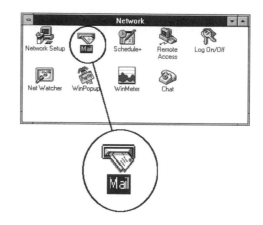

Figure BD3.19.
The Inbox window, with the mail that MyNET sent.

☐ Double-click the message.

> *Mail responds by displaying the complete message (see Figure BD3.20).*

☐ Double-click the microphone icon to play the WAV file (this is the attachment that you sent via MyNET).

Figure BD3.20.
Displaying the message that was sent by MyNET.

The Visual Implementation of the MyNET Program

Now that you know what the MyNET program is supposed to do, you can write the program.

☐ Select New Project from the File menu of Visual Basic and save the new project as follows: Save the new form as MyNET.FRM inside the C:\EXPROG\BD3 directory and save the new project file as MyNET.MAK inside the C:\EXPROG\BD3 directory.

The MyNET program utilizes the MSMAPI.VBX control from the Professional Edition of Visual Basic 3.0. Therefore, you need to add this VBX control to your project:

☐ Select Add File from the File menu of Visual Basic and select the file C:\Windows\System\MSMAPI.VBX.

> *Visual Basic responds by adding the MSMAPI.VBX control to your project. Figure BD3.21 shows the two icons that Visual Basic added to the Toolbox after adding the MSMAPI.VBX control.*

Figure BD3.21.
The icons of the MSMAPI.VBX control.

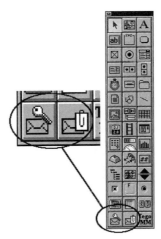

☐ Implement the frmMyNET form according to the specifications in Table BD3.1. When you finish implementing the form, it should look like the one shown in Figure BD3.22.

Table BD3.1 instructs you to place the MapiSession and MapiMessages controls inside the form. In Figure BD3.21, the left control is the MapiSession control, and the right control is the MapiMessages control.

Table BD3.1. The properties table of the frmMyNET form.

Object	Property	Setting
Form	**Name**	**frmMyNET**
	BackColor	(light gray)
	Caption	The MyNET Program
	Height	5700
	Icon	C:\VB\Icons\Mail\Mail01a.ICO
	Left	
		1020
	Top	1140
	Width	7485
Command Button	**Name**	**cmdExit**
	Caption	E&xit
	Height	495
	Left	120
	Top	4560
	Width	1215
Command Button	**Name**	**cmdSetAttachment**
	Caption	Set &Attachment
	FontBold	-1-True
	FontName	MS Sans Serif
	FontSize	12
	Height	495
	Left	1560
	Top	4200
	Width	4575
Command Button	**Name**	**cmdSelectAddress**
	Caption	Select A&ddress
	FontBold	-1-True
	FontName	MS Sans Serif
	FontSize	12
	Height	1095
	Left	4560

Object	Property	Setting
	Top	360
	Width	2415
Common Dialog Box	**Name**	**CMDialog1**
	CancelError	-1-True
	Left	6480
	Top	4680
Command Button	**Name**	**cmdSend**
	Caption	&Send Message
	FontBold	-1-True
	FontName	MS Sans Serif
	FontSize	12
	Height	495
	Left	1560
	Top	4680
	Width	4575
MapiMessages	**Name**	**MapiMessages1**
	Left	3360
	Top	1560
MapiSession	**Name**	**MapiSession1**
	Left	2520
	Top	1560
Command Button	**Name**	**cmdLogOnOFF**
	Caption	&Log ON
	Height	1095
	Left	240
	Top	360
	Width	1215
Text Box	**Name**	**txtMessage**
	Height	1815
	Left	240
	MultiLine	-1-True

BD3

continues

Table BD3.1. continued

Object	Property	Setting
	ScrollBars	3-Both
	Text	(empty)
	Top	2040
	Width	6855
Label	**Name**	**lblMessage**
	BackColor	(light gray)
	Caption	Message to send:
	Height	255
	Left	240
	Top	1800
	Width	1695

Figure BD3.22.
*The frmMyNET form
(in design mode).*

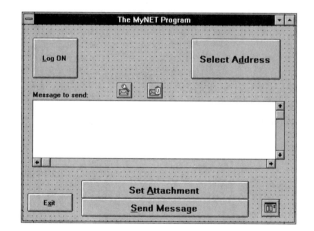

Entering the Code of the General Declarations Section of the frmMyNET Form

You'll now enter the code of the general declarations section.

☐ Type the following code inside the general declarations section of the frmMyNET form:

```
Option Explicit

Dim gAddress
Dim gAttach
Dim gSend
```

The code you typed declares three general variables. As you'll soon see, these variables serve as flags in the MyNET program.

Attaching Code to the *Load* Event of the Form

You'll now attach code to the Load event of the form.

☐ Type the following code inside the Form_Load() procedure:

```
Sub Form_Load ()

    gAddress = 0
    gAttach = 0
    gSend = 0

End Sub
```

Upon startup of the program the flags are set to 0.

BD3

Attaching Code to the *Click* Event of the Log ON/OFF Button

You'll now attach code to the cmdLogOnOFF button. As you'll soon see, this button serves as the Log ON button and as the Log OFF button.

☐ Type the following code inside the cmdLogOnOFF_Click() procedure of the frmMyNET form:

```
Sub cmdLogOnOFF_Click ()

    If cmdLogOnOFF.Caption = "&Log ON" Then
        '''''''''''''''''''''''''''
        ' User is now logging On
        '''''''''''''''''''''''''''  '
        ' Ask the user for password and account name
        MapiSession1.LogonUI = True

        On Error GoTo DidNotLogOn

        ' Log on
        MapiSession1.Action = 1

        MapiMessages1.SessionID = MapiSession1.SessionID

        cmdLogOnOFF.Caption = "&Log OFF"
        gAddress = 1
        gAttach = 0
        gSend = 0

    Else
        ' User is now logging Off
        MapiSession1.Action = 2
```

```
          MapiMessages1.SessionID = 0

          cmdLogOnOFF.Caption = "&Log ON"
          gAddress = 0
          gAttach = 0
          gSend = 0

      End If
      Exit Sub

DidNotLogOn:
      MsgBox "Did Not Log On"
      gAddress = 0
      gAttach = 0
      gSend = 0
      Exit Sub

End Sub
```

The code you typed starts with an If…Else statement:

```
If cmdLogOnOFF.Caption = "&Log ON" Then

      ' User is now logging ON

Else

      ' User is now logging OFF

End If
```

The code under the If statement is executed when the Caption property of the button is &Log ON (that is, the user clicked the Log ON button).

The code under the Else is executed when the Caption property of the button is &Log OFF (that is, the user clicked the Log OFF button).

The code under the If statement sets the LogonUI property of the MapiSession1 control to True:

```
MapiSession1.LogonUI = True
```

When you set the LogonUI property to True, a dialog box appears. This dialog box asks the user to type the mailbox name and the password. (If you set the LogonUI property of the MAPI Session control to False, the dialog box will not be displayed.)

The next statement sets an error trap:

```
On Error GoTo DidNotLogOn
```

That is, if an error occurs due to the execution of the next statements, the program will immediately jump to the DidNotLogOn line. Here is the code under the DidNotLogOn line (placed at the end of the procedure):

```
DidNotLogOn:
   MsgBox "Did Not Log On"
   gAddress = 0
   gAttach = 0
   gSend = 0
   Exit Sub
```

As you can see, when an error occurs, a message box is displayed with the message Did Not Log On, and the three general variables are set to 0.

The next statement you typed after the On Error statement is this:

```
MapiSession1.Action = 1
```

When you set the Action property of the MAPI Session control to 1, an attempt will be made to log on. The logon will be based on the settings of the UserName and Password properties of the MAPI Session control (the MapiSession1 control).

The next statement sets the SessionID property of the MapiMessages1 control to the SessionID property of the MapiSession1 control:

```
MapiMessages1.SessionID = MapiSession1.SessionID
```

Recall that you logged on by setting the Action property of the MapiSession1 control to 1. If an error occurs, the program immediately jumps to the error line indicated by the trapping line, and the procedure is terminated. If no error occurs, the logon is successful, and the SessionID property of the MapiSession1 control is updated automatically with a number that represents the session identification number. The preceding statement assigned the SessionID property of the MapiMessages1 control to the value of the SessionID property of the MapiSession1 control.

The next statement sets the Caption property of the button to &Log OFF:

```
cmdLogOnOFF.Caption = "&Log OFF"
```

That is, from now on, the button serves as a Log OFF button.

The last three statements set the value of the general variables:

```
gAddress = 1
gAttach = 0
gSend = 0
```

gAddress is set to 1, because now the user is logged on, and therefore the user can now select the address to which the mail should be sent.

The gAttach flag is set to 0, because you don't want the user to click the Set Attachment button yet. When the gAttach flag is equal to 1, the corresponding button is enabled, and when the flag is equal to 0 the corresponding button is disabled.

The gAddress flag corresponds to the Select Address button, the gAttach flag corresponds to the Set Attachment button, and the gSend flag corresponds to the Send Message button.

The code under the `Else` statement is responsible for logging off. Recall that this code is executed whenever the user clicks the Log OFF button.

The first statement under the `Else` is this:

```
MapiSession1.Action = 2
```

When the Action property of MapiSession1 is set to 2, a log off operation is performed.

Because the user logged off, the next statement sets the SessionID property of the MapiMessages1 control to 0:

```
MapiMessages1.SessionID = 0
```

Finally, the Caption property of the button is set to &Log ON:

```
cmdLogOnOFF.Caption = "&Log ON"
```

Then all the flags are set to 0:

```
gAddress = 0
gAttach = 0
gSend = 0
```

Attaching Code to the *Click* Event of the Exit Button

You'll now attach code to the `Click` event of the Exit button.

☐ Type the following code inside the `cmdExit_Click()` procedure of the frmMyNET form:

```
Sub cmdExit_Click ()

        ' User is now logging Off
        MapiSession1.Action = 2
        MapiMessages1.SessionID = 0
        End

End Sub
```

The code you typed performs a Log off operation, and then the program terminates.

Attaching Code to the *Click* Event of the Select Address Button

You'll now attach code to the `Click` event of the Select Address button.

☐ Type the following code inside the `cmdSelectAddress_Click()` procedure of the frmMyNET form:

```
Sub cmdSelectAddress_Click ()
```

```
   If gAddress = 0 Then

      MsgBox "Please Log ON before selecting an address."
      Exit Sub

   End If


   MapiMessages1.MsgIndex = -1
   MapiMessages1.AddressEditFieldCount = 1


   On Error GoTo ActionError

   '' 11 is the MESSAGE_SHOWADBOOK
   MapiMessages1.Action = 11

   gSend = 1
   gAttach = 1

   Exit Sub

ActionError:
  MsgBox "Error"
  gAddress = 0
  gSend = 0
  gAttach = 0
  Exit Sub
```

End Sub

The code you typed uses an `If` statement to examine whether it is okay to select an address:

```
If gAddress = 0 Then

      MsgBox "Please Log ON before selecting an address."
      Exit Sub

End If
```

Recall that if the logon was successful, the gAddress flag is set to 1. So if gAddress is equal to 0, the user is not logged on, and therefore the program refuses to select an address.

If the user is logged on, the rest of the code inside the cmdSelectAddress_Click() procedure lets the user selects an address.

The MsgIndex property of the MapiMessages1 control is set to -1:

```
MapiMessages1.MsgIndex = -1
```

The value -1 indicates that the message under consideration is an outgoing message.

The user selects an address from a dialog box (see Figure BD3.16). The AddressEditFieldCount property of the MapiMessages control determines what edit fields will be shown in the Select Address dialog box.

The code you typed sets the AddressEditFieldCount property to 1:

```
MapiMessages1.AddressEditFieldCount = 1
```

This means that the To edit box is present in the Select Address dialog box. So the user can either highlight an address in the top edit box and then click the Add button to select the To address, or type the To address (inside the lower edit box of Figure BD3.16).

An error trap is set:

```
On Error GoTo ActionError
```

The next statement sets the Action property of the MapiMessages1 control to 11:

```
MapiMessages1.Action = 11
```

The preceding statement displays the Select Address dialog box (Figure BD3.16).

If an error occurred during the process of selecting an address, the error is trapped, and the program immediately jumps to the ActionError line:

```
ActionError:
  MsgBox "Error"
  gAddress = 0
  gSend = 0
  gAttach = 0
  Exit Sub
```

Because an error occurred, all the flags are set to 0, and the procedure terminates.

If no error occurred, the gSend and gAttach flags are set to 1, because now the user can attach a file to the message and send the message:

```
gSend = 1
gAttach = 1
```

Attaching Code to the *Click* Event of the Set Attachment Button

You'll now attach code to the Click event of the Set Attachment button.

☐ Type the following code inside the cmdSetAttachment_Click() procedure of the frmMyNET form:

```
Sub cmdSetAttachment_Click ()

If gAttach = 0 Then
   MsgBox "Please log ON and select an address before attaching."
   Exit Sub
End If

CMDialog1.DialogTitle = "Attach a File to your message"
```

```
CMDialog1.Filter = "All Files(*.*)¦*.*¦Test Files(*.txt)
➡ ¦*.txt¦WAV Files (*.wav)¦*.wav"

    On Error GoTo DialogError

    CMDialog1.Action = 1

MapiMessages1.AttachmentIndex = MapiMessages1.AttachmentCount

MapiMessages1.AttachmentName = CMDialog1.Filetitle
MapiMessages1.AttachmentPathName = CMDialog1.Filename
MapiMessages1.AttachmentPosition = MapiMessages1.AttachmentIndex

' 0 is MAPI_ATT_File
MapiMessages1.AttachmentType = 0

gSend = 1

Exit Sub

DialogError:
    MsgBox "Error", 64, "No File was attached"
    gAddress = 0
    gSend = 0
    gAttach = 0
    Exit Sub

End Sub
```

The code you typed uses an `If` statement to examine whether it is okay to execute the rest of the statements inside the `cmdSetAttachment_Click()` procedure:

```
If gAttach = 0 Then
    MsgBox "Please log ON and select an address before attaching."
    Exit Sub
End If
```

That is, it is okay to attach a file to the message, provided that the gAttach variable is not equal to 0. Recall that you set gAttach to 1 after the user sets the address.

The rest of the statements inside the `cmdSetAttachment_Click()` procedure let the user select a file that will be attached to the message.

The title of the dialog box that lets the user select a file is set:

```
CMDialog1.DialogTitle = "Attach a File to your message"
```

The Filter property of the common dialog box is set:

```
CMDialog1.Filter =  "All Files(*.*)¦*.*¦Test Files(*.txt)
➡ ¦*.txt¦WAV Files (*.wav)¦*.wav"
```

An error trap is set:

```
On Error GoTo DialogError
```

Then the common dialog box is displayed:

```
CMDialog1.Action = 1
```

At this point, the selected file is stored as the FileTitle and FileName properties of the common dialog box.

Now the process of attaching the selected file to the message begins.

The AttachmentCount property indicates the number of attachments. The AttachmentIndex property indicates an index number for the attachment. You have to set the value of the AttachmentIndex property based on the value of the AttachmentCount property as follows:

```
MapiMessages1.AttachmentIndex = MapiMessages1.AttachmentCount
```

The AttachmentName and AttachementPathName properties specify the name and path of the file that will be attached. Because the attached file was selected with the common dialog box, the following statements are used:

```
MapiMessages1.AttachmentName = CMDialog1.Filetitle
MapiMessages1.AttachmentPathName = CMDialog1.Filename
```

The AttachmentPosition property is set based on the AttachmentIndex property:

```
MapiMessages1.AttachmentPosition = MapiMessages1.AttachmentIndex
```

Finally, the AttachmentType property is set:

```
MapiMessages1.AttachmentType = 0
```

When the AttachmentType property is set to 0, the attached file is data. Other possible values for the AttachmentType property are 1 and 2. 1 means that the attachment is an embedded OLE, and 2 means that the attachment is a static OLE.

Attaching Code to the *Click* Event of the Send Message Button

You'll now attach code to the Click event of the Send Message button.

☐ Type the following code inside the cmdSend_Click() procedure of the frmMyNET form:

```
Sub cmdSend_Click ()

If gSend = 0 Then
   MsgBox "Please log ON and select an address before sending"
   Exit Sub
End If
```

```
    MapiMessages1.MsgNoteText = " " + txtMessage.Text

    On Error GoTo SendError

    '''3 is the MESSAGE_SEND action
    MapiMessages1.Action = 3
    Exit Sub

SendError:
    gAddress = 0
    gSend = 0
    gAttach = 0
    MsgBox "Error. No mail was sent"
    Exit Sub
```

End Sub

BD3

The code you typed examines the gSend flag to see if it is okay to send the message:

```
If gSend = 0 Then
    MsgBox "Please log ON and select an address before sending"
    Exit Sub
End If
```

If it is okay to send, the rest of the statements inside the cmdSend_Click() procedure are executed.

The MsgNoteTest property contains the text message. Because you want the contents of the txtMessage text box to be sent, the MsgNoteTest property is set as follows:

```
MapiMessages1.MsgNoteText = " " + txtMessage.Text
```

An error trap is set:

```
On Error GoTo SendError
```

Finally, the message is sent:

```
MapiMessages1.Action = 3
```

☐ Experiment with the MyNET program and verify its proper operation.

Summary

In this chapter you have learned the basics of network hardware.

In this chapter you have also learned how to utilize the MSMAPI.VBX control that is included with the Professional Edition of Visual Basic 3.0. You have learned that you can use this control for e-mail communication with other PCs over the network.

Q&A

Q **I have read in this chapter about different topologies, about the shielded cables, and so on. Do I know everything I need to know about network hardware?**

A Well, like everything else, there are always additional things to know. For example, although the shielded cables for connecting PCs are the most commonly used, your salesperson might try to sell you the so-called twisted pair unshielded wires. What are these wires? These are the same type of wires used by the telephone company to connect telephones. As implied by the name, the unshielded wires are not shielded, and they are very inexpensive. In fact, these wires are probably the most inexpensive wires one can purchase. So the advantage of purchasing these wires is that they cost very little. The disadvantage of using these wires is that in a noisy environment (for example, a room where you have a lot of electrical equipment) the other electrical equipment might generate electrical noise that will be "injected" into the unshielded wires. If you are connecting only several PCs, trust us, use shielded wires! However, if you are connecting hundreds of PCs, then using unshielded wires can save you thousands of dollars, and you can start thinking about whether it is worthwhile to use unshielded wires.

Q **I can use Mail for sending mail. Why would I need to write a Visual Basic program that sends mail?**

A You *can* use Mail to send mail. However, there are many situations in which it is not appropriate to send mail via Mail. For example, suppose a salesperson needs to send information to the accounting department. The salesperson would be able to be more efficient if he/she were concentrating on his/her job, presenting the product, talking to the customers, and so on. It would be unrealistic to ask the sales person to operate the Mail program during a sales session. If during the sales session the salesperson needs to send mail, the process of transmitting the mail should be as painless as possible. You can write a Visual Basic program (similar to the MyNET program) that makes life easier. To begin with, the process of sending the message can be accomplished by simply clicking a single button (that is, you'll perform the logon task and all the other tasks inside the Click event procedure of a single button). Also, your code can let the user send mail by letting the user click various option buttons and check boxes. For example, suppose that the salesperson needs to receive the latest pricing information (and that this type of message is mailed by the salesperson daily). Instead of drafting such a message, your Visual Basic program can display list boxes that let the user draft the message by simply making selections with the mouse. Your Visual Basic code can "translate" the user's input into a text message and send the message.

This chapter has just scratched the surface of the MSMAPI.VBX control. Just as you are able to send mail by writing a Visual Basic program, you can display received

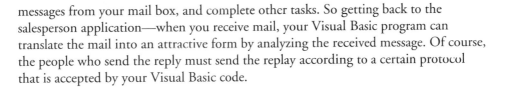

messages from your mail box, and complete other tasks. So getting back to the salesperson application—when you receive mail, your Visual Basic program can translate the mail into an attractive form by analyzing the received message. Of course, the people who send the reply must send the replay according to a certain protocol that is accepted by your Visual Basic code.

Quiz

1. When you set the LogonUI property of the MapiSession control to True, as in the following statement:

   ```
   MapiSession1.LogonUI = True
   ```

   a dialog box will pop up. This dialog box lets the user type the mailbox name and the password.

   a. True

   b. False

2. When you set the LogonUI property of the MapiSession control to False as in the following statement:

   ```
   MapiSession1.LogonUI = False
   ```

   the dialog box that lets the user type the mailbox name and the password will not pop up.

   a. True

   b. False

3. If you set the LogonUI property to False, there is no need to supply a mailbox name and password.

   a. True

   b. False

4. If the dialog box is not displayed, the user does not have to type the mailbox name and the password. So how is the security mechanism implemented?

Exercise

Modify the MyNET program so that it will enable/disable the buttons according to the user's action. For example, upon startup of the program, only the Exit and Log On buttons should be enabled. After a successful logon, the Select Address button should be enabled (but the Set Attachment and the Send Message buttons should be disabled, because the user did not yet select an address).

Quiz Answers

1. a
2. a
3. b
4. You have to set the UserName and Password properties during design time, or from within the code. In any case, you'll have to set these properties prior to setting the Action property to 1.

Exercise Answer

As you saw in this chapter, general variables were used to enable/disable the buttons. For example, if the user tries to send the message without first logging on and selecting an address, a message box is displayed:

```
Sub cmdSend_Click ()


If gSend = 0 Then
    MsgBox "Please log ON and select an address before sending"
    Exit Sub
End If

...
...
...


End Sub
```

Alternatively, you can disable the Send Message button at design time. Once the user logs on and selects an address, you can enable the button as follows:

```
cmdSendMessage.Enabled = True
```

In a similar manner, enable/disable the Set Address and Set Attachment buttons.

Here is, for example, the modified `cmdLogOnOFF_Click()` procedure:

```
Sub cmdLogOnOFF_Click ()

If cmdLogOnOFF.Caption = "&Log ON" Then
    ''''''''''''''''''''''''''''''''''''
    ' User is now logging On
    ''''''''''''''''''''''''''''''''''' '
    ' Ask the user for password and account name
    MapiSession1.LogonUI = True

    On Error GoTo DidNotLogOn

    ' Log on
```

```
        MapiSession1.Action = 1

        MapiMessages1.SessionID = MapiSession1.SessionID

        cmdLogOnOFF.Caption = "&Log OFF"
        ''' gAddress = 1
        ''' gAttach = 0
        ''' gSend = 0
        cmdSelectAddress.Enable = True
        cmdSetAttachment.Enabled = True
        cmdSendMessage.Enabled = True

    Else
        ' User is now logging Off
        MapiSession1.Action = 2
        MapiMessages1.SessionID = 0

        cmdLogOnOFF.Caption = "&Log ON"
        ''' gAddress = 0
        ''' gAttach = 0
        ''' gSend = 0
        cmdSelectAddress.Enable = False
        cmdSetAttachment.Enabled = False
        cmdSendMessage.Enabled = False

    End If
    Exit Sub

DidNotLogOn:
    MsgBox "Did Not Log On"
    ''' gAddress = 0
    ''' gAttach = 0
    ''' gSend = 0
    cmdSelectAddress.Enable = False
    cmdSetAttachment.Enabled = False
    cmdSendMessage.Enabled = False
    Exit Sub

End Sub
```

BD3

Bonus Day 4

Virtual Reality

In this chapter you'll learn about the interesting topic of virtual reality.

What Is Virtual Reality?

A virtual reality program is a program that simulates a three-dimensional environment. That is, the program creates an illusion that makes the user feel as if he/she is moving inside a 3D environment.

Nowadays many software companies categorize their game programs as virtual reality–based programs. The game program displays a room, and the user can move inside the room by using the arrow keys of the keyboard or by using the mouse. As the user goes forward, backward, and in the other directions inside the room, the screen displays different views of the room. The user feels that he/she is moving inside the room.

A more expensive virtual reality apparatus may include a pair of goggles. The goggles have two miniature monitors in them. In addition to the goggles, the user is attached to the computer via a set of sensors that sense the user's movements. So instead of using the mouse to move around the room, the sensors detect the user's movements, and accordingly, the program displays different views inside the goggles. Figure BD4.1 is a schematic diagram showing a virtual reality apparatus in which the user uses goggles and the user is attached to the computer through sensors.

Figure BD4.1.
A virtual reality apparatus.

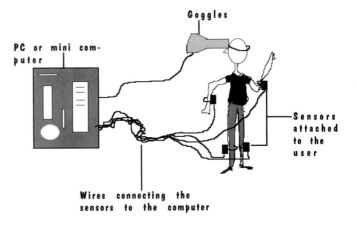

In this chapter you'll implement a virtual reality program that uses the mouse and the keyboard as the devices that tell the program about the user's movements inside a room, and the screen serves to display the various views of the room.

Note: In recent years, people have come to associate virtual reality technology with games. As stated, a virtual reality game can be implemented by using the standard devices of the PC (screen, mouse, keyboard, joystick). Alternatively, the virtual reality game can be implemented by using an expensive apparatus. For example, many amusement parks offer the use of such an apparatus; for a small fee you'll be attached to sensors, you'll use goggles, and through a toy gun that has sensors attached to it, you'll be able to "shoot" at bad creatures. The virtual reality program senses the directions in which you shoot via the sensors that are attached to the gun and to your body.

Besides games, virtual reality has some very serious applications. For example, the Air Force and many airlines are using a virtual reality apparatus that teaches student pilots how to fly. The virtual reality apparatus looks and feels like a real aircraft. This is commonly known as a flight simulator. The user can "fly" a virtual plane, and the program displays the instruments exactly as they are displayed in real flight. This way, the flight does not cost fuel, a real aircraft is not needed for the exercise, and students' mistakes are not fatal.

Lately, virtual reality technology has been applied to various medical fields, where students can practice complex operations on virtual patients.

BD4

The Room Program

The Room program demonstrates how you can use Visual Basic to create a virtual reality program that lets your user travel inside a 3D room.

Before writing the Room program yourself, review its specifications.

Upon startup of the Room program, the window shown in Figure BD4.2 appears.

Figure BD4.2.
The Room program.

Virtual Reality

As shown in Figure BD4.2, the Room program displays a room. At this point you see the left portion of the room. You can display different views of the room by using the down, up, left, and right arrow keys on your keyboard.

If you press the right arrow key several times, the Room program displays the window shown in Figure BD4.3. As shown in Figure BD4.3, you now can see the right portion of the room, which contains a window on the right wall.

Figure BD4.3.

The Room program after you move to the right side of the room.

During the time the user changes the picture from the one shown in Figure BD4.2 to the one shown in Figure BD4.3, the Room program displays all the pictures in between these two positions. For example, Figures BD4.4 and BD4.5 show the pictures that the user views while the right arrow key is down.

Figure BD4.4.

The Room program after you move a little bit to the right.

Figure BD4.5.

The Room program after you move additional distance to the right.

In a similar manner, the user can get farther away from the picture on the wall by pressing the down arrow key, and the user can get closer to the picture on the wall by pressing the up arrow key. Figures BD4.6 and BD4.7 show different views of the room when the user presses the down arrow key.

Figure BD4.6.
Moving a little bit away from the picture on the wall.

Figure BD4.7.
Moving farther away from the picture on the wall.

BD4

Now that you know what the Room program is supposed to do, you can implement it.

The Visual Implementation of the Room Program

You'll now visually implement the frmRoom form of the Room program.

☐ Select New Project from the File menu of Visual Basic, and save the new project as follows: Save the new form as Room.frm inside the C:\EXPROG\BD4 directory and save the new project file as Room.MAK inside the C:\EXPROG\BD4 directory.

☐ Implement the frmRoom form according to the specifications in Table BD4.1. When you finish implementing the form, it should look like the one shown in Figure BD4.8. Table BD4.2 instructs you to set the Picture property of the imgRoom image to Room01.BMP. The Room01.BMP picture is shown in Figure BD4.9. You can use Paintbrush to draw something like Figure BD4.9 by yourself. When drawing the picture with Paintbrush, start by selecting Image Attributes from the Options menu, and set the image size to Width=284 pixels and Height=326 pixels. Then draw the picture, and save the picture as a BMP file.

Table BD4.1. The properties table of the frmRoom form.

Object	Property	Setting
Form	**Name**	**frmRoom**
	BackColor	(black)
	BorderStyle	1-Fixed Single
	Caption	The Room Program
	Height	3900
	Icon	C:\EXPROG\ICONS\Room.ICO (or use your own icon)
	Left	2145
	MaxButton	0-False
	Top	1095
	Width	2565
Image	**Name**	**imgRoom**
	Height	4905
	Left	0
	Picture	C:\EXPROG\BMP\Room01.BMP
	Top	0
	Width	4275

Figure BD4.8.
The frmRoom form
(in design mode).

Attaching Code to the *KeyDown* Event of the Form

You'll now attach code to the KeyDown event of the form.

Figure BD4.9.
The Room01.BMP picture.

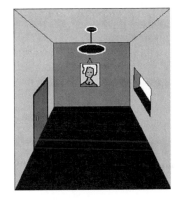

☐ Type the following code inside the `Form_KeyDown()` procedure of the frmRoom form:

```
Sub Form_KeyDown (keycode As Integer, Shift As Integer)

    If keycode = 39 Then
        ' Right arrow key was pressed
        If imgRoom.Left < -1800 Then
            Beep
            Exit Sub
        End If
        imgRoom.Move imgRoom.Left - 10

    End If

    If keycode = 37 Then
        ' Left arrow key was pressed
        If imgRoom.Left > 0 Then
            Beep
            Exit Sub
        End If

        imgRoom.Move imgRoom.Left + 10

    End If

    If keycode = 38 Then
        ' Up arrow key was pressed
        If imgRoom.Top > 0 Then
            Beep
            Exit Sub
        End If

        imgRoom.Move imgRoom.Left, imgRoom.Top + 10

    End If

    If keycode = 40 Then
        ' Down arrow key was pressed
        If imgRoom.Top < -1400 Then
```

BD4

```
        Beep
        Exit Sub
    End If

    imgRoom.Move imgRoom.Left, imgRoom.Top - 10

  End If


End Sub
```

The code you typed detects which key was pressed, and the picture is displayed according to the key that was pressed.

The first parameter of the `Form_KeyDown()` procedure is keycode:

```
Sub Form_KeyDown (keycode As Integer, Shift As Integer)

    .......
    .......
    .......
End Sub
```

That is, when the user presses a key on the keyboard, the `Form_KeyDown()` procedure is executed. The keycode parameter is automatically updated with a number that represents the pressed key.

The first `If` statement checks whether the pressed key is the right arrow key:

```
If keycode = 39 Then
    ' Right arrow key was pressed
    If imgRoom.Left < -1800 Then
       Beep
       Exit Sub
    End If
    imgRoom.Move imgRoom.Left - 10
End If
```

The integer 39 represents the right arrow key. So the `If` statement is satisfied when the user presses the right arrow key. The code under this `If` statement checks whether the upper-left corner of the image is less then 1800 units from the upper-left corner of the form. If this is the case, the program beeps, and the procedure terminates:

```
If imgRoom.Left < -1800 Then
   Beep
   Exit Sub
End If
```

If the preceding `If` statement is not satisfied, the image is moved 10 units to the left:

```
imgRoom.Move imgRoom.Left - 10
```

That is, from the point of view of the user, a different view of the room is displayed. This process is shown in Figure BD4.10.

Figure BD4.10.
Moving the picture 10 units to the left.

The picture on the right side of Figure BD4.10 is the initial picture (before the user presses the right arrow key). The user sees only the portion of the image that is enclosed by a rectangle in Figure BD4.10. This rectangle represents the area of the frmRoom form.

Once the right arrow key is pressed, the image is moved 10 units to the left of its previous position (see the left picture of Figure BD4.10). Because the area of the frmRoom form remains the same, the user now sees parts of the room that were not displayed prior to pressing the right arrow key.

BD4

The next If statement inside the Form_KeyDown() procedure checks whether the pressed key is the left arrow key:

```
If keycode = 37 Then
   ' Left arrow key was pressed
   If imgRoom.Left > 0 Then
      Beep
      Exit Sub
   End If

   imgRoom.Move imgRoom.Left + 10

End If
```

When keycode is equal to 37, it means that the user pressed the left arrow key. The code that is executed when the user presses the left arrow key is similar to the code that is executed when the user presses the right arrow key. However, now the image is moved 10 units to the left:

```
imgRoom.Move imgRoom.Left + 10
```

Also, because you don't want to move the image too much to the left, an If statement makes sure that the upper-left corner of the image does not exceed 0:

```
If imgRoom.Left > 0 Then
        Beep
        Exit Sub
     End If
```

When keycode is equal to 38, it means that the up arrow key is pressed. Here is the If statement that moved the image 10 units up:

```
If keycode = 38 Then
    ' Up arrow key was pressed
    If imgRoom.Top > 0 Then
        Beep
        Exit Sub
    End If

    imgRoom.Move imgRoom.Left, imgRoom.Top + 10

End If
```

When keycode is equal to 40, it means that the down arrow key is pressed. Here is the If statement that moved the image 10 units down:

```
If keycode = 40 Then
    ' Down arrow key was pressed
    If imgRoom.Top < -1400 Then
        Beep
        Exit Sub
    End If

    imgRoom.Move imgRoom.Left, imgRoom.Top - 10

End If
```

Figure BD4.11 shows a rectangle that represents the area of the frmRoom form. The right side of the figure is the initial position (before the user presses the down arrow key). The left side of Figure BD4.11 shows that the image was moved up 10 units in reference to the frmRoom area.

Figure BD4.11.
Moving the picture 10 units in the vertical direction.

☐ Execute the Room program and experiment with the down, up, right, and left arrow keys to see different views of the room.

The Room02 Program

The Room program illustrates how you can display different portions of the image by using the Move method on the image.

The first parameter of the Move method is the new X coordinate of the top-left corner of the image, and the second parameter of the Move method is the new Y coordinate of the top-left corner of the image. You can take advantage of the third and fourth parameters of the Move method. The third parameter of the Move method is the new width of the image, and the fourth parameter of the Move method is the new height of the image. By simultaneously changing the four parameters of the Move method, you can create some impressive movements inside the room. The Room02 program illustrates how this is accomplished.

Before writing the Room02 program yourself, review its specifications.

Upon startup of the Room02 program, the window shown in Figure BD4.12 is displayed.

Figure BD4.12.
The Room02 program.

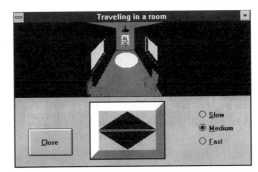

The control with the two arrow icons on it is the Spin.VBX control. The spin control works as follows:

- Clicking the up arrow icon of the spin control and keeping the left mouse button pressed down on the up arrow icon is equivalent to generating several click events.
- Clicking the down arrow icon of the spin control and keeping the left mouse button pressed down on the down arrow icon is equivalent to generating several click events.

The Spin.VBX control is part of the Professional Edition of Visual Basic 3.0.

Note: Even if you don't have the Professional Edition of Visual Basic 3.0, it is recommended that you read the rest of this chapter. However, instead of using the spin control, you will have to use two pushbuttons. One pushbutton will serve as

the up arrow icon of the spin control, and the other pushbutton will serve as the down arrow icon of the spin control.

The advantage of using the spin control is that to generate several click events, you have to click the mouse on the arrow icon of the spin control only once. Thereafter, as long as you keep the left button of the mouse pressed down, click events will occur periodically.

Upon clicking the up-arrow icon of the spin control, the picture of the room will be displayed as if the user is advancing toward the picture on the wall. Figures BD4.13 and BD4.14 show two different views of traveling toward the picture on the wall.

Figure BD4.13.
Getting a little closer to the picture on the wall.

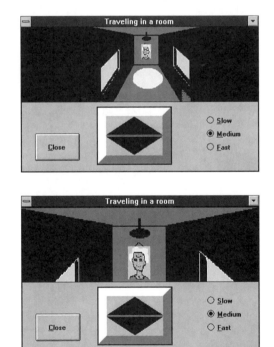

Figure BD4.14.
Reaching the picture on the wall.

The Room02 program has three option buttons: Slow, Medium, and Fast. The setting of these option buttons determines how fast the program responds to clicking the spin control.

Now that you know what the Room02 program is supposed to do, you can write it.

The Visual Implementation of the Room02 Program

You'll now visually implement the frmRoom form of the Room02 program.

☐ Select New Project from the File menu of Visual Basic and save the new project as follows: Save the new form as Room02.frm inside the C:\EXPROG\BD4 directory and save the new project file as Room02.mak inside the C:\EXPROG\BD4 directory.

☐ Implement the frmRoom form according to the specifications in Table BD4.2. When you finish implementing the form, it should look like the one shown in Figure BD4.15. Table BD4.2 instructs you to set the Picture property of the imgRoom image control to C:\EXPROG\BMP\Room02.BMP. Use Paintbrush to draw a picture similar to the picture shown in Figure BD4.16. When using Paintbrush to draw the picture, start by using the Image Attributes item from the Options menu of Paintbrush to set the size of the BMP picture to Width=392 pixels and Height=318 pixels, draw your picture, and then save the picture as a BMP file. Table BD4.2 instructs you to place the spin control inside the frmRoom form of the Room02 program. The icon of the Spin.VBX controls as it appears inside the Toolbox is shown in Figure BD4.17. Table BD4.2 instructs you to place three option button controls inside the frmRoom form. These option buttons are an array of option buttons with three elements in the array.

Table BD4.2. The properties table of the Room02 program.

Object	Property	Setting
Form	**Name**	**frmRoom**
	BackColor	(gray)
	BorderStyle	1-Fixed Single
	Caption	Traveling in a room
	Height	4305
	Icon	C:\EXPORG\ICONS\ROOM.ICO (or use an appropriate icon)
	Left	1440
	MaxButton	0-False
	Top	1335
	Width	6585
Picture Box	**Name**	**picStatus**
	Align	2-Align Bottom
	BackColor	(light gray)

continues

Table BD4.2. continued

Object	Property	Setting
Picture Box	**Name**	**picStatus**
	Height	1890
	Left	0
	Top	2010
	Width	6465
Option Button	**Name**	**optMove**
	BackColor	(light gray)
	Caption	&Slow
	Height	255
	Index	0
	Left	5040
	Top	360
	Width	855
Option Button	**Name**	**optMove**
	BackColor	(light gray)
	Caption	&Medium
	Height	255
	Index	1
	Left	5040
	Top	720
	Value	-1-True
	Width	975
Option Button	**Name**	**optMove**
	BackColor	(light gray)
	Caption	&Fast
	Height	255
	Index	2
	Left	5040
	Top	1080
	Width	855

Object	Property	Setting
Command Button	Name	**cmdClose**
	Caption	&Close
	Height	735
	Left	360
	Top	840
	Width	1215
Spin Button	**Name**	**Spin1**
	BackColor	(light gray)
	BorderThickness	2
	Delay	50
	Height	1575
	Left	2040
	ShadowBackColor	(light gray)
	TdThickness	15
	Top	120
	Width	2055
Image	**Name**	**imgRoom**
	Stretch	-1-True
	Height	2295
	Left	1920
	Picture	C:\EXPROG\BMP\ROOM02.BMP (or draw your own picture with Paintbrush)
	Top	0
	Width	2295

Figure BD4.15.
The frmRoom form of the Room02 program (in design mode).

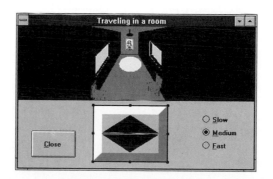

Figure BD4.16.
The Room02.BMP picture.

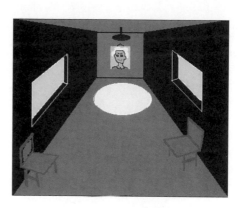

Figure BD4.17.
The icon of the Spin.VBX control.

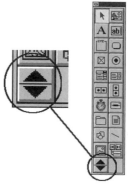

Entering the Code of the General Declarations Section of the Room02 Program

You'll now type code inside the general declarations section of the frmRoom form of the Room02 program.

☐ Type the following code inside the general declarations section of the frmRoom form:

```
Option Explicit

Dim gMinRoomWidth
Dim gMinRoomHeight

Dim gMaxRoomWidth
Dim gMaxRoomHeight
```

```
Dim gRoomWidth
Dim gRoomHeight

Dim gInc
```

The code you typed declares various variables inside the general declarations section. These variables are accessible by any procedure of the form.

Attaching Code to the *Load* Procedure of the frmRoom Form

You'll now attach code to the Load event of the form.

☐ Type the following code inside the Form_Load() procedure of the frmRoom form of the Room02 program:

```
Sub Form_Load ()

    gMinRoomWidth = imgRoom.Width
    gMinRoomHeight = imgRoom.Height

    gMaxRoomWidth = imgRoom.Width * 3
    gMaxRoomHeight = imgRoom.Height * 3

    gRoomWidth = imgRoom.Width
    gRoomHeight = imgRoom.Height

    gInc = 400

End Sub
```

The code you typed initializes the general variables that you declared inside the general declarations section.

Attaching Code to the *Click* Event of the Close Button

You'll now attach code to the Click event of the Close button.

☐ Type the following code inside the cmdClose_Click() procedure:

```
Sub cmdClose_Click ()

    Unload frmRoom

End Sub
```

The code you typed executes the Unload method on the frmRoom form. This means that when you click the Close button, the Room02 program terminates. (You could use the End statement instead of the Unload method.)

Attaching Code to the *Click* Event of the Option Buttons Array of Controls

You'll now attach code to the Click event of the option button array of controls. Recall that during design time you placed three option buttons inside the frmRoom form. The first option button is optMove(0) (the Slow option button), the second option button is optMove(1) (the Medium option button), and the third option button is OptMove(2) (the Fast option button).

☐ Type the following code inside the optMove_Click() procedure of the frmRoom form of the Room02 program:

```
Sub optMove_Click (Index As Integer)

    Select Case Index
            Case 0
                gInc = 50
            Case 1
                gInc = 400
            Case 2
                gInc = 1000
    End Select

End Sub
```

The code you typed uses a Select Case statement to determine which option button was clicked. The parameter of the optMove_Click() procedure is Index. This parameter indicates which element of the optMove array of option buttons was clicked.

Depending on which option button was clicked, the general variable gInc is updated. For example, if the user clicked the Medium option button, gInc is set to 400. As you'll soon see, gInc determines how fast the program moves the picture when the user clicks the spin control.

Attaching Code to the *SpinDown* Event of the Spin Control

You'll now attach code to the SpinDown event of the spin control. Recall that during design time you set the Delay property of the spin control to 50. This means that once the user clicks the down arrow icon of the spin control and keeps holding the left button of the mouse on the down arrow icon of the spin control, the Spin1_SpinDown() procedure is automatically executed every 50 milliseconds.

☐ Type the following code inside the Spin1_SpinDown() procedure:

```
Sub Spin1_SpinDown ()

    gRoomWidth = gRoomWidth - gInc
    gRoomHeight = gRoomHeight - gInc

    If gRoomWidth < gMinRoomWidth Then
       gRoomWidth = gMinRoomWidth
       gRoomHeight = gMinRoomHeight
    End If


    imgRoom.Move Int((frmRoom.Width - imgRoom.Width) / 2),
                      ➥ 0, gRoomWidth, gRoomHeight

End Sub
```

The code you typed decreases the value of the variable gRoomWidth by gInc, and it decreases the value of the gRoomHeight variable by gInc:

```
    gRoomWidth = gRoomWidth - gInc
    gRoomHeight = gRoomHeight - gInc
```

Recall that inside the Form_Load() procedure you initialized the gRoomWidth and gRoomHeight variables according to the width and height of the image control.

An If statement is then executed to make sure that the variables you decreased were not decreased too much:

```
    If gRoomWidth < gMinRoomWidth Then
       gRoomWidth = gMinRoomWidth
       gRoomHeight = gMinRoomHeight
    End If
```

Finally, the Move method is executed:

```
imgRoom.Move Int((frmRoom.Width - imgRoom.Width) / 2), 0, gRoomWidth, gRoomHeight
```

Note the four parameters of the Move method. The first parameter is the new X coordinate of the upper-left corner of the image. This X coordinate is set to the following:

```
Int((frmRoom.Width - imgRoom.Width)/2)
```

In other words, the X coordinate of the image is set so that the image is placed at the center of the frmRoom form.

The second parameter of the Move method is 0. This means that the Y coordinate of the upper-left corner of the image is at the top of the form.

The third parameter of the Move method is the following:

```
gRoomWidth
```

The third parameter is the new width of the image. You already decreased the value of gRoomWidth by gInc. This means that the image will have a width equal to the previous width of the image, minus gInc.

Similarly, the fourth parameter of the Move method is the following:

gRoomHeight

This means that the new height of the image is decreased by gInc (because you decreased gHeight by gInc).

So when the user clicks the down arrow of the spin control, the image remains at the center of the frmRoom form, but the width and height of the form are decreased. This gives the user the impression that the image is getting farther away from the user.

Attaching Code to the *SpinUp* Event of the Spin Control

You'll now attach code to the SpinUp event of the spin control. This event occurs whenever the user clicks the up arrow icon of the spin control. If the user keeps the left mouse button pressed on the up arrow icon of the spin control, the Spin1_SpinUp() procedure is executed automatically every 50 milliseconds (because you set the Delay property of the spin control to 50).

☐ Type the following code inside the Spin1_SpinUp() procedure:

```
Sub Spin1_SpinUp ()

    gRoomWidth = gRoomWidth + gInc
    gRoomHeight = gRoomHeight + gInc

    If gRoomWidth > gMaxRoomWidth Then
        gRoomWidth = gMaxRoomWidth
        gRoomHeight = gMaxRoomHeight
    End If


    imgRoom.Move Int((frmRoom.Width - imgRoom.Width) / 2),
                  ➥ 0, gRoomWidth, gRoomHeight

End Sub
```

The code you typed is very similar to the code you typed inside the Spin1_SpinDown() procedure. However, now you increase the gRoomWidth and gRoomHeight variables by gInc. This gives the user the impression that the image is getting closer.

☐ Execute the Room02 program and experiment with it.

☐ Terminate the Room02 program by clicking the Close button.

Note: The Room and Room02 programs that you have written in this chapter illustrate how easy it is to write virtual reality programs with Visual Basic.

Although these programs were illustrated by using the keyboard and the spin control, you can let the user use the mouse for "traveling" inside the room. To let the user "travel" inside the room by using the mouse, you have to use the imgRoom_MouseMove() procedure. Note that the imgRoom_MouseMove() procedure has the following parameters:

```
Sub imgRoom_MouseMove (Button As Integer, Shift As Integer,
                    ➡ X As Single, Y As Single)


    .......
    .......
    .......


End Sub
```

The Button parameter of the Form_MouseMove() procedure indicates which button was pressed when the mouse was moved.

If you want to move the pictures only if the mouse was moved while the mouse button was pressed, you'll have to use the following If statement:

```
Sub imgRoom_MouseMove (Button As Integer, Shift As Integer,
                    ➡ X As Single, Y As Single)


If (Button And 1 = 1) Then
        .......
        ... Write here code that is executed
        ... whenever the user moves
        ... the mouse while the mouse button
        ... is pressed down.
        .......
End If


End Sub
```

Note that the imgRoom_MouseMove() procedure has the X and Y parameters as its third and fourth parameters. These parameters tell you the X,Y coordinates of the mouse cursor at the time that the imgRoom_MouseMove() procedure is executed. You can store the values of these coordinates inside a static or general variable, and during the next execution of the imgRoom_MouseMove() procedure, you can compare

the previous X,Y coordinates with the current X,Y coordinates. Based on the comparison, you can make a determination of whether the user moved the mouse forward, backward, to the left, to the right, or diagonally.

You can further enhance the Room programs by letting the user rotate inside the room. To rotate the picture, you'll have to use an additional BMP picture. For example, if you are using the `MouseMove` event to determine how to move the picture, and you discover that the user is trying to rotate the picture with the mouse, then you can start displaying a new BMP picture. For example, if the user is trying to rotate to the left, then set a new picture to the Picture property of the image control. From now on the user will "face" the new BMP picture.

Figure BD4.18 shows the BMP picture the user will see after rotating to the right. As shown, now the user faces the window on the wall.

Figure BD4.18.
Facing the window on the wall.

Summary

In this chapter you have learned what virtual reality is and how you can implement virtual reality programs with Visual Basic. Basically, your virtual reality program has to display images in different views based on user activity.

Q&A

Q In Figure BD4.1, the computer used for the virtual reality apparatus is a PC or mini computer. Why would you want to use a mini computer for virtual reality?

A Sometimes the virtual reality applications requires an expensive, fast computer. For example, a very sophisticated flight simulator might display the different views that the pilot would see during an actual flight. In addition, the flight simulator has to fly the aircraft based on the user's settings of the instruments, as well as based on

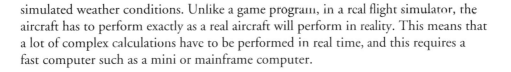

simulated weather conditions. Unlike a game program, in a real flight simulator, the aircraft has to perform exactly as a real aircraft will perform in reality. This means that a lot of complex calculations have to be performed in real time, and this requires a fast computer such as a mini or mainframe computer.

Quiz

1. How many parameters does the Move method have?
   a. 2
   b. 4
2. Explain the function of the first parameter of the Move method.
3. Explain the function of the second parameter of the Move method.
4. Explain the function of the third parameter of the Move method.
5. Explain the function of the fourth parameter of the Move method.

Exercise

Add code to the Room program so that whenever the user moves the mouse inside the image while the left button of the mouse is pressed the PC beeps.

Quiz Answers

1. b
2. The first parameter of the Move method indicates the X coordinate for the new location of the upper-left corner of the image. The upper-left corner of the image is referenced to the upper-left corner of the form.
3. The second parameter of the Move method indicates the Y coordinate for the new location of the upper-left corner of the image. The upper-left corner of the image is referenced to the upper-left corner of the form.
4. The third parameter of the Move method is an optional parameter. This parameter indicates the new width of the image.
5. The fourth parameter of the Move method is an optional parameter. This parameter indicates the new height of the image.

Exercise Answer

Add the following code to the Room program so that whenever the user moves the mouse inside the image while the left button of the mouse is pressed the PC beeps:

☐ Add the following code inside the `imgRoom_MouseMove()` procedure:

```
Sub imgRoom_MouseMove (Button As Integer, Shift As Integer,
          ➥ X As Single, Y As Single)

If (Button And 1) = 1 Then
    Beep
End If


End Sub
```

Note the X,Y parameters of the procedure. These parameters tell you the current locations of the mouse cursor. You can store these coordinates in general variables, and on the next execution of this procedure, you can compare the new X,Y coordinates with the old X,Y coordinates. This way, you'll be able to determine how the mouse was moved.

Bonus Day

5+

Games

Games? Yes! People like to play computer games, and as you'll see in this chapter, writing game programs with Visual Basic is easy and fun.

The Cards Program

The Cards program demonstrates how you can write a card game program with Visual Basic.

Borland International sells a package called Borland Visual Solutions Pack for Windows. As implied by its name, this package contains various VBX controls. You can use these VBX controls in programs such as Visual Basic, Visual C++, Borland C++, and other programming packages that can utilize VBX controls.

The Cards program that you'll now write utilizes the MHCD200.VBX control that is part of the Borland Visual Solutions Pack. This control was designed to help you write card game programs with great ease. As it turns out, to use the MHCD200.VBX control, you also need the MHCARDS.DLL file (also from the Borland Visual Solutions Pack).

Your first step, therefore, is to make sure that the MHCD200.VBX file and the MHCARDS.DLL file are inside your \Windows\System directory:

☐ Make sure that the MHCD200.VBX and MHCARDS.DLL files are inside your \Windows\System directory. (The installation program of the Visual Solutions Pack copied these files to your \Windows\System directory.) If for some reason these files do not reside inside your \Windows\System directory, you have to copy these files manually from the disk of the Borland Visual Solutions Pack.

> **Note:** Even if you currently do not have the Borland Visual Solutions Pack, it is recommended that you read this chapter because you'll be able to learn how game programs are implemented with Visual Basic. You'll learn about some logic issues that you'll have to consider and implement when designing game programs. After reading this chapter, you may find it worthwhile to purchase the Visual Solutions Pack for further extending the power of your Visual Basic product.

The Specifications of the Cards Program

Before writing the Cards program yourself, review its specifications.

Upon startup of the Cards program, the window shown in Figure BD5.1 appears.

Figure BD5.1.
Shuffling the cards.

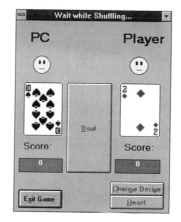

Note that the caption of the Cards program window contains the text Wait while Shuffling...

For a few seconds the Cards program shuffles the cards, and then the window shown in Figure BD5.2 appears.

Figure BD5.2.
The window of the Cards program after the cards have been shuffled.

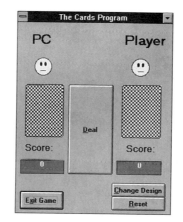

As you can see from Figure BD5.2, the score is now 0:0. That is, the Cards program lets the player play against the PC. Because you just started the Cards program, the score right now is 0 points for the player and 0 points for the PC.

Before starting to play the Cards program, verify that you like the design on the back of the cards.

☐ Click the Change Design button.

> *The Cards program responds by changing the design of the cards' backs. Figures BD5.3 through BD5.12 show some of the card back designs.*

Figure BD5.3.
The blue hatch design.

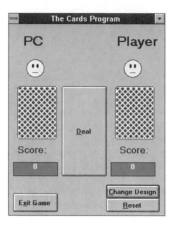

Figure BD5.4.
The robot design.

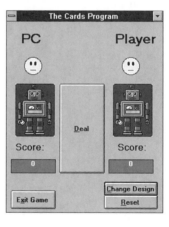

Figure BD5.5.
The roses design.

Figure BD5.6.
One leaves design.

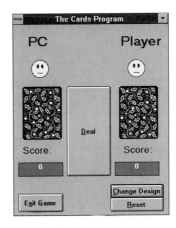

Figure BD5.7.
Another leaves design.

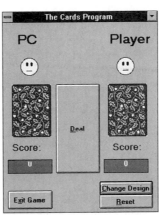

BD5

Figure BD5.8.
The fish design.

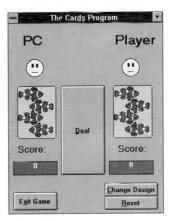

Figure BD5.9.
The conch design.

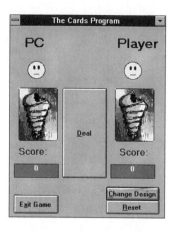

Figure BD5.10.
The castle design.

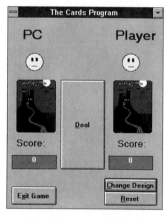

Figure BD5.11.
The beach design.

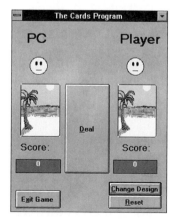

Figure BD5.12.
The hand design.

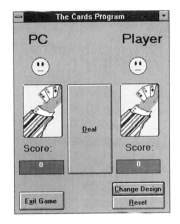

As stated, upon startup of the Cards program, the program shuffles the cards, and during the shuffling the user sees random cards displayed on the screen.

After the shuffling, the reader can click the Deal button to start a game. Once the Deal button is clicked, two cards are dealt—one for the PC and one for the player. Note the face icon that appears above the cards. This face indicates who won the deal! For example, if the PC won, the face above the PC's card smiles, while the face above the player's card remains grim. Whoever won gets 100 points, and the score text is updated. For example, Figure BD5.13 shows the Cards window after several rounds of play. As shown, the current score of the PC is 400, and the current score of the player is 300. In the last deal, the PC got the king of clubs card, and the player got the 6 of spades card.

Figure BD5.13.
After playing several times.

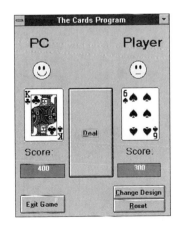

At any time the user can click the Reset button to start the game over. In this case, the program shuffles the cards, and the score is reset to 0:0.

To exit the game, the user clicks the Exit button.

As you'll soon see, when playing against the computer, the cards are dealt in an honest, random manner. That is, the PC has the same chance of winning the game as the player. Nevertheless (for the sole purpose of fun), you can design a "backdoor" mechanism to the game. That is, you can impress your friends with your "good luck" by incorporating a secret backdoor in the game that lets the player win in each deal. The following paragraphs explain how the backdoor mechanism works.

To win constantly, double-click the area between the text PC and the text Player that appears at the top of the Cards window. As a result, a small line appears between the Exit Game button and the Reset button. This small line is just a small visual indication that the game is currently in a cheating mode (see Figure BD5.14).

Figure BD5.14.
The Cards game in a cheating mode.

To take the game from cheating mode back to honest mode, double-click again the area between the PC and Player labels.

> **Note:** Once you finish writing the Cards program, you'll be able to continue enhancing the game yourself. Remember that it is a game, your game! Use your imagination to further enhance the game. For example, add the TegoMM.VBX multimedia control to the form. When the player loses, play the audio phrase "you lose." When the player wins, play the audio phrase "you win."

The Visual Implementation of the Cards Program

You'll now visually implement the frmCards form of the Cards program.

☐ Select New Project from the File menu and save the new project as follows: Save the new form file as C:\EXPROG\BD5\Cards.FRM and save the new project file as C:\EXPROG\BD5\Cards.MAK.

> **Note:** The Cards program uses the MHCD200.VBX control and the MHCARDS.DLL file. These files include pictures (the pictures of the cards), and you may therefore experience memory problems during design time if your project includes too many VBX controls. Therefore, remove all the VBX controls from the project window.
>
> To remove a VBX control from the project window do the following:
>
> ☐ Display the project window (by selecting Project from the Window menu).
>
> ☐ Inside the project window highlight the VBX control you want to delete from the project.
>
> ☐ Select Remove File from the File menu.
>
> An alternate way (and a much easier way) to remove the VBX controls from your project is the following:
>
> ☐ Terminate Visual Basic (select Exit from the File menu).
>
> ☐ Use Notepad to load the C:\EXPROG\BD5\Cards.MAK file.
>
> ☐ Delete all the lines that contain the name of a file with a .VBX file extension.
>
> ☐ Save the file.
>
> ☐ Start Visual Basic, load the Cards.MAK project, and note that now the project does not contain any VBX files.

BD5

The Cards program uses the MHCD200.VBX control. Here is how you add this control to your project:

☐ Select Add File from the File menu and select the C:\Windows\System\MHCD200.VBX file.

Your project window should now look like the one shown in Figure BD5.15, and the Toolbox should contain the card control, as shown in Figure BD5.16.

Figure BD5.15.
The project window
of Cards.MAK.

Figure BD5.16.
The card control.

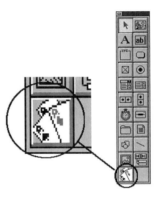

☐ Implement the frmCards form according to the specifications in Table BD5.1. When you finish implementing the form, it should look like the one shown in Figure BD5.17.

Table BD5.1. The properties table of the frmCards form.

Object	Property	Setting
Form	**Name**	**frmCards**
	BackColor	(light gray)
	BorderStyle	1-Fixed Single
	Caption	The Cards Program
	Height	5550
	Icon	C:\EXPROG\ICONS\MyCard.ICO (or use an icon that is appropriate for the Cards program)
	Left	1290

Object	Property	Setting
	MaxButton	0-False
	Top	1140
	Width	4350
MHCD200.VBX	**Name**	**crdPlayer**
	Autosize	-1-True
	Height	1425
	Left	2880
	Top	1680
	Width	1065
MHCD200.VBX	**Name**	**crdPC**
	Autosize	-1-True
	Height	1425
	Left	240
	Top	1680
	Width	1065
Timer	**Name**	**tmrShuffle**
	Interval	150
	Left	1680
	Top	4320
Command Button	**Name**	**cmdReset**
	Caption	&Reset
	Height	375
	Left	2640
	Top	4680
	Width	1455
Command Button	**Name**	**cmdChangeDesign**
	Caption	&Change Design
	Height	375
	Left	2640
	Top	4320
	Width	1455

continues

Table BD5.1. continued

Object	Property	Setting
Command Button	**Name**	**cmdDeal**
	Caption	&Deal
	Height	2415
	Left	1440
	Top	1680
	Width	1215
Command Button	**Name**	**cmdExit**
	Caption	E&xit Game
	Height	495
	Left	120
	Top	4560
	Width	1215
Line	**Name**	**linBackDoor**
	Visible	0-False
	X1	1920
	X2	1800
	Y1	4920
	Y2	4800
Image	**Name**	**imgBackDoor**
	Height	735
	Left	1200
	Picture	(none)
	Top	240
	Width	1575
Label	**Name**	**lblPlayer**
	Alignment	2-Center
	BackColor	(light gray)
	Caption	Player
	FontSize	18
	Height	495

Object	Property	Setting
	Left	2880
	Top	240
	Width	1215
Label	**Name**	**lblPlayerScore**
	Alignment	2-Center
	BackColor	(dark gray)
	BorderStyle	1-Fixed Single
	Caption	0
	ForeColor	(white)
	Height	375
	Left	2760
	Top	3720
	Width	1215
Label	**Name**	**lblPCScore**
	Alignment	2-Center
	BackColor	(dark gray)
	BorderStyle	1-Fixed Single
	Caption	0
	ForeColor	(white)
	Height	375
	Left	120
	Top	3720
	Width	1215
Image	**Name**	**imgWin**
	Height	480
	Left	2040
	Picture	C:\VB\ICONS\MISC\Face2.ICO
	Top	1080
	Visible	0-False
	Width	480

BD5

continues

Table BD5.1. continued

Object	Property	Setting
Image	**Name**	**imgLose**
	Height	480
	Left	1560
	Picture	C:\VB\ICONS\MISC\Face1.ICO
	Top	1080
	Visible	0-False
	Width	480
Image	**Name**	**imgPlayer**
	Height	480
	Left	3120
	Picture	C:\VB\ICONS\MISC\Face1.ICO
	Top	960
	Width	480
Image	**Name**	**imgPC**
	Height	480
	Left	480
	Picture	C:\VB\ICONS\MISC\Face1.ICO
	Top	960
	Width	480
Label	**Name**	**lblPC**
	Alignment	2-Center
	BackColor	(light gray)
	Caption	PC
	FontSize	18
	Height	495
	Left	240
	Top	240
	Width	855
Label	**Name**	**lblPlayScoreHead**
	BackColor	(gray)

Object	Property	Setting
	Caption	Score:
	FontSize	12
	Height	375
	Left	3000
	Top	3240
	Width	975
Label	**Name**	**lblPCScoreHead**
	BackColor	(light gray)
	Caption	Score:
	FontSize	12
	Height	375
	Left	240
	Top	3240
	Width	855

Figure BD5.17.
The frmCards form
(in design mode).

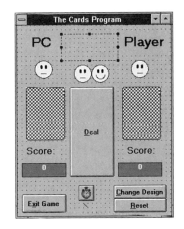

The General Declarations Section of the frmCards Form

You'll now declare several general variables inside the general declarations section of the frmCards form.

☐ Type the following code inside the general declarations section of the frmCards form:

```
Option Explicit
Dim gPCScore
Dim gPlayerScore
Dim gShuffle
Dim gBackDoor
```

The code you typed declares four general variables. Because these variables are declared inside the general declarations section, they are accessible from any procedure of the frmCards form.

Attaching Code to the *Load* Event of the frmCards Form

You'll now attach code to the Load event of the frmCards form.

☐ Type the following code inside the Form_Load() procedure of the frmCards form:

```
Sub Form_Load ()

    gPCScore = 0
    gPlayerScore = 0

    gShuffle = 1

    gBackDoor = 0

End Sub
```

The code that you typed sets the initial values of the general (global) variables.

Attaching Code to the *Click* Event of the Change Design Button

You'll now attach code to the Click event of the Change Design button. Recall that when the user clicks the Change Design button, the cards should be displayed with a new back design.

☐ Type the following code inside the cmdChangeDesign_Click() procedure of the frmCards form:

```
Sub cmdChangeDesign_Click ()

    Static CurrentBack

    crdPC.Value = 0
    crdPlayer.Value = 0

    CurrentBack = CurrentBack + 1
    If CurrentBack = 13 Then
        CurrentBack = 0
    End If
```

```
    crdPC.CardBack = CurrentBack
    crdPlayer.CardBack = CurrentBack

End Sub
```

The code you typed declares a static variable:

```
Static CurrentBack
```

Upon creation of the variable, `CurrentBack` is equal to 0. During the execution of the `cmdChangeDesign_Click()` procedure, the value of `CurrentBack` changes. The next time the procedure is executed, the value of `CurrentDesign` retains its value from the last execution of this procedure.

The next two statements set the Value property of the card control to 0:

```
crdPC.Value = 0
crdPlayer.Value = 0
```

When the Value property of the card control is set to 0, the card is displayed with its back shown. So the card of the PC and the card of the player are both shown with their backs up. But what is the design on the back? The design is determined by the CardBack property of the card control. Here are the possible values for the CardBack property of the card control:

Setting of the CardBack Property	Design of the Card Back
0	Red Checks
1	Blue Checks
2	Red Hatch
3	Blue Hatch
4	Robot
5	Roses
6	Leaves 1
7	Leaves 2
8	Fish
9	Conch
10	Castle
11	Beach
12	Hand

The value of the static variable `CurrentBack` is increased by 1:

```
CurrentBack = CurrentBack + 1
```

As you'll soon see, the value of the variable `CurrentBack` is then assigned to the CardBack property of the card control. But because the value of the CardBack property must be an integer between 0 and 12, an If statement is used to verify that the value of `CurrentBack` does not exceed 12:

```
If CurrentBack = 13 Then
   CurrentBack = 0
End If
```

Finally, the CardBack property of the card control is set to the value of the `CurrentBack` variable:

```
crdPC.CardBack = CurrentBack
crdPlayer.CardBack = CurrentBack
```

Attaching Code to the *Click* Event of the Exit Button of the frmCards Button

You'll now attach code to the `Click` event of the Exit button.

☐ Type the following code inside the `cmdExit_Click()` procedure of the frmCards form:

```
Sub cmdExit_Click ()

    End

End Sub
```

Attaching Code to the *Click* Event of the Deal Button

You'll now attach code to the `Click` event of the Deal button.

☐ Type the following code inside the `cmdDeal_Click()` procedure of the frmCards form:

```
Sub cmdDeal_Click ()

    Dim PCCardValue
    Dim PlayerCardValue

    ' Deal a card to the PC
    Randomize
    crdPC.Value = Int(Rnd * 13) + 1
    crdPC.Suit = Int(Rnd * 4)
    If crdPC.Value = 1 Then
        PCCardValue = 14 + crdPC.Suit / 10
    Else
        PCCardValue = crdPC.Value + crdPC.Suit / 10
    End If

    ' Deal an honest card to the Player
    Randomize
    crdPlayer.Value = Int(Rnd * 13) + 1
    crdPlayer.Suit = Int(Rnd * 4)
    If crdPlayer.Value = 1 Then
        PlayerCardValue = 14 + crdPlayer.Suit / 10
    Else
        PlayerCardValue = crdPlayer.Value + crdPlayer.Suit / 10
    End If
```

```
If PlayerCardValue > PCCardValue Then

    imgPC.Picture = imgLose.Picture
    imgPlayer.Picture = imgWin.Picture
    gPlayerScore = gPlayerScore + 100
    lblPlayerScore = Str(gPlayerScore)

End If

If PlayerCardValue < PCCardValue And gBackDoor = 0 Then

    imgPC.Picture = imgWin.Picture
    imgPlayer.Picture = imgLose.Picture

    gPCScore = gPCScore + 100
    lblPCScore.Caption = Str(gPCScore)

End If


If PlayerCardValue = PCCardValue And gBackDoor = 0 Then

    imgPC.Picture = imgLose.Picture
    imgPlayer.Picture = imgLose.Picture

End If

If PlayerCardValue <= PCCardValue And gBackDoor = 1 Then

    If crdPC.Value = 1 Or crdPC.Value = 13 Then
        crdPC.Value = 12
        crdPC.Suit = Int(Rnd * 4)
        crdPlayer.Value = 13
        crdPlayer.Suit = Int(Rnd * 4)
        PCCardValue = crdPC.Value + crdPC.Suit / 10
        PlayerCardValue = crdPlayer.Value + crdPlayer.Suit / 10
    Else
        crdPlayer.Value = crdPC.Value + 1
        PCCardValue = crdPC.Value + crdPC.Suit / 10
        PlayerCardValue = crdPlayer.Value + crdPlayer.Suit / 10
    End If

    imgPC.Picture = imgLose.Picture
    imgPlayer.Picture = imgWin.Picture
    gPlayerScore = gPlayerScore + 100
    lblPlayerScore = Str(gPlayerScore)

End If
```

End Sub

At first glance, the code you typed might appear complicated, but it is actually easy.

Two local variables are declared:

```
Dim PCCardValue
Dim PlayerCardValue
```

A card is dealt to the PC:

```
' Deal a card to the PC
Randomize
crdPC.Value = Int(Rnd * 13) + 1
crdPC.Suit = Int(Rnd * 4)
If crdPC.Value = 1 Then
   PCCardValue = 14 + crdPC.Suit / 10
Else
   PCCardValue = crdPC.Value + crdPC.Suit / 10
End If
```

As previously stated, when the Value property of the card control is set to 0, the card is displayed with its back up. The other possible values for the Value property of the card control are the following:

Setting of the Value Property	Face Value of the Card
0	(back of the card is shown)
1	Ace
2-10	Deuce through ten
11	Jack
12	Queen
13	King

The Randomize statement is executed:

```
Randomize
```

Randomize is executed because the next statement uses the Rnd function to generate a random number. Randomize causes the Rnd function to generate a different random number each time the program is executed.

The next statement sets the Value property of the crdPC card to a random number between 1 and 13:

```
crdPC.Value = Int(Rnd * 13) + 1
```

Recall that the Value property can be an integer between 0 and 13. To display a card, you have to set the Value property of the card to an integer between 1 and 13.

The next statement sets the Suit property of the card control to an integer between 0 and 3:

```
crdPC.Suit = Int(Rnd * 4)
```

The Suit property determines the suit of the card:

Setting of the Suit Property	Meaning
0	Clubs
1	Diamond
2	Hearts
3	Spades

For example, if you set the Value property of the card control to 6 and the Suit property to 0, the card is displayed as the 6 of clubs.

Later in this procedure you are going to compare the PC's card with the player's card. In this game, you want the ace to be a stronger card than the king. However, an ace is a card with a Value property equal to 1. So you need to perform some translations. Also, the suit of the card should be a factor that determines which card is strongest. In this game, you set the spades cards as stronger than the hearts cards, the hearts cards stronger than the diamonds cards, and the diamonds cards stronger than the clubs cards. For example, the 10 of diamonds is stronger than the 10 of clubs.

So you need to translate the face value of the card to an absolute number. This is accomplished with the following block of statements:

```
If crdPC.Value = 1 Then
    PCCardValue = 14 + crdPC.Suit / 10
Else
    PCCardValue = crdPC.Value + crdPC.Suit / 10
End If
```

That is, translate the ace to 14. Also, the Suit property is divided by 10, and the result of the division is added to the Value property. For example, if Value is equal to 6 and Suit is equal to 3, PCCardValue is equal to 6+3/10=6.3. If Value is equal to 6 and Suit is equal to 0, PCCardValue is equal to 6+0/10=6.0. Similarly, if Value is equal to 1 and Suit is equal to 2, PCCardValue is sct to 14+2/10=14.2

The next block of statements deals a card to the player:

```
' Deal an honest card to the Player
Randomize
crdPlayer.Value = Int(Rnd * 13) + 1
crdPlayer.Suit = Int(Rnd * 4)
If crdPlayer.Value = 1 Then
    PlayerCardValue = 14 + crdPlayer.Suit / 10
Else
    PlayerCardValue = crdPlayer.Value + crdPlayer.Suit / 10
End If
```

The preceding statements deal the player a card in the same manner in which a card was dealt to the PC. Who will have a stronger card? It is completely random! Maybe the PC will be lucky, or maybe the player will be lucky!

The next block of statements is an If statement that checks whether the player wins:

```
If PlayerCardValue > PCCardValue Then

    imgPC.Picture = imgLose.Picture
    imgPlayer.Picture = imgWin.Picture
    gPlayerScore = gPlayerScore + 100
    lblPlayerScore = Str(gPlayerScore)

End If
```

The **If** condition is satisfied if the value of the **PlayerCardValue** variable is larger than the **PCCardValue** variable. If the condition is satisfied, it means that the player won, and the Picture property of the imgPC image (the image above the PC's card) is changed to the Picture property of the imgLose image:

```
imgPC.Picture = imgLose.Picture
```

Recall that during design time you set the Visible property of the imgLose control to False. This means that during runtime the imgLose image is not displayed. But when the PC loses, the losing face image is transferred to the image that is displayed above the PC's card.

Similarly, the image above the player's card is changed to a smiling face:

```
imgPlayer.Picture = imgWin.Picture
```

Finally, the **gPlayerScore** variable is increased by 100:

```
gPlayerScore = gPlayerScore + 100
```

gPlayerScore is a variable that contains the number of points of the player. Because the player won, the **gPlayerScore** variable is increased by 100. Finally, the label that displays the score of the player is updated:

```
lblPlayerScore = Str(gPlayerScore)
```

The next **If** statement deals with the case in which the player lost the deal:

```
If PlayerCardValue < PCCardValue And gBackDoor = 0 Then

    imgPC.Picture = imgWin.Picture
    imgPlayer.Picture = imgLose.Picture

    gPCScore = gPCScore + 100
    lblPCScore.Caption = Str(gPCScore)

End If
```

Note that the **If** condition is satisfied provided that the player lost and that the player did not place the game in a cheating mode. That is, **gBackDoor** is a flag that indicates whether the game is in an honest or a cheating mode. When **gBackDoor** is equal to 0, the game is in honest mode. The code under the preceding **If** statement grants the PC 100 points and changes the images accordingly. The PC gets a smiling face, and the player gets a losing face.

The next If statement checks whether the PC and the player got identical cards:

```
If PlayerCardValue = PCCardValue And gBackDoor = 0 Then

    imgPC.Picture = imgLose.Picture
    imgPlayer.Picture = imgLose.Picture

End If
```

The preceding statements do not award any points (nobody won), and both the PC and the player get a losing face image.

The last block of statement deals with the case in which the PC won, but you want to change the player's card to a winning card because the game is in a cheating mode (gBackDoor is equal to 1):

```
If PlayerCardValue <= PCCardValue And gBackDoor = 1 Then

    If crdPC.Value = 1 Or crdPC.Value = 13 Then
        crdPC.Value = 12
        crdPC.Suit = Int(Rnd * 4)
        crdPlayer.Value = 13
        crdPlayer.Suit = Int(Rnd * 4)
        PCCardValue = crdPC.Value + crdPC.Suit / 10
        PlayerCardValue = crdPlayer.Value + crdPlayer.Suit / 10
    Else
        crdPlayer.Value = crdPC.Value + 1
        PCCardValue = crdPC.Value + crdPC.Suit / 10
        PlayerCardValue = crdPlayer.Value + crdPlayer.Suit / 10
    End If

    imgPC.Picture = imgLose.Picture
    imgPlayer.Picture = imgWin.Picture
    gPlayerScore = gPlayerScore + 100
    lblPlayerScore = Str(gPlayerScore)

End If
```

An inner If…Else statement checks whether the PC card is an ace or a king. If this is the case, the card is changed to a queen, and the player's card is set as a king.

```
If crdPC.Value = 1 Or crdPC.Value = 13 Then
    crdPC.Value = 12
    crdPC.Suit = Int(Rnd * 4)
    crdPlayer.Value = 13
    crdPlayer.Suit = Int(Rnd * 4)
    PCCardValue = crdPC.Value + crdPC.Suit / 10
    PlayerCardValue = crdPlayer.Value + crdPlayer.Suit / 10
Else
    crdPlayer.Value = crdPC.Value + 1
    PCCardValue = crdPC.Value + crdPC.Suit / 10
    PlayerCardValue = crdPlayer.Value + crdPlayer.Suit / 10
End If
```

BD5

885

If the PC's card is not an ace or a king, the `Else` code is executed. The code under the `Else` sets the player's card to a card with a face value greater than the PC's card.

Then the player's score is increased, and the player's image is changed to a smiling face.

Attaching Code to the *Click* Event of the Reset Button

You'll now attach code to the Reset button of the frmCards form.

☐ Type the following code inside the `cmdReset_Click()` procedure of the frmCards form:

```
Sub cmdReset_Click ()

    gPCScore = 0
    gPlayerScore = 0

    lblPCScore.Caption = Str(gPCScore)
    lblPlayerScore.Caption = Str(gPlayerScore)

    ' Enable shuffling
    gShuffle = 1

End Sub
```

The code you typed initializes the scores of the PC and the player to 0:

```
gPCScore = 0
gPlayerScore = 0
lblPCScore.Caption = Str(gPCScore)
lblPlayerScore.Caption = Str(gPlayerScore)
```

Then the `gShuffle` variable is set to 1:

```
' Enable shuffling
gShuffle = 1
```

As you'll see later in this chapter, when `gShuffle` is equal to 1, the program shuffles the cards. Therefore, once the user clicks the Reset button, the cards are shuffled.

Attaching Code to the *DblClick* Event of the imgBackDoor Image

You'll now attach code to the `imgBackDoor_DblClick()` procedure of the frmCards form.

☐ Type the following code inside the `imgBackDoor_DblClick()` procedure of the frmCards form:

```
Sub imgBackDoor_DblClick ()

    If gBackDoor = 1 Then
       gBackDoor - 0
       linBackDoor.Visible = False
    Else
       gBackDoor = 1
       linBackDoor.Visible = True
    End If

End Sub
```

Recall that if currently the Cards program is not in a cheating mode, double-clicking the imgBackDoor image causes the program to enter a cheating mode. imgBackDoor is an image with no picture in it. Therefore, nobody but you the programmer knows about the existence of this image control.

DO	DON'T

DON'T set the Visible property of this image control to False because when the Visible property of the image control is set to False, the control does not generate the Click or DblClick event.

DON'T place any picture inside the imgBackDoor image because you don't want the user to know that this image control exists.

An If…Else statement toggles the value of the gBackDoor variable and the Visible property of the line control:

```
    If gBackDoor = 1 Then
       gBackDoor = 0
       linBackDoor.Visible = False
    Else
       gBackDoor = 1
       linBackDoor.Visible = True
    End If
```

So if currently the value of gBackDoor is 0, after you double-click the imgBackDoor image the variable gBackDoor is set to 1 and the line control is made visible. Likewise, if currently the value of gBackDoor is 1, after you double-click the imgBackDoor image the variable gBackDoor is set to 0 and the line control is made invisible. Remember that the line control is just a visual indication for you to determine whether the game is in a cheating mode. Naturally, you want to make the line control as small as possible, because you don't want other people to realize that whenever the line appears, the player wins consistently.

Attaching Code to the *Timer* Event of the Timer Control

You'll now attach code to the Timer event of the tmrShffle control.

Remember that whenever the gShuffle variable is set to 1 the Cards program shuffles the cards. Inside the Form_Load() procedure you set gShuffle to 1 because you want the program to shuffle the cards when the program starts. Also, inside the cmdReset_Click() procedure you set the gShuffle variable to 1 because you want to shuffle the cards after the user clicks the Reset button.

Before going any further, you should know that this business of shuffling the cards is performed for cosmetic reasons only! That is, there is no reason to shuffle the cards. In reality, you shuffle cards so that you'll be able to draw random cards. Inside the cmdDeal_Click() procedure you implemented random card drawing by using the Randomize and Rnd statements. Nevertheless, this is a game, and people want to see the cards shuffled before a new game, so go ahead and implement a shuffle mechanism.

☐ Type the following code inside the tmrShuffle_Timer() procedure of the frmCards form:

```
Sub tmrShuffle_Timer ()

    Static ShuffleInProgress

    If gShuffle = 0 Then
       Exit Sub
    End If


    cmdDeal.Enabled = False
    cmdChangeDesign.Enabled = False
    cmdReset.Enabled = False
    frmCards.Caption = "Wait while Shuffling..."

    ShuffleInProgress = ShuffleInProgress + 1
    If ShuffleInProgress = 25 Then
       frmCards.Caption = "The Cards Program"
       ShuffleInProgress = 0
       gShuffle = 0
       cmdDeal.Enabled = True
       cmdChangeDesign.Enabled = True
       cmdReset.Enabled = True
       crdPlayer.Value = 0
       crdPC.Value = 0

       Exit Sub
    End If


    ' Deal a card to the PC
    Randomize
    crdPC.Value = Int(Rnd * 13) + 1
```

```
    crdPC.Suit = Int(Rnd * 4)

    Randomize
    crdPlayer.Value = Int(Rnd * 13) + 1
    crdPlayer.Suit = Int(Rnd * 4)
```

End Sub

During design time you placed a timer control inside the frmCards form and set its Interval property to 150. This means that the `tmrShuffle_Timer()` procedure is executed automatically every 150 milliseconds.

The code you typed declares a static variable:

```
Static ShuffleInProgress
```

An `If` statement is executed to determine whether the rest of the statements inside the `tmrShuffle_Click()` procedure should be executed:

```
    If gShuffle = 0 Then
        Exit Sub
    End If
```

That is, if `gShuffle` is equal to 0, no shuffling is performed.

During the shuffling you don't want the user to be able to press any button (except the Exit button), so you disable the buttons:

```
    cmdDeal.Enabled = False
    cmdChangeDesign.Enabled = False
    cmdReset.Enabled = False
```

Also, during the shuffling the Caption property of the form is changed so that the user will know what's happening:

```
    frmCards.Caption = "Wait while Shuffling..."
```

DO	DON'T

DO display the message `Wait while Shuffling...` by using a label control.

The static variable `ShuffleInProgress` is then increased by 1:

```
    ShuffleInProgress = ShuffleInProgress + 1
```

An `If` statement makes sure that the `ShuffleInProgress` variable does not exceed 24:

```
    If ShuffleInProgress = 25 Then
        frmCards.Caption = "The Cards Program"
        ShuffleInProgress = 0
        gShuffle = 0
```

BD5

```
        cmdDeal.Enabled = True
        cmdChangeDesign.Enabled = True
        cmdReset.Enabled = True
        crdPlayer.Value = 0
        crdPC.Value = 0

        Exit Sub
    End If
```

That is, you want 25 shuffles (from `ShuffleInProgress` equal to 0 up to `ShuffleInProgress` equal to 24). Every 150 milliseconds the `tmrShuffle_Timer()` procedure is executed. Because `ShuffleInProgress` is declared as a static variable, its value remains for the next execution of this procedure. Once `ShuffleInProgress` reaches a value of 25, the code inside the `If` statement is executed. This code changes the Caption property of the form back to The Cards Program:

```
frmCards.Caption = "The Cards Program"
```

The `ShuffleInProgress` variable is initialized back to 0 (for the next shuffle):

```
        ShuffleInProgress = 0
```

`gShuffle` is initialized back to 0 (so the program will no longer perform shuffling):

```
        gShuffle = 0
```

The buttons are enabled:

```
        cmdDeal.Enabled = True
        cmdChangeDesign.Enabled = True
        cmdReset.Enabled = True
```

The cards are displayed with their backs up:

```
        crdPlayer.Value = 0
        crdPC.Value = 0
```

Finally, the procedure is terminated:

```
        Exit Sub
```

If `ShuffleInProgress` has not yet reached 25, the rest of the statements inside the `tmrShuffle_Timer()` are executed. These statements deal a random card to the PC and to the player:

```
' Deal a card to the PC
    Randomize
    crdPC.Value = Int(Rnd * 13) + 1
    crdPC.Suit = Int(Rnd * 4)

    Randomize
    crdPlayer.Value = Int(Rnd * 13) + 1
    crdPlayer.Suit = Int(Rnd * 4)
```

☐ Experiment with the Cards program and then click its Exit button to terminate it.

Enhancing the Cards Program

The Cards program has an infinite number of cards in it. That is, the deck of cards never runs out of cards. In reality, however, a deck has 52 cards, and the same card cannot appear twice in the same deck.

You can write card programs that use finite numbers of cards. For example, if you design a game that uses a single deck of 52 cards, then you can construct an array of numbers with 52 elements in it. Each element represents a unique card.

For example, you can use the same technique that was used in the Cards program to represent the absolute values of the cards. That is, 2.0 represents the 2 of clubs, 2.1 represents the 2 of diamonds, and so on.

When you start the program, your Form_Load() procedure should shuffle the cards. In this case, the shuffling is real (not for cosmetic reasons), and the array should be filled in a random order.

When dealing the first card, your program will select the first element of the array (which contains a random card). When dealing the second card, your program should select the second element of the array and so on. Eventually, your program will deal all the elements of the array (which means that the entire deck of cards was dealt already).

The Dice Program

The Dice program demonstrates how to write a program that lets the user play a dice game.

Before writing the Dice program, review its specifications.

Upon startup of the Dice program, the window shown in Figure BD5.18 appears.

Figure BD5.18.
The Dice program.

The player uses the scroll bar to select an integer between 1 and 6. The label below the scroll bar displays the selected number. The player clicks the Try Your Luck button. As a result, the die displays several numbers (as if the die is rolling), and finally, the die lands on one of its sides.

BD5

If the player guessed the right number, the Dice program displays the window shown in Figure BD5.19. If the player guessed the wrong number, the window shown in Figure BD5.20 appears.

Figure BD5.19.
Guessing the correct number.

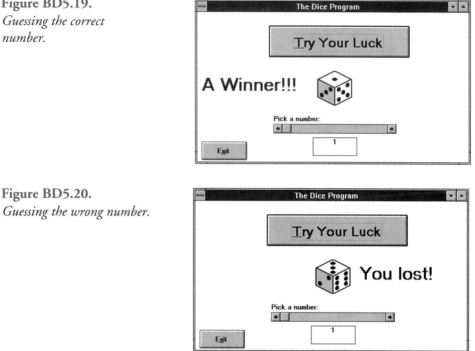

Figure BD5.20.
Guessing the wrong number.

The Visual Implementation of the Dice Program

You'll now visually implement the frmDice form of the Dice program.

☐ Implement the frmDice form according to the specifications in Table BD5.2. When you finish implementing the form, it should look like the one shown in Figure BD5.21.

Table BD5.2. The properties table of the frmDice form.

Object	Property	Setting
Form	**Name**	**frmDice**
	Caption	The Dice Program
	Height	4425

Object	Property	Setting
	Icon	C:\EXPROG\ICONS\MyDice.ICO (or use an appropriate icon)
	Left	1035
	Top	1140
	Width	7485
Timer	**Name**	**tmrTry**
	Interval	50
	Left	6240
	Top	3360
Command Button	**Name**	**cmdTry**
	Caption	&Try Your Luck
	FontSize	18
	Height	855
	Left	1920
	Top	360
	Width	3855
Command Button	**Name**	**cmdExit**
	Caption	E&xit
	Height	495
	Left	120
	Top	3480
	Width	1215
HScrollBar	**Name**	**hsbPickANumber**
	Height	255
	Left	2040
	Max	6
	Min	1
	Top	3000
	Value	1
	Width	3375

continues

Table BD5.2. continued

Object	Property	Setting
MHDC200.VBX	**Name**	**Dice**
	AutoSize	-1-True
	Height	960
	Left	3240
	Top	1560
	Value	1
	Width	960
Label	**Name**	**lblWin**
	Caption	A Winner!!!
	FontSize	24
	Height	495
	Left	120
	Top	1680
	Visible	0-False
	Width	2895
Label	**Name**	**lblLose**
	Caption	You lost!
	FontSize	24
	Height	495
	Left	4440
	Top	1680
	Visible	0-False
	Width	2655
Label	**Name**	**lblHeader**
	Caption	Pick a number:
	Height	255
	Left	2040
	Top	2760
	Width	1695
Label	**Name**	**lblNumber**

Object	Property	Setting
	Alignment	2-Center
	BorderStyle	1-Fixed Single
	Caption	1
	Height	495
	Left	3120
	Top	3360
	Width	1215

Figure BD5.21.
The frmDice form
(in design mode).

The General Declarations Section of the frmDice Form

You'll now attach code to the general declarations section of the frmDice form.

☐ Type the following code inside the general declarations section of the frmDice form:

```
Option Explicit
Dim gTryYourLuck
```

Attaching Code to the *Click* Event of the Exit Button

You'll now attach code to the Click event of the Exit button.

☐ Type the following code inside the cmdExit_Click() procedure of the frmDice form:

```
Sub cmdExit_Click ()

    End

End Sub
```

Attaching Code to the *Load* Event of the frmDice Form

You'll now attach code to the Load event of the frmDice form.

☐ Type the following code inside the Form_Load() procedure of the frmDice form:

```
Sub Form_Load ()

    gTryYourLuck = 0

End Sub
```

The code you typed initializes the gTryYourLuck variable to 0. You declared this variable inside the general declarations section of the form. Therefore, this variable is accessible from any procedure of the frmDice from.

Attaching Code to the *Change* Event of the Horizontal Scroll Bar

You'll now attach code to the Change event of the horizontal scroll bar.

☐ Type the following code inside the hsbPickANumber_Change() procedure:

```
Sub hsbPickANumber_Change ()

    lblNumber.Caption = Str(hsbPickANumber.Value)

End Sub
```

The Change event occurs whenever the user changes the scroll bar position. The code you typed updates the Caption property of the lblNumber label with the Value property of the scroll bar. So when the user changes the scroll bar's position, the label displays the current Value property of the scroll bar.

Attaching Code to the *Scroll* Event of the Scroll Bar

You'll now attach code to the Scroll event of the scroll bar.

☐ Type the following code inside the hsbPickANumber_Scroll() procedure of the frmDice form:

```
Sub hsbPickANumber_Scroll ()

    lblNumber.Caption = Str(hsbPickANumber.Value)

End Sub
```

The code you typed is identical to the code you typed inside the hsbPickANumber_Change()
procedure. So when the user drags the thumb tab of the scroll bar, the label immediately displays
the current position of the scroll bar.

Attaching Code to the *Click* Event of the Try Your Luck Button

You'll now attach code to the Click event of the Try Your Luck button of the frmDice form.

☐ Type the following code inside the cmdTry_Click() procedure of the frmDice form:

```
Sub cmdTry_Click ()

    Randomize
    lblWin.Visible = False
    lblLose.Visible = False

    gTryYourLuck = 1

End Sub
```

The code you typed executes the Randomize statement:

```
Randomize
```

As you'll soon see, the Dice program uses the Rnd() function to generate a random number (that
will be assigned to the Value property of the die). By using the Randomize statement, you are
assuring that a fresh random number is generated whenever the Dice program is executed.

The next two statements set the Visible properties of the lblWin and lblLose labels to False:

```
lblWin.Visible = False
lblLose.Visible = False
```

That is, the user just clicked the Try Your Luck button. So these labels are removed. As you'll
soon see, based on the outcome of tossing the dice, either the lblWin label is made visible or the
lblLose label is made visible.

The last statement inside the cmdTry_Click() procedure sets the gTryYourLuck variable to 1:

```
gTryYourLuck = 1
```

gTryYourLuck serves as a flag that indicates that die tossing is in progress.

Attaching Code to the *Timer* Event of the Timer Control

You'll now attach code to the Timer event of the tmrTry timer. Recall that during design time
you set the Interval property of the timer to 50. This means that every 50 milliseconds the
tmrTry_Timer() procedure is executed.

897

☐ Type the following code inside the `tmrTry_Timer()` procedure of the frmDice form:

```
Sub tmrTry_Timer ()

    Static StillGoing

    If gTryYourLuck = 0 Then Exit Sub


    StillGoing = StillGoing + 1
    If StillGoing = 20 Then
        StillGoing = 0
        gTryYourLuck = 0
        If hsbPickANumber.Value = Dice.Value Then
            lblWin.Visible = True
        Else
            lblLose.Visible = True
        End If
        Exit Sub
    End If

    Dice.Value = Int(Rnd * 6) + 1

End Sub
```

The code you typed declares a static variable:

```
    Static StillGoing
```

Next, an `If` statement is executed to examine the value of the `gTryYourLuck` flag:

```
    If gTryYourLuck = 0 Then Exit Sub
```

Recall that inside the `cmdTry_Click()` procedure you set the value of this flag to 1. So if the user did not click the Try Your Luck button, the rest of the statements inside the `tmrTry_Timer()` procedure are not executed because the `If` condition is satisfied.

If `gTryYourLuck` is equal to 1, the rest of the statements inside the `tmrTry_Timer()` procedure are executed.

The static variable `StillGoing` is increased by 1:

```
    StillGoing = StillGoing + 1
```

`StillGoing` is a variable that keeps track of how many times the `tmrTry_Timer()` procedure is executed. An `If` statement is executed to make sure that `StillGoing` does not exceed 20:

```
    If StillGoing = 20 Then
        ...................
        ... This code is executed when StillGoing
        ... is equal to 20.
        ...................
    End If
```

If `StillGoing` is not equal to 20, the statements under the `If` are not executed. The next statement to be executed is therefore the following:

```
Dice.Value = Int(Rnd * 6) + 1
```

The preceding statement assigns a random integer between 0 and 6 to the Value property of the die. This causes the die to be displayed according to the Value property. For example, if Value equals 2, the die is shown with two dots on its upper side.

On the next execution of the `tmrTry_Timer()` procedure, `StillGoing` is increased by 1. The `If` statement will not be satisfied because `StillGoing` is not equal to 20 yet. So, again, this statement:

```
    Dice.Value = Int(Rnd * 6) + 1
```

is executed, setting the Value property of the die to a new random number. This process repeats itself 20 times. So after the user clicks the Try Your Luck button, the Value property of the die is changed 20 times. This gives the illusion that the die is rolling. Eventually, `StillGoing` is equal to 20, and the `If` condition is satisfied:

```
    If  StillGoing = 20 Then
        StillGoing = 0
        gTryYourLuck = 0
        If hsbPickANumber.Value = Dice.Value Then
            lblWin.Visible = True
        Flse
            lblLose.Visible = True
        End If
        Exit Sub
    End If
```

The code under the `If` statement sets the value of `StillGoing` to 0:

```
    StillGoing = 0
```

So the next time the user clicks the Try Your Luck button, `StillGoing` will again serve as a counter that counts from 0 to 20.

The `gTryYourLuck` flag is set to 0:

```
    gTryYourLuck = 0
```

So the next time the `tmrTry_Timer()` procedure is executed, the first `If` statement inside the `tmrTry_Timer()` procedure will prevent the execution of the rest of the statements inside the `tmrTry_Timer()` procedure (that is, no shuffling will occur).

An `If` statement is then executed to examine whether the user guessed the correct number:

```
        If hsbPickANumber.Value = Dice.Value Then
            lblWin.Visible = True
        Else
```

```
            lblLose.Visible = True
        End If
```

If the user guessed the correct number, the lblWin label is made visible (see Figure BD5.19). On the other hand, if the user guessed the wrong number, the lblLose label is made visible (see Figure BD5.20).

The last statement under the If statement causes the termination of the tmrTry_Timer() procedure:

```
Exit Sub
```

☐ Execute the Dice program.

☐ Experiment with the Dice program and then click its Exit button to terminate the program.

Enhancing the Dice Program

You can further enhance the Dice program by letting the player gamble. If the player guessed the right number, his/her scores are increased. If the player guessed the wrong number, his/her scores are decreased.

You can also place two dice inside the form, and "toss" the two dice (by assigning random values to the Value properties of the dice).

If you plan to include a gambling mechanism when playing with two dice, the player will have to guess a number that is the sum of the two dice.

Remember that your program has to reward the winner in a fair manner. For example, there is a smaller chance that the sum of the two dice will be 2 than that the sum of the two dice will be 7. This is because there is only one possible combination in which the sum of the two dice is 2 (that is, when both dice have the value of 1). On the other hand, there are several combinations for having the sum of the two dice equal to 7 (for example: 1+6, 2+5, 3+4, and so on).

A player that guessed the number 2 took a greater risk, and if he/she guessed correctly, the reward should be greater than for correctly guessing the number 7 for example.

Summary

In this chapter you have learned how to design game programs with Visual Basic. Basically, to design games you need the "toys" of the games. In this chapter, the toys of the games that you used were the controls from the Borland Visual Solutions Pack. Once you have the toys, writing the game program is no different from writing any other Visual Basic application.

Q&A

Q   Can I place additional cards inside the form? For example, I want to place 10 cards inside the form for the purpose of playing poker against the PC. The PC will be dealt five cards, and the player will be dealt five cards.

A   Yes, you can place additional cards. Simply place additional card controls inside the form.

Quiz

1. To display a card with a face value of ace which of the following statements would you use?

    a. `crdMyCard.Value= "Ace"`

    b. `crdMyCard.Value= Ace`

    c. `crdMyCard.Value = 1`

    d. `crdMyCard.Value = 14`

2. Which of the following statements generates a random integer between 0 and 3?

    a. `MyRandom = Int(Rnd * 4)`

    b. `MyRandom = Int(Rnd *3) + 1`

Exercise

Enhance the Cards program so that it makes several audio announcements during its execution.

BD5

Quiz Answers

1. c

2. The correct answer is a.

    The `Rnd()` function generates a number between 0 and 1 but less than 1. So `Rnd * 4` generates a number between 0 and 4 but less than 4.

    The `Int()` function converts the number that is supplied as its parameter into an integer. So this statement:

    `MyRandom = Int(Rnd * 4)`

    generates a random integer between 0 and 3.

    Similarly, `Rnd * 3` generates a number between 0 and 3 but less than 3. Converting the returned number into an integer with the `Int()` function means that `Int(Rnd * 3)` returns one of the numbers 0, 1, or 2.

Exercise Answer

Place the TegoMM.VBX multimedia control inside the form. You can now use your imagination to play audio during the course of the program. For example, during the shuffling, play the phrase "Now shuffling. Please wait."

When the player wins, play the audio phrase "You win." If the player wins again, play the phrase "You win again."

To determine a sequential winning, you'll have to maintain another static variable. For example, inside the cmdDeal_Click() procedure you can declare the static variable WinAgain as follows:

```
Static WinAgain
```

When the player loses, set the value of WinAgain to 0:

```
WinAgain = 0
```

When the player wins, increase the value of WinAgain by 1:

```
WinAgain = WinAgain + 1
```

Before exiting the cmdDeal_Click() procedure, use an If statement to determine the value of WinAgain:

```
If WinAgain > 1 Then
    .....................
    ... player won again
    .....................
Else
```

Under the If statement you can place code that plays an audio phrase telling the player that he/she won again.

Bonus Day

6+

Miscellaneous Powerful Controls

In this chapter you'll learn about various powerful VBX controls that you can use with Visual Basic. As you'll soon see, the controls that are discussed in this chapters are VBX controls included with the Professional Edition of Visual Basic 3.0. (These controls are not included with the Standard Edition of Visual Basic 3.0.)

3D Controls

Microsoft markets Visual Basic Version 3.0 in two ways: the Standard Edition and the Professional Edition. The Professional Edition contains additional VBX controls that are not shipped with the Standard Edition. One of the controls that is shipped with the Professional Edition but is not shipped with the Standard Edition is the THREED.VBX control. You'll now learn how to use the THREED.VBX control in your Visual Basic application.

> **Note:** Even if you don't own the Professional Edition, it is recommended that you read this chapter because by reading it you'll be able to see additional possible capabilities of Visual Basic. After reading this chapter you might find it worthwhile to purchase the Professional Edition of Visual Basic.
>
> Note that if you already own the Standard Edition of Visual Basic 3.0 and you decide to upgrade the product to the Professional Edition, it might be worthwhile for you to first investigate whether Microsoft offers any upgrade sales. (That is, you are upgrading Visual Basic 3.0 from the Standard Edition to the Professional Edition.)

The Pentium Program

The Pentium program demonstrates how to utilize the 3D controls that come with the Professional Edition of Visual Basic 3.0. As you'll soon see, there is nothing new about these 3D controls. The main difference between the 3D controls of the Professional Edition and the standard controls of the Standard Edition is that the 3D controls are prettier. Yes, they were designed for cosmetic reasons only. Nevertheless, don't underestimate the power of cosmetics in Windows applications. Your users expect your Windows application to be attractive.

> **Note:** At the time of the writing of this chapter, the news media started to discuss the problem of the floating point unit (FPU) of the Pentium CPU chip.
>
> In this chapter you'll write a simple program that checks the FPU of your Pentium. As you'll soon see, if you are not using a Pentium, the program will report that

everything is okay. If you are using a Pentium that does not have a problem, the program will again report that everything is okay.

If you are using a Pentium that has a problem with its FPU, the program will detect the problem.

Before writing the Pentium program, review its specifications.

Upon startup of the Pentium program, the window shown in Figure BD6.1 appears.

Figure BD6.1.
The initial window of the Pentium program.

```
┌─────────────────────────────────────────────────────┐
│ ▬             The Pentium Program            ▼ ▲     │
├─────────────────────────────────────────────────────┤
│                                                       │
│     ( 4,195,835 / 3,145,727 ) * 3,145,727 =          │
│                                                       │
│   The Correct Answer       You Got                    │
│                                                       │
│       4195835          =                              │
│                                                       │
│   ┌──────┐      ┌───────────┐      ┌──────┐          │
│   │  ✂   │      │     ÷     │      │ Reset│          │
│   │ Exit │      │Check Division│   └──────┘          │
│   └──────┘      └───────────┘                        │
└─────────────────────────────────────────────────────┘
```

As shown in Figure BD6.1, the Pentium program will perform a very simple calculation:

```
(4,195,835/3,145,727)*3,145,727
```

Of course, the answer should be 4,195,835. Indeed, a non-Pentium CPU and a Pentium with a correct FPU will report the correct answer. However, a Pentium with a problematic FPU will report an incorrect answer.

To exit the Pentium program, click the Exit button. Note that the Exit button has a picture in it (a picture of an ax cutting a cable).

When you click the Check Division button, the Pentium program will perform the division calculations. The result of the division is displayed inside the You Got 3D frame control. If the result is the correct one, the user sees the equals sign between the The Correct Answer frame and the You Got frame (see Figure BD6.2). If the result of the division is incorrect, the user will see a flashing red X over the equals sign (see Figure BD6.3).

Although you can't see it in the black-and-white pictures in Figures BD6.1, BD6.2, and BD6.3, the caption of the Reset button is shown in red.

BD6

Figure BD6.2.
The window of the Pentium program when the correct result is obtained.

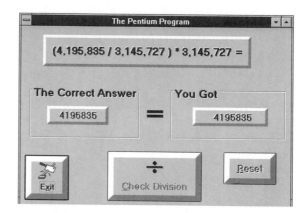

Figure BD6.3.
The window of the Pentium program when the incorrect result is obtained.

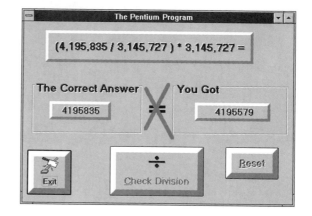

When the user clicks the Reset button, the number inside the You Got frame is erased so the user can start the experiment all over again.

The important thing to note about the Pentium program is that its various controls are three-dimensional (3D) controls.

Now that you know what the Pentium program is supposed to do, you can write it.

The Visual Implementation of the Pentium Program

You'll now visually implement the frmPentium form of the Pentium program.

☐ Select New Project from the File menu and save the new project as follows: Save the new form as Pentium.frm inside the C:\EXPROG\BD6 directory and save the new project file as Pentium.mak inside the C:\EXPROG\BD6 directory.

The Pentium project uses the THREED.VBX control of the Professional Edition of Visual Basic 3.0. Therefore, you must make sure that the THREED.VBX control appears inside the Toolbox. Figure BD6.4 shows the THREED.VBX controls. As shown in Figure BD6.4, once you add the THREED.VBX control to your project, six 3D controls appear in the Toolbox.

Figure BD6.4.
*The THREED.VBX
controls.*

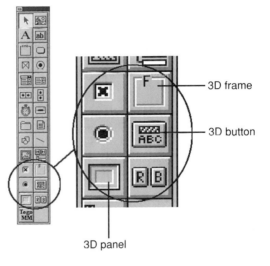

3D frame

3D button

3D panel

If your project does not contain the THREED.VBX controls, complete the following steps to add the control to your project:

☐ Select Add File from the File menu of Visual Basic.

☐ Add the file \Windows\System\THREED.VBX.

Once you add the THREED.VBX file to your project, the controls shown in Figure BD6.4 appear in your Toolbox, and the THREED.VBX file appears in your project window.

You can now visually implement the frmPentium form.

☐ Implement the form of the Pentium program according to the specifications in Table BD6.1. When you finish implementing the form, it should look like the one shown in Figure BD6.5.

BD6

Table BD6.1. The properties table of the frmPentium form.

Object	Property	Setting
Form	**Name**	**frmPentium**
	BackColor	(light gray)
	Caption	The Pentium Program

Table BD6.1. continued

Object	Property	Setting
	Height	5295
	Icon	C:\VB\Icons\Misc\Misc21.ICO
	Left	1035
	Top	1140
	Width	7485
3D Command Button	**Name**	**cmdReset**
	BevelWidth	10
	Caption	&Reset
	Font3D	4-Inset w/heavy shading
	FontSize	12
	ForeColor	(red)
	Height	855
	Left	5520
	Top	3360
	Width	1455
Timer	**Name**	**tmrTimer**
	Interval	250
	Left	5640
	Top	4320
3D Frame	**Name**	**fraYouGot**
	Caption	You Got
	Font3D	4-Inset w/heavy shading
	FontSize	13.5
	Height	1455
	Left	4080
	Top	1560
	Width	3135
3D Panel	**Name**	**pnlResult**
	BackColor	(light gray)
	BevelWidth	5

Object	Property	Setting
	Caption	(empty)
	Font3D	2-Raised w/heavy shading
	FontSize	12
	Height	495
	Left	600
	Top	600
	Width	2055
3D Frame	**Name**	**fraCorrect**
	Caption	The Correct Answer
	Font3D	4-Inset w/heavy shading
	FontSize	13.5
	Height	1455
	Left	240
	Top	1560
	Width	3015
3D Panel	**Name**	**pnlCorrect**
	BackColor	(light gray)
	BevelWidth	5
	Caption	4195835
	Font3D	2-Raised w/heavy shading
	FontSize	12
	Height	495
	Left	480
	Top	600
	Width	1695
3D Panel	**Name**	**pnlA**
	BackColor	(light gray)
	BevelWidth	5
	Caption	(4,195,835 / 3,145,727) * 3,145,727 =
	Font3D	2-Raised w/heavy shading

continues

Table BD6.1. continued

Object	Property	Setting
	FontSize	13.5
	Height	855
	Left	600
	Top	240
	Width	5655
3D Command Button	**Name**	**cmdExit**
	BevelWidth	10
	Caption	E&xit
	Font3D	4-Inset w/heavy shading
	FontSize	9.75
	Height	1215
	Left	120
	Picture	C:\VB\Icons\Comm\NET11.ICO
	Top	3480
	Width	1215
3D Command Button	**Name**	**cmdCheckIt**
	BevelWidth	10
	Caption	&Check Division
	Font3D	1-Raised w/light shading
	FontSize	12
	Height	1335
	Left	2400
	Picture	C:\VB\Icons\Misc\Misc21.ICO
	Top	3360
	Width	2535
Line	**Name**	**linLine1**
	BorderWidth	5
	X1	3480
	X2	3840

Object	Property	Setting
	Y1	2280
	Y2	2280
Line	**Name**	**linLine2**
	BorderWidth	5
	X1	3480
	X2	3840
	Y1	2400
	Y2	2400
Line	**Name**	**linLine3**
	BorderColor	(red)
	BorderWidth	7
	Visible	0-False
	X1	3360
	X2	4080
	Y1	1800
	Y2	3120
Line	**Name**	**linLine4**
	BorderColor	(red)
	BorderWidth	7
	Visible	0-False
	X1	3960
	X2	3360
	Y1	1680
	Y2	2880

BD6

Entering the Code of the General Declarations Section of the frmPentium Form

You'll now attach code to the general declarations section of the frmPentium form.

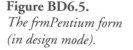

Figure BD6.5.
The frmPentium form
(in design mode).

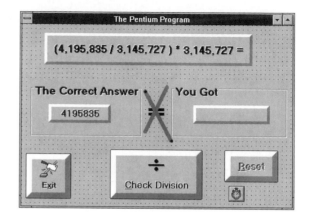

☐ Type the following code inside the general declarations section of the frmPentium form:

```
Option Explicit

Dim gReplacePentium
Dim gDisplayResult
```

Attaching Code to the *Load* Event of the Form

You'll now attach code to the Load event of the form.

☐ Type the following code inside the Form_Load() procedure:

```
Sub Form_Load ()

    gReplacePentium = 0
    gDisplayResult = 0

End Sub
```

The code you typed initializes the general variables. You'll soon understand the purpose that these variables serve in the program.

Attaching Code to the *Click* Event of the Exit Button

You'll now attach code to the Click event of the Exit 3D command button.

☐ Type the following code inside the cmdExit_Click() procedure of the frmPentium form:

```
Sub cmdExit_Click ()

    End

End Sub
```

Attaching Code to the *Click* Event of the Check It 3D Button

You'll now attach code to the Click event of the CheckIt 3D command button.

☐ Type the following code inside the cmdCheckIt_Click() procedure of the frmPentium form:

```
Sub cmdCheckIt_Click ()

   Dim Result

   Result = (4195835 / 3145727) * 3145727
   pnlResult.Caption = Str(Result)

   If Result <> 4195835 Then
      gReplacePentium = 1
   Else
      gReplacePentium = 0
   End If

   gDisplayResult = 1
   cmdCheckIt.Enabled = False

End Sub
```

The code you typed declared a local variable:

```
Dim Result
```

The Result variable is then assigned with the following value:

```
Result = (4195835 / 3145727) * 3145727
```

As you know, the result should be 4195835.

The Caption property of the pnlResult 3D panel control is then set so that the panel control displays the result:

```
   pnlResult.Caption = Str(Result)
```

As you can see from the preceding statement, the 3D panel control can be thought as a 3D label. Note that during design time you set the BevelWidth property of the pnlResult control to 5. This property determines the thickness of the control in the Z-direction.

As stated, the result of the calculations should be 4195835. An If statement is executed to check whether the result obtained is the correct result:

```
   If Result <> 4195835 Then
      gReplacePentium = 1
   Else
      gReplacePentium = 0
   End If
```

The general variable `gReplacePentium` serves as a flag. If `gReplacePentium` is equal to 1, the obtained result is incorrect.

The general variable `gDisplayResult` is then set to 1:

```
gDisplayResult = 1
```

This variable serves as a flag that indicates that the calculations had been performed, and it is now time to display the result. As you'll soon see, setting the `gDisplayResult` variable to 1 causes the Pentium program to display the results in an impressive manner.

Finally, the Check It 3D button is disabled:

```
cmdCheckIt.Fnabled = False
```

Attaching Code to the *Click* Event of the Reset Button

You'll now attach code to the `Click` event of the Reset 3D button.

☐ Type the following code inside the `cmdReset_Click()` procedure of the frmPentium form:

```
Sub cmdReset_Click ()

    gDisplayResult = 0
    gReplacePentium = 0
    pnlResult.Caption = ""
    linLine3.Visible = False
    linLine4.Visible = False
    cmdCheckIt.Enabled = True

End Sub
```

The code you typed sets the general variables back to 0:

```
gDisplayResult = 0
gReplacePentium = 0
```

The `Caption` property of the 3D panel that displays the result of the division is made empty:

```
pnlResult.Caption = ""
```

The two control lines that serve as the X over the equals sign (see Figure BD6.3) are made invisible:

```
linLine3.Visible = False
linLine4.Visible = False
```

Finally, the cmdCheckIt 3D command button is enabled:

```
cmdCheckIt.Enabled = True
```

Attaching Code to the *Timer* Event of the Timer

You'll now attach code to the `Timer` event of the timer. Recall that during design time you set the Interval property of the tmrTimer control to 250. This means that the `tmrTimer_Timer()` procedure is executed automatically every 250 milliseconds.

☐ Type the following code inside the `tmrTimer_Timer()` procedure of the frmPentium form:

```
Sub tmrTimer_Timer ()

    Static BlinkResult

    If gDisplayResult = 0 Or gReplacePentium = 0 Then
       Exit Sub
    End If


    If BlinkResult = 0 Then
       BlinkResult = 1
       linLine3.Visible = False
       linLine4.Visible = False
    Else
       BlinkResult = 0
       linLine3.Visible = True
       linLine4.Visible = True
    End If

End Sub
```

The code you typed is responsible for displaying the result. Of course, you can use a label control that displays a message, but the Pentium program displays the results in a more impressive manner.

A static variable is declared:

```
Static BlinkResult
```

An `If` statement is executed to determine whether there is a need to flash the red X over the equals sign (see Figure BD6.3):

```
    If gDisplayResult = 0 Or gReplacePentium = 0 Then
       Exit Sub
    End If
```

If `gDisplayResult` is equal to 0 or if `gReplacePentium` is equal to 0, there is no need to flash the red X, and the `tmrTimer_Timer()` procedure is terminated.

If there is a need to flash the red X, the `tmrTimer_Timer()` procedure is not terminated by the preceding `If` statement, and the procedure continues executing the rest of the statements in this procedure.

An `If…Else` statement is executed to cause the red X to blink:

```
If BlinkResult = 0 Then
    BlinkResult = 1
    linLine3.Visible = False
    linLine4.Visible = False
Else
    BlinkResult = 0
    linLine3.Visible = True
    linLine4.Visible = True
End If
```

Recall that the `BlinkResult` variable is a static variable. When the `tmrTimer_Timer()` procedure is executed for the first time, `BlinkResult` is equal to 0. The preceding `If` statement is satisfied, and `BlinkResult` is set to 1. On the next execution of `tmrTimer_Timer()`, `BlinkResult` is equal to 1 (because a static variable retains its value from the last execution of the procedure). The code under the `Else` is executed, which makes `BlinkResult` equal to 0 again. This process repeats itself every 250 milliseconds. The values of `BlinkResult` are 0,1,0,1,0,….

The red X is blinking because you set the Visible properties of the line controls to False, True, False, True, False, True,….

☐ Execute the Pentium program and experiment with it. When the Pentium program is executed by a CPU that does not have a problem with its FPU, the red X will not appear. If you execute the Pentium program in a PC that has a Pentium chip with a faulty FPU, the red X will blink.

The Gauge Program

There are several ways to display information to your users in Windows. For example, a label control can display a message to the user. Sometimes you'll need to display certain numeric data. Again, you can display the number with a label control. But in some cases, it is appropriate to display to the user a whole range of numbers so the user will get a visual feeling of how large or small the number is.

For example, you can design an installation program that installs files into your user's hard drive. During the installation, it makes sense to display the status of the installation's progress. During the installation, the user can determine how the installation is progressing by observing the percentage of files that have been installed already. You can do this, for example, by displaying a scroll bar. The extreme left of the scroll bar signifies the 0 percent level, and the extreme right side of the scroll bar represents the 100 percent level. During the installation, you can set the Value property of the scroll bar according to the percentage of files that have been installed.

The preceding solution of using a scroll bar for providing the user with a visual way of indicating how a certain process is progressing is fine. However, users typically think of a scroll bar as a control for inputting data, not as a control for outputting data. A better control for displaying

progress information is the gauge control. The Gauge program illustrates how you can take advantage of the GAUGE.VBX gauge control that comes with the Professional Edition of Visual Basic 3.0.

Before writing the Gauge program yourself, review its specifications.

Upon startup of the Gauge program, the window shown in Figure BD6.6 appears.

Figure BD6.6.
The Gauge program.

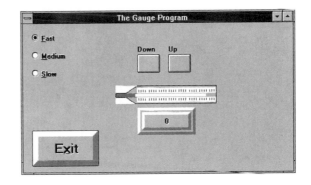

The gauge shown in Figure BD6.6 indicates that the current value is 0. To increase the value of the gauge, the user has to click the Up button. Once the user clicks the Up button, the gauge starts increasing its value. Figure BD6.7 shows the gauge when its value reaches 34. Figure BD6.8 shows the gauge after it has reached its maximum value.

Figure BD6.7.
The gauge control, indicating that the current value is 34.

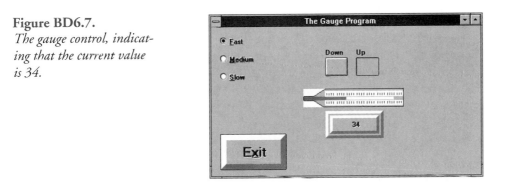

BD6

The Up and Down buttons are very interesting buttons. When you press the Up button, the Up button remains pressed! In Figure BD6.6, the Up and Down buttons are both not pressed. This means that the gauge does not change its value.

In Figure BD6.7 the Down button is not pressed, but the Up button is pressed. This means that the gauge increases its value. You can unpress the Up button by clicking it again. If you did not click the Up button and let the gauge increase its value to the maximum, the Gauge program pops out the Up button when the gauge control reaches its maximum value.

Figure BD6.8.

The gauge control, indicating that the current value is 100 (the maximum value).

Pressing the Down button causes the gauge control to decrease its value. If during the time the gauge control decreases its value the user clicks the Down button to unpress the Down button, the gauge control will stop decreasing the gauge value. The minimum value of the gauge is 0. Once the gauge reaches its minimum value, the Down button pops out.

> **Note:** The Up and Down buttons are called 3D group buttons. In the Gauge program there are two buttons in the group: the Up button and the Down button. The group buttons work like this: You cannot have more than one button pressed. That is, you can have the Up button pressed, or you can have the Down button pressed, but you can't have both buttons pressed. In this aspect, the group buttons behave like option buttons. For example, if currently the Up button is pressed and you click the Down button, the Up button will pop out, and the Down button will be pressed. However, unlike option buttons where one of the option buttons must be selected, you can have all the group buttons unpressed. To unpress a group button, you have to click the button.

As shown in Figure BD6.6, you can control the speed at which the gauge control changes its value by selecting the Fast, Medium, or Slow 3D option buttons.

Now that you know what the Gauge program is supposed to do, you can write it.

The Visual Implementation of the frmGauge Form

You'll now implement the frmGauge form. The frmGauge form uses two VBX controls from the Professional Edition of Visual Basic 3.0: THREED.VBX and GAUGE.VBX.

Once you install the THREED.VBX control into your project, six 3D controls appear in your Toolbox (see Figure BD6.4). The icon that has a picture of two buttons in it is the group button control.

☐ Select New Project from the File menu, and save the new project as follows: Save the new form as Gauge.frm inside the C:\EXPROG\BD6 directory and save the new project file as Gauge.mak inside the C:\EXPROG\BD6 directory.

If your Toolbox does not contain the 3D controls and you are using the Professional Edition of Visual Basic 3.0, add the THREED.VBX control to your project as follows:

☐ Select Add File from the File menu, and add the C:\Windows\System\THREED.VBX control.

If your Toolbox does not contain the gauge control and you are using the Professional Edition of Visual Basic 3.0, add the GAUGE.VBX control to your project as follows:

☐ Select Add File from the File menu, and add the C:\Windows\System\GAUGE.VBX control.

The Gauge.VBX control appears in the Toolbox, as shown in Figure BD6.9.

Figure BD6.9.
The Gauge.VBX control inside the Toolbox.

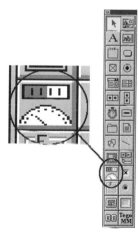

BD6

☐ Implement the frmGauge form according to the specifications in Table BD6.2. When you finish implementing the form, it should look like the one shown in Figure BD6.10. Table BD6.2 instructs you to place three 3D option buttons inside the frmGauge form. These three option buttons all have the same Name property (optSpeed), which means that these three option buttons are an array of controls. The first option button (the Fast option button) is the first element in the array of controls: optSpeed(0). The second option button (the Medium option button) is the second element in the array of controls: optSpeed(1). The third option button (the Slow option button) is the third element in the array of controls: optSpeed(2).

Table BD6.2. The properties table of the frmGauge form.

Object	Property	Setting
Form	**Name**	**frmGauge**
	BackColor	(light gray)
	Caption	The Gauge Program
	Height	4425
	Icon	C:\EXPROG\Icons\MyGauge.ICO
	Left	1020
	Top	1140
	Width	7485
3D Panel	**Name**	**pnlValue**
	BackColor	(light gray)
	BevelInner	2-Raised
	BevelWidth	5
	Caption	"0"
	Font3D	4-Inset w/heavy shading
	Height	735
	Left	3120
	Top	2280
	Width	1575
Timer	**Name**	**tmrTimer**
	Interval	100
	Left	5760
	Top	3240
3D Command Button	**Name**	**cmdExit**
	BevelWidth	10
	Caption	E&xit
	Font3D	4-Inset w/heavy shading
	FontSize	18

Object	Property	Setting
	Height	975
	Left	240
	Top	2880
	Width	1815
3D Option Button	**Name**	**optSpeed**
	Caption	&Fast
	Font3D	2-Raised w/heavy shading
	Height	495
	Index	0
	Left	240
	Top	120
	Value	-1-True
	Width	1215
3D Option Button	**Name**	**optSpeed**
	Caprion	&Slow
	Font3D	2-Raised w/heavy shading
	Height	495
	Index	2
	Left	240
	Top	1080
	Width	1215
3D Option Button	**Name**	**optSpeed**
	Caption	&Medium
	Font3D	2-Raised w/heavy shading
	Height	495
	Index	1
	Left	240
	Top	600
	Width	1215

BD6

continues

Table BD6.2. continued

Object	Property	Setting
3D Group Button	**Name**	**cmdUp**
	AutoSize	0-None
	BackColor	(light gray)
	Height	495
	Left	3960
	Top	840
	Width	615
3D Group Button	**Name**	**cmdDown**
	AutoSize	0-None
	BackColor	(light gray)
	Height	495
	Left	3120
	Top	840
	Width	615
Label	**Name**	**lblDown**
	BackColor	(light gray)
	Caption	Down
	Height	255
	Left	3120
	Top	600
	Width	615
Label	**Name**	**lblUp**
	BackColor	(light gray)
	Caption	Up
	Height	255
	Left	3960
	Top	600
	Width	375
Gauge.VBX	**Name**	**Gauge1**
	Autosize	-1-True

Object	Property	Setting
	BackColor	(light gray)
	ForeColor	(red)
	Height	495
	InnerBottom	20
	InnerLeft	35
	InnerRight	20
	InnerTop	20
	Left	2520
	Max	100
	Min	0
	NeedleWidth	1
	Picture	C:\VB\Bitmaps\gauge\Horz.BMP
	Style	0-Horizontal Bar
	Top	1680
	Value	0
	Width	2745

Figure BD6.10.
*The frmGauge form
(in design mode).*

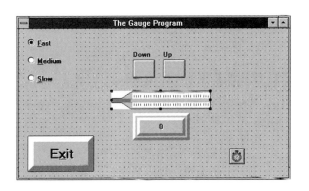

BD6

Table BD6.2 instructs you to place the gauge control inside the frmGauge form, and then to set the properties of the gauge control.

The BackColor property of the gauge control is set to light gray. Take a look at Figure BD6.11. The original area, which will be filled as the value of the gauge increased, is light gray.

Table BD6.2 instructs you to set the ForeColor property of the gauge control to red. Take a look at Figure BD6.11. As the gauge control increases in value, a red "fluid" fills the gauge.

Figure BD6.11.

The BackColor and ForeColor properties of the gauge control.

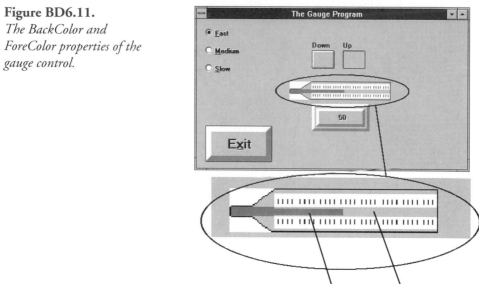

Fill with red over light gray

The Value property serves the same role as the Value property of the scroll bar. That is, the Value property indicates that current value of the gauge.

In Table BD6.2 you set the Value property to 0 because you want the value of the gauge control to be 0 upon startup of the program. The Min and Max properties of the gauge control serve the same role as the Min and Max properties of the scroll bar. That is, Min and Max indicate the minimum and maximum values of the control.

The Style property of the gauge control is set to 0-Horizontal Bar. This means that as the Value property of the gauge control increases, a horizontal bar is drawn. It is important to understand that the thermometer that you see in the Gauge program is just the cosmetic representation of the gauge control. As far as the gauge control is concerned, a horizontal bar will be drawn according to the Value property of the control (this is shown in Figure BD6.12). Because you set the ForeColor property of the control to red, the horizontal bar is drawn in red.

But what is the starting point of the horizontal bar and what is the endpoint of the horizontal bar? The starting point and endpoint of the horizontal bar are set with the InnerBottom, InnerLeft, InnerRight, and InnerTop properties. In Table BD6.2 you set these properties as follows: InnerBottom is 20, InnerLeft is 35, InnerRight is 20, and InnerTop is 20.

In the following discussion, the preceding four properties will be referred to as the Inner properties of the gauge control.

The Inner properties define the horizontal bar as it appears in its maximum value (when it is completely filled). Figure BD6.13 illustrates that these coordinates are referenced to the rectangle that encloses the gauge control.

Figure BD6.12.

A horizontal bar is drawn according to the Value property of the gauge control.

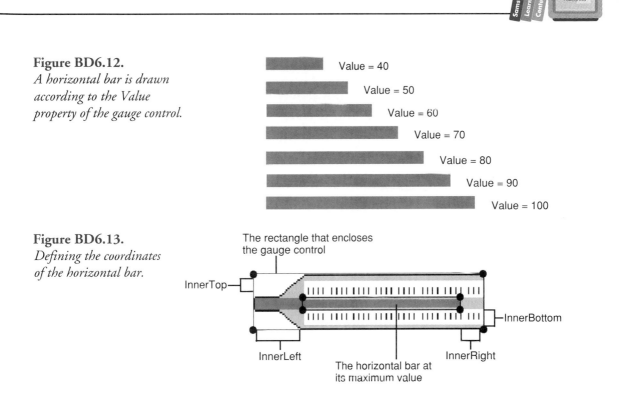

Value = 40

Value = 50

Value = 60

Value = 70

Value = 80

Value = 90

Value = 100

Figure BD6.13.

Defining the coordinates of the horizontal bar.

The rectangle that encloses the gauge control

InnerTop

InnerLeft

The horizontal bar at its maximum value

InnerBottom

InnerRight

The entire gauge control is enclosed by a rectangle. This rectangle is defined by the Width and Height properties of the gauge control. The Width and Height properties of the gauge control are not different from the Width and Height properties of any other VBX control.

The Inner properties define the coordinates of the horizontal bar. The Inner properties are defined referenced to the rectangle that encloses the gauge control. Look at Figure BD6.13 and note that the vertical distance between the upper-left corner of the rectangle that encloses the gauge control and the upper-left corner of the rectangle that is being filled is InnerTop. In Table BD6.2 you set InnerTop to 20. This means that the vertical distance is 20. In a similar way, the horizontal distance between the upper-left corner of the rectangle that encloses the gauge control and the upper-left corner of the horizontal bar that is being filled is InnerLeft.

The lower-right corner of the horizontal bar that is being filled (at its maximum position) is referenced to the lower-right corner of the rectangle that encloses the gauge control. As shown in Figure BD6.13, the vertical distance between these two points is InnerBottom, and the horizontal distance is InnerRight.

Note that the Left and Top properties of the gauge control are referenced to the upper-left corner of the form (just as any other controls would be).

So the Inner properties define the size and location of the horizontal bar when it is completely filled. It is the responsibility of the gauge control to fill the horizontal bar according to the Value

BD6

property. For example, when the Value property of the gauge control is 100 (the maximum value), the rectangle is drawn as shown in Figure BD6.13. When the Value property of the gauge control is 50, the rectangle is drawn as shown in Figure BD6.14. As shown in Figure BD6.14, only half of the horizontal bar is filled when the Value property is set to 50. This is because you set the Min property to 0 and the Max property to 100. This means that when Value is equal to 50, the horizontal bar is filled halfway.

Figure BD6.14.

The horizontal bar when the Value property of the gauge control is 50 and when it is 25.

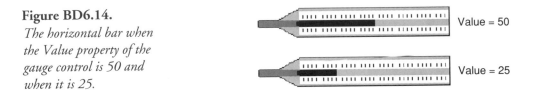

You set the Picture property of the gauge control to C:\VB\Bitmaps\gauge\Horz.BMP. (When designing gauge controls, you can use some of the bitmaps that come with the Professional Edition of Visual Basic 3.0, or you can design your own gauge BMP files.)

As shown in Figure BD6.15, on the upper-right side of the Paintbrush window you can see the Cursor Position window. This Cursor Position window enables you to see the coordinates of the mouse cursor. For example, in Figure BD6.15 the mouse cursor is 74 pixels to the right of the upper-left corner of the picture, and it is 16 pixels below the upper-right corner of the picture. To display the Cursor Position window, select Cursor Position from the View menu of Paintbrush. Why do you need the Cursor Position window of Paintbrush? When you are using the BMP files that come with the Professional Edition of Visual Basic 3.0 (or when you are using your own BMP pictures), you have to figure out the Inner properties, and the easiest way to figure out the values of the Inner properties is by using this feature of Paintbrush.

Note: You should understand that you can supply your own BMP pictures as the picture of the gauge control. For example, Figure BD6.16 shows a BMP picture that can be used as the picture for the gauge control. The picture shows the nose of Pinocchio as the horizontal bar that changes while the Value property of the gauge control increases.

Attaching Code to the *Click* Event of the Exit Button

You'll now attach code to the Click event of the Exit button.

Figure BD6.15.
*Loading the
C:\VB\Bitmaps\Gauge
\HORZ.BMP picture with
Paintbrush.*

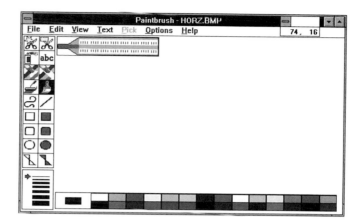

Figure BD6.16.
*The nose of Pinocchio grows
as the Value property of the
gauge control increases.*

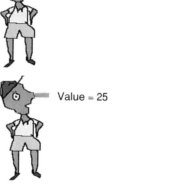
Value = 100

Value = 25

☐ Type the following code inside the cmdExit_Click() procedure of the frmGauge form:

```
Sub cmdExit_Click ()

    End

End Sub
```

BD6

The code you typed terminates the Gauge program whenever the user clicks the Exit button. Note that during design time you did not assign a picture to the Picture property of the 3D Exit button. However, as demonstrated with the Pentium, you can set the Picture property to a picture that gives the user a visual indication that this button is the Exit button.

Attaching Code to the Speed Option Button Control Array

Recall that during design time you placed an array of option buttons inside the frmGauge form. You'll now attach code to the Click event of the array of option buttons.

☐ Type the following code inside the optSpeed_Click() procedure of the frmGauge form:

```
Sub optSpeed_Click (Index As Integer, Value As Integer)

    Select Case Index
        Case 0
            ' Fast
            tmrTimer.Interval = 100
        Case 1
            ' Medium
            tmrTimer.Interval = 500
        Case 2
            ' Slow
            tmrTimer.Interval = 1000
    End Select

End Sub
```

The code you typed uses a Select Case statement to determine which option button was clicked. Note that the first parameter of the optSpeed_Click() procedure is Index. This parameter indicates which option button was clicked. According to the option button that was clicked, the Interval property of the timer control is set:

```
Select Case Index
        Case 0
            ' Fast
            tmrTimer.Interval = 100
        Case 1
            ' Medium
            tmrTimer.Interval = 500
        Case 2
            ' Slow
            tmrTimer.Interval = 1000
End Select
```

As you'll soon see, the Interval property of the tmrTimer control determines how fast the Value property of the gauge control is increased or decreased.

Attaching Code to the *Timer* Event of the tmrTimer Control

You'll now attach code to the Timer event of the tmrTimer control. This code is responsible for increasing or decreasing the Value property of the gauge control.

☐ Type the following code inside the `tmrTimer_Timer()` procedure of the frmGuage form:

```
Sub tmrTimer_Timer ()

    If cmdUp.Value = True Then
        Gauge1.Value = Gauge1.Value + 1
        pnlValue.Caption = Str(Gauge1.Value)
        If Gauge1.Value = 100 Then
            cmdUp.Value = False
        End If
    End If

    If cmdDown.Value = True Then
        Gauge1.Value = Gauge1.Value - 1
        pnlValue.Caption = Str(Gauge1.Value)
        If Gauge1.Value = 0 Then
            cmdDown.Value = False
        End If
    End If

End Sub
```

The code you typed uses an `If` statement to determine whether the Value property of the cmdUp group button is pressed:

```
    If cmdUp.Value = True Then
        Gauge1.Value = Gauge1.Value + 1
        pnlValue.Caption = Str(Gauge1.Value)
        If Gauge1.Value = 100 Then
            cmdUp.Value = False
        End If
    End If
```

The preceding `If` statement is satisfied provided that the cmdUp group button is pressed. If this is the case, the Value property of the gauge control is increased by 1:

```
Gauge1.Value = Gauge1.Value + 1
```

The Caption property of the 3D panel control is set to indicate the current value of the gauge's Value property:

```
pnlValue.Caption = Str(Gauge1.Value)
```

Finally, an `If` statement is executed to make sure that the Value property of the gauge control does not exceed 100:

```
If Gauge1.Value = 100 Then
    cmdUp.Value = False
End If
```

Note that if the Value property of the gauge control is 100, the Value property of the Up group button is set to False, which means that the button pops out:

```
cmdUp.Value = False
```

BD6

The next `If` statement takes care of the case in which the Down button is pressed:

```
If cmdDown.Value = True Then
   Gauge1.Value = Gauge1.Value - 1
   pnlValue.Caption = Str(Gauge1.Value)
   If Gauge1.Value = 0 Then
      cmdDown.Value = False
   End If
End If
```

The preceding code is similar to the code that is executed when the Up group button is pressed. However, because now the Down group button is pressed, the Value property of the gauge control is decreased, and the inner `If` statement verifies that the Value property of the gauge does not decrease below 0.

☐ Execute the Gauge program and experiment with the Up group button, the Down group button, and the option buttons. Then click the Exit button to terminate the program.

The Style property of the gauge control is set to 0-Horizontal Bar in Table BD6.2.

Here are the four possible settings for the Style property of the gauge control:

> 0-Horizontal Bar
> 1-Vertical Bar
> 2-Semi Needle
> 3-Full Needle

The Gauge program uses a gauge control with the Style property set to 0-Horizontal Bar. As shown in Figure BD6.14, this means that as you increase the Value property of the gauge control, a rectangle is filled in the horizontal direction.

If you set the Style property to 1-Vertical Bar, a vertical bar will be filled in the vertical direction as the Value property of the gauge control is increased (see Figure BD6.17).

If you set the Style property to 2-Semi Needle, as the Value property of the gauge control is increased, a needle is drawn and the needle rotates according to the Value property (see Figure BD6.18). That is, when Value is at its minimum, the needle points to the left, and when the Value property is at its maximum, the needle points to the right.

If you set the Style property to 3-Full Needle, as the Value property of the gauge control is increased, a needle is drawn, and the needle rotates according to the Value property (see Figure BD6.19). That is, when the Value property is at its minimum, the needle points to the left. As the Value property increases, the needle rotates clockwise. The needle will complete a full circle when the Value property reaches its maximum value.

Note that for all the possible settings of the Style property the Inner properties define the rectangle in which the horizontal/vertical bar is advancing or the needle is rotating.

When setting the Style property to 2 or 3, you can set the NeedleWidth property for determining the width of the needle. For example, setting the NeedleWidth property to 1 causes the gauge control to draw the needle with a width of 1 pixel, setting the NeedleWidth property to 2 causes the gauge control to draw the needle with a width of 2 pixels, and so on.

Figure BD6.17.
A gauge control with the Style property set to 1-Vertical Bar.

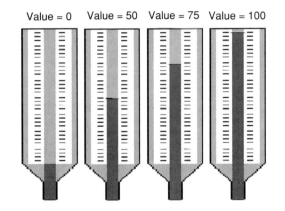

Figure BD6.18.
A gauge control with the Style property set to 2-Semi Needle.

Figure BD6.19.

A gauge control with the Style property set to 3-Full Needle.

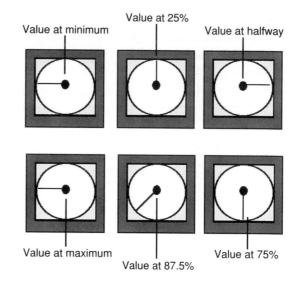

Summary

In this chapter you have learned how to use 3D controls and how to use the gauge control. As you have learned, these controls are very similar to the standard controls that you use with Visual Basic. However, by using the 3D controls, for example, you can make your Visual Basic programs better looking than when using the standard controls.

Q&A

Q When I installed the THREED.VBX control into a project, six 3D controls were added to the Toolbox. The Pentium program uses the 3D command button, 3D frame, and 3D panel. The Gauge program uses the 3D option button, the 3D option button, and the group buttons. What about the 3D check box?

A As you saw in the Pentium program, the 3D command button is very similar to the standard command button. The only difference is that unlike a standard command button, the 3D command button has several cosmetic aspects to it. For example, you can attach pictures to the 3D command buttons (as you did with the cmdExit 3D command button of the Pentium program).

Similarly, the 3D option button serves the same role as the standard option button, only the 3D option button is prettier. The 3D check box serves the same role as the standard check box.

Generally, the standard controls work the same way as the 3D controls. However, be aware of some differences between the standard controls and the 3D controls. For

example, the Value property of the standard check box can be set to 0-Unchecked, to 1-Checked, and to 2-Unavailable. On the other hand, the 3D check box can be set to either True-Checked or False-Unchecked. You cannot set the Value of the 3D check box to Unavailable.

Q Should I use 3D controls or standard controls in my Visual Basic programs?

A As you have seen in this chapter, programs written with 3D controls are more attractive than those written with standard controls. If you want your programs to look good, use 3D controls.

Quiz

1. The group command button serves the same role as the option button.

    a. True

    b. False

2. The settings of the Inner properties of the gauge control can be best determined by using which of the following:

    a. Paintbrush

    b. Guessing—trial and error

Exercise

The Up group button of the Gauge program does not have a caption on it. Therefore, in this chapter a label was placed above the cmdUp button to indicate that this is the Up button (see Figure BD6.6). Similarly, the Down group button of the Gauge program does not have a caption on it, and therefore a label control was used. Make it better! That is, modify the Gauge program so that the user will see a better visual indication for the purpose of these group buttons. (Hint: The group buttons do not have a Caption property. They do, however, have various Picture properties.)

BD6

Quiz Answers

1. b (When you place, for example, two option buttons inside the form, one of these option buttons must be selected at any given time. On the other hand, when you place two group buttons inside the form, you may have only one of the buttons pressed, or you may have none of the group buttons pressed.)

2. a

Exercise Answer

The group command button has several Picture properties. For example, the PictureUp property determines which picture is displayed inside the button when the button is not pressed. The PictureDn property determines which picture is displayed inside the button when the button is pressed.

You can use Paintbrush to draw small BMP pictures and then to set the various Picture properties of the group button controls to the picture you drew with Paintbrush. Alternatively, you can use the icons that are supplied with Visual Basic as the pictures. For example, the \VB\Icons\Arrows directory contain various icons that are appropriate as the pictures of the group command buttons of the Gauge program.

Bonus Day

7+

Creating Your
Own DLLs
for Visual Basic

One of the best and most powerful features of Visual Basic is its ability to utilize third-party software modules. The designers of Visual Basic realized that during the course of developing programs with Visual Basic you'll need more features and programming power that are included in the off-the-box package. In such cases, you can utilize dynamic linked library (DLL) files and VBX controls. In this chapter you'll learn how to create your own DLLs for Visual Basic.

Note: As stated, Visual Basic enables you to incorporate DLLs and VBXs into your Visual Basic projects. In this chapter you'll learn how to design your own DLLs. For more information on learning how to design your own VBX controls, see the Sams Publishing book *Master Visual Basic 3* by Gurewich and Gurewich.

Using DLLs

Occasionally, you'll need a feature in your Visual Basic program that does not exist in the out-of-the-box Visual Basic package. In such cases, you have to "add" this feature to Visual Basic by using a DLL.

Windows contains many DLL functions that you can use from within Visual Basic. For example, Windows contains DLL functions that let you determine the path of the \Windows\System directory and let you determine the amount of free space in the system, as well as many other DLL functions. In fact, currently there are well over 700 documented DLL functions in Windows. Naturally, you don't need to use all of these, because the designers of Visual Basic incorporated most of the Windows DLL functions into Visual Basic.

For example, one of the DLL functions of Windows causes the speaker to beep. However, it is much more convenient to use the Beep statement of Visual Basic than to use an external DLL function. Sometimes, though, you'll need to use a feature that does not exist in Visual Basic, nor in any of the Windows DLL functions.

You can also write your own DLL functions. However, to write a DLL function, you need to know how to use the C programming language, and you need to use a C compiler. The rest of this chapter shows how to write your own DLL functions by using the Microsoft Visual C/C++ compiler.

Note: You cannot write DLLs with Visual Basic. In this chapter you'll write a DLL by using the C programming language and by using the Microsoft Visual C++ package.

This chapter assumes that you are familiar with the C programming language and that you own the Microsoft Visual C++ package.

Files Needed for Creating a DLL

To create your own DLL you'll need to use three "skeleton" files: GenDLL.C, GenDLL.H, and GenDLL.DEF. These files are listed in Listing BD7.1, Listing BD7.2, and Listing BD7.3.

☐ Create the directory C:\EXPROG\GenDLL.

☐ Use a text editor to type the code in Listing BD7.1, and save the file as GenDLL.C inside the C:\EXPROG\GenDLL directory.

Listing BD7.1. The GenDLL.C file.

```
//-----------------------------------------------------
// GenDLL.C
//-----------------------------------------------------
// Contains code for Generic DLL.
//
// Use the following files as templates for building your
// own DLL:
//
// - GenDLL.C (this file)
// - GenDLL.H
// - GenDLL.DEF
//-----------------------------------------------------

#include <windows.h>
#include "GENDLL.H"

//-----------------------------------------------------
// Global Variables
//-----------------------------------------------------
HANDLE hmodDLL;


//-----------------------------------------------------
// Prototypes
//-----------------------------------------------------

//-----------------------------------------------------
// Initialize library. This routine is called when the
// first client loads the DLL.
//-----------------------------------------------------
int FAR PASCAL LibMain
(
    HANDLE hModule,
```

continues

Listing BD7.1. continued

```c
        WORD    wDataSeg,
        WORD    cbHeapSize,
        LPSTR   lpszCmdLine
    )
    {
        // Avoid warnings on unused formal parameters
        wDataSeg    = wDataSeg;
        cbHeapSize  = cbHeapSize;
        lpszCmdLine = lpszCmdLine;

        hmodDLL = hModule;

        return 1;
    }




    //----------------------------------------------------
    // WEP
    //----------------------------------------------------
    // C7 and QCWIN provide default WEP:
    //----------------------------------------------------
    #if (_MSC_VER < 610)

    int FAR PASCAL WEP(int fSystemExit);

    //----------------------------------------------------
    // For Windows 3.0 it is recommended that the WEP
    // function reside in a FIXED code segment and be
    // exported as RESIDENTNAME.  This is accomplished
    // using the alloc_text pragma below and the related
    // EXPORTS and SEGMENTS directives in the .DEF file.
    //
    // Read the comments section documenting the WEP
    // function in the Windows 3.1 SDK "Programmers
    // Reference, Volume 2: Functions" before placing
    // any additional code in the WEP routine for a
    // Windows 3.0 DLL.
    //----------------------------------------------------
    #pragma alloc_text(WEP_TEXT,WEP)

    //----------------------------------------------------
    // Performs cleanup tasks when the DLL is unloaded.
    // WEP() is called automatically by Windows when the DLL
    // is unloaded (no remaining tasks still have the DLL
    // loaded). It is strongly recommended that a DLL have a
    // WEP() function, even if it does nothing but returns
    // success (1), as in this example.
    //----------------------------------------------------
    int FAR PASCAL WEP
    (
        int fSystemExit
    )
```

```
{
    // Avoid warnings on unused formal parameters
    fSystemExit = fSystemExit;

    return 1;
}
#endif // C6

//-------------------------------------------------------
```

☐ Use a text editor to type the code in Listing BD7.2, and save the file as GenDLL.H inside the C:\EXPROG\GenDLL directory.

Listing BD7.2. The GenDLL.H file.

```
//-------------------------------------------------------
// GenDLL.H
//-------------------------------------------------------
// Contains code for Generic DLL.
//
// Use the following files as templates for building your
// own DLL:
//
// - GenDLL.C
// - GenDLL.H (this file)
// - GenDLL.DEF
//-------------------------------------------------------
```

☐ Use a text editor to type the code in Listing BD7.3, and save the file as GenDLL.DEF inside the C:\EXPROG\GenDLL directory.

Listing BD7.3. The GenDLL.DEF file.

```
;-------------------------------------------------------
; GenDLL.DEF
;-------------------------------------------------------
; The DEF file for Generic DLL.
;
; Use the following files as templates for building your
; own DLL:
;
; - GenDLL.C
; - GenDLL.H
; - GenDLL.DEF (this file)
;
;-------------------------------------------------------
LIBRARY          GENDLL
EXETYPE          WINDOWS
DESCRIPTION      'Visual Basic Generic DLL'

CODE             MOVEABLE
DATA             MOVEABLE SINGLE
```

continues

Listing BD7.3. continued

```
HEAPSIZE        2048

EXPORTS
  WEP       [064]1      RESIDENTNAME


SEGMENTS
  WEP_TEXT FIXED

;- - - - - - - - - - - - - - - - - - - - - - - - - - - - - - - - - - - - - - - - - - - - - - - - -
```

In the following sections you'll customize the three skeleton files to make a DLL. Therefore, you need to copy the three skeleton files to the C:\EXPROG\BD7 directory:

☐ Create the C:\EXPROG\BD7 directory.

☐ Copy the GenDLL.C, GenDLL.H, and GenDLL.DEF files from the C:\EXPROG\GenDLL directory to the C:\EXPROG\BD7 directory.

☐ Rename the files inside the C:\EXPROG\BD7 directory as follows: Rename GenDLL.C to MyDLL.C, rename GenDLL.H to MyDLL.H, and rename GenDLL.DEF to MyDLL.DEF.

Your C:\EXPROG\BD7 directory should now contain the following files: MyDLL.C, MyDLL.H, and MyDLL.DEF.

Using the Visual C++ Compiler to Create a DLL

You'll now use the Microsoft Visual C++ compiler to create your DLL.

☐ Double-click the Visual C++ icon from the group of program icons in the Microsoft Visual C++ group of programs (see Figure BD7.1).

Windows responds by executing the Microsoft Visual C++ program and displaying the window shown in Figure BD7.2.

☐ Select New from the Project window.

Visual C++ responds by displaying the New Project dialog box (see Figure BD7.3).

Currently, the new project is set so that Visual C++ will generate a regular EXE program (as indicated by the Project Type box of Figure BD7.3).

☐ Click the arrow icon that appears to the right of the Project Type box and select the Windows dynamic-link library (.DLL) item from the list that drops down.

Figure BD7.1.
Starting Visual C++.

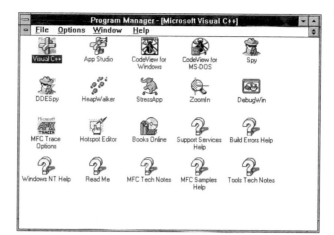

Figure BD7.2.
The main Visual C++ window.

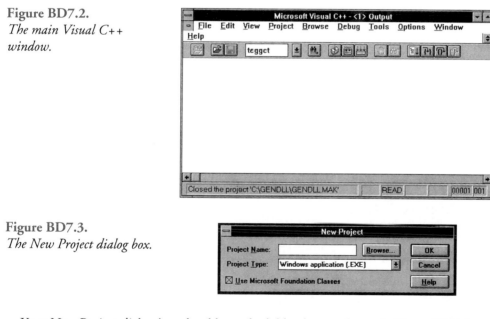

Figure BD7.3.
The New Project dialog box.

Your New Project dialog box should now look like the one shown in Figure BD7.4.

☐ Click the Browse button of the New Project dialog box.

   Visual C++ responds by displaying the Browse dialog box.

☐ Select the C:\EXPROG\BD7 directory, and type MyDLL.MAK inside the File Name box.

Your Browse dialog box should now look like the one shown in Figure BD7.5.

Figure BD7.4.
The New Project dialog box set to generate a DLL file.

Figure BD7.5.
Setting the new project as C:\EXPROG\BD7 \MyDLL.mak.

☐ Click the OK button of the Browse dialog box.

> *Visual C++ responds by closing the Browse dialog box and returning to the New Project dialog box (see Figure BD7.6).*

Figure BD7.6.
The new project set to C:\EXPROG\BD7 \MyDLL.mak. This project will generate a DLL file called MyDLL.DLL.

☐ Click the OK button of the New Project dialog box.

> *Visual C++ responds by displaying the Edit dialog box (see Figure BD7.7).*

Figure BD7.7.
The Edit dialog box.

You'll use the Edit dialog box to add the files that belong to this project.

☐ Select the C:\EXPROG\BD7\MyDLL.C file and click the Add button of the Edit dialog box.

☐ Select the C:\EXPROG\BD7\MyDLL.DEF and click the Add button of the Edit dialog box.

Your Edit dialog box should now look like the one shown in Figure BD7.8.

Figure BD7.8.
Adding MyDLL.C and
MyDLL.DEF to the project.

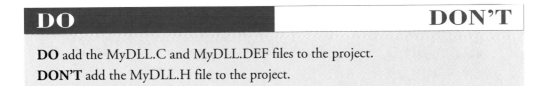

DO   **DON'T**

DO add the MyDLL.C and MyDLL.DEF files to the project.
DON'T add the MyDLL.H file to the project.

☐ Click the Close button of the Edit dialog box.

Visual C++ responds by returning to the main window of Visual C++.

Customizing the MyDLL.C File
In the following steps you'll customize the MyDLL.C file.

☐ Select Open from the File menu and load the C:\EXPROG\BD7\MyDLL.C file.

Visual C++ responds by loading the MyDLL.C file (see Figure BD7.9).

The MyDLL.C file that you loaded is the old GenDLL.C file that you copied to the C:\EXPROG\BD7 directory. You'll now customize this file.

Figure BD7.9.
Loading the MyDLL.C file.

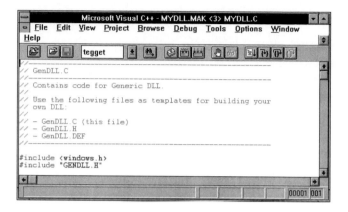

☐ Modify the MyDLL.C file by replacing each occurrence of the word GenDLL with the word MyDLL.

MyDLL.DLL, which you are now writing, will contain a DLL function called MyBeep() and a DLL function called MyDelay().

☐ In the prototype section of the MyDLL.C file type the prototype of the MyBeep() function and the prototype of the MyDelay() function. After adding the prototypes, the Prototype section inside the MyDLL.C file should look like this:

```
//-----------------------------------------------
// Prototypes
//-----------------------------------------------

int FAR PASCAL _export MyBeep ( void );
int FAR PASCAL _export MyDelay ( long );
```

The code you typed declares the prototypes of the MyBeep() and the MyDelay() functions that will be available from your Visual Basic programs.

Note that the functions are declared as FAR PASCAL _export functions. By declaring the functions as such, other Windows programs will be able to use these functions. In other words, you declare the functions as DLL functions.

Writing the *MyBeep()* DLL Function

You'll now write the MyBeep() function:

☐ Add the following code at the end of the MyDLL.C file:

```
int  FAR PASCAL _export MyBeep (void)
{

MessageBeep((WORD)-1);
```

```
return 1;
}
```

The code you typed uses the Windows API `MessageBeep()` function to cause the PC speaker to beep.

Writing the *MyDelay()* DLL Function

You'll now write the `MyDelay()` function:

☐ Add the following code at the end of the MyDLL.C file:

```
int FAR PASCAL _export MyDelay ( long wait)
{

DWORD goal;

goal = (DWORD)wait + GetTickCount();

while (goal > GetTickCount() )
        ;

return 1;

}
```

Your MyDLL.C file should now look like this:

```
//------------------------------------------------------
// MyDLL.C
//------------------------------------------------------
// Contains code for Generic DLL.
//
// Use the following files as templates for building your
// own DLL:
//
// - MyDLL.C (this file)
// - MyDLL.H
// - MyDLL.DEF
//------------------------------------------------------

#include <windows.h>
#include "MYDLL.H"


//------------------------------------------------------
// Global Variables
//------------------------------------------------------
HANDLE hmodDLL;


//------------------------------------------------------
// Prototypes
//------------------------------------------------------
int FAR PASCAL _export MyBeep ( void );
int FAR PASCAL _export MyDelay ( long );
```

```
//---------------------------------------------------
// Initialize library. This routine is called when the
// first client loads the DLL.
//---------------------------------------------------
int FAR PASCAL LibMain
(
    HANDLE hModule,
    WORD   wDataSeg,
    WORD   cbHeapSize,
    LPSTR  lpszCmdLine
)
{
    // Avoid warnings on unused formal parameters
    wDataSeg    = wDataSeg;
    cbHeapSize  = cbHeapSize;
    lpszCmdLine = lpszCmdLine;

    hmodDLL = hModule;

    return 1;
}




//---------------------------------------------------
// WEP
//---------------------------------------------------
// C7 and QCWIN provide default WEP:
//---------------------------------------------------
#if (_MSC_VER < 610)

int FAR PASCAL WEP(int fSystemExit);


//---------------------------------------------------
// For Windows 3.0 it is recommended that the WEP
// function reside in a FIXED code segment and be
// exported as RESIDENTNAME.  This is accomplished
// using the alloc_text pragma below and the related
// EXPORTS and SEGMENTS directives in the .DEF file.
//
// Read the comments section documenting the WEP
// function in the Windows 3.1 SDK "Programmers
// Reference, Volume 2: Functions" before placing
// any additional code in the WEP routine for a
// Windows 3.0 DLL.
//---------------------------------------------------
#pragma alloc_text(WEP_TEXT,WEP)


//---------------------------------------------------
// Performs cleanup tasks when the DLL is unloaded.
// WEP() is called automatically by Windows when the DLL
// is unloaded (no remaining tasks still have the DLL
// loaded). It is strongly recommended that a DLL have a
// WEP() function, even if it does nothing but returns
// success (1), as in this example.
```

```
//-------------------------------------------------
int FAR PASCAL WEP
(
    int fSystemExit
)
{
    // Avoid warnings on unused formal parameters
    fSystemExit = fSystemExit;

    return 1;
}
#endif // C6

//-------------------------------------------------


int  FAR PASCAL _export MyBeep (void)
{

MessageBeep((WORD)-1);

return 1;
}

int FAR PASCAL _export MyDelay ( long wait)
{

DWORD goal;

goal = (DWORD)wait + GetTickCount();

while (goal > GetTickCount() )
        ;

return 1;

}
```

☐ Select Save from the File menu.

Visual C++ responds by saving the file MyDLL.C.

Customizing the MyDLL.H File

Typically, you'll have to customize the MyDLL.H file.

☐ Select Open from the File menu and load the file C:\EXPROG\BD7\MyDLL.H.

☐ Replace each occurrence of the text GenDLL with the text MyDLL.

Your MyDLL.H file should look like this:

```
//-------------------------------------------------
// MyDLL.H
//-------------------------------------------------
// Contains code for Generic DLL.
```

```
//
// Use the following files as templates for building your
// own DLL:
//
// - MyDLL.C
// - MyDLL.H (this file)
// - MyDLL.DEF
//-------------------------------------------------------
```

☐ Select Save from the File menu to save the MyDLL.H file.

Customizing the MyDLL.DEF File

Typically, you'll have to customize the MyDLL.DEF file.

☐ Select Open from the File menu and load the C:\EXPROG\BD7\MyDLL.DEF file.

☐ Replace each occurrence of the GenDLL text with the MyDLL text.

☐ Under the EXPORT section of the MyDLL.DEF file add the name of the DLL functions:

```
EXPORTS
    WEP        [064]1        RESIDENTNAME
    MyBeep
    MyDelay
```

Your MyDLL.DEF file should look like this:

```
;-------------------------------------------------------
; MyDLL.DEF
;-------------------------------------------------------
; The DEF file for Generic DLL.
;
; Use the following files as templates for building your
; own DLL:
;
; - MyDLL.C
; - MyDLL.H
; - MyDLL.DEF (this file)
;
;-------------------------------------------------------

LIBRARY          MYDLL
EXETYPE          WINDOWS
DESCRIPTION      'Visual Basic Generic DLL'

CODE             MOVEABLE
DATA             MOVEABLE SINGLE

HEAPSIZE         2048

EXPORTS
    WEP        [064]1        RESIDENTNAME
    MyBeep
    MyDelay
```

```
SEGMENTS
  WEP_TEXT FIXED
```

; -

☐ Select Save from the File menu to save the file MyDLL.DEF.

Generating the MyDLL.DLL File

☐ Select Rebuild All MyDLL.DLL from the Project menu.

> *Visual C++ responds by compiling and linking the files, and after a while the MyDLL.DLL is created in your C:\EXPROG\BD7 directory.*

To terminate the Visual C++ program do the following:

☐ Select Exit from the File menu of Visual C++.

☐ Use the File Manager program of Windows to copy the MyDLL.DLL file (which you just created) from the C:\EXPROG\BD7 directory to the \Windows\System directory.

Testing the MyDLL.DLL File

You have successfully generated the MyDLL.DLL file and copied it to your C:\Windows\System directory. You'll now create a Visual Basic program that makes use of this DLL.

> **Note:** In the previous section you were instructed to copy the file MyDLL.DLL to your \Windows\System directory.
>
> A program that uses a DLL will search for the DLL file in the current directory (the same directory in which the application resides). If the DLL file does not exist in the current directory, the application will look for the DLL file in the \Windows directory, in the \Windows\System directory, and in the directories of the DOS path.
>
> It is a good idea to place your DLL files inside the \Windows\System directory because this way many applications can share the same DLL file.

☐ Start Visual Basic.

☐ Select New Project from the File menu and save the new project: Save the new form as TestDLL.FRM inside the C:\EXPROG\BD7 directory and save the new project file as TestDLL.MAK inside the C:\EXPROG\BD7 directory.

☐ Implement the frmTestDLL form according to the specifications in Table BD7.1. When you finish building the form, it should look like the one shown in Figure BD7.10.

Table BD7.1. The properties table of the frmTestDLL form.

Object	Property	Setting
Form	Name	frmTestDLL
	Caption	The TestDLL Program
	Height	4425
	Icon	C:\EXPROG\ICONS\TestDLL.ICO (or use your own icon)
	Left	1035
	Top	1140
	Width	7485
Command Button	Name	cmdTestDLL
	Caption	&Test DLL
	Height	1575
	Left	2040
	Top	1800
	Width	3615
Command Button	Name	cmdExit
	Caption	E&xit
	Height	495
	Left	120
	Top	3360
	Width	1215

Figure BD7.10.
The frmTestDLL form (in design mode).

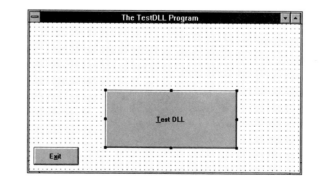

The *cmdExit_Click()* Procedure of the frmTestDLL Form

☐ Type the following code inside the `cmdExit_Click()` procedure of the frmTestDLL form:

```
Sub cmdExit_Click ()

    End

End Sub
```

Declaring the DLL Functions

The TestDLL program uses the `MyBeep()` and the `MyDelay()` DLL functions from the MyDLL.DLL file. This means that you must declare the `MyBeep()` function inside the general declarations section of the frmTestDLL form.

☐ Declare the `MyBeep()` and the `MyDelay()` functions from the file MyDLL.DLL inside the general declaration section of the frmTestDLL form. After you declare these DLL functions, the general declarations section should look like this:

```
Option Explicit
Declare Function MyBeep Lib "MyDLL.DLL" () As Integer
Declare Function MyDelay Lib "MyDLL.DLL" (ByVal wait As Long) As Integer
```

The *cmdTestDLL()* Procedure of the frmTestDLL Form

☐ Type the following code inside the `cmdTestDLL_Click()` procedure of the frmTestDLL form:

```
Sub cmdTestDLL_Click ()

    Dim Dummy

    Dummy = MyBeep()

    Dummy = MyDelay(1000)

    Dummy = MyBeep()

End Sub
```

The code you typed declares a dummy variable:

```
Dim Dummy
```

Then the `MyBeep()` DLL function is executed:

```
Dummy = MyBeep()
```

BD7

951

Then a 1-second (1000-millisecond) delay is executed:

```
Dummy = MyDelay(1000)
```

Then another beep is played:

```
Dummy = MyBeep()
```

So whenever the user clicks the Test DLL button, the MyBeep() DLL function is executed, which causes the PC speaker to beep twice with a 1-second delay in between the beeps.

> **Note:** Note that the MyBeep() DLL function was written for the sake of illustrating how you can write a DLL function. That is, Visual Basic has a Beep statement that is already implemented in Visual Basic, and you should use it.
>
> However, the MyDelay() DLL function is useful, because there is no such function in Visual Basic.

☐ Select Save Project from the File menu.

☐ Select Start from the Run menu.

Visual Basic responds by executing the TestDLL program and displaying the window shown in Figure BD7.11.

Figure BD7.11.
Testing the DLL with Visual Basic.

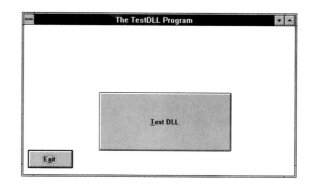

☐ Click the Test DLL button.

The TestDLL program responds by beeping twice with a 1-second delay between the beeps.

☐ Experiment with the TestDLL program and then click its Exit button to terminate the program.

Summary

In this chapter you have learned how to create your own DLLs for Visual Basic. As you have seen, you create DLLs by using the Microsoft Visual C++ compiler. As you have learned, you cannot create DLLs by using the Visual Basic programming language. That is, you must use the C programming language to write and generate the DLL, and once you finish implementing the DLL, you can use the DLL from within your Visual Basic programs.

Q&A

Q Must I use the C programming language for writing DLLs?

A Yes. You can't use Visual Basic to write DLLs.

Q Now I know how to create DLLs. How can I create VBX controls?

A You can read the Sams Publishing book *Master Visual Basic 3* by Gurewich and Gurewich. This book includes an elaborate discussion and tutorials on how to create and design VBX controls.

Quiz

1. When writing your own DLLs, there are three files that serve as the skeleton files. What are they?

2. After creating the DLL, it is best to copy the DLL to the following directory:

   a. \Windows\System

   b. C:\EXPROG\BD7

   c. The root directory of C:

Exercise

Use the material of this chapter to create some DLLs.

Quiz Answers

1. GenDLL.C, GenDLL.H, and GenDLL.DEF.

2. a

BD7

Exercise Answer

To create DLLs, just follow the tutorial that was presented in this chapter. As you can see, creating DLLs is a simple matter of following the step-by-step instructions.

Index

files

SAMS
Learning
Center

SAMS
PUBLISHING

Graphics menu commands

SAMS
Learning
Center

SAMS
PUBLISHING

MyNET.MAK file

Sams
Learning
Center

SAMS
PUBLISHING

procedures

SAMS
Learning
Center

SAMS
PUBLISHING

procedures

Sams
Learning
Center

SAMS
PUBLISHING

properties tables

Write # statement

Sams
Learning
Center

SAMS
PUBLISHING

PLUG YOURSELF INTO...

THE MACMILLAN INFORMATION SUPERLIBRARY™

Free information and vast computer resources from the world's leading computer book publisher—online!

FIND THE BOOKS THAT ARE RIGHT FOR YOU!

A complete online catalog, plus sample chapters and tables of contents give you an in-depth look at *all* of our books, including hard-to-find titles. It's the best way to find the books you need!

- **STAY INFORMED** with the latest computer industry news through our online newsletter, press releases, and customized Information SuperLibrary Reports.

- **GET FAST ANSWERS** to your questions about MCP books and software.

- **VISIT** our online bookstore for the latest information and editions!

- **COMMUNICATE** with our expert authors through e-mail and conferences.

- **DOWNLOAD SOFTWARE** from the immense MCP library:
    - Source code and files from MCP books
    - The best shareware, freeware, and demos

- **DISCOVER HOT SPOTS** on other parts of the Internet.

- **WIN BOOKS** in ongoing contests and giveaways!

TO PLUG INTO MCP: ➔ WORLD WIDE WEB: **http://www.mcp.com**

GOPHER: gopher.mcp.com

FTP: ftp.mcp.com

| Home Page | What's New | Bookstore | Reference Desk | Software Library | Macmillan Overview | Talk to Us |

Disk Offer

Teach Yourself Visual Basic in 21 Days, Bestseller Edition

You can purchase the book's special companion disks (two 3 1/2" disks) for only $15. The two disks contain the following:

- [ ] All the programs of the book, with complete source code.
- [ ] WAV files, MIDI files, and BMP files that are required for the multimedia programs.
- [ ] The limited version of the TegoMM.VBX multimedia control. This limited version of the multimedia control enables you to execute the multimedia programs that are discussed in this book. (You'll be able to play only supplied WAV and MIDI files.)

The easiest way to order the disks is to call 1-800-428-5331 between 9:00 a.m. and 5:00 p.m. EST. For fastest service, please have your credit card available.

To order the two disks by mail, complete this form and mail it to:

Sams Publishing
Sales Department—Disk Offer
Teach Yourself Visual Basic in 21 Days, Bestseller Edition
201 West 103rd Street
Indianapolis, IN 46290

Special Offer

The Full TegoMM.VBX Advanced Multimedia Control

You can order the full version of the TegoMM.VBX multimedia control, which enables you to play WAV files through the PC's built-in speaker, directly from TegoSoft, Inc.

As discussed in the bonus week chapters of this book, the TegoMM.VBX control lets you play and record WAV files through a sound card, play MIDI files, play movie AVI files, play CD audio, and detect whether the PC has a sound card installed in it. If no sound card is installed in the PC, you can play the WAV files through the PC speaker without any additional hardware or software.

The TegoMM.VBX multimedia control can perform other multimedia tasks such as letting your user use a joystick, letting you write programs that access each and every sample of WAV files (for the purpose of manipulating the WAV files and performing a variety of sound effects), and completing other powerful multimedia tasks.

The price of the full version of the TegoMM.VBX multimedia control is $29.95, plus $5.00 shipping and handling. New York State residents, please add the appropriate sales tax.

To order, send check or money order to:

TegoSoft, Inc.
Box 389
Bellmore, NY 11710
Phone: (516)783-4824

When ordering outside the United States, please send a check or money order in U.S. dollars, drawn from a U.S. bank.

Add to Your Sams Library Today with the Best Books for Programming, Operating Systems, and New Technologies

The easiest way to order is to pick up the phone and call
1-800-428-5331
between 9:00 a.m. and 5:00 p.m. EST.
For faster service please have your credit card available.

ISBN	Quantity	Description of Item	Unit Cost	Total Cost
0-672-30534-8		Teach Yourself Visual C++ 2 in 21 Days, Third Edition	$29.99	
0-672-30553-4		Absolute Beginner's Guide to Networking, Second Edition	$22.00	
0-672-30509-7		Graphics Programming with Visual Basic	$35.00	
0-672-30562-3		Teach Yourself Game Programming in 21 Days	$39.99	
0-672-30466-X		The Internet Unleashed (book/disk)	$44.95	
0-672-30617-4		The World Wide Web Unleashed	$35.00	
0-672-30570-4		PC Graphics Unleashed (book/CD-ROM)	$49.99	
0-672-30595-X		Education on the Internet	$25.00	
0-672-30413-9		Multimedia Madness, Deluxe Edition! (book/disk/CD-ROM)	$55.00	
0-672-30638-7		Super CD-ROM Madness! (book/CD-ROM)	$39.99	
0-672-30590-9		The Magic of Interactive Entertainment, Second Edition (book/CD-ROM)	$44.95	
❏ 3 ¹⁄₂" Disk		Shipping and Handling: See information below.		
❏ 5 ¹⁄₄" Disk		TOTAL		

Shipping and Handling: $4.00 for the first book, and $1.75 for each additional book. Floppy disk: add $1.75 for shipping and handling. If you need to have it NOW, we can ship product to you in 24 hours for an additional charge of approximately $18.00, and you will receive your item overnight or in two days. Overseas shipping and handling adds $2.00 per book and $8.00 for up to three disks. Prices subject to change. Call for availability and pricing information on latest editions.

201 W. 103rd Street, Indianapolis, Indiana 46290

1-800-428-5331 — Orders   1-800-835-3202 — FAX   1-800-858-7674 — Customer Service

Book ISBN 0-672-30715-4